AF663477

GAUTAMA : THE NYĀYA PHILOSOPHY

Gautama
THE NYĀYA PHILOSOPHY

N.S. JUNANKAR

MOTILAL BANARSIDASS PUBLISHERS
PRIVATE LIMITED • DELHI

2nd Reprint: Delhi, 2018
First Edition: Delhi, 1978

ISBN: 978-81-208-0896-6

<u>*Also available at:*</u>

MOTILAL BANARSIDASS

41 U.A. Bungalow Road, Jawahar Nagar, Delhi 110 007
1B, Jyoti Studio Compound, Kennedy Bridge, Nana Chowk, Mumbai 400 007
203 Royapettah High Road, Mylapore, Chennai 600 004
236, 9th Main III Block, Jayanagar, Bengaluru 560 011
8 Camac Street, Kolkata 700 017
Ashok Rajpath, Patna 800 004
Chowk, Varanasi 221 001

MLBD Cataloging-in-Publication Data
Gautama : The Nyāya Philosophy
by N.S. Junankar
Includes Notes, Bibliography, Index
ISBN : 978-81-208-0896-6
I. Gautama II. Nyaya
III. Indian Philosophy IV. N.S. Junankar

Printed in India

by RP Jain at NAB Printing Unit,
A-44, Naraina Industrial Area, Phase I, New Delhi–110028
and published by JP Jain for Motilal Banarsidass Publishers (P) Ltd,
41 U.A. Bungalow Road, Jawahar Nagar, Delhi-110007

TO

My Mother

Who suffered for her sense of justice and generous impulse

CONTENTS

Preface ix
Acknowledgements xiv
Abbreviations xvii
A Guide to References xix
Introduction xxxix

PART ONE : CENTRAL THEME 1

1. Categories (*padārtha*) 3

PART TWO : THEORY OF COGNITION 7

2. Pramāṇa 9
3. Perception (*pratyakṣa*) 45
4. Inference (*anumāna*) 114
5. Analogy (*upamāna*) 141
6. Word (*śabda*) 146

PART THREE : CONCEPT OF PROOF 195

7. Doubt (*saṃśaya*) 197
8. The Objective (*prayojana*) 213
9. Established tenet (*siddhānta*) 214
10. *Avayava* (member) 217
11. The fallacy of the hetu (*hetvābhāsa*) 264
12. Disputation (*tarka*) 287
13. Ascertainment (*nirṇaya*) 291

PART FOUR : TECHNIQUE OF REFUTATION 295

14. Discourse (*kathā*) 297
15. Quibble (*chala*) 306
16. Legitimate objection (*jāti*) 309
17. Deficiency (*nigrahasthāna*) 329
18. Doctrines of other philosophers (*prāvāduka*) 342

PART FIVE : OBJECT OF COGNITION (*Prameya*) :

SELF (*ātman*), its equipment, career and destiny 371

19. Self (*ātman*) 373
20. Body (*śarīra*) 399

21. *Buddhi* 409
22. Activity (*pravṛtti*) 423
23. Defect (*doṣa*) 425
24. State after death (*pretyabhāva*) 430
25. Result (*phala*) 432
26. Pain (*duḥkha*) 438
27. Release (*apavarga*) 441

PART SIX: SOURCE OF *SAMSĀRA* 453

28. Misapprehension (*mithyājñāna*) and knowledge of the true nature of things (*tattvajñāna*) 455

PART SEVEN: REFLECTIONS ON THE NYĀYA SYSTEM 473

29. Reflections on the Nyāya System 475
Notes 577
Appendix 631
Selective Bibliography 637
General Index 649

PREFACE

Within the last few decades much has been published in the West on Indian logic and epistemology. Many works, too many to be listed here, written by Indian logicians have been translated into European languages; a considerable number of essays and treatises on the subjects has appeared with or without recourse to primary sources. Moreover, Western authors of books and manuals on logic in general who some years ago would not have dreamt of including in their works chapters on Indian logic, now offer hospitality, as a matter of course, to this field of study and, though with varying competence, treat it on par with Western logic.

On the other hand, several Indian scholars, familiar with Sanskrit and with the heritage of Indian logic and epistemology, and well versed in Western philosophy, ancient and modern, have made valuable contributions to a better understanding of the methods and modes of Indian thinking.

These combined efforts have resulted in the often successful presentation of the idiosyncratic problems involved in this particular area of Indian endeavour. The use of modern formulae and terminology in the exposition and the interpretation of the Indian logical and epistemological systems has rendered these subjects more palatable to the Western philosopher and has won them, for better or for worse, a safe place in this sector of philosophical research. Let it be said that with the fairly recent outbreak of scepticism regarding the infallibility of Aristotelian logic and theories of cognition, the attempts at the modernisation of the Indian systems have been readily acceptable; much more so than would have been the case at the time when logic could stand the test of its validity only when gauged against the authority of Aristotle. Nobody is likely to subscribe any longer to Vidyabhusana's proposition that "the Hindu logician owed the idea of syllogism to the influence of Aristotle," even if such a proposition is narrowed down to no more than the origin of Indian syllogism.

It is perhaps natural that since its inception the interest in Indian logic and epistemology has found almost exclusively its expression in the authors' strict and limited adherence to the boundaries outlined by the subject. Translations of, and the treatises on, Indian logical works have been limited to the confines of analyses of the elements and means of cognition and the methods by which these elements and means could be applied to the processes of arriving at a valid cognition established within the framework of the respectively acknowledged ontological systems.

While Dr. Junankar's present work adheres to the postulates of this type of analysis by offering occasional translation or relevant summaries of the Nyāyasūtra and its most important commentaries, the emphasis of his analysis goes beyond the mere exegesis of the logical and epistemological data. This is what makes his investigation into the Nyāya system new and original. Presenting in a *par excellence* scholarly manner the data as they are given in the apposite Sanskrit texts, Dr. Junankar has by far not tried to eschew the task of probing into the validity of these data from the philosophical viewpoint; having done this he has attempted to enquire into the socio-ethical environment within the context of which such and no other data had been established as the unchallengeable criteria constituting the true means of cognition, and into the validity of such cognition as attainable by the employment of these and no other means.

Consequently the uniqueness of Dr. Junankar's treatment of the Nyāya system lies in the fact that, while not swerving from the factual presentation of the body of arguments contained in the texts, he uses this very textual material as the instrument for his enquiry into the validity of these arguments and the foundations of the Nyāya philosophers' claim to their veracity. He does not stop here; he wants to know what type of society it was that induced its leading philosophers to the selection of a particular kind of laws and regulations to govern man's reasoning and what were the motivations inveigling man to abide by the precepts so arbitrarily imposed on him.

Answers to these questions within the framework of Indian tradition are tortuous and complex and the author has fully realized that it is this framework within the confines of which the enquiry has to be pursued. A purely modern and scientific enquiry (as we now understand it) would be one-sided and rather confound than clarify the issue. The author's awareness of this dilemma adds to the fascination of the book. Dr. Junankar had to choose between the role of yet another commentator and that of a historian. It seems that he has successfully found a compromise between these two commitments, and it is up to the reader to judge the soundness and the validity of the compromise at which he has arrived. If the author's exegesis is found to be controversial, such controversy can only add to the interest of the problems involved and underline their complexity.

Thus Dr. Junankar's critique appears to concern itself primarily with the question of the reliability of the essential data, ontological, epistemological and metaphysical, purporting to form the basic foundation of the structure and the course of the logical apparatus and the ensuing theories of cognition. The Nyāya system claims to be an intrinsically empirical system accepting the duality of the subject and object of cognition. Consequently the Naiyāyika would be expected to lay down principles strictly commensurate with cognitive criteria emerging from experience. While not challenging this fundamental claim of the Naiyāyikas, the author is baffled by the scope which the concept of experience is given by the Nyāya; as a sequel to that Dr. Junankar cannot refrain from wondering how much credibility can be afforded to experience unless the latter is treated as the necessary premises of logic and epistemology underlying man's relationship between the extraneous world and himself. This doubt, as has been indicated before, concerns not only the philosophical aspects of the reasons why the Naiyāyika has chosen to treat experience in a manner defying in a way its 'normal' terms of reference, but also probes into the socio-political implications of that choice. For Dr. Junankar the motives underlying that choice are closely and structurally intertwined.

The position of the Naiyāyika, presented in simplest terms is as follows: He has adopted four pramāṇas, means of cognition: perception, inference, word (verbal communication), and analogy. The adoption of these instruments of cognition was supported by the understanding that they are irrevocable and unchallengeable as they are founded on the actual order of events and the structure of the universe embracing the concrete and psychological phenomena. In other words, while they serve as means of acquiring all aspects of knowledge, their own validity does not postulate any proof from outside and has to be accepted without further questioning. Perception, the pramāṇa heading all other pramāṇas, is thus valid on two counts: on the acceptance of the fact that it arises from the contact between senses (including the mind) and the object; secondly, perception is the means of acquiring knowledge by way of insight, an *union mistique* of the enlightened individual, the āpta, with the structure of the universe. Since such a non-sensory perception is by nature infallible, it is the foundation underlying the true interrelation between subject and object; it *eo ipso* verifies the law governing such interrelation. Those who do not have the gift or powers of such intuitive cognition and can but rely on the sense-object contact, have to accept the reliability of the enlightened being as a guide and dogma, which require no further proof and indeed defy any attempt at such a proof. The enlightened person's, or shall we say, the expert's content of perception is communicated by him to the rank and file by means of language (word = *śabda*) which in itself is listed in the table of the pramāṇas as a valid instrument of cognition. Furthermore, the āpta's word is deemed to be the reflection of his 'vision' which, in turn, is said to be based on actual experience typologically identical with the perception of a person gained on the sensory everyday-empirical level. In this manner the āpta's word dictates, as it were, the kind of experience that the ordinary person will undergo within the set of logical and epistemological rules constructed by the āpta. Briefly, the ordinary man will in a way have to subject his mental and psychological apparatus to the processes laid down by the authority of the enlightened person or persons, whose mystic experience is to guarantee the veracity and authenticity of the events apprehended and the rules guiding the acts of apprehension. With the acceptance of the āpta's authority on the philosophical, social and soteriological level the person is bound to follow that set of rules which, whether or not consistent with the postulates of science or in concert with his own actual experience, has become a dogma to be followed by those who adopt the Nyāya system. It is thus only natural that a modern thinker will ask himself how far mysticism can be reconciled with empiricism. The primary concern, however, will be one involving the foundation of empirical thinking: are behaviour and phenomena subjected to the body of dogmas and injunctions or are the latter subservient to evidence gained by experience; if so, where lie the limits of experience ?

It is only within the context of Indian traditional thinking that the answer to these questions can be attempted. And in this vein Dr. Junankar has tried, successfully, I think, to challenge the roots of the Nyāya concept of empiricism, and to explore the social implications of an intellectual feudalism entailing the philosophical and dogmatic strictures imposed by the spiritual élite on their more or less captive audience. His concern about this state of affairs puts him above the mere curiosity of a chronicler, as he is not convinced that a Nyāya-like intellectual élitarism is absent from contemporary India.

In his endeavour Dr. Junankar has trodden on delicate grounds: his treatment of the subject and his conclusions are evocative. A student of Sanskrit and historian of Indian philosophy may be tempted to challenge his hypotheses; he may find that the logical or, more so, metaphysical theories constitute a sufficient reason to render the Naiyāyika ratiocination internally consistent in the light of the established Indian tradition preceding or deriving from the Nyāya system. It can also be expected and, indeed, hoped that the treatment of the Nyāyadarśana in this book will be a stimulant to those who will want to tackle logic and epistemology of India not merely within the specialized confines, but pursue the study further, as the author of this book has done, within the framework of its broad context.

Whatever influence Dr. Junankar's book may carry, it has been written by a man, whose well-informed approach, scholarship, honesty and force of conviction should mark an important step in the treatment of the Nyāya logic and epistemology.

Arnold Kunst

ACKNOWLEDGEMENTS

I have been working on a research project, the principles and systems of Indian Logic for some time past, but it was only in 1965 that I was able to leave my official career and devote undivided attention to the study of the Nyāya system.

In making this switch a large number of my friends lent their valuable support in numerous ways. Professor A. J. Ayer, Professor H. H. Price and Professor T. Burrow who saw my synopsis on the subject encouraged me to pursue the research project. Sir Peter Noble, Sir Eric Ashby, Sir Christopher Cox, Sir Douglas Logan and Professor C. H. Philips explored ways and means of enabling me to undertake this work.

As a cumulative result of these efforts the Principal of the University of London invited the support of the Leverhulme Trust Fund for this research and Professor C. H. Philips agreed to have me at the School of Oriental and African Studies for this work. I was not strictly eligible for assistance under the Trust's Research Awards Scheme according to the rules which confine such awards to British subjects resident in the United Kingdom. However, in view of the importance of the subject and of the support lent by the Principal of the University of London and the Director of the School of Oriental and African Studies the Leverhulme Trust awarded me a research fellowship for three years and this fellowship was subsequently extended by two years to complete the work on the recommendation of the Director based on the progress of my research as seen by Dr. A. V. Kunst and Professor H. H. Price. The former Directors of the Leverhulme Trust, Sir Miles Clifford and Lord Murray of Newhaven, took personal interest in my research project and throughout treated me with great sympathy and understanding. I am most grateful to the Trustees and those mentioned above for the opportunity they have given me for working on my research project.

I am also grateful to the General Secretary, Mr. K. D. D. Henderson and the Trustees of the Spalding Trust for the grant in aid they gave me in 1971 for completing the present study. As in the case of the Leverhulme Trust, Dr. A. V. Kunst supported my request to the Trust.

During this period I have had opportunities of discussing aspects of my work with various scholars in the United Kingdom. Professor H. H. Price read a part of my manuscript and I have had several luncheon discussions with him regarding certain problems in the Nyāya system which are similar to those in Western philosophy. These discussions have been helpful to me in preparing my comments on the Nyāya system and I am most grateful to Professor Price both for his advice and hospitality.

Professor T. Burrow read a part of my manuscript and I also discussed it with him. I am thankful to him for his suggestions.

Almost from the day I began my work at the School of Oriental and African Studies, Dr. A. V. Kunst went out of his way to help me in every possible way. He has not only read the entire manuscript line by line but also discussed it line by line on countless occasions at his home and outside. It is impossible for me to spell out the items of his advice, assistance and encouragement which have gone into the preparation of the manuscript and if this study has any merit, the credit for it is entirely due to him.... I owe him a tremendous debt of gratitude not only for his techincal assistance but also generous hospitality. Through our countless meetings Mrs. Kunst and Dr. Kunst have played wonderful hosts. Their gifts of head and heart have been a perpetual source of comfort and encouragement to me and my family, and they have given the best of these to us at all times and most graciously.

The Director and Staff of the School of Oriental and African Studies have treated me as one of them and I had every opportunity of participating in the life of the academic community. The Librarian and the Staff of the School's Library gave me every facility which any research worker could have asked for. I am most grateful to all of them for this breakthrough into the intellectual life of a British University.

My thanks are also due to the Librarian of the India Office Library for the special facilities he extended to me for my research as well as to the staff of the Library for their courtesy and kindness.

My thanks are due to Mrs. V. Williams and her typists for having done most of my typing work. They had to deal not only with a difficult subject but also to cope with my handwriting.

After a long period of trials and tribulations in the official career it has not been easy to settle down to a life of peaceful pursuit of research. In this process my wife and children have played an important part and I must express my appreciation of all that they have done for me during these years.

ABBREVIATIONS

(Particulars about books mentioned are given in the Selective Bibliography.)

Bibl Ind	Edition of the *Nyāyavārtika* of Uddyotakara by V. P. Dvivedin, Calcutta, 1907.
BL	*Buddhist Logic* by Th. Stcherbatsky.
BOS	Bulletin of the School of Oriental and African Studies.
GOS	Gaekwad's Oriental Series.
Hattori	*Dignāga, On Perception* by Masaaki Haṭtori.
HIL	*A History of Indian Logic* by S. C. Vidyabhusana.
ILES	*Indian Logic in the Early Schools* by H. N. Randle.
Ingalls	*Materials for the study of Navya-Nyāya Logic* by D. H. H. Ingalls.
Jha	Translation of the *Nyāya Sūtra*, *Nyāyabhāṣya* and *Nyāyavārtika* by Ganganath Jha.
LS	*Laṅkāvatāra Sūtra*, edited by Bunyiu Nanjio.
Matilal	*The Navya-Nyāya Doctrine of Negation* by B. K. Matilal.
MK	*Mūlamādhyamika Kārikās* of Nāgārjuna, edited by Louis de la Vallée Poussin.
MV	*Mādhyamikavṛtti* (*Prasannapadā*) of Candrakīrti as given in Louis de la Vallée Poussin's edition of *Mūlamādhyamika Kārikās*.
NBh	*Nyāyabhāṣya* of Vātsyāyana.
NS	*Nyāya Sūtra* of Gautama.
NV	*Nyāyavārtika* of Uddyotakara.
NVTT	*Nyāyavārtikatātparyaṭīkā* of Vācaspati.
Pre-D.	*Pre-Diṅnāga Buddhist Texts on Logic from Chinese Sources* by G. Tucci.
SBE	*Sacred Books of the East*.
SBH	*Sacred Books of the Hindus*: When SBH is not followed by the number of Volume, it indicates the edition of the *Nyāya Sūtra* of Gautama by S. C. Vidyabhusana.
VS	*Vaiśeṣika Sūtra* of Kaṇāda.

VSS *The Vizianagram Sanskrit Series:*
When VSS is not followed by the number of Volume, it indicates Tailanga's edition of the *Nyāya Sūtras* of Gautama, Vātsyāyana's *Bhāṣya* and extracts from the *Nyāyavārtika* and the *Tātparyaṭīkā.*

WZKSO Wiener Zeitschrift für die Kunde Süd- und Ostasiens.

A GUIDE TO REFERENCES

1. The following editions have been used for reference. [SBH, VSS and Bibl Ind are used as abbreviations for the first three editions respectively].

(i) *The Nyāya Sūtras of Gotama*, translated by S. C. Vidyabhusana, Sacred Books of the Hindus, Volume VIII, Allahabad: The Panini Office, 1930.

(ii) *The Nyāya Sūtras with Vātsyāyana's Bhāshya and extracts from the Nyāyavārtika and the Tātparyaṭīkā*, edited by G. S. Tailanga, The Vizianagram Sanskrit Series, Volume IX, Benares: E. J. Lazarus & Co., 1896.

(iii) *The Nyāyavārtika of Uddyotakara*, edited by Vindhyeśvari Prasāda Dvivedin (Dube), Bibliotheca Indica, Calcutta, 1907.

(iv) *Nyāyavārtikatātparyaṭīkā* by Vācaspati Miśra, edited by R. S. Dravida, Kashi Sanskrit Series, 24, Benares: Chowkhamba Sanskrit Series Office, 1925.

2. The aphorisms given in SBH do not tally with those in VSS and Bibl Ind. There are two reasons for this: (a) Some of the aphorisms in SBH appear as parts of NBh in VSS or of NV in Bibl Ind; those which are given as aphorisms in VSS or in Bibl Ind are not so given as SBH. (b) There are misprints in different editions.

On some of the aphorisms Vātsyāyana and Uddyotakara have combined their comments.

To ensure uniformity of reference the number of an aphorism as given in SBH has been used and the same number has been used for NBh, NV and NVTT. In indicating the number of aphorisms misprints have been corrected. Although Vātsyāyana and Uddyotakara have combined their comments on some of the aphorisms, the number of the aphorism in SBH has been used for both NBh and NV; so that the comments can be seen as relevant to the aphorism concerned.

The following tables and notes will enable the reader to identify the references in the various editions.

3. The misprints in the numbering of the aphorisms in SBH and VSS have been corrected in the references in the text as indicated in the following tables I and II.

TABLE I

NS Misprints in SBH			Errata			Remarks
Book	Chapter	Aphorism	Book	Chapter	Aphorism	
I	1	3	I	1	33	
II	1	1-28	II	2	1-28	The misprints refer to the aphorisms under the heading Book II, Chapter II.
II	1	3	II	2	33	
III		64	III	1	64	
III	1	6	III	1	69	

TABLE II

NS *Misprints in VSS*			*Errata*			*Remarks*
Book	*Chapter*	*Aphorism*	*Book*	*Chapter*	*Aphorism*	
II	1	1-4	II	2	1-4	On the top of pp. 101-03
II	2	35	II	2	36	Two aphorisms are numbered 35. The second 35 should be 36.
II	2	36-51	II	2	37-52	Each number of the aphorism from the printed 36 which is wrong has to be increased by one.
IV	1	49	IV	1	39	This misprint refers to the number after IV. 1, 38, p. 209.

4. The corresponding numbers of the aphorisms in the three editions after the misprints have been corrected are given in the following table III.

TABLE III

NS-SBH			NS-VSS			NS-Bibl Ind			Remarks
Book	*Chapter*	*Aphorism*	*Book*	*Chapter*	*Aphorism*	*Book*	*Chapter*	*Aphorism*	
I	1	1-41	I	1	1-41	I	1	1-41	
I	2	1-20	I	1	1-20	I	1	42-61	
II	1	1-24	II	1	1-24	II	1	1-24	
II	1	25	II	1	25	II	1	Part of NV II. 1,24	
II	1	26	II	1	26	II	1	Part of NV II. 1,24	
II	1	27	II	1	27	II	1	25	
II	1	28-52	II	1	28-52	II	1	26-50	
II	1	53	II	1	Part of NBh II. 1, 52	II	1	51	
II	1	54-69	II	1	53-68	II	1	52-67	
II	2	1-12	II	2	1-12	II	2	1-12	

TABLE III (*contd.*)

II	2	13	II	2	Part of NBh II. 2, 12	II	2	13
II	2	14-28	II	2	13-27	II	2	14-28
II	2	29	II	2	Part of NBh II. 2, 27	II	2	29
II	2	30-37	II	2	28-35	II	2	30-37
II	2	38	II	2	36	II	2	38
II	2	39-48	II	2	37-46	II	2	39-48
II	2	49-51	II	2	Part of NBh II. 2,46	II	2	49-51
II	2	52-60	II	2	47-55	II	2	52-60
II	2	61	II	2	56	II	2	Part of NV II. 2, 60
II	2	62-71	II	2	57-66	II	2	61-70
III	1	1-52	III	1	1-52	III	1	1-52
III	1	53-54	III	1	Part of NBh III. 1,52	III	1	Part of NV III. 1,52
III	1	55	III	1	Part of NBh			Part of NV

TABLE III (*contd.*)

NS-SBH			*NS-VSS*			*NS-Bibl Ind*			*Remakrs*
Book	*Chapter*	*Aphorism*	*Book*	*Chapter*	*Aphorism*	*Book*	*Chapter*	*Aphorism*	
					III. 1,52			III. 1,52	
III	1	56-63	III	1	53-60	III	1	53-60	
III	1	64	III	1	61-62	III	1	61-62	SBH aphorism is split into two.
III	1	65-66	III	1	63-64	III	1	63-64	
III	1	67	III	1	65	III	1	Part of NV III 1,64	
III	1	68-75	III	1	66-73	III	1	65-72	
III	2	1-9	III	2	1-9	III	2	1-9	
III	2	10	III	2	Part of NBh III. 2,9	Not	given		
III	2	11-38	III	2	10-37	III	2	10-37	
III	2	39	III	2	38	Not	given		
III	2	40-45	III	2	39-44	III	2	38-43	

TABLE III (*contd.*)

III	2	46	III	2	Part of NBh III. 2,44		Not	given	
III	2	47-48	III	2	45-46	III	2	44-45	
Not	given		III	2	47	Not	given		
III	2	49-71	III	2	48-70	III	2	46-68	
III	2	72	III	2	71	III	2	Part of NV III. 2,68	
III	2	73	III	2	72	III	2	69	
III	2	74	III	2	73	Not	given		NV comments cover the substance of the aphorism
III	2	75-78	III	2	74-77	III	2	70-73	
IV	1	1-60	IV	1	1-60	IV	1	1-60	
IV	1	61	IV	1	Part of NBh IV.1, 60	IV	1	61	
IV	1	62	IV	1	61	IV	1	62	
Not	given		IV	1	62	IV	1	63	Aphorisms in VSS and Bibl Ind are the same.
IV	1	63-68	IV	1	63-68	IV	1	64-69	
IV	2	1-50	IV	2	1-50	IV	2	1-50	
Not	given		IV	2	51	IV	2	51	
V	1	1-48	V	1	1-48	V	1	1-48	

TABLE III (*contd.*)

NS-SBH			*NS-VSS*			*NS-Bibl Ind*			*Remarks*
Book	*Chapter*	*Aphorism*	*Book*	*Chapter*	*Aphorism*	*Book*	*Chapter*	*Aphorism*	
V	2	1-14	V	2	1-14	V	2	1-14	
V	2	15	V	2	Part of NBh V. 2, 14	V	2	15	
V	2	16-25	V	2	15-24	V	2	16-25	

5. In VSS there are eighty-one passages printed in bold type as parts of NBh as given in the following Table IV. They look like aphorisms and some of them as indicated in the Remarks column are given as aphorisms in SBH.

The reference number of NBh in VSS is the corresponding NS number in SBH.

The aphorism numbered III. 2,47 in VSS is not given as an aphorism in SBH.

TABLE IV

NS-SBH			*Number of passages as parts of NBh in VSS*	*Remarks*
Book	*Chapter*	*Aphorism*		
	Introductory		3	
I	1	22	16	
II	1	6	1	
II	1	11	3	
II	1	19	7	
II	1	31	1	
II	1	32	1	
II	1	36	11	
II	2	14	4	
II	2	41	6	
II	2	48	3	These three passages are NS II. 2,49-51 in SBH.
III	1	2	1	
III	1	52	3	These three passages are NS III. 1,53-55.
III	2	3	3	
III	2	9	1	This passage is NS III. 2,10.
III	2	17	2	
III	2	33	1	
III	2	35	2	
III	2	40	1	
III	2	45	1	The latter part of this passage is NS III. 2,45 in SBH.

TABLE IV (*contd.*)

NS-SBH			*Number of passages as parts of NBh in VSS*	*Remarks*
Book	*Chapter*	*Aphorism*		
III	2	47	1	This number is of the aphorism in VSS. The aphorism is not given in SBH.
III	2	51	1	
IV	1	32	2	
IV	1	36	1	
IV	1	37	1	
IV	1	40	1	
IV	1	60	4	One of these passages is NS IV. 1,61.
IV	1	62	1	This number is of the aphorism in VSS. The aphorism is not given in SBH.
IV	1	64	1	
IV	2	12	1	
IV	2	14	1	
IV	2	22	1	
IV	2	32-33	2	These two aphorisms are printed one after the other and there is combined NBh on them in VSS.
IV	2	34	1	
V	1	26	1	

6. The aphorisms in SBH printed as parts of NBh in small type in VSS are given in the following Table V.

TABLE V

NS-SBH			*Printed as parts of NBh in VSS*			*Remarks*
Book	*Chapter*	*Aphorism*	*Book*	*Chapter*	*Aphorism*	
II	1	53	II	1	52	
II	2	13	II	2	12	
II	2	29	II	2	28	
V	2	15	V	2	14	

7. Vātsyāyana and Uddyotakara have given combined comments on various aphorisms as indicated in the following two tables VI and VII.

Such aphorisms are printed one after the other except where the aphorisms are parts of NBh and NV. The reference number of NBh and NV is the corresponding number of NS in SBH.

TABLE VI

NS-SBH			NBh-VSS			Remarks
Book	*Chapter*	*Aphorism*	*Book*	*Chapter*	*Aphorism*	
II	1	52-53	II	1	52	Aphorism II. 1,53 in SBH is part of NBh II. 1,52.
II	2	12-13	II	2	12	Aphorism II. 2,13 in SBH is part of NBh II. 2,12 in VSS.
II	2	28-29	II	2	28	Aphorism II. 2,29 in SBH is part of NBh II. 2,28.
II	2	48-51	II	2	48	Aphorisms II. 2,49-51 in SBH are parts of NBh II. 2,48 in VSS.
IV	2	10-11	IV	2	10-11	
IV	2	42-43	IV	2	42-43	

TABLE VII

NS-SBH			NS-NV-Bibl Ind			Remarks
Book	Chapter	Aphorism	Book	Chapter	Aphorism	
I	1	13-14	I	1	13-14	
I	2	10-13	I	2	10-13	
I	2	15-16	I	2	15-16	
II	1	2-3	II	1	2-3	
II	1	11-12	II	1	11-12	
II	1	24-26	II	1	24	Aphorisms II. 1,25 & 26 are parts of NV II. 1,24.
II	1	44-45	II	1	44-45	
II	1	46-48	II	1	46-48	
II	1	61-62	II	1	61-62	
II	2	6-7	II	2	6-7	
II	2	12-13	II	2	12-13	
II	2	23-24	II	2	23-24	
II	2	25-26	II	2	25-26	
II	2	27-28	II	2	27-28	
II	2	49-51	II	2	46-47	
II	2	60-61	II	2	60	Aphorism II. 2,60 in SBH is printed as part of NV II. 2,60.
III	1	15-16	III	1	15-16	
III	1	52-55	III	1	52	Aphorisms III. 1, 53, 54

TABLE VII (*contd.*)

NS-SBH			*NS-NV-Bibl Ind*			*Remarks*
Book	*Chapter*	*Aphorism*	*Book*	*Chapter*	*Aphorism*	
						& 55 in SBH are parts of NV III. 1,52.
III	1	64	III	1	64	Aphorism III. 1,64 in SBH is split into two III. 1,61 & 62 in Bibl Ind; these are printed one after the other.
III	1	66-67	III	1	66	Aphorism III. 1,67 in SBH is part of III. 1,66 in Bibl Ind.
III	2	11-12	III	2	11-12	
III	2	21-22	III	2	21-22	
III	2	33-35	III	2	33-35	
III	2	42-43	III	2	42-43	
III	2	47-48	III	2	47-48	
III	2	55-56	III	2	55-56	
III	2	71-72	III	2	71	Aphorism III. 2,72 in SBH is part of NV III. 2.71 in Bibl Ind.
III	2	73-74	III	2	73	Substance of aphorism III. 2,74 in SBH is covered by NV III. 2,73.

TABLE VII (*contd.*)

IV	1	14-15	IV	1	14-15	
IV	1	61-62	IV	1	61-62	
IV	2	19-20	IV	2	19-20	
IV	2	24-25	IV	2	24-25	
IV	2	30-31	IV	2	30-31	
IV	2	32-34	IV	2	32-34	
IV	2	42-44	IV	2	42-44	
V	1	30-32	V	1	30-32	
V	1	33-34	V	1	33-34	

8. There are minor variations in the texts of some of the aphorisms in the three editions. These variations have no significant bearing on the meanings of the aphorisms concerned as given in SBH.

9. The subject of the *Nyāya Sūtra* is the knowledge of the sixteen categories (*padārtha*) mentioned in NS I. 1,1. It also deals with the doctrines of other philosophers (*prāvāduka*) and misapprehension (*mithyājñāna*).

Tables VIII and IX show the distribution of the aphorisms devoted to these topics. Some of the categories are divided into sub-categories. In view of the importance of the categories of *pramāṇa* and *prameya* the aphorisms dealing with them have also been given in the Table.

References to the other sub-categories are given in the main text.

TABLE VIII Categories (*padārtha*) (I. 1,1)

(1) Instrument or means of cognition (*pramāṇa*)
I.1,3
II.1, 8-19
II. 2,1-12

Perception	Inference	Analogy	Word
(*pratyakṣa*) I. 1,4 II. 1,20-36 III. 1,30-50 IV. 2, 4-37	(*anumāna*) I. 1,5 II. 1,37-38 III. 1,39-43: In these aphorisms objection to the reality of past, present and future is discussed. According to Vātsyāyana this objection refers to the Nyāya view of inference as referring to past, present and future objects. Similar objection is discussed in connection with the validity of pramāṇa II. 1,8-19.	(*upamāna*) I. 1,6 II. 1,44-48	(*śabda*) I. 1,7 & 8 II. 1,49-69 II. 2,13-71

Table VIII (*contd.*)

(2) Object of Cognition (*prameya*)

Self (*ātman*) I	Body (*śarīra*) II	Sense-organs (*indriya*) III	Object (*artha*) IV	*Buddhi* V	Mind (*manas*) VI
I.1,10 III. 1,1-6 III. 1,12-27	I.1,11 III.1,28&29 III. 2,64-78 IV. 1,11-13	I. 1,12 III. 1,7-11 III. 1,51-75	I. 1,14 Objects [of sense] are properties (*guṇa*) of five elements mentioned in NS I. 1,13	I. 1,15 III. 2,1-59	I. 1,16 III. 2,60-63
Activity (*pravṛtti*) VII	Defect (*doṣa*) VIII	State after death (*pretyabhāva*) IX	Result (*phala*) X	Pain (*duḥkha*) XI	Release (*apavarga*) XII
I. 1,17 IV. 1,1	I. 1,18 IV. 1;2-9	I. 1,19 IV. 1,10	I. 1,20 IV. 1,44-54	I. 1,21 IV. 1,55-58	I. 1,22 IV. 1,5968-

TABLE VIII (*contd.*)

(3) Doubt	(4) The Objective	(5) Familiar Instance	(6) Established Tenet	(7) Member	(8) Disputation	(9) Ascertainment	(10) Discussion
(*saṃśaya*)	(*prayojana*)	(*dṛṣṭānta*)	(*siddhānta*)	(*avayava*)	(*tarka*)	(*nirṇaya*)	(*vāda*)
1,23 II.1,1-7	I. 1,24	I. 1,25	I. 1,26-31	I. 1,32-9	I. 1,40	I. 1,41	I. 2,1

(11) Rejoinder	(12) Cavil	(13) Fallacy of the hetu	(14) Quibble	(15) Legitimate Objection	(16) Deficiency
(*jalpa*)	(*vitaṇḍā*)	(*hetvābhāsa*)	(*chala*)	(*jāti*)	(*nigraha-sthāna*)
I. 2,2	I. 2,3	I. 2,4-9 V. 2,25	I. 2,10-17	I. 2,18 & 20 V. 1,1-43	I 2,19 & 20 V. 2,1-25

TABLE IX

Doctrines of other philosophers (*prāvāduka*)	Misapprehension (*mithyājñāna*)	Knowledge of the true nature of things (*tattvajñāna*)
IV. 1,14-43	I. 1,2 IV. 2,1-3 IV. 2,38-51	I. 1,1 (Categories are also listed in the aphorism).

INTRODUCTION

In this study I have discussed and analysed the doctrines of the Nyāya system as formulated by Gautama in his *Nyāya Sūtra* and explained by Vātsyāyana in his *Nyāyabhāṣya* and by Uddyotakara in his *Nyāyavārtika*. I have referred to the *Nyāyavārtikatātparyaṭīkā* of Vācaspati for clarification of doubtful points. The exposition and analysis follow closely the original Sanskrit texts of the three works mentioned above. I have consulted the translation of these texts and studies based on them wherever appropriate. Regarding the texts used and references given in this book a guide has been included for the convenience of the reader.

According to the commentators Gautama follows the standard method of exposition appropriate to a *śāstra* (scripture). This method consists of enunciation (*uddeśa*), definition (*lakṣaṇa*) and examination (*parīkṣā*). Accordingly, Gautama has first enumerated his sixteen categories together with sub-categories in certain cases; they are then defined; and at the end they are subjected to a detailed scrutiny. The scrutiny is generally intended to dispel a doubt or refute a contrary view. It may however be mentioned that Gautama has not always conformed to the standard mentioned above.

The *Nyaya Sūtra* contains five *adhyāyas* (books); each *adhyāya* consists of *ānhikas* (chapters); each *ānhika* has a number of *sūtras* (aphorisms). According to the standard method mentioned above Gautama has discussed his categories and subcategories in different parts of his work. The commentators follow his treatment. Generally this discussion involves refutation of contrary views. Since the commentators refer not only to such views as are mentioned by Gautama but also to later developments the exposition tends to become complicated. In order to highlight the basic doctrines and arguments of the Naiyāyikas and opponents I have classified the themes of the *Nyāya Sūtra* under the following main heads:

i. Central Theme
ii. Theory of Cognition
iii. Concept of Proof

iv. Technique of Refutation
v. Objects of Cognition (*prameya*); Self (*ātman*), its equipment, career and destiny
vi. Source of *Saṃsāra*

According to the conventional estimate of the Nyāya system, Gautama is said to have furnished a conceptual framework of most of Indian thought. It is hoped that the method of treatment adopted in this study and the comments I have made on the entire Nyāya system will help the reader in the understanding of the essential features of the conceptual framework.

In spite of a great deal of literature now available on Indian subjects it is unfortunate that some misconception about Indian philosophy still persists. In a fascinating and somewhat unconventional study of Western Philosophy Anthony Flew has observed: 'For philosophy, as the word is understood here, is concerned first, last and all time with arguments. (It is, incidentally, because most of what is labelled *Eastern Philosophy* is not so concerned — rather than for any reasons of European parochialism — that this book draws no materials from any sources east of Suez..)'.[1]

On any reasonable concept of what an argument is, the Nyāya system must be treated as philosophy. In fact, the typical Indian philosopher was, by training and mode of life, dedicated to argument, even to the extent of demonstrating what may seem to be *prima facie* indemonstrable. His premises may sound incredible but once the premises are conceded his conclusions are inevitable. The problems like those of knowledge, certainty, meaning of words or inductive proof, which have figured prominently in modern Western Philosophy, were examined with remarkable skill and rigour, even though the Indian philosophers had none of the advantages of sophisticated techniques which a modern philosopher has at his command.

In a recent study on Greek Philosophy W. K. C. Guthrie not only rejects the comparison between Parmenides and the Indian concept of 'the cosmic illusion of Māyā' but goes on to remark in a footnote: 'But in truth the motives and methods of the Indian schools, and the theological and mystical background of their thought, are so utterly different from those of the Greeks that there is little profit in the comparison'.[2] Such a summary disposal of the tremendous intellectual achievement of centuries in a footnote is hardly justified. It is true that many writers have regarded the Vedānta as the philosophy of India *par excellence* or emphasized intuition, spirituality and mysticism as the distinctive characteristics of Indian thought. This is no longer regarded as a correct judgment on Indian thought. So far as the Nyāya system is concerned, none of these characteristics can be said to have played an important part in the actual exposition of the various doctrines. I venture to express the belief that the present analysis of the system will enable the reader to assess the Nyāya system in a proper perspective as free from the cliches still so often associated with the evaluation of the Indian logic and epistemology.

Regarding the authors of the Nyāya works, we have no authentic information about their intellectual and social background or their lives. According to some scholars Gautama belongs to the second century A.D., Vātsyāyana to the fourth, the fifth or the sixth century and Uddyotakara to the seventh. As far as is known, these authors have written only one work each. Perhaps even these works, like some of modern scientific research, were the products of collective effort of teachers and their disciples but bore the names of the teachers only.

PART ONE : CENTRAL THEME

1

CATEGORIES (*Padārtha*)

According to Gautama there are sixteen categories (NS I. 1,1).

1. *Pramāṇa* (means or instrument of cognition)
2. *Prameya* (object of cognition)
3. *Saṃśaya* (doubt)
4. *Prayojana* (the objective)
5. *Dṛṣṭānta* (familiar instance)
6. *Siddhānta* (established tenet)
7. *Avayava* (member)
8. *Tarka* (disputation)
9. *Nirṇaya* (ascertainment)
10. *Vāda* (discussion)
11. *Jalpa* (rejoinder)
12. *Vitaṇḍā* (cavil)
13. *Hetvābhāsa* (fallacy of the hetu)
14. *Chala* (quibble)
15. *Jāti* (legitimate objection)
16. *Nigrahasthāna* (deficiency)

According to the commentators,[1] the sixteen categories of Gautama are *padārthas*. This Sanskrit word literally signifies the meaning of a word. According to Gautama the meaning of a word consists of individual (*vyakti*) configuration (*ākṛti*) and universal (*jāti*). Each of the sixteen words or names used must therefore have a threefold meaning. The Naiyāyikas have not explained how these names can be understood in this fashion nor is it easy to see how they can have such a meaning.

While Gautama seems to have accorded equal status to the sixteen categories, the commentators have attempted to modify this status. They have suggested that the fourteen categories following the second, *prameya*, are virtually included under the second category. This reduction in the category status must be regarded as an innovation in the scheme of Gautama.

Gautama himself has not clarified his position with regard to the nature of *padārtha*. The commentators have however furnished the clarification. The *padārthas* are said to represent '*sat*', i.e., ultimate existence or reality; they provide a classification of all that exists or is real.

This concept of the *padārthas* cannot be applied to the individual *padārthas* in any intelligible sense. If the *padārthas* constitute a geography of ultimate existence, the Nyāya notion of ontology must be rather odd. The four pramāṇas accepted by Gautama—perception, inference, analogy and word—constitute what is generally regarded as the theory of knowledge. *Saṃśaya, prayojana, siddhānta, avayava, hetvābhāsa, tarka* and *nirṇaya* constitute what can best be described as the concept of proof; these *padārthas* are partly psychological, partly epistemological and partly logical. *Vāda* is religious, scriptural and philosophical discourse and *jalpa, vitaṇḍā, chala, jāti* and *nigrahasthāna* constitute what is really a technique of refutation. Both the concept of proof and the technique of refutation are meant to operate within the broad framework of *siddhānta*. The former is designed to confirm the *siddhānta* while the latter is really intended for the demolition of heresy. Armed with the appropriate concept of proof and the technique of refutation the philosopher is expected to defend the truth and demolish the untruth. Such *padārthas* cannot be accorded the kind of ontological status which the commentators have in view.

This leaves us with the second *padārtha, prameya*.

According to Gautama there are nine *prameyas*: *ātman* (self), *śarīra* (body), *indriya* (sense-organ), *artha* (object), *buddhi* (apprehension), *manas* (mind), *pravṛtti* (activity), *doṣa* (defect), *pretyabhāva* (state after death), *phala* (result), and *apavarga* (release). Broadly speaking, according to Gautama both *ātman* and *artha* can be said to exist in a proper sense; they represent the principle of consciousness or the entity endowed with consciousness and the physical world respectively. *Śarīra, indriya, buddhi* and *manas* represent the physical and mental outfit of *ātman*. None of these *prameyas* is considered permanent or even a desirable acquisition. *Pravṛtti, doṣa, pretyabhāva, phala* and *duḥkha* represent the involvement of *ātman* in *saṃsāra*. In fact these together with the physical and mental outfit constitute *saṃsāra*. While the involvement of *ātman* in *saṃsāra* has no beginning it has an end. It is thus contingent, not logically necessary. What is thus contingent cannot be accorded the ontological status proposed by the Naiyāyikas.

The ninth *prameya, apavarga,* represents the consummation of the highest objective of *ātman*. It is the termination of *saṃsāra* and attainment of what the *ātman* has always been but obscured by its own misapprehension. Like *saṃsāra,* misapprehension is contingent, not logically necessary. It has no beginning but an end and there must be some *ātmans* who have already attained *apavarga* or are on the way to that attainment. But for an indefinite number of *ātmans, apavarga* must be a distant goal attainable only after a prolonged experience of torment and torture which *saṃsāra* is said to entail. Thus *apavarga* is neither a universal nor a logically necessary property of *ātman*. In fact it depends upon one's access to the true nature of the sixteen *padārthas* of Gautama. It is obvious that this access cannot be easily available to every *ātman* unless, of course, it has found its way in *saṃsāra* after Gautama has propounded his system and even more importantly, in that human embodiment a particular *ātman* (i.e., individual) has accepted the system. It would therefore seem that even *apavarga* cannot be accorded an ontological status except perhaps as an achievement of those fortunate *ātmans* who have had the benefit of the instruction of Gautama.

It is perhaps because of some such considerations at the back of their minds that the commentators have tried to convince us that the real purpose of Gautama is stated not so much in the opening aphorism where the knowledge of the true nature of the sixteen *padārthas* is said to lead to the attainment of *niḥśreyasa* (supreme felicity) but in the second aphorism where Gautama states the stage in a process of annihilation where *apavarga* is attained; *apavarga* follows on the successive annihilation of pain, birth, activity, defect and *mithyājñāna* (misapprehension). But, as already pointed out, this merely states the empirical fact, i.e., *apavarga* is historically attained after the annihilation of the five things mentioned. The first four of these are included among the nine *prameyas* and what is said about *saṃsāra* is a *pari passu* application to them in this context. Like *saṃsāra,* misapprehension is not a necessary property of *ātman*. It is true that like *saṃsāra*, misapprehension has no beginning, but it is equally true that like *saṃsāra*, it has an end. *Tattvajñāna* (knowledge of the true nature of the sixteen *padārthas*) destroys this misapprehension and clears the way for the attainment of *apavarga*. While such knowledge is available from the time of Gautama, its attainment is not inevitable; in the last analysis it is problematic. What is thus problematic cannot be regarded as an ultimate feature of existence. It will not be out of place to mention here that the notion of *apavarga* as absence of pain cannot be established by any of the four pramāṇas.

In the light of what has been said above it would seem that all the *padārthas* of Gautama cannot be accorded the glorified status of existence or reality. Nor can they be regarded as conducive to the attainment of *niḥśreyasa* if that *niḥśreyasa* is to be identified with *apavarga*.

But this view of the *padārthas* does not detract from the importance of the Nyāya system. It is generally agreed that this system furnished a conceptional framework within which Indian philosophical discourse was conducted. In this sense Gautama has the same place in Indian thought which Aristotle had in Western thought until recently.

PART TWO : THEORY OF COGNITION

2

PRAMĀṆA

Introductory

Indian philosophy presents a variety of opinions regarding the sources or means of cognition—pramāṇas. Different schools recognize different number and kinds of pramāṇa and their position is as follows:[1] The Cārvākas, who are the foremost materialists, recognize one pramāṇa—perception. The Vaiśeṣikas and the Buddhists admit two—perception and inference. The Sāṃkhyas and a branch of the Naiyāyikas add one to these two—word or verbal testimony (*śabda*). The Naiyāyikas have four pramāṇas : analogy, together with the above three. The Pūrva Mīmāṃsā school of Prabhākara recognize five pramāṇas : implication (*arthāpatti*), in addition to the above four. The Pūrva Mīmāṃsā school of Kumārila Bhaṭṭa and the Vedānta admit six pramāṇas: absence or negation (*abhāva*), together with the above five. The Paurāṇikas recognize eight pramāṇas : possibility or inclusion (*saṃbhava*) and historical tradition (*aitihya*), together with the above six.

According to the Jains there are five kinds of knowledge :[2] ordinary cognition obtained by sense-perception (*mati*), scriptural knowledge (*śruti*), knolwedge of things even at a distance of time and space (*avadhi*), knowledge of thoughts of others' (*manaḥ-paryaya*) and ominscience (*kevala*). The first two are called indirect (*parokṣa*), because they are obtained with the external help of the senses or scripture. The last three are direct (*pratyakṣa*) because they are obtained directly by the soul, without any external help of the senses including the mind or the scripture or without internal help, i.e. by the subsidence, destruction and operation of knowledge—obscuring karma. These two, direct and indirect knowledge, are recognized as two pramāṇas.

As already mentioned, the Naiyāyikas recognize four independent or distinct pramāṇas. Gautama also mentions four additional pramāṇas (viz. historical tradition, inclusion, implication and absence), but he rejects them as independent pramāṇas as they can be subsumed under one or the other of his four pramāṇas. The theory of pramāṇa is the pivot of the Nyāya system and, in fact, it is often described as *pramāṇa śāstra* (treatise on pramāṇa). Pramāṇa heads the list of Gautama's sixteen categories and the categories of pramāṇa and *prameya* (object of cognition) have a pre-eminent position in the scheme. In the final analysis the other fourteen categories can be subsumed under one or the other of these two categories. In this list there are three other categories which are intimately connected with the doctrine of pramāṇa, viz. member (*avayava*), fallacy of the hetu or literally spurious cause or reason (*hetvābhāsa*) and familiar instance (*dṛṣṭānta*). The member category represents a form of reasoning in which the four pramāṇas recognized by Gautama are reflected and spurious cause or reason represents those faults or defects which vitiate reasoning. If the reasoning reflects pramāṇas, the faults are the faults of pramāṇas; these are spurious pramāṇas (*pramāṇābhāsa*). The third category of familiar instance is connected with one of the members of reasoning called 'example' (*udāharaṇa*) and one of the pramāṇas, perception. But as a category, it has a status equivalent to that of the other categories connected with the doctrine of pramāṇa.

The formal recognition or non-recognition of different pramāṇas does not necessarily mean that these are not used in the course of the exposition of the system to which the philosophers are committed or of the refutation of the systems to which they are opposed. Moreover, the fact of recognition or non-recognition does not bind the philosophers to similar consequences in their doctrines. For instance, all Indian systems are agreed upon perception as a pramāṇa and at least one of them, the Nyāya, would go as far as to say that all valid cognition is ultimately based on perception. If the materialists can be said to have recognized inference—as it is now believed—this agreement extends to two pramāṇas. In the ordinary way we would expect that any philosophical speculation which was founded on this twin basis would be characterized by broad agreement on fundamentals. But in fact the philosophers are divided on a large number of issues. They do not even agree on the nature, object and fruit (result) of the pramāṇas they seem to have accepted. Instead of consensus philosophy we have the utmost divergences between different systems and even within the technically one system. What they lack in doctrinal consensus they have made good in their social and ethical philosophy. The sophisticated doctrines remained more or less confined to the sophisticated philosophers while their social and ethical doctrines, whether original or borrowed from other sources, percolated to the average man in a form which is too well-known to require any special elaboration in the present context.

I. The Nature and Scope of the Pramana

As already mentioned, pramāṇa is the first in the list of the categories, but curiously enough, Gautama has not defined it in any of his aphorisms. This omission has been made good by the commentators in their introductory comments. These comments provide a framework for the Nyāya doctrine and in view of their importance these are given, as far as possible, in conformity with the language they have used.

According to Vātsyāyana, the pramāṇa is a means of cognizing things, and this is quite evident from the etymology of the word itself (NBh I. 1,3). The pramāṇas must be regarded as rightly effective, because it is only when a thing is known by means of a pramāṇa that it has the power to arouse fruitful and effective activity (*pramāṇataḥ arthapratipattau pravṛttisāmarthyāt arthavat pramāṇam*).[3] There can be no cognition of things except through a pramāṇa nor can fruitful exertion be aroused except when things have been cognized. It is only when the cognizer has apprehended a thing by means of a pramāṇa that he desires either to accept or reject it. The activity of the cognizer stimulated by this desire to accept or reject the thing is known as 'activity' (*pravṛtti*). This activity is said to be 'fruitful' when it becomes related to its fruit (*phalānubandha*); that is to say, when the cognizer undertakes the activity after having desired to acquire or get rid of the thing and, by that activity, actually acquires or discards it (the thing), his activity becomes fruitful; this constitutes the power (*sāmarthya*) of the activity.

The real nature of things (*tattva*) is nothing but 'existence' (*sat*) in the case of that which exists and 'non-existence' (*asat*) in the case of that which does not exist. When 'existence' is apprehended as 'existence' and is therefore apprehended as what it really is and not as something of a contrary nature, i.e. as 'non-existence' (*aviparīta*), then that which is thus apprehended constitutes the 'true nature (*tattva*) of that existence'. Similarly, when 'non-existence' is apprehended as 'non-existence' and is therefore apprehended as what it is (i.e. non-existence) and not as of a contrary nature, then that which is thus apprehended constitutes the true nature (*tattva*) of that non-existence.

The thing (*artha*) which is cognized by means of the pramāṇa is of four kinds : (1) pleasure, (2) source or cause of pleasure (*sukhahetu*), (3) pain, and (4) source or cause of pain (*duḥkha-hetu*). These things are innumerable (*aparisaṃkhyeya*), because living creatures are innumerable. It is only when the pramāṇa duly operates with regard to a thing (*arthavat*) that due success comes to the cognizer (*pramātṛ*), the object of cognition (*prameya*) and cognition itself (*pramiti*). The pramāṇa is therefore the most effective means of cognition.

The cognizer is one who is stimulated to activity by the desire to accept or reject the thing; that by means of which the cognizer obtains the right cognition of the thing is called the 'pramāṇa'; that thing which is rightly known is called the 'object of cognition' (*prameya*). The knowledge of the object (*arthavijñāna*) is called 'right cognition' (*pramiti*). There is no other possibility of any object being duly cognized unless these four factors are present.

The next question considered by Vātsyāyana is: How is it possible to apprehend non-existence by means of a pramāṇa ? This is possible, says the commentator, because when the existence is apprehended the non-existence is not apprehended, and this is like what happens in the case of the lamp. When the lamp illumines, and renders visible, something that is visible, that which is not apprehended in the same manner as that visible thing, is regarded as non-existent. The mental process in this case is as follows: If the thing had existed, it would have been apprehended; as it is not apprehended, it must be concluded not to exist. Exactly the same is the case with the apprehension of non-existence by means of a pramāṇa. When an existent thing is apprehended by means of a pramāṇa, and, at the same time, that which is not (i.e. non-existence) is not apprehended, the conclusion is that this latter does not exist. As in the case of the lamp, the mental process is as follows: 'If the thing had existed, it would have been apprehended; as it is not apprehended, it must be concluded not to exist.' Thus in both cases we find that there is apprehension of the non-existent, only at the time when there is apprehension of the existent thing. This clearly shows that the same pramāṇa which illumines (*prakāśayati*) the existent thing also illumines the non-existent; it is only by means of the pramāṇa whereby that which exists is apprehended, that we apprehend also the non-existence of the non-existent. And it is this existence (*sat*) that Gautama has described in his *Nyāya Sūtra* by means of a collection (*vyūḍha*) of sixteen. These are the sixteen categories of Gautama.

The opening statement of Vātsyāyana is explained by Uddyotakara and his explanation throws further light on what the pramāṇa stands for in the Nyāya system.

1. The purpose of the *Nyāya Sūtra* of Gautama is to enable us to attain supreme felicity through the knowledge of his sixteen categories. When Vātsyāyana says that the pramāṇa must be regarded as rightly effective, he is only reiterating the connection of this Nyāya treatise with its purpose; this is what the treatise actually does.

The treatise or scripture (*śāstra*) in this context denotes a coordinated aggregate or collection of words descriptive of the pramāṇas and other categories (*śāstraṃ punaḥ pramāṇādivācakasamūho vyūhaviśiṣṭaḥ*). A word is an aggregate (*samūha*) of *varṇas* (phonemes); an aggregate of words forms a lecture (*prakarana*); an aggregate of lectures forms a daily lesson (*ānhika*); an aggregate of lessons forms a discourse (*adhyāya*); the aggregate of five discourses constitutes the scripture, the *Nyāya Sūtra* of Gautama. This scripture describes the sixteen categories but the real purpose is to ensure the highest good of men (*puruṣaśreyas*). What distinguishes a scripture of this kind from other works is that it explains the real nature of such objects as are not truly cognized by the ordinary means of knowledge, viz., perception and inference. The subject-matter of the scripture is thus the real nature of things not known by ordinary means. And the man who is authorised to study the scripture is that disciple who is equipped with the inner power.[4]

Men are divided into four classes: those who have right knowledge (wise or learned); those who are devoid of such knowledge; those in a state of doubt as regards the true nature of things; and those who have perverse or distorted views. From amongst these four classes, only those belonging to the first class are qualified to teach; those who fall within the ambit of the other three classes stand in need of knowledge and have therefore to be taught. In cases where such men depend upon the contact of the sense-organs with objects, they learn through perception; where they depend upon perception and remembrance of certain marks or characteristics of things, they learn through inference; where they need instruction in matters which cannot be known through perception and inference, the scripture steps in and imparts knowledge.

The 'good of man' (*puruṣaśreyas*) is of two kinds: pleasure and cessation of pain; pleasure is the seen good and cessation of pain is the unseen good.

The cessation of pain can be partial or complete. The partial cessation is brought about by the removal of temporary agencies (*sādhana*) of pain like a thorn, and the complete or absolute cessation by the removal of all the twenty-one kinds of pain (viz. the body, the six sense-organs and the six kinds of cognition, pleasure and pain). Of these the body is regarded as 'pain' because it is the abode of all painful experiences; the sense-organs, the objects and cognitions are so regarded, because they are the agency (*sādhana*) of painful experiences; pleasure is pain, because it is always accompanied by or subordinate to pain; and pain is regarded as pain by its very nature (*svarūpa*).

The removal of all these different kinds of pain is possible only when such agencies (*sādhana*) as merit (*dharma*) and demerit (*adharma*) are abandoned; merit and demerit are abandoned when they are not produced; those that are produced are abandoned when they are exhausted as a result of the person having undergone all painful and pleasant experiences—experiences which are the results of the merit and demerit mentioned above.

Like the cessation of pain, the cessation of pleasure, which is to be regarded as pain, also constitutes the good of man. Men are of two kinds: those that are possessed by attachment and those that are free from attachment. Attachment consists of desire for objects and non-attachment of the absence of all desire for objects. According to this two-fold division, human activity is also of two kinds. The activity of those who are altogether free from attachment is of only one kind, namely, for the purpose of avoiding the undesirable; these men have only one motive in undertaking any activity, expressed in the form 'May I avoid the undesirable' and they have no desire to acquire any object. But the case of those who are not free from attachment is different. Their activity is directed towards the attainment of the desirable and the avoidance of the undesirable. Further, this activity may or may not bring about its fruit. If a man obtains what he wants or avoids what he wants to avoid, the activity which he undertakes for the purpose leads to the attainment of the result; if he does not obtain what he seeks to obtain or to avoid what he wishes to avoid, the activity that he undertakes for the purpose does not lead to the attainment of the result.

2. Another way to look at the efficiency of the pramāṇa is to classify activity under two heads: according as the pramāṇa leading to the activity is effective or not effective (*tataḥ punaḥ pravṛttir dvaividhyaṃ pramāṇasyārthavad anarthakatvāt*). The true pramāṇa is effective, because through it objects are cognized as they are; the false pramāṇa, on the other hand, is called pramāṇa in a figurative or secondary sense, because it resembles the true pramāṇa in a certain general characteristic. The general feature which allows us to treat the false pramāṇa as a pramaṇa at all, is that both the true pramāṇa and the false pramāṇa enable us to apprehend the general features (*sāmānya*). In view of this two-foldness of the pramāṇas, the activity is effective when one acts after cognizing one's object by means of a true pramāṇa and it is ineffective when one acts after apprehending one's object by means of the false pramāṇas.

3. According to Vātsyāyana, the pramāṇa leads to an effective activity only when a thing is known by a pramāṇa. Against this view it is urged that as there is mutual dependence between the pramāṇa and the activity, neither can be established. If the cognition of the thing by the pramāṇa comes first, how can there be any such definite cognition until its capacity to give rise to fruitful action has been ascertained? If, on the other hand, what comes first is the knowledge of the capability of giving rise to fruitful action, how can there be any

activity or exertion for acquiring or discarding an object unless the object has been cognized ? This objection of mutual dependence (*parasparāpekṣitvād ubhayāsiddhi*), according to Vātsyāyana, can be easily met. There would be force in this objection if the world had a beginning. In fact, the world has no beginning and such mutual dependence is necessarily implied in numerous worldly processes. Hence it is not right to take objection to any one process on this ground alone.

4. According to Uddyotakara, another interpretation of Vātsyāyana's opening statement is to underline the supreme importance (*prādhānya*) of the pramāṇa amongst the four objects (*artha*). The four objects are:

(a) That which has to be avoided (*heya*), viz. pain and the cause of pain (viz. ignorance [*avidyā*]) and desire (*tṛṣṇā*), merit and demerit;

(b) the means of avoiding that which has to be avoided (*hānopāya*), viz. the knowledge of the true nature of things (*tattvajñāna*), i.e. the knowledge of things as they really are;

(c) that which provides the means mentioned under the second above, viz. scripture (*śāstra*);

(d) that which is sought to be attained, viz. emancipation or absence of pain.

Another way of looking at the situation in which the pramāṇa is treated is to give it the highest priority among the four factors involved in cognition: the pramāṇa itself, object of cognition, cognizer and cognition.

The supreme importance of the pramāṇa amongst the set of the four objects is due to the fact that it is the direct cause of the highest good; amongst the set of the four factors involved in cognition the importance is due to the fact that the other three factors depend for their very existence upon the pramāṇa.

Having given various possible interpretations of Vātsyāyana's opening statement, Uddyotakara proceeds to analyse the statement, word by word, and in the course of this analysis he throws further light on the concept of the pramāṇa in the Nyāya system.

(a) The pramāṇa is regarded as 'cause' of cognition because it is from the pramāṇa that the cognition proceeds. It is regarded as 'instrument' because the cognition of objects is accomplished by means of pramāṇas; it is the most efficient means of producing cognitions.

(b) The pramāṇa is the cause of cognition and the character of pramāṇa consists in its being the cause of cognition.

It may be objected that this definition of pramāṇa is not right, because it can apply to the other factors of cognition, the cognizer and the object of cognition. These two are also causes of cognition (*upalabdhihetu*) and since they share this common character with pramāṇa, they too should be endowed with the character of pramāṇa. If the definition is not intended to cover these two factors, it is necessary to indicate the difference between pramāṇa on the one hand, and the cognizer and the object of cognition on the other.

There is, replies Uddyotakara, a difference between the two. The function of the cognizer and the object of cognition lies in, and is duly fulfilled by, the setting of the pramāṇa into activity. The pramāṇa as the instrument, on the other hand, does not have its function fulfilled except when it produces the cognition. And it is for this reason that the pramāṇa, and not the cognizer and the object of cognition, is regarded as the real cause of cognition.

An objection might be raised: if the pramāṇa itself is produced by the cognizer and the object of cognition, the operation of the pramāṇa is itself without any instrument whatsoever. This would be an absurd situation, as without the intervening agency of an instrument, no cognizer (or agent) can operate upon anything. This is not so, says Uddyotakara, because the contact of the sense-organ with the object would be the requisite instrument;[5] it is through the instrumentality of this contact that the pramāṇa is brought into existence by the cognizer and the object of cognition. If, in the bringing about of the pramāṇa, the cognizer and the object of cognition depend upon the contact of the sense-organ with the object, what do they depend upon in the bringing about of this contact (which itself is treated as a pramāṇa or an instrument of cognition)? In this matter they depend upon the sense-organ; the series of agents and instruments goes on *ad infinitum*; what comes afterwards depends upon what has gone before it, and so on; the dependence of the agent upon the instrument can be traced back, without beginning.

Another objection raised against this concept of the pramāṇa is that if the pramāṇa is brought into existence by the cognizer and the object of cognition, then these latter two must exist before the pramāṇa is produced. Until the pramāṇa is there, no person can be known as the 'cognizer' nor can any object be known as the 'object of cognition'. Thus it is not possible for either the cognizer or the object of cognition to have existence prior to the appearance of the pramāṇa. The reason for this is that the words pramāṇa, *prameya* and *pramātṛ* have some sort of practical relation to the action of cognizing. It is not possible for any substance *per se* or mere action *per se* to be a *kāraka* (i.e., a word bearing a practical relation to an action). In fact all words denoting practical relation are used with reference to that which is operative towards the accomplishment of the principal action concerned; they are so operative because they are the substratum of auxiliary actions that lead to that final or principal action (NV I. 1,1).

This argument, which is discussed at length in connection with the validity of the pramāṇas, is countered by a different view of the *kāraka* words. These words are no doubt related to action, but this does not mean that they are used only when actually related to the action at the time when it takes place. In fact, they are used, like the word '*pācaka*' (cook), with reference to the action in the past, the present and the future. If such words were to be used only with reference to the action at the time when they are used, then they could never be used when such action was absent. But we do find such usage. The reason for this usage lies in the potency (*sāmarthya*) of the words themselves. This potency is present at all times. In view of this there is no incongruity in the assertion that the pramāṇa is brought into existence by the cognizer and the object of cognition.

5. Another distinction between pramāṇa on the one hand, and *pramātṛ* and *prameya* on the other, is that the pramāṇa is the most efficient cause of cognition (*sādhakatama*). Consequently, there is no danger of any confusion between them. This characterisation of pramāṇa, says Uddyotakara, is not mere verbal jugglery but certainly has a meaning. No fewer than seven meanings are given.

Since these meanings are not all distinct they are briefly

summarized and not enumerated. The most efficient cause is that presence and absence of which regulates the presence and absence of the effect. When the cognizer and the object of cognition are absent, cognition naturally does not appear; it is only when the former two are present that the cognition occurs; but at the same time it does not follow that it must occur. However, when the pramāṇa is present, the cognition must occur. Accordingly the pramāṇa has primary importance (*atiśaya*) as the most efficient cause.

Even if the two factors, the cognizer and the object of cognition, are present, they do not have any causal efficiency (*kartṛtva*) towards the production of cognition until the pramāṇa appears. In the case of substance, for example, it is the final contact of the component particles which produces that substance. Similarly, pramāṇa is the last to occur in the production of cognition. The fact that cognition follows the pramāṇa immediately also makes the latter the most efficient cause.

Uddyotakara has another kind of contact which makes the pramāṇa the most efficient cause. The contact between the mind and the self is present in all forms of cognition, but it is the pramāṇa which indicates or specifies the contact that leads to a specific cognition.

The production of cognition has two types of cause, the general (*sādhāraṇa*) and the specific (*asādhāraṇa*). The cognizer is a cause which holds good for every cognition, perceptional, inferential, analogic and verbal; equally the object of cognition is a general cause as it is the same in its cognition by all men. But the pramāṇa pertains to each individual cognition that is produced; and it is therefore the principal cause of cognition. It is this predominance (*prādhānya*) that makes it the most efficient cause.

Uddyotakara considers the following Buddhist objection: "Since objects of different pramāṇas are distinct from one another, it is not right to speak of the various pramāṇas as pramāṇa. Each pramāṇa has a distinct object (*viśiṣṭaviṣaya*): sense-perception has for its object specific individuality (*viśeṣa*); inference has generality (*sāmānya*) as its object. Sense-perception cannot apprehend generality nor can inference apprehend specific individuality. And these are the only two pramāṇas."

Uddyotakara answers the objection as follows: In the first place, there are not two but four pramāṇas. Secondly, the objects apprehended are not of two kinds but of three, viz. generality, individuality and uniqueness, (*tadvat*). Thirdly, there is a convergence of pramāṇas (*pramāṇasaṃplava*) as one and the same object is cognized by more than one pramāṇa. For example, the sense-organs, being instruments whereby things are being revealed, are pramāṇas. Among these we find that while each of them has its own specific object, there are many objects common to a number of the sense-organs. Odour, for instance, is the specific object of the olfactory organ, but the earth is perceived by the two senses, the nose and the eye; the cognition of being (*sattā*) and of 'quality-ness' (*guṇatva*) are produced by all the sense-organs.

Object (artha)

The explanation of pramāṇa as given by Vātsyāyana refers to the cognition of the object proceeding from pramāṇa. According to Uddyotakara, the significance of the word 'object' in this context is twofold: In the first place it excludes the cognition which has the pramāṇa for its object. It is only when a person cognizes something as desirable that he undertakes any activity. Secondly, it excludes the cognition of such objects as deserve to be disregarded. The cognition of such objects does not urge the man to undertake any activity; what does urge him to activity is the cognition of the object as the source of either pleasure or pain.

In the account of the pramāṇa, both the words, object (*artha*) and pramāṇa, are essential. It is true that it is only the cognition of an object that can lead to fruitful activity. This implies the agency of pramāṇas without which no cognition can arise. In ordinary usage, we find the word 'pramāṇa' used indiscriminately; sometimes it is used with reference to the true pramāṇas and sometimes it is applied to the spurious pramāṇas (*pramāṇābhāsa*), which are nonetheless called 'pramāṇa' on account of their similarity to the true pramāṇas.

The use of the word '*artha*' in the explanation given by Vātsyāyana, says Uddyotakara, has often been misinterpreted by others. For example, some hold that it means all objects that are desired while others consider that it stands for innumerable (*aparisaṃkhyeya*) objects. Both these interpretations, according to Uddyotakara, are not right: What is really intended is 'purpose' (*prayojana*), and not 'object' (*viṣaya*). The purposes which are served by a pramāṇa cannot be enumerated.

Four Factors of Cognition

According to Vātsyāyana, the act of cognition involves four factors, the cognizer, the object of cognition, the instrument or means of cognition and the cognition. Amongst these the cognizer is the first to be mentioned. This cognizer, according to Uddyotakara, is dependent upon himself (*svatantra*). This dependence can be interpreted in four ways: (a) The cognizer is the consumer of the fruits produced by the active agencies pertaining to the action of cognition; it is the cognizer who is related to such results. (b) It is the cognizer in whom inheres the action proceeding from all the agencies concerned; the cognizer is the substratum of such action. (c) The cognizer sets the agencies concerned into motion. (d) The cognizer is urged to activity by these agencies. The cognizer as agent operates the agencies whose potency has been duly ascertained.

It is through these four factors that things become capable of being acquired or disregarded. The dependence involved in this matter consists in the fact that it is only when a certain thing has been duly cognized as being a source of pleasure or pain that it becomes capable of being used (i.e. either acquired or disregarded); or, when it is cognized as being a source of neither pleasure nor pain that it becomes capable of being disregarded (NV Introductory).

Real Nature of Things (tattva)

According to Vātsyāyana, the real nature of things depends upon the four factors of cognition and this real nature is nothing but 'being' as it is and 'non-being' as it is not. Uddyotakara develops this theme as follows:

Real nature (*tattva*), says Uddyotakara, is that which constitutes the basis of a certain thing being cognized in its essence; there is something in every object by virtue of which the object comes to be known as it is, and it is this something that constitutes the real nature of that object (NV I. 1,1).

Being and non-being are different in character. The former constitutes the object of cognition independently, by itself, while the latter constitutes the object of cognition only through something else, viz. absence. For instance, odour is present in earth but absent in water; the absence of odour in water is apprehended only because of its presence in earth.

The operation of the pramāṇa, as Vātsyāyana has already stated, can be explained on the analogy of the lamp. The lamp makes known things that are present and also those that are not present. What a person does in this situation is as follows: "If there was any perceptible thing, except these I see, I would have perceived it; but since I do not perceive it, it is not in the room." Similarly, if a thing is cognizable, it is cognized by the pramāṇa; but since it is not so cognized, it does not exist.

According to Vātsyāyana, what Gautama has described in his first aphorism on the sixteen categories is the entity (*sat*), and according to Gautama it is the knowledge of the true nature of these categories which can lead to supreme felicity. As 'that' (*tat*) in the word '*tattva*', according to Uddyotakara, covers both entity (*sat*) and non-entity (*asat*), then the question that needs to be considered is whether Gautama has described both the entity and the non-entity in his opening aphorism. The commentator undoubtedly finds himself in a tight corner and the answer he gives is somewhat confusing.

The non-entities, says Uddyotakara, are not described by Gautama, because they are never apprehended by themselves. We may, however, treat the aphorism as if it does describe only those non-entities as well, which are helpful in the attainment of the highest good; he has omitted only those that are not so helpful and therefore not included amongst the four 'purposes of man'. Gautama has done exactly the same thing in the case of the positive entities; only those which are conducive to the attainment of the highest good have been described and others have been ignored (NV Introductory).

The real difficulty that the commentators face is that while Gautama says that the supreme felicity (*niḥśreyasa*) can be attained by the knowledge of his sixteen categories, he does not say that it is necessary for emancipation nor does he mention emancipation in his opening aphorism. According to Vātsyāyana, the sixteen categories enumerated by Gautama in the first aphorism are the categories for the true knowledge of which the *Nyāya Sūtra* has been composed. The aphorism should be taken as stating in brief the purport of the whole treatise. This purport is that the supreme felicity is attained by the knowledge of the essence or true nature of such objects as the self. This same idea is further elaborated in the second aphorism where it is stated that "pain, birth, activity, defect and misapprehension (wrong notion)—on the successive annihilation of these in the reverse order, there follows release", and the sense of this aphorism is that the supreme felicity is attained when one has rightly understood the real nature of (a) that which is fit to be discarded (*heya*) (e.g. pain), along with its causes (i.e. ignorance and desire, merit and demerit, as leading to pain); (b) that which is absolutely destructive of pain (*hāna*) (i.e. true knowledge); (c) the means (*upāya*) of its destruction (viz. scripture); and (d) the goals to be attained (*adhigantavya*) (i.e. supreme felicity). These four classes or kinds of objects (*artha*) are dealt with in treatises of this nature (i.e. like the *Nyāya Sūtra*) (NBh I. 1,1). This is the practice of the sciences of the *ātman* and of the great teachers. These four classes of objects are called '*arthapadāni*' (NV I. 1,2).

The supreme felicity (*niḥśreyasa*), according to Uddyotakara, is of two kinds: seen or perceptible (*dṛṣṭa*) and unseen or imperceptible (*adṛṣṭa*). What follows from the knowledge of the sixteen categories is the seen felicity. Whenever anyone of the categories is cognized, it does not fail to bring about the idea of acquiring, rejecting or indifference, and all this is seen. But the imperceptible felicity—and this is the highest—follows only from the knowledge of the self and other objects of cognition. This was the intention of Gautama, as it is clear from his separate mention of the objects of the pramāṇas (*prameya*) in a separate aphorism (NV I. 1,1).

Convergence of Pramanas (pramanasamplava)

In view of the fact that there is more than one pramāṇa, Vātsyāyana raises the question of their mode of operation: Do the pramāṇas operate in combination or in isolation from one another ? Or, as the question is phrased, have the pramāṇas their object in common or is their operation confined to their respective objects?

As a matter of fact, says Vātsyāyana, we find both ways of operation. For instance, in the case of the self (which is one of the objects of pramāṇa), we witness the following operation:

(a) First we know from the advice of a reliable person (*āptopadeśa*) that the self exists. (b) Next the inference operates upon it, when it is asserted that the marks of the self are desire, aversion, effort, pleasure, pain and consciousness. This is the definition of the self as given by Gautama (NS I. 1,10). We infer the existence of the self from these marks. (c) The self is also perceived by a peculiar contact of the self with the mind. This perception is the result of yogic concentration (*yogasamādhi*) and only a yogin can have such a perception.

Another instance of the combined operation is that of fire: (a) When a reliable person says that 'there is fire here', we have the cognition of fire from this advice. (b) Drawing nearer to the place of the fire, if we see smoke, we infer, from this, the existence of fire. (c) Coming to the place of the fire itself, we directly perceive the fire.

In both instances of the self and the fire, the communication of the reliable person (or *śabdapramāṇa*), inference (*anumāna*) and perception combine to operate upon one and the same object (NBh I. 1,3).

In the case of certain things we find that a thing is amenable to only one particular pramāṇa. For example, that 'the *Agnihotra*—this is the name of a sacrifice—should be performed by one desiring heaven', one can know only from the words of the Veda. An ordinary man does not know of any signs of heaven from which he can infer the existence of heaven nor can he perceive it directly. Another instance is that of the source of sound. We hear the sound of thunder and from this we infer the source, thunder; in this neither perception nor scripture (*āgama*) operates; in so far as thunder is concerned, only inference operates. In the case of our hand we have direct perception (NBh I. 1,3).

In his introductory exposition of the pramāṇa doctrine, Uddyotakara, as we have seen, has mentioned the possibilities of several pramāṇas operating upon one object as well as upon many objects. Each sense-organ, for instance, has its own specific object, while there are many objects common to a number of these organs. The sense-organs in this context are the pramāṇas. In this context the commentator mentions the following objection to this Nyāya concept. If the object has already been cognized by the agency of one pramāṇa, the other pramāṇa would be absolutely useless; if the latter pramāṇa were to bring about the cognition of that same object which had already been cognized by the agency of the former pramāṇa, then its operation would be as useless and superfluous as the pounding of the grain that has already been pounded.

This objection, according to Uddyotakara, is based on a misunderstanding of what is meant by the convergence of pramāṇas. This convergence does not mean that the object cognized by means of inference and other pramāṇas is of the same kind as that cognized by means of sense-perception. When an object is cognized by sense-perception, it is connected with the sense-organ; when the same object is cognized by inference, it is not connected with the sense-organ; when the same object is cognized only as bearing a certain name (*saṃjñāsaṃjñisaṃbandhapratipatti*), the cognition is obtained through the pramāṇa, analogy (*upamāna*); when the same object is cognized by trustworthy assertion (*śabdollekha*) the cognition is obtained through the agency of the scripture (*āgama*). When the pramāṇas operate on different objects, there is a distinct line of demarcation between them. Even though these frequently combine to operate, several pramāṇas are not useless. For there are cases where there is no such convergence of pramāṇas (Introductory NV).

II. Validity of the Pramanas

In the examination of pramāṇas in general, Gautama deals with the various objections[6] raised against their validity on the ground that they cannot be connected with the three times. He devotes twelve aphorisms to this subject (NS II. 1,8-19) and these are as follows:

Objections

(1) Perception and other pramāṇas are not established, as they are impossible at all the three times (NS II. 1,8).

(2) If pramāṇa already existed, it could not have arisen from the contact of the sense-organ with its object (NS II. 1,9).

(3) If pramāṇa comes into existence after the object of cognition has come into existence, the object of cognition is not established by the pramāṇas (NS II. 1,10).

(4) If the two came into existence simultaneously, then, inasmuch as each cognition (*buddhi*) is restricted to its own object, there can be no succession (*kramabhāva*) of cognitions (NS II. 1,11).

Reply

(1) Since it is impossible to connect the pramāṇas with the three times [retorts Gautama] the denial of the pramāṇas is equally impossible (NS II. 1,12).

(2) Moreover, the denial itself cannot be established if all the pramāṇas are denied (NS II. 1,13).

(3) [If, alternatively, the objector says that] his denial is based on a certain pramāṇa, then there is no denial of the validity of the pramāṇa (NS II. 1,14).

(4) The pramāṇas are established in the manner in which a musical instrument is established by its sound, and the establishing of the pramāṇas is not affected by the objection concerning the three times (NS II. 1,15).

(5) An object of cognition is established in the same way as a weighing balance (NS II. 1,16).

Objection

(1) If the pramāṇas are established by means of pramāṇas, then these latter will require other pramāṇas for their establishment (NS II. 1,17).

(2) Or, if a pramāṇa does not require another pramāṇa for its establishment, then the object of cognition could be established without any pramāṇa (NS II. 1,18).

Reply

It is not so; the pramāṇas are recognized in the same way as a lamp is accepted as illumining its object (NS II. 1,19).

(1) *Objection*

Vātsyāyana explains the objection as follows: The character

of pramāṇa cannot be attributed to perception, etc., because it is impossible to connect them with any of the three times; it is not possible for them to precede, synchronise with, or follow the objects cognized. For example, if perception, which is the cognition of such objects as colour, etc., already exists, and the objects come into existence after it, then perception cannot be said to be produced by the sense-object contact. If the pramāṇa comes into existence after its object (*prameya*), how can the object be cognized and thus become an object of cognition? It is only when a thing is cognized by a pramāṇa that it becomes established as an object of cognition. If the pramāṇa and its object both come into existence simultaneously there can be no necessity of a sequence among cognitions. Various objects of sense-perception can exist at one and the same time, e.g. colour and smell exist in a flower at the same time. As a matter of fact, all such cognitions with reference to their respective objects are found to appear one after the other. If we hold that perception is simultaneous with its object, we will have to admit that the colour and the smell can be perceived at one and the same time, i.e. our perception of colour will have to be treated as simultaneous with our perception of smell. This is absurd because two acts of perception or two cognitions cannot take place at one and the same time. Each cognition pertains to, or is restricted to, its own object. Since there is an order of succession in our cognitions, perception cannot be regarded as simultaneous with its object. Besides, even if such a sequence is accepted as essential, it would be contrary to Gautama's view that the presence of mind is indicated by the non-simultaneity of cognitions.

These three are the only possibilities in regard to the existence (or relation) of the pramāṇa and object of cognition (*prameya*). Since each one of them can be realized, perception and other pramāṇas cannot be regarded as pramāṇa (NBh II. 1, 1-8).

Reply

Vātsyāyana explains Gautama's reply as follows: This objection is based upon a misconception. As a matter of fact, the cause of apprehension (*upalabdhihetu*) and the object of apprehension (*upalabdhiviṣaya*) do not follow any definite rule or order; there is no such restriction that the former should come into existence before or simultaneously with, or after, the latter. It is therefore necessary to treat each case as we find it and state the position accordingly. The following examples illustrate this absence of any definite rule about the cause of apprehension and object of apprehension.

(1) In some cases the cause appears first and the object afterwards; e.g. in the case of the apprehension of things which come into existence while the sun is shining, the sunlight which is the cause of apprehension exists already and the objects come into existence afterwards.

(2) In some cases the object comes first and the cause afterwards, e.g. the lamp just lit, which is the cause, illumines and makes perceptible objects already in existence. Another striking example is that of a hidden musical instrument and its sound. In this case we find that by means of the sound, which comes into existence after the musical instrument, we infer the existence of the musical instrument which has been in existence prior to the sound. Here it is the musical instrument that is to be made known and the sound is the means by which it is made known. The inference is that the lute is being played or that the flute is being played; the particular instrument is inferred by the peculiarity of the sound produced by it. Thus in this case we apprehend the object (e.g. the musical instrument) which has a prior existence, by means of sound, which comes into existence after the object. The pramāṇa follows the object of cognition.[7]

(3) In some cases the cause of apprehension and the object of apprehension come into existence simultaneously, e.g. the apprehension of fire is brought about by means of smoke.

In view of these illustrations it is obvious that there is no fixed rule or order regarding the manner in which the cause of apprehension (viz. pramāṇa) and the object of apprehension (viz. *prameya*) should appear. And from this it follows that the argument from the impossibility of a relation with the three times (*traikālyāsiddhi*) has no basis in fact (NBh II. 1,11).

Uddyotakara comments on this objection as follows: The proposition—'The character of pramāṇas cannot belong to the pramāṇas recognized in the Nyāya system, because it is impossible to connect them with any of the three times' is untenable. In the first place, the hetu, 'the impossibility of connecting them with any of the three times', is not one which is perceived. Secondly, the proposition involves a contradiction between its own terms. It can only mean that pramāṇas do not indicate the existence of their objects, which is self-contradictory. To name them as pramāṇas and then assert that they do not indicate the existence of things is like the assertion 'this thing is not known'. To call it 'this thing' and then to say 'it is not known' is obviously self-contradictory. Certainly, the expression pramāṇa would be meaningless if it did not indicate the existence of things.

Further, to deny to the pramāṇas the character of being pramāṇa does not amount to the denial of pramāṇas themselves; it is a denial of their particular character only, viz. the character of being pramāṇa (*pramāṇatva*). The character of being pramāṇa is a property (*dharma*) and in denying this property, it may be argued, the denial of the things possessing that property is implied. This is not right, as the property is not independent of that of which it is the property. Besides, if the pramāṇas do not exist, there is no way of establishing their non-existence; the pramāṇas are our only means of establishing their existence.

Further, to deny some pramāṇas would imply that there are others that are admitted. On the other hand, if it is maintained that there are no pramāṇas, an argument becomes self-contradictory.

If the opponent contends that what he is denying is only the character of being pramāṇa (*pramāṇatva*) and not the very existence of pramāṇas, this would mean that the existence of a pramāṇa is distinct from its *pramāṇatva*. But then the distinction cannot be justified.

In the argument of the opponent the hetu, the impossibility of connecting the pramāṇas with any of the three times (*traikālyāsiddhi*), is not co-substrate (*vyadhikaraṇa*) with the subject of the proposition, viz. the pramāṇas. The impossibility (*asiddhi*) belongs to the three times (*traikālya*) and not to the pramāṇas which are the subject of the proposition. If the hetu means that the pramāṇas do not serve their purpose at any of the three times, then the hetu is superfluous; the proposition means that the so-called pramāṇas do not serve their purpose. Thus the hetu does not prove the proposition[8] (NV II. 1,11).

2. *Objection*

According to Vātsyāyana, the second objection urged against the Nyāya position is as follows: if the pramāṇa is regarded as coming into existence after the object of cognition has come into existence, then, at the time when the pramāṇa is not actually bringing about the apprehension of an object, the object cannot be called the object of cognition (NBh II. 1,11).

Reply

According to Vātsyāyana, this objection, if pressed, would destroy the basis of ordinary linguistic expressions. The application of a name to the three times rests on the possibility of the requisite operation at all the three times. The application of the name 'pramāṇa' is due to the fact that what is so named is the cause of apprehension, and this fact pertains to all the three times. When we give the name pramāṇa to the cause of apprehension, we use one of the three expressions: (a) This has brought about the apprehension; (b) this brings about the apprehension; (c) this will bring about the apprehension. Since the hetus of naming pertain to all the three times, past, present and future, the name also should be taken as pertaining to all the three times. Similarly, when we use the name '*prameya*' (object of cognition) what is meant is that it has been apprehended, it is apprehended, or it will be apprehended (NBh II. 1,11).

3. *Objection*

Vātsyāyana states the objection against the Nyāya view as follows: The assertion that the pramāṇas cannot be regarded as pramāṇas as it is impossible to connect them with any of the three times (i.e. past, present and future) seems to suggest that the objector denies the pramāṇa altogether.

Reply

Anyone who denies the pramāṇa altogether should be asked: What is meant to be accomplished by such a denial? If it is meant to set aside the possibility (*saṃbhava*) of the pramāṇas, the possibility of the pramāṇas is really accepted; for it is only what exists that can be set aside. Since there is a possibility of the pramāṇas, they cannot be denied altogether. If the denial is meant to make known the impossibility of the pramāṇas, then the denial itself becomes endowed with the character of pramāṇa; the denial becomes the cause of the apprehension of the impossibility of pramāṇas (NBh II. 1,11).

If all pramāṇas are denied, the denial itself cannot be established. The hetu for the denial of the pramāṇas is 'because they cannot be connected with any of the three times'. To corroborate this hetu an example (*udāharaṇa*) is required. An example can only be furnished through perception, which is itself a pramāṇa. If even perception is denied, the so-called hetu ceases to be hetu altogether; and as a result, the whole argument collapses.

4. *Objection*

Vātsyāyana explains the objection as follows: The denial of the pramāṇas, it is urged, can be invested with the character of pramāṇa (NBh II. 1,12).

Reply

Explaining the reply Vātsyāyana says that this argument goes against the basis of the opponent's own objection to the Nyāya view. If the denial exists before the thing denied, what is there that could be denied ? If the denial followed the thing denied, then the thing cannot be denied; for the denial is not in existence. If the denial and the thing denied came into existence simultaneously, the denial would be absolutely futile; for the thing has already been recognised as 'denied'. Thus the assertion of the objector, embodying as it does a denial, is found to be impossible. And the denial being impossible, it is established that the pramāṇas are genuine pramāṇas (NBh II. 1,12).

If the contention of the opponent means that the character of pramāṇa really belongs to the pramāṇas that are embodied in his own argument, then he cannot refuse to accept the same character of pramāṇa also in these pramāṇas embodied in the reasoning that may be used against him. This means that the opponent cannot deny all pramāṇas, as there is really no difference in the two sets of pramāṇas. And if this is his position, there is no justification for his denial of these pramāṇas (NBh II. 1, 14).

According to Uddyotakara, the denial advocated by the opponent is not possible with regard to the three times. He has already admitted that the denial, 'the pramāṇas do not serve any useful purpose' has the character of pramāṇa and he cannot therefore use it against the Nyāya view without involving himself in a self-contradiction. But the point and the counter-point in this debate do not stop here. The objector contends that by urging, as the Naiyāyika does, that the denial is not possible, as it cannot be connected with the three times, then the Naiyāyika must admit the force of his own contention that 'the pramāṇas cannot be regarded as pramāṇas, because they cannot be connected with any of the three times'. This contention, says Uddyotakara, is not valid for the simple reason that what he has done is merely to show that the reasoning of the objector is contrary to the latter's own doctrine. When the objector says that what cannot serve its purpose at any of the three times cannot be regarded as a cause (*sādhaka*), he thereby accepts the position of a man, says Uddyotakara, who wishes to burn other people by the fire in his own hand; but in fact, he will only burn his own fingers! Further, the denial that the objector makes in the form 'the pramāṇas do not accomplish their purpose' can mean either the denial of the efficiency of the pramāṇas or of their very existence. If it is the former, the existence of the pramāṇas is not really denied.

In this debate, says Uddyotakara, there are two assertions: (1) the pramāṇas cannot be regarded as pramāṇa, because they cannot be connected with any of the three times; (2) the pramāṇas should be regarded as pramāṇas, because they are connected with the three times. If these assertions mean the same thing, says Uddyotakara, it is better to have the second assertion; we do not have the two negatives of the first and thus it is much simpler and shorter. Further, if we know that these two assertions in fact mean the same thing, we can only do so by a pramāṇa. But then the position of the opponent becomes self-contradictory. If we do not know it by a pramāṇa but by some other means, then that 'other means' would also be a pramāṇa. In that case the difference amounts to one of nomenclature only.

Further, when the opponent speaks of the non-existence of pramāṇas, to whom and how does he do it ? Who, then, is the speaker ? If he says 'he is telling it to one who does not know it, and the speaker is one who knows it', we have to ask him how he knows it. If he knows it by a pramāṇa, then he admits the pramāṇa and his position becomes self-contradictory. If he knows it by some other means, this means will have to be cognized by some pramāṇa. Further, how does he know the difference between the speaker and the listener ? If he knows the difference, he has to admit the existence of the pramāṇa whereby he knows the difference. If he does not know the difference, he cannot explain how and whom he has addressed. In either case his position becomes absurd or self-contradictory. Last but not least, if the pramāṇas do not exist as the opponent maintains, how does he know that they do not exist ? If he offers pramāṇas in support of his contention, he stultifies himself; if he does not, his purpose cannot be accomplished. Thus the more we examine the arguments of the opponent, says Uddyotakara, the more do we find them crumbling away !

Pramāṇa and prameya as noun functions (*kāraka*)

(1) According to Vātsyāyana, the names pramāṇa and *prameya*, are applied according to circumstances. Such application depends upon certain causes that determine the name. Such a cause in the case in question consists in the fact that (a) that which is the means of bringing about a cognition is called 'pramāṇa'; (b) that which is the object cognized is called '*prameya*'; and (c) when that which, though itself a cognized object, happens to be a means of cognition of something else, then that something may be called pramāṇa and *prameya*. This is clearly brought out in the illustration of a weighing balance given by Gautama (NS II. 1,16). The weighing balance is called 'pramāṇa' when it is the means of bringing about the cognition of the exact weight of the thing weighed; the object weighed, e.g. gold, is called '*prameya*'; but when the object thus weighed, gold, is made the means of testing another balance, then in the cognition of the accuracy of this second balance, it becomes the pramāṇa and this second balance becomes the *prameya*.

This convention regarding the application of the names, pramāṇa and *prameya*, according to circumstance, applies to all objects mentioned by the philosophers (*tantrārtha*). For instance, Gautama has included the self among the *prameyas* because it is an object of cognition. But it is the cognizer (*pramātṛ*) also, because with reference to the action of cognizing, it is the self-dependent agent. Similarly, apprehension (*buddhi*) is pramāṇa because it is the means of cognizing things; it becomes *prameya* when it is itself cognized; when it is neither the means nor the object of any cognition, it comes to be known as mere apprehension (*pramiti*). The same convention applies to other objects mentioned by Gautama (NBh II. 1,16).

The words pramāṇa and *prameya* are *kāraka* words, i.e. they are expressive of action and declension. The word pramāṇa is the instrument of cognition and *prameya* its object. As words expressive of the noun function, they conform to the nature of nouns. The expression 'noun function' is applied neither to the mere substance nor to the mere action, but to that which, while being endowed with a particular action of its own, becomes the means of the accomplishment of the principal action. Since the words pramāṇa and *prameya* imply noun functions, they cannot renounce what is in the nature of these functions (NBh II. 1,16).

That this is the nature and significance of *kāraka* words can be illustrated by their declension. The nominative, for instance, applies neither to the substance alone nor to the action alone but to that which, independently by itself, becomes the means by which the act is performed. For example, when we say 'the tree stands' the 'tree' is called the nominative (*kartṛ*) because in regard to its own action of standing, it is independent (*svatantra*); in the sentence 'He sees the tree', the same 'tree' is called the object (*karma*) because it is that which is most desired to be got at by the action of 'seeing'; in the sentence 'He indicates the moon by the tree', the same tree is called 'instrument' (*karaṇa*) because it is the means by which the moon is pointed out; in the sentence 'He is pouring water for the tree' the tree is called the dative (*saṃpradāna*) because it is that which is the target for the pouring of water; in the sentence 'The leaf falls from the tree' the tree is called the ablative (*upādāna*) because it is what remains stationary while it is the leaves that move. When we say 'Birds are on the tree' the tree is the locative (*adhikaraṇa*) because it is the support of the birds.

The grammatical concepts explained by Vātsyāyana have been worked out in detail by Uddyotakara. His exposition is of interest, but since it would divert our attention from the main trend of argument, it is given in the Appendix.

Pramāṇas and anavasthā (infinite regress)

The Nyāya concept of pramāṇa and *prameya* as names of agencies (*kāraka*) and their application according to circumstances is challenged on the following grounds:

Perception and other pramāṇas are pramāṇas as they are causes of the action of cognizing and they are also *prameyas* as they are the objects of the action of cognizing. We have such assertions as 'I know this by perception', 'I know this by inference', 'I know this by analogy', and 'I know this by scripture' (*āgama*). In these assertions perception, inference, analogy and scripture figure as 'pramāṇa'. We have also such assertions as 'My cognition is perceptional', 'My cognition is inferential', 'My cognition is analogical' and 'My cognition is scriptural'. In these assertions perception, inference, analogy and scripture are apprehended as '*prameya*'. Similarly, perception and other pramāṇas, when defined, become known and thus become objects of cognition.

In this context the question that needs to be considered is: Is this cognition of perception and other pramāṇas brought about by the instrumentality of another set of pramāṇas or without other pramāṇas ? If perception and other pramāṇas are apprehended by means of the pramāṇas, this means that the pramāṇas by means of which they are apprehended are distinct from perception and other pramāṇas. This involves *anavasthā* (infinite regress): one pramāṇa will have to be apprehended by another, this latter again by means of another, and so on, *ad infinitum.* The infinite regress does not really arise in this case. But if it did, we would be faced with the prospect of a total abolition of all pramāṇas (*sarvapramāṇa-vilopa*). If the pramāṇas are not to lead to their own respective cognition, there is no reason why they should operate with regard to the objects of cognition (*prameya*) such as the self,etc. These two cases are exactly alike (NBh II. 1,18).

That the objection of *anavasthā* is not valid can be illustrated by the similarity between the cognition of a pramāṇa and the light of a lamp. The light of the lamp, when it is an aid to an act of perception, is a pramāṇa in the perception of a visible object, but it is itself also cognized by another perception through its contact with the eye. That is to say, the light is a pramāṇa when an object is seen with its help and is a *prameya* when it is itself seen. Similarly, from the knowledge of the fact that the presence and absence of seeing are in accordance with the presence and the absence of the lamp, this lamp is inferred as the cause of seeing. Here the lamp is cognized by inference. When we hear the expression 'Fetch a lamp into a dark room', we cognize the lamp by means of trustworthy or reliable assertion (*āptopadeśa*).

In the case of the lamplight we thus find that though a pramāṇa, it is itself cognized by means of perception and other pramāṇas. In the same fashion perception and the other pramāṇas are cognized by means of perception and the other pramāṇas, and not by means of other pramāṇas. For instance, perception involves the following factors: (a) the sense-organ, (b) the objects perceived, (c) the sense-object contact, and (d) the cognition produced by this sense-object contact. Each one of these factors is cognized by means of pramāṇas: (a) the sense-organs are cognized by means of the inference based on the fact that each sense apprehends the object within the sphere of its capacity. The inference is in the form: the visual sense-organ exists, because we have the cognition of colour, which could not be possible except by means of the visual organ. (b) The objects are perceived by the pramāṇa of perception. (c) The sense-object contacts are cognized by the inference based upon obstructions (*āvaraṇa*). The inference is in the form: The perception must be due to actual sense-object contact, because we find that there is absence of perception whenever sense-object contact is absent by reason of obstructions to such contact. (d) The cognition produced by the sense-object contact is apprehended, just like pleasure, etc., through its inherence in the self as accompanied by a special contact of the mind with the cognizing self. Similarly, every other pramāṇa can be analysed and it will be found that the various factors involved are cognized by one or the other of the four pramāṇas of Gautama.

From this analysis of the instance of the light of the lamp, it is thus clear that the lamp-light itself is visible and it also is the means by which other visible things are seen; in the former case it is called the object of cognition and in the latter the pramāṇa. It follows that according to circumstances the same thing may be called an object of cognition or a pramāṇa. The similarity with the lamp shows that the cognition of pramāṇas is brought about neither by a different set of pramāṇas nor without the assistance of the pramāṇa altogether.

It may be argued that perception, etc., cannot be apprehended by perception, etc. themselves, as a thing is always apprehended by means of something other than itself but not by itself. This objection is not valid as in reality individual things differ from each other but they are similar in virtue of their generic character (*lakṣaṇasāmānya*). The character of perception, for example, belongs to, and covers many individual things, viz. individual perceptions. In the case of inference, we have the cognition of water in the well by means of water itself drawn from that well. The same is the case with the cognizing self and the mind. When we have such cognitions as 'I am happy', or 'I am unhappy', we find that the cognizing self is apprehended by itself. When we say that the non-simultaneity of cognitions is indicative of the mind, it means that the inference proving the existence of the mind is brought about by means of the mind itself.

It may be argued that when it comes to the question of cognition of oneself and one's mind, circumstances are different. The cognizing self does not cognize itself (i.e. becomes an object of cognition). The circumstances are different, says Vātsyāyana, but that does not alter the position. When the cognizer cognizes himself or his mind cognizes itself, he or it does so exactly in the same manner as when he cognizes or the mind apprehends other things. This mode of operation is exactly the same as that of perception.

Furthermore, there is no possibility of there being anything that cannot be apprehended by the four pramāṇas. As a matter of fact, no one can indicate any such thing, for the simple reason that everything, existing as well as non-existing, is actually found to be apprehended by the four pramāṇas. This is an undisputed fact of ordinary experience (NBh II. 1.19).

The instance of the lamplight cited by Gautama, as we have

seen, is meant to establish the proposition that the pramāṇas are cognized by themselves. Some philosophers have apparently mistaken the purpose of the instance. They have detached it from Gautama's proposition and interpreted his aphorism on the subject to mean that just as the lamplight is seen without the light of any other lamp, so also are the pramāṇas apprehended without other pramāṇas.

In this argument the independence of the pramāṇas is based upon the fact that the perception of one lamp does not require another. If this be so, says Vātsyāyana, we might as well say that the pramāṇa is superfluous for the apprehension of the object of cognition. Thus if the instance of the lamplight is understood in the proper context of Gautama's aphorism, then there is no danger of infinite regress. If perception and other pramāṇas are apprehended by perception and other pramāṇas, this can be explained by the fact that all these pramāṇas are sometimes objects of cognition and at other times are instruments of cognition. It is only on the basis of the actual recognition of this difference that it is possible for us to carry on all our business for the purpose of acquiring merit, prosperity, happiness and emancipation and also for the purpose of avoiding the opposites. Ordinary usage can be explained on this basis (NBh II. 1,19).

III. Status of four additional Pramanas

According to Gautama there are four distinct pramāṇas but there are other philosophers who recognize additional pramāṇas. Gautama mentions four such additional pramāṇas, viz. historical tradition (*aitihya*), implication (*arthāpatti*), inclusion (*saṃbhava*) and absence (*abhāva*), without explaining them. Vātsyāyana has, however, explained each of them as follows:

(1) *Historical Tradition*

When an assertion in the form 'So they say' is handed down in a regular order and the exact person who made the assertion is not known, we have the 'historical tradition' as a pramāṇa (NBh II. 2,1). 'So they say' of Vātsyāyana becomes 'So the old men say' for Uddyotakara (NV II. 2,1).

(2) *Implication*

The Sanskrit term for implication, *arthāpatti,* means getting at a thing or fact on the basis of another thing or fact. When a certain fact having been asserted, another fact is implied, we have the pramāṇa known as 'implication'. For instance, when it is asserted that 'if there are no clouds there is no rain', what is implied is that 'if there are clouds, there is rain' (NBh II. 2,1).

(3) *Inclusion*

When the cognition of the presence of one thing follows from the cognition of another thing, which is invariably concomitant with the former, we have the pramāṇa called 'inclusion'. For instance, from the cognition of the presence of the 'quarter maund' follows that of the presence of the 'two seers and a half'; and from the cognition of the 'two seers and a half' follows the cognition of the presence of the 'seer' (NBh II. 2,1).

(4) *Absence*

Absence is contrary to what is present. For instance, the absence of raining conveys the presence of the contact of the clouds with the high winds. It is only when there is some such obstruction that there is no action of raining, which would otherwise take place by reason of the force of gravity in the drops (NBh II. 2,1).

This pramāṇa is further explained by Uddyotakara as follows:

Absence is based upon the cognition of the opposite to what is present. When there is an obstacle in the shape of the contact of clouds with high winds, the effect of gravity is counteracted and there is no rainfall. Consequently, when it is found that no rain fell one recognizes the presence of the contrary, viz. the contact of clouds with high winds (NV II. 2,1).

The recognition of the additional four pramāṇas, says Gautama, is no contradiction, since historical tradition is not different from verbal testimony (*śabda*) and implication, inclusion and absence are not different from inference (NS II. 2,2). Gautama has defined verbal testimony as the assertion of a reliable person and this definition, says Vātsyāyana, covers historical tradition. The difference between the two, as he puts it, is obliterated by their similarity. Unless historical tradition is known to have originated from a reliable person, it is not accepted as a pramāṇa. Inference consists in the cognition, through the perceptible, of the imperceptible related to it and precisely the same is the case with implication, inclusion and absence.

What happens in the case of implication is this: on our cognizing what is asserted in a certain statement, there arises also a cognition of what is not asserted in it; this latter cognition is the result of the relation of the opposition (*pratyanīkabhāva*) between what is asserted and what is not asserted. Or, as Uddyotakara puts it, what constitutes the subject of implication is the affirmation of one thing on the basis of the denial of another thing. For example, when there is the negative statement 'the man does not eat in the day' what is implied is the affirmative statement 'he eats at night' (NBh & NV II. 2,2).

In the case of inclusion, what happens is this: The composite and the component being related to each other by the relation of invariable concomitance, the cognition of the former gives rise to the cognition of the latter. Thus, it is but a case of inference. So far as absence is concerned, what happens is this: of two things, one is found to be present while the other is not present and the contrast between the present and the absent is well-known. If it is then observed that a certain effect does not come about even when its cause is present, we infer that there must be something obstructing the operation of the cause. Absence, says Vātsyāyana, is thus nothing but inference. According to Uddyotakara, both inclusion and absence, like implication, belong to the *sāmānyatodṛṣṭa* type of inference.

These additional four pramāṇas are undoubtedly 'pramāṇas but the Nyāya view is that these are not distinct pramāṇas. And thus there is no contradiction, as Gautama says, between the opinion of the philosophers who advocate these pramāṇas and his own view that there are four pramāṇas (NS & NBh II. 2,3).

Implication

Gautama considers the following objection: implication cannot be treated as a pramāṇa because it leads to uncertainty (NS II. 2,3). The assertion that 'there is rain when there are clouds', when it is made on the basis of another assertion that there is no rain when there are no clouds, is not valid. As a matter of fact, sometimes it so happens that even though clouds are present there is no rain (NBh II. 2,3).

If there is any uncertainty, says Gautama, in reply, it is because what is not implication is treated as implication (NS II. 2,4). According to Vātsyāyana, the objection is based on a complete misunderstanding of the general principle that underlies implication as a pramāṇa. From the assertion that when the cause is absent the effect is not present, we presume its obverse that when the cause is present, the effect is present. Existence is the obverse of non-existence. Certainly, this presumption that the effect is produced when the cause is present is never found to fail in any single instance; that is to say, there is not a single instance where the effect is produced when the cause is not present. It is not, therefore, right to treat presumption as uncertain. In a situation where the effect does not appear even when the cause is present — and this is due to causal operation being obstructed by something, this is indeed the characteristic of all causes, but this is not what the pramāṇa of implication is about. The object of an implication is: The effect is produced when the cause is present, i.e. the production of the effect is never unconcomitant with the presence of the cause. In view of this, it is obvious that when the opponent denies the character of pramāṇa to implication, he is thinking of those instances of implication which are not really implication (NBh II. 2,4).

Further, the denial itself, says Gautama, is invalid because it leads to uncertainty (NS II. 2,5). The denial is in the form of the sentence 'Implication is not a pramāṇa as it is uncertain'. What this sentence denies, says Vātsyāyana, is the fact that implication is a pramāṇa and not that the implication as such exists. Consequently, this denial itself becomes uncertain, and therefore is invalid (NBh II. 2,5).

It may be argued that certainty regarding the existence of implication as such does not amount to a certainty regarding that implication as a pramāṇa (NBh II. 2,6). If the denial is valid, says Gautama in reply, there can be no invalidity in implication (NS II. 2,6). What is involved in implication is that the cause remains a cause whether or not the effect is produced; for there can be an obstruction in the production of the effect (NBh II. 2,6). Without knowing what is meant by invalidity or uncertainty, the opponent asserts that presumption cannot be regarded as a pramāṇa as it is uncertain.[9] And this, says Uddyotakara, is nothing better than the babble of a lunatic and can be dismissed with the contempt that it deserves. (NV II. 2,6) !

Absence (abhāva)

According to Gautama absence is not a distinct pramāṇa. His views on the subject take the form of refutation of the arguments which are advanced to establish it as a pramāṇa.

Objection

Absence is not a pramāṇa, because it is not an object of cognition (NS II. 2,7).

Reply

Where several [pieces of cloth] are marked, since there are those unmarked which are marked out by the absence of marks, absence is established as an object of cognition (NS II. 2,8).

[If the objector says that] there can be no absence without the thing [first] being present, [Gautama replies] no, because the mark can be [present] on something else (NS II. 2,9).

[The objector retorts] But the presence [or establishment] of the marks [on the marked pieces] is no reason for there being [an absence of them] on the unmarked pieces of cloth (NS II. 2,10).

[Gautama answers] No, [the absence of the marks] is established by the presence of the marks [elsewhere] (NS II. 2,11).

[The answer continues] Also, because there can be an absence [of a thing] prior to its production (NS II. 2,12).

The objections and Gautama's answers are further explained by the commentators as follows:

(1) Regarding the first objection, i.e. there is nothing which can be cognized through the instrument of absence, it is our ordinary experience, says Vātsyāyana, that many objects are indeed cognized by means of this pramāṇa. It is, therefore, sheer impudence on the part of the opponent to deny this status to non-existence (NBh II. 2,7).[10]

Of the vast number of things cognized by this means, only a

few of them are indicated. Suppose there are a number of things some of which have a specific mark and others have none. A man is asked to fetch those things which bear no mark. In this situation he can identify the things which bear no mark and fetch them as ordered. The absence of marks is thus clearly an indication of his cognition.

(2) The second objection of the opponent is that where a certain thing, having existed, ceases to exist, there alone its non-existence is possible. In the case of the unmarked pieces of cloth where the marks have never existed, however, the marks cannot be said to have ceased to exist after having existed there. Now then can any non-existence of these marks be possible in this case? This objection, says Vātsyāyana, can be simply answered. What happens in this case is that the man who has been asked to fetch the unmarked pieces of cloth sees the presence of marks in certain pieces; on perceiving the absence of marks in these other pieces, he cognizes the unmarked pieces (NBh II. 2,9).

This objection, as Uddyotakara remarks, is based upon a misunderstanding of Gautama's view. What is suggested is not that a thing is non-existent where it exists but that when the man perceives the marked pieces of cloth, he recognizes others by the absence of marks (NBh & NV II. 2,9).

(3) The third objection raised by the opponent is that the Nyāya view is self-contradictory. The presence of the marks is in the marked pieces of the cloth. The absence of these marks present in the marked pieces is in the unmarked pieces. How can this absence or non-existence be the cause of any cognition? What we maintain, says Vātsyāyana, is not that there is absence or non-existence of these marks that are present but something entirely different. The marks are present in some pieces of cloth and not present in others. When a person, looking for these marks, does not find them present in these latter pieces, he comes to recognize them by means of that absence or non-existence of the marks. It is thus that the non-existence becomes an instrument of cognition (NBh II. 2,10 & 11). Further, such non-existence is quite possible. In fact, non-existence is of two kinds: non-existence of a thing before it has come into existence and non-existence of a thing, due to its destruction, after it has come into existence. The

non-existence of the marks that obtains in the unmarked pieces of cloth is that of the former kind (NBh II. 2,12). This kind of non-existence is quite conceivable, while the second kind is obviously impossible. The marks cannot be destroyed where they have never existed (NV II. 2,12).

3

PERCEPTION (*pratyakṣa*)

Introductory

Gautama deals with the problem of perception in its various aspects and these are discussed under the following heads:

- I Definition
- II Cognitive apparatus
  - A Sense-organs (*indriya*)
  - B Mind (*manas*)
  - C Contact (*sannikarṣa*)
- III Non-inferential character of perception
- IV Object (Substance) as distinct from qualities
- V Reality of objects: objections examined
- VI Composite and Components
- VII Contents of the Universe

The definition of perception as given by Gautama has proved to be highly controversial primarily because it unequivocally includes sense-object contact as the cause of perceptual cognition. Since perception is the foundation of all cognition, *prima facie* it would demolish the whole superstructure of doctrines and beliefs which lie at the root of much of Indian speculation. But the controversy has taken the shape that it did for two reasons: first, Gautama appears to be directly opposed to some of the Buddhist doctrines; second, the commentators try to attribute to Gautama the views which he never held or if he did they were never quite definite.

The cognitive apparatus as outlined by Gautama is important in that the physical basis of this apparatus diverts epistemological investigations from the directions which they have taken in modern times. The attack on the sense-object contact mentioned in the definition leads Gautama to clarify his views on other factors in perception, mind and self, and mind-sense and mind-self contact. It is true that perception strictly occurs in the self, as cognition is the quality of self which, in turn, is considered to be substance (*ātman* = *dravya*). But almost the entire epistemic argument can be said to terminate with the mind on the one hand and the external object on the other. The problem of the self is not discussed in this context and for the reason just stated, it does not materially detract from our understanding of perception. In fact, the mind is the double of the self and the Naiyāyika is prepared to say that the difference between the two is one of idiom rather than substance. In this connection it may be mentioned that the nature of the cognitive apparatus eliminates the issues connected with extreme scepticism about the senses and their role in the perceptual processes.

The non-inferential character of perceptual object and its existence or reality as independent of the mind or the self revolve round the time-honoured notion of substance and quality or the notion of composite and its components. There the debate is primarily between those Buddhists who in a way accept the atoms but deny the reality of the object which is composed of them and the Naiyāyikas who accept the atoms but insist on the emergence of a distinct and novel object from the combination of atoms. This is really a debate about what I would call second-order problems and the upshot of the debate is to find a suitable means for the description of the data which both parties seem to accept.

As is known, the problem of perception is linked up with our knowledge and status of the external world. The Naiyāyikas have listed a variety of items as components of the universe, for example substance and quality, and according to them all such items exist and are real. But it would seem that there are really two entities which can be regarded as ultimate and independent, viz. atom and self. Each is what the other is not and thus there is an unbridgeable gap between them. The Naiyāyikas attempt to bridge the gap by assigning an extraordinary function to the mind. As it will be evident from what I shall be saying on the section concerned, the ghost planted in the atomic machine is not really the self but the mind. This is one of the most ambiguous entities in the Nyāya scheme because it is bound up with the classical karma theory. On that theory rests the entire empirical existence of one's self and its painful entanglement in life and experience. And it is on this slender basis of the mind and its function that the whole superstructure of misery and liberation from it rests.

I. Definition

According to Gautama perception is the first of the four pramāṇas, and it is the basis on which the other pramāṇas operate. It is superior to inferential, analogical and verbal cognitions, says Vātsyāyana, because with it our desire for certain knowledge is fulfilled. When a man seeks the knowledge of a thing, for instance fire, he is informed about it by a reliable person and thus he obtains a verbal cognition. But this does not satisfy him and he seeks further confirmation. He obtains some confirmation through inference, but it is only when he sees the thing with his own eyes that his search for knowledge ends; his desire for knowledge is fulfilled and he does not seek for any other kind of confirmation. Thus whenever he has to depend upon the operation of several pramāṇas, perception offers him a cognition which is superior to all others obtained by other means. Of course, the question of superiority, says Uddyotakara, can arise when more than one pramāṇa is involved. Like the pramāṇa of word, perception operates on a vast field of objects, but the reason why perception is most important is that it precedes all pramāṇas. Gautama was therefore fully justified in putting perception first in his list of four pramāṇas (NBh & NV I. 1,3).

Gautama defines perception as follows:

"Perception is that cognition which arises from the contact of the sense-organ with its object, and which is unnamable [not expressible in words], not erroneous, and definitive. (NS I.. 1,4).[1]

Sense-object contact

According to Vātsyāyana this characteristic of perception conforms to the etymological meaning of the Sanskrit word for perception, *pratyakṣa*.[2] It means the operation of the visual organ with reference to its object, viz. colour. This term is extended to cover all kinds of sense-perception (NBh I. 1,4). Perception may be in the form of the operation of sense-object contact or of cognition. When it is the former the result of the pramāṇa is in the form of cognition called perception. When, however, the pramāṇa is in the form of cognition, the result of the pramāṇa is expressed in the attitudes of acceptance, rejection or indifference to the object perceived (NBh I. 1,3). Thus the result of pramāṇa (*pramāṇa phala*) is different from the pramāṇa itself.

The reference to the sense-object contact in the definition, says Gautama, is not intended to exclude other contacts. Cognition is a quality of self (*ātman* = *dravya*). In every form of cognition the contact of the mind with the self is involved, and perception being a form of cognition, this contact is present whenever perception occurs. Similarly, the contact of the mind with the sense-organ is also present. The property of the mind is that it cannot grasp more than one sensation at a time and the sense-object contact alone cannot therefore produce perception without the mind-sense contact. But the reason why the sense-object contact has been singled out is that it is an efficient cause (*nimitta*) of perception. And this is confirmed by our everyday experience. These questions are discussed in the section on the cognitive apparatus.[3]

Unnamable (*avyapadeśya*)

Vātsyāyana introduces the explanation of this characteristic of perception with the observation that it is meant to distinguish Gautama's view from the following opinion held by some philosophers. In so far as the object is concerned, there are [for each of them] words capable of naming them; with these words objects are connected. Owing to this connection between [words and] the objects communication [of the result of perception is possible]. Because of the contact between the senses and the objects there arises cognition such as "this is colour". The expression "colour", "taste", etc. are names of the objects [but not of the cognition]. By these words denoting the objects [— an opponent may say —] the cognition [and not just its objects] is being expressed in words, and so there arises the undesirable contingency that we are confronted with a *śabda-pramāṇa* [rather than the *pratykṣa-pramāṇa*]. [To ward off such an implication Vātsyāyana says: *pratyakṣa*] has no verbal expression.

The cognition of an object, when it occurs, does not take into account the connection between the word [denoting the name] and the object; it (the cognition) is verbally expressed [at a subsequent stage]. When the connection between the word and the object is realized [*ex post*], then and only then follows the process of "name-giving", i.e. the word [is used] which is the appellation of the object. When the object [as connected with its name] is grasped, then that cognition of this [so connected] object is the same as that attained beforehand [i.e. when the name-object connection was ignored]. But there is no verbal communication [at this stage] due to absence [in the *pratyakṣa*] of any speculative operation. [The word used] for the object which is not knowable [when *pratyakṣa* operates] is a [vicarious] name of a concept [rather than that of the object itself]; it is *rūpam iti* (colour — as it were).

And so at the time of the cognition of an object the word denoting that cognition is not being used; it is being used when [this cognition] is communicated [to others]. Consequently the [mere] cognition of an object is void of words being [only] a matter of contact between the sense and the object (NBh I. 1,4).

Not erroneous (*avyabhicāri*)

According to Vātsyāyana this characteristic is meant to exclude an erroneous cognition from the purview of the pramāṇa of perception, as this exclusion cannot be accomplished by the first two characteristics viz. sense-object contact and unnamable. For instance, in summer the rays of the sun get mixed up with the heat-rays radiating from the earth's surface and when these two together come into contact with the eye of the observer, he sees at a distance a mirage. This is an erroneous cognition. Cognition of 'that in what is not that' is characterized as erroneous, while cognition of 'that in what is that' is non-erroneous. This is why perception is non-erroneous cognition (NBh I. 1,4).[4] In the case of the mirage the error, says Uddyotakara, lies not in the object as some philosophers believe but in the cognition itself. It is not that the rays are not rays nor that the flickering is not flickering; there is no error in the object. The cognition which, instead of occurring as the cognition of the flickering rays, occurs as the cognition of water, i.e. the cognition of 'that' in what is not that; the error lies in the cognition. There is no water here, and yet we have the cognition of water. This erroneous cognition is due to the defect in the perceiving organ (NV I. 1,4).

Definitive (*vyavaṣāyātmaka*)

According to Vātsyāyana this characteristic is meant to exclude doubtful cognitions from the purview of the pramāṇa of perception. For instance, when a man observes from a distance and sees an object rising from the earth, his cognition is in the form 'this object is smoke or this object is dust'. This is a doubtful cognition but produced by sense-object contact, If only the first characteristic, sense-object contact, were to be kept in the definition, such doubtful cognitions would have to be accepted as pramāṇa. It is to exclude such cognitions that Gautama has added the characteristic, 'definitive'. A cognition must be absolutely definite in order to qualify for the status of pramāṇa.

If all doubtful cognitions are produced by the mind-self contact only, it is argued against this interpretation, then they would stand excluded by the sense-object contact; and in that case the present characteristic is unnecessary for the purpose. Vātsyāyana rejects this argument on the following grounds. It is only when a man has actually seen an object with his own eyes that he has a doubtful cognition whether this object that he sees is smoke or dust. Further, just as in true perception the object which is apprehended with the sense-organ is precisely the object which is apprehended with the mind, so in the case of doubtful cognition it is because he has failed to have certain apprehension with the sense-organs that he fails to have certain apprehension with the mind. This failure to have certain apprehension with the mind is preceded by the failure to have certain apprehension with the sense-organs; it is a state of mere hesitation or wavering with reference to the specific character of the object. And this is what constitutes doubt (*saṃśaya*). It is therefore evident that the kind of doubtful cognition that needs to be excluded from the purview of the pramāṇa of perception cannot arise unless there has been a previous contact of the object with the sense-organ. Likewise, in the case of all objects of perception ascertainment of the specific character of any of these objects comes through the sense-organs, as it is quite obvious from the fact that when the sense-organ is injured, no such ascertainment can take place.

In his comment on Gautama's definition Uddyotakara makes two observations: (a) All the characteristics mentioned by

Gautama collectively constitute the definition of perception. (b) It is quite appropriate to mention a cause in a definition: to state a cause of a thing produced is to state its defining characteristic. But it is not necessary to state all the causal factors in a definition; it is enough to refer to that causal factor which is exclusively concerned with the production of a thing defined. Such a characteristic is its cause because it does produce the thing concerned; it is its defining characteristic because it distinguishes the thing defined from the things of a homogeneous class as from the things of a heterogeneous class. In the present case sense-object contact is exclusively involved in the production of perception; it is therefore the cause of perception. This contact distinguishes it from things both homogeneous and heterogeneous with it (NV II. 1,20).

Apart from these observations on Gautama's definition, Uddyotakara criticizes five definitions of perception and his comments on two Buddhist definitions[5] are given below.

Buddhist definitions

1. The first definition, which is attributed to Vasubandhu, is "Perception is a cognition (produced) from that object" (*Tato arthād vijñānaṃ pratyakṣaṃ*). It is interpreted in two ways:

(a) If a certain cognition, which is designated according to the name of a certain object, is produced only from that object (*tata eva*) and not from any other object (*nārthāntarāt*), then that cognition is perception. The object of cognition is not a single entity. Although many atoms may combine to appear as a single entity, the single entity cannot produce any cognition. It is the individual atoms that form the cause of a cognition, and the cognition is constituted by many representations, each of which is produced from an atom. Thus when the atoms, which are represented in a cognition, are homogeneous ones, there appears in the cognition as the totality of their representations the form of an object, as in the case of the "cognition of blue". But when the collection of homogeneous atoms is treated as the object, the form that appears in a cognition is not the sum total of representations of atoms but is the product of conceptual construction (*kalpanā*) as, for instance, the "cognition of a jar". Thus the cognition of the jar is a wrong cognition (*saṃvṛtijñāna*) of an empirical object and therefore not a right cognition. Hence the cognition of an object does not proceed from that after which it is named and is thus excluded from the definition of perception.

(b) The second interpretation is: The inferential cognition is ruled out by the definition of perception, because the inferential cognition of fire, for example, is produced not from fire alone but from smoke and the remembrance of the relation between fire and smoke. When fire is inferred from smoke, the resulting cognition of fire is neither a cognition of smoke nor a cognition of the invariable concomitance between smoke and fire. The smoke and its invariable concomitance with fire are certainly regarded as the objects during the process of inference, but they are no longer the objects when the cognition of fire arises. If the past objects — smoke, etc., for example — are to be regarded as the objects of the cognition of fire, then recollection, which is caused by the past object, must also be regarded as a kind of perception because it is designated according to the name of that object. If the absence of the object in recollection were the reason for excluding it from perception, then neither the smoke nor its invariable concomitance with fire would be regarded as the object of the cognition of fire.

Uddyotakara criticizes this definition on several grounds. In the first place the word 'object' (*artha*) in the definition is superfluous. If we said merely that the cognition proceeds from 'that' (*tat*), it would mean 'from that object'. Since the exclusion of inferential and other cognitions from perception is based upon the word 'object', the elimination of this word from the definition does not help in excluding these cognitions. If the purpose is to exclude empirical cognition (*saṃvṛtijñāna*), this too cannot be served by definition. The explanation that is offered by the Buddhist is: the cognition of the jar proceeds from the qualities such as colour, but is called after the jar as the 'cognition of the jar'; hence it does not proceed from that after which it is named; and thus such cognitions are excluded from the definition. This explanation is not right, because the cognition that proceeds from colour, etc., is never called the 'cognition of the jar'; the cognition proceeding from colour is always named after colour and the cognition proceeding from the jar is named after the jar. Hence there is no such possibility of confusing the two cognitions which are named after their own specific objects. If the contention is that the jar is nothing but colour, etc., this is like building castles in the air. The correct position is that the jar is something different from its qualities. Every cognition proceeds from its own object. It is suggested that the word '*tataḥ*' (from that) serves the purpose of excluding wrong cognition as such a cognition proceeds from 'an object which is not that' after which it is named. This suggestion is based on a complete misunderstanding. It is not that the wrong cognition proceeds from an object which is not 'that'; it only appears in a form which does not belong to the real object which is in contact with the sense-organ. For instance, when a conch-shell is wrongly perceived as silver, this wrong cognition is not produced by what is *not-shell*; there is no doubt that the object whose contact gives rise to the cognition is the shell itself. What really happens is that the cognition is in the form of something (silver) which the actual object (shell) is not. Hence the wrong cognition, not proceeding from that which is not 'not-that', cannot be excluded from the definition.

In view of these considerations the first two words in the definition '*tat*' (that) and '*arthāt*' (from the object) are futile. And if we are left only with the third word '*vijñāna*' (cognition), this would cease to be a definition. If mere cognition were the definition of perception, then all cognitions would be perception. But even if we accept the definition as it is meant by the Buddhist, it would not cover perception. The object which is apprehended is cause and the apprehension of that object which is its effect could not be present at one and the same time. The cause precedes effect and therefore the apprehension of an object which is the effect of a cause that has ceased to exist cannot be regarded as perception, for perception is the apprehension of an object that is present. The Buddhist definition leads therefore to an absurd situation where we have to say that we perceive an object which is past.

2. The second definition, which is attributed to Dignāga, is : "Perception is free from mental construction" (*Kalpanā-poḍhaṃ pratyakṣam*). It is explained as follows : The characteristic feature of mental construction (*kalpanā*) consists in the association of immediate awareness with a word. A thing

which in itself is essentially inexpressible comes to be expressed by a word only when it is associated with a name and other characteristics. Mental construction means nothing but the process of associating five characteristics. Dignāga divides the five characteristics into five categories which function in five kinds of words. In the case of arbitrary words (*yadṛcchā-śabda*, proper nouns), a thing (*artha*) distinguished by a name (*nāman*) is expressed by a word, e.g. *Ḍittha.* In the case of genus words (*jātiśabda*, common nouns), a thing distinguished by a genus is expressed by a word, e.g. *go* (cow). In the case of quality-words (*guṇaśabda*), a thing distinguished by a quality is expressed by a word, e.g. *śukla* (white). In the case of action-words (*kriyāśabda*, adjectives), a thing distinguished by an action is expressed by a word, e.g. *pācaka* (cook). In the case of substance-words (*dravyaśabda*), a thing distinguished by a substance is expressed by a word, e.g. *daṇḍin* (a staff-bearer) or *viṣāṇin* (a horn-bearer).

Dignāga mentions two other views: (a) What is expressed by action-words and substance-words is a thing distinguished by a relationship such as that of an action to its agent, that of a substance to its possessor. (b) What is expressed in all these cases is a thing qualified by words which denote no real entity (*arthaśūnyaśabda*).

In any case that which is devoid of such mental construction is perception.

Dignāga appears to have adopted the classification from the grammarians. Patañjali classifies words into four categories: genus-words, quality-words, action-words and arbitrary words. As regards substance-words, he does not mention this term, but the fact that Dignāga identifies *viṣāṇin* as a *dravya* shows that his explanation is based upon Patañjali's *Mahābhāṣya.*

Praśastapāda also classifies the qualities (*viśeṣaṇa*) of *savikalpakapratyakṣa* into five categories, but his categories differ from those employed by Dignāga, inasmuch as they are based on the Vaiśeṣka doctrines.[6]

According to Uddyotakara Dignāga's definition is open to several objections. If perception is inexpressible, its definition cannot be expressed in words: neither the words individually nor the entire definition (*kalpanāpoḍhaṃ pratyakṣam*) can denote perception; if, on the other hand, it can be so expressed, it cannot be free from mental construction. If the expression "free from mental construction" were held to mean "inexpressible in its specific feature", then everything would be regarded as perception, because a word expresses only the general feature of a thing and not its specific feature. No educated person, says Uddyotakara, would dream of expressing the specific feature of a thing, as this is opposed to all conventions. But this does not mean that a thing is inexpressible because its specific feature is inexpressible; for instance, we do speak of a *Brāhmaṇa* by the word "man", although this word does not express his specific feature. Moreover, it would be self-contradictory to say that the specific feature of perception is expressed in the words "mental construction", since these words signify that the specific feature of perception is inexpressible. And if the Buddhist persists in saying that the specific feature of perception is inexpressible, then this would not only apply to perception but to the entire universe; for no object is spoken of in its specific form. If the Buddhist says that "mental construction" is only a conventional expression for the specific form of perception without any literal meaning of its own, the position remains as self-contradictory as before. It is self-contradictory to say that the specific form of a thing cannot be spoken of by any word and yet the specific form of perception is expressed in the words "mental construction". Lastly, if the expression "mental construction" signifies nothing, then the definition would have to be regarded as utterly uselsss. And not expressing anything at all, says Uddyotakara, is exactly like the dream of a dumb person ! The more the definition of Dignāga is examined, concludes the commentator, the more incapable it turns out to be of bearing the scrutiny of reasoning (*nyāya*) (NV I. 1,4).

II Cognitive Apparatus

A. Sense-organs

According to Gautama perception involves sense-object contact. His views on the nature, origin and function of the sense-organs are an important element in his theory of perception. These are mainly based on his philosophical doctrines, although certain facts of experience are occasionally produced in their support.[1]

The reason why Gautama has undertaken this investigation is that ordinary special criteria for determining numerical identity and diversity cannot be easily applied in the case of the sense-organs. According to Vātsyāyana we find that when different places are occupied, there are several substances; but when a composite substance occupies several places, it is still regarded as a single substance. The sense-organs occupy different places and it is therefore necessary to evolve suitable criteria in order to determine the exact number of the sense-organs.

According to Gautama the sense-organs and sense-objects are 'objects of cognition'. Each sense-organ is produced from one material element; it is restricted to one sense-object and the sense-object is itself the property of the element from which the sense-organ is produced. The initial production of the sense-organs and their sense-objects for each embodiment of a being is according to the karma of that being to whom they belong; these are designed to serve its purpose.

There are five sense-organs, five sense-objects, five elements and their five properties; there is mutual correspondence amongst them. Nose is the sense-organ; it is produced from earth; its object is smell which is also the property of earth. Tongue is the sense-organ; it is produced from water; its object is taste which is also the property of water. Eye is the sense-organ; it is produced from light; its object is colour which is also the property of light. Skin is the sense-organ; it is produced from air; its object is touch which is also the property of air. Ear is the sense-organ; it is produced from ākāśa or more strictly, it is ākāśa itself; its object is sound which is also the property of ākāśa. (NS I. 1,13-14).

Proofs for five sense organs

Gautama establishes his position with regard to the number of the sense-organs in two stages. First, he rejects the view that there is only one sense-organ, the tactual organ, of which the other senses are modifications, and then proceeds to his theory of five sense-organs and their composition.

(a) According to the doctrine of the unitary sense-organ the skin pervades all the sense-organs, so that when it is present there is perception and when it is absent there is no perception at all. Gautama criticises this doctrine on the following grounds:

If the tactual organ were the only sense-organ it would be able to apprehend all sensible objects; colour would be perceived by the blind or sound by the deaf. As this is not true, the tactual sense-organ cannot be the only organ.

It is argued that the various sense-organs are nothing but special parts of the tactual sense-organ. The different kinds of sensible objects are perceived through these parts, so that when these particular parts are destroyed the corresponding sensible objects are not perceived. The blind fail to see colours or the deaf fail to hear sounds, because the parts of the tactual organ in the eye or the ear-hole have been destroyed.

Gautama rejects this argument as self-contradictory. If the perception of colour, sound, etc. is held to be brought about by different parts of the tactual organ, then it goes against the doctrine of the unitary tactual organ. Are the so-called special parts of the tactual organ of the nature of sense-organs or not ? If they are, then there is a plurality of sense-organs. If they are not, then colours, sounds, etc., cannot be regarded as perceptible by senses.

Further, the tactual organ cannot be treated as the only sense-organ because, if this were true, there would be simultaneous perception of colour, sound, etc. The self would come in contact with the mind, the mind with the tactual organ, and the tactual organ with colour, sound, etc. But such simultaneous perception is impossible. Moreover, the doctrine of a single sense-organ involves a contradiction. The single sense-organ can apprehend only those objects which it comes in contact with; but it cannot apprehend distant objects. However, we perceive colour and sound from a great distance. If these were perceived through the tactual organ without coming into contact with it, it should operate uniformly for all other sense organs; or it should not operate in this fashion for any of the sense-organs.

But it may be argued that the tactual organ does require contact in the case of touch but not in the case of sound and colour. If this were so, we should be able to see both hidden and unhidden colours; but this does not happen; nor can we explain perception of colour near the observer and non-perception of colour at a distance. Moreover, if the tactual organ is the only sense-organ, its derangement or destruction would make all perception impossible. But in fact we find that even if one sense-organ is deranged or destroyed, we can perceive through the other sense-organs. (NS & NBh III. 1, 52-56).

(b) Having thus rejected the doctrine of a single tactual sense-organ as both self-contradictory and contrary to the facts of perception, Gautama proceeds to establish his main thesis that there are five sense-organs. His arguments as explained by Vātsyāyana are as follows:

In the first place, the existence of five sense-organs is inferred from five distinct objects (*artha*) or purposes (*prayojana*), viz. touch, colour, taste, odour and sound. These five distinct objects require distinct sense-organs for their apprehension. Touch, for example, is apprehended by the tactual organ; but it does not apprehend colour. So we infer the existence of the visual organ which serves the purpose of apprehending colour. Similarly, the existence of the other sense-organs can be established.

The argument based on purpose, according to Uddyotakara, can also be stated as an argument based on instrument (*karaṇa*). An observer confronted with a variety of sensible objects is like a craftsman who is proficient in several crafts. Such a craftsman uses an appropriate implement for the work of each craft; when one job is finished with the help of one implement he undertakes another job with the help of another implement (NV III. 1,58). The function of each sense-organ is distinct and it can only be performed by that sense-organ, and not by another. Thus the existence of five sense-organs is established by inference from five kinds of the activities of the sense-organs.

It is argued that this inference from five sense-objects is not conclusive. We have many more kinds of objects than five; e.g. there are three kinds of touch, hot, cool and lukewarm.

This argument has no force, as such kinds of sense-objects are grouped under their respective kinds. These kinds of touch come under one genus, touch, so that when we experience a cool touch, there is no need for the assumption of an instrument other than the tactual organ. As a matter of fact, several kinds of touch are actually experienced by the tactual organ. Similarly, varieties of other sense-objects can be explained.

It is urged that if different kinds of sense-objects can be grouped under five types, they can also be grouped under a single genus, 'object' (*viṣaya*); in that case we might settle for one sense-organ. This objection has no force, because, as a matter of fact, the scope of sense-objects cannot be determined through such a genus. On the other hand, we do find that the five types of sense-objects are adequate for explaining the varieties of perceptual experience.

The second argument is that the existence of the five sense-organs is inferred from the five-fold character of the marks corresponding to apprehension, site, operation, form and constitutent (NS III. 1,62).

First, there are five different kinds of apprehension, visual, auditory, etc., from which we infer the existence of five sense-organs. In fact, it is because of the power of the literal signification of the names of various kinds of perception that we learn to define the various sense-organs as instruments of apprehending their respective objects.

Secondly, there are five sense-organs corresponding to five sites; for example, the tactual organ, which is indicated by the apprehension of touch, has its seat throughout the body. The diversity of sense-organs is proved from the diversity of their locations. Things with distinct locations are always found to be distinct, as in the case of numerous jars. If the whole body were to be treated as the seat of all the sense-organs, then no one could be deaf or blind. But if the different sense-organs are held to have different sites, the site of one organ being destroyed, the other organs may remain intact; a blind or deaf person need not therefore be deprived of all the sense-organs. This clearly shows that the sense-organs are different from their sites.

Thirdly, the five sense-organs involve different processes. The visual organ, which is of the nature of fire or light, goes out of the pupil to objects endowed with colour. The other four sense-organs come in contact with their respective objects resting in their own sites; they do not move out to their objects like the visual organ. This argument shows that they apprehend their objects by coming in direct contact with them.

Fourthly, the five sense-objects have different forms and these are determined by their different magnitudes. The olfactory, gustatory and tactory organs have the magnitude of their sites;

they are coextensive with their sites. The visual organ, though located in the pupil, moves out of it and pervades its object. Thus it is not coextensive with its site but with the field of vision. The auditory organ is nothing but ākāśa; ākāśa is all-pervading and contrary to what one would expect, we do not hear all sounds because the organ is limited in size and operates according to the karma of the person concerned. The auditory organ renders audible only particular sounds by reason of its substratum and the karma of one to whom the organ belongs.

Lastly, the five sense-organs have their origin in five material elements. The olfactory organ is made of earth and apprehends smell which is its characteristic property. The gustatory organ is made up of water and apprehends taste which is its characteristic property. The visual organ is made of light and apprehends colour which is its characteristic property. And the auditory organ is nothing but ākāśa and apprehends sound which is its characteristic property. A sense-organ apprehends the distinctive property of that element which enters into its constitution. (NS & NBh III. 1, 59-63).

The elements except ākāśa have more than one property, but this can be easily reconciled with the constitution and function of the sense-organs. The sense-organ is distinguished from its corresponding element by its fineness or excellence, and it apprehends that property which is preponderant in the corresponding element.

A sense-organ is what it is, because it is endowed with its property. It cannot apprehend its own property because the property is its own integral part. Whenever an object is apprehended, it is apprehended as associated with a property; in the case of the sense-organ no such attending property is possible. Nothing can operate upon itself. There is one exception to this, i.e. the auditory organ. In the case of the other four organs it is only as possessed of their specific properties that the corresponding elements constitute their respective sense-organs; in the case of the auditory organ it is the ākāśa by its very nature that constitutes the organ. Further, in the case of the other four organs the fact that they apprehend their specific properties cannot be established by perception or inference. But in the case of the auditory organ we do know, by inference based on elimination (*pariśeṣa*), that it apprehends sound and that sound is a property of ākāśa. Among the substances that could be regarded as the auditory organ are the self and the mind. The former is the hearer and cannot therefore be the instrument of hearing. The mind is imperishable. If the mind were the auditory organ, deafness would be inexplicable. Thus for this purpose both the self and the mind are ruled out and we are left with the auditory organ which alone can apprehend sound. Amongst the five elements earth, air, water and fire have the capacity to constitute their respective sense-organs, but they do not have such capacity to constitute the auditory organ. Hence it is only ākāśa that can constitute the organ. (NS & NBh III. 1, 58-75).

Double visual organ

The concept of five sense-organs seems to be contrary to Gautama's acceptance of a double visual organ. One of the arguments for the distinction of self from the physical and mental complex is that what is perceived by the left eye is recognised by the right eye. When we connect two successive cognitions with the same object, we have what is called recognition. This implies that there is a double visual organ. It is objected that the notion of a double visual organ is wrong; all that happens is that we see two ends or parts of a single visual organ divided by the nasal bone. Gautama rejects this criticism on the ground that when one eye is destroyed the other may remain intact. In a dead man's skull we see two holes where the two eyes existed previously. If there was one organ this would be impossible. Further, there is the pheonmenon of double vision. When one eye is pressed with the finger, the contact of the visual ray with the object is interrupted; as a result we see two objects instead of one. When the pressure is released the object is again seen as one. Besides there is no certainty that the destruction of or obstruction to one eye will lead to a similar condition in the other.

It is argued that the destruction of a component part does not mean the destruction of the composite substance of which it is the part; for example, when the branches of a tree are cut off, the tree continues to stand. Gautama rejects this illustration as irrelevant. A composite substance does not continue after its components are destroyed. If it did it would be eternal;

this is absurd. What really happens is that the composite substance is itself destroyed when its parts are destroyed and that it remains intact when its parts are not destroyed. In the case of the tree the tree continues to exist but only in a mutilated form when its branches are cut off. (NS & NBh III. 1, 7-11).

Uddyotakara disagrees with the view of a double visual organ. The visual organ is really one and the same with two black pupils as its two substrata. While the visual organ is itself made of the element of light, the pupils are made of earth; they function like the windows in a room; when one window is closed, things are seen through another. The notion of the dual visual organ is like that of a double object when we see two ends of a long thing intercepted by something in the middle and mistake it for two things (NV III. 1,11).

According to the Nyāya theory of material elements earth, air, water and fire have more than one property; ākāśa has only one property, sound. Although the four sense-organs have their origin in the material elements with more than one property, they apprehend one property only. This is due to the fact that one property is found in a large measure in one element and the sense-organ is therefore characterised by that property in the element from which it is produced. For example, the olfactory organ is characterised by odour which is found in a large measure in the earth from which it is produced. It is because of this that the sense-organs are not able to apprehend more than one property; each apprehends a specific property. This also explains the difference between the sense-organs and the elements. The sense-organs, though composed of these elements, are different from them, because they have a finer or excellent texture. This refinement or excellence is governed by the karma of man.

As already mentioned, to this general pattern of our cognitive apparatus there is one exception: the property of sound is both a property of ākāśa and of the auditory organ. Ākāśa constitutes, by its very nature, the auditory organ, and not as having the property of sound. In the case of the other sense-organs the position is different, as these organs are made of the corresponding elements.

In the case of the other sense-organs neither perception nor inference can establish that they can apprehend their own properties. But in the case of the ākāśa of the auditory organ, as already mentioned, we do know, by inference based on elimination (*pariśeṣa*) that sound is apprehended by it and that it is the property of ākāśa. Among the substances that could be regarded as the auditory organ are the self and the mind. The former is a hearer and cannot therefore be treated as an instrument of hearing. The mind is imperishable and if it were the auditory organ, deafness would be impossible. The four elements have the capacity to constitute the four sense-organs but they do not have the capacity to constitute the auditory organ. Thus it is established that ākāśa constitutes the auditory organ and sound is the property of both. The other four sense-organs are what they are, because they are endowed with their own properties.

These are their integral parts and cannot therefore be apprehended by the sense-organs themselves (NS III. 1, 71-75).

B. Mind (manas)

In the scheme of perception we have four entities or factors: object, sense, mind and self, and three contacts: sense-object, sense-mind and mind-self. In this context it is first necessary to establish the existence of the mind and then show that although the mind is not specifically mentioned by Gautama in this context it has a part to play in the theory of cognition.

Existence of Mind

According to Gautama, it is the non-appearance of simultaneous cognitions that is the mark of the mind. Vātsyāyana provides a list of additional marks: remembrance, inference, scripture (*āgama*), doubt, illumination (*pratibhā*), and conception (*ūhā*), dream, intuitive knowledge (*prajñā*), perception of pleasure, desire, etc. These marks are not produced by the external senses and therefore require some other organ to account for their production. We find that even though several sensible objects are in contact with their respective sense-organs at one and the same time, there is no simultaneous cognition of these objects. From this fact we infer that there is some instrumental cause (*nimitta*) other than the sense-organs, because with its assistance and its contact with the sense-organs cognitions can appear but without this assistance and contact cognitions do not appear. If the sense-object contact alone were able, independently of the mind-sense contact, to produce cognitions, we should have simultaneous production of cognitions. But this does not happen. Hence this cause (and not the sense-organs) is the mind. This mind is, in its turn, in contact with the sense-organs (NS I. 1,16).

The above-mentioned procedure for establishing the existence of the mind creates several difficulties. One of them is that the marks mentioned by Vātsyāyana do not subsist in the mind but in the self. According to Uddyotakara the answer to this difficulty is that they are marks of the mind not because they subsist in it but because they are actions (*kriyā*). These actions are different from other actions, for example, the cognition of odour, and therefore need an instrument other than the external senses. Further, though pleasure and the like are different from the objects of the external senses, they are nonetheless objects of cognition; so they need an instrument or an organ for the production of their cognitions. Such an operational instrument is the mind.

There is another difficulty. If non-appearance of simultaneous cognitions is a property of cognitions, how can it be indicative of the mind's existence ? If a property could be indicative of a thing even when it is not related to the thing, then anything could be indicative of anything; for example, we could say that the self exists because the crow is black. This difficulty, it is suggested, can be met in the following way : We have such inferences as when we see a new earthen pot or a potter's wheel, this *seeing* of the pot does not subsist in the potter but indicates his existence. Uddyotakara rejects this explanation on the ground that what the fact of *seeing* the pot or the wheel indicates is not the potter but the place (*deśa*) as qualified by the presence (*sadbhāva*) of the potter. Thus the inference is not from a property unrelated to a thing to that thing but from a property related to it.

The fact of the matter, says Uddyotakara, is that the mark of non-production is not totally unrelated to the mind. Such a relation can be shown if we make non-production as the subject of our inference. The inference can be formulated in two ways: (1) The cognitions of colour, etc., do not appear simultaneously;

for instance, in the case of a man well-versed in handicrafts, although several implements are before him at one and the same time, they do not produce several objects such as a chariot, etc., for these implements stand in need of the operation of his hands. Similarly, since the sense-organs do not produce simultaneous cognitions they stand in need of some other instrument. (2) We can make the sense-organs the subject of our inference and state the inference as follows. The sense-organs stand in need of another instrument for all their operations, because, like the axe and the like, they never operate simultaneously.

If the sense-organs cannot apprehend several objects simultaneously because they need another instrument, it may be asked, why should we not have simultaneous cognition of such objects as are in contact with the same sense-organ? For instance, when we see a white cow walking, all the three objects, the white colour, the animal and its motion, are in contact with the visual organs. Why can't we have the cognition "the white cow is walking" ? This latter difficulty, according to Uddyotakara, cannot be met by saying that we do not cognize several such objects at one and the same time because we do not wish to do so. If in one case we have such a desire we can have another desire in another case; for example, for simultaneous cognition of several other objects. Besides there are cases where, even though the desire is there, there are no simultaneous cognitions. The presence or absence of desire cannot explain the fact of non-simultaneous production of cognitions. And if it did, there would be no need to have the mind at all.

Nor can we explain this phenomenon by reference to the self. The self is in contact with more than one sense-organ at one and the same time and may supervise their operations. For instance, a boy, says Vācaspati, simultaneously accompanies his teacher, carries his jug and repeats his lessons — all at one and the same time. In this instance the self of the boy in this case does bring about several effects when several causes are present. The supervision by the self cannot therefore explain the phenomenon. The real explanation, says Uddyotakara, lies in the very nature of the instrument. Even though the instruments are related to several objects, they never perform more than one action at a time; and even though the self may supervise their operations, this cannot explain the situation (NV & NVTT I. 1,16).

If all marks cited for the existence of the mind are equally applicable to the self, how can we distinguish the mind from the self ? To this Gautama had already given an answer: since the instruments of cognition can only belong to the cognizer, it is merely a nominal difference to apply the name 'mind' to that which is really the self. Further, according to Vātsyāyana, this is amply vouched for by such expressions as 'He sees with the eye'. Similarly, the mind also is known only as an instrument by means of which the cognizer becomes aware of all objects. If the cognizer could operate without an instrument, he might as well have perceived sense-objects without instruments. And this means that we would have to dispense with all the senses, internal and external. Further, it is not quite true that all the marks are equally applicable to the self and the mind. In fact, there are different sense-objects and different conceptual objects. For instance, we infer the visual organ from visual cognition, as we infer the existence of the mind from perception of pleasure and the like as well as from the fact of non-simultaneous production of cognition. Once the existence of the cognizer is accepted, the dispute boils down to one of nomenclature. It seems as though some people find unpalatable the very idea of calling the cognizer by his proper name, 'self' (NBh III. 1, 17-18).

According to Uddyotakara, although the mind is characterized by non-simultaneity of cognitions, it can be said to be directly apprehended by perception. In the case of one who has direct perception of the mind, the instrument of that perception is the mind-self contact as assisted by the merit born of Yogic practices. In the case of the cognition of the self also the mind-self contact is the instrument and it can be explained in the same way. The exact nature of the merit of the Yogin, says Uddyotakara, is beyond our comprehension; he does not therefore wish to explain how the merit of the Yogin assists in the cognition of the mind (NV III. 1, 18).

Having thus proved the existence of the mind as an internal instrument, Gautama proceeds to demonstrate that the mind cannot be the seat of consciousness or cognition. It is characterized by subservience to the self and incapacity to reap the fruits of another's deeds (NS III. 2,41). Like the material substances or sense-organs, it has no consciousness, for desire and the like are the marks of the self. Like them, it is dependent on something else; it is only under the impulse of the self's effort that it can perform the actions of sustaining, propelling and pattern-making (*vyūhana*). If these actions were performed independently of the self, this would be contrary to the concept of the body as being under the control of the self. Another reason why the mind cannot be the seat of consciousness is its incapacity to experience the fruits of deeds of another self. What is conscious is independent. If consciousness belonged to the mind, to the sense-organs or to material substances, these would become independent agents of all activity. Activity produces merit and demerit which, in their turn, produce rebirth. The fruits of the deeds performed by these independent agents are bound to appear in future births. But since these agents would already have perished at death, there would be only the self left to consume these fruits. This would not be right. If, however, we treat the self as conscious and these agents as unconscious, the self remains as an independent agent with the instruments under his control. And in that case it is but proper that the self should consume the fruits of his own deeds. Thus Vātsyāyana explains Gautama's reasons for depriving the mind of the seat of cognition (NBh III. 2,41).

According to Gautama there can be only one mind in one body on account of non-simultaneity of cognitions. This non-simultaneity is twofold: (a) the non-simultaneity of cognitions produced by the same sense-organ and (b) the non-simultaneity of cognitions produced by several sense-organs. The former is due to the fact that one instrument can, by its very nature, accomplish one thing at a time and has therefore no bearing on the present problem. It is the latter that shows why there can be only one mind in one body. If there were several minds, they would be in contact with several sense-organs; and thus simultaneous cognitions would be possible. But this cannot be so. Hence it is established that since cognitions appear only one after another, and more than one cognition can never occur at one and the same time, there is only one mind in one body (NBh III. 2,60).

Gautama criticizes the following objection. We do apprehend several acts (*kriyā*) simultaneously. For instance, when the pupil sees the teacher going into the forest, he has several cognitions: this teacher reads, walks, hears sounds, remembers his destination, etc. He does not notice that these acts are successive and his cognitions must therefore be regarded as simultaneous. This apprehension of simultaneity among cognitions, says Gautama, is due to the fact that the mind comes in contact with different senses in rapid succession; it is like the apprehension of a circle of firebrand (NS III. 2,62). When the circle moves rapidly, there is a succession among several cognitions of the fire; but because it moves with extreme rapidity, we perceive a continuity in the circle of fire, i.e. a single continuous circle of fire. Similarly, it is because of the rapidity of actions and cognitions that they are perceived as simultaneous while the sequence is not perceived. There is undisputed evidence in favour of this explanation. Everyone knows directly that cognitions due to several sense-organs appear one after another in rapid succession. Hence Vātsyāyana concludes that there can be only one mind in one body (NBh III. 2,62).

The reason for one mind in one body, says Gautama, is also the reason for its being an atom (NS III. 2,63). If the mind were something larger than an atom, it could come in contact with several organs at one and the same time. Thus the fact that our cognitions are successive and not simultaneous proves both the propositions: there is only one mind in one body and the mind is an atom (NS III. 2,63).

Contact of Mind

Gautama has already mentioned sense-object contact as the first characteristic of perception. This creates a doubt as to whether the mind and self have any part to play in the theory of cognition. In this connection Gautama answers the following objections:[2]

1. *Objection*

The definition of perception is untenable because the definition is incomplete (NS II. 1,20).

Perception cannot arise unless there is contact between self and mind (NS II. 1,21).

If this were so, direction (*dik*), place, time and ākāśa would also have to be mentioned (NS II. 1,22).

Reply

The self has not been excluded from the definition, inasmuch as knowledge is a mark of the self (NS II. 1,23).

The mind, too, has not been omitted from the definition as non-simultaneity of cognitions is its mark (NS II. 1,24).

Inasmuch as only the one contact of a sense-organ with its object constitutes the efficient cause (*nimitta*) of perception, this contact has been mentioned separately in the definition (NS II. 1,25).

The contact of the sense-organ with the object is the efficient cause, as perception is produced even when one is asleep or preoccupied with other things (NŚ II. 1,26).

By the sense-organs and their objects are also indicated the special kinds of cognition (NS II. 1,27).

2. *Objection*

According to Vātsyāyana the following objection is aimed at the instances of perception mentioned in NS II. 1,26 above.

[The perception in the case of one who is asleep or whose mind is preoccupied with other things] is not a valid hetu, as it involves self-contradiction [i.e. it denies that the mind-sense contact is involved in perception] (NS II. 1,28).

Reply

There is no self-contradiction; as [in the instances cited, perception] is due to the special force of a particular object (NS II. 1,29).

Vātsyāyana explains the first objection mentioned by Gautama as follows: The definition of perception is incomplete because sense-object contact alone cannot account for the occurrence of perception. Furthermore, perception cannot arise if mind-self contact is absent nor can it arise if direction, place, time and ākāśa are absent.

According to Gautama cognition is a quality of self and its occurrence depends upon mind-self contact. This contact should also be regarded as the cause of perception if sense-object contact is the cause of perception. Secondly, since

Gautama holds that sense-object contact cannot function independently of mind-sense contact, the mind-self contact should also be treated as the cause of perception. If sense-object contact did not depend upon mind-sense contact, we would have simultaneous cognitions; this is opposed to Gautama's description of the mind as characterized by non-simultaneity of cognitions. Thirdly, if sense-object contact is treated as a cause of perception simply because perception occurs when this contact is present, then direction, place, ākāśá and time should also be regarded as causes, for they are eternal and present everywhere. Even if they are not given that status, some explanation is due for their exclusion from the definition of perception (NBh II. 1,20-22).

As already mentioned, Gautama's answer is that it is precisely because congition is a mark of self that the self is not excluded from perception. As Vātsyāyana puts it, cognition is a mark because it is a quality. Since cognition is produced by contact, it follows that the self must be in contact with something which, in the present case, can only be the mind. And this contact is involved not only in perception but also in all forms of cognition. In view of this it is really not necessary to mention it in the definition. In mentioning sense-object contact what is intended is not that it alone is the cause but that it is a cause specific to perception; it is a cause which marks perception out from inferential and other forms of cognition.

As regards the mind-sense contact, Gautama says that this is also involved in perception because he regards the mind as characterized by non-simultaneity of cognition. If sense-object contact could function independently of mind-sense contact, we would be confronted with simultaneous occurrence of various congitions. Gautama has not mentioned this contact in the definition, says Vātsyāyana, because the sense-object contact has already done the job of distinguishing perception from other forms of cognition (NBh I. 1,4 & II. 1,23 & 24).[3]

The suggestion that direction, place, time and ākāśa should be treated as the cause of perception is based on the argument that since cognitions occur when they are present they should be regarded as the cause of cognition. This is not possible, says Uddyotakara, because direction, etc., have no power or capacity to produce cognition. It is true that they are eternal and present everywhere, but this proximity is something which cannot be avoided. If such factors are to be treated as cause, there must be some special reasons for it. For instance, the hot touch of light is not regarded as the cause of the perception of its colours, though it is present at the time; but the colour of the light is regarded as the cause of its perception because it has the capacity to produce that perception.[4] In the case of direction, place, time and ākāśa we have positive concomitance in that cognitions appear when these factors are present, but we cannot have negative concomitance; i.e. cognitions do not appear when these factors are absent. But in the case of the object, sense-organ, mind and self we have both positive and negative concomitance. It is therefore right to regard their contact as the cause of perception (NV II. 1,22).

Vātsyāyana explains at some length the instances of perception mentioned by Gautama and their bearing on this subject. When a man goes to sleep determined to wake up at a particular time, he does wake up at that time. In this case the mind-self contact is the principal factor while mind-sense and sense-object contacts are subordinate factors. But if the man wakes up because of a loud noise, his perception of sound is due to its force. In this case the sense-object contact is the principal factor while the mind-sense and mind-self contacts are subordinate.

When a man's mind is preoccupied with other things we have a different situation. For instance, if such a person wishes to perceive a particular thing when his mind is engaged in perceiving another, he directs his mind to contact that thing and thus becomes aware of it. Here the mind-self contact is the principal factor while the mind-sense and sense-object contacts are minor. But sometimes such a person is forced to perceive an object without any desire or effort on his part, and in that case the sense-object contact becomes the principal factor while the other two contacts play a subordinate part. These instances clearly show that whenever perception occurs the sense-object contact must be present (NBh II. 1,26).[5]

Regarding the second objection (NS II. 1,28), Vātsyāyana says that the instances of perception during sleep or when one's mind is preoccupied with other things, would seem to indicate that perception is brought about by sense-object contact only.

But, then, this contradicts Gautama's concept of the mind and the role of the mind-sense contact in perception (NBh II. 1,27 & 28). There is no such contradiction because all that Gautama has said is that perception in these cases is due to the force of objects. This force can obviously affect sense-object contact and not the mind-sense contact. This former contact is therefore the more important of the two (NBh II. 1,27).

In the case where a man is asleep or his mind is preoccupied, there is obviously on his part no effort or desire to perceive. Since Gautama holds that perception must have the contact of the mind for its cause, the role of the mind in such cases, asks the objector, needs an explanation.

Vātsyāyana replies that the action of the mind is due to the quality of self known as *adṛṣṭa* (literally 'unseen'). This quality, says Uddyotakara, is known as *saṃskāra* which is the effect of merit and demerit. In ordinary cognition what impels the mind to establish contact is the quality of the self, 'effort' (*prayatna*), i.e. that quality of the self which is brought about by its desire. Similarly, there is in the self another quality, *adṛṣṭa*, which impels the mind to establish contact with the sense-organ even when there is no desire or effort on its part.

Vātsyāyana establishes the existence of the quality of *adṛṣṭa* in the following fashion. If the mind were not impelled by this force, there would be no mind-sense contact; in the absence of the contact there would be no possibility of having any cognition whatsoever. But if there were no cognition, the quality would become totally ineffective. It is, however, essential that this quality of *adṛṣṭa* should operate on all things such as substances, qualities and actions; for otherwise, there would be no agency which could produce the initial activity either in the four atoms of the four elements or in the minds at the beginning of creation. And if there were no such activity, there would be no possibility of any such thing being produced as the body, the sense-organs and the objects. Thus the quality of *adṛṣṭa* which is a product of merit and demerit explains not only our cognitive experience but also the entire creation of the physical and cognitive apparatus of living beings and the objects on which it operates (NBh and NV II. 1,27).[6]

Another reason which underlines the importance of sense-object contact, says Gautama, is that our individual cognitions are named after the sense-organs and their objects (NS II. 1,27). We have five kinds of perception, says Vātsyāyana, because we have five sense-organs and each individual perception is named after the sense-organ and the object concerned, e.g. visual perception or colour-perception (NBh II. 1,27). Everything, says Uddyotakara, is named after that which is peculiar to itself, e.g. barley-sprout. When a barley-seed bursts into a sprout, this is due to various causes such as the seed, the season of the year, etc. But the plant is named the barley-sprout as it appears (NV I. 1,4).

Vātsyāyana mentions another objection to the sense-object contact theory. In the list of five organs Gautama has not included the mind. If perception is produced by sense-object contact, the definition would not be applicable to the perception of the qualities of self such as cognition, pleasure, pain, etc., for the perception of these qualities cannot be said to be produced by the sense-object contact.[7] Vātsyāyana replies that the mind, whose contact with the self is the generic cause of all cognition, is as good a sense-organ as the five sense-organs.[8] But the reason that prompted Gautama to exclude it from the list of sense-organs is the fact that there are certain differences in their properties. These differences are the following: The five sense-organs (a) are composed of material elements, (b) are each confined to a specific class of objects, and (c) are organs endowed with the qualities which they apprehend. The mind, on the other hand, is not composed of any material element, operates on all objects without any restriction, and is not endowed with the qualities it apprehends. Moreover, it is the mind which makes it impossible for cognitions to be simultaneous. And that it is a sense-organ is learned from another philosophical system. In support of this argument Vātsyāyana observes that Gautama was only following the accepted methodological principle (*tantrayukti*) that 'a view of others which is not rejected is accepted'.[9] As Uddyotakara remarks, the objector is ignorant of the ways of philosophers.

To sum up, the controversy regarding the inclusion of sense-object contact in the definition of perception leads to three definite conclusions. In the first place it is not necessary to mention all the characteristics of a thing defined; it is enough to state that characteristic which distinguishes the thing from all like and unlike things. When expressed in the language of causation, in referring to a cause of a thing produced it is not necessary to specify all the conditions that are involved in its production; it is sufficient to state that condition which is specific to the thing, i.e., its efficient cause. In defining perception as Gautama did it was not his intention to include all the characteristics or causes of perception but only that characteristic or cause which is specific to perception, viz., sense-object contact. In every cognition there are other entities like the mind or the self and their contact enters into the causes of cognition. But where ordinary explanation will not succeed the Naiyāyika is prepared to invoke the *adṛṣṭa* or *saṃskāra*. This is the classical karma doctrine.

C. *Sense-object contact* (*sannikarṣa*)

According to Gautama, sense-object contact is the first characteristic of perception, and all the sense-organs apprehend their objects only when they come into contact with them. The Buddhists hold the view that the tactual, gustatory and olfactory organs apprehend their objects when they come into contact with them; the visual and auditory organs do so without such contact. The Jains hold that only the visual organ apprehends its object without coming into contact with it; it apprehends the object at a distance with the help of light.

Gautama considers the following objections raised against his theory of sense-object contact: there is really no proof for the existence of visual ray; even if such a ray did exist the visual organ could be said to apprehend its object without coming into contact with it, on the ground that when glass, mica or crystal intervene between the eye and the object the latter can be perceived.

(a) *Visual Ray*

According to Gautama an objection is raised against the existence of the visual light on the ground that it is not perceived. By its very nature, light is endowed with colour and touch. If the ray did exist, it should have been perceived in the same manner as the light of the lamp is perceived. Perception of a thing is due to its being possessed of certain magnitude, being a composite and endowed with colour. All the conditions for the perception of light are present: the visual organ has magnitude; light is endowed with colour and touch; the visual organ, if it was made of light, cannot be without colour. Since the visual ray is not perceived in spite of the presence of all the conditions for perception, its existence cannot be established on the basis of inference (NS, NBh & NV III. 1,33).

Gautama rejects this objection saying that a thing may not be perceived but may nonetheless exist; what is not known by perception may be known by inference (NS III. 1,34). We do not see the other side of the moon or the lower part of the earth but neither is regarded as non-existent; we know their existence by inference (NBh III. 1,34). Secondly, perception depends upon the special character of the substance and its qualities. For instance, the molecule of water in the atmosphere, which is in actual contact with the visual organ, is perceived, but its quality, coolness, is not perceived. It is from the presence of such molecules that the winter has two seasons known as *hemanta* and *śiśira*. Similarly, the colour of the molecule of light in the atmosphere is not perceived but the quality of light, warmth, is perceived. It is from the presence of the molecules of light that the summer has two seasons known as *vasanta* and *grīṣma* (NBh III. 1,35). Thirdly, colour is perceived only when it inheres in a substance and possesses a special characteristic, manifestation (*udbhava*). This special characteristic is absent in the visual ray; the ray is not therefore perceived (NS III. 1,36). Fourthly, light, according to Vātsyāyana, has a diversity of character. It is of four kinds: (a) it is perceived both by the visual and tactual organs, e.g. the rays of the sun; (b) its colour is manifest but its touch is not, e.g. the rays of lamp-light are seen but their touch is not apprehended by the tactual organ; (c) its colour is not apprehended by the tactual organ; its colour is not manifest but its touch is, e.g. light in the heated water is perceived by the tactual organ but not by the visual organ; (d) light is apprehended neither by the visual nor by the tactual organ. And this light is the visual ray. This four-fold character of light is fully endorsed by Uddyotakara (NBh & NV III. 1,36). Fifthly, the non-perception of the visual ray is similar to that of the light of the stars (NS III. 1,39). The light of the stars is not perceived during the day because neither its colour nor touch is manifest. It is because of such special reasons that the visual ray is not perceived. It is only when a thing is not perceived at all nor are there any special reasons for its non-perception, that we would be justified in denying its non-existence (NS III. 1,39).

If this is so, why can we not say that the stone also has light because it is suppressed ? We cannot say so because the light of the stone is not perceived at night (NS III. 1,40) or at all times and by all means of cognition (NBh III. 1,40). The reason why the visual ray is not seen is not because it is suppressed or over-powered by the ray of an external light such as the light of the sun, but because it lacks the characteristic of manifestation. It is only if a thing has such a characteristic that it can be suppressed or over-powered (NS & NBh III. 1,42).

Sixthly, we do see a ray of light in the eyes of the animals like cats wandering by night, and from this we can infer that other living beings must also have the ray (NS & NBh III. 1,43).

Seventhly, if the eye did not have the ray, it could not perceive any object. But since the eye does perceive objects the ray does exist. Further, since the eye requires the aid of external light for the perception of objects it follows that the ray does not have the property of manifestation (NS & NBh III. 1,41).

Apart from these reasons, there are various well-known facts and usages to justify the existence of the visual ray. The sense-organs are not themselves perceptible by themselves. In regard to certain objects the operation of the visual organ is obstructed. If the visual ray had its colour manifested, then when such light-rays fall upon any perceived object that object would be burnt, as on the contact of fire. This is the only light that has its colour manifested. When several light-rays fall upon an object at one and the same time, these rays would hide the object from view. As a matter of fact, this does not happen (NBh & NV III. 1,37).

Uddyotakara states the inference for the existence of the visual ray as follows:

(i) The eye possesses light because, being a substance, it forms a necessary factor in the special set of causes that bring about the perception of colour, like the lamp.

(ii) The visual organ is possessed of light because, being a substance and being endowed with a special aptitude, it renders perceptible things placed behind transparent things, like the lamp (NV III. 1,42).

(b) *Contact of the visual organ with the object*

According to Vātsyāyana the opponent's argument is wrong on several counts when he says that an object is perceived even when glass or mica intervenes between the eye and the object. Firstly, the visual ray does come into contact with the object as the intervening glass or mica does not obstruct the passage of the ray. Equally, the apprehension of an object screened by a crystal is like that of a reflected image in a mirror of water. When a man looks into a mirror, the rays from his eyes enter the mirror and are turned back; then they come into contact with his own face and its form and colour are perceived. This perception of the reflected image is possible because such objects are, by nature, transparent. The visual ray cannot reach an object hidden behind a wall but can reach an object screened by transparent things like glass or mirror for the simple reason that the former is not transparent while the latter are. This is an actual state of affairs and it is not open to us to question it. It is not possible, says Gautama, to impose commands or prohibitions on things perceived or inferred. Every pramāṇa, says Vātsyāyana, apprehends things as they really exist, with their true nature and as possessed of their properties. It would not be right to argue, for example, that just as the colour is visible to the eye, so should smell also be visible, or as the cognition of fire arises from that of smoke so should the cognition of water also arise from that of smoke, or like the cognition of water, the cognition of fire should not arise from that of smoke. It is entirely wrong to argue that as the wall obstructs the visual ray, so should the glass, or as the glass does not obstruct the visual ray, so the wall should not. Whether there is obstruction or non-obstruction is a matter to be determined by perception or non-perception of the phenomenon, and inference. Thus the sense-object contact theory is fully justified, also in the case of the visual organ (NS & NBh III. 1,37 & 50).

Uddyotakara considers the following four objections raised against the contact theory with special reference to visual perception.[10]

1. The opponents argue that the eye cannot come into contact with an object, (*hetu*) because it cannot apprehend objects at a distance (*sāntaragrahaṇāt*=*hetu*). This hetu is explained in two ways: (a) The pupil of the eye is made up of a material

element and operates with the aid of a material element (visual ray). The pupil depends for its operation on the part of the owner of the pupil and his previous karma conducive to visual perception. Situated as the pupil is in the eye it cannot therefore be said to come into contact with the object. (b) In the case of the nose and other sense-organs which operate by coming into contact with objects, the objects are not apprehended because they are at a distance. But in the case of the eye objects at a distance are apprehended.

Uddyotakara refutes the opponents' argument: The hetu can mean either (a) the apprehension of that which, being at a distance, is not got at or (b) the apprehension of the object along with the distance.

(a) On the first interpretation the opponents' argument comes to this: The eye cannot operate by getting at the object because it apprehends objects without getting at them. The hetu is not different from the proposition to be proved. (b) If the second interpretation is accepted, one is entitled to ask: What is that distance which is apprehended by the eye along with the object? Is it ākāśa or some other substance or mere absence? The distance cannot be regarded as ākāśa for the latter is not an object of visual perception. Ākāśa has no colour. If the distance is a substance with colour, there could be no apprehension of the object; such a substance would obstruct the apprehension. The distance cannot be regarded as absence because the latter can never be apprehended independently. Absence resides in its locus and cannot therefore be apprehended independently of the locus. If the absence means that which is apprehended (independently but) as pertaining to the object with colour, then the hetu becomes inconclusive.

(b) If the hetu means the apprehension in the form 'this is distant', it cannot prove the proposition; for the cause of this awareness is the distance between the eye and the object, and not the distance between the eye and the object. Distance is determined with reference to the body of the cognizer. When the body and the sense-organ are in contact with the object, the latter is regarded as near; when the object is in contact with the sense-organ only, we regard it as far.

Uddyotakara does not comment on the karma aspect of the opponents' argument.

2. The opponents contend that the eye apprehends things larger and smaller than itself. Uddyotakara says that all that is necessary for perception of things of varying dimensions is mere connection of the eye with objects; it is not necessary for the entire thing to be in contact with the eye. According to Vācaspati the visual ray goes on expanding outwards, spreading wider as it proceeds farther, and thus illumines objects of varying dimensions. This is just like the light of the lamp. Originally centred round the wick, it spreads gradually in expanding circles, and thus illumines objects of varying sizes.

3. The opponents argue that there is no contact between the eye and the object because there is mention of direction (*dik*). The direction, says Uddyotakara, is determined with reference to the body of the perceiver and not to his sense-organs. When both the body and the sense-organs are in contact with the object perceived, there is no reference to the direction nor is there any notion of the thing being near or far. But when the object is in contact with the sense-organ only, and not with the body, we have notions of direction, proximity, remoteness, etc. These notions are relative to the perceiver's body and depend upon the number of conjunctions of the sense-organ, which is in contact with the object, with the points of space intervening between the body and the object.

4. The opponents say that we see the branch of a tree which is close to us at the same time as we see the moon which is far away. According to Uddyotakara no sane person believes that the apprehension of the tree is simultaneous with that of the moon. There is a difference in the time of these two apprehensions and the idea of simultaneity is due to the non-apprehension of this difference; just as when we prick a hundred petals of a lotus with a needle, we apprehend as if all of them are being pricked simultaneously only because we do not notice the difference amongst the moments of different pricking. This non-apprehension is known by inference based on the impossibility of obstruction. If the eye were to apprehend its object without coming into contact with it, walls or screens would have no power of obstructing our vision of objects hidden behind them. Moreover, we see things near us and do not see those far away. If there was no contact between the visual organ and the object, this could not be explained.

The opponents argue: objects hidden behind a wall are not seen because they are not capable of being seen; things are apprehended because they are objects of apprehension, and not otherwise. Thus the argument from obstruction has no bearing on the sense-object contact theory.

Uddyotakara rejects this argument on the ground that nothing can be an object of perception without some sort of connection. Apart from such a connection, what can this 'becoming an object of perception' mean ? Thus there is really no difference of opinion as regards the facts of the case; it is only a difference of idiom.

Having thus rejected the various arguments of the opponent Uddyotakara formulates the following inference for the sense-object contact theory: The eye operates by getting at its object because it is a sense-organ like the nose, etc. The nose, etc. have been found to operate by getting at their objects. The eye also is a sense-organ. Therefore the eye operates by getting at its object. The same inference can be formulated by making 'all sense-organs' its subject.

If, in spite of these cogent proofs, the opponent persists in his erroneous view, Uddyotakara reminds him of the general principle regarding the causal process. If causes can produce their effects by themselves, without getting at one another, without having any power or force added on to them, how is it that effects are not produced at all times and in all places ? For instance, the potter's stick, his wheel, etc., can produce a pot only when they are in contact with the material of which the pot is made (NV I. 1,4).

Six kinds of sense-object contact

Apart from meeting the criticism of the opponents, Uddyotakara was perhaps the first to formulate a systematic theory of six kinds of sense-object relation.[11] These are explained by him as follows:

(i) *Contact* (*saṃyoga*)

Contact takes place only between two substances. For instance, when a jar is seen, the jar as having the quality of colour is the object; the visual organ is another object; the connection between the two is one of contact.

(ii) *Inherence in that which is in contact* (*saṃyuktasamavāya*).

In the perception of the colour of the jar, the contact of the eye with the colour is of the nature of inherence in that which is in contact. The colour is a quality which subsists in the jar and this subsistence (*vṛtti*) is of the form of inherence.

(iii) *Inherence in that which inheres in that which is in contact* (*saṃyuktasamavetasamavāya*)

In the perception of the genus of the quality of colour, the contact is of this type. The genus of colour inheres in the colour and the colour inheres in the jar which is in contact with the eye.

(iv) *Inherence* (*samavāya*)

In the perception of sound, sound which is the quality of ākāśa inheres in the ākāśa of the ear by which it is apprehended. The contact is of the form of inherence.

Sound produces other sounds. Each of these sets out another sound, till there is produced a sound in that part of ākāśa which is enclosed in the eardrum. This sound is perceived through inherence.

(v) *Inherence in that which inheres* (*samavetasamavāya*)

When we perceive a genus of a quality independently of the substance, the contact is of this type. The genus of sound inheres in sound, which inheres in the ākāśa of auditory organ. The perception of this genus is independent of the substance, ākāśa, of which it is a quality, and the contact is of this type.

(vi) *Relation of qualificand-qualifier* (*viśeṣaṇaviśeṣyabhāva*)

When we perceive the absence of the jar on the floor, this type of contact is involved. The eye is in contact with the floor in which resides the qualifier of the absence (*abhāva*) of the jar.

The perception of inherence also involves this type of contact. Inherence is the qualifier of that which is inherent.

The sense-object contact mentioned in the definition of perception covers all these varieties of contact (NV I. 1,4).

I Non-Inferential Character of Perception

According to Gautama perception is non-inferential in

character. He develops his theory in answer to the following objection:

Objection

Perception is inference because it apprehends only a part [of the object] (NS II. 1,30).

Reply

Not so, for [the objector] admits that there is perception of at least that part which is actually apprehended (NS II. 1,31).

Moreover, the apprehension is not only of a part, for that part is a part of a composite (NS II. 1,32).

According to Vātsyāyana the argument on which the objection mentioned above is based is as follows: The Naiyāyika holds that the cognition, "This is a tree", which arises from the contact of the object with the sense-organ, is a case of perception. But what really happens is that one sees only a part nearest to oneself, and certainly that one part is not the tree. And from the apprehension of this part one infers the tree. This inference of the tree is exactly like the inference of fire from smoke.

In answer to this objection Vātsyāyana poses the question as to how the object that is said to be inferred is made up. The opponent says that such an object can be constituted in two ways: (a) either it is an aggregate of parts or (b) it is a composite substance produced out of component parts but distinct from them. In the former case the object inferred from the apprehension of one part will have to be the component parts other than the part apprehended. In the latter case it will have to be the composite substance as different from its parts (NBh II. 1,30).

(a) On either method of composition, says Vātsyāyana, the inference of the object from the apprehension of one of its parts is impossible. If the tree in the perception under consideration is not different from the parts, and it is regarded only as an aggregate of the parts, the cognition of the tree as such will be an impossibility. For the tree is neither the parts directly perceived nor those that are not perceived but are said to be inferred. Thus the tree is neither perceived nor can it be regarded as inferred (NBh II. 1,30).

If such a cognition of the tree were to arise, adds Uddyotakara, it could arise only with reference to what is non-tree; the cognition would therefore have no basis. Further, if there is no composite substance, it is meaningless to speak about parts, for 'part' is but a name for the component of a composite substance.

The objector contends that the name 'part' is given to 'one place' (*ekadeśa*) — the term used by Gautama in reference to this view. But a place is only a container or a receptacle, and in the present instance the only thing of which the place could be the substratum is the composite substance. If the objector denies the substance, he must also deny the so-called 'one place' as the meaning of 'part'.

According to Uddyotakara the objector offers another interpretation: Things are said to be component parts if they are in constant juxtaposition without being causally connected. Juxtaposition (*pratyāsatti*) without causal connection, says Uddyotakara, is contrary to the nature of things. Such juxtaposition is possible in the following three ways and in each of them causal connection is involved. A number of causes such as clay, potter's wheel, cooperate to produce a common effect, the jar. A number of effects are produced by a single set of causes like colour, taste, and odour along with the jar. Of the two things, one is the cause and the other is the effect, e.g. fire and smoke. Thus the objector, observes Uddyotakara, has really a poor insight into the nature of what juxtaposition means! (NV II. 1,31).

The objector argues that when one perceives the front part, one infers from it the hind part; thus the cognition of the tree results from the remembrance of several parts perceived and inferred. But in that case the resulting cognition, says Vātsyāyana, is a case of remembrance and not of inference. In fact, it cannot be either (NBh II. 1,30).

Neither the front part nor the hind part is the tree, and no cognition of the tree can be produced, says Uddyotakara, by the remembrance of what is not the tree. Remembrance is that cognition of a thing which appears as accompanied by a previous cognition, e.g. I am the one by whom the colour of this object had been perceived before and by whom its taste is now perceived. Since the hind part in the case of the tree was previously inferred from the perception of the front part, the objector is only entitled to say that these two parts have been remembered. Neither of these parts is the tree nor does the tree exist. Even if such a notion of the tree could be said to arise with reference to these parts which do not, of themselves, constitute the tree, the cognition of the tree would be a cognition of a thing as what it is not.

Further, under this view the tree cannot be really inferred at all. In the argument that from the perception of the front part one infers the hind part we cannot discover what exactly is the subject of the inference. If the objector states his inference in the form "This is a tree, because it has a front part", the inference of the tree is equally impossible. Since the objector does not accept the tree as an object perceived there is no subject for the inference — a subject of which 'having the front part' could be predicated. All that is perceived is merely the front part, and until the tree is perceived, the predicate cannot be attributed to it. The objector suggests that the inference may take the form "This front part has the hind part". This is surely absurd, as the front part cannot be said to have the hind part. And if one part can belong to another part, this latter becomes the composite whole — a composite having that other part. This is directly opposed to the objector's view (NV II. 1,30).

(b) According to the second view as to how the object is made up, what is inferred is the tree as different from the parts of which it is composed. Such an inference, says Vātsyāyana, is impossible. It is necessary for inference that the inferential mark (*liṅga* = hetu) and the thing to be inferred must be first perceived as directly associated with each other. In the present case the tree as related to its part perceived could not have been perceived. But if such a relation has been perceived, the tree must also have been perceived. Thus the inference of a composite substance as different from its parts is completely untenable (NBh II. 1,30). A thing which has never been perceived, adds Uddyotakara, can never be inferred (NV II. 1,30).

The correct position on this subject, says Gautama, is that we perceive not only one component part but also a composite whole which is different from its component parts (NS II. 1,32). Since this composite occupies the same point in space as the component part, all the conditions which make the component part perceptible can equally make the composite perceptible. Thus when the component is perceived the composite is also perceived. It is true that all the component parts of a composite object are not actually perceived nor does the object subsist entirely in any of the parts that are perceived. But this difficulty, says Vātsyāyana, can be easily met. In the first place, the terms like 'entire' (*kṛtsna*) or 'non-entire' (*akṛtsna*) are not applicable to what is a single object; the composite object is neither 'entire' nor 'non-entire' but a single object. The term 'entire' applies to a number of things when they are meant collectively, without any one of them being left out; the term 'non-entire' applies only to some one or a few of the number of things. In the case of the composite we cannot therefore say that while some parts are seen others are not. It has no parts apart from its components, nor is it of the same nature as its component parts. The character of the composite substance is such that it is perceived along with those parts that are perceived, and it is not perceived along with those that are not perceived on account of obstruction. But this does not alter the character of the composite; it is single and not divided; the distinction between the perceived and unperceived parts does not amount to a distinction between the composite as subsisting in the perceived parts and the composite as subsisting in the unperceived parts (NBh. II. 1,32). One may see a man with a sword and not see him with a stick, says Vācaspati, but the man is the same in both cases.

Commenting on this subject, Uddyotakara observes that if the composite object were to subsist entirely in that part which is being perceived, there would be no need for other component parts. Further, if it were to consist of a single component part, it could never be perceived, as the conditions of perceptibility are magnitude (*mahattva*), multiplicity of constituent causes (*kāraṇabahutva*) and aggregation (*pracaya*). Moreover, such a composite would be incapable of disruption as it has no components into which it could be disrupted. Thus the composite cannot be said to subsist entirely in any single component. The composite cannot be said to subsist partially in any single component, because it has no parts apart from its constituent causes. If such a composite were perceived in its parts it would have to be described as subsisting entirely in each of these parts. Nor can there be perception of all its parts, as some parts are hidden from view by others. Thus the composite cannot be said to subsist entirely in its component parts. It is because of these difficulties that the mode of subsistence of the composite in its components is so difficult to grasp; all that can be said is that the components are the substratum and the composite the superstratum (NV II. 1,32).

The entire argument about the inferential character is based upon the cognition of a component part. This cognition cannot be without an object, i.e. the part. Hence to accept this object as perceived is to accept perception as distinct from inference. Since the cognition of the part is a perceptual cognition, says Gautama, perception must be accepted as a pramāṇa. The initial cognition of a single part cannot itself be inferential. For there can be no hetu for such an inference. The only hetu that could be used is the cognition of another part, and to establish this latter cognition as inferential we will need another hetu in the form of still another inferential cognition of another part, and so on. To avert this infinite regress, we have to postulate the cognition of the component part as pure perception (NBh II. 1,31).

Inference is always preceded by perception and involves remembrance of the relation between the sign and the significate. Perception involves no such remembrance. Inference deals with objects, past, present and future, but perception is concerned with objects present only. Inference has several varieties while perception has no such varieties. Thus Uddyotakara shows how one is radically different from the other (NV II. 1,31).

IV Object (Substance) as Distinct from Qualities

According to Uddyotakara the Buddhist view is that substance and qualities cannot be distinguished. This view is directly opposed to the Nyāya concept of a substance as a substratum of qualities and separate from the qualities. One of the arguments by which Gautama proves self as separate from the aggregate of body and sense-organs is that a single object is apprehended by sight and touch (NS III. 1,1). This fact of apprehension establishes not only the unity of the object of cognition but also the unity of the self. In this context Uddyotakara examines the Buddhist objection to Nyāya position.

According to the Buddhist, what we actually apprehend is

only touch by the tactual organ and colour by the visual organ, and not one single object or substance possessing the qualities of touch and colour. Uddyotakara asks the Buddhist to explain: how does one know that colour or touch is actually apprehended by the sense-organs concerned ? If he says that we actually find that the cognition produced by the visual organ is qualified by colour or the cognition produced by the tactual organ is qualified by touch, then his argument against the Nyāya position will not stand. As a matter of fact, whenever we apprehend an object by means of the visual and tactual organs, say a jar, the object we cognize is the jar; our cognition is qualified by the jar, and is of the jar. We have also the further evidence of perception of objects when their qualities are not actually apprehended. For instance, when a row of cranes is flying across the sky at night, we do not perceive their colour and other qualities, but we do have perception of their being birds (NV III. 1,1).

The Buddhist suggests that the so-called notion of a substance can be explained as the perception of qualities of colour, etc. as arranged in different shapes. This suggestion, says Uddyotakara, is based on a complete misunderstanding of what shape actually means. To say that an object has a particular shape (*ākāra*) is to say that it resembles something different from itself. For instance, when we speak of the man having the shape of a pillar, we mean that he has the shape of a thing, the pillar, which is not man; that is, the word 'shape' in this context means the resemblance of the pillar to the man; and this resemblance is possible only when the man and the pillar are both well-known entities. As the Buddhist does not accept the existence of real substances like a cow, horse, etc. there cannot arise specific notions of the shape of those substances caused by qualities, colour, touch, etc. If the Buddhist were to suggest that the different notions of the cow, horse, etc. are caused by different arrangements or configurations (*saṃsthāna*), the answer of Uddyotakara would be: if these different arrangements are identical with colour, etc., they cannot explain the difference in our cognitions; if, on the other hand, they are regarded as different from colour, etc., it amounts to the acceptance of a separate substance by another name, i.e. arrangement (*saṃsthāna*) (NV I. 1,13 & 14).[1]

V Reality of Objects: Objections Examined

Gautama discusses two objections to the reality of objects and these objections and his answer to them are as follows:[1]

1. *Objection*

Objects are separated from their corresponding concepts. [Objects as they exist] are not apprehended because they are separated from their corresponding concepts, in the same way as cloth is not apprehended when separated from its threads (NS IV. 2,26).

Reply

The hetu [in the above objection] is not valid as it is self-contradictory (NS IV. 2,27).

The cloth is not apprehended separately from its threads because it resides in them (NS IV. 2,28).

Objects are apprehended by means of pramāṇa (NS IV. 2,29).

The non-existence of objects is established neither by means of pramāṇa nor without it (NS IV. 2,30).

2. *Objection*

The notion of pramāṇa and the *prameya* is like that of dream and of object of dream (NS IV. 2,31).

Or, it is like the notions of illusion (*māyā*), celestial town and mirage (NS IV. 2,32).

Reply

This cannot be proved because the objection does not contain a hetu (NS IV. 2,33).

The notion of dream objects is like that of objects of remembrance and desire (*saṅkalpa*) (NS IV. 2,34).

Wrong apprehension [of objects] is destroyed by the apprehension of the true nature [of the objects], just as our notion of object in a dream is destroyed on [our waking up] (NS IV. 2,35).

Wrong apprehension cannot be denied as its cause exists (NS IV. 2,36).

Wrong apprehension is twofold on account of the distinction between the object as it really is (*tattva*) and the object as it is apprehended (*pradhāna*) (NS IV. 2,37).

1. Vātsyāyana explains the first objection: According to the Nyāya view, objects exist because we have concepts of them. Since these concepts are wrong, there is no justification for saying that the objects of these concepts exist. If we had right concepts, we would be able to apprehend objects as they are. For instance, when we think separately of each thread of the cloth — as 'this is a thread', 'this is another thread', etc. — we do not perceive in it anything other than the thread, which could constitute the object of our concept of the cloth. The concept of the cloth is therefore wrong. Our concepts of objects are exactly like the concept of the cloth and these concepts are therefore equally wrong (NBh IV. 12, 25 & 26).

Explaining Gautama's reply, Vātsyāyana says that the above objection is based upon the premise that the analysis of existing things (*bhāva*) is possible. If this premise is right, the objector would not be justified in saying that we do not apprehend the objects as they are; if, on the other hand, we do apprehend things as they are through the analysis of our concepts, the objector must abandon his premise. Thus the objection is self-contradictory. Secondly, the effect is based on cause and cannot therefore be apprehended apart from it. As is well known, two things are apprehended separately only when one does not subsist in the other. All ordinary objects are composites of non-perceptible components (atoms), and it is through our analysis of the notions of the composites that they are apprehended as separate from their components (atoms). Thirdly, the analysis of things through the medium of our notions is the analysis of those things which, as declared by the scriptures, are involved in actions of living beings and are cognized and proved by means of the pramāṇas. All that the analysis does is to enable us to determine whether a certain thing exists or does not exist or whether we apprehend it as what it is or as what it is not; it cannot prove that nothing exists (NBh IV. 2,29). Whether we depend upon pramāṇa or not, this position cannot be altered. If pramāṇa could prove that nothing exists, it would be self-contradictory; if the absence of pramāṇa could prove that nothing exists, that could equally prove that everything exists (NBh IV. 2,30).[2]

2. According to Vātsyāyana, the second objection mentioned by Gautama is that our notion of pramāṇas and objects cognized

by means of them is like that of dream and dream objects. Objects which we dream in our sleep do not exist but we have their wrong notion (*abhimāna*). Similarly, pramāṇas or objects cognized by means of these pramāṇas can be compared to our notions of magical phenomena, celestial cities or a mirage (NBh IV. 2, 31-32).

Vātsyāyana explains Gautama's answer in the following way. In the first place, there is no reason to believe that what we dream does not exist. It is true that when we wake up we do not see the things we dreamt, but this fact can lead to a conclusion contrary to the conclusion of the objector. If we can prove that dream objects are unreal because we do not apprehend them on waking up, then the objector must accept that things are real because they are apprehended during our waking state. But if the objector were to suggest that whether or not we apprehend things in dream or in waking state they are equally non-existent, then non-apprehension cannot prove anything. For instance, when we do not apprehend colour in the absence of a lamp, what justifies our attributing of non-apprehension of colour to the absence of the lamp is the fact that colour exists and would have been perceived if the lamp were present.

Secondly, the objector cannot really explain the diversity of our dreams. For instance, we may dream of an object which is pleasant or unpleasant or neither; sometimes one may not dream at all. This diversity of dream cognitions can only be explained if there are real causes for the occurrence of various dream cognitions.

On the subject of dreams and dream objects some of the observations of Uddyotakara are interesting. If there were no distinction between dream and waking states, the distinction between merit and demerit would be jeopardized. For instance, we do not ordinarily regard incest committed in dream as a sin, but if the opponent of the Nyāya view were right, we would have to treat incest committed by a person when he is awake in the same way. It would be no excuse to say that in one case one was asleep while in the other one was awake, for we would have no means of ascertaining that it is the sleep that has caused the mental derangement leading to the act of incest in the dream. Another observation of the commentator is that the diversity of dream cognitions cannot be explained, as is suggested by the opponent, by invoking the karma doctrine. For instance, at the time of death one man dreams of a river as full of water while another dreams of the same river as full of blood and pus. These different dreams cannot be said to be due to the impressions (*vāsanās*) left by the karma of each of these men for the simple reason that different dreams can be produced only by different causes, i.e. real objects, and not by internal causes like the impressions (NV IV. 2,34).

Thirdly, the dream objects, says Vātsyāyana, are like those of remembrance and desire. All such objects have been previously apprehended and the cognitions concerned do not justify the non-existence of these objects. A dream cognition refers to an object previously apprehended in the waking state, and when the sleeping man wakes up from his dream, he recognizes the dream cognition as 'this is what I saw in my dream'. It is only in relation to the cognition in waking state that he determines the dream cognition as unreal. If there were no difference between these two states, the contention that the notion of pramāṇas and objects cognized by means of them are like the notions of things in a dream becomes meaningless; for the basis of the notion of a thing as what it is not (i.e. a wrong notion) is based upon the notion of a thing as what it is. The notion of things in a dream, for instance, 'I have seen an elephant' can only rest upon some real prototype, i.e. the cognition of a real elephant. This is like the wrong notion of a pillar as man. Unless one has seen a real man, one can have no notion of man in regard to the pillar (NBh IV. 2,34).

Fourthly, the objector has misunderstood the significance of what is meant by the destruction of wrong apprehension by right apprehension. When one has the notion of man with regard to the pillar, it is a wrong apprehension, i.e. apprehension of the thing as what it is not. But when one has the notion of the pillar with regard to the pillar, this is right apprehension, i.e. apprehension of the thing as what it is. What is set aside by the right apprehension is the wrong apprehension and not the object. In the case of magical phenomena, celestial cities and mirages, we have the cognition of things as what they are not; and these wrong cognitions also are set aside by right cognitions. With the necessary equipment, the magician takes up a real substance similar to that whose illusion he intends to produce and it is with reference to this real substance that he produces the wrong apprehension in another person. Either snow or some such real substance actually assumes the shape of a town and those who see it from a distance have the notion of it as 'town'; this is quite obvious from the fact that such a wrong notion does not appear when there is no such substance as snow. When the rays of the sun begin to flicker on coming into contact with the heat radiating from the earth's surface, we have the notion of water in regard to the flickering of the rays on account of the perception of the common quality of flickering; this is evident from the fact that when we draw near or when the rays of the sun are not there, no such mirage arises. In all such cases of wrong apprehension there is some sort of real entity at the bottom somewhere, and no wrong cognition is entirely baseless.

Moreover, there is a distinct difference in the character of the cognitions. The apprehension by the magician is of magical phenomena as unreal while the audience sees these phenomena as real. The man distant from the snow or the flickering rays regards them as real while the man nearer to them has no such apprehension at all. The man in a dream treats the objects he dreams as real and when he wakes up, he recognizes them as unreal. This diversity of cognitions and attitudes towards objects of cognitions would be inexplicable if everything were non-existent, and as such without any name or character (NBh IV. 2,35 & 36).

Last, but not least, the wrong apprehension exists as much as its object exists, because we cognize both the existence of the wrong apprehension and its cause. Every one has wrong apprehension, and is actually aware of it as such. When we have a wrong apprehension of the pillar as man, the real object (*tattva*) is the pillar and what is apprehended is the man (*pradhāna*). It is because there are these two distinct objects that the perception of similarity between them produces the wrong apprehension of the pillar as the man. In fact, wrong apprehensions can arise only in regard to similar objects, because they are produced by the perception of similarity.

As regards various objects of sense-perception like colour, odour, etc. and other objects of cognition, there are no two things involved — in the shape of the real object and what is actually apprehended. Consequently the question of perception of properties common to them does not arise. The apprehensions of these objects cannot therefore be regarded as wrong apprehensions; in fact, these must be regarded as right apprehensions.

In view of these considerations Vātsyāyana concludes that the contention of the opponent that notions of the pramāṇas and of objects cognized by them are wrong notions is absolutely unjustified. Objects are therefore real and our apprehensions of these objects are right apprehensions (NBh IV. 2,37).

In addition to the two objections rejected by Gautama, Uddyotakara mentions a third view which is equally opposed to the Nyāya concept of the reality of objects. According to this view objects are not different from consciousness (*citta*) because they are apprehended in the same way as our feelings, etc. (*vedanā*) are. Feelings have no existence apart from consciousness, and similarly, objects also must be regarded as having no existence separate from consciousness (NV IV. 2,33).

This view, says Uddyotakara, is wrong because it stems from confusion between feeling and cognition. Pleasure and pain are undoubtedly feelings but they are in the nature of objects apprehended. But cognition (*jñāna*) itself is the act of apprehending (*grahaṇa*), and certainly apprehension is different from the object of apprehension. Even if we were to concede that cognition is the same as feeling, the opponent cannot produce any instance to show that the apprehension and its object are one and the same thing. The act (*kriyā*) of apprehending and its object (*karma*) can never be one and the same. The contention of the opponent is thus contrary to the evidence furnished by pramāṇas (NV IV. 2,33).

Another criticism that can be made against this view is that it destroys the very basis of reasoned argument. If there were nothing external to consciousness, how could we have anything like proof and refutation ? Consciousness of one man is never apprehended by another man and no proposition can therefore be proved or refuted by one man for the benefit of another. The situation cannot be improved if we regard consciousness itself as having the form of words (*śabdākāra*). Of the two things one thing can be conceived as having the form of another only when there is a similarity between them and that similarity is perceived. But if there is nothing apart from consciousness, there can be no such real entity as 'word', and consequently the expression 'consciousness has the form of words' becomes meaningless. The only way to save the situation is to admit that there are real objects external to consciousness, and this, of course, is directly opposed to the proposition of the opponent.

In summing up his criticism Uddyotakara says: "Objects are different from my consciousness (a) because they are possessed of generic and specific properties, like the consciousness appearing in another person, (b) because they are capable of being apprehended by pramāṇas." Another reason added by Uddyotakara is that the objects of apprehension are brought about by merit. One may perform a deed in one body and the fruit may appear in another body. For instance, a man who performs a sacrifice for the birth of a son obtains the fruit of his deed in another body. The son is born long after the deed and in a place other than the father's body. This instance might be construed to mean that the action resides in one substratum while the fruit resides in another. The answer of Uddyotakara is that the deed and its fruit have the same substratum, the self of the performer of the deed. It is the pleasure of having the son which is the fruit and there is therefore no difficulty in locating the deed and the fruit in the same self. And, of course, the deed is good and so is the fruit. Thus the objects apprehended can be said to be preceded or produced by merit (NV IV. 2, 32 & 34).

VI Composite and Component

Gautama deals with the following objection which is raised against his concept of the composite (*avayavin*) in the context of perception.[1]

(1) Since apprehension (*vidyā* = *upalabdhi*) and non-apprehension are each of two kinds, there arises a doubt (NS IV. 2,4).

(2) There is no room for doubt, as the hetus are well established (NS IV. 2,5).

Objection

(3) There is, [says the objector], no room for doubt on account of the impossibility of subsisting (NS IV. 2, 6).

(4) The composite is absent because its components subsist in it neither wholly (*kṛtsna*) nor partially (*ekadeśa*) (NS IV. 2,7).

(5) Also because the composite does not subsist in its components (NS IV. 2,8).

(6) In the absence of such subsistence there is no composite as separate from its components (NS IV. 2,9).

(7) And the components are not the composite (NS IV. 2,10).

Reply

(8) There is no room for any such objection as the term 'diversity' (*bheda*) cannot be used in reference to 'one' (*eka*) which is devoid of diversity (NS IV. 2,11).

(9) Further, the hetu is a non-hetu (unreasonable) because even if one component could subsist in another, [the composite could not subsist in it] (NS IV. 2,12).

According to Vātsyāyana the doubt which Gautama has mentioned is as follows: Apprehension and non-apprehension are of two kinds: we apprehend things that exist and things that do not exist. For instance, there is apprehension of what is present, i.e. we see water in the tank; there is also apprehension of what is not present, i.e. we perceive water in the mirage. There is non-apprehension of what is present, i.e. we do not perceive a long-buried treasure; there is also non-apprehension of what is not present, i.e. we do not perceive what is absent. Thus whether we apprehend the composite or not, there is a doubt as to whether the composite exists or does not. Although Gautama has already established, beyond all doubt, the existence of the composite as different from its components, he introduces [what is] a Buddhist objection in the following way: one could also say that there is no doubt because it is impossible for the composite to subsist in any way whatsoever (NBh IV. 2,4).

Vātsyāyana elaborates this objection as follows:

(a) Each single component cannot subsist either in the entire (*kṛtsna*) composite or only in a 'part' (*ekadeśa*) of the composite. The subsistence in the entire composite is not possible because both the composite and the component are not of the same size, and because there can be no connection between the composite and the component. The partial subsistence of the composite in the component is not possible because the composite has no parts separate from the components (NBh IV. 2,7).

(b) The entire composite cannot subsist in each one of the components or partially in all the components. The first alternative is not possible because the composite and the components are of different sizes; further, in that case we would be confronted with the possibility of the composite being reduced to a single substance. The second alternative is not possible as the composite has no parts other than the components (NBh IV. 2.8).

(c) The composite cannot subsist apart from the components because it is not so perceived. Such a composite would be eternal, as every substance which has no constituent parts for its substratum is eternal. And this is impossible (NBh IV. 2,9).

(d) The composite cannot be regarded as a mere property of the components, because the composite is never perceived apart from its components; further, there can be no connection of the property with that which has that property. If the property (the composite) could be perceived apart from that which has the property (component) the composite would be eternal. And this is impossible (NBh IV. 2,10).

Vātsyāyana explains the answer of Gautama to the Buddhist objection as follows: The expression 'entire' denotes all individuals and the expression 'a part' denotes some; these two expressions denote diversity (*bheda*). The composite is a single entity devoid of diversity, and these expressions cannot therefore be applied to the composite. Secondly, the hetu on which the Buddhist argument is based is no hetu at all. His argument is: The composite cannot subsist partially in its components, because it has no parts other than the components that it has (= *hetu*). Even if the parts of the composite were actually different from the components, the meaning of the composite subsisting partially in its components would be that one part or component subsists in another part or component, and not that the composite subsists in its components. If the composite is regarded as something different from the components, then even if it had parts other than those components this would not mean that it is the composite that subsists in the components; hence it would not mean that the composite subsists partially in the components. The hetu given by the Buddhist cannot therefore prove his proposition. What is meant by the composite subsisting in its components, says Vātsyāyana, is not that it subsists in them wholly or partially but that it subsists in them in the manner of the container subsisting in the contained or the one (composite) subsisting in the many (components). When one of the two things cannot have existence apart from the other, the former is called 'superstratum' (*ādheya*) and the latter 'substratum' (*ādhāra*). The composite is the superstratum and the components are the substratum. The composite is an effect-substance and it can have no existence apart from its cause-substance. But this is not the case with the cause-substance. It can exist apart from the effect-substance. What has been proved to be true of non-eternal things can be inferred to be true with regard to eternal things (NBh IV. 2, 11 & 12). This relation between the composite and its components is a peculiar relation of inherence (*samavāya*). All that a philosopher can do, says Uddyotakara, is to describe the relation as it actually exists (NV II. 1,32; IV. 2,12).

One of the objections to the Nyāya view of the composite arises in the context of what is known as the problem of variegated colour (*citrarūpa*) of the composite.[2] The Naiyāyika believes that colour (or any quality) of a composite (effect) is different from that of its parts (cause). For instance, the colour of a cloth is different from that of its threads. The causes of the two are also different. The inherent cause of the qualities of a substance, i.e. colour of the cloth, is the cloth itself, while its non-inherent cause is the colour of the threads which are the cause of the cloth. The difficulty in this view of causation arises when a cloth is produced from threads of different colours, e.g. blue, red, yellow and white. Obviously, the effect (cloth) will also have all these colours. In this connection it may be mentioned that qualities are of two kinds. Some like contact (*saṃyoga*) reside only at a particular point in their substrata, while others like colour pervade the whole of the substratum. In the case of a cloth of variegated colours, however, the various colours, blue etc., reside in particular parts, and therefore they will be the colours of those parts only. Obviously, the various colours cannot be the colours of the cloth, because each one of them does not pervade the whole of the cloth, and also because the cloth must have a colour different from that of its parts (threads). If the cloth is different from the threads, its variegated colour cannot be explained on the basis of the Nyāya view of the composite.

Uddyotakara meets this objection by a simple device: the cloth has only one colour, called variegated colour (*citrarūpa*). This colour is both one and many; it is a variegated colour which consists of many colours, blue, yellow, etc. A thing can be regarded as the substratum of only that colour which is perceived in it. The colour of the cloth perceived is the variegated colour. The colour of the components is exactly that which is perceived in them. The colours of the threads are the colours perceived in them, blue, yellow, etc. The expression 'variegated' (*citra*) itself denotes both one and many; we have both expressions 'variegated colour', which is in singular number and 'variegated colours', which is in plural. If one colour cannot be said to be variegated, several colours cannot also be said to be variegated; for several variegated colours are nothing but the collection of a number of individual colours. If several non-variegated colours can make a variegated colour, this amounts to saying that the non-variegated becomes variegated. This is as self-contradictory as the assertion that non-white is white. If the contention is that the non-variegated colours of the threads combine to produce the variegated colour of the cloth, this is quite acceptable. The cloth, says Uddyotakara, has only one colour known as variegated colour (*citrarūpa*), which consists of many individual colours, blue, yellow, etc.

The concept of variegated colour leads to another difficulty. For instance, what would be the position if one of the two sides of a cloth is variegated and the other is not ? The cloth which consists of one side of a variegated colour and the other of a non-variegated colour is a cloth of variegated colour; so that it is reasonable to expect that just as we perceive a variegated colour in the side that has the colour we should also perceive a variegated colour in the side that does not have it. We do not perceive such a variegated colour, says Uddyotakara, because one variegated colour is not productive of another; how can the variegated colour of one side produce another variegated colour in the whole cloth ? All that we can say is that the two colours of the two sides combine to produce a new colour in the whole cloth: and this is exactly the colour that we perceive. If the cloth had no colour, it could not be seen. The perception of the cloth cannot be said to be due to the colour of its parts; if perception of one thing could be due to the colour of another thing, we would have seen the air, which is colourless, through the colour in fire (NV IV. 2,12)!

Defence of the atom

(1) According to Gautama, if the opponents' contention were right, the composite and the components should continue till the time of *pralaya* (total annihilation). But there can be no such annihilation because the atoms exist. And the atom is that which is not capable of being further divided (NS IV. 2,15 & 17).

Vātsyāyana explains Gautama's position: If there are difficulties in the subsistence of the composite in its components, these difficulties would be applicable to the subsistence of the components in their own components; for the components have their own components. These difficulties should lead either to the denial of the existence of all things or to a stage where there is nothing but the mere atom which has no components. In the former case there is nothing to perceive; in the latter nothing can be perceived because the atom is imperceptible. If there is no perception of anything whatsoever, the very basis of the opponents' argument is destroyed.

The kind of difficulties envisaged by the opponent cease at the atomic stage. The atom has no components and is therefore not divisible into further components. For instance, when we divide a clod of earth into parts, we reach smaller and smaller particles; this division must come to an end at that part of the clod than which there could be no smaller part; this part is therefore the smallest part possible; it is that very thing than which there is nothing smaller that is what is known as the atom (NBh IV. 2,15).

(2) Gautama mentions the following objection: The notion of the indivisible atom cannot be accepted because the atom is permeated by ākāśa (NS IV. 2,18). If ākāśa is all-pervasive, it must permeate the atom from both inside and outside the atom; being so permeated the atom must be made up of parts; and being so made up it must be non-eternal (NBh IV. 2,18). If, on the other hand, the atom is not so permeated, ākāśa cannot be regarded as all-pervasive (NBh IV. 2,19).

Gautama's answer is that the expressions 'inside' and 'outside' are only applicable to the parts of things produced from the atoms; these cannot apply to the atom which is not an effect or a product (NS IV. 2,20). The term 'inside', says Vātsyāyana, stands for those constituent parts of a thing which are hidden from view by other constituent parts, and the term 'outside' for those constituent parts of the thing which hide the hidden constituent parts and which are themselves not hidden from view. Hence these terms are applicable only to that which is a product or an effect. The atom is not a product or an effect and is therefore partless. Hence the use of such terms in reference to the atom is absolutely unjustified (NBh IV. 2,20).

Ākāśa is regarded as all-pervasive, says Gautama, because its properties, viz. sound and contact (*saṃyoga*), are all-pervasive (NS IV. 2,20). Sounds that are produced anywhere are found to pervade ākāśa and subsist in it. Similarly, the contacts with minds, atoms and their products are also found to pervade ākāśa. These two properties of ākāśa thus make it all-pervasive (NS IV. 2,21).

(3) [It may be objected why ākāśa being all-pervading, does not obstruct the objects moving in it, and cause their disruption, just as water obstructs a boat, and gets disrupted or transfigured by its movement (NVTT IV. 2,21).] Gautama replies that there is an absence of pattern (*avyūha*). Moreover, absence of pattern, non-obstruction (*aviṣṭambha*), and all-pervasiveness are the properties of ākāśa (NS IV. 2,22). Only things which have parts and tangible can break up or obstruct.

(4) Gautama mentions another objection: An atom, inasmuch as it is corporeal (i.e. having a limited measure) must have a shape (*saṃsthāna*), and consequently it must have component parts (NS IV. 2,23). A shape is only a particular arrangement of component parts and can only belong to such things as are limited and tangible. Atoms also have such a shape; they are globular (NBh IV. 2,23). Similarly, an atom is connected with other atoms (NS IV. 2,24). When an atom intervenes between two other atoms and becomes connected with them it produces separation between them. From this it is inferred that the two parts of the intervening atom are connected with the two atoms. Similarly, it can also be connected on all sides with other atoms. Thus the atom must have parts (NBh IV. 2,24).

The answer of Gautama to all such objections is that this kind of argument leads to an infinite regress (*anavasthā*) and to endless splitting (NS IV. 2,25). The process of division cannot be carried on till the object divided disappears. If such an infinite regress were accepted, says Vātsyāyana, it would mean that in every object there are endless component substances; this in turn would mean that we would have to abandon our notions of diverse dimensions or weight, and that after the disruption of the component parts of the atom, the composite and the component would have to be regarded as having equal dimensions. Hence the infinite regress which the opponent forces upon things must be rejected and the concept of the partless atom accepted (NBh IV. 2,24 & 25).

As regards the argument that the atom must have parts because it is connected with other atoms (i.e. the atom can bring about separation only if it is tangible, and conjunction not pervading over the whole of its substratum only if it is divisible into parts), Vātsyāyana points out that while it is true that the atom is tangible, the separation that the intervening atom causes between the two atoms is due to the fact that it constitutes an obstacle in the way of these two atoms coming together; it is not due to the atom itself being made up of parts (NBh IV. 2, 24 & 25).

Non-perception of objects

According to Gautama, if there were no composite there would be nothing for us to perceive (NS II. 1,33). The Buddhist contends that there can be perception even when there is no composite. For instance, one whose vision is dimmed may not be able to perceive a single hair but can certainly see a collection of hairs (NS IV. 2,13). All that we require is a collection (*samūha*) of atoms and not a composite.

In answer Gautama says that distinct or indistinct perception depends upon the efficiency of the sense-organs; these never go beyond the range of their respective objects, nor can they operate upon what is not their object (NS IV. 2,14). However efficient the sense-organ may be, it can never perceive odour, which is not the specific object of visual perception; however dull or inefficient it may become, it cannot but apprehend its own specific object. It may be that a person whose vision is not good cannot see the hairs singly, but can see them in an aggregate. In either case the object is basically perceptible. But the case of the atom is radically different. The atom is beyond the reach of the sense-organs altogether, and consequently, it can never become the object of perception. If an aggregate of atoms could be perceived it would mean that the sense-organs have operated upon something which is not their object at all. And since these philosophers do not accept any object other than the atoms, the Nyāya argument stands; if there is no composite there can be no perception at all.

Consistent with its doctrine, the Buddhist objection comes to this: The atoms which are individually non-perceptible become perceptible when they are collected together. When the atoms are separated they cease to be perceived. An object that we actually perceive is nothing but an aggregate (*saṃcaya*) of atoms. This argument, says Vātsyāyana, is based upon an erroneous view of what the aggregate means. The aggregate is in the nature of contact (*saṃyoga*), and the contact of things, which are themselves non-perceptible, can never be perceived. When we perceive a contact in the form 'this thing is in contact with that thing', what we perceive is only the contact of things that are themselves perceptible and never a contact of things that are beyond the reach of the sense-organs. Further, in the case of things that are perceptible to our sense-organs, whenever such things are not perceived there is always something in the nature of an obstruction that prevents their perception. In the case of the atom there is no such question of any deficiency in our sense-organs or obstruction to normal perception for the simple reason that the atom is non-perceptible. An object which is composed of non-perceptible atoms becomes perceptible, concludes Vātsyāyana, because it is a new object that is produced when the atoms come together (NBh IV. 2,14). As Uddyotakara puts it, the imperceptible atoms cannot become perceptible unless some specific characteristic (*viśeṣa*) is produced in them (NV IV. 2,14).

If we deny the composite, the Buddhist argues, we need not be in a situation, as feared by the Naiyāyika, where perception is impossible; what is perceived is an aggregate of atoms. Vātsyāyana replies that this does not do justice to the facts of perception. Since we have a notion of 'one substance', the question remains: what does it refer to ? If it refers to a non-diverse or single thing, then this thing is different from its diverse components. And this is exactly the Nyāya position. If it refers to diverse or separate things (or components), then it would amount to saying that the many things are perceived as one. We do not have any such notion as that of one in regard to the many, and therefore this suggestion must be rejected (NBh II. 1,36).

The Buddhist disputes this Nyāya view and says that we do have such notions as 'army' or 'forest' (NS II. 1,36). We have the notion of a single thing in the case of the army or the forest because the diversity of their components is not apprehended owing to such extraneous factors as their remoteness from the observer. Similarly, when the atoms are collected together, their diversity or distinctness is not perceived, and because of this non-perception there arises a notion of one in regard to the many atoms.

Gautama replies that in the case of the atoms such a unitary notion is impossible because they are non-perceptible (NS II. 1,36). Explaining this reply, Vātsyāyana says that the unitary notion that we have in the case of the army or the forest is only a figurative notion (*bhāktapratyaya*). The diversity of the components of the army or the forest is ordinarily perceptible but is not perceived owing to extraneous circumstances like the distance of the observer. Similarly, when there are several trees, the particular species (*jāti*) to which each tree belongs is such as is ordinarily perceptible but is not perceived owing to distance. In these cases diverse things are themselves perceived but their diversity or distinctness is not perceived. It is this non-perception which gives rise to a unitary notion in a secondary or figurative sense. But in the case of the atoms no unitary notion of a figurative character can arise because there can be no such non-perception of their diversity as they are themselves not perceptible (NBh II. 1,36).

The figurative notion, says Uddyotakara, is based upon *bhakti*, which literally means "that which is divided by two"; it refers to the similarity of a thing to that which it is not. For instance, when one sees the "dull intelligence of the ploughman", one speaks of him as a 'bull'. Uddyotakara further remarks that the unitary notion in the case of the atoms cannot be regarded as analogical (*upamānapratyaya*), because there is no similarity between that which is really as it is conceived (i.e. what is really one) and that which is not really so (i.e. many, not one). For instance, in the analogical notion "The boy is a lion" the word 'lion' stands for behaving like the lion; it is bravery that constitutes the basis of comparison. In the case of the atoms there is no such basis of comparison. The analogical notion is different from the figurative in that in the former the idea of difference between the two things is not completely lost as it is in the case of the latter.

The Buddhist comes forward with another solution to the problem. The atoms are many but as their diversity is not perceived they are regarded as one. Such a notion of one with regard to many may be regarded as a notion of something (i.e. many atoms) as what it is not (i.e. one), like that of the post as man. This solution, says Vātsyāyana, is equally untenable. The notion of something as what it is not depends upon the principal (*pradhāna*) notion of what it is. If there is a former notion it only establishes the existence of the latter. The basis of a wrong notion can only be a right notion, so that the notion of the many as one proves the reality of the notion of the really one as one; and this proves the existence of a really single object as distinct from its components. In the case of the wrong notion of the post as man, the principal notion is that of real man as man; it is only because of this notion that a notion of man can arise in regard to the post from the perception of certain points of similarity between the man and the post.

So far the Buddhist has argued his case on the basis of visual perception. He now says that we have evidence of principal unitary notions in the case of other sense-organs.[3] For instance, all sounds are one and the same and are therefore conceived as one. This is a case of really non-diverse things conceived as one — a true unitary conception which can furnish the prototype for the unitary conception in regard to the diverse atoms. Vātsyāyana replies that this kind of reasoning cannot prove the proposition of the Buddhist. The point at issue is whether in the case of the atoms in the aggregate there is a notion of something as what it is not, like the notion of the post as man or whether there is the actual state of things as represented by the unitary notion. That the sound is really one or there is a unitary notion in regard to sound can help only if this instance is cited in support of some special hetu. No such hetu has been offered by the Buddhist; in the absence of a hetu, the multiplication of instances can only add to uncertainty (NBh II. 1,36).

The Nyāya position on the question whether the unitary notion in the case of atoms can be regarded as figurative or analogical or wrong is summed up by Uddyotakara as follows: Wrong notions are due to perception of similarity and non-perception of difference. The perception of similarity imposes a contrary character upon a thing wrongly conceived. In the case of the atoms there can be neither perception of similarity nor non-perception of difference, as they are non-perceptible; consequently, there can be no imposition of a contrary character. In the absence of the cause the effect, wrong notion, would not be possible (NV II. 1,36).

As Gautama has observed, there would be non-perception of all things in the absence of the composite. Such things, says Vātsyāyana, are substance, quality, action, universal, particular, and inherence. A substance in its atomic condition is non-perceptible. If there were no substance in the form of a composite, there would be no objects of perception. Substances and other things mentioned above are found to be objects of perception and are perceived as such. But if they had no substratum in the form of the composite, they could not be apprehended. We have such apprehensions as 'this is a jar, dark in colour, one in number, large in size, conjoined (with something else), moving, existing, and made of clay.' Every one of these, colour, etc., is a property of some composite substance. Since we do have the apprehension of all these things, there must be such a thing as a composite, apart from the components (NBh II. 1,34). Uddyotakara adds that as perception is the basis of all pramāṇas, to deny perceptual objects is as good as denying objects of all the pramāṇas; this means the end of all pramāṇas and their operations. But since the fact that there is apprehension of things by pramāṇas cannot be disputed there must be such a thing as the composite (NV II. 1,34).

Not only is there a composite but it is also distinct or separate from its components. This is confirmed, says Gautama, by the fact that the operations like holding or pulling are possible only because the composite is distinct from its components (NS II. 1,35). A jar, for instance, can be pulled or held because it is distinct from its components. A thing is said to be held when one part of it is held and it is prevented from moving to another place; in holding a part of the object, one holds the thing itself, and on account of this holding, the whole object is prevented from moving to another place. This is what constitutes the operation of holding. Pulling is that operation in which one part of the thing being caught, the thing itself is made to move to another place. This is how people use these terms and this is what they mean. The operations of holding and pulling are possible only in the case of composites and never in the case of the non-composites. For instance, neither ākāśa, which is a non-composite substance, nor an atom, which is a purely component substance, can be held or pulled. Of course, not every composite substance can be held or pulled, for example, a heap of dust. All that is meant, says Uddyotakara, is that there can be no such operations of holding or pulling apart from the composites (NV II. 1,34).

According to Vātsyāyana, if the composite is denied, everything — substance, quality, motion, universal, particular and inherence would cease to be objects of our apprehension. If the composite is not regarded as different from the components, well-known notions such as magnitude (*parimāṇa*), contact (*saṃyoga*), movement (*spanda*) and class (*jāti*) would also be impossible. Vātsyāyana explains this as follows:

A unitary notion is the notion of something as what it really is. Whenever it arises, it must be regarded as arising in connection with what the thing really is. The specific hetu for this is that this notion has the same locus as the notion of magnitude.[4] In fact, the two notions — 'this is large' and 'this is one' — belong to the same object and therefore have the same locus. And from this fact, it is known that what is large is one. The Buddhist contends that this notion of magnitude can be regarded as a predominant property (*atiśaya*) of the aggregate of atoms. But this would be a wrong notion, says Vātsyāyana, because atoms have no magnitude. Since a wrong notion presupposes a right notion, there must be a right notion of magnitude in regard to something that really has the magnitude. And this proves that there must be some such substance as has magnitude. The Buddhist suggests that such notions as 'sound is large (*mahat*)' or 'sound is small (*aṇu*)' might serve as a prototype for the notion of magnitude. This would not be right, says Vātsyāyana, because these notions have nothing to do with magnitude. When we say 'sound is large or small', we mean that it is loud (*tīvra*) and faint (*manda*). These notions are unlike those of substances like fruits; we know their exact magnitude. The magnitude in such cases is perceptible while this is not possible in the case of either atoms or sounds.

The notion 'these two things are in contact' involves the cognition of contact having the same substratum as the notion of duality (*dvitva*); it proves that there are two things in contact. The substratum of this notion of contact cannot be an aggregate of atoms as suggested by the Buddhist for the following reason. The aggregate (*samudāya*) is either one combination (*prāpti*) of several component atoms or many combinations of a single substance. When we have a notion of two things being in contact, we have no such notion that two combinations are in contact, or contact subsists in many combinations of things. Both alternatives are therefore untenable. The two things which are in contact cannot be the atoms because the atoms are not perceptible. Thus the composite must be separate from the components.

It is argued that contact is nothing but proximity (*pratyāsatti*) which amounts to an obstruction (*pratighāta*); it is not something different from the objects in contact. This is not right, says Vātsyāyana, because contact does produce in the things in contact something entirely different from them. For instance, contact between the stick and the drum produces sound. Unless an entirely distinct quality, contact, is produced in the two things in contact, it would not be possible to ascertain the cause of the sound. Contact is thus a quality, distinct from the things in contact, and it is actually perceived as such. This is also confirmed by ordinary usage.

If the composite is denied, the notion of classes cannot be explained. The classes are the bases of our comprehensive or all-inclusive notions (*pratyayānuvṛtti*). For instance, the notion of horse is restricted in its application only to particular animals and not to others, because they belong to the class 'horse'. Since such classes exist, they must have a substratum without which they cannot be manifested or perceived.

The substratum of the class, it is suggested, can be the atoms arranged in a certain manner. The question now arises: Is the atom, to which this capacity to manifest the class belongs, itself in contact with perceiving sense-organ or not ? That is, when a particular class is cognized, is it or is it not cognized as subsisting in aggregates of atoms that are themselves in contact with the perceiving organ ? Since the entire aggregate of atoms, say a tree, cannot be perceived at a time, we are faced with the following situation: If it is perceived in the unperceived atoms, then the unperceived atoms should be perceived so as to manifest the class. If, on the other hand, it is perceived in the perceived atoms, it cannot be manifested in the unperceived atoms. If the class is regarded as manifested by that part of the thing which is perceived, then that part will be the substratum of the class. This would mean that when a certain aggregate of atoms is perceived, there is a diversity of things in that group; that part of the aggregate which is perceived is one thing and that which is not perceived another. Thus none of the alternatives is satisfactory and the only reasonable conclusion is that there is a distinct substance subsisting in the aggregate of atoms. And this is the composite as something different from its components (NBh II. 1,36).

On this entire undertaking of Gautama to establish the composite as different from the components Uddyotakara sums up the Nyāya position in the following way. If it is the composite that is to be established, such an effort can lead to no satisfactory result. If the opponent denies the very existence of the composite, no marks or properties can be indicated to establish its existence. The properties reside in their substratum and one who denies the substratum itself cannot be persuaded by means of its properties or by any reasonable arguments. Nor is there any room for difference of opinion with regard to the composite. Different opinion means contrary notion; contrary notion consists in imposing upon a thing a property contrary to the other property; such an imposition is possible if there is some degree of similarity between two things having contrary properties and non-perception of difference between them. If, therefore, the composite is not accepted, there can be no difference of opinion or contrary conception. But if the opponent wishes to prove that the composite is non-different from the components, it is for him to produce the pramāṇas; for without pramāṇa there can be no cognition.

It is in this perspective of the task that Uddyotakara takes up the brief of his opponent and deals with no less than his thirteen arguments. His refutation is interesting for the kind of argumentation prevalent in his time and since it does not add much to the exposition of the issues involved it has been left out (NV II. 1,33).

Contents of the Universe

According to the commentators the entities that fill our universe are literally innumerable and no wise philosophers can hope to enumerate them all. A selection on some rational or convincing basis becomes imperative. There is a deep-rooted tradition in Indian thought that the great sages or founders of systems have only one supreme aim, and that is to enable us to attain salvation or release provided, of course, their instructions are carried out both in letter and spirit. Accordingly, in his opening aphorism Gautama declares that the knowledge of the true nature of his sixteen categories leads to the attainment of supreme felicity (*niḥśreyasa*) which is equated with final release (*apavarga*). The commentators suggest that what is really required for release is the knowledge of Gautama's objects of cognition, and it is this knowledge which can put an end to our empirical existence. This provides a good enough basis for selection from a vast variety of things in the universe, and accordingly, Gautama has selected twelve such objects for treatment in his *Nyāya Sūtra*. These objects revolve round the self and its historical career in the universe. In a sense, if we treat each one of these objects as a class, they can be said to exhaust the universe; for we have amongst them not only the bio-physical equipment and cognitive and emotional apparatus of human beings but also what are called objects of sense (*artha*). Since the cognition of the whole universe is essentially perceptible, this amounts to stating a class of objects which can take care of the physical world.

Since the list of objects of cognition is an open list, the commentators make their own additions. For instance, Vātsyāyana says that there are many other objects like substance, quality, action, universal, particular and inherence (NBh I. 1,9). Uddyotakara is somewhat perturbed at the omission of pleasure from the list, but he has an explanation. Gautama was anxious to emphasize the need for treating everything as pain. Pleasure, of course, is a fact and it has been listed amongst the marks of self. In another context the commentator mentions that the objects of cognition on which pramāṇas operate are three: universals, particulars and things possessed of these (NV I. 1,3).

As already mentioned, there is a class of sense-objects (*artha*). Like the objects of cognition, these are also innumerable and consistent with the overall basis of selection. Gautama has selected those sense-objects for treatment which are relevant to our empirical existence and release. Here our senses provide an easy solution. There are five senses each of which specializes in a particular kind of perception, and this function they perform because they are endowed with an appropriate quality and are produced from an element which has a similar endowment. In the Nyāya language there are five qualities of five senses and five objects of sense, and these five objects are the qualities of the five elements. The position of the auditory organ, and sound which is its quality and object, and ākāśa of which it is made up, is somewhat privileged in this scheme. The auditory perception has also a special connection with the karma of the self. So far as the physical world is concerned, it consists of four material elements (viz. earth, air, water and fire) and ākāśa which pervades the entire universe. The perceptible world of matter is composed of these four elements; ordinary objects are composed of these elements.

But in the scheme of existence these elements have only a derivative status. The real constituents of the physical world are the atoms of four kinds corresponding to four elements. These atoms are partless and because they are partless, they are eternal. Strictly speaking, the existence of the atom is established on the basis of analysis of our sense-experience. Whatever is perceptible is found to be a composite or complex entity having parts, and if we go on dividing the broad categories of things until we can divide no more, we reach a stage where we must stop; that is an atom. If we did not stop at some stage, we would be faced either with an infinite regress or with a situation where the thing to be divided will have vanished into nothing. Thus we reach an irreducible entity, viz. the atom, which is of four kinds. Ordinary objects are perishable precisely because they have parts, and their constituents are the atoms which are themselves partless and therefore indestructible. The relation between the atoms and their products is one of support and supported. The atoms provide the support and the products rest upon this support. This is the famous relation of inherence which subsists between the composite and the components; the composites inhere in its components. But it is a distinct entity — distinct from its components. By their very nature atoms are non-perceptible but the objects produced from them are perceptible. One of the great epistemic problems in the Nyāya system is: how does the non-perceptible become perceptible ?

An atom cannot act singly. At least two atoms are required to set the process of production going.

In the first stage we have a dyad and the combination of three dyads (i.e. a triad) is the beginning of gross objects. The atoms are in motion or set in motion and they furnish the universe with the kind of objects which the self needs to unfold its historical career according to its karma.

Like the atoms and their products, their qualities also exist and are innumerable. Gautama's list of five qualities is therefore open to further additions. These qualities are restricted to their corresponding sense-organs but there are other qualities which are not so restricted. These are the genus of quality (*guṇatva*), being (*sattā*) and absence (*abhāva*). In fact they are apprehended by all the senses. Following Uddyotakara's description of the coalescence of pramāṇas, this coalescence may be called the theory of the coalescence of senses (*indriya-saṃplava*). The commentator also mentions the following qualities of substance, viz. number, measure, contact, separation, priority, posteriority, viscidity, velocity, motion, universal. Inherence, which is the fundamental relation between the composite and its components, is not a quality of substances, but the commentator wishes to treat it as a quality because it is a property of substances (NV I. 1,13 & 14).

If the atom is the ultimate constituent of the physical universe which has its being in all-pervading ākāśa, there is another ultimate constituent of the total universe, the self. Like the atom, it is partless, and strictly non-perceptible; the selves are also innumerable. But unlike the atom, the self is not regarded as a constituent of other complex entities. The atom, though itself partless, can be a part of a complex substance, and though it is itself eternal or indestructible its products are all perishable, i.e. they are disrupted into their constituent atoms periodically according to the rhythm of creation and destruction of the universe. The self is undoubtedly partless and eternal but its qualities are all perishable. In fact their perishability is the *sine qua non* of all our endeavour to obtain final release. In this sense the qualities of the self are like the products of atoms. But the striking characteristic of the self is that it is an agent in a fashion in which no atom can be. The body, the senses, the sensible qualities and objects are its instruments and the self is the manipulator. The instruments are fashioned not out of its own stuff but out of the physical world of atoms. These instruments are tailored to the whole scheme of its career; the scheme which covers its entire empirical existence till it attains release is to experience pleasures and pains commensurate with its karma — a compound of merit and demerit which results from good and bad deeds done by it in its long journey through the universe.

Despite efforts to introduce extra-sensory perception, the basic doctrine of Gautama is that self is inferred from its perceptible marks. Like the atom, it has also innumerable qualities, and one can say that the qualities Gautama has selected for treatment are relevant to the broad purpose of the *Nyāya Sūtra*, viz. treatment of the entanglement of the self in the historical process and its termination in final release. These qualities or marks of the self are: desire, aversion, effort, pleasure, pain and cognition. This is, of course, an open list, but what the commentators have done is to give the self another extraordinary quality named '*adṛṣṭa*' (literally unseen). It is that quality which explains the kind of equipment which the self will have from time to time according to the karma generated by it and which enables it to have appropriate cognitive and affective experience commensurate with that karma. It is this unseen power which moulds its historical career, and if only it could listen to Gautama's advice, it may be free from all its worldly ailments.

Like the atom, the self is a substance; and like it, it has its qualities. The relation between a substance and its qualities is also inherence as it is between the composite and its components. The qualities inhere in the substance of which they are the qualities. The self is the support of its cognitive and other qualities.

As already mentioned, the self can operate only through instruments. Its nearest instruments are three: mind, senses and body. The body is the seat of the senses, sense-objects and action or activity. The five senses are the windows of the self to the external world. These senses receive countless messages, but if the self had to deal with them all, there would be utter chaos in its mental life. In order to prevent such a situation, there is another instrument which mediates between the self and the senses, and that is the mind (*manas*). It ensures orderly presentation of the reports from the senses and passes them on to the self where they become conscious experiences. It also acts as its chief instrument for directing and controlling the operations of the senses. It is atomic because if it were not, there would be confusion in the relation between it and the self. For all practical purposes the mind is really the double of self. In this capacity as the agent of the self and the receiving and transmitting station from the outer world its role is highly important. It is through the mind that the self can be said to reap the harvest of its past deeds. The mind, the senses and the body are the tool kit of the self and the force which drives them into action is the karma of the self. This is the mysterious unseen force. In the Cartesian scheme, to use the famous description of Ryle, the soul is the ghost in the machine; in the Nyāya scheme of the atom and the self, the mind is the ghost, planted in the tool kit under the direct control and supervision of the self, and with the whole universe as a theatre for its operations.

4

INFERENCE (*anumāna*)

Inference is the second pramāṇa in Gautama's list and he has devoted the following three aphorisms to the subject:

Inference is knowledge which is preceded by perception and is of three kinds; *pūrvavat*, *śeṣavat* and *sāmānyato dṛṣṭa* (NS I. 1,5).

Objection

Inference is not a pramāṇa, as it errs in certain cases on account of obstruction, destruction and similarity (NS II. 1,37).

Reply

It is not so, because it (inference) is based on an object other than the part, fear and similarity (NS II. 1,38).

I. Nature and Scope of Inference

The sixteen categories of Gautama, says Vātsyāyana, can be included under either the pramāṇas or the *prameyas* — the two categories with which Gautama's list begins. Why, then, it may be asked, has Gautama enunciated the other fourteen categories ? The answer of Vātsyāyana reveals both the man and his approach. For the good of living beings the four branches of learning have been provided: each of these deals with a distinct set of objects and each has its own distinct method of treatment. Amongst these four branches the fourth '*ānvīkṣikī*' ('investigation') is also called '*nyāya*'. The other three branches, which the commentator does not even mention by name are usually said to be the three Vedas, agriculture, and polity.

In view of these four distinct departments of learning with their own distinctive methods of treatment it was necessary for Gautama to state separately the fourteen categories. For, if these were not so stated, it would appear as if the *nyāya* is nothing but that department of learning which is concerned with the supreme spirit or soul, like the *Upaniṣad*. Thus the separate enunciation of the fourteen categories, according to the commentator, distinguishes the *nyāya* from the other departments.

Having thus vindicated the separate enunciation, Vātsyāyana proceeds to show that the fourteen categories are an integral part of the *nyāya* or the *nyāyavidyā*. Doubt, the first of the fourteen categories, constitutes the very basis of the process of reasoning. When we are trying to ascertain the true nature of things, we have a doubt: this doubt appears in the form 'or'— 'is the thing this or that?' It is an uncertain idea that we have of things; when we are in such a doubt, we consider the two sides of the question, and this is what constitutes the process of reasoning. When we have ascertained the true nature of things, we have what is called ascertainment (*nirṇaya*), the ninth category in Gautama's list. Consideration of the two sides of the question constitutes the very basis of the process of reasoning, and since this begins with a doubt, doubt is an integral factor of any treatise on *nyāya*. The uncertain idea of things, which is doubt, is certainly an object of cognition, and can be regarded as covered by the second category. But since it is an integral part of reasoning, its separate enunciation as a category, says Vātsyāyana, is fully justified.

Similarly, we can explain the separate enunciation of the category, objective (*prayojana*). Objective is what urges a man to undertake activity; the activity is undertaken to obtain or acquire things. Thus obejective affects all living beings, all actions and all branches of learning. It follows that this forms the basis of all reasoning or investigation. Reasoning means examination of things by pramāṇas, i.e. inference based upon perception and upon the authority of the scripture. Inference cannot be contrary to perception and scripture; that inference which is contrary to them is false reasoning. This inference is called '*nyāya*'; it is also called *ānvīkṣā* (investigation), because it consists in reviewing a thing previously cognized by perception and by the scriptural authority; this whole operation of investigation is called '*ānvīkṣikī*', '*nyāyavidyā*' and '*nyāyaśāstra*' (NBh I. 1,1).

On this subject some of the observations made by Uddyotakara deserve mention. As we have seen, Vātsyāyana had not dealt with the four branches of learning in detail. Uddyotakara gives some information about these branches. The Vedic triad (*trayī*) deals with such subjects as sacrifice; agriculture (*vārtā*) deals with the plough, the cart and similar subjects; polity (*daṇḍanīti*) is concerned with the distinct duties of the king and ministers; the science of investigation (*ānvīkṣikī*) examines the distinct categories such as doubt, etc. If these categories were not mentioned separately, the science of investigation would be regarded merely as a science of the *ātman*. If it were treated as a science of the *ātman* only, it would be nothing more than the *Upaniṣads*. Consequently it would have to be included in the Vedic triad. But this would result in the reduction of the four branches of learning to three only. And this, of course, could not be tolerated. It is for this reason that the fourteen categories beginning with doubt have been mentioned separately.

Another observation of the commentator in this context is that reasoning consists in the due ascertainment of the real nature of things by means of all the pramāṇas collectively. When any single pramāṇa brings about the cognition of a thing, it is not called reasoning; it is only when all the pramāṇas operate collectively to bring about cognition, that it is called 'reasoning'. And it is because this reasoning produces valid cognition that this form of reasoning, says Uddyotakara, is the highest form of reasoning (NV I. 1,1).

A pramāṇa, according to Vātsyāyana, can operate singly or in combination with other pramāṇas. Inference also operates in these two ways : for instance, we infer the cause of the sound of thunder from the hearing of the sound; in the inferential cognition of thunder neither perception nor scripture operates. This illustrates the operation of inference when it operates by itself. A combined operation of the pramāṇas can be illustrated as follows : it is by means of the instruction of an authoritative person (āpta) that the existence of the self is apprehended; on this self the inference operates when it is asserted that the marks of the self are desire, aversion, effort, pleasure and pain. The self is perceived by means of a peculiar contact of itself with the mind. Another instance is the case of fire: in this case when an āpta says 'there is fire', the existence of fire is apprehended by means of the instruction of the āpta; having thus got the information, one goes nearer to the place of the fire, and if one perceives the smoke coming from the place, one infers the existence of fire; when one actually reaches the place of fire, one directly sees the fire (NBh I. 1,3).

A. Definition of inference

Vātsyāyana explains Gauṭama's definition of inference as follows: Inference consists of subsequent measurement of an object by a measuring sign (NBh I. 1,3). This conforms to the etymology of *anumāna* (*anu* = after; *māna* = measuring). When Gautama says that inference is that which is preceded by perception he means the perception of the relation between the sign and the significate as well as the perception of the sign itself; and the perception of the relation between the sign and the significate also implies the recollection of the sign. Thus it is by means of recollection and perception of the sign that the non-perceived object is inferred. (NBh I. 1,5).

The etymological explanation of Vātsyāyana, it is objected, is not right because it does not yield proper results. According to it inference becomes entirely fûtile, as the object which is sought to be known by it is already known. This objection has no force, replies Uddyotakara, because inference is 'the cognition obtained through the sign'. The result of inference is in the form of the 'idea of the object rejected, accepted or disregarded'. In fact, in the case of all pramāṇas, when the word pramāṇa pertains to itself, it denotes or accomplishes its own being and is the same as cognition (*pramiti*). But when it bears upon something else, the word denotes instrumentality. Thus in the former case the result is rejection, acceptance or disregarding, and in the latter case it is in the form of resultant cognition. When the word 'pramāṇa' is treated as an abstract noun as in the first case, the result, i.e. rejection, etc., can follow *only after* the object has been cognized. It is obvious that *only after* the object has been cognized that we can have such ideas as 'this should be chosen' or 'this should be disregarded'. Thus the charge of futility cannot be sustained (NV I. 1,3).

The word '*anumāna*' means that by which something is inferred (*anumiyate anena*). The suffix *anu* has the force of the instrumental. In the smoke-fire inference perception is the instrument which is concerned with the sign and it leads to the cognition of something not yet perceived. How can the instrument which is concerned with one thing produce the cognition of another thing ? How can the instrument, pestle for instance, which falls upon paddy, produce the pounding of the grains of *śyāmāka* ? According to some philosophers there is really no difficulty here, as there is no such fixed rule that the resulting action (*kriyā*) must bear upon the same object upon which the instrument operates; for example, when a tree is cut by an axe, the axe operates upon the tree but it is the parts of the tree that keep on falling.

In some cases we find that both the instrument and the resulting action pertain to the same thing; for example, the cooking pertains to the rice-grains and the resulting action of being cooked also pertains to the same grains. In some cases again, the thing itself is both the agent and the instrument, and the resulting action also bears upon the same thing; for instance, when we say 'the tree is standing' we mean that it is by itself that the tree stands; the action of standing is performed without any other instrument. Similarly, in some cases the action bears upon an object entirely different from that upon which the instrument operates. In some cases again it does happen that the action bears upon the same object as the pramāṇa, when, for instance, the same object is cognized on which it operates. This happens when the resultant cognition itself is regarded as the pramāṇa, and what follows this pramāṇa is the acceptance, rejection or disregarding of the object cognized; in this case the instrumental cognition and the resulting acceptance, etc., both bear upon the same object. And in that case what is meant by the object being further cognized is that it comes to be regarded as accepted, rejected or disregarded.

Neither the objection nor the explanation offered by the philosophers, says Uddyotakara, is right. For there is no difference between the object of the pramāṇa and the object of the result (*pramāṇaphalayor viṣayabhedānabhyupagamāt*).

As already mentioned, inference is preceded by two perceptions.[1] What happens in the case of inference is as follows: When a man wishes to acquire inferential cognition, he perceives the sign for the second time. This perception arouses the impression left in his mind by the former perception, which leads him to remember the relation between the sign and the significate. In the light of this recollection, when he again perceives the sign, this last perception, which follows the former two perceptions and the subsequent recollection, leads to inferential cognition. This entire operation, says Uddyotakara, is known as *parāmarśa*. The various factors involved in this operation are all equally necessary for inferential cognition, but it is the consideration of the sign which is the most important. Its supreme importance lies in the fact that it is followed immediately by inferential cognition[2] (NV I. 1,5).

B. Examination of rival definitions

Uddyotakara examines and rejects the following four definitions of inference. The first three are attributed to the Buddhist logician Dignāga[3] and the fourth belongs to the Sāmkhya system.

(1) Definition: Inference is the perception of the thing which is invariably concomitant for one who knows it (*nāntarīyakārthadarśanaṃ tadvido 'numānam*).

Uddyotakara rejects this definition on the following three grounds: First, the word 'thing' in the definition is superfluous because what is concomitant cannot but be a thing. Second, the compound *nāntarīyakārtha* cannot be explained in any satisfactory manner. This is a grammatical objection. Third, the expression 'for one who knows it' (i.e. who knows that the thing perceived is invariably concomitant with it) is superfluous. There can be no idea of anything being concomitant unless the person using it knows it to be so. For example, people living in the *Nārikeladvīpa* where no fire is known, if they happen to see smoke, cannot have the idea of its being concomitant with fire.

(2) Definition: The cognition of the property of invariable concomitance is the hetu (*avinābhāvidharmopadarśanaṃ hetuḥ*).

Like the word 'thing' in the previous definition, the word 'property' in this definition is superfluous. Further, the inference mentioned by the advocates of this definition — 'there is smoke because there is fire' — is impossible.

(3) Definition: Inference is that which (i.e. hetu) is present where the subject of inference and that which is homogeneous are present, and which is absent where the subject is absent (*anumeye 'tha tattulye sadbhāvo nāstitā 'satītyanumānam*).

According to Uddyotakara this definition is defective because it is either too wide or too narrow. (a) It is too wide because it applies also to that which subsists in only part of the subject of inference. For instance, according to this definition the inference 'Atoms are non-eternal because they have odour, like the jar' would be valid. In fact, it is invalid because odour is present in the atoms of earth and is not present where these atoms are not present. This difficulty cannot be met by saying that what the definition states is that the hetu should be present wherever atoms are present. For what subsists in a part of the subject is also its property, just as what subsists in a part of that which is unlike the subject (vipakṣa) is also its property. When a certain thing subsists in a part of the subject we cannot deny that it subsists in the subject. Similarly, when a certain thing subsists in a part of that which is unlike it we do not think that it does not subsist in the latter (vipakṣa).

The advocates of the definition argue that if we construe the expression *anumeye sadbhāvaḥ* as *anumeye sadbhāva eva* (i.e. that which, i.e. hetu, is present where the subject of inference is present is construed as that which, i.e. hetu, is present *only* where the subject of inference is present), the definition cannot be regarded as too wide. This explanation, says Uddyotakara, cannot save the definition because there is no satisfactory way of interpreting the significance of 'only' (*eva*). The revised expression can mean either that the hetu subsists *only* in the subject of inference or that the hetu must subsist in the subject of inference. In the former case the assertion would mean that the hetu subsists in the subject of inference and that it is not impossible for the hetu to subsist in it. But this does not mean that the hetu should not be one which is present in the part of the subject of inference. The second interpretation, i.e. the hetu must subsist in the subject, suggests that there is invariable concomitance between the two. But in the valid inference, for instance the smoke-fire, the fire wherein the hetu (i.e. smoke) subsists at the time of inference is entirely different from that wherein the invariable concomitance between the fire and the smoke has been observed. Thus the expression '*anumeye sadbhāvaḥ*' is unsatisfactory.

The expression *tattulye sadbhāvaḥ* (i.e. that which subsists n that which is homogeneous = belonging to the same genus as the subject of inference) is equally unsatisfactory. Where the subject of inference, fire for example, is observed, there is always the possibility of the hetu being present in the subject of inference, the homogeneous example and the heterogeneous example. But the expression merely says that the hetu is present in the homogeneous example and not that it is invariably concomitant with it. It is the latter that we need for a valid inference. As in the case of the first expression, no modification on similar lines can improve the position.

Similarly, the last part of the definition *nāstitā 'sati* (i.e. the hetu should not be present where the subject is absent) makes no sense. That which does not exist is a non-entity; surely, the non-entity cannot be the substratum of the hetu. As in the case of the previous two expressions, there is no way of improving the expression.

If the definition is taken as a whole, it becomes too narrow. The two kinds of positive hetus are covered by only the first two expressions; the negative hetu is covered by only the first and third expressions. And yet both these hetus are accepted as true hetus. For instance, those who do not regard sound as eternal accept the following two hetus as valid: 'because it is a product' and 'because it is preceded by effort'. But they fulfil only the conditions indicated by the first two expressions. Since there is no heterogeneous example in this case, the condition indicated by the third expression cannot be fulfilled. In the inference 'the living body is not soulless as otherwise it would be without the life-breath' the hetu is negative and fulfils only the conditions indicated by the first and third expressions. In this case there is no homogeneous example and therefore it cannot fulfil the condition indicated by the second expression. And yet the hetu is accepted as perfectly valid. Thus the definition taken as a whole is too narrow.

(4) Definition: Inference is the establishment of that which remains from one perceptible relation (*saṃbandhād ekasmāt pratyakṣāc cheṣasiddhir anumānam iti lakṣaṇam*).

This definition is interpreted in two ways: (a) 'where there is a relationship (between two things) from a single perception (of the sign), the cognition of the other (thing = subject) that arises is inference', or (b) out of a single perceptible relationship the cognition of the subject that arises is inference.

The first version is wrong because inference does not proceed from a single perception. The second interpretation is wrong because when the observer draws an inference, what he actually perceives is not the relationship but only the sign (hetu). The relationship cannot be said to have been perceived beforehand because in that case we would have to treat as inference the cognition that one had when the sign was actually perceived. And surely, this is absurd. Further, the inference which the advocates of this definition themselves accept as valid cannot fit in with it. For instance, they infer the cool or warm touch from the colour of a thing, which is quite right. But since according to their doctrine everything is undergoing modifications there can be no relationship between any two things (NV I. 1,5).

C. Inference and its relation to perception and āgama *(scripture)*

Inference, says Vātsyāyana, should be based on perception and scripture. It should not be contrary, explains Uddyotakara, to perception and scripture. As a matter of fact, we find that when what is known by inference is corroborated by perception and *āgama*, the knowledge thus acquired becomes clearer. When inference is contrary to perception and scripture, says Vātsyāyana, it is not true reasoning; it is false reasoning (*nyāyābhāsa*). This false reasoning, according to Uddyotakara, is known as '*nyāya-viplava*' ('confusion of reasoning' or 'muddle'). This confusion arises when there is no mutual corroboration amongst these pramāṇas. Those who seek pecuniary gain, adoration or fame put forward such confused reasoning and this is what constitutes spurious doctrine (NBh & NV I. 1,1).

(i) *Inference contrary to perception*

As an example of this inference, we have: 'Fire is not hot because it is a product, like the jar'. It concerns a thing which is not fit for inference; for the thing has been rejected or negatived (NV I. 1,1).

According to some philosophers, the inference, 'sound is not audible because it is a product', is contrary to perception. Inaudibility is a function of the sense-organ of hearing and the functioning of sense-organs, as we know, is beyond the reach of the senses. Hence audibility can never be an object of perception. If audibility is not an object of perception, an inference of inaudibility cannot be contrary to perception (NV I. 1,1).

(ii) *Inference contrary to scripture*

As an example of this inference the following is cited: "The human skull is sacred because it is a part of the animal body, like the conch shell." How can this inference be treated as contrary to scripture ? When a person asserts that the human skull is sacred, he should explain the meaning of sacredness. If it means that if a man touches the skull no sin accrues to him, he should be asked to indicate for what man there is no sin in touching the skull. Now, if he says that it is he himself to whom no sin accrues by the touch, then he is quite right; for he has a scriptural authority for himself in this matter (i.e. the skull is sacred for him according to his scripture). But if such a person were to assert that it is the believer in the Vedas to whom no sin would accrue by the touching of the skull, the assertion that the skull is sacred would be a clear case of contradiction with scripture; for the believers in the Vedas accept the authority of their Vedas and according to the Vedas the skull is not sacred.

Can we establish the sacredness of the skull by inference pure and simple, independently of scriptural authority ? The assertion 'the human skull is sacred' is in the nature of a specific statement; as a specific statement it implies the negation or exclusion of all other things. Hence it is necessary for the person who makes the statement to indicate what is not sacred. Obviously, this cannot be done by one who rejects all scriptures, as scripture is the only guide on sacredness and non-sacredness. The position does not improve if the assertion is taken to imply that all things are sacred. But then the inference becomes invalid, as there can be no corroborative instance; for all things have been included in the subject of the inference (NV I. 1,1).

According to Vātsyāyana inference should not be contrary to perception and scripture. It may be asked: Can it be contrary to analogy (*upamāna*) or inference itself ? The former is quite possible, says Uddyotakara, while the latter is impossible. Analogy consists in the cognition of similarity which depends upon remembrance due to impressions left by scripture. Since analogy involves both the pramāṇas, perception and scripture, it follows that what should not be contrary to perception and scripture should not be contrary to analogy as well. The position regarding the second possibility, inference being contrary to inference, is different. As a matter of fact, it is not possible that with regard to one and the same thing, there should be two inferences, fully equipped with positive and negative instances. Since there is no such possibility, inference can never be contrary to inference. But from this it does not follow that inference cannot be contrary to perception. As a matter of fact, we do find that an inference fully equipped with positive and negative instances is actually rejected by perception (NV I. 1,1).

According to Vātsyāyana, the difference between perception and inference is that while the former deals with things present the latter deals with things present as well as not present. As a matter of fact, inference is applicable to all the times; by means of inference we apprehend things past, present and future: we infer, for instance, (a) that such and such a thing existed; (b) that such and such a thing is present; (c) that such and such a thing will happen. The past and the future are not present and hence inference is spoken of as pertaining to the present as well as the non-present (NBh I. 1,5).

The difference between perception and inference as stated by Vātsyāyana, says Uddyotakara, has been questioned as follows:

Is this distinction based upon the difference of the properties or of the objects ? If the latter, the difficulty is that there can be no inherence (*samavāya*) with reference to objects that are *not-present*; for inference never operates upon a thing, according to the Naiyāyika, which is not already cognized in a general or a specific way; no such cognition is possible with regard to things that are not-present. If, on the other hand, the distinction is based upon the difference of the objects, the following points arise: There are three kinds of properties: (a) those that are affirmed; (b) those that are denied; (c) those that are independent. For instance, (a) there is odourousness which is affirmed of the earth; (b) the same property is denied of substances other than the earth; (c) there is no relation of inherence subsisting between things that are independent of each other.

Another question is raised, and this concerns the relation of inherence: between object and quality: how can inherence itself be regarded as independent ? It is independent because there is no further inherence by which the former inherence should subsist in the inherent things. Whenever one thing subsists in another, it does so through some relation, and as a matter of fact, for inherence there can be no further inherence that could be the relation through which the former could subsist in the inherent things. If there were such further inherence of the former inherence, there would be no end to the assumption of such inherences; and if there is to be a limit somewhere to these assumptions, it would be best to have the limit at the very first inherence and treat it as independent (or self-sufficient).

What is the basis for the assertion that inherence is independent ? Do we accept it on faith (or trust) or is there any reasoning in support of it ? Undoubtedly, there is reasoning, and it is as follows:

(i) Inherence is independent because it is denoted by a word expressive of the relation that subsists in the five categories (viz. substance, quality, action, generality and specific individuality), just like the atom which is regarded as independent, because it is spoken of as subsisting in the five categories.

(ii) Or, inherence is independent because it is all-pervasive, and being so, it is present in every specific instance; for example, the qualities of self inhere in every individual self.

If inherence were dependent on something else, it could depend upon the effect only. This would mean that inherence could exist before the effect came into existence and thus it would be without any substratum. This would also amount to inherence having the cause as its substratum. It is well-known that inherence is a relation that subsists between the cause and its effect and hence if it is to be dependent upon that effect, it cannot exist before the effect appears. In that case we would not be able to determine the particular relation of inherence in their case. For whenever one thing subsists in another, it does so in a particular form of relation.

Inherence, it may be suggested, is a kind of approach or contact (*saṃyoga*). This cannot be so, as it involves a contradiction. When the contact is said to subsist, does this subsistence mean a property of contact or of the effect ? According to this line of argument, it should be a property of the effect, and not of the contact. Since there are other numerous effects to which this contact belongs, the relationship of inherence must apply to these other effects as well. On the other hand, if the subsistence were a property of the contact, then this contact would stand in need of a further contact, so as to establish the relation of inherence with these effects, so on and on; thus we will have an infinite regress (*anavasthā*). Such an endless assumption of contacts would be unjustifiable, as there is no pramāṇa in support of it. If it is suggested that inherence subsists through another inherence, this would be against the scripture (*śāstra*) which says that the nature of inherence is explained by its mere nature (*tattvaṃbhāva*)

Another objection is that a relation of inherence continues to exist even when the effect in which inherence subsists as a relation has ceased to exist. But there is no pramāṇa in support of this contention. When the relation ceases to exist, all that ceases to exist is the circumstances that rendered the inherence cognizable (*khyātinimitta*) and not the inherence itself. For inherence is not an effect and as such, cannot cease to exist. That it is not an effect is inferred from the fact of every effect having a substratum. If inherence were an effect, it could only be produced along with the effect; in that case, this latter effect would be without a substratum at the moment when it is produced, as it can subsist in its substratum only through inherence, which, on the initial assumption of this reasoning, is not yet produced. If it is argued, however, that inherence can be produced before the effect, then it will have to be explained as to what the inherence belongs to at the time when it is produced; for the effect has not yet come into existence.

The upshot of this whole objection to the Nyāya concept is that if inherence pertains to things not present, we do not know which of the three kinds of properties are meant. The answer of Uddyotakara is unusually brief : Inherence pertains to properties that are denied, and not to those that are affirmed or to those that are independent; only things which are not present, i.e. past and future things, can be denied at the time when the inherence appears. It is true that we have such affirmative expressions as '*ghaṭo bhavati*' ('the jar is being produced'), where the verb '*bhavati*' is synonymous with '*jāyate*' (i.e. is being produced). It may therefore seem that since the jar that is being produced is not present, we actually affirm that which is certainly not present. This, says Uddyotakara, is not right, as what is said in the expression is not 'the jar is being produced' (*ghaṭo jāyate*) but 'the jar is known' (*ghaṭo vidyate*). For the verb '*bhavati*' in this expression is synonymous with '*vidyate*' (is known). When we affirm the existence of the jar in the process of production, the word 'jar' stands for the several parts of the jar; since these parts have already been constructed and are thus accomplished entities already, this is sufficient for the purpose of a thing being recognised as 'jar' and of being spoken of as existing (*bhavati*, i.e. *vidyate*) (NV I. 1,5).

II. Three Kinds of Inference

While Gautama has provided some kind of definition of inference, he is silent on the three kinds of inference which he has mentioned by name in his aphorism. This omission seems to have been observed by some philosophers, and Vātsyāyana, faithful to the master that he is, first defends the omission and then proceeds to fill in the gap. It is true, he says, that since the bare mention of the three names is sufficient to indicate that there are three kinds of inference, the expression 'of three kinds' (*trividham*) could have been dropped from the aphorism. But Gautama thought, according to the commentator, that he had already compressed — and compressed in its entirety — in a short aphorism what is really a very vast subject, viz. inference; any further abridgement would have been undesirable. In fact, this method of treatment has been adopted by Gautama; for example, in the case of the categories *siddhānta*, *chala*, *śabda*, etc., Gautama is always in favour of conciseness but he uses different forms of conciseness as the occasion demands. Thus Vātsyāyana explains the omission (NBh I. 1,5).

Vātsyāyana offers two alternative interpretations of the three kinds of inference without stating which of the two or both alternatives are the Nyāyā view. Uddyotakara goes further and suggests four possible interpretations but, like his predecessor, leaves the choice open. However, he examines several objections to each kind of inference and vindicates the Nyāya position which primarily concerns the recognition of the threefold inference. In what follows the views of the two commentators are given:

Interpretaions of the three kinds of inference

A. Vātsyāyana's interpretations :

(1) *Pūrvavat*

(a) The *pūrvavat* inference is one in which the effect is

inferred from the cause, e.g., when we see clouds rising, we infer that there will be rain.

(b) The *pūrvavat* inference is that in which, out of two things perceived on some former occasion, the one that is not perceived (at the time of inference) is inferred from the perception of the other, e.g., when fire is inferred from smoke (NBh I. 1,5).

(2) *Śeṣavat*

(a) The *śeṣavat* inference is that in which the cause is inferred from the effect, e.g., when we see that the river is full and the current is swifter, we infer that there was rain.

(b) The word '*śeṣavat*' means that which remains. Hence the *śeṣavat* inference is one in which, with regard to an object, some of the postulated properties being eliminated, and this elimination not applying to other postulated properties, we have the cognition of those that remain uneliminated, e.g., with regard to sound (*śabda*) we find that it is an entity (*sat*) and is non-eternal; these two properties, being an entity and being non-eternal, are found to be common to substances, qualities and actions only, their presence in sound distinguishing it from the remaining categories of generality, particularity and inherence (all of which three are entities but eternal); we have a doubt as to whether sound is a substance, a quality or an action and we then reason as follows:

(i) Sound cannot be a substance, because it inheres in a single substance (ākāśa). (There is no substance which inheres in only one substance; substances are either not inherent in any substance (e.g. the atoms), or they are inherent in more than one substance (e.g. the jar which inheres in more than one atom).

(ii) Sound is not an action, because it is the originator of another sound. (It thus gives rise to something that is of its own kind). This is never the case with any action, which produces effects unlike itself (e.g. action produces some kind of conjunction or disjunction).

By this process of elimination we arrive at the cognition that 'what remains must be it'; in the present case we have the cognition that sound is a quality (NBh I. 1,5).

(3) *Sāmānyato dṛṣṭa*

(a) Vātsyāyana does not give any general explanation of this kind of inference but merely gives an example: we have generally observed that we see a thing in a place different from where we saw it before only when it has moved; from this fact of general observation we infer the movement of the sun, even though we cannot perceive it. This is the *sāmānyato dṛṣṭa* inference.

(b) When the relation between the sign and the significate is non-perceptible, the non-perceptible significate is inferred from the similarity of the sign to something else; e.g. the self is inferred from desire, etc. Desire, etc., are qualities, and qualities reside in substance. From this we infer that that (substance) in which these qualities of desire, etc. reside is the self (NBh I. 1,5).

B. Uddyotakara's interpretations :

(1) *Positive anvayi*)

When that which (i.e. hetu) subsists in the subject of the inference and in the objects which are homogeneous, and which is absent from the objects which are heterogeneous, we have the positive inference. An example of this type of inference is the reasoning of the philosopher who regards all things to be non-eternal. 'Sound is non-eternal because it is a product'.

Negative (*vyatireki*)

When that which (i.e. hetu) subsists in the subject of the inference in the case of which there is no object of heterogeneous class, and which does not subsist in the subject when the probandum is absent, we have the negative inference. For example, 'the living body is not soulless because it would be lifeless'.

In the case of this inference a homogeneous example is not possible. The probandum is the negation of 'soullessness' and this cannot be present anywhere except in the living body, which is already the subject.

Positive-cum-negative (*anvayavyatireki*)

When that which (i.e. hetu) subsists in the subject of the inference and the homogeneous objects, and does not subsist in the heterogeneous objects, we have the positive-cum-negative inference. For example, sound is non-eternal because, though it has both the generic and specific character, it is perceived by the external organ of ordinary human beings, like the jar.

This inference is based on the property of sound. This property subsists in sound and homogeneous things, like the jar for instance, and is not present in eternal things such as ākāśa (NV I. 1,5).

(2) *Pūrvavat*

In the word *'pūrvavat' 'pūrva'* is related to the probandum; *'pūrvavat'* therefore means that which is concomitant with the probandum.

Śeśavat

In the word *'śeṣavat'* the word *'śeṣa'* stands for the objects which belong to the same class as the probandum. *'Śeṣavat'* therefore means that which is related to that class of objects.

Sāmānyato dṛṣṭa

The word *'sāmānyato dṛṣṭa'* means that which is related to objects which are not perceptible. Further, this inference should not be contrary to the scripture or perception.

The *pūrvavat* inference is concerned with an explicit probandum whereas the *śeṣavat* is concerned with the class of homogeneous objects.

(3) When Gautama says that inference is of three kinds, according to Uddyotakara, he has in mind the aspects of hetu = *liṅga* : whether it fulfils the conditions of being popularly known, or objectively true, or certain.[4] The popularly known sign is that which is concomitant with the probandum; the objectively true hetu is that which subsists in other things belonging to the same class to which the probandum belongs; the certain hetu is that which is never found apart from the things belonging to the same class.

(4) The reference to the three kinds of inference, says Uddyotakara, may be taken as restricting the number of inferences; that is to say, the various kinds of inference are included under the three kinds that are actually mentioned by Gautama, viz. *pūrvavat, śeṣavat* and *sāmānyato dṛṣṭa.*

Inference can be spoken of as being of various kinds as follows:

(i) *Anvayavyatireki* inference is of two kinds:

(a) that in which the hetu is present in things where the probandum is present; (b) that in which the hetu is absent as well as present in such things.

(ii) *Anvayi* inference is of the same two kinds.

(iii) *Vyatireki* inference is of one kind only, as in this case we cannot have any such thing in which the probandum is absent.

Again, these five kinds of inference come to be of fifteen kinds, according as each of them pertains to the past, the present or the future. These fifteen kinds again come to be sixty, according as they become addressed to the four kinds of persons (viz. one who already accepts the conclusion, one who does not accept the conclusion, one who is doubtful on the point, and one who accepts the contrary of the conclusion). Of these again there are countless sub-divisions.

Examination of Objections to the Three Kinds of Inference

A

In his examination of inference Gautama states the following objection to his theory of inference: "Inference is not a pramāṇa, as it errs in view of obstruction, destruction and resemblance" (NS II. 1,37). His reply is: "Not so, because [the inferences are based upon] something other than the part, fear and similarity" (NS II. 1,38).

According to Vātsyāyana, the real significance of the objection mentioned by Gautama is that in no case inference can provide cognition of an object. The commentator's reply is that the instances of inference cited by the opponent are wrong inferences because in each case the hetu is not specific. When one tries to infer a specific thing on the basis of an unspecific hetu, the inference is bound to be wrong. But then the fault lies not with the pramāṇa of inference but with the person who draws such inferences. It is not that inference is not a valid pramāṇa but the inferences drawn in the instances are wrong because they are based on unspecified hetu.

In the instance of the *pūrvavat* inference it is quite right to infer that the rain will come if it is based upon the fact of commotion of a large number of ants with their eggs and not merely of a few. But if we were to infer that the rain will come on the basis of a few ants running away, the inference would be false; for the ants may be running away because their nests have been demolished.

As regards the instance of the *śeṣavat* inference, when we infer that the rain-god has rained in the regions above the river, we do so on the basis of the perception of several facts: the water level has increased, the stream is flowing more swiftly, etc. But if we were to infer that the rain-god has rained on the basis of the mere fact that the river is full, the inference would be false; for the river may be full because there is some obstruction in its course.

As regards the instance of the *sāmānyato dṛṣṭa*, when we infer the presence of the peacock from the sound we hear, we do so from the specific sound which is associated with that bird. The serpents draw such correct inferences. But if we were to infer the presence of the bird from any sound, the inference would be wrong (NBh II. 1,37 & 38).

Apart from the arguments so far urged against the objection, Uddyotakara subjects the statement 'Inference is not a pramāṇa' (*anumānam apramāṇam*) to a detailed scrutiny. This assertion, says the commentator, is wrong for the following reasons:

(a) The two terms of the proposition are contradictory to each other. The term '*anumānam*' (inference) is the name of that relation (of concomitance) which brings about the cognition of things beyond the reach of the senses, while the term '*apramāṇam*' (that which is not a pramāṇa, i.e. not pramāṇa) is that which does not bring about that cognition. One and the same thing cannot be affirmed and denied in regard to anything.

(b) There is a contradiction between the proposition and the hetu. The proposition is in the form 'Inference is not a pramāṇa,' and the hetu is in the form 'because of falsity, in view of obstruction, destruction and resemblance'. This means that that which is false cannot be a pramāṇa. What is the meaning of the assertion 'Inference is not a pramāṇa' ? Is it intended to deny the character of being a pramāṇa in regard to all inference or only in regard to some inferences ? If the proposition is 'all inferences are devoid of the character of being a pramāṇa', then the hetu is one that resides only in a part of the subject. For 'all inferences' is the subject in the proposition and certainly 'falsity' does not belong to all inferences. In the present argument the objector cannot himself affirm the falsity of the inference which establishes the fact of inference not being a pramāṇa, for this is nothing but his own inference. Thus there is no proof for the falsity of the hetu 'falsity', which is intended to prove the invalidity of all inference; the hetu therefore turns out to be one which is not necessarily concomitant with the whole of the subject, 'all inferences'. If, on the other hand, the proposition is in the form 'that inference which is beset with falsity cannot be a pramāṇa', another hetu will be required; for falsity which is a part of the proposition cannot serve as a hetu. But in that case, the argument would be superfluous. Certainly that which is beset with falsity is never treated as a pramāṇa (NV II. 1,38).

B

According to Uddyotakara, several objections have been raised against the Nyāya view regarding the three kinds of inference mentioned by Gautama and Vātsyāyana. In what follows these objections and the commentator's answers are given (NV I. 1,5):

(1) Regarding the name of the first kind of inference, *pūrvavat*, a question is raised: What is it that is *pūrvavat* ? The cause or the effect ? If the word '*pūrva*' means that which has a *pūrva* (antecedent), then it is the effect that must be the *pūrvavat*; in that case it is a contradiction in terms to say that the *pūrvavat* inference is the inference of the effect from the cause. It is true that the word '*pūrvavat*' means that which has a *pūrva* (antecedent), says Uddyotakara, but from this it does not follow that it must be the effect that is so. The name is applied to the cognition, and the cognition is certainly 'that which has the antecedent' for its object. Thus the meaning is: 'that from the cognition of which (i.e. the cause) follows the inference of the effect'. Similarly, the name *śeṣavat* applies to the cognition of that which comes after, and so on.

Alternatively, the *pūrvavat* may mean that as one has perceived the thing by means of sense-perception, so also one has cognized the same thing by means of inference as before, *pūrvavat*.

(2) Objections against the first interpretation of Vātsyāyana.

The following objections are raised against the first interpretation of the three kinds of inference given by Vātsyāyana.

(a) *Pūrvavat*

The assertion 'the effect is inferred from the perception of cause' can mean (a) either, on seeing the cause one cognizes the presence of the effect, (b) or, 'where the cause is, there the effect is'. The first is not true, as no man in his senses cognizes the effect on seeing the cause. The second is not true, as the cause and the effect occupy different points of space; e.g., the yarns (the cause of cloth) are inherent in the component fibres, while the cloth inheres in the yarns. Further, to assert that 'the effect is inferred from the perception of the cause' is contrary to the concept of inference, as this reasoning (or inference) would operate upon a thing that is not known. And the essence of inference is that it does not operate either on what is fully known or what is not known. Thus on either interpretation the whole fabric of inference would be destroyed.

This objection, says Uddyotakara, is totally irrelevant. It is not the Nyāya view that 'the presence of the effect is inferred from the perception of the cause' or that 'where the effect is, there the cause is'. The correct view is: what is inferred is the effect as the qualifying property of the cause. And this is certainly not destructive of the essence of inference. According to Uddyotakara the example of the *pūrvavat* inference given by Vātsyāyana should be stated in the following form: "Being accompanied, as they are, by dark rumbling, having many rows of cranes flying (about or through them), flashing with lightning, these clouds are endowed with rain, just like other clouds."

(b) *Śeṣvat*

A similar objection to the *śeṣavat* inference can be met in the above fashion; what is inferred is the cause as a qualifying property of the effect (lit. as a limb of the effect). The word '*śeṣa*' in the *śeṣavat* means 'effect'. Both cause and effect have been indicated as instruments of inferential cognition, and in the *pūrvavat* inference the cause has been indicated as the instrument. Therefore, of the two, the effect remains as the one which has not been used as the instrument of cognition. Thus the effect comes to be spoken of as '*śeṣa*' (what remains).

Regarding the example of the *śeṣavat* inference given by Vātsyāyana, it is objected that the rise of water, which is in the stream, cannot bring about the inferential cognition of rain in the regions above the stream, as these two, i.e. the rise of water and the rain, are in totally different places.

This objection, says Uddyotakara, has no foundation. It is not the rise of water in the river which is the instrument leading up to the inferential cognition of the rain in the regions above the stream. What happens is that by means of the rise, which is a quality of the river, we infer the connection of the river itself with some place towards its source, where rain must have fallen. And the inference can be stated in the following form:

"This river stream is connected with a place near its source where the rain had fallen, as there is swiftness of current as well as the floating of pieces of wood."

Since the question of the time of the rain has not been raised against this inference, the future or the past tense may be used.[5]

(c) *Sāmānyato dṛṣṭa*

The *sāmānyato dṛṣṭa* inference, says Uddyotakara, is that in which an object is cognized as qualified by and or invariably concomitant with a specific character and not as the cause. Thus we get the inferential cognition of water from the cranes.

Having thus explained this type of inference, Uddyotakara proceeds to examine the objections that are raised against Vātsyāyana's first interpretation of the inference.

According to some people we have the *sāmānyato dṛṣṭa* inference, when we infer the movement of the sun in the example given by Vātsyāyana. If this means that the inference is in the form 'the sun moves' (i.e. we infer the movement of the sun), then we must ask: How is that movement cognized ? In this case there would be no connecting or relating mark nor can we infer a thing which is not related to a mark. And if this were possible, anything could be inferred by means of anything. The change of position, it may be argued, can serve as the mark, but this is not possible as no one has ever seen with his own eyes the sun's going from one place to another. The other place where the sun is said to go must be either ākāśa or a particular direction: since both ākāśa and that direction are imperceptible[6]—and there is no other way of perceiving them—it is not right to assert that there is the perception of the sun's going from one place to another. The cognition of the movement is all the more impossible, as in all cases what is actually seen of the sun is only the disc. And it is not right to draw an inference from the perception of the object by itself.

Further, even if we were to assume that the movement of the sun is perceived because it is something that has the capacity of being perceived, the sun's reaching of another place could never be perceptible. Change of place is something beyond the reach of the senses; the conjunction of two things (viz. the sun and the place), one of which (the sun) is perceptible and the other (place) imperceptible, cannot be perceived. And the sun's going from one place to another is nothing more than its conjunction with a place. If from his perception of the sun's going to another place, Devdatta can infer the movement of the sun and treat it as an instance of the *sāmānyato dṛṣṭa*, an inference of this kind would be of the movement not only of the sun but also of many other things. Why should he not, then, infer that he himself is moving ?

Uddyotakara replies to this criticism of Vātsyāyana as follows: We do not infer, in the instance under discussion, the movement of the sun directly; but we first infer that the sun goes to another place and from this fact, we infer the movement of the sun.

The first inference, the sun's getting from one place to another, takes the following form: The sun is a substance which never waxes or wanes; yet it goes to another place. When it is seen in the east, it is in front of the observer even though he has not changed his position. This is exactly like what happens in the case of a jewel. As the jewel is turned round, the observer sees that side of it which is towards him even though he has himself not moved at all. Thus the conditions for the inference of movement are fulfilled.

Some people, says Uddyotakara, try to meet the criticism of Vātsyāyana in a different way. They argue: Direction is perceptible because it is pointed at and indicated by means of the finger—like the moon. According to the commentator, this inference is not right, because direction, being colourless, is not perceptible by external sense-organs. What is actually indicated by the finger is not the direction but the trees and such other things connected with definite directions. And it is these which are figuratively spoken of and indicated as direction. In this case what really happens is this: A certain point happens to be perceived along with the (rising) sun; the name 'east' comes to be applied to that point which is thus connected with the sun; then, when any other thing, a tree for instance, is perceived along with the rising sun, this other thing also comes to be spoken of as in the 'east'; thus when people indicate the 'east' with their finger, they do so with reference to the tree and such other things, to which the name is applied figuratively.

(3) Objections against the second interpretation of Vātsyāyana :

(i) *Pūrvavat*

Vātsyāyana has given the following example of the *pūrvavat* inference in his second interpretation: 'Fire is inferred from smoke'. The question that needs to be considered, says Uddyotakara, is: What is it that is cognized by means of smoke ? (a) Is it the fire ? (b) Or, the particular place where the fire is ? (c) Or, the existence of the fire ? (d) Or, the particular place along with the fire ?

(a) It cannot be that the fire is cognized, as the relation of *dharma* (quality) and *dharmin* (qualified object) is not possible. The fire is not the quality of the smoke, nor the smoke of the fire. Further, the fire is something that is already known, and therefore does not need to be inferred. Hence it cannot be rightly regarded as the object of inference. (b) These objections apply to the view that what is inferred is existence and (c) to the view that it is the particular place that is inferred. Both existence and place are already known. (d) The fourth answer, the particular place along with the fire, is no less unsatisfactory, as the smoke is not a quality of that place containing fire. Besides the relation of the fire to a place is not unknown.

It is suggested that the inference can be stated in the form: 'This place contains fire'; in this inference what is inferred is a particular place as containing fire, and not merely a place in general. This suggestion is not tenable, as, according to the general position of the Buddhist, the actual place is never perceived. Nor is the smoke perceived and it cannot therefore bring about the cognition of fire, as according to their theory, everything is imperceptible. Thus any particular place cannot be regarded as the object of inference, and to assert that 'this place contains fire' is meaningless.

As a matter of fact, the smoke does bring about the cognition of fire, argues the Buddhist, by reason of its invariable concomitance with it. If this assertion means that there is an invariable concomitance between smoke and fire and on account of this concomitance, when one sees the smoke one naturally apprehends the presence of fire, it cannot be accepted as true. The invariable concomitance between smoke and fire can be interpreted in three ways: (a) The smoke and fire are related to each other as cause and effect. (b) The two are related by the relation of 'inherence'. (c) The two are related by mere relationship in general.

(a) Regarding the first alternative, which the Buddhist accepts, Uddyotakara contends that the fire and the smoke do not inhere in each other; the fire does not inhere in the smoke nor the smoke in the fire. In fact, each of them inheres in its own particular cause, which is neither fire nor smoke. Thus the invariable concomitance cannot consist of the relation of cause and effect.

(b) Regarding the second alternative, Uddyotakara observes: There is no single object of which both fire and smoke are the material cause and therefore they cannot inhere in that object. There is no object which can be the material cause of both smoke and fire and therefore there is no object which can inhere in them. There is no object which can inhere in itself.

(c) If the inference were formulated as 'there is some relation between smoke and fire', such an inference would not be right, for no such relationship is really known. In fact, the smoke is actually perceived even in the absence of fire. Can this concomitance be treated as some kind of coexistence (*sāhacarya*), as there is in the case of colour and touch? This is not possible, as fire and smoke do not always coexist. The same reasoning holds against the inference that may be formulated as 'wherever there is smoke, there is fire'.

As none of these alternative explanations is tenable, we are forced into a position where we must conclude that fire is not inferred from smoke. But this is against a fact accepted by everyone. There is, says Uddyotakara, a way out of this impasse. What really happens in the case of the inference of fire from smoke is this: when we see certain peculiarities of smoke we infer the presence of smoke as qualified by fire. The fire becomes a qualification of smoke, simply because the fire is subordinate to the smoke. This is inferred by means of certain specific features of the smoke. At the time of inference we perceive both the smoke as well as its specific features, such as the continuity of its upward rising, volume, etc.; what these features, as belonging to the smoke, lead us to infer is some such qualification of smoke as is not already known. It is a fact noticed in all inferences that all these specific qualifications of the object being inferred, which are already known, serve as the means of bringing about the cognition of that thing; e.g. in the case of sound, its two specific features (viz. it is an entity and it is a product) are well known; what is not obvious is its further specific features of non-eternality; when we infer the sound, we therefore infer it as qualified by its non-eternality (hitherto unknown).

(ii) *Śeṣavat*

An objection is raised against Vātsyāyana's example of the *śeṣavat* inference in his second interpretation. The hetu is too exclusive, as it is absent both in the probandum and in that which is heterogeneous; that is to say, the character of a sound originating another sound is one that is not found either in action or non-action. The origination of one sound by another sound is not a case of action or non-action because one thing produces another dissimilar thing.

This objection is not valid, says Uddyotakara, because when sound is said to be the originator of another sound, what is meant is that it produces a sound like itself. Thus this latter character is present in what is non-action. Hence the inference is correct.

(iii) *Sāmānyato dṛṣṭa*

An objection is raised against the second interpretation of the *sāmānyato dṛṣṭa* inference as given by Vātsyāyana: What is meant by saying that the relation between the sign and the significate is imperceptible ? Does it mean that it is not perceived at the time when the inference is drawn or that it is never perceived ? If it means the former, the qualifier (*viśeṣaṇa*) does not help in distinguishing this kind of inference from the *pūrvavat* and *śeṣavat* inferences. In all inferences the relation is not perceived at the time when they are actually made. The qualifier is therefore useless. If the relation is never perceived, there are two objections: in such a case where the relation has never been perceived, how can any inference operate ? Secondly, this assertion contradicts the view of Vātsyāyana that it is impossible for any inference to apply to such things as have been never perceived or to those that are already well known.

This objection, says Uddyotakara, is not valid, because what is inferred in the smoke-fire inference, is not fire by itself, which is, of course, perceptible, but fire as the qualifier of smoke. And certainly, the fire as such is not perceived at the time when the inference is drawn and has got to be inferred.

Thus the *sāmānyato dṛṣṭa* inference is that which, from the perception of a certain property of an object, leads to the cognition of that object. For example, when desire, aversion, etc. are inferred as belonging to the self, desire etc. are the objects of inference and the self becomes their qualifier (*dharma*); in this form of inference what is perceived is the property as belonging to the self, i.e. desire, etc., as belonging to the self; then this inference takes the following form: "Desire, etc. are dependent upon something else, because they are qualities, like colour."

This inference, it is argued, merely leads to the cognition that desire, etc. belong to something else; how do we get at the conclusion that they belong to the self ? We get at this latter conclusion, says Uddyotakara, by means of elimination: first of all, we know that desire, etc. cannot belong to the earth and other similar substances, because they can be perceived only by the self, and are not perceived by means of any external organ. In the case of properties belonging to the earth and other similar substances, we find that they can be perceived by the person who draws the inference as well as by other persons, and further that the properties are perceived by means of external organs of perception. Desire, etc., on the other hand, are such as are perceived only by the self, and that also by means of the internal organ of perception. This proves that these cannot belong to earth, water, fire, air, or ākāśa. Secondly, we also know that they cannot belong to direction (*dik*), time and mind, because like these three substances themselves, their properties also are imperceptible. Apart from these eight substances, there is no other substance except the self. Hence the only possible conclusion is: Desire, etc. must belong to the self.

5

ANALOGY (*upamāna*)

The third pramāṇa recognized by Gautama is *upamāna* (analogy). According to him, analogy is "the means of proving that which is to be proved from a well-known similarity" (NS I. 1,6). Vātsyāyana explains this definition: Analogy is that which makes known what is to be made known, from similarity with an object that is already well known; e.g. the assertion 'as the cow so the *gavaya*' (*yathā gaur evaṃ gavayaḥ*) i.e. the animal called '*gavaya*' is just like the cow. When a person finds similarity with the cow, he actually perceives the object (i.e. *gavaya*) that was referred to in the analogical statement; he then has the cognition that the word '*gavaya*' is the name of the animal; and thus he comes to realize that the particular name is connected with the particular object. We have similar analogies in ordinary life. For instance, a person is told that the herb called the 'bean-leaf' is like a bean; on seeing afterwards a herb like the bean he realizes that it is the herb to which the name 'bean-leaf' applies and collects it for medicinal purposes. Such analogies are of great practical value (NBh I. 1,6).

In his comment on the list of Gautama's pramāṇas, Vātsyāyana has observed that analogy consists in the cognition of approximation (*sāmīpya*) which, in this context, means connection of similarity. This observation apparently contradicts the concept of analogy as the cognition of the connection of a thing with its name. According to Uddyotakara, there is no such contradiction; for the cognition of the connection of a thing with its name is obtained by means of the cognition of similarity (NBh & NV I. 1,3). What Vātsyāyana is thinking of is analogy as an instrument or a means and not as an analogical cognition, and the cognition of similarity is undoubtedly such a means of analogical cognition.

The two commentators differ regarding the *means* of analogical cognition. According to Vātsyāyana, it is the analogical statement that is the means of cognition — the statement which is remembered when a person perceives an object that has been referred to in the statement. Uddyotakara maintains that the means is the cognition of similarity as aided by the memory of a reliable analogical statement. In the illustration just given, when a person has heard the analogical statement he knows that there is a similarity between the cow and the *gavaya*; on some future occasion, he sees the *gavaya* and perceives its similarity with the cow and he recognizes the connection of the animal with the name '*gavaya*' (NV I. 1,6).

Gautama refers to the following two objections to his concept of analogy.

(1) Similarity can be complete, preponderant or slight, and on the basis of such similarity analogy cannot be established (NS II. 1,44).

(2) Analogy consists in the establishment of apprehension by non-apprehension (NS II. 1,46).

Gautama answers these two objections as follows:

[The first objection] is not valid for analogy is based upon well-known similarity (NS II. 1,45).

[The second objection is not valid for the following reasons:] (a) It is not in the unperceived *gavaya* that we perceive the object of analogy. (b) Analogy is established through the compendinous expression 'As...so' (*tatheti*) (NS II. 1,47 & 48).

Vātsyāyana explains the first objection: If similarity is complete, there is no analogy; no one says 'a cow is like a cow'. Nor can analogy be based upon preponderant similarity; for no one asserts 'bull is like a buffalo'. Nor again can analogy be based upon slight similarity; otherwise everything would be like everything.

There is no question of complete, most or little similarity in analogy at all; where there is well-known similarity, there is analogy. Since there is a causal relation between the resemblances and the cognition of the connection of a thing with its name, says Vātsyāyana, analogy cannot be denied (NBh II. 1,44 & 45).

Uddyotakara answers the present objection in a different way. In the first place, it is not right for the objector to say that there can be no analogy based on complete, preponderant or slight similarity. Since he does not admit any kind of analogy at all, he should have said 'analogy is not a means of valid cognition'. Secondly, what the Naiyāyika considers as the basis of analogy is such similarity and dissimilarity as are well known. Hence the argument based upon the extent of resemblance has no bearing on the Nyāya view of analogy. In fact, since there is a causal relation between the resemblance cognized and the connection of a thing with its name, there can be no question of denying analogy at all. Uddyotakra goes even further and asserts that analogy is quite possible even in the three cases of resemblance mentioned by the objector. When there is complete resemblance, even to the extent of absolute identity, we have such analogical assertions; for instance, when an action is compared with itself, we have such a statement as 'the battle between Rāma and Rāvaṇa is like the battle between these two heroes alone.' We say 'the buffalo is like a cow'; here we are concerned with the strength of the two animals and the resemblance between them is preponderant. When we are considering the mere existence of a thing, for instance, the existence of the Meru mountain, we say 'the existence of the Meru is like that of the grain of oil-seed'; here the resemblance between the mountain and the seed is obviously very slight. On these various grounds the objection is thus unjustified (NV II. 1,45).

(2) According to Vātsyāyana the second objection is: Analogy is really inference because it proves by means of something perceived something which is not perceived; the cognition of the unperceived *gavaya* is effected by means of the perceived cow (NBh II. 1,46).

Vātsyāyana explains Gautama's reply:

(a) A person who has seen the cow and has been informed about the resemblance between the cow and the *gavaya*, comes to perceive an animal resembling the cow, and then arrives at the cognition 'this is *gavaya*' in which he recognizes the definite application of the name '*gavaya*'. In this process of analogical cognition there is no question of the *gavaya* as something unperceived. We apprehend that a *gavaya* which is perceived is a *gavaya*. This is quite different from inference: in inferential cognition we infer the existence of fire which, when the inference is being formulated, is not perceived at all. Another difference between analogy and inference is that the analogical statement is made for the benefit of another person.[1] The person who makes the statement knows both the objects between which there is resemblance while the person who hears it does not know one of them, viz. the object that is described as resembling an object that is already known; that is, in the present case he knows the cow but not the *gavaya*. It is argued that the author of the analogical statement should also have analogical cognition. Surely, such a person does not need any such cognition, says Vātsyāyana, because what is to be accomplished by analogy has already been accomplished in his case on the basis of well-known resemblance (NBh II. 1,47).

(b) . Analogy is always stated in the form 'as...so' by means of which the common property constituting resemblance is expressed, e.g. 'as the cow, so the *gavaya*' (NBh II. 1,48). According to Uddyotakara, inference is never expressed in a similar form; e.g. 'as the smoke, so the fire' (NV II. 1,48).

Uddyotakara mentions the objection raised by Dignāga. The latter has argued in his *Pramāṇasamuccaya* that analogy is not different from either perception or word. When one apprehends both the cow and the *gavaya*, then one acquires the knowledge that 'this is like that' from perception. When, again, one hears that 'the *gavaya* is like the cow' then it is merely on hearing this that one understands that some of the properties of the cow are pesent in the *gavaya* and some are absent; otherwise the expression 'as...so' (*yathā tathā*) — 'the *gavaya* is like the cow' — would not have been used. All that one apprehends is that the *gavaya* bears preponderant resemblance to the cow (NV I. 1,6).

Uddyotakara's reply to this objection is that Dignāga has not understood the aphorism of Gautama on analogy. Dignāga seems to think that the same cognition apprehends the similarity of the cow in the *gavaya* as well as the presence of the *gavaya*. What Gautama means is something entirely different. In analogy what follows from the cognition of the similarity of the *gavaya* to the cow is the cognition of the connection of that animal with the name. It is neither by means of word (*āgama*) nor by that of perception that one can cognize the fact of a certain animal being '*gavaya*'.[2] The mere perceptional cognition of resemblance only without the words 'the *gavaya* is like the cow' does not constitute analogy. Nor do mere words, without the cognition of resemblance, constitute analogy. Hence it is a pramāṇa quite distinct from perception and word. In confusing analogy with these two pramāṇas, adds Uddyotakara, Dignāga has shown indeed a poor insight into the nature of pramāṇas.

As Gautama and Vātsyāyana have already shown, analogy is a pramāṇa as distinct from inference. What produces analogical cognition is the perceptional cognition of resemblance as aided by the recollection of the connection between a thing and its name as originally learnt from words. This process is quite different from that of inferential cognition (NV I. 1,6; II 1,47 & 48).

6

WORD (*śabda*)

Introductory

In its widest sense, the word *śabda* means a sound. But in a narrower sense it means a sound used as a symbol for the expression of some meaning. In this sense it stands for a "word". In the context of the pramāṇa doctrine *śabda* means word or words as the source of knowledge; it corresponds, therefore, to "authority" or "testimony". *Śabdapramāṇa* means knowledge derived from the authority of word or words.

The examination of the *śabdapramāṇa* inevitably involves the refutation of rival doctrines and the main opponents of Gautama in this field are the Mīmāṃsakas and the Buddhists. The significance of this debate lies not so much in Gautama's criticism of the arguments used by the opponents for the vindication of the authority of the Veda but in his attempt to furnish a more plausible justification for the acceptance of the Vedic authority.

Gautama has discussed the various aspects of the *śabdapramāṇa* in the following order: nature of word, specific word (*śabdaviśeṣa*), non-eternality of word, modification of sound (*śabdavikāra*) and word and meaning. His views as explained by the commentators on each of these aspects are given below:

I. Nature of World

A. *Definition and kinds of word*

Gautama defines the pramāṇa of word and its two kinds as follows:

Word is communication of āpta[1] (NS I. 1,7).

It is of two kinds: that which refers to the object which is perceived and that which refers to the object which is not perceived (NS. I. 1,8).

Vātsyāyana explains the definition of the pramāṇa in the following way: Word is that by which an object is spoken of or made known (NBh I. 1,3). In his direct comment on Gautama's definition he explains what an āpta is. An āpta is one who has direct or intuitive knowledge of things, who wishes to make known the things as he has seen them, and who is capable of speaking about them. And the word āpta itself means one who operates through the direct or intuitive knowledge of things. This is a common characteristic of all āptas, whether they are sages, *āryas* or *mlecchas*. All human activity is regulated according to the advice of āptas. In fact, the activities of gods, men and animals, says the commentator, are regulated by the four pramāṇas recognized by Gautama; they cannot be regulated otherwise.

In making the twofold classification of the *śabdapramāṇa*, says Vātsyāyana, Gautama wished to make his position quite clear.[2] The assertions of the sages and ordinary people are concerned with things seen in this world and with those that are only indirectly known to exist in the other world. The pramāṇa of word is not confined to the former only. As is known, the pramāṇa can operate on things which are not directly perceived; for instance, inference deals with such unperceived things. According to Uddyotakara, the twofold classification may be taken with reference to the nature of things on which the pramāṇa operates or of the speakers who give advice. In the former case it refers to things perceived and those inferred; in the latter case it refers to the speakers who speak about things perceived and those who speak about things not perceived. In this connection the commentator also adds that both perception and word operate on a very wide range of things; they deal with generic and specific properties and things that possess these properties (NBh & NV.I. 1,7 & 8).

B. *Is word Inference ?*

In his detailed examination Gautama considers the view that word is inference as follows:

1. *Objection*

Word is inference because the object indicated by it is not perceived but inferred, because cognitions [yielded by the words] do not involve two different processes and also because the connection [between word and object, which is apprehended both in inference and *śabdapramāṇa*] is the same.

Reply

Right cognition of an object arises from word on the strength of the communication of an āpta. The cognition of connection does not arise from the pramāṇa [of word]. The connection [between a word and the object cognized by it] is absent, as we do not find [words like food, etc. accompanied by the actions of] filling, etc. (NS II. 1,49-54).

2. *Objection*

The following objection is raised against the answer given above:

It cannot be denied that there is a definite arrangement between words and objects.

Reply

This is not right, as right cognition of objects denoted by words is based upon convention (*samaya*). Moreover, no uniformity of connection between words and objects denoted by them [is observed among] different castes (NS II. 1,55-57).

1. According to Vātsyāyana, the first objection mentioned by Gautama is as follows: The subsequent inferential cognition arises only when there is a relationship between the sign and the significate, and the relationship has been previously apprehended. Similarly, in the case of word an object is apprehended by means of a word that has been previously apprehended. And this subsequent verbal cognition arises only when there is a relationship between the word and the object and this relationship has been previously apprehended. Thus the cognitive processes involved in the operation of inference and of word are exactly the same. Since the processes are the same, it follows that inference and word cannot be treated as independent pramāṇas; in fact word is nothing but inference (NBh II. 1, 49-51).

Explaining the answer of Gautama to the objection, Vātsyāyana observes that the cognition of an object denoted by a word is correct not simply because it arises from the word but because the word is uttered by an āpta. This is quite evident from the fact that there is no such correct cognition when a word is not uttered by an āpta. For instance, when words like heaven, celestial nymphs, ocean, human settlements, etc., are uttered the objects corresponding to those words cannot be perceived; but we have the correct cognitions of these objects not simply because there are such words but because they have been uttered by an āpta. And such correct cognitions cannot be obtained when the words are not uttered by an āpta. Thus the cognitive processes involved in inference and word are different.

As regards the argument of the objector that there is a connection between a word and an object, it is undoubtedly true, says Vātsyāyana, that there is such a connection between them; but the connection is of the type that is conveyed in an expression like 'this is *of* this (*asya idam*), i.e. this object is denoted by this word. The connection that could make verbal cognition inferential is one of contact[3] between a word and an object, and it is this connection that must be rejected; for the simple reason that it cannot be cognized by any pramāṇa. We cannot perceive such a contact, because the word is heard through the ear while the object cannot be apprehended by that organ. In fact, contact can be perceived only when objects in contact are apprehended by the ear. Nor can the contact be established by inference. We cannot say that the object goes over to the word; for if it did go over when the word 'food' is uttered, the mouth where it is uttered should be filled with food; when the word 'fire' or 'hatchet' is uttered, the mouth should be burnt or split. If the whole animal, cow, entered the mouth on utterance of the word 'cow', adds Uddyotakara, no one would care to utter such a word. And a modern Indian might be tempted to say that the cows would still be with us but without their sanctity!

To escape from the difficulties in the contact theory, various suggestions are made, but each one of them, says Uddyotakara, is untenable. For instance, he says, it is suggested that a word which is eternal goes over to the place where the thing exists. This would mean that the word when uttered produces a series of words like itself until the final word reaches the place where the thing is. This is self-contradictory, because the word which is eternal cannot be said to go over to the place in the form of a series of words produced one after the other. Nor can it be said to come into existence at the place where the thing is. Apart from being self-contradictory, this is impossible because the causes of its production (e.g. effort) are inside the body and the thing is outside. It may now be suggested that every single word is pervasive in its character, and comes to be manifested. This means that all words continue to exist eternally, in a pervasive form, and they become manifested when the relevant instrumental causes (such as the action of the organ of utterance, effort, etc.) are present. If this were the case, it would be possible to cognize all things when any single word is heard. For what would lead to the manifestation of one word would also lead to the manifestation of all words, as all words are equally pervasive in their character. If, however, the existence of a word in a pervasive form means that it pervades over its own denotation, even then there would be the possibility that whenever the word 'cow', for instance, is uttered, that word would become manifested to all persons in the world wherever they may be, and all of them would have the cognition of all the cows. This difficulty cannot be got over by saying that the word is like a universal (*sāmānya*); even though the universal pervades all its component individuals, it is not cognized all over the world but only in that particular place where the special circumstances are present to make it cognizable; similarly, though the word pervades its entire denotation, its manifestation is restricted to particular places. This suggestion cannot be accepted for several reasons. In the case of the universal what leads to its manifestation is the cognition of its substratum, i.e. an individual belonging to that universal; in the case of the word, however, there is no cognition of its substratum which could lead to its manifestation. Secondly, the word does not subsist in the individual in the manner in which the universal subsists in its constituent individuals. If it did subsist in the thing denoted by it, any one should recognize the corresponding word on seeing that thing without any previous knowledge of the convention on their relation, just as one recognizes the universal 'cow-ness' on seeing any individual cow. Thirdly, the word is a quality of ākāśa and it cannot therefore inhere in anything else but ākāśa. We cannot say that the word and the thing denoted inhere in a common substratum, because nothing can be produced out of them.

In view of these considerations no eternal connection between word and its denotation can be established by inference. The connection cannot be known by analogy, as no such relation can be the object of analogy. It cannot be said to be cognized by means of word itself, for this is what is now on the anvil (NV II. 1,54).

2. Vātsyāyana explains the second objection mentioned by Gautama as follows: It is observed that there is a fixed arrangement whereby the cognitions of certain things arise from certain words. From this we infer that what causes such an arrangement is some kind of relation between the words and the things denoted by them. If there were no such relation, we would have a cognition of an object from a word itself. Since this does not happen, the existence of the relation cannot be denied.

Explaining Gautama's reply, Vātsyāyana observes that the fact that certain words produce certain cognitions is due not to any natural relation but to convention (*samaya*). It is this kind of conventional connection between a word and an object that is conveyed in the statement 'this is of this,', i.e. this object is denoted by this word, and as already mentioned, this is the correct view.

This convention, says the commentator, is of the nature of an ordinance which determines the denotation of words; it lays down injunctions like "Such and such a thing shall be denoted or spoken of by such and such a word". In fact, it is only when this ordinance is known that a cognition can arise from the use of a word; when it is not known, even though the word is heard when uttered, it does not give rise to any cognition. Even those who believe in a fixed relatiohship cannot dispute these facts. Ordinary people learn the convention by observing the use of words in ordinary parlance.

To preserve and protect this convention the science of grammar has been created. It explains and determines both forms of speech: the use of single words and the use of sentences. Words denote objects and a sentence which is a collection of words denotes the entire collection of objects denoted by those words.

Another reason why the relation between a word and an object is conventional and not natural (*svābhāvika*), is the diversity of objects denoted by the same words. In fact, the sages, *āryas* and *mlecchas* make use of words for expressing things in any way they like (*yathā kāmam*). For instance, the word '*yava*', according to Vācaspati, is used by the *āryas* to denote barley, and by the *mlecchas* to denote long-pepper. If the connection was natural, such arbitrary uses of words would be impossible. For instance, light which has a natural relation to the illumination of things and to the making of colour perceptible, never fails to perform this function among any particular people. Light makes colour visible, and not a thousand artists, says Vācaspati, can establish a connection between light and taste. The diversity of usage in the case of words among different castes or peoples can be explained only on the basis of convention, which can vary among different people.

In view of these considerations there is no justification for the theory of contact or natural relation between word and object (NBh & NVTT II. 1,55-58).

3. Apart from the comments already mentioned, Uddyotakara has examined the following *Pūrvamīmāṃsā* and Buddhist objections to Gautama's definition.

(a) Uddyotakara mentions the following *Pūrvamīmāṃsā* argument against the Nyāya view of words. According to the Naiyāyika an āpta is one who has direct or intuitive knowledge of things, and it is his statement or assertion that constitutes the pramāṇa of word. If this were so, says the objector, no transaction could be conducted on the basis of any assertion regarding heaven, deity, etc.; for these cannot be perceived at all. It is therefore more appropriate to define the pramāṇa as a reliable assertion rather than the assertion of a reliable person.

This objection, says Uddyotakara, does not really impair the Nyāya position. What the Naiyāyika says is not that heaven and the like are perceptible to ordinary people but that they are perceptible to some people. The reason why they are perceptible to some persons and not to others is that they have certain generic and specific properties. These things subsist in a certain substratum; whatever is so subsistent in a substratum must be perceptible to some person. They are for the sake of others; whatever is for the sake of others must be perceptible to some person. They are things, and are spoken of in the scripture;

whatever is a thing and is spoken of must be perceptible to someone; as we find in the case of a jar and similar things. They are not eternal; whatever is not eternal must be perceptible to someone.

In this connection Uddyotakara raises the question whether merit and demerit which constitute *apūrva*[4] are eternal or non-eternal. If they were eternal, we would not be able to die. It is only because they are non-eternal that death is possible. This phenomenon can be explained in the following way: merit and demerit of a man are destroyed when all their fruits have been experienced by him; since nothing is left to yield any further fruit, his mind leaves one body and moves on into another. Thus there can be birth and death according to one's merit and demerit. Uddyotakara examines the theory of *apūrva* at some length but since it has no further bearing on the subject of the present pramāṇa, his views are not dealt with.

(b) As is known, the Buddhists do not recognize word as a pramāṇa at all. Their objection is as follows.[5] The assertion of a reliable person can mean either that the person making the assertion is reliable or that the thing asserted is really as it has been asserted to be. If the person who spoke the word is reliable, it is a mere inference. We infer that the reliable person's words agree with reality from that common property of agreement which belongs to all statements made by reliable persons. We have learnt from experience that the statements of reliable persons are true, and we apply this generalisation to the case of this particular statement. The cognition is therefore inferential. If, on the other hand, the thing is as it is asserted to be, this is a mere perception; the agreement of the statement of the speaker with reality can be verified only when one actually perceives the actual state of the thing to be as it is asserted to be.

This Buddhist objection, says Uddyotakara, is based upon a complete misunderstanding of Gautama's definition. The pramāṇa of word would be inference if it is the word aided by the reliability of the speaker which makes the object known; it would be perception if the agreement of the assertion with reality is meant to be verified by perception. This is not what Gautama has in view; what Gautam means is that in regard to things connected with the senses and those not connected with them, we have a cognition indicated by a word. It is this cognition that constitutes the word pramāṇa. Uddyotakara therefore rejects the Buddhist criticism as completely irrelevant.

4. As already mentioned, Vātsyāyana has examined the inferential theory of the word pramāṇa. In this connection Uddyotakara first establishes word as a pramāṇa and then proceeds to reinforce the Nyāya position on its independent status by rejecting further objections.

(a) Uddyotakara examines the question whether a word is eligible for the status of pramāṇa at all. It may be argued that even though the word is present, if it is not heard it does not lead to any cognition. It cannot have any object of its own to operate upon, as all objects are already cognized either by perception or inference. It is very much like a jar for the following reasons: it is not of the nature of cognition; it is perceptible by the external organ; it does not subsist in the self; and it is a quality of ākāśa. On these various grounds it may be disputed whether a word is a pramāṇa at all.

Uddyotakara replies as follows: The word that constitutes the pramāṇa is not any word but a word that is actually heard, and such a word does lead to cognition. It has already been pointed out that this pramāṇa does have its own objects apart from those of perception and inference The comparison with the jar is unjustified, because the reasons advanced are really not conclusive. For instance, all that can be said of the jar can be said of a lamp, but it does function as a pramāṇa because it helps in seeing things illumined by its light. Word is undoubtedly a property of ākāśa, but that is no bar to its being a pramāṇa; for instance, dimension (*parimāṇa*) is a property of ākāśa but it does lead to the cognition of magnitude (*mahat*). Thus none of the arguments can dislodge word from its status of pramāṇa (NV II. 1,49).

(b) Having thus established the status of word, Uddyotakara examines the following arguments in favour of reducing word to inference. These are in addition to those mentioned by Vātsyāyana in connection with the first objection mentioned by Gautama. Word depends upon remembrance in bringing about the cognition of its object. It applies to all the three times, past, present and future. It involves positive and negative concomitance; that is, when the word 'jar' is uttered we have the cognition of the jar, and when it is not uttered we have no such cognition. The object cognized by means of a word is such as is not cognized by means of perception. All of these characterize inference and therefore word is nothing but inference.

These arguments, says Uddyotakara, cannot establish the proposition, because the hetus are all inconclusive (NV II. 1,47 and 49).

II. Specific Word (*śabdaviśeṣa*)

A. *Indictment of the Veda*

In the following aphorisms Gautama examines the charges against the pramāṇa of word with special reference to the Veda.

Objection

That [word] cannot be regarded as a pramāṇa, because it has the faults of untruth, discrepancy and repetition (NS II. 1,58).

Reply

Not so; [the alleged untruth] is due to deficiencies in the act, the agent and the means (NS II. 1,59).

Discrepancy would occur if there were alteration of the time agreed upon (NS II. 1,60).

[There is no fault in repeating], because reiteration occurs [in the Veda] (NS II. 1,61].

Also because the Vedic utterances are divided on the basis of the things [they deal with] (NS II. 1,62):

The Vedic utterances are employed as injunctions, descriptions and reiterations (NS II. 1,63).

The injunction is that which prescribes [an act] (NS II. 1,64).

The descriptions are valedictory, laudatory, illustrative and narrative (NS II. 1,65).

When the injunction and that which is enjoined are repeated, this constitutes reiteration (NS II. 1,66).

Objection (to the above definition of reiteration)

There is no difference between reiteration and repetition, as both consist in the repetition of the same words (NS II. 1,67).

Reply

[They are] not the same, as reiteration is like the instruction to go faster (NS II. 1,68).

Like the reliability of *mantras* and Āyurveda, the reliability of the Veda is based upon the reliability of the āptas [i.e. their authors] (NS II. 1,69).

According to Vātsyāyana the objections mentioned by Gautama do not refer to the pramāṇa of word as such but its specific instance, the Veda. But if these objections are sound the validity of the main pramāṇa would be impugned. Hence Gautama has dealt with them.

According to Vātsyāyana, the charge of untruth arises in the following way: There is a *mantra* saying that one who desires a son should perform a sacrifice. But we find that even if such a sacrifice is performed, no son is born. Now the birth of a son is a visible thing, and if the *mantra* bearing on such a visible thing turns out to be false, other texts bearing on invisible objects — for instance, 'one should perform the *Agnihotra* sacrifice' (for the attainment of heaven) are also false.

This charge of untruth, says Vātsyāyana, can be answered in the following way: What the *mantra* in question says is that the parents, when connected with the sacrifice, give birth to a son. This involves three factors: agent, instrument or means and act. The parents are the agents, sacrifice the means and connection with the sacrifice the act. When these three factors are good, the son is born; but when they are defective, no son is born. The defects of the agent consist in his being immoral or his being ignorant of what is to be done; the instrument is defective when the material offered is not duly consecrated or has been descrated; or when the *mantra* is not properly recited or when the fee for the sacrifice has been acquired by unfair means or is too small or consists of unapproved material.

The defects in the three factors involved in the sacrifice explain why even when the sacrifice is performed the son is not born. In addition, the commentator adds defects in the act of procreation itself presumably as a supplement. The act is defective when the method of sexual intercourse is wrong; the agent is defective when there are uterine diseases or defective semen; and the instrument is defective in the manner already described in connection with the sacrifice.

The *mantra*, says Vātsyāyana, is like an ordinary injunction. Neither can be regarded as guilty of untruth. If everything is all right, the result is accomplished; if the result does not appear, it is due to various defects. Thus the charge of untruth against the Veda is unfounded (NBh II. 1,58 & 59).

Vācaspati goes even further in this defence of the Veda and his explanation is worthy of mention. When the sacrifice is said to bring about the son's birth, it does not mean that there is any such positive and negative concomitance between the sacrifice and the son's birth as 'whenever the sacrifice is performed the son is born' or 'whenever the sacrifice is not performed the son is not born'. What is meant is that the scripture (*āgama*) lays down that the sacrifice assists in the son's birth. On the basis of the reliability of such a scriptural text one can say that in cases where sons are born without the performance of the sacrifice, the birth must be the effect of the sacrifice performed in a previous life; and if, even when there is no deficiency in any factor, the performance should fail to bring about the son's birth, it must be attributed to some invisible obstruction that has neutralized the force initiated by the sacrificial performance (NVTT II. 1,59).

Discrepancy

The charge of discrepancy[1] is explained by Vātsyāyana as follows: What is enjoined by one *mantra* is discrepant with what is enjoined by another. For instance, there are such *mantras* as require a person to offer oblation before or after sunrise or when the stars are shining and the sun is not visible. Regarding these three times for the oblations, there are corresponding deprecatory texts; oblations offered at three different times are eaten by different kinds of dogs. The simple answer to this accusation is that once a person has agreed to offer an oblation at a certain time, the time that he has accepted should not be altered. The texts in question are meant to carry disapproval of alterations in the procedure already adopted. Thus the charge of discrepancy is unfounded (NBh I. 1,58 & 60).

Repetition

According to Vātsyāyana this charge of repetitiveness arises in the following way: There are *mantras* which lay down repetition; for instance, 'One should repeat three times the first verse, and three times the final verse'. Surely, such assertions, says the objector, can come only from a demented person.

Vātsyāyana replies that what constitutes repetitiveness is repetition without a purpose. When there is repetition with a purpose we have reiteration and not repetition. In the instance cited by the opponent the purpose of repeated recitation of the verses is to enable the person who recites them to attack the enemy whom he hates and who hates him (NBh II. 1,58 & 60). There is a real case of repetition, adds Uddyotakara, when the same thing is mentioned again, without the addition of any further qualification; but when it is mentioned again but with additional qualifications, it is a case of reiteration (NV II. 1,60). Thus the charge of repetition is unjustified.

B. *The Veda as pramāṇa*

Having thus answered the opponent's indictment of the Veda, Vātsyāyana proceeds to explain the positive arguments[2] offered by Gautama in spuport of the Veda as the pramāṇa of word. (i) The first argument is that the *Brāhmaṇa* (i.e. the ritual part of the Veda) is divided on the basis of the various purposes served by the texts in it. The Vedic texts are employed as injunction, description and repetition and their respective purposes are to command a particular course of action, to persuade a person to implement the command and reiterate the command or what is commanded in order to emphasize the need for implementing the command exactly in the manner in which it requires. The whole purpose of these various kinds of texts is to ensure compliance with the commands mentioned therein by a variety of means ranging from fear to cajolery. In other words the *Brāhmaṇas* consist of a command structure and an elaborate technique for its translation into practical action. The texts promise certain fruits to those who carry out the commands contained therein, and there is a fool-proof and knave-proof guarantee for their success. It is this guaranteed success which makes these Vedic texts the pramāṇa of word. This assurance is no theoretical business; it has a solid basis in fact. Whenever the commands have been carried out without any blemish or deficiency they are known to have produced the appropriate result. They have always worked and it is certain they will always work. Thus the Vedic texts have twofold credibility: they are the utterances of men who are reliable; what they promise is always fulfilled.

This is true not only of the Vedic texts. According to Vātsyāyana, all that is said of these texts is true of ordinary speech. Like the Vedic texts, ordinary statements are of three kinds — injunctive, descriptive and reiterative. For instance, 'one should cook rice' is an injunction; 'Long life, glory, strength, pleasure and intelligence — all these reside in food' is descriptive; we have a reiteration in the following form: 'cook, cook, please' (NBh II. 1,66).

The real significance of the acceptance of the Vedic authority lies not so much in the recognition of the Veda as the pramāṇa of word but in the various uses of the Vedic texts which those who accept the Veda intend to make. The views of Gautama as explained by the commentators are briefly summarized below.

The Veda has two main divisions:[8] *Saṃhitā* and *Brāhmaṇa*. The *Brāhmaṇa* texts are subdivided into three parts: injunction, description and reiteration according to the purposes they serve. The injunction is that which prescribes a course of action. It is either mandatory or permissive. For instance, 'one who desires to attain heaven should offer the *Agnihotra* oblations'. This is an instance of the mandatory injunction. Description is of four kinds: valedictory, deprecatory, illustrative and narrative. The valedictory description is that text which eulogizes a certain injunction. Such a text serves two purposes: it inspires faith in what is thus eulogized; it persuades a person to perform an act on hearing that the fruit follows from such an act. For instance, there is a text: 'By the *Sarvajit* sacrifice gods conquered all; there is nothing so efficacious as the *Sarvajit* sacrifice, as it enables us to obtain everything and vanquish everyone, etc.'. This text is not a straight-forward command but the sacrifice is extolled in such a way that one is persuaded to perform it. The deprecatory description is that text which describes undesirable consequences of a certain act, and its purpose is to dissuade a person from performing an act deprecated; for instance: 'The *Jyotiṣṭoma* is the foremost of all sacrifices; one who, without performing this sacrifice, performs another sacrifice, falls into a pit, the act perishes and the man is destroyed, etc.'

The narrative description is that text which prescribes a course of action commended on account of its antiquity or tradition; for instance: 'Thus it is that the *brāhmaṇas* have adopted, in their hymns, the *bahipṣavamāna sāma* hymns, thinking that in so doing they were performing the sacrifices, etc.'. The illustrative and narrative texts are regarded as descriptive for two reasons: first, they are connected with valedictory or deprecatory texts; second, they indicate something connected with some other injunction.

Reiteration is repetition — with a purpose of injunction and of that which is enjoined by it. The former is verbal reiteration and the latter objective reiteration. The objective reiteration is praise of the act or deprecation of the omitting of the act enjoined in an injunction or a prescribed supplementary course of action; sometimes reiteration indicates the sequence of two acts (NBh II. 1,62-66). 'Sound is non-eternal, non-eternal' is an instance of verbal repetition; 'Sound is non-eternal; it has the property of extinction' is an instance of objective reiteration (NV II. 1,66).

(ii) The second argument of Gautama on this subject is that the character of pramāṇa (*prāmāṇya*) of the Veda is like that of the *mantras* and the Āyurveda (medical scripture) and that in both cases it is due to the character of pramāṇa of the āptas who have composed them. Vātsyāyana explains this argument at length in the following manner. The medical scripture declares that by doing a particular thing one obtains a particular desirable object, and by not doing a particular thing, one avoids a particular undesirable object; when one acts accordingly, the object turns out to be exactly as declared; this is what constitutes the character of pramāṇa in the case of the medical scripture; the scripture deals with things as they are and not as they are not. In the case of the *mantras* also their character of pramāṇa has a similar basis. Whenever they are used for the purpose of averting such evils as poison, ghosts and thunderbolt, they are found effective in producing that result; these *mantras* therefore deal with the things as they are and not as they are not.

This character of pramāṇa of the medical scripture and the *mantras* is the product of the character of pramāṇa which the āptas have. This latter character consists in the following. The āptas have a direct or intuitive perception of *dharma* (i.e. the true nature of things), compassion for living beings and desire to describe things as they really exist. They know what should be acquired and the method of acquiring it, and what should be avoided and the method of avoiding it. This constitutes their direct perception of the true nature of things. They have the following feelings about living things: "These poor creatures are themselves ignorant and have no other means except instruction available to them for knowing things; they cannot perform desirable acts or avoid undesirable acts until they have knowledge of the true nature of things; unless they act accordingly, it cannot be well with them; and there is no one (except myself) who would help them in this matter; well, I am therefore going to instruct them about things as they exist and as I know them; having listened to these instructions, these creatures will understand things as they are, and thus acquire what should be acquired and avoid what should be avoided." It is on this threefold basis that the instruction of āptas proceeds; when an act is known on this threefold character of pramāṇa of the āpta, and is performed accordingly, it fulfils the purpose which it is meant to fulfil. From this it follows that the instruction of āptas is a pramāṇa; and thus the āptas themselves become pramāṇa.

The Āyurveda is that part of the Veda which deals with visible things. It has already been established that the instruction of the āpta contained in the Āyurveda is pramāṇa. From this fact we infer that the character of pramāṇa belongs to those parts of the Veda which deal with invisible things. And the hetu which guarantees the inference is the same in both cases — the character of pramāṇa of the āpta. These parts of the Veda also deal with visible things, e.g. 'one who desires to acquire a village should perform sacrifices'. On seeing that this comes true, we can infer, from this also, that the other Vedic texts have the character of pramāṇa, which deal with invisible things.

In ordinary matters of everyday life also, a large amount of business is conducted on the basis of the advice of reliable persons. As before, the character of pramāṇa of such ordinary persons is based upon the same three conditions: they have knowledge of things as they are, sympathy for others and desire to describe things as they are; on the basis of these three qualifications the advice of these āptas is regarded as pramāṇa.

That part of the Veda which deals with invisible things is the work of the same seers and exponents (or speakers) as the Āyurveda. On this ground also, we infer that that part of the Veda, like the Āyurveda, has the character of pramāṇa (NBh II. 1,69).

(iii) The Nyāya concept of the character of pramāṇa of the Vedic texts is different from that of the Pūrvamīmāṃśā. According to the latter's view, it is due to their eternality. Vātsyāyana criticizes this Pūrvamīmāṃsā objection in the following manner.

The character of pramāṇa which words have in denoting objects, says the commentator, is due not to their eternality but to their denoting power. For if it were due to eternality, all things would be denoted by all words; there would be no such restriction as a particular word having a particular denotation.

The opponent retorts that if words are not eternal, they will have no power to signify anything at all. Vātsyāyana replies that this is not true. Words in ordinary use do denote objects, but they are not eternal. The opponent insists that all words, both Vedic and ordinary, are eternal. To this Vātsyāyana replies that in that case it would not be possible to explain the discrepancy between statement and fact as we find in the case of statements of those who are not āptas; in fact, since every word is eternal it should be pramāṇa. The opponent says that such words cannot be eternal, but then Vātsyāyana asks him to explain the difference between the assertion of an āpta and that of an untruthful person in ordinary speech; that is, he must tell us why the latter assertion is not eternal. Further, in the case of proper names their character of pramāṇa depends upon their denoting the objects denoted by them. This denotation is determined in accordance with the convention on the application of a particular name to a particular object; it is therefore convention and not eternality which explains the correct apprehension of objects denoted by their respective proper names.

The eternality of the Veda does not mean the eternality of the words in the Veda; all that this can mean, says Vātsyāyana, is that there is a continuity of tradition, practice and use; these are through all the ages, past and future. As Uddyotakara explains, the same Vedic texts have been handed down by a long tradition extending over several ages and it is on this basis that ordinary people assert that the Veda is eternal. Such statements are exactly like the assertion 'mountains and rivers are eternal'. What is true of the Vedas is also true of the assertions of Manu and other ancient authors. The opponent might ask that the eternality of the Veda cannot be explained in terms of the continuity of tradition. Uddyotakara replies that the arguments advanced by the Nāiyāyikas are unassailable; when one speaks of the eternality of the Vedas one is using only a figurative expression — 'eternality' standing for 'continuity of tradition' (NV II. 1,69).

In the light of the detailed arguments mentioned above, Vātsyāyana concludes that the character of pramāṇa that Vedic and ordinary words have, can be explained on the same basis; it is due to the character of pramāṇa of āpta in both cases (NBh II. 1,69).

According to Uddyotakara, the Pūrvamīmāṃsā argument — as the Veda is eternal, it cannot be composed by any person; its character of pramāṇa is due to eternality — is not sound, because the hetu eternality is not an established fact. Words have the character of pramāṇa, retorts the opponent, not because they are eternal but because they bring about cognition of objects of cognition. According to some philosophers, this line of reasoning can be answered in the following way: no pramāṇa is eternal; since Vedic texts are pramāṇa they cannot be eternal. Uddyotakara rejects this reply, as the word pramāṇa denotes the entire group (*samudāya*) of eternal and non-eternal things; for instance, the lamp which is non-eternal is a pramāṇa, and the atom which is eternal is a pramāṇa for establishing the existence of composite things. Hence the hetu — because the pramāṇa is not eternal — cannot prove the non-eternality of the Veda.

The correct answer to the Pūrvamīmāṃsā is as follows:

Vedic texts are non-eternal, (a) because they are divided according to the purposes served by them; and in this respect they are just like ordinary assertions. If the ordinary assertions were eternal, no such division would be possible; (b) because the Vedic assertion consists of *varṇas* as are ordinary assertions; *varṇas* are non-eternal; (c) because while the Vedic texts belong to a class (*sāmānya*) and possess specific individuality (*viśeṣa*), they are apprehended by the auditory organs as are the ordinary assertions.

The opponent argues that words are uttered not for one's own cognition but for making things known to other persons. In view of this cognition from a word would be possible only if it were eternal; if it were non-eternal, it would disappear as soon as uttered; so that each time when a person hears a word, it would be a new word never heard before, and certainly no cognition can arise from a word that has not been heard; for instance, when an inhabitant of the *Nārikela* Island hears the word 'cow' which he has never heard before, he does not have any cognition of the animal. Anyone who holds words to be non-eternal will be in such a predicament: all words would be words heard for the first time and there would be no certainty that he could obtain any cognition from words.

This argument, says Uddyotakara, is based on a false hetu; momentary things like a lamp do bring about the cognition of things — even those which come into existence for the first time. This instance, objects the opponent, is not analogous to the case in question; it is through its connection with the thing lighted that the lamp renders that thing perceptible. And the word is not so connected and cannot therefore produce cognition of anything. It is true, says Uddyotakara, that no such connection is perceived, but the relation between the word and its denotation is that of the denoter and the denoted. This relation is based on convention and learnt from ordinary usage. Such a convention has no beginning in time for the simple reason that the world has no beginning (NV II. 1,69).

III. Non-Eternality of Sound

A. *Examination of the theories of sound*

According to Gautama the pramāṇa of word is a specific kind of word, viz. the assertion of an āpta. This implies that there are different kinds of words. Further, there are conflicting theories of word supported by conflicting hetus. There are four such theories in the field: (1) The Mīmāṃsaka view: Sound is a quality of ākāśa; it is all-pervading and eternal; being eternal it is liable to manifestation only. (2) The Sāṃkhya view: Sound coexists in tangible substances along with colour and other qualities; it is liable to manifestation only. (3) The Vaiśeṣika view: Sound is the quality of ākāśa, and is liable to production and destruction like *buddhi* (intelligence). (4) The Buddhist view: Sound is produced by vibrations in the elements; it does not subsist in anything; it is liable to production and destruction (NBh II. 2,12). The Nyāya view on this subject is: Sound is a quality of ākāśa and is non-eternal. It is liable to production and destruction. If sound were eternal, it could not account for the facts of our auditory experience, and in that case no satisfactory explanation could be given of the so-called manifestation. Every sound consists of a series of sounds and is heard when the last of the series reaches the ear which also is composed of ākāśa. The main attack of the Naiyāyika is levelled against the Mīmāṃsakas who are the champions of the eternalist school.

Gautama has devoted no less than twenty-eight aphorisms to the controversy about the nature of sound. He states his own view and then proceeds to deal with the various objections.

[Sound is not eternal] because it has a beginning and is apprehended by sense-organ and is deemed to be a product (NS II. 2,14).

Objection

[The three hetus mentioned above are not valid] because the absence of a jar [after it has been destroyed] and the universal of the jar [jar-ness] are eternal, and eternal things are also deemed to be products (NS II. 2,15).

Reply

Inasmuch as there is a difference between meaning proper (*tattva*) and indirect or figurative meaning (*bhākta*) of the term 'eternal', the hetus are not untrue (NS II. 2,16).

[The apprehension of sound by the sense-organ has been mentioned only as leading to] the specific inference of the series [of sounds] (NS II. 2,17).

Because what the term '*pradeśa*' denotes is the substance which is the cause (NS II. 2,18).

According to Gautama sound is non-eternal (i) because it has a beginning, (ii) because it is apprehended by sense-organ, and (iii) because it is spoken of as a product. Vātsyāyana explains the views of Gautama as follows:

(i) The first hetu means that sound has a cause. It is observed that what has a cause is non-eternal. To say that sound has a cause is to say that it is liable to origination; that is, after having come into existence, it ceases to exist. It is therefore non-eternal in this sense (NBh II. 2,14).

It is objected that this hetu of Gautama is not true in all cases. For instance, when a jar is destroyed, its destruction has undoubtedly a cause; it ceases to exist only when the clay-particles are disrupted. But once the jar has been destroyed, that same jar can never come into existence again. Thus the absence of the jar has a beginning but no end; that is, it is eternal (NBh II. 2,15).

The objection is not valid, says Vātsyāyana, because it ignores the distinction between what is eternal and what is not eternal. What is meant by the thing being 'eternal' is that it is a thing which is not subject to origination and destruction; the question of absence does not arise at all. In this primary sense the destruction of the jar cannot be said to be eternal. However, it can be said to be eternal in a figurative or secondary sense; having existed, the jar has ceased to exist and never comes into existence again (NBh II. 2,16).

While Vātsyāyana has explained the position in the context of destruction, Uddyotakara explains it in the context of prior absence as well. The term 'eternality' means that the thing has such existence as is not conditioned by two limits, beginning and end, and the contrary of this constitutes non-eternality. When the absence of the jar is regarded as eternal in a figurative sense, this means that its absence is not observed at two times: first the destruction of the jar, which is a kind of absence, was not present before the jar came into existence nor is it present while the jar actually exists; second, prior absence is not found while the jar exists nor after its destruction has been accomplished (NV II. 2,16).

(ii) The second hetu for the non-eternality of sound is that it is apprehended through the contact of the sense-organ. The significance of this hetu is to make it quite clear that sound is a product and not a manifestation of something eternal. When a piece of wood, for example, is being cut, its sound is heard at a distance even after the impact of the axe on the wood has ceased. This is possible because there is a series of sounds. The impact of the axe produces the initial sound; this latter sets up a series of sounds; when the last of the series reaches the ear, it is this sound that is actually heard. Thus even though the impact has ceased we can hear the sound long afterwards. But if this impact were to serve merely to manifest something that is eternal (i.e. eternal sound) and not actually to produce the initial sound, this would not be right; for it is never the case that the thing manifested is apprehended after the agent which manifests it has ceased (NBh II. 2,14).

According to Uddyotakara the initial sound produced by conjunction and disjunction produces other sounds in all directions, like the filaments of the *kadamba* flower; from each of these latter there proceeds another sound, and from the latter another, and so on, each of these being duller than its predecessor. This series of sounds goes on being produced till there is an obstacle in its vehicle (i.e. air). The last of this series, having become too attenuated, loses the capacity of producing a further sound, by reason of some sort of obstacle; thus the series of sounds comes to an end. Of such a series of sounds that alone which reaches the ākāśa in the ear of the hearer is apprehended; no other sound is apprehended. If sound were eternal, there would be no production of the series of sounds; if there were no series the sound would not be heard. It is therefore wrong to say that eternal sound is manifested (NV II. 2,14).

It is objected that the second hetu, apprehension through sense-organ, like the first, is not universally true. The universal (*sāmānya*) of a thing, though eternal, is apprehended through sense-organs (NBh II. 2,15). According to Vātsyāyana, this objection is based upon a misunderstanding of Gautama's intention. Sound is non-eternal not simply because it is apprehended by a sense-organ but because this fact leads to the inference that in every instance of sound apprehended there is a series of sounds; and the series means that each of the sounds in it is non-eternal (NBh II. 2,17).

(iii) The third hetu for the non-eternality of sound is that it is spoken of as a product. We say sound is loud or soft, as we say pain is acute or dull. Only a product can be spoken of in this fashion. It is argued that loudness or softness belongs to the manifesting impact and not to the sound itself. This is just like the case of colour: the colour remains the same but its apprehension becomes brighter or duller by the light that manifests it. This explanation cannot be accepted, says Vātsyāyana, because in the case of sound there is the phenomenon of suppression (*abhibhava*). It is only when the sound of a drum is loud that it suppresses the softer sound of a lute, and not when it has been deadened. This suppression cannot be ascribed to the apprehension of the sound itself. If the two sounds — the loud sound and the soft sound — were the same in both cases, the former should always suppress the latter; this is contrary to our experience. But if the two sounds are regarded as different, the suppression of one by the other can be explained. Moreover, if the sounds are manifested in the same place as their manifesting agency, there can be no such phenomenon as suppression. The sound of the drum which is in the drum cannot eclipse the sound of the lute which is in the lute. If these could get at each other even without any contact, there should be suppression of all sounds. According to this theory, the sound of the drum at any one place should suppress the sound of the lute nearby but also the sound of all lutes that may be sounded at the time anywhere — in all regions of the world! But if there are two different series of sounds — one of the drum and the other of the lute — a loud sound can suppress a soft sound if they reach the ear at the same time. (NBh II. 2,14.)

An objection is raised against the third hetu: Even eternal things are spoken of as non-eternal; for instance, we speak of a part of ākāśa or of self, as we speak of a part of a tree or a blanket. Ākāśa and self are eternal, and if Gautama's hetu was right, these would be regarded as non-eternal. Thus this hetu, like the first two, also is not true in all instances (NBh II. 2,15).

According to Vātsyāyana, this objection is based upon a confusion between two different senses in which the word '*pradeśa*' is used. When it is used in relation to ākāśa or self, it does not denote its inherent cause, as it does in the case of the tree or the blanket. That self or ākāśa has no inherent cause can be ascertained by any of the pramāṇas. The word '*pradeśa*' in the expression 'part of ākāśa' means that contact of any substance of limited extension does not pervade over the entire ākāśa; it subsists in it without pervading over the whole of it. Herein lies the similarity between ākāśa and ordinary products: the contact between two berries, for instance, does not pervade over the entire berries. And on the basis of this similarity the word 'part' is used in a secondary or figurative sense.

It may now be asked how the Naiyāyika maintains two different positions: the properties of loudness or softness are said to belong to sound in reality, and not figuratively, and in the present argument the word *'pradeśa'* is said to be used indirectly rather than directly.

It is the practice of Gautama in several sections, says Vātsyāyana, to establish certain truths in the belief that these can be learnt from the doctrine of his *śāstra.* This *śāstra* — doctrine consists of inferential reasonings with numerous implications. The truths — ākāśa or self has no parts and loudness and softness are real properties of sound — can be learnt from the *Nyāya Sūtra* and this is their authority (NBh II. 2,18).

Some of the observations made by Uddyotakara on this subject are of interest. When there are two things — one of them not quite the same as the other — and if some similarity is found between them, this similarity constitutes the basis of their being treated figuratively as the same. This basis is known as *bhakti,* because it is divided between the two things concerned. When we say 'part of ākāśa' the character of 'part' is imposed upon what is really not a part. This imposition is based upon the similarity of ākāśa to things that have real parts, in the sense that its contact does not pervade over the whole of it. Even though ākāśa has no parts, the contact is not deprived of its substratum; it subsists in the ākāśa itself.

Pervasion or non-pervasion, says Uddyotakara, means nothing more than subsistence or non-subsistence in the substratum. When a jar is seen, its colour is seen; this shows that colour is pervasive. Pleasure is not apprehended whenever self is apprehended; or sound is not apprehended whenever ākāśa is apprehended; this proves that pleasure and sound are non-pervasive qualities. When a few cows are perceived, the universal of the cow 'cow-ness' is perceived; this shows that the universal is pervasive. When only one of the two things in contact is perceived, the contact is not perceived; this shows that contact is not pervasive. Whether a thing is pervasive or not depends upon its being apprehended or not apprehended on the apprehension of its substratum (NV II. 2,18).

Gautama offers the following positive argument in support of the non-eternality of sound and deals with the objections raised against it.

[Sound is non-eternal] because there is non-apprehension of it before it is uttered and also because there is non-apprehension of obstruction [that could explain the non-apprehension of the sound] (NS II. 2,19].

Objection

Obstruction exists because there is non-apprehension of the non-apprehension of obstruction (NS II. 2,20).

If [you assert] non-apprehension of obstruction exists even though there is non-apprehension of the non-apprehension then the mere non-apprehension of obstruction cannot prove the non-existence of the obstruction (NS II. 2,21).

Reply

This is no hetu, because non-apprehension is of the nature of the negation of apprehension (NS II. 2,22).

According to Vātsyāyana, the eternalist may be asked: how does one know whether a thing exists or not ? He would say: a thing exists when it is apprehended by means of a pramāṇa and a thing does not exist when it is not apprehended by means of a pramāṇa. In that case the eternalist will have to accept the argument of Gautama that sound does not exist because it is not apprehended before its utterance. This non-apprehension cannot be attributed to any obstruction. For example, it cannot be said that sound is not heard either because it is not close to the sense-organ or there is something intervening between the sound and the sense-organ.

The utterance of sound, objects the eternalist, serves only to manifest it and this explains why, prior to utterance, sound, though existing, is not apprehended. What utterance means is this: when there is a desire on the part of a speaker to speak, he makes an effort; this effort raises the wind in his body; this wind rises and strikes the throat, etc.; it is this impact (*pratighāta*) of the wind that produces the manifestation of particular varṇa-sounds.

This explanation, says Vātsyāyana, proves exactly the opposite. As already mentioned, the impact is only a specific form of contact. Consequently the non-apprehension of sound is due not to the absence of the manifesting agent but to the sheer absence of the sound. The fact that sound is heard only when it is uttered shows that it comes into existence when it is heard and that it has ceased to exist when it is not heard. Thus if the sound is not heard it is always due to its sheer non-existence (NBh II. 2,19).

According to Vātsyāyana, Gautama deals with positive arguments of the eternalist in his aphorisms, NS II. 2,23-40. His views are briefly summarised in the light of the explanation given by the commentators.

(a) The eternalist says that sound is eternal because it is intangible. This hetu is not conclusive because it is found that the atom is intangible but eternal while action is intangible but non-eternal (NBh II. 2,23-25).

(b) Another hetu given by the eternalist is that sound that is imparted persists; for example, the sound imparted by a teacher to his pupil. This is not right because sound is not audible in the space intervening between the teacher and the pupil. The eternalist argues that the persistence of sound is indicated by the fact that it makes teaching possible. It is true that the word-sounds are taught, but 'being taught' admits of two interpretations: the sound that originally subsisted in the teacher goes over to the pupil or the pupil only imitates what he finds in the teacher, as is the case with the teaching of dancing. Thus the hetu is doubtful.

(c) The eternalist argues that repetition can prove eternality of sound if not the fact of instruction. What one reads several times must persist during all that time. The argument from repetition is doubtful as the term is used in the case of the same thing repeated and of different things repeated. In the latter case the use is figurative. For instance, we say dance twice; here there are two acts but we ask for the repetition of one and the same dance. Thus the fact of repetition does not indicate that the same sound persists (NBh II. 2,30).

(d) In the context of repetition the eternalist, according to Gautama, raises the following objection: "When a thing is different, it is different from something that is not different [from it]; and what is different must be non-different from itself; therefore, there is nothing that can be regarded as different (*anyathābhāva*) (NS II. 2,32). Explaining this objection, Vātsyāyana says that the contention of the eternalist is that what the Naiyāyika regards as different is non-different from itself; consequently there can be no possibility of anything being entirely different. It follows that the Nyāya view that the term 'repetition' is used figuratively also in cases where the things concerned are 'different' is not right (NBh II. 2,32).

To this objection Gautama replies: In the absence of the conception of difference there can be none of non-difference, as the two conceptions are mutually dependent (NS II. 2,33). If the eternalist believes the different to be non-different, says Vātsyāyana, he cannot reject the conception of difference. In fact, the word non-different (*ananya*) is a compound consisting of two words: 'different' and the negative particle 'non'. If the second term of the compound is denied, there is nothing with which the negative particle is compounded; in fact, the two terms 'different' and 'non-different' can function only in relation to each other (NBh II. 2,33).

(e) In this connection a question is raised: People have such notions as "this is the word 'cow' " whenever we hear the word. This uniform notion cannot be explained except on the basis that there is some one sound to which this refers. Such notions cannot be wrong; for if they were wrong, the notion produced by that word-sound in regard to the animal cow would be wrong also; this, however, is not so. This is not like the notion of fire which can be wrong when it is based upon a mistaken perception of smoke. Thus the notion the people have in regard to the word 'cow' is right; and this proves that the said word-sound is abiding, and not ephemeral.

Uddyotakara's reply as explained by Vācaspatiis: It is true — and this is accepted by the questioner and himself — that the notions of the cow that we have are diverse, even though all these notions are regarded as 'the idea of the cow'. Similarly, it is reasonable to suppose that the various words 'cow' may be regarded as the word 'cow' but they are in fact diverse. What makes such a comprehensive notion of 'idea of the cow' possible — the notion which includes all individual ideas of cow — is the generic concept 'idea of cow'; this idea is based upon the fact that there are certain points common to all ideas of cow. Similarly, what makes the comprehensive notion of the word 'cow' — the notion which includes all cases of the utterance of that word — is the generic concept of the word 'cow', based upon the fact that there are certain points of similarity between all the individual utterances of the word 'cow'. The concept of identity in such cases is based upon similarity (*sāmānya*) (NV & NVTT II. 2,33).

(f) The eternalist argues that sound is eternal because we perceive no cause for its destruction. What is non-eternal is destroyed by a cause; for instance, a stone is destroyed by the disintegration of its constituents. Sound is non-eternal and should have a cause for its destruction. Since such a cause is not perceived it is eternal (NBh II. 2,34).

The Nyāya reply is as follows: the cause of destruction is actually perceived and therefore the hetu of the eternalist is false. As already explained, in the case of every sound there is a series of sounds in which each preceding sound produced by conjunction and disjunction is destroyed by every succeeding sound. The last sound in the series is destroyed when there is the conjunction or impact of an obstructing substance. We can stop the sound of a bell by our hands (NBh II. 2,35-37).

If the mere fact that the cause of destruction is not perceived were to prove that a thing is eternal, it is objected, then the hearing of a sound should be eternal like the sound itself. A thing is eternal, says Gautama, only if it continues to exist and if we cannot perceive any cause why it should cease (NS & NBh II. 2,38).

(g) The Sāṃkhya philosopher raises an objection: according to the Naiyāyika sound subsists in a substance other than that which touches the bell. If so, it cannot be stopped by the touch subsisting in something totally different. If sound, though subsisting in a different substratum, were stopped by the touch, then it would mean that a single touch can stop the sound of all bells. Hence sound subsists in the same substratum with the contact of the bell and the hand: that is, sound subsists in the air where the vibrations subsist, and in ākāśa.

This objection has no force, says Vātsyāyana, as the substratum of sound, ākāśa, is intangible: the sound-series is perceived even at a time where there is no perception of anything having colour and other qualities. This clearly shows that sound has for its substratum a substance which is intangible and all-pervading, viz. ākāśa.

In each tangible thing there is only one kind of smell, taste, touch or colour. If sound were to coexist in any tangible substance along with other qualities and constitute an aggregate, it will have to be of one kind only. But sound is of various kinds; for instance, when sound appears in a musical instrument, it is of various kinds such as loud, soft, and even the sound of the same kind may vary in degrees. Such diversities are possible only if there are several sounds and they are produced; and not if there is a single sound and that single sound is itself a manifestation. Hence sound cannot be said to manifest, as it subsists in each substance along with colour and other qualities[1] (NBh & NV II. 2,39 & 40).

B. *What is non-eternality (anityatā)?*

According to Uddyotakara the main issue in the debate on the eternality and non-eternality of sound is: what is it by virtue of which a thing becomes non-eternal ? His own view is that non-eternality is something positive; a thing is non-eternal when it does not have continuous or absolute existence. In this context his comments[2] on some of the views opposed to his are given below:

(i) According to some philosophers non-eternality consists in prior non-existence and prior non-destruction; that is, a thing is non-eternal which has these two. Uddyotakara rejects this notion on the following grounds: (a) When a thing exists it does not have prior non-existence nor prior destruction; it cannot therefore be related to that which does not exist. Further, this notion means that the thing has prior non-existence before it has come into existence and has prior destruction after it has ceased to exist; this is absurd. (b) Previous non-existence and previous destruction denote sheer absence, but non-eternality denotes something positive; a thing is non-eternal when it has the property of not having absolute (*atyanta*) existence. This is also evident from the fact that the term (*anityatā*) is an abstract noun.

(ii) Another notion of non-eternality is: non-eternality of a thing consists in the absence of the cause of its destruction.

The commentator rejects this notion on the following grounds: A thing is described as non-eternal even when the cause of its destruction is not actually present; e.g. a jar is described as non-eternal even before it has been disrupted into its constituent particles. Further, to say that the cause of the destruction of a thing is present does not amount to saying that the thing has destruction. However, in such expressions as 'the body has the character of being destructible' (*vināśavac charīram*), all that it means is that the destruction of the body is inevitable or absolutely certain; destruction which is not actually present is figuratively spoken of the body.

(iii) According to the Sāṃkhya the notion of non-eternality is: When all the conditions of apprehension of a thing are present, and in its own form the thing, having completely disappeared from view, is absolutely not apprehended — that thing is called 'non-eternal'. This notion is contrary to the doctrine of the Sāṃkhya philosophers: there is nothing which is absolutely not apprehended. Since everything that is manifested is a product of the primordial matter and is non-different from it in the Sāṃkhya system, some product or other is bound to be apprehended. Besides no disappearance of a thing is possible unless some new element is introduced into it (NV II. 2,14).

IV. Modification of Sound (*śabdavikāra*)

In his aphorisms on the non-eternality of sound Gautama claims to have established the nature of sound. He now proceeds to examine the nature of *varṇas* (phonemes).

As we have seen, Gautama has refuted the Sāṃkhya theory of sound that it is manifested as coexisting with colour and other qualities. These philosophers, however, persist in their theory of modification and argue: Sound may not be eternal in the sense that it continues to exist in a modified form, but it could be regarded as eternal in the sense that it continues to exist and undergo modifications. This is exactly like the primordial matter (*prakṛti*) which is regarded as eternal, though it is modified into various evolutes. In support of the eternality of sound the Sāṃkhya philosophers cite the grammatical rules of *sandhi* according to which *varṇas* undergo modifications. It is to demolish this theory of modification, says Vācaspati, that Gautama has embarked upon its examination. His own view on *sandhi* is that what happens in this process is not modification of one *varṇa* into another but substitution of one *varṇa* by another (NVTT II. 2,41).

Sound, says Vātsyāyana, is of two kinds: *varṇa* and *dhvani* (sound as such). Regarding the former, there is doubt because there are two interpretations of what happens when final and initial *varṇas* are combined: modification (*vikāra*) and substitution (*ādeśa*). For instance, in the expression *dadhyatra*, *i*, the last *varṇa* of *dadhi*, is combined with *a*, the first *varṇa* of *atra* and the result of the combination is *ya* and the combined word *dadhyatra*. According to the modification theory, *i* is modified into *y*; the *i* renounces its own character and acquires the character of *y*. According to the substitution theory, *y* is substituted in place of *i*; the *i* having been used, it gives up its place and in the place thus vacated, *ya* (i.e. *i*+*a*) comes to be used. In view of these conflicting views Gautama has examined this subject in his aphorisms NS II. 2,41-59, with a view to vindicating his own preference for the substitution theory. His arguments as explained by Vātsyāyana are given below.

Gautama's first objection to the modification theory is that if *varṇas* underwent modification an augmentation in the original cause would be accompanied by a corresponding augmentation in its modification. But in the presnt case, whether the preceding *varṇa*, *i*, is short or long, in combination with the initial *a* *ya* which is always substituted is *ya*. The objector contends that the argument is not valid because modifications are found to be less than, equal to, and greater than, the original cause. Gautama rejects this contention on the ground that the modifications which he has mentioned are those which originate from different causes. A modification may not vary concomitantly with its cause but if the original cause is different the modification should be different. In fact, we have a counter-example: when a horse is harnessed in place of a bull to carry a load, the horse is not treated as a modification of the bull.

An objection is raised: The difference between a *varṇa* and its modification is similar to that between a substance and its modification. In the case of substances the modification differs from the original, even though both are substances. Similarly, in the case of *varṇas* the modification differs from the original, even though both equally are *varṇas.* This is not right, says Gautama in reply, because the character of modification is not found in the case of *varṇas.* When a substance undergoes modification, the character of being a substance remains the same; only one pattern of the substance disappears and another comes into existence and this latter patternis called 'modification'. For instance, when a ring is made from gold, gold remains gold but it has acquired only a new pattern in place of its original pattern. In the case of *varṇas,* on the other hand, there is no such *varṇa*-character which could remain constant and yet undergo modification. This is exactly like the case of the horse and the bull mentioned before. Both are undoubtedly substances but one is not the modification of another because their characters are different.

Another argument in favour of the substitution theory, says Gautama, is that things which have undergone modifications cannot revert to their original form; for instance, the curd cannot again become milk. It is true that gold, for instance, renounces the form of the ear-ring, takes the form of the bracelet, again renounces the form of the latter and takes the form of the ear-ring. But throughout this process gold does not abandon its character of being gold. A *varṇa,* say *i,* does not have the character of *i*-ness (*ittva*). Since it does not have such a genuine character it cannot be said to renounce one form and acquire another. Thus what happens in the case of substances, says Gautama, cannot be said to happen in the case of *varṇas.*

The objector continues: The generic character of *varṇa* is never absent from the modification of the *varṇa.* Gautama replies: a property (*dharma*) belongs to that which has a generic character (*sāmānya*), and not to the generic character itself. In the case of gold we can say that the ear-ring and the bracelet are forms or properties of gold; they are not properties of the generic character of being gold. In the case of *varṇas* we cannot say that a particular *varṇa* is a property of anything nor can we say that it is a property of the generic character of being such a *varṇa.*

Gautama gives another argument against the modification theory. If the *varṇas* were eternal they could not be modified; if they were non-eternal they could not continue long enough to provide a basis for modification. The eternalist argues: It is quite possible for eternal *varṇas* to undergo modification as some of the eternal things are beyond the reach of our senses while others are not: moreover, even if the *varṇas* were non-eternal, their modification could be perceived as they themselves would be perceptible. The character of modification, says Gautama in reply, is incompatible with eternality and the so-called modification appears at a time subsequent to the destruction of its original.

Another argument against the modification theory is that while in the case of real modification there is a definite rule regarding the original cause, there is no such rule in the case of the *varṇas*. For instance, milk is always the original material of curd and not *vice versa*, but in the case of *varṇas* it cannot be said that a particular *varṇa* is always the original base of another.

The argument based on the absence of rule (*aniyama*) is questioned by the opponent: it is not right to say that there is no rule because the absence of rule is itself in the nature of a rule. This objection is not right, says Gautama, because rule and absence of rule are contradictory. The absence of rule may be uniform in its application but it cannot have the essential character of the rule. What is important, says Vātsyāyana, is that uniformity and non-uniformity, which are opposed to each other, cannot be predicated of one and the same thing. Rule and absence of rule are not synonymous.

What appears as the modification of *varṇas*, says Gautama in conclusion, is that there is a change in one or the other of the following forms: acquisition of a different property, suppression, diminution, curtailment and coalescence. According to Vātsyāyana, what really happens is not that one *varṇa* is the effect of another which is its cause or one *varṇa* is modified into another, but that a cognate *varṇa* is substituted; that is, one cognate *varṇa* is used when the utterance of another has ceased, and this substitution is made in diverse forms. If this is all that the opponent means by his modification theory, adds the commentator ironically, he is prepared to accept the statement that '*varṇas* undergo modifications' (NS & NBh II. 2, 41-59).

V. Word and Meaning

A. *Examination of theories of meaning*

Having established the theory of substitution of *varṇas*, Gautama proceeds to deal with the problem of word and meaning in twelve aphorisms (NS II. 2, 60-71). In this context he defines *pada* (word) as '*varṇas* ending with an affix' (NS II. 2,60).[1] According to Vātsyāyana affixes are of two kinds: noun-affixes and verb-affixes. Words ending with noun-affixes are nouns and words ending with verb-affixes are verbs. Both indeclinables and prepositions are to be treated as words, though they do not end in affixes.[2] Only words can produce cognition of things, and indeclinables and prepositions produce such cognition (NBh II. 2,60). According to Vācaspati, Gautama's definition of word is meant to distinguish his position from that of the grammarians who hold the explosion theory (*sphoṭa*). A word consists of *varṇas* only, and not of any such abstract thing like *sphoṭa* (NVTT II. 2,60).

If words consist of *varṇas*, how do we cognize a thing on hearing the word ? We cognize the thing, says Uddyotakara on hearing the last *varṇa* of its corresponding word as aided by the recollection of preceding *varṇas* (NV II. 2,60).

According to the commentators, Gautama discusses the theories of the meaning of noun-words only, because they are not only numerous but our usage depends upon them. "There is doubt," says Gautama, "because a word is used indirectly or metaphorically in reference to an individual (*vyakti*), a configuration (*ākṛti*) and a universal (*jāti*), which are presented side by side." This doubt arises because philosophers regard one or the other of these three as the meaning of the word and Gautama therefore proceeds to refute the theories which conflict with his own position.

(1) *Individual*

According to Gautama the opponent's theory of meaning is: "The word signifies the individual because it is only in respect of individuals that the following words can be used metaphorically: that, collection, giving, possession, number, enlargement, contraction, colour, compound and propagation" (NS II. 2,62).

Vātsyāyana explains this theory in the following way: In the expression 'that cow is standing', the term 'that' can be used only in reference to an individual cow, and not to the class of cows. Similarly, it is only in respect of individuals that we can use such expressions as 'collection of cows', 'he gives the cow'. In none of these expressions can there be reference to the class of cows (NBh II. 2,62).

Gautama rejects this theory of the opponent on two grounds:

(a) "This is not right because there is no determination of the individual" (NS II. 2,63);

(b) "In the case of *brāhmaṇa*, scaffold, mat, king, flour, sandal-wood, the Ganges, cart, food and man, though these are not directly signified they are figuratively signified respectively on account of association, location, purpose, behaviour, measure, containing, proximity, conjunction, means (or cause) and supremacy" (NS II. 2,64).

Vātsyāyana explains Gautama's reply to this opponent as follows:

(a) When we say 'that cow is standing', what is denoted by the word 'cow' is not the individual by itself, without any qualification, but the individual as qualified by the class to which it belongs (NBh II. 2,63). If the word denoted the individual only, says Uddyotakara, we would have cognition of any individual and not of the particular individual (NV II. 2,63).

(b) If the word does not denote an individual, how can we refer to an individual in the various expressions under consideration ? The answer is : When Gautama says that one thing is spoken of as another which is not the same as that, he means that a thing is spoken of by means of a word which does not directly signify it. For instance, we say 'feed the staff'. Here the word staff signifies the *brāhmaṇa* accompanied by the staff by reason of association. The word 'staff', says Uddyotakara, signifies the staff because it belongs to the class of staffs; this class subsists in the staff; the connection of the *brāhmaṇa* with the staff as related to that particular class, is due to association; when the *brāhmaṇa* is spoken of as the 'staff', there is imposed upon the *brāhmaṇa* that class which subsists in the staff with which the *brāhmaṇa* is connected; thus the word 'staff' figuratively signifies the *brāhmaṇa* (NBh II. 2,64).

(2) *Configuration*

According to Gautama the opponent's theory of configuration is: The word signifies configuration as the determiation of the essential nature of a thing depends upon the configuration (NS II. 2,65). Vātsyāyana explains the theory : The configuration of a thing consists in a definite arrangement of its components and of components of these components. It is only when this arrangement has been apprehended that we can determine the essential nature of the thing; for instance, whether the thing is a cow or a horse. Hence the word can be taken as signifying only that the apprehension of which leads to the determination of the exact nature of the thing spoken of (NBh II. 2,65).

Gautama has not directly criticized this theory, as he has done in the case of the individual theory. Vātsyāyana has, however, given his criticism in the light of the definition of configuration as given by Gautama. A thing is spoken of as the 'cow' as qualified by the class 'cow-ness' only when it is really related to that class. What can be related to a class is an individual substance composed of definitely arranged components, and not the configuration of the substance itself (NBh II. 2,65).

(3) *Universal*

According to Gautama the opponent's theory of the universal is : "The word signifies the universal because immolation, etc., cannot be performed on the cow of clay even though it is endowed with individuality and configuration" (NS II. 2,66). Vātsyāyana explains : We have such expressions as 'wash the cow', 'bring the cow'. None of these expressions refers to the cow made of clay. The clay-cow has both individuality and configuration, but does not belong to the class of cows. It is because of the absence of this class in the clay-cow that the various actions mentioned in the expressions are not applicable to the clay-cow. Hence the word signifies a universal (NBh II. 2,66).

Gautama rejects this theory: "This is not right because the manifestation of a universal depends on individuality and configuration" (NS II. 2,67). There can be no apprehension of a universal by itself, says Vātsyāyana, unless the individuality and configuration have been apprehended. Hence the universal cannot be regarded as constituting the denotation of a word (NBh II. 2,67).

Gautama reiterates his view that "the meaning of a word is an individual, a universal and a configuration" (NS II. 2,68). It follows that the three theories of meaning are all one-sided. According to Vātsyāyana, there is no hard and fast rule that one or the other of the three aspects of meaning is a principal or subordinate factor. It all depends upon the intention of the person using the expression. For instance, when a person uses a nominal word to emphasize the difference of a thing from other things and when the cognition produced by the word is one of the distinctive features of that thing, then the individual is a principal factor and the universal and the configuration are subordinate factors. But if the individual is not meant to be emphasized, and the resultant cognition is one of a universal, then the universal is a principal factor and the other two aspects are subordinate factors. Similarly, one or the other factor becomes principal or subordinate. Instances of such varying degrees of predominance and subordination can be found in our ordinary usage. When we say 'make a cow out of rice-flour', it is the configuration that is a principal factor and the other two are subordinate.

According to Vātsyāyana, these aspects are known from the fact that each one of them has a distinctive character of its own. These distinctive characters are described by Gautama as follows:

"An individual," says Gautama, "is that which has a definite form and is the abode of specific qualities" (NS II. 2,69). An individual is any substance which is apprehended by the sense-organs as a limited abode of colour, taste, smell, touch, weight, solidity, fluidity and elasticity or momentum (*saṃskāra*) (NBh II. 2,69).[3] "The configuration," says Gautama, "is that which indicates the universal and its marks" (NS II. 2,70). According to Vātsyāyana, this configuration is nothing apart from the definite arrangement of the components of an object and the components of these components. The universal, cow-ness for instance, is indicated by the particular arrangement of head and feet that a cow has. If a universal is not indicated, it means that there is no configuration at all. In such cases configuration does not constitute part of the meaning of the nominal word (NBh II. 2,70). For instance, in the case of clay and gold, the universal is indicated by the particular colour, and not by configuration. The universal '*brāhmaṇa*-hood' is indicated by birth; the universals of butter, oil, etc., are indicated either by odour or taste (NVTT II. 2,70). As Uddyotakara observes, all configurations indicate universals but not all universals are indicated by configurations.

The third component of meaning, universal, is defined by Gautama as "that whose nature is to produce the same notion" (NS II. 2,71).[4] Vātsyāyana explains: "That which produces the same notion in regard to different things (or loci), which does not distinguish several things from one another, and which is an instrumental cause of the comprehensive notion of several things — such a thing is *sāmānya*. That which distinguishes some things and does not distinguish others is a specific *sāmānya*. And this is the universal (*jāti*)" (NBh II. 2,71).

On this subject of the universal Uddyotakara has made a number of observations and these are summarized below.

The universal is that which is the hetu (cause) of the comprehensive notion of several different things. For instance, 'these are bowls' is a comprehensive notion and 'these are not bowls' is an exclusive notion. In this connection what is important to note is that while the universal is always the cause of the notion of sameness (*samānapratyaya*) there is no rule that the notion of sameness cannot be produced by anything but the universal. This is quite evident from the fact that even when the universal is absent the notion of sameness is present; for example, the word 'cook' does represent a notion of sameness but cook is not a universal (NV II. 2,71). The word represents a predominant factor in the cause of cooking. This predominance belongs to all persons who perform the act of cooking and therefore the term is applied to them (NV II. 2,66). The universal is eternal. It produces the notion of sameness with regard to its cause, i.e. that by which it is manifested. For instance, the universal 'cow-ness' is not manifested except through the object (i.e. the animal) possessed of the dewlap, etc. The eternality of the universal is thus quite compatible with its having a cause for its manifestation.

The universal is all-pervading (*sarvagata*) in the sense that it pervades its own objects. For instance, the universal 'cow-ness' pervades the cows but not the clay-cow; for the same simple reason that while both the cow and the clay-cow have an individuality and a configuration, the universal 'cow-ness' is present in former and absent in the latter; the clay-cow is not a real cow. But the word cow is actually used in the word clay-cow because of the similarity of configuration or shape.

It is objected that there can be no such entity as a universal apart from the individual objects. How can such an entity exist in the space intervening between objects ? Uddyotakara replies that none of the alternatives open to the objector is tenable. The intervening space can be ākāśa, absence or something else. Since ākāśa is not the cow, it is not surprising that the 'cow-ness' is not found there. Similarly, the other alternatives can be shown to be untenable. Further, since we have a specific notion of the universal apart from the notion of individual objects, there must be a cause for its production other than these objects. For instance, we have a concept of blueness with regard to several objects, which is based upon something different from these objects themselves. The notion of sameness cannot be based on the similarity of configuration, for the configuration is as specific as the individual object itself. Just as one individual object does not subsist in another, so also the configuration that is present in one object cannot be present in another. And if one and the same configuration can be present in different objects, this amounts to the acceptance of the universal; then the difference is only verbal.

It is argued that the mere presence of a comprehensive notion is not a valid ground for postulating the presence of the universal as different from individual objects. For instance, we say the universal 'cow-ness' subsists in the cow, the universal 'horse-ness' subsists in the horse; we thus speak of several universals as universals. Thus the mere presence or absence of the notion of sameness is not a valid ground for postulating the universal.

Uddyotakara replies that the comprehensive notion that we have with regard to several universals such as cow-ness, horse-ness, etc., has a basis. If this objection means that there can be no universal in the universal or the particular in the particular, this is quite correct. In fact, this is the Vaiśeṣika position.

The notion of the same substance that we have with regard to substances is one that has the universal of substance for its distinctive qualification, but this is not the case with the universal and particular. The intention of the Vaiśeṣika philosopher is not to deny that the notion of sameness that we have in regard to universals is without foundation. But if the objector wishes to know how the notion of sameness is conceived with regard to several universals — or, how several universals are conceived as universal — Uddyotakara answers that its cause is the congregation of several entities (*anekārthasamavāyi*). The universal of 'cow-ness' is conceived as a universal because it subsists in several cows. Similarly, the universal of the universal, universalness, subsists in several entities like cow-ness, horse-ness, etc. Thus the notion of sameness with regard to the various universals can be explained.

The following objection is raised: if a universal subsists in each individual, does it subsist in the individual in its entirety or in parts ? If it subsists entirely, it becomes as specific as the individual itself; then it ceases to be a universal. If it subsists in parts, it is not the case of one subsisting in many; this would mean that there are parts (*pradeśa*), one subsisting in one individual. Regarding these parts themselves, the question arises as to whether they are generic in character or not. If they are generic, this becomes the case of one subsisting in one; then the universal ceases to be the one that subsists in the many. If, on the other hand, the parts are not generic, it is meaningless to say that the parts of the universal subsist in the individuals.

Uddyotakara replies that this whole objection is based on a complete misunderstanding. When in regard to a group or a composite the whole of the group or the composite is meant to be spoken of — nothing of it is to be excluded — then alone is the composite referred to as a 'whole' in relation to its components or to a group in relation to its members. And the term 'part' refers to one of the components or the members. Since the universal is neither a composite nor a group, the objection has no bearing on the relation between it and the individuals in which it subsists. But if the question is whether one subsists in many in its entirety or in parts, then it becomes self-contradictory: If the one subsists in the many in its entirety, then it is the case of the many subsisting in the many; each entire thing being a separate entity. On the other hand, if the one subsisting in the many were to subsist in parts only, even that would not be the case of one subsisting in many; this would also be the case of many subsisting in many.

The relation between the universal and the individuals, says Uddyotakara, is one of substratum and superstratum, known as inherence (*samavāya*). The universal subsists in the individuals by the relation of inherence; the universal is the superstratum and the individuals substrata. Subsistence means inherence which is the basis of our notion of one thing abiding in another.

An objection is raised: Does the universal, say cow-ness, subsist in the cow or in the non-cow ? If it subsists in the former, then this means that the cow is a cow even without the subsistence of the universal cow-ness; the postulation of the universal is therefore useless. If the universal subsists in the non-cow, then the horse and other animals which also belong to the category of the non-cow would have the universal of 'cow-ness' subsisting in them; thus they would be liable to be regarded as cow. These are the only two alternatives in this case. Hence the comprehensive notion in question cannot be based on the universal of cow-ness.

Uddyotakara replies that a thing is neither a cow nor a non-cow before the universal of 'cow-ness' has come in. Both these notions of the cow and the non-cow refer to qualified things; and a notion of the qualified thing is not possible unless the qualifier is there. In the present case, prior to its connection with the universal of 'cow-ness', the thing itself (i.e. the animal) does not exist at all; that which does not exist cannot be spoken of as 'cow' or as 'non-cow'; and whenever the thing is there it is connected with the universal of 'cow-ness'. The objection raised in this context is similar to the question whether the connection of the character of being (*sattā*) is what exists or what does not exist. As a matter of fact, the connection of this character is neither with an existing thing nor with a non-existing thing; whenever a thing exists it is connected with the character of being (NV II. 2,66).

According to the Buddhist, the word for the universal cannot denote diverse individuals. Since he does not recognize the universal he cannot strictly use the expression 'the word for the universal'. Here the word 'word' is a qualifier of the qualificand 'universal', and unless the qualificand is accepted the qualifier is useless. Secondly, if the word for the universal did signify diverse individuals, it would cease to be a word for the universal; for a word which signifies one thing cannot be regarded as a word signifying another thing. If diverse individuals were signified by words for the universal, they would no longer be diverse individuals. In fact, diverse individuals must be regarded as signified by totally different words; for if they are not signified by words for the universal nor by other words, then they are not signified by both kinds of words. In view of these circumstances the only course open to the Buddhist is to say that words express nothing. But, then, it is not only self-contradictory to use words to convey their inexpressiveness but also there can be no means of speaking about things.

In the light of these various considerations Uddyotakara concludes that there is such a thing as the universal. It subsists in different things in which it is meant to. It does not subsist in things in which it is not meant to. For instance, the 'cow-ness' subsists in the cows, and not in the clay-cow. It is because of this absence that the clay-cow is a clay-cow and not a cow. Hence the word cow signifies the universal 'cow-ness' and the latter subsists in the cows (NV II. 2,66).

B. *Paradigm of* sat *(existence or being)*

Apart from vindicating the universal aspect of meaning, Uddyotakara meets the Buddhist objection to the three-fold nature of meaning with reference to the paradigm of the word '*sat*' (existence or being). In what follows a brief account of this discussion is given.

The Buddhists maintain that the word *sat* (existence) cannot be regarded as signifying a universal for the following reason: *sat* has the widest denotation as it applies to everything that exists. Substance (*dravya*) is one of the numerous existing things and has therefore less denotation than that of *sat*. When we say '*sat dravyam*' (*sat* is substance), both words are in the nominative and yet have unequal denotations. This is against ordinary usage. If two words have the same case, it is understood that they denote the same thing. Thus the fact that there is coextensiveness (*sāmānādhikaraṇya*) clearly shows that the word *sat* cannot denote the universal with the widest denotation. It may be argued that the coextensiveness can be explained by taking the word *sat* to mean *sattā* (character of being), since this character subsists in substances, etc. But in that case *sat* ceases to be independent and therefore will have to subsist in something else; that is, it becomes a quality. This is also against usage. We do not find a word denoting a substance with quality taking the same case as a word denoting a quality; in fact, the cases must be different, e.g. *śaṅkhasya śauklyam* (whiteness of conch-shell) — in this expression the first word denoting a substance is in the genitive and the second denoting a quality in the nominative. On these gounds the word *sat* cannot be said to signify a particular relation.

In reply to this Buddhist objection Uddyotakara remarks that the word *sat* has two meanings: its principal meaning is the things that exist and its secondary meaning is the character of being (*sattā*). In the expression *sat dravyam* the word is used in the first sense; both the words are coextensive because they mean one and the same thing. When it is used in the second sense, there cannot be any coextensiveness; for instance, we do not say *sattā dravyam* (the character of being is substance). In the expression *śaṅkhasya śauklyam* cited by the Buddhist, it is but right that the two words should not have the same case. Thus the Buddhist objection based on the impossibility of coextensiveness is unfounded.

Further, the Buddhist has himself used the word *sattā*. If the word *sattā* does not denote *sattā*, he is guilty of self-contradiction. He has also used the words substance, etc. in connection with *sat* and obviously he understands what they mean. If he says that he has only assumed that the words have certain meanings, he has betrayed his ignorance of what assumption means. For instance, the post is not the same as the man but they are similar in certain respects; when one sees the post and imposes the properties of man on it, one conceives of it as man; this is what constitutes assumption. If the words in question are 'assumed' by the Buddhist, he must indicate the principal basis of his assumption; for certainly there can be no assumption without a principal basis.

The Buddhist contention that the word *sat* cannot denote a particular relation has no bearing on the subject. The relation is denoted not by the word *sat* but by relative words. Relation is a quality and *sat* is not a word denoting a quality; nor can there be any coextensiveness between a word denoting quality and a word denoting substance.

The Buddhist raises another objection: How can one word '*sat*' be related to innumerable objects ? Unless such a relation is clearly understood, we cannot have a correct cognition of the objects denoted by the word. If, to escape from this difficulty, the word is held to be expressive of the particular forms of objects, it would lead to an anomalous position: when the word *sat* is uttered, the resulting cognition would be wavering or uncertain in its character, as pertaining to substances, qualities and actions all of which have the character of being (*sattā*) denoted by the word *sat*. And a denotation that leads to such a wavering cognition cannot be regarded as the right denotation. *Sat* cannot therefore be said to denote particular objects.

Uddyotakara replies that his position is not that the word for the universal of *sat* (*sattā*) denotes diverse individuals, but that the word *sat* denotes substance, quality and action not in an unqualified form but as qualified by the character of being. We apply the word *sat* to things in which we perceive *sattā*, and certainly *sattā* is one only, the same universal pervading all the things.

Uddyotakara further points out that the Buddhist argument is faulty. The argument is: The word *sat* cannot denote substance, quality and action, because objects are innumerable. The innumerability (*ānantya*) belongs to the objects and not to the subject of the argument 'the word *sat*'. The hetu is thus not valid. If the proposition is 'innumerable individuals are not denotable by words expressive of universals', then no corroborative example, positive or negative, can be given; for all diverse individuals are already included in the proposition. Nor can the example be 'what is denoted by words expressive of universal is not found to be innumerable', as for the Buddhist the very notion of universal is baseless.

Another objection raised by the Buddhist is: The word *sat* cannot be regarded as denotative of only that which is endowed with universal (*jātimat*), because it is not independent. Its absence of independence is evident in two ways: (a) the word *sat* does not produce the cognition of the jar and other things endowed with *sattā*, and on account of this we should not have the expressions in which the word *sat* and an object have the same case, e.g. *sad ghaṭaḥ* (*sat* is a jar). (b) The word *sat* primarily signifies *sattā* and while signifying that, it is applied indirectly to something else. Certainly, when a word, while denoting one thing, is applied to something else, it cannot be regarded as denoting the latter; e.g. when the word 'scaffolding' applies figuratively to the man on the scaffolding, it cannot be said to denote the man.

This difficulty cannot be got over by saying that the notion of the universal is transferred to the thing endowed with the universal. Such a transfer can be effected if there is a similarity of properties. For instance, the word 'master' can be applied to the servant when the latter has the properties of the former or the crystal is said to be blue when the blue colour of a flower is reflected in it. In the case of *sat* and the things denoted by it we cannot say that *sattā* is transferred to them because of similarity of properties. Further, in the present case the cognition of the individual does not arise after that of *sattā*, as we generally find in the case of indirect application. Nor can *sattā* be said to be transferred by reflection as in the case of the blue crystal, for in that case the cognition would be a wrong one. Last but not least, what is directly signified and what is indirectly signified cannot be cognized simultaneously; for no two cognitions can appear at one and the same time.

Uddyotakara replies to the objection in the following way: In the first place, the words *sat* and *ghaṭa* signify one and the same thing. Unless these words signified one and the same thing, there would be no question of coextensiveness. Coextensiveness means that the words which have the same case signify one and the same object. Secondly, the word *sat* is an object-word (*bhedaśabda*). That alone can be said to be denoted by it the cognition of which proceeds from that word. The word *sat* signifies three things: *sattā* (*summum genus*), the presence or connection of *sattā* by virtue of which substance, quality and action are regarded as *sat*, and things other than these three. Amongst these the substance is the principal factor, while *sattā* and its connection are regarded as subordinate factors. The nature of the factor depends upon the effect produced. Whenever *sattā* produces an effect it does so through a particular thing; so that the thing is regarded as the principal and *sattā* as the subordinate factor. This is particularly so, because when *sattā* is present the principal thing is cognized as *sat*, and when it is absent it cannot be cognized as *sat*. Thus it is not right to say that the word *sat* does not produce the cognition of the jar and other things endowed with the universal *sattā*.

As regards the Buddhist contention that the word *sat* primarily signifies *sattā* and while denoting it, is applied indirectly to that which is endowed with *sattā*, it shows his ignorance of the meaning of the word *sat*. As already mentioned, its primary signification is substance, quality and action.

As regards the transfer of the universal *sattā* to the thing endowed with the universal, this question does not arise at all. In the case of the master and the servant it is not that the conception of the master is transferred to the servant. All that happens is that when one finds the servant to be grave and agreeable like the master, one applies to him the word 'master' in a figurative sense. But in so far as the word *sattā* is concerned, it is never applied to substance, etc. However, when the word stands for the existence of existing things, the existing things are indirectly signified by the word, as qualifiers or subordinate factors. In this case the fact of the things being qualifiers constitutes the basis of the secondary meaning.

The Buddhist contention that the transfer of *sattā* to the thing endowed with the universal is similar to that of the transfer of colour to the crystal is unfounded. When the white crystal is said to have become blue, the blue colour does not really subsist in it; it is merely superimposed on it. The cognition of the blue colour is therefore erroneous. There is no question of such false superimposition in the present case.

The Buddhist argument that there is no sequence of cognitions nor can there be any simultaneity of cognitions is also unfounded. The cognition of *sattā* itself pertains to its indicator, viz. substance itself, and therefore both the substance and *sattā* are cognized in one and the same cognition (NV II. 2, 68).

Criticism of the apoha *theory*

According to Uddyotakara, the *apoha* theory of meaning held by the Buddhist is: "The object denoted by a word is the negation of objects denoted by other words." (*anyaśabdārthā-*

pohaḥ śabdārthaḥ). Uddyotakara criticizes this theory on the following grounds:

(i) If words have positive meaning, then alone on the basis of its cognition it can be negatived by means of another word. For instance, until one knows the cow, one cannot have any idea of the cow in the form that the word 'cow' denotes what is not non-cow, nor of the non-cow; thus both the ideas of the cow and non-cow are impossible without a previous cognition of the cow.

(ii) When the word cow is said to mean the *apoha* of other things, i.e. what is not non-cow, is this something in the nature of presence or absence ? If it is the former, is it the cow or non-cow ? If it is the cow, this is against the Buddhist concept of *apoha.* If it is the non-cow, this shows a wonderful insight into the meaning of words. If the cow means something in the nature of absence, it cannot be the subject of injunction or cognition. No one understands anything negative on hearing the word cow. In fact, the meaning of a word is always recognized through the cognition produced by it.

(iii) *Apoha* (exclusion) is an action (*kriyā*) and as such its object needs to be indicated. It is explained as 'not being the non-cow'. Now , is the object of this the cow or the non-cow ? If it is the cow, there cannot be the absence of cow in the cow itself. If, on the other hand, the object is the non-cow, how can the *apoha* of the non-cow lead to the cognition of cow ?

(iv) None of the alternatives possible under the *apoha* theory is tenable. Is the *apoha* of the non-cow in the cow (a) different or non-different from the cow ? If it is different, does it or does it not reside in the cow ? If it does reside in it, it becomes a quality.; the word cow denotes a quality, and not the cow — the animal. And then there can be no such co-ordination as that is expressed in the words 'the cow is sitting'; a quality cannot sit ! If, on the other hand, the *apoha* of the non-cow in the cow does not reside in the cow, then the genitive in the expression *goḥ apohaḥ* (the *apoha* of the cow) has no significance. (b) If the *apoha* of the non-cow in the cow is non-different from the cow, then it is the same as the cow; in that case the postulation of the *apoha* is useless. Thus all the possible alternatives are not admissible.

(v) Is this *apoha* postulated by the Buddhist one and the same in regard to everything or different with each individual thing ?

If it is one and the same, and is related to several cows, then it is not different from the universal (*jāti*) postulated by the Naiyāyika. But if it is many, it is as innumerable as the individual objects themselves; in that case the meaning of the word cannot be understood.

(vi) Is this *apoha* (a) capable of being denoted or (b) not so capable by the word *apoha* ? (a) In the former case it is contrary to the theory of *apoha*; or else, it leads to infinite regress; for if the *apoha* is held to mean the *apoha* of the non-*apoha*, then the meaning of the latter will consist of a further *apoha*, and so on. (b) If, on the other hand, the *apoha* is not denotable by any word at all, then the Buddhist assertion "the word means the *apoha* of what is signified by other words" is meaningless.

(vii) In the case of words where there are two exclusive collections it may be true that when one is affirmed the other is denied; for instance, when the word 'cow' is heard, the cow is affirmed and non-cow is denied. But the *apoha* theory cannot provide satisfactory explanation for the meaning of all words: (a) The word 'all' (*sarva*) cannot be said to mean the denial of not-all (*asarva*), as there is no such thing as not-all. The 'all' consists of one, two, etc., and if these latter are excluded from 'all', then there is nothing left to constitute 'all'; for according to the Buddhist the whole has no existence apart from its components. What is true of 'all' is true of all words which denote a collection (*samudāya*). (b) In the case of the words like 'many' (i.e. not-one — *aneka*), the generic conception of the many can only be explained if the particulars to which it applies are cognized; the cognition of a particular cannot arise from the mere general *apoha* of other particulars. (c) In the compound words like 'blue lotus' (*nīlotpalam*) the word 'blue' is placed first and the word lotus second, because the former is a qualifier of the second. According to the *apoha* theory, the word blue means the exclusion of the non-blue and the word lotus the exclusion of the non-lotus. Both words become equally principal and this, in turn, makes the relation of qualifier and qualificand impossible, as the former is subordinate and the latter principal in that relation. Further, the expression 'blue lotus' means that one and the same thing is both blue and lotus. This community of locus (*sāmānādhikaraṇya*) cannot be explained on the basis of the *apoha* theory. If the word 'blue' means the exclusion of non-blue and the word 'lotus' the exclusion of not-lotus, these two exclusions cannot have one and the same locus. But if words are held to denote positive entities, there is no such difficulty in explaining the community of locus. The two words 'blue' and 'lotus' mean that the universal of substance and the quality blue subsist in one and the same substance lotus (NV II. 2,68).

PART THREE : CONCEPT OF PROOF

7

DOUBT (*saṃśaya*)

I

According to Vātsyāyana the third category of doubt in Gautama's list is really included under the second, *prameya*, as an object of cognition. However, it has been given independent status because it is the basis of all reasoning. While wrong cognition has an important place in the Nyāya scheme of things, it is doubt and not wrong cognition that has been accorded that status, says Uddyotakara, because one would make an effort to obtain right cognition only if one were in doubt and not under the influence of wrong cognition.

According to Vātsyāyana, we employ reasoning when we are in doubt about things and not when things are unknown or duly ascertained. On any question under investigation we have a view opposed to it, a counter-view. Consequently we have doubt as to whether a thing is or is not. The consideration of these two alternatives constitutes the process of reasoning and ascertainment of the true nature of the thing in question. Thus the category of doubt is connected with another category of Gautama, ascertainment (*nirṇaya*) (NBh I. 1,41).

While deliberation over the two sides of a question, i.e. *pro* and *contra*, is essential for the ascertainment of the true nature of a thing, every case of ascertainment need not be preceded by such deliberation. In the case of discussion (*vāda*) and scripture (*śāstra*) we have ascertainment without any doubt at all. Furthermore, only in the case of disputation (*tarka*) investigation is preceded by doubt.

Clarifying this role of doubt Uddyotakara remarks that scripture is concerned with things which have been duly ascertained and established; hence there is no question of any doubt about them. When such things are discussed, those who engage in discussion have no doubt about them; for they are thoroughly conversant with the respective doctrines as given in their respective scriptures. For instance, in the scripture the arguments for and against the eternality of things are examined and the question is definitely settled; in discussion also these arguments are examined and their effectiveness determined. It is this kind of investigation which is preceded by doubt, and not ascertainment of the true nature of things (NBh & NV I. 1,1).

Doubt is an uncertain cognition about the nature of a particular object. As its etymology shows, it means the property of being asleep or that by which the *ātman* is made to sleep or by the force of which the *ātman* appears as if it were asleep. In doubt there is non-ascertainment of the true nature of things. Nevertheless, it is a form of cognition because it makes itself known. Doubt is itself apprehended and therefore correctly called '*pratyaya*' (apprehension) in conformity with its etymological derivation[1] (NV I. 1,23).

II

Gautama defines doubt as follows: 'Doubt is a conflicting judgment [about the true nature of an object] depending upon [the cognition of] of a distinguishing characteristic [of that object]. It arises from [the cognition of] a similar characteristic (*samānadharma*), a characteristic of many things (*anekadharma*), conflicting views and lack of uniformity in apprehension and non-apprehension' (NS I. 1,23).[2]

The explanation of the definition as given by the commentators is as follows. Vātsyāyana's explanation of the first two forms of doubt is indicated by (a) and Uddyotakara's by (b).

(1) *Doubt arising from a similar characteristic*

(a) When a person sees a similar characteristic (*samānadharma*) of a post and a man on perceiving uprightness and width, he wants to find out a distinguishing characteristic (*viśeṣa*); in that stage he has a cognition which is not definite as to whether the object is a man or a post; it is this notion (*buddhi*) which produces doubt. This kind of doubt is therefore that wavering judgment arising from the cognition of the similar property and depending upon the distinguishing property (NBh I. 1,23).

(b) The expression *samānadharma* means *sādhāraṇadharma* = *sādraśya*. Similarity cannot be regarded as *guṇa* (quality) because the latter is not common (*sādhāraṇa*); it subsists in a single substance; what is thus limited to one thing cannot be common. The similarity cannot be regarded as *sāmānya* (universal) because it does not subsist in a substance but in a quality; for instance, the universal of uprightness subsists not in the upright substance but in the quality, the particular uprightness. The universal of uprightness which subsists in the quality of uprightness cannot create doubt in regard to the substance.

It is true that the quality is definitely known; and consequently the universal of the quality is also known. Though these are known they do not prevent the emergence of doubt; for doubt is based on similarity. The doubtful notion is in the form: 'the two things, a man and a post, which I had seen before, possessed the quality of uprightness; the quality that I am now seeing is one that is similar to that quality.'

In this context when the similarity is mentioned this means the apprehension of similarity. The reference to the dependence on the distinguishing characteristic means that the characteristic is not apprehended.

One and the same characteristic (*dharma*) cannot both be similar (*samāna*) and function as an excluding agency (*vyavacchedahetu*); for the characteristic that can function as such an agency must subsist in all homogeneous things but must not subsist in anything heterogeneous. This is not what is meant by a similar characteristic (*sādhāraṇadharma*). A characteristic that is similar is one which subsists not only in all homogeneous things but also in heterogeneous things (NV I. 1,23).

(2) *Doubt arising from a characteristic of many things*

(a) The term '*aneka*' (diverse) denotes all homogeneous and heterogeneous things. Doubt arises from the apprehension of a distinguishing characteristic (*viśeṣa*) which distinguishes the thing in question from the homogeneous and heterogeneous things. For instance, the distinguishing characteristic (*viśeṣa*) of sound is being produced by disjunction. The apprehension of this characteristic generates the doubt as to whether sound is a substance, a quality or an action. Since the characteristic can distinguish the thing in question from homogeneous and heterogeneous things, there arises doubt as to whether (i) sound is distinguished by the characteristic from qualities and actions if it were a substance; (ii) it is a quality distinguished from substance and action; (iii) it is an action distinguished by that characteristic from substance and quality. In this case there is the absence of the apprehension of such other characteristic as would enable us to determine whether the sound is a substance, a quality or an action.

Sound has the universal (*sāmānya*) of being. No universal can subsist in universal, *viśeṣa* (individuality) and inherence (*samavāya*). By reason of this characteristic, i.e. having the universal of being, sound is distinguished from the universal, individuality and inherence. Substance, quality and action have the universal of being, in common with sound, but sound has the characteristic of being produced by disjunction of objects, which does not belong to substance, quality or action (NBh I. 1,23).

(b) Some logicians argue that since Gautama has already mentioned *samānadharma* as a source of doubt, the expression *anekadharma* should be taken to mean its contrary, *asamāna-dharma*. Uddyotakara disagrees with the suggestion on the following two grounds. (i) This suggested expression would not give the sense of the characteristic being excluded from diverse objects (*anekasmād vyāvṛtto dharmaḥ*), which can be obtained only from the expression *anekadharma*. (ii) Gautama may have preferred his expression to the one suggested for reasons of brevity; the expression *samānānekadharma* contains one letter less than the expression *samānāsamānadharma* which he would have to use.

These logicians argue that if *anekadharma* means only *asādhāraṇadharma* — and if this is what leads to doubt with regard to a thing — then the following reasoning should be regarded as doubtful. The living body is not without *jīva*, because if it were, it would be without breathing, etc. Breathing belongs to the living body only. Such an argument is regarded as perfectly valid.

This objection, says Uddyotakara, does not have any bearing on the Nyāya view at all. Even in the case of the first kind of doubt based upon *samānadharma*, doubt does not arise simply because the characteristic is present in all things, for there can be no question of there being any failure in the universality (*anvaya*) of such a characteristic. Similarly, in the case of a characteristic, not present in things other than the one in question, such a characteristic may be present in that thing only; but it is the failure or otherwise in the general absence in other things that produces doubt; when there occurs the failure of the general absence, the characteristic becomes a source of doubt; otherwise there is a well ascertained cognition.

Both in the first and the second kind of doubt there is failure (*vyabhicāra*), but there is this difference between the two forms of doubt: in the first there is failure of what is affirmed and in the second of what is denied: in the first what is similar (*samāna-dharma*) is the presence of the characteristic in question and in the second the absence of the characteristic.

Some logicians interpret the expression '*anekadharma*' as the characteristic of diverse things (*anekasya dharmaḥ*) or as the diverse characteristic (*aneko dharmaḥ*). For instance, the characteristic of being produced by conjunction is the characteristic of diverse things such as substance, quality and action; the characteristics, e.g. being produced by conjunction, being without qualities and being without action, are diverse characteristics. Both types of characteristics subsist in sound; so that from the apprehension of such characteristics subsisting in sound there arises doubt as to whether sound is a substance, a quality or an action.

The commentator rejects this latter interpretation on the ground that this kind of doubt is already covered by the first interpretation. The expression '*samānadharma*' means the one characteristic that subsists in diverse things, as well as the diverse characteristics that subsist in any thing.

According to the commentator the expression under consideration can be interpreted in two ways: (i) *asādhāraṇadharma*, i.e. the characteristic that belongs to the thing itself (*yathā svaṃ so 'yaṃ anekadharmaḥ*): such a characteristic can be described as '*anekadharma*' because it distinguishes the thing in question from 'diverse' things, i.e. homogeneous and hetergeneous things. (ii) the characteristic which is the cause of the notion of the 'same' and 'diverse' (*ekānekapratyayahetu*): the notion that 'this is the same, this is diverse' (*idam ekam anekam*). The basis of the notion of 'sameness' is *abheda* (non-difference); the basis of the notion of diversity is the distinguishing characteristic (*viśeṣadharma*), e.g. the characteristic of sound, being produced by disjunction.

Some logicians explain the expression *anekadharma* as follows: the negative particle in the word '*aneka*' signifies preclusion (*paryudāsa*); hence the expression means the presence of two such characteristics as are not variable (*avyabhicāridharma*) i.e. *aneka* is other than *eka*, so that the expression signifies the presence of two such invariable characteristics as are mutually opposed (*viruddha*). This is illustrated in a reasoning known as *pratitarka*: sound is eternal because it is audible (=hetu); sound is non-eternal because it is a product (=hetu). The two hetus are equally effective in proving eternality and non-eternality respectively. Since two such contradictory properties cannot subsist in one and the same thing we have a doubtful cognition about sound.

Uddyotakara rejects this interpretation on the following grounds. If two properties are invariably present and also contradictory, they cannot subsist in one and the same thing. For this would mean that one and the same thing has two forms (*rūpa*): that is, it is of two intrinsic natures; this is impossible. Further, the kind of reasoning proposed is not right If the person who produces the counter-argument claims that it is as valid as the argument, since he has accepted the argument he cannot put forward the counter-argument which is directly opposed to it; it stands rejected because it contradicts the argument.[3] If, however, he says that his counter-argument is as inconclusive as the argument, he has condemned his own claim.

Further, if two opposed properties could subsist in one and the same thing, they would cease to be opposed. Opposition (*viruddha*) can mean (i) impossibility of coexistence of the properties (*sahāsaṃbhava*) or (ii) realization of two opposite things (*viruddhārthasādhakatva*) or (iii) the intrinsic forms of the properties (*svarūpa*). The first is not found to be the case. The second is not right because one and the same thing cannot have two intrinsic forms. If the two different intrinsic forms of two properties were to constitute opposition, there could be no annulment of anything at all. Opposition is possible only if the properties have the same intrinsic natures. Since being audible and being a product have different intrinsic natures there can be no opposition between them. And in that case no doubt can arise at all. Thus the third interpretation is as untenable as the first two.

Suppose opposition between the two properties is possible and it leads to doubt as to whether sound is eternal or non-eternal. This doubt will have arisen from the apprehension of the individual forms (*viśeṣa*) of these properties. But doubt arises when general characteristics are apprehended and the individual characteristics have yet to be apprehended. Thus the supposition does not improve matters for the opponent.

The opponent argues that the doubt has arisen because there is a conflict between the two inferences about sound; such a conflict can be resolved by perception. This is not possible, says the commentator, because neither eternality nor non-eternality can be apprehended by perception. The conflict cannot be resolved by scriputre (*āgama*) for it is in the scripture that the subject of eternality or non-eternality of sound is being considered. Thus we are still left with the doubt about the true nature of sound. If such a doubt were left unresolved, reasonings like 'apprehension is non-eternal because it is a product' would not yield right cognition. If the property of being a product cannot establish the non-eternality of sound, it cannot be expected to prove the non-eternality of apprehension. In fact this would make it impossible to prove the non-eternality of anything at all. Thus the reasoning (*nyāya*) of the opponent vitiates all such inferences. A reasoning which strikes at the very root of all inference cannot be regarded as proper reasoning at all.

The Buddhist argues that since everything is non-eternal the compatibility of the two opposite properties makes no difference to his view. The Buddhist, says Uddyotakara, does not really know what is involved in 'annulment' (*bādhā*). When the Buddhist asserts that there is nothing eternal he is objecting to the particular argument of his opponent who believes in eternality. In the Buddhist philosophy itself one could find instances where contradictory properties are said to be concomitant. Where such state of affairs prevails there must be doubt, and where there is doubt it must be resolved.

In the case of sound the properties of audibility and being a product are actually found to be invariably concomitant. On this basis we cannot therefore say whether the sound is eternal or non-eternal. But we do make such assertions as sound is eternal, sound is non-eternal. Thus it is not right to say that the compatibility of two contradictory properties can function as a source of doubt.

When one finds two such properties in a single thing, one should ponder over and ascertain the comparative strength (*sāmarthya*) of the two properties. When such an effort is made it will be found that the property which can lead to a correct cognition is the one that indicates the non-eternality of sound. Eternality of sound is opposed to all the well-known pramāṇas (NV I. 1,23).

(3) *Doubt arising from conflicting views*

This kind of doubt consists in attributing two incompatible properties to one and the same thing. Such incompatibility means that the properties in question are mutually opposed or destructive or incapable of co-existing in one and the same thing. For instance, we have two views: *ātman* exists and *ātman* does not exist. Existence and non-existence cannot be attributed to one and the same thing nor do we have a hetu which would prove one and disprove the other. In such cases we cannot determine the true nature of the object concerned. We have therefore a doubtful cognition (NBh I. 1,23).

(4) *Doubt arising from lack of uniformity in apprehension*

Lack of uniformity in our apprehension of an object is another source of doubtful cognition. For instance, we see real water in a tank and water in a mirage which does not exist. When in any particular case of apprehension of water we do not find a suitable pramāṇa to determine the true nature of the object in question, we have a doubtful cognition as to whether the object is real water or unreal water (NBh I. 1,23).

(5) *Doubt arising from lack of uniformity in non-apprehension*

Lack of uniformity in our non-apprehension of an object is also a source of doubtful cognition. For instance, we do not apprehend an object that exists, e.g. water in the roots of a tree, or an object that does not exist at all, e.g. an object that is not produced at all or that has been destroyed. When we do not apprehend an object we are doubtful whether what is apprehended exists or does not exist at all. In such doubtful cognitions, as in the fourth kind of doubt, we do not find a property which would enable us to decide one way or the other (NBh I. 1,23).

The first three kinds of doubt, viz. doubt arising from a similar characteristic, doubt arising from a characteristic of many things and doubt arising from conflicting views, says Vātsyāyana, depend upon the object apprehended and the last two upon the cognizer. The various kinds of doubtful cognition have been mentioned separately on the basis of this distinction (NBh I. 1,23).

According to Uddyotakara doubt is not of five kinds but only of three kinds. He does not accept the fourth and fifth kinds of doubt. The lack of uniformity is necessary in the first three kinds of doubt; for instance, in the case of the first kind of doubt there is lack of uniformity in what is apprehended and what is not apprehended. This cannot therefore be regarded as an independent cause. Further, it will not be right to say that doubt arises because apprehension and non-apprehension are of two kinds. This is contrary to ordinary experience (*loka*). If doubt were to arise in this way, there would be doubt about everything. Since what we perceive is of two kinds, real and unreal, the doubt could never be removed. It is no use saying that it would be removed by the subsequent apprehension of the individual features (*viśeṣa*); for in this case also what is apprehended would be of two kinds, real and unreal. And this would mean that there could be no end to any doubt at all.

What is true of apprehension is equally true of non-apprehension being of two kinds. One would never be free from fear and suspicion. For instance, when a person enters a room, even though he may not see a serpent, he would have to doubt: does the house contain a serpent or not ? No place will be safe if we accept the two kinds of non-apprehension as the source of doubt.

Further, it is not possible to give a reasonable basis for the five-fold classification. If the different kinds of doubt are based on the difference in the causes of doubt, then these kinds should not be five but innumerable; for the causes of doubt are innumerable. If the difference is said to be based on the difference in the intrinsic nature (*svabhāva*) of the doubts, this is quite untenable; for every doubt is of one and the same nature (*svarūpa*) (NV I. 1,23).

According to the commentator the cognition of *samāna-dharma*, the cognition of *anekadharma* and the desire to find *viśeṣa* — all these three are involved in every form of doubt (NV I. 1,23).

According to Uddyotakara the Nyāya definition of doubt is really the same as that of the Vaiśeṣika.[4] But he rejects the following Buddhist definition :[5]

'Doubt is that wavering judgment which proceeds from the perception of similarity by one who wishes to find out the specific property of a thing.'

What is it, asks the commentator, with regard to which there is doubt if the similarity is already apprehended ? If the Buddhist says that it is with regard to an object, he contradicts himself; for he does not accept an object apart from its properties. Further, if the object and its property are regarded as totally different from each other, then what is apprehended and ascertained in the present case is the property, and the object is absolutely unknown; hence no doubt can arise with regard to that object. If, to escape from this predicament, the Buddhist says that similarity means an object that has the property (*dharmin*), this is not right; for similarity, which is an abstract noun, denotes the property of being similar, and not an object. And in that case the perception of one, i.e. property, cannot give rise to doubt about another, i.e. object. If, on the other hand, the Buddhist says there is no difference between the object and its properties, there can be no doubt; for the definite cognition of the property would mean that the object is also definitely known (NV I. 1,23).

III

Gautama mentions that the various sources of doubt he has included in his definition are challenged by his opponents. He does not give any detailed information about the objections. All that he says is this: Regarding the third source of doubt, the objector says that there is certainty in cognition. Regarding the fourth and the fifth sources the objector argues that the lack of uniformity in apprehension and non-apprehension is itself uniform. Moreover, there is the possibility of an interminable doubt on account of the constancy (*sātatya*) of the cause of doubt.

To these various objections Gautama's brief reply is: 'The determinate cognition [of the similar and of the distinguishing characteristics of an object] are certainly the causes of doubt because of the dependence on [i.e. want of cognition of] the individual characteristic of the object (*viśeṣa*) nor is there any possibility of interminable doubt.' He concludes the detailed examination of doubt with the advice that wherever doubt is raised a rejoinder should be given as the occasion requires (NS II. 1, 1-7).[6]

In what follows, the objections and the Nyāya reply are given in the light of the explanations given by the commentators. The commentator can be easily identified by the references given.

(1) *Doubt based on the cognition of the similar characteristic*
Objection

(a) Doubt arises from the definite cognition of a similar characteristic and not merely from the characteristic itself. The cause of doubt is that characteristic which is cognized. (b) Doubt does not arise from the mere cognition of a similar characteristic and the things possessing that characteristic; for instance, when the observer has the apprehension, 'I perceive a similar characteristic of two things', he has no doubt at all at that time. (c) Doubt does not arise when the two things are different, that is, doubt cannot arise in regard to one thing when what is apprehended is a totally different thing; for instance, when the similarity of one thing, colour, is apprehended, there is no doubt about another thing, touch. (d) *Adhyavasāya*, which means determination of a thing (*arthāvadhāraṇa*), cannot lead to doubt, which means non-determinate cognition of a thing (*anavadhāraṇajñāna*). There is no similarity of form (*sārūpya*) between cause and effect. (e) Doubt can never arise from the cognition of the characteristics of any one out of the two things (NBh II. 1, 1 & 6).

(f) Doubt cannot arise with regard to things perceived and not perceived. It cannot arise with regard to the former, because what is perceived is known with certainty; nor can it arise with regard to the latter for the simple reason that the things are not perceived.

(g) Doubt does not always arise from the cognition of a similar characteristic; for instance, when we apprehend the characteristic of being a product in sound, we have no doubt; on the contrary, we are convinced that it is non-eternal.

(h) It is not right to say that doubt arises only when there is cognition of similar characteristics, for doubt does arise in other circumstances; for instance, when we find two mutually opposed characteristics in a thing as in the case of the fallacy of *prakaraṇasama* we do not know the true nature of that thing.

(i) It is not right to say that a property is similar if it subsists in only one thing; such a property cannot be called similar (NV II. 1,1).

Reply

(a) What is the cause of doubt is not the similar characteristic but its cognition. Although Gautama has not explicitly stated this in his definition it is implied when we say 'fire is inferred from smoke', we mean that fire is inferred from the apprehension of smoke. When a term indicates an object it also denotes the apprehension of that object. The expression *samānadharma* means determinate cognition of *samānadharma* (NBh II. 1,6).

(b) What is intended is that the apprehension of the similar characteristic and the things possessing it occurs before the appearance of doubt. The notion in the observer's mind is: 'I am now apprehending a similar characteristic of two things known to me; I am not now apprehending any characteristic that belongs to one of them specifically (*viśeṣa*). How can I find some characteristic which will enable me to be certain about one thing or the other ?' Such a doubt does not cease merely on the apprehension of a similar property which brings to his mind the characteristic and the thing possessing that characteristic (NBh II. 1,6).

(c) The Naiyāyika does not hold that the mere determination of one thing is the cause of doubt about another (NBh II. 1,6). It is the apprehension of a thing having a similar property (*aviśiṣṭadharma*) which leads to doubt about that same thing, because the individual characteristics (*viśeṣaviśiṣṭadharma*) of that thing are not apprehended at that time (NV II. 1,6).

(d) The objection regarding the similarity of cause and

effect is based on a misunderstanding of what constitutes this similarity. It means that the presence and absence of the effect are in accordance with the presence and absence of the cause; further, when it is found that if of two things one comes into existence, the other also comes into existence, and if the former does not come into existence, the latter also does not come into existence, then the former is called the 'cause' and the latter the 'effect'. Such similarity is certainly found between doubt and its cause (NBh II. 1,6).

The similarity of cause and effect in the case of doubt means that the apprehension of a thing, i.e. the cause, and doubt, i.e. the effect, are both wanting in the apprehension of individual characteristics (*viśeṣa*) of anything; just as the individual characteristic of a thing is not apprehended in the apprehension of a similar characteristic, so also it is not apprehended in doubt (NV II. 1,6).

(e) According to the Nyāya view doubt is that wavering judgment which is wanting in the cognition of the individual characteristic of a thing. Such a characteristic can only be a characteristic of one of two things. If this is a cognition of such a characteristic there would be no doubt at all (NBh II. 1,6).

(f) This objection is based on misunderstanding. The Nyāya view is not that doubt appears with regard to one thing, when what is definitely apprehended is an entirely different thing; what is intended is that when a thing is apprehended in a general way (*sāmānyataḥ*), there arises doubt which is essentially of the nature of non-determination of the individual characteristic (*viśeṣa*) of a particular thing (NV II. 1,6).

(g) This objection is also based on misunderstanding. A similar characteristic means the characteristic that subsists in the thing intended and also in other than homogeneous things. Being a product is not a similar characteristic of sound in the sense which the objector understands but in the sense which the Naiyāyika favours as mentioned above (NV II. 1,6).

(h) The Naiyāyika does not accept the instance cited by the objector as a case of doubt. He also does not accept that the apprehension of mutually opposed characteristics as subsisting in one and the same thing can be a source of doubt. Nor is it the Nyāya view that doubt can arise only from the cognition of similar characteristics, for Gautama has recognized various other causes of doubt in his definition.

(i) The characteristic that subsists only in one thing cannot be called similar; for instance, the characteristic of tallness is perceived as subsisting only in one thing, the post, and this is not a characteristic which can be regarded as similar (NV II. 1,6).

(2) *Doubt based on the characteristic of many things*

Objection

The objections raised against the first kind of doubt are urged against the second (NBh II. 1,1).

Reply

The answer given to the objections to the first kind of doubt is also valid for the objections to the second (NBh II. 1,6). Vātsyāyana remarks that doubt can never arise from the cognition of any one out of two things; on the contrary, it leads to determinate cognition of that one thing (NBh II. 1,1).

(3) *Doubt based on conflicting views*

Objection

The objection to the third kind of doubt takes three forms:

(a) Doubt does not arise merely from the diversity of views. It arises in the person who observes such diversity.

(b) Doubt cannot arise from the certain cognition of the fact that some people find that *ātman* exists while others think that it does not exist.

(c) Diversity of opinion is nothing but the certain cognition by two persons in regard to two opposite views (NBh II. 1,2 & 3).

Reply

The expression 'diversity of views' (*pṛthakpravāda*) stands for contradictory assertions regarding one and the same thing. What produces doubt is the cognition of such assertions by an observer, as helped by the non-cognition of any special feature (*viśeṣa*) in favour of one or the other. In this situation the observer is obviously unable to decide the true nature of the thing under consideration.

When the objector says that there is certain cognition in the minds of persons holding diverse views he is evading the issue. The objector has only given a different name (i.e. *sampratipatti*) to an uncertain cognition in the mind of the observer, which is what is under consideration; there is genuine doubt in such cases. Such an argument can only delude the ignorant. (NBh II. 1,6).

(4 & 5) *Doubt based on the lack of uniformity in apprehension and non-apprehension*

Objection

An observer recognizes that there can be no uniformity in the apprehension of a thing as having a certain characteristic and also that there can be no uniformity in the apprehension of a thing as not having a certain characteristic. This is what constitutes the lack of uniformity in apprehension and non-apprehension. But when each of such facts is duly ascertained there can be no room for doubt. Moreover, the lack of uniformity which is regarded as the cause of doubt is in itself quite uniform. Since there is uniformity in the lack of uniformity, it follows that this cannot be a case of the lack of uniformity at all. If, on the other hand, the lack of uniformity is not quite uniform in its own character, this would mean that it is not really a lack of uniformity at all. Thus in both versions of the lack of uniformity it is impossible to have doubt at all (NBh II. 1,2 & 4).

Reply

In the way the objection is framed the objector admits that there is such a thing as the 'cause (*nimitta*) of doubt' and also that it is essentially of the nature of the lack of uniformity. All that he has done is to give it a different name 'lack of uniformity'. To call a thing by a different name without altering the thing signified is futile. Uniformity is uniformity and does not become lack of uniformity, because it is, in itself, uniformity.

The objector does not deny that doubt is produced by the apprehension and non-apprehension regarding the existence and non-existence of the thing about which there is the doubt, as accompanied by the fact of a specific feature (*viśeṣa*) in favour of either not being available. In so far as this lack of uniformity retains this character the objector has conceded the substance of doubt. Thus even though a different name has been given this has not proved anything different from the Nyāya view of doubt in such cases (NBh II. 1,6).

(6) *Objection*

The Naiyāyika holds that doubt arises from cognition of similar characteristic. Inasmuch as the cognition of similarity does not cease to exist—it cannot cease because the cause of the cognition, the similar characteristic, does not cease to exist—the doubt, which is the effect of this cause, cannot cease to exist. For instance, even while one is pondering over a certain thing, this thing does not cease to be apprehended as possessing the characteristic that it always has. If the cause continues, so must its effect. Thus doubt which proceeds from such sources must be interminable (*atyanta*) (NBh II. 1,5).

Reply

Since the doubt is produced not from the similar characteristic, etc., but by the determinate cognition of such characteristics, assisted by the remembrance of the individual characteristics (*viśeṣa*), hence there is no danger of any doubt being interminable (NBh II. 1,6). Nor is there any contingency of there being no doubt at all (NV II. 1,6).

On the subject of doubt and the objections raised against it the final advice of Gautama is as follows: Wherever investigation (*parīkṣā*) is preceded by doubt—either in a *śāstra* or a controversy (*kathā*) the opponent will try to deny the very existence of doubt. In such cases he should be refuted with the answers that Gautama has furnished. Doubt is involved in all investigations and it is for this reason that he has subjected this question to a detailed scrutiny before embarking upon the examination of other topics such as pramāṇa (NBh II. 1,7). This is Gautama's instruction to the students of the Nyāya (NV II. 1,7).

8

THE OBJECTIVE (*prayojana*)

The Objective, which is the fourth category, is defined by Gautama as 'that which operates with reference to an object' (NS I. 1,24).

An object (*artha*) is something to be acquired or discarded; when a person decides whether he should acquire or discard it, he adopts the means of acquiring or discarding it; such an object is called '*prayojana*' because it constitutes the cause of that activity of the person. It is said to be aimed at only when the person has decided in the form 'I shall acquire it' or 'I shall discard it' (NBh I. 1,24).

This objective inspires all living beings in their actions and their pursuits of learning; it is the basis of all Nyāya, i.e. the investigation of things by means of pramāṇas. It is well known that discussion and rejoinder have a purpose; the former aims at the truth and the latter at the defect of an opponent. But there is some doubt about cavil. According to some philosophers, cavil consists in mere fault-finding and is therefore devoid of any purpose. This, says Vātsyāyana, is not right for even a person who resorts to cavil has a purpose. If he says that he wishes to maintain a particular standpoint or establish a tenet, he cannot be said to indulge in cavil; for only a person who has no definite position to uphold can be regarded as resorting to cavil. But if he does not have such a purpose, he cannot be considered as a responsible investigator or an ordinary person who means business; he must be dismissed, says Uddyotakara, as a madcap, if he now declares his purpose to be the demonstration of how his opponent's position is untenable.

According to Uddyotakara, what induces man to act is not the traditional four objects, viz: *dharma*, wealth, eroticism and liberation, but pleasure and pain. When a person knows that a particular object is the cause of pleasure or pain he makes an effort to acquire or discard it. This is what induces human activity and therefore is its objective (NBh & NV I. 1,1).

9

ESTABLISHED TENET (*siddhānta*)

According to Vātsyāyana, the sixth category of established tenet is an object of cognition and therefore included under the second category of *prameya.* The reason why Gautama has mentioned it separately as a category is that the three categories of discussion (*vāda*), rejoinder (*jalpa*) and cavil (*vitaṇḍā*) can operate only if there are a number of established tenets (NB I. 1,1).

According to Gautama, an established tenet is a tenet which rests on the authority of a certain school, hypothesis, or implication (NS I. 1,26). Vātsyāyana explains:[1] There are four distinct kinds of established tenet: (1) conviction based upon the direct assertion of an object in a school of philosophy which in this context stands for the teachings about objects connected with one another: (a) the tenet common to all schools and (b) the tenet peculiar to one school, both of which are mentioned in (NS I. 1,27). (2) Conviction based on implication, and not direct assertion. (3) Provisional acceptance of an object not duly determined (NBh I. 1,26).

According to Uddyotakara, the Buddhists argue that the so-called four kinds of the established tenet are nothing better than different kinds of proposition (pakṣa) which is put forward either directly on the authority of a school of philosophy or by implication. Others suggest that *siddhānta* is only a synonym for pakṣa.

This objection, replies Uddyotakara, is untenable. The established tenet is something which is regarded as fully established or proved; when the same is put forward with the firm conviction of its being so established, this assertion is called 'pakṣa'. Thus the pakṣa is that by means of which a certain fact is put forward as an object to be proved by one disputant to another. Hence the word 'pakṣa' which denotes an *instrument,* cannot be the synonym for 'established tenet' which denotes the *object,* i.e. *siddhānta.*

If two such words were to be treated as synonyms, the word '*paraśu*' (axe) would have to be regarded as synonymous with the word '*chedana*' (cutting). In fact, the axe is called an 'axe' simply when it stands by itself, not operated upon by any action of man; when the same axe is used to cut wood, it is called the 'cutting instrument'. The use of the two words thus depends respectively upon the absence and presence of operation by man. All such *kāraka* words which denote any sort of instrumentality do not denote either the object alone or the action alone by itself; they denote the object as accomplishing a certain act, endowed with a particular activity or operation.

What do the Buddhists mean, asks Uddyotakara, when they say that the established tenet and the pakṣa are synonymous terms ? If they mean that 'pakṣa' is the genus (*sāmānya*) which includes 'established tenet', this is not possible; for the former does not include the latter, i.e. while the former is something put forward for discussion, the latter is something already established. A real genus, for instance 'being' , includes substance, quality and action, because it has wider extension; being of a wider extension it constitutes the genus. If the Buddhists mean that 'pakṣa' and 'established tenet' are synonymous, then the latter would have to be regarded as probandum. This is self-contradictory.

In view of these considerations the Buddhist objection against the fourfold division of the established tenet is unfounded. For instance, how can the Buddhists deny the existence of an established tenet common to all schools of philosophy without giving some reasoning (*nyāya*) ? If they give any reasoning, they have admitted at least one established tenet common to all schools, viz: reasoning. If they refuse to give any reasoning, then mere denial can prove nothing (NV I. 1,31).

Four Kinds of Established Tenet

According to Gautama, (1) established tenet common to all schools (*sarvatantra*) is a tenet which is not opposed by any school and is claimed by at least one school; e.g. objects are cognized by pramāṇas. (2) Established tenet peculiar to some school (*pratitantra*) is a tenet which is accepted by similar schools but rejected by opposite Schools; e.g. what does not exist cannot come into existence. (3) The tenet based on provisional acceptance (*adhikaraṇa*) is a tenet, if accepted as established, leads to the acceptance of another e.g. when the fact that the cognizer is distinct from the body is proved by the fact that one and the same object is apprehended by the visual and tactual organs, the following facts are subordinate to or implied by it:

(a) there are more sense-organs than one;
(b) they operate upon specific objects;
(c) their existence is indicated by the apprehension of their objects;
(d) they are the instruments which bring about cognitions by the cognizer;
(e) the substratum of quality is a substance other than the qualities of colour, etc.
(f) conscious beings cognize only specific objects. All these propositions are proved by the fact that the cognizer is distinct from the body.

(4) Tenet based on implication (*abhyupagama*) is a tenet which is accepted without investigation but which follows from the investigation of its specific features; e.g. it is accepted, without investigation, that sound is a substance, and then an inquiry is commenced as to whether it has the distinguishing property of eternality or non-eternality. This kind of tenet is put forward by those who wish to show off their own superior intellect, without any respect for the intellect of others (NS & NBh I. 27-31).

10

AVAYAVA (Member)

I

Avayava is the seventh category in Gautama's list sandwiched between the category of established tenet (*siddhānta*) which precedes it, and the category of disputation (*tarka*). Gautama has not himself furnished any definition or explanation of this category, but he has given the list of five members and defined each of them. In all, he has devoted eight aphorisms to this entire subject, which has come to be treated as his most significant contribution to Indian thought. Much of the explanation or comment on the aphorisms is based on linguistic considerations or arguments and therefore the Sanskrit text of these aphorisms is essential for the understanding of the comments. Although the English translation of the aphorisms except one is given in the subsequent exposition, the entire statement of Gautama on this subject is given below for ready reference.

(1) The members are the proposition, the hetu, the example, the confirmation and the conclusion (*Pratijñāhetūdāharaṇopanayanigamanāni avayavāḥ.* NS. I 1,32).

(2) The proposition (*pratijñā*) is the declaration of what is to be proved. (*Sādhyanirdeśaḥ pratijñā* NS I. 1,33).

(3) The hetu is the means of establishing what is to be proved on the basis of similarity to (a) homogeneous or (b) heterogeneous example.

[(a) *Udāharaṇasādharmyāt sādhyasādhanaṃ hetuḥ.* NS I. 1, 34; (b) *Tathā vaidharmyāt.* NS I. 1,35].

(4) An example (*udāharaṇa*) is a familiar instance which, through its (a) homogeneity or (b) its heterogeneity to the probandum, has or has not the same quality as what is to be proved (probandum).

[(a) *Sādhyasādharmyāt taddharmabhāvī dṛṣṭānta udāharaṇam.* NS I. 1,36; (b) *Tad viparyayād vā.* NS I. 1,37].

(5) The confirmation (*upanaya*) is in the form of a resumé of what is to be proved on the strength of the example: 'This is so' or 'this is not so'. (*Udāharaṇāpekṣas tathety upasaṃhāro na tatheti vā sādhyasya upanayaḥ*. NS I. 1,38).

(6) The conclusion (*nigamana*) is the re-stating of the proposition with reference to the hetu. (*Hetvapadeśāt pratijñāyāḥ punarvacanam nigamanam*. NS I. 1,39).

Vātsyāyana has explained the category of member as follows: When an object to be proved is expressed in a collection of words, the five members are called '*avayavas*' (members) with reference to that collection. This collection also represents an assembly of the pramāṇas; for instance, *āgama* (scripture) is found in the proposition; inference in the hetu; perception in the example; analogy in the confirmation; the 'conclusion' is the demonstration of the power of these pramāṇas with reference to one and the same object. It is thus that such a collection of words represents the highest form of reasoning (*paramanyāya*). It is through this reasoning that the three categories, discussion, rejoinder and cavil can operate, and not otherwise; the determination of the true nature of things depends upon it. In view of these considerations the five members of reasoning expressed by means of words are really included in the second category. However, such categories have been mentioned separately (NBh I. 1,1).

According to Uddyotakara, the members are the various parts of a statement. And the statement is the cause of obtaining the knowledge (or idea) of an object as qualified by, or related to, a quality. When words are used, we have a cognition of the word denoting an object; when this cognition is taken along with the remembrance that is afforded by the other word denoting certain qualities of that object—by the help of that remembrance we obtain the cognition of that object as qualified by, or related to, that quality; and that which causes the obtaining of the knowledge of the object so qualified, is known as 'statement' (*vākya*). It is the 'parts' (*deśa*) of such a statement that constitute the members mentioned above.

How many of these parts are there ? As many, says Uddyotakara, as are necessary for the proving of the object; the proving of the object consists in demonstrating that the object has the particular character.

The proposition, according to Vātsyāyana, embodies *āgama*. The *āgama* determines the true nature of things, but the object of the proposition is something that is yet to be determined. There is, says Uddyotakara, no contradiction here, because what is sought to be proved is precisely what is known from the *āgama*; that is to say, the proposition embodies *āgama* in so far as one makes known to another person what one has oneself known by means of the *āgama*. Similarly, the embodiment by the other members of the other pramāṇas can be explained.

When Vātsyāyana describes hetu as inference, it is to be taken in a secondary sense. Inference in this context stands for the mere perception of the mark; that is to say, the second perception of the mark that is available to us when we assert its presence in the significate. This is the second perception, the first perception being at the time when we recognize the relation of the mark to the significate. This second perception activates the recollection of the relation, which was perceived on a previous occasion, and thus it functions as the cause of this activation. It is because of this functioning as the cause that the hetu is called hetu. And it is this hetu that is spoken of as inference in a secondary sense.

In the same manner the example is spoken of as embodying perception, because it presents the object of remembrance as if it were perceived here and now. Thus the example is in complete accord with what has been directly perceived before. It is like perception itself. To say this is to say that it is as well known as the previous perception.

Similarly, the confirmation is spoken of as embodying the pramāṇa of analogy. The object of analogy cannot be presented through perception and consequently through the example. But the confirmation is spoken of as analogy, because its character is attributed to that aspect of analogy which consists of the cognition; 'as that, so this' (*yathā tatheti*); that is to say, analogy depends upon the assertion 'as that, so this'—consisting in the perception of similarity between 'that' and 'this'; this analogy comes about after due comprehension of the assertion 'as that, so this', and is assisted by perception, *āgama* and remembrance.

The fifth member, *nigamana*, literally means that by means of which the five members are tied to a single object. Since the five statements bear upon the same object, they are treated as one single statement, while each of them is dependent upon what is expressed by another statement.

The members, according to Vātsyāyana, constitute the highest form of reasoning. Each of the members which exhibit the operation of the various pramāṇas does not convince the opponent; but when all of them are put forward as one statement, they do succeed in convincing him. According to Uddyotakara, this is what is meant when these members are described as the highest form of reasoning.

What exactly is the status of the members *vis-à-vis* the pramāṇas ? Are they included among Gautama's pramāṇas or are they other than those mentioned by him ? If the former, there is no need to mention the members as a separate category; if the latter, they should have been mentioned in the list of the pramāṇas. The members, says Uddyotakara, are not distinct from the pramāṇas, and yet these have been separately mentioned in the Nyāya list of categories for two reasons: first, it is only these, when taken together as collectively constituting a statement, that bring conviction to the opponent; secondly, it is only as distinct from the Nyāya pramāṇas that the members function as causes for the operation of the three categories of discussion, rejoinder and cavil; in this capacity, they support the arrangement of the nature of things; i.e. they function as the cause or means of obtaining the cognition of the qualification of things (NV I. 1,1).

Ten Members of Reasoning

According to Vātsyāyana, some of the Naiyāyikas add five members to those mentioned by Gautama.[1] These additional five members are : (1) Desire to know (*jijñāsā*), (2) Doubt (*saṃśaya*), (3) Efficacy (*śakyaprāpti*), (4) Objective (*prayojana*) and (5) Removal of doubt (*saṃśayavyudāsa*).

Vātsyāyana rejects this view on the following grounds : (1) The desire to know is only that which brings forward the purpose meant to be accomplished by the cognition of a thing not yet cognized. When a person comes to know the thing in its true character, he will either abandon or acquire or treat it with indifference; so that these attitudes serve the purposes for which the knowledge of the true nature of the thing is sought. Certainly this cannot constitute what is understood as proof.

(2) In doubt, which constitutes the basis of the desire to know, we have apprehension of objects which exclude each other. Of such objects only one can be true. Hence doubt cannot be treated as part of proof. (3) Since pramāṇa is meant to ensure correct apprehension of the appropriate object, it is not necessary to include in the statement an additional member for the apprehension of the object of cognition. But this cannot be part of the statement put forward for the accomplishment of the apprehension, in the manner in which the proposition constitutes part of it. Hence what the pramāṇa can do is already provided for in the first member (proposition). It follows that the efficacy of the pramāṇas is furnished in that member. (4) As regards the objective, it consists in the ascertainment of the true nature of the thing sought to be known. This is the fruit, and not a part, of the statement towards its efficacy. (5) The removal of doubt consists in the setting forth of a counter-proposition and then denying it. This only tends to lend support to the negation of what is sought to be proved. Hence it cannot be regarded as part of the structure of proof.

Thus these five additional members suggested by some of the Naiyāyikas cannot be regarded as *parts* of the sructure of proof. But they are useful in so far as they assist in the ascertainment of the object to be proved. The five members mentioned by Gautama, however, are *parts* of the structure of proof (NBh I, 1,32).

There are some Naiyāyikas, according to Uddyotakara, who believe that proof should have three members, while others, as already mentioned by Vātsyāyana, hold that it should have ten. Like Vātsyāyana, Uddyotakara subscribes to the five member proof of Gautama but rejects the five additional members with a different set of arguments.

(1) The desire to know and other members are not members of the proof, because they do not help in proving the proposition to the opponent. Only such members of a proof can be accepted as members if each of which, by itself, serves to prove an object not proved by another member; these members should combine to constitute a single statement and thus serve to accomplish the desired purpose of proving the proposition to the opponent. The five additional members do not carry conviction with the opponent. Hence they cannot be regarded as genuine members.

(2) The person who puts forward any proposition must have definitely certain knowledge of what he is putting forward, and it is only when he is thus convinced that he can attempt to prove his proposition. Such a person cannot possibly have any desire to know the proposition or have doubt in the matter. The objective and the efficacy of the proof are implied by the mere fact of proving. No one ever seeks to prove what is impossible or useless. Hence objective and efficacy cannot be regarded as members of a proof.

(3) The five additional members initiate discussion. Unless there is a desire to know, there can be no discussion. Hence these members are to be treated as stimulants rather than members of the proof.

Uddyotakara adds that in this context the whole effort of Gautama is to describe what helps in the proving of a proposition to the opponent, what are mentioned are only the statements of the proposition and of the other members (NV I. 1,32).

II

In what follows each member of the proof as mentioned by Gautama and explained by the commentators is discussed.

First Member : The Proposition (*pratijñā*)

The proposition as defined by Gautama is the declaration of what is to be proved (NS I. 1,33). As elaborated by Vātsyāyana, the definition is : The proposition is that declaration which states an object as qualified by a property—the object so qualified to be made known or proved. This is the significance of the term *sādhya* (probandum) in Gautama's aphorism. As an illustration of the proposition we have 'Sound is non-eternal' (NBh I. 1,33).

In his comments Uddyotakara examines the following objections raised against the Nyāya definition as well as rival definitions offered by other philosophers (NV I. 1,33).

Examination of Objections

(1) An objection is raised against the definition of the pro-

position: the object is something established, as proving a property. How can, then, what is established be regarded as something to be established ? This objection is not tenable, says Uddyotakara, because it is not an object by itself that is to be established but an object as qualified by a property that is to be established.

If the property is yet to be made known, says the objector, it cannot serve as a qualifier; if it is a qualifier, it cannot be something yet to be established. As a matter of fact, that which is not known can never serve as a qualifier; every object is qualified by a property that has been established and not by a property yet to be established.

It is quite true, says Uddyotakara, that that which is not known cannot be a qualifier. In the illustration of the proposition 'Sound is non-eternal', non-eternality is quite well known, but it is known as subsisting in the jar. And what is to be made known is that same property as belonging to sound.

In that case, the objector continues, what is to be proved is not sound but the non-eternality of sound. This objection is not tenable either. What is to be proved, according to the Naiyāyikas, is neither the object, i.e., sound, by itself, nor the property of non-eternality itself, but that relation of the qualifier and the qualified which subsists between the object and the property, the latter being already known as belonging to some other object. That is to say, what is to be proved consists of both. The object is already known in a general form, but is not known in a particular instance. The inference does demonstrate a particular fact in regard to the object in question; it sets aside the doubt which is always in the form: Does this property of non-eternality belong to sound or to something else ? Thus what is to be proved in the illustration is the non-eternality as subsisting in sound. This property is connected with such properties as being a product and the like. Thus it is quite correct to say that what is to be demonstrated is the object qualified by a property and this is to be demonstrated. And the assertion of that which is to be demonstrated constitutes the proposition.

(2) Another objection is raised against the definition. If it means that what is to be proved is a mere declaration of what

is intended to be proved, then the proposition is not the declaration of what is to be proved. If every proposition were the declaration of what is intended to be proved, then such declaration of what is to be proved would be tantamount to proposition. If, of on the other hand, the converse were true, then every declaration of what is intended to be proved would be tantamount to proposition. In either case the definition would be too wide or too narrow. A good definition cannot be too wide or too narrow. To avoid these difficulties, if the definition is taken as denoting neither of the two interpretations it becomes meaning less. And apart from these three interpretations, no other interpretation is possible. Hence the definition is defective.

This entire objection is based upon the principle: 'In the case of a sentence or a statement which is liable to be taken in its wider or narrower scope, if only one of these constructions is accepted the position is untenable. If neither of these is accepted, the sentence becomes meaningless.'

The principle that every sentence must have a wider or narrower scope, says Uddyotakara, cannot be applied to every sentence. For instance, when a cowherd indicates the path by saying 'this is the path leading to the city of *Śrughna*,' in this sentence we do not find any further need for any more specification of its sense. The quest for specific determination arises only when out of a number of objects conveyed by the sentence we have to specify any one of these objects; without such a specification the sentence would lead to undesirable consequences. And this is according to ordinary usage. (3) Another objection raised against the definition is that it is applicable also to such a hetu and such a familiar instance (*dṛṣṭānta*) as bring about the proof. For example, the hetu in the inference 'sound is eternal because it is visible', and the *dṛṣṭānta* in the inference 'sound is eternal because it is not tangible, like cognition', are not established and are in need of being established. As such, they should be called the probandum (*sādhya*). And their declaration is, in fact, the declaration of what is to be proved.

To this objection Uddyotakara offers no less than seven answers. These are as follows:

(a) The definition of the proposition as the declaration of the probandum means that it is the declaration indicating the acceptance of the object as qualified by a property to be established. The objection is therefore based on a misunderstanding of the definition. As regards the two illustrations cited by the objector, 'because it is visible' and 'because it is not tangible, like cognition', they constitute the *mention* of the properties, i.e. visibility and eternality; but they do not constitute the probandum.

The objector argues that the expression, the declaration of the probandum, really means the non-declaration of what is not probandum; so that when Gautama uses the expression 'the declaration of the probandum', he means the non-declaration of what is *asādhya* (*not-sādhya*). In reply to this objection, Uddyotakara says that any *sādhya* must exclude every *asādhya*. However, *asādhya* could have two meanings: first, it would mean *siddha* (something that has already been established); second, it would mean *asādhya* (i.e. something the proof of which is impossible). It is true that in the illustrations under consideration both the properties, the visibility of sound and the eternality of cognition, would belong to the second category of *asādhya*, and, therefore, these are anyhow not included within the scope of the declaration of the probandum.

The objector argues: In a case where such properties of sound, for example 'being a product', etc., which are regarded as established by one of the two parties to a discussion, are put forward as *sādhya*, then the mention of such a property would be the declaration of the *sādhya*, and this would be regarded as a proposition. This objection, says Uddyotakara, can be interpreted in two ways: If the proposition is 'the property of being a product is *sādhya*', it is the mere mention of that property; but what we need in a proposition is an object as qualified by a property which has to be proved and not just its mention. However, if, according to the objector, the proposition is 'sound is a product', then this is exactly what the Nyāya concept of proposition is.

The objector has identified the non-statement of the non-probandum with the statement of the probandum. Such an identification is wrong. One can, however, make a positive or a negative statement as the occasion demands.

(b) The definition of the proposition does not mean the declaration of a mere probandum; it means the declaration of that probandum which represents a *siddhānta* (established tenet); the word *sādhya* in the definition is meant to be qualified by the word *siddhānta*. That this is the intention of Gautama, says Uddyotakara, is quite clear from the sequence of categories in the *Nyāya Sūtra*; the mention of the *avayava* (member) follows immediately after that of the *siddhānta*.

If this was the intention, asks the objector, why has Gautama not defined the proposition as 'the declaration of that' (*tan nirdeśaḥ pratijñā*) ? The pronoun that (*tat*) would refer to the '*siddhānta*'. The *siddhānta* is of four kinds, and amongst these is the *siddhānta* common to all schools of philosophy (*sarvatantra-siddhānta*). This latter *siddhānta* cannot be obviously included under the present definition. The word *sādhya* in the definition represents that *siddhānta* only which has to be established, and not that which is accepted by all.

Such exclusion of the *sarvatantra*, continues the objector, could be effected by force of circumstances; the *sarvatantra* needs no proof, while the other three kinds do. For example, in the assertion 'Feed the Brahmins', the assertion can only operate within certain limits, as it is impossible to feed all the Brahmins. If the force of circumstances can be admitted in such cases, says Uddyotakara, then in that case the objector might as well ask Gautama not to say anything at all; even the words '*tan nirdeśaḥ pratijñā*' should not be used; instead *pratijñā pratijñā* would suffice. This, says Uddyotakara, would be absurd.

(c) The definition of the proposition is intended to include such qualifying factors as the desire to know that give rise to discussion; the word '*sādhya*' means that object with regard to which there is desire to know, and the declaration of such a '*sādhya*' is the proposition.

(d) The commentator has given an etymological explanation of the root and the suffix in the term *sādhya*.

(e) The property of the accusative (*karma*) is entirely different from that of the instrumental (*karaṇa*). The property of the former is that it is most desired by the subject, while the property of the latter is that it is the means. And certainly, the property of the one can never become the property of the other. In the case under discussion, 'sound is eternal because it is visible', the word '*sādhya*' denotes the object, while the word '*cakṣuṣā*' (by means of eyes) denotes the instrument. Hence there is no justification for treating the latter as '*sādhya*', and for extending the definition to it.

(f) Things are divided between three distinct groups: probandum (what is to be proved). *asiddha* (what has not been proved) and *siddha* (what has been proved). *Sādhya* is regarded as something to be established by one of the two parties, and is addressed to another party as the object of proof. *Asiddha* is something that has not yet been accepted by either party. *Siddha* is something that is accepted by both parties. In view of this difference between the three groups the term '*sādhya*' used by Gautama in the definition cannot be said to apply to what is *asiddha* or *siddha*. If objects to which the term *sādhya* does not apply were to be included in the denotation of *sādhya*, then all objects — even those which have been proved and accepted by both parties — could be regarded as coming under the definition of the proposition. And surely, this would be absurd !

(g) In the definition of the proposition, the word '*sādhya*' must stand for the object of the proposition and of the other members; for it is only an object, which, as qualified by a well-known property, constitutes the object of the proposition and the other members of the reasoning — that comes to be established as the substratum of some other property. This clearly means that neither the hetu nor the *dṛṣṭānta* is something that is to be established.

Examination of rival definitions

From the detailed examination of the third objection it is quite clear, says Uddyotakara, that the opponents have no grounds to reject the Nyāya definition. But some of these people insist that unless the term '*sādhya*' is qualified by 'desired' (*iṣṭa*), the definition would be applicable to the hetu and the *dṛṣṭānta*. These philosophers therefore offer various definitions of the proposition and call it 'pakṣa' and in this context Uddyotakara proceeds to examine these definitions as follows:

(1) *Definition*

Pakṣa is that which is desired to be proved (*pakṣo yaḥ sādhayitum iṣṭaḥ*).

Comment

The definition is defective for the following reasons:

(a) The addition of the word 'desired' is entirely useless. The wrong hetu and the *dṛṣṭānta* are both excluded by the term *sādhya*=pakṣa and it would not therefore do to say that the addition is meant for their exclusion. Further, the qualification of being desired follows from the fact that the pakṣa is the object to be established.

The advocates of the definition contend that the word '*iṣṭa*' serves the purpose of excluding the *undesired* propositions, such as 'Words are not expressive', 'Fire is not hot'. Every one of such *undesired* propositions, says Uddyotakara, can be shown to be either contrary to their own assertions or to some other pramāṇa; so that any effort for the purpose of excluding such propositions is uncalled for. The proposition 'Words are not expressive' is clearly self-contradictory; what is asserted is the inexpressiveness of words and yet it is words that are used to express the idea of inexpressiveness.

The proposition 'Fire is not hot' is contrary to well-ascertained facts of perception. However, some people wrongly cite the proposition 'Sound is not perceived by the auditory organ' as an example of 'contrary to perception'. The functioning of the sense-organ is not amenable to sense-perception. As a matter of fact, the operations of the sense-organs are beyond the reach of the sense-organs themselves; so that no one can ever have any such perceptional knowledge as that 'such and such a thing is perceived or not perceived by the sense-organ'. The functioning of the sense-organs is a matter of inference from the fact that perception, say of colour, appears when the organ operates and does not appear when it does not operate. Hence this is not a proper example of 'contrary to perception'.

The opponents cite the proposition 'Sound is eternal' as an example of 'contrary to the scripture' because that proposition is directly against the Vaiśeṣika doctrine. This, says Uddyotakara, is not a proper example of 'contrary to the scripture'. The Vaiśeṣika accepts the non-eternality of sound not on the basis of scripture but on the basis of inference from such facts as sound undergoing modifications through its cause, etc. The Vaiśeṣika accepts the non-eternality of sound, argues the opponent, on the strength of what is declared in the aphorism of Kaṇāda, and thus the proposition becomes contrary to the scripture. In that case even the proposition 'the jar is eternal' may well be regarded as 'contrary to the scripture'. A correct example of 'contrary to the scripture' is 'Wine should be drunk by the Brahmins'.

Another illustration of the 'undesired' proposition cited by the opponents is: 'The śaśi is not *candra* (*candraḥ na śaśi*), as this is contrary to a well-known fact.' The expression 'contrary to a well-known fact', says Uddyotakara, makes no sense. A well-known fact is a fact that is cognized by one of the pramāṇas; to be 'contrary to a well-known fact' is therefore nothing more than being 'contrary to the pramāṇas'. The illustration cited above is really one of a proposition 'contrary to inference'. The only well-known fact to which the proposition is contrary is the fact that the word '*candra*', is a name for śaśi; but this fact is known only by means of inference based upon ordinary usage; whenever the older man used the word '*candra*', the younger man always understood it to mean the moon. Thus the illustration is a case of the proposition 'contrary to the pramāṇas', which has been previously rejected as it is not covered by the definition. Thus the qualifying word 'desired' is entirely superfluous.

The opponent argues that what he means by the addition of the word '*iṣṭa*' is the inclusion of what is intended to be proved. This line of argument, says Uddyotakara, does not improve the opponent's position. No man ever seeks to prove what he does not desire or intend to prove; even in cases where a man seeks to prove an undesired thing through fear, he cannot be said to be proving what he does not desire to prove. By the act of proving he avoids the contingency that he fears, and this avoidance is, for him at that time, what is desired by him. On this ground as well, the addition of the word '*iṣṭa*' is useless.

The entire basis of the objection, says Uddyotakara, is highly improper. The various defects attributed to the definition of the proposition such as self-contradiction are defects neither of the object nor of the assertion embodied in the proposition; they pertain to the person who makes the assertion, while the object remains the same whether it is affirmed or negated. As we know, the defects of the agent are attributed to him on account of his actions and come to be figuratively attributed to actions even when they are really the defects of the agent.

Inasmuch as the assertion speaks of the object, which figures at the same time as its subject, the objector suggests that the defects of the assertion might as well be regarded as the defects of the subject.

The hetu and various other things spoken of in the members of the inference also are only subjects in some form or other, and their defects would have to be treated as defects of the subject. In that case, says Uddyotakara, we will have to reject such statements as 'there is a deficiency in the subject or the hetu'.

In view of this the objector might as well lump together all defects under the heading 'defects of the subjects'. The objector argues that this contingency can be easily avoided. The subject appears, in the reasoning, as an object to be proved; the defects of the object may defile the subject because the object is *expressed* by the subject and not proved by it. Accordingly, there is nothing to show that the defects of the hetu are the defects of the subject. So far as the defects of the assertion are concerned, these can be attributed to the subject on the grounds mentioned above. Thus the relation of that which expresses and that which is expressed and the relation of that which proves and that which is to be proved are sufficient to enable us to restrict the defiling by defects of the assertion to the subject, and not extend the defiling to the hetu.

This argument, says Uddyotakara, cannot be accepted. So long as direct signification of anything is possible, its indirect signification is not permissible. For example, when the assertion 'the platforms are crying out' is made, it is quite obvious that no platforms can cry out. This is why we reject the direct signification of the sentence and take the word 'platforms' in its indirect sense of men occupying the platforms. The question of applying indirect meaning arises only when direct meaning does not make any sense. In the case under discussion these considerations do not obtain; it is quite possible to say that the assertion is defective. Hence the question of indirect meaning does not really arise.

(2) *Definition*

'The pakṣa is that which is desired in the course of an enquiry' (*vicāraṇīyām iṣṭo 'rthaḥ pakṣaḥ*).

Comment

This definition, according to Uddyotakara, is defective on two grounds: (a) The addition of the word 'desired' (*iṣṭa*), as we have seen elsewhere, is useless. (b) If 'enquiry' consists in the presentation of arguments for and against a proposition, then there must be, in this enquiry, an aggregation of several things: so that it cannot be known what is desired as what; it cannot be ascertained whether what is desired is desired as what has been established, or as what proves, or as what refutes, or as what has been refuted.

It may be suggested that 'enquiry stands for doubt'; when we speak of the enquiry as to whether the *ātman* exists or not, then the expression 'doubt in regard to the existence or non-existence of the *ātman*', is synonymous with the expression 'the enquiry as to the existence and non-existence of the *ātman*'. This suggestion, says Uddyotakara, is not proper, as the word 'enquiry' does not signify 'doubt' nor does the word 'doubt' signify 'enquiry'. In fact, the name 'enquiry' is given to that process of presentation of arguments for and against two contradictory opinions, which follows after the doubt has arisen on a point, and which terminates with the ascertainment of one of these opinions. Certainly this process cannot be called 'doubt', as doubt is 'uncertain cognition'. In a discussion there is no doubt, because there is certainty in the minds of their respective exponents, who engage in a discussion only when they have a firm conviction in regard to the opinion held by themselves.

(3) *Definition*

'Pakṣa is that which is desired to be proved, and which is not obstructed by anything to the contrary' (*sādhyatvenepsitaḥ pakṣo viruddhārthanirākṛtaḥ*).

Comment

The expression 'that which is desired' serves the purpose of excluding what is not desired, and, therefore, the expression 'which is not obstructed by anything to the contrary' is superfluous. In the other definitions emanating from the same Buddhist source — 'pakṣa is that which is desired to be proved', — the qualification 'desired' (*iṣṭa*) is accepted as serving the purpose of excluding the undesirable pakṣa, and since this is the position of the opponents, it should hold good in the present case as well. If it is suggested that the second qualification, 'which is not obstructed by anything to the contrary' serves to preclude the defects of the pakṣa, then the first qualification 'desired' is superfluous; and if both these qualifications are necessary to preclude the defects of the pakṣa, then the second qualification should have been attached to the expression: 'Pakṣa is that which is desired to be proved'. Thus the definition is too diffuse, i.e. it contains superfluous qualifications, or it is too narrow.

(4) *Definition*

'Pakṣa is that which a person himself desires to prove' (*svayaṃ sādhyatvenepsitaḥ*).

Comment

The expression 'a person himself' should not have been introduced in the definition, since where there is action, it always has an agent. For example, when it is said that 'the, agent is cutting the tree', it is naturally implied that he is doing it himself. Similarly, when a certain thing is proved by a person, it is naturally implied that it is proved by himself. The author of the definition has shown how the definitions of other logicians contain superfluous expressions, but it seems, says Uddyotakara, that he has lost sight of this fault in his own definition.

The author of *Vādavidhānaṭīkā*, argues that it is necessary to say that a person himself proves because without the expression 'himself' it may be understood that the proving is done either by the person himself or he has it done by some one else. Uddyotakara replies that the author could have used a different word for proving.

Another justification is suggested for the qualification 'by himself': The qualification is intended to indicate that the proposition that the man desires to establish is independent of the scripture (*śāstra*). This is not right, says Uddyotakara, because what one has to prove is a probandum warranted by one's own scripture and one cannot therefore expect someone else to prove it for oneself. Secondly, the doctrine itself cannot be contrary to perception and scriptural authority. If the proposition that is established is independent of the scripture, this means that it is contrary to the pramāṇas. And a proposition that is not so supported cannot be accepted by any person in his senses, nor would it be right to seek to advocate such a proposition.

(5) *Definition*

'The proposition is the utterance of the *sādhya*' (*sādhyābhidhānaṃ pratijñā*). This definition is given in the *Vādavidhi*.

Comment

Since the definition is put forward with reference to the pakṣa that has been spoken of before by the author of the *Vādavidhi*, the introduction of the word '*sādhya*' in the definition becomes superfluous; this pakṣa could be referred to simply by the pronoun '*tat*' and the definition should be stated as 'the proposition is the utterance of the pronoun that' (*tad abhidhānaṃ pratijñā*). If, on the other hand, the definition has no reference to the pakṣa and is meant to be independent by itself, then the objections that have been raised against the Nyāya definition by these logicians can be equally raised against this definition itself. For, taken by itself, the mention of the *sādhya* in the definition is the same as the assertion of the *sādhya* in Gautama's definition.

These logicians say that the answers given by Uddyotakara can be used to support their own definition. This, says Uddyotakara, is completely out of order. These logicians, when they put forward their objections, fully accept the force and validity of these objections. But his own position is different; he docs not admit these arguments at all. For instance, when a man says to another person 'Your mother is bad because she is a woman', that person could reply, 'being a woman is not a reason for being bad; a woman is said to be bad only by reason of her relations with men other than her husband'. This answer would be quite effective in setting aside the charge against the mother of the second man. But such an answer would not be effective against the mother of the first man who originally sought to prove the bad character of the mother of the second man on the ground of her being a woman. For, according to him being a woman is a reason for being of bad character. If he were now to answer that what proves a bad character is not being a woman but having relations with men other than her husband, he contradicts his own assertion that a certain woman is bad because she is a woman. Similarly, if the logicians were now to accept as true the Nyāyà answers against their objection (viz. the definition of the proposition as the declaration of *sādhya* becomes applicable to the hetu and the *dṛṣṭānta*), they would be courting self-contradiction. Thus this definition, like the other definitions, must be rejected as unsatisfactory.

In view of the unsatisfactory nature of the various definitions of the proposition in the field, the Nyāya definition, concludes Uddyotakara, is free from all faults.

Second Member : The Hetu

The second member of inference is defined by Gautama in the following two aphorisms:

(1) Hetu is the means for proving what is to be proved on the basis of (a) homogeneity or (b) heterogeneity of the example (NS I. 1,34 & 35).

Gautama's definition of the hetu is explained by Vātsyāyana as follows:

That which makes known the property to be established through its similarity to the example is the hetu: when one notices a certain property in that which is to be proved, and notices the same property in the example as well, and then states that property as proving (that which is to be proved) — this statement of the said property is the hetu. For instance, in the inference 'sound is non-eternal because it has the character of having an origin'. The statement 'because it has the character of having an origin' is the hetu. It is perceived that whatever has the character of having an origin is non-eternal (NBh I. 1,34).

This is not the entire definition. The hetu is also that which is the means of establishing that which is to be proved through its dissimilarity with the example. The illustration of this is: Sound is non-eternal because it has the character of having an origin; such substances as *ātman* are eternal because they do not have the character of having an origin (NBh I. 1,35).

Commenting on the illustration of the hetu given by Vātsyāyana, 'Sound is non-eternal because it has the character of being produced', Uddyotakara explains what exactly is meant by 'non-eternal'. Non-eternal is what has non-eternality. Non-eternality itself consists in being connected with a thing characterised by prior and posterior non-existence.

That which has '*utpatti*' (production) for its *dharma* (character or property) is said to be '*utpattidharmaka*' (having the character of being produced). The '*utpatti*' (production) consists in the precluding of the absolute existence and the absolute non-existence of what did not exist before; that is to say, when a thing is qualified by non-existence (i.e. it did not exist before) and is afterwards found to come into existence, there is, with regard to that thing, preclusion of such absolute existence as is found in the case of ākāśa and also of absolute non-existence as is found in the case of things which have no existence at all, e.g. sky-lotus.

Components of the definition of the hetu

Uddyotakara examines the components of Gautama's definition of the hetu and a brief account of this examination is given below.

Similarity with the example (*udāharaṇasādharmya*)

The similarity with the example means that the property that subsists in that which is to be established, subsists, in the same way, in the example: the property that subsists in that which is to be proved is not the same as that which subsists in the example; it cannot be the same because that property which subsists in one thing cannot subsist elsewhere, i.e. the property of one thing cannot subsist in another thing; but the property similar to it may be spoken of as the same.

If Gautama had spoken in reference to hetu of mere 'similarity',[2] this would no doubt have been sufficient to indicate what is actually meant. But this would not have served the purpose of excluding what was not meant. The use of the expression 'similarity to the example' ('*udāharaṇasādharmya*'), ensures that the property which does not belong to an example should be excluded from the purview of the hetu. Alternatively, we can say that this exclusion is obtained by means of restriction; the expression 'similarity to the example' may be taken as emphasising two restrictions: (a) similar property must belong to the example only; (b) there should be similarity only, and not dissimilarity as well.

To what should the example have similarity ? The similarity, says Uddyotakara, must be to that which is to be proved, as what is to be proved constitutes the principal subject in the inference and also because it is next to the subject in the formulation.

When the hetu is spoken of as the property similar to the example, we have the hetu with its two and its three characteristics. The hetu with its two characteristics accommodates those philosophers who produce inferences without the vipakṣa; the hetu with its three characteristics accommodates those who produce inferences with the vipakṣa. There are properties similar to those which what are not included as examples in the formulation have, but these need not be taken into account.

With these characteristics we obtain four kinds of hetu: (1) Two are affirmative-negative: the Vaiśeṣika inference 'Sound is non-eternal (a) because it is a product, and (b) because having both genus and species, it (sound) is perceptible by the external sense-organ.' The first hetu, 'because it is a product', subsists in the entire sapakṣa; the second, 'because having genus and species, it is perceptible by the external sense-organ', subsists only in a part of the sapakṣa. (2) Two are purely affirmative: the inference of the philosopher who holds that everything is non-eternal, 'sound is non-eternal' (a) because it is knowable, and (b) because it is non-corporeal. The first hetu, 'because it is knowable', subsists in the entire sapakṣa; the second, 'because it is incorporeal', subsists only in a part of the sapakṣa. Thus the two kinds of the affirmative-negative hetu and the two kinds of the affirmative hetu give us a total of four kinds of hetu.

Having thus determined the exact nature of the hetu according to Gautama's definition we can exclude *hetvābhāsas* (fallacies of the hetu). For instance, when the characteristic of hetu that it is similar to the example only is mentioned, we exclude the *viparyayahetu* (contradictory hetu) and the *anaikāntikahetu* (inconclusive hetu); when the characteristic of the hetu that it is similar only to the example is mentioned, we exclude that hetu which does not subsist in that which is to be proved, and also that which subsists in only a part of that which is to be proved. The contradictory hetu is illustrated in the inference: 'This animal is a horse (= proposition), because it has horns' (= hetu); the inconclusive hetu in the reasoning: 'This is a cow

(= proposition), because it has horns' (= hetu); the hetu not subsisting in that which is to be proved in the inference: 'Sound is noneternal (= proposition), because it is visible (= hetu); the hetu subsisting only in a part of that which is to be established in the reasoning 'Atoms are non-eternal (= proposition), because they have odour' (= hetu).

Examination of Objections

Uddyotakara then examines three objections to the Nyāya definition of the hetu. Two of them, although significant, are largely of a grammatical character and therefore need not be mentioned here. The third objection runs as follows: It is the similar property that is not invariably concomitant with what is to be proved is invariably concomitant. Hence in the definition it is not the expression stating the property but the property itself that should have been mentioned. The qualification does not govern the expression but the property.

Uddyotakara replies: As a matter of fact, a statement can be governed in the same way as any other object. We find objects to be both eternal and non-eternal, corporeal and non-corporeal. The same can be said of statements. For example, one man asks — 'what does this man say ?' — and he is answered — 'he says that it is a cow' (*gaur iti*); here the particle '*iti*' serves the purpose of singling out the expression 'cow' from all other expressions. In trying to find fault with others, says the commentator, the objector only succeeds in lowering himself in the estimation of the people.

Dissimilarity with the example (udāharaṇavaidharmy)

As in the case of 'the similarity with the example only', the dissimilarity is also meant to be 'the dissimilarity with the example only', and not to what is non-example — to the example there should be dissimilarity only, and not similarity.

The reasoning illustrating the similarity with the example and that illustrating the dissimilarity, which have been cited by Vātsyāyana, differ only in form and not in their meaning. Mere difference in form does not make things different. It is true that in each of the examples a different object is mentioned; jar and *ātman*. But this does not mean that the hetus are different.

According to Uddyotakara, the correct example of a heterogeneous hetu is as follows: 'This living body is not without a soul (*jīva*), because if it were so it would be without breath'; it is only what is found to be without soul that is accepted by both parties to be without breath; as a matter of fact, the living body is not found to be without breath; hence the conclusion is that it is not without a soul.

As already mentioned, Gautama has stated the nature of hetu in two aphorisms. It follows from them, says Uddyotakara, that the hetu is of two kinds: affirmative (*vīta*) and negative (*avīta*). The distinguishing feature of the former is that it determines, by itself, the object; the object is affirmed by it. The latter proceeds only by way of refutation of the views of other persons; the object is negated by it.

The affirmative hetu can be said to determine or make known the object by means of hetu-example concomitance; so does the negative hetu. How can the negative hetu, it may be asked, perform this function in the same manner as the affirmative one ? If this were so, how is it that 'knowability' is not accepted as hetu for establishing the object (for example, the *ātman*), when the concomitance has the power of establishing and making things known. 'Knowability' cannot so function, says Uddyotakara, because of its non-concomitance with the example or its non-universal character; it is not concomitant with all knowable objects, as all knowable things are not either with or without *ātman*. It is therefore evident that what is necessary for proving an object is not just concomitance but the fulfilment of the condition that such concomitance must be invariable and derive from its universality. The same conditions of concomitance must be fulfilled in the case of the negative hetu. In the example stated — Everything that is without soul has also been found without breath, etc., — the hetu precludes the absence of breath from all living beings. Thus the absence of the soul also becomes precluded by virtue of the infallibility of the concomitance between the absence of soul and the absence of life-breath.

Can we say that all that this reasoning proves is the absence of breath from the living body rather than the preclusion of the absence of soul ? Such an argument would mean that necessary concomitance fails in regard to the probandum. It is criticized as fallacious. If this is the criticism, then the universal affirmative can be said to be fallacious with equal justification; for example, even though sound is a product, it may be said to be eternal, and such a juxtaposition of two incompatible properties renders the hetu dubious and fallacious. Every inferential conclusion is primarily open to doubt. If the presence of such doubt renders the hetu fallacious, the entire inferential process will collapse. And if the failure of concomitance renders inference nugatory, the fallacy would be one of *bādha* (annulment) and not of 'fallibility' (*vyabhicāra*).

In view of these considerations the position regarding the two kinds of the hetu is this: Just as in the case of the universal affirmative hetu, the perception of one property leads to the inference of the presence of another property which is invariably concomitant with the former property, so also in the case of the negative hetu, the perception of the absence of one property leads to the inference of the absence of another property which is invariably concomitant with the former.

If the absence of one property is inferred from the absence of another — and the absence thus inferred proves the presence of the soul in the living body — the particular body should be regarded as inhabited by all the souls. According to the Nyāya reasoning the absence of want of breath leads to the inference of the absence of *Non-Ḍittha* (i.e. the presence of a particular personality, *Ḍittha*), and one could therefore argue as follows: This particular body is not without the personality (or soul) of *Ḍittha*; for, if it were so, it would be without the breath; a similar argument can be used for any other person.

This argument of the objector, says Uddyotakara, is not right, because none of the alternatives admissible under it can be accepted. For example, the following question may be put to the objector: Does or does not the word '*Ḍittha*' signify something whose distinctive functions are definitely known ? If the word expresses one whose distinctive functions are definitely known, then it stands only for a particular personality; in that case the difference is only verbal. If, on the other hand, it denotes something whose distinctive functions are not definitely known, then its absence cannot be established. And yet it is this absence that constitutes the principal factor in the reasoning. It is therefore clear that the objector has really not understood the nature of the negative hetu; there is no justification for any such absurd position that one living body contains all personalities.

What is said in his refutation of the objection, says Uddyotakara, should not be understood to mean that a correct conclusion can be obtained if we have a hetu that merely fulfils the condition that it does not subsist where the pakṣa is absent. If the specific property (*asādhāraṇadharma*) were a true hetu, then the following reasoning would have to be treated as correct: 'The earth is eternal (=proposition), because it has odour' (=hetu). It is true that a 'too exclusive' hetu can be heterogeneous, but a hetu can never be too wide; in the argument mentioned above, the property of having odour is one that is too wide because it subsists in eternal as well as in non-eternal substances (viz. in the eternal earth-atom and in the non-eternal jar). It is for this reason that in the case of the negative as well as the affirmative hetu, it is not mere negation and affirmation but their unfailing character that gives the true hetu.

Can we treat a specific property as a true hetu, which subsists only in the pakṣa ? In such a case there is neither anything where the pakṣa subsists, or nothing where it would not subsist; therefore, there is no possibility of any failure of concomitance. For Instance, in the argument 'Everything is eternal (=proposition), because it exists' (=hetu), the property of existence is one that subsists in everything, and its concomitance must therefore be unfailing. This property is specific in the sense that it is not excluded from everything. Therefore from the fact that from 'everything' nothing can be excluded there is no negative hetu for this particular case.

For this same reason, that property cannot be regarded as a true hetu which would subsist in a part of the subject, and in whose case there is neither no thing where the pakṣa would subsist, nor any thing where the pakṣa would be absent; e.g. the hetu in the reasoning 'every thing is eternal (=proposition), because it is immaterial' (=hetu) is not a true hetu.

Can we regard that property as the true hetu which subsists in a part of the pakṣa and which, though there is no thing where the pakṣa is present, is still excluded from a thing where the pakṣa is absent ? If a reasoning was placed before a non-eternalist — speech and mind are eternal (=proposition), because they are audible (=hetu) — he cannot really reject it because the hetu conforms to the conditions mentioned above.

This kind of hetu, says Uddyotakara, cannot be accepted as true hetu, because in such a case there is no possibility of finding a heterogeneous example which would necessitate a negative hetu.

Thus we find, says Uddyotakara, that the affirmative and negative hetus are both such as are well known to all persons, —even to a child. Anyone who says that these two hetus are not distinct means of making things known, adds the commentator, must be an idiot!

Examination of Buddhist definitions

Uddyotakara examines the following four definitions of the hetu given by the Buddhists.

(1) *Definition*

Hetu is that which cannot qualify any object within the scope of the heterogeneous class (vipakṣa) (*hetur vipakṣād viśeṣaḥ*).

The definition is explained as follows: If the hetu were defined simply as that which is distinct, every property other than the one covered by the definition would be eligible for functioning as a hetu.

To exclude the undesirable hetu, it is necessary to add the phrase 'from the vipakṣa'; so that the true hetu is that which cannot qualify any object within the scope of the heterogeneous class. With the hetu so defined anything and everything which is not covered by the vipakṣa could be included. Furthermore, even such properties as subsist in a part of the vipakṣa would have to be treated as valid hetus. For example, in the reasoning 'this is a cow (=proposition), because it has horns' (=hetu), 'having horns' would have to be treated as a valid hetu. To exclude such hetus, it is necessary to emphasise further that the property should be one that is never included in a heterogeneous class.

Thus the definition applies to both the affirmative and negative hetus, the characteristics of which are: subsisting in the pakṣa, and in the sapakṣa and not subsisting in the vipakṣa.

Comments

The definition is open to the following objections:

(i) Though the definition does not succeed in indicating the three characteristics of the hetu, it excludes that which, though subsisting in a part of the sapakṣa, yet fulfils all the three conditions of the valid hetu. If the definition is simply that the hetu is that which qualifies an object in the heterogeneous class, then the hetu is one which is merely excluded from the sphere of the vipakṣa. This certainly excludes that which subsists in a part of the sapakṣa, as this latter is distinct, not from the vipakṣa only, but also from a part of the sapakṣa.

The advocate of the definition argues that the exclusion of the hetu subsisting in a part of the vipakṣa is meant to indicate that the hetu can be a true hetu if it is at any time distinct from the sapakṣa; e.g. the hetu in the reasoning 'this is a horse because it has horns'. The hetu that has been cited, 'being a product of effort', in the reasoning for establishing the non-eternality of sound, is not one that never functions outside the scope of the homogeneous class of objects.

If this explanation is accepted, says Uddyotakara, the interpretation of the definition, that which cannot qualify any object within the scope of the heterogeneous class of objects, will have to be rejected. Properties like the character of being a product of effort, are not such as are excluded from the sphere of the vipakṣa only; they are excluded from a part of the sapakṣa as well.

The advocate of the definition suggests that both the emphasized forms have their use. If the hetu is found only in one part of the sapakṣa, it can mean that the other part where the hetu is not found is not covered by the definition. In that case, says Uddyotakara, just as that which subsists in a part of the sapakṣa is accepted as a valid hetu, so would be also that which subsists in only a part of the pakṣa; the same consideration which makes for the validity of the hetu subsisting only in a part of the sapakṣa, will also establish the validity of the hetu which equally subsists in a part of the pakṣa only; e.g. the hetu in the reasoning — 'the atoms are eternal (= proposition), because they have odour' (= hetu).[3] Thus if the two interpretations of the definition are accepted, in an inference where the hetu is the property of being produced this hetu would not be valid; if the suggestion of the advocate mentioned above is accepted, then the validity of the hetu that he wishes to ensure, e.g. 'being produced by effort' is undoubtedly ensured; but then the validity of the hetu that he wishes to reject, e.g. 'having odour', has to be accepted. Thus the exclusion of the desirable and the inclusion of the undesirable hetu vitiates the definition.

The advocate of the definition contends that this objection of the Naiyāyika can be fully met if we add to the definition the qualification 'the hetu should subsist in the pakṣa'. This qualification would exclude the subsistence of the hetu in a part of the pakṣa only.

This line of argument, says Uddyotakara, cannot meet the situation. All that the addition of the further qualification does is to exclude the hetus like visibility of sound or atom which do not subsist in either of them. But it cannot exclude the hetu which subsists in a part of the pakṣa only. What subsists in a part of the pakṣa cannot be said to be not subsisting in the pakṣa; similarly, what subsists in a part of the vipakṣa cannot be said to be non-subsisting in the vipakṣa. Thus the suggested method cannot remove the undesirable contingency.

The advocate argues that the desired exclusion can be obtained by saying that the hetu subsisting in a part of the pakṣa can be excluded if we add the qualification 'subsists in the pakṣa'. The qualification, says Uddyotakara, can be (a) either the hetu must subsist in the pakṣa, or (b) the hetu should subsist in the pakṣa only, and in either form the position is not tenable.

(a) Regarding the first form, one may ask: What is exactly the significance of this qualification? Does it indicate the possibility of hetu subsisting in the pakṣa? Or, does it preclude the impossibility of its subsistence? As a matter of fact, we can obtain the indication of possibility and the preclusion of impossibility, even without this qualification. The qualification cannot therefore be regarded as serving either of these two purposes. Nor can it serve the purpose of excluding the hetu which subsists only in a part of the pakṣa, even if we accept that it does exclude that which is absolutely non-existent in the pakṣa.

What the qualification does, persists the advocate, is to indicate invariable concomitance; that is, the hetu must subsist in the pakṣa and never be absent from it. Even if we grant this, says Uddyotakara, we must ask the advocate: What is the use of the expression 'subsisting in the sapakṣa'? The condition prescribed by this expression is already fulfilled by the qualification which conveys invariable concomitance. The fact that the qualification is given in the form — 'it must subsist in the pakṣa' — clearly indicates that the pakṣa is restricted; hence it has to be restricted by means of the emphasising particle *eva* (only). When the property is unrestricted, it means that there is an uncertainty about its concomitance being precise or too wide; obviously, there can be concomitance in the case of the vipakṣa as much as in the case of the sapakṣa.

(b) The second form of the qualification — the hetu subsists in the pakṣa only — does not yield any better results. This involves the rejection of both the other expressions — 'the pakṣa subsists in the sapakṣa' and 'the pakṣa does not subsist in the vipakṣa' — on the following grounds:

The emphasis now is on the subsistence of the hetu in the pakṣa only. It is therefore absurd to say that it should subsist in the sapakṣa. No one ever says 'Feed Devadatta only and also Yajñadatta', as the first expression is useless. The second expression is already implied under the present form of emphasis. When one says that the hetu subsists in the pakṣa only, it certainly follows that it does not subsist in anything else. Further, the qualification that the hetu subsists in the pakṣa only, does not exclude that which subsists in a part only of the subject. The emphasized form therefore does not serve the purpose for which it has been stated.

If it is suggested that the expression 'subsisting in the sapakṣa' is also added for the purpose of emphasizing that the hetu must subsist in the sapakṣa and that it should subsist in the sapakṣa only — then we must ask: What is achieved by means of this emphasis ? If it implies mere possibility of subsistence in the sapakṣa, then this possibility can be obtained even without the qualification, by the simple unqualified assertion that it subsists in the sapakṣa. If, on the other hand, it implies the invariable concomitance of the hetu with the sapakṣa, then it would mean that what subsists in only a part of the sapakṣa is not a valid hetu. Further, the qualified expression — the hetu should subsist in the sapakṣa only — leads to the rejection of the other two expressions — 'the hetu subsists in the pakṣa' and 'the hetu does not subsist in the vipakṣa'.

Lastly, if it is held that the expression 'not subsisting in the vipakṣa' is also meant to be for the purpose of emphasis, then we must ask: What is emphasized here ? It is meant, says the advocate of the definition, to underline that the hetu should be non-subsistent in the vapakṣa and that it must be non-subsistent in the vipakṣa only. In the latter case we will have to accept as valid the hetu in the reasoning that 'this is a cow because it has horns'; the hetu, having horns, is non-subsistent only in the vipakṣa, as all these animals that are hornless are also not-cows. Obviously, the hetu cannot be valid, as the class of hornless animals which is vipaksa includes animals other than cows. In the former case the expression 'the hetu subsists in the sapakṣa' becomes superfluous. Of the three expressions the first 'subsisting in the pakṣa' is for the purpose of denoting invariable concomitance; the third, 'the hetu does not subsist in the vipakṣa' is for the exclusion of what subsists in a part of the vipakṣa; the second expression 'the hetu subsists in the sapakṣa' has no useful function to perform. Thus the addition of a separate expression is superfluous.

In view of these considerations the definition as a whole, concludes Uddyotakara, is open to the following three objections: It involves (a) the acceptance of the validity of the invalid hetu, (b) the rejection of the validity of the valid hetu, (c) the rejection of other objects concomitant with what is desirable.

(ii) The definition of the hetu as distinct from the vipakṣa, says Uddyotakara, cannot justify the practice of the advocates of the definition. For example, the hetu that is put forward for proving the non-eternality of every thing from the point of view of the Buddhist (Sautrāntika) cannot fit in with this definition. If every thing is non-eternal, there can be no thing where non-eternality can be said to be absent. The Buddhist should therefore explain what he means by the term 'vipakṣa' used in the definition. If no such thing as vipakṣa is possible, says Uddyotakara, no meaning can be attached to the term 'vipakṣa' as used by the Buddhist. Again, when no vipakṣa is possible, and every hetu, such as 'being a product' and the like, is such as is always present in the pakṣa and in the sapakṣa, it is difficult to determine from what such a hetu can be excluded. In fact, the property of being a product, under the circumstances, should be spoken of as '*sāmānya*' (general) and not as *viśeṣa* (particular). Thus it makes no sense to say that the hetu is that which cannot qualify any object in the scope of the heterogeneous class.

(iii) A Buddhist writer of the Commentary (*Vārttika*) on the definition of hetu has stated as follows:[4]

Out of the seven possible definitions of the hetu six have to be excluded; consequently, we are left with the seventh definition only, i.e. hetu with three characteristics. The exclusion of the six is necessitated by the rejection of those definitions which contain one or two terms. The seven possible definitions of the hetu as cited by the commentator are as follows: (1) The hetu should subsist in the pakṣa only; (2) It should be fulfilled in the sapakṣa only; (3) It should be non-subsistent in the vipakṣa only; (4) It should subsist in the pakṣa, and be fulfilled in the sapakṣa; (5) It should subsist in the pakṣa, and not subsist in the vipakṣa; (6) It should be fulfilled in the sapakṣa and not subsist in the vipakṣa; (7) While subsisting in the pakṣa, and also in the sapakṣa, it should not subsist in the vipakṣa.

This entire exclusion of definitions with one or two terms as advocated by the Buddhist commentator, says Uddyotakara, is not right, because we do have hetus covered by these six excluded definitions which are valid. For example, for the Buddhist who does not accept any thing as eternal, the hetus 'being a product' and 'being a product of effort' are valid and they possess only the characteristics expressed by two terms, i.e. they subsist in the pakṣa, and they subsist also in sapakṣa; the third condition, not subsisting in the vipakṣa is not possible; as for one who accepts no thing as eternal, there can be no vipakṣa for proving the non-eternality of things. If the definition with three terms is the only one which is admitted, then both the valid hetus mentioned above will have to be rejected. Further, the negative hetu that we have in such reasonings as 'the living body is without personality (*nirātmaka*), as if it were so it would be without life', will also have to be rejected as invalid; for this also has only two characteristics; the character of subsisting in the sapakṣa in this case is impossible, as there can be no living body without life.

In the light of this detailed examination of the Buddhist definition of the hetu 'that which cannot qualify any object within the scope of the heterogeneous class', Uddyotakara concludes that it either imparts the character of the valid hetu to that which is not really so, or it excludes that which is really so, or it contradicts the Buddhist doctrine.

(2) *Definition*

The hetu is that which subsists in the sapakṣa in two ways, and which does not subsist in the vipakṣa (*yaḥ samānajātīye dvedhā cāsaṅstadatyayaḥ*). Its subsistence in the sapakṣa is in two ways: (a) entirely and (b) partially.

According to the Buddhists a valid hetu must fulfil three conditions: (a) subsistence in the pakṣa, (b) subsistence in the sapakṣa and (c) non-subsistence in the vipakṣa. The entire and partial subsistence covers the first two conditions and thus the definition given above is claimed by the Buddhists to guarantee a correct hetu.

Comment

The Buddhist definition, says Uddyotakara, does not guarantee a correct hetu with its three characteristics on the following grounds.

There is no word in the definition to indicate that the hetu should subsist in the pakṣa. It is true that the advocates of this definition have declared that practically every hetu, valid or invalid alike, must subsist in the pakṣa; but even this assertion does not mean that it is only what subsists in the pakṣa that can be a hetu; all that it means is that what does not subsist in the pakṣa is not a hetu, either valid or invalid. This, the Buddhist argues, is certainly obtained by implication: when the words of the assertion are construed to mean that what does not subsist in the pakṣa cannot be a hetu, valid or invalid, it is certainly implied that the hetu, valid as well as invalid, must subsist in the pakṣa. It is true, says Uddyotakara, that the idea that it should subsist in the pakṣa is obtained by implication; but there is nothing to imply that this subsistence is invariable. All that the sentence means is that what does not subsist in the pakṣa cannot be a hetu, and this, in turn, can only imply that every hetu may subsist in the pakṣa. The possibility of such subsistence is twofold: invariable (i.e. every hetu must subsist in the pakṣa only), or not invariable (i.e. it may subsist in the pakṣa, but also in the vipakṣa). If the definition merely indicated the twofold possibility, it would imply that even an undesirable hetu would have to be accepted as true, even though it does not necessarily subsist in the whole of the pakṣa.

The validity of a hetu subsisting in part of the pakṣa only, says the Buddhist, is certainly not implied; when it is distinctly stated that the hetu must subsist in the pakṣa, such hetu alone is implied as true, and certainly that which subsists in part of the pakṣa only, cannot be said to be one that must subsist in the pakṣa. This, says Uddyotakara, is not right; when the Buddhist emphasizes that the hetu must subsist in the pakṣa, what he has in view is the contingency of a fallacy of the hetu and not so much the hetu itself; he means merely to differentiate between valid and invalid hetu. The latter would have to be excluded as a hetu since it does not subsist in the whole of the pakṣa.

If the intention of the Buddhist is to emphasize both the exclusion of the partially subsisting hetu and the differentiation between the valid and invalid hetus, then he should have used the phrase that the hetu should subsist in the pakṣa and the sapakṣa. For when the Buddhist has already emphasized the invariable concomitance, he has stated that the pakṣa as predicated by the hetu is already determined. It is only when there is no such determining with regard to the predicating hetu that there is a twofold possibility of its subsisting in the sapakṣa and the vipakṣa.

The Buddhist insists that in order to avoid a contingency whereby the definition might cover an undesirable hetu, it is necessary to add the qualification that it should not subsist in the vipakṣa. But then, asks Uddyotakara, what is the justification for the qualification that it should subsist in the sapakṣa ? If it is for the purpose of indicating the possibility of the hetu subsisting in the sapakṣa, this indication of mere possibility would keep it undetermined. In fact, mere possibility of subsistence would imply both entire and partial subsistence. Under the circumstances, no useful purpose is served by keeping this expression of wide denotation, when entire subsistence, which is duly determined, is what is implied by the non-subsistence in the vipakṣa. In any case, the phrase in 'two ways' is redundant, as to say that a thing subsists obviously means that it subsists entirely or partially.

The phrase 'subsisting in the sapakṣa', argues the Buddhist, is added for the sake of accuracy. This argument, says Uddyotakara, is as unhelpful as the others. If the emphasis means that the hetu must be subsisting in the sapakṣa, the hetu such as the property of being produced by effort, used by the Buddhist to establish the non-eternality of things, will not be valid; for this property is present in some and not present in other non-eternal things. Such a property will have to be excluded wherever it does not subsist in all cases of the sapakṣa. For example, it makes no sense to say 'Feed the Brahmins only and the Kṣatriyas also'. If, on the other hand, the hetu is restricted to its subsistence in the sapakṣa only, then the other two qualifications are unnecessary, as one of them is, in fact, contrary to the sense of the qualification in question, and the other is already implied by the subsistence in the sapakṣa.

If the Buddhist intends to lay emphasis on the phrase 'in two ways', we must ask: what is the meaning of this emphasis? Does it mean that the twofold subsistence is in the sapakṣa only, or that it should subsist in the sapakṣa in two ways? If it means that the hetu should subsist in two ways in the sapakṣa only, and nothing else — then the twofoldness does not pertain either to any other pakṣa or to the vipakṣa. In that case the Buddhist should not keep the expression in his definition, 'subsisting in the sapakṣa'. This subsistence is already implied, *ex hypothesi*, by the emphasis laid upon the phrase 'in two ways'. As regards the possibility of the subsistence of the hetu in the sapakṣa, this also is already implied in the very first qualification, viz. the hetu should subsist in the pakṣa. Further, since the phrase 'in two ways', according to the Buddhist, precludes the twofoldness of the subsistence in another pakṣa and that of non-subsistence in the vipakṣa, the phrase itself implies the possibility of subsistence in the sapakṣa. And this means that the qualification 'subsisting in the sapakṣa' becomes superfluous.

In order to avoid unnecessary fuss about every single word of the definition, says the Buddhist, let us not insist on the problem of the twofold subsistence of the hetu in the sapakṣa only. Even so, replies Uddyotakara, the two phrases in the definition, i.e. 'subsisting in the sapakṣa' and 'in two ways', will have to be rejected. This makes the Buddhist look like a man who is trying to push his goitre in only succeeds in having his eye balls protruding. So, if he emphasizes the phrase 'in two ways', explaining it to mean that the hetu should subsist in the sapakṣa in two ways only — he will have to reject such valid hetus as 'being a product'; for such hetus do not subsist 'in two ways only' (i.e. the property of 'being a product' subsists in non-eternal things in only one way, i.e. in their entirety, and never in part).

Further, in insisting on the definition with three terms, the Buddhist excludes that hetu which fulfils only two conditions — the same hetu which he himself has accepted as valid in his system. Under his own definition, the negative hetu ceases to be true hetu, as it does not subsist in the sapakṣa in two ways. Since the validity of the negative hetu has been so laboriously established by the Buddhists themselves, they cannot now reject it because of the difficulties they encounter. If, in order to avoid all these difficulties, no emphasis is to be laid on any of the terms of the definition, then the Buddhist might as well accept such hetus as subsist in only a part of the pakṣa or anywhere else.

(3) *Definition*

The hetu is that which subsists in the pakṣa and is concomitant with a part of it (*etena grāhyadharmas tadaṁsena vyāpto hetuḥ*).

Comment

The arguments given against the second definition equally hold good against this definition. This definition, as it stands, does not take pakṣa into account, and this is a serious defect in any definition of the hetu. Secondly, the expression '*asan tadatyaye*' is exactly similar to the expresssion '*vipakṣe nāsti*' of the previous definition; and it is therefore open to all those objections that have been raised against it.

(4) *Definition*

The hetu is that which is indicative of the presence of a character which is never apart from like things (*tādṛg avinābhāvidharmopadarśanaṃ hetuḥ*).

Explanation

Here the form 'which is never non-concomitant with homogeneous things' indicates the following characteristics: not subsisting in the vipakṣa and subsisting in the sapakṣa; the term 'indicative of the presence' denotes presence in the pakṣa; thus we get the hetu with its three characteristics.

Comment

It is true that the expression 'which is never non-concomitant with homogeneous things' indicates that the property does not subsist in the vipakṣa. But it does not indicate that it does subsist in the sapakṣa. When the property does not subsist in the vipakṣa, it does not necessarily follow that it subsists in the sapakṣa. In the absence of any expression which can indicate this subsistence in the sapakṣa, we would have to treat audibility as a true hetu for establishing the non-eternality of sound, as audibility never subsists apart from non-eternal things; the only condition that can exclude such unique or singular hetus from the scope of the true hetus, viz. it should subsist in the sapakṣa, is absent from the definition.

Even if we were to accept that the expression 'never non-concomitant with homogeneous things' does indicate 'subsistence in homogeneous things' what is there to indicate that the hetu must subsist in the pakṣa itself ? It cannot be argued that this indication is provided by the word '*upadarśana*'. Such a word has certainly no power to imply that it is indicative of presence in the pakṣa or elsewhere.

If the word is not indicative of presence in the pakṣa, asks the Buddhist, where else could the presence be of which it would be indicative ? Wherever there might be a possibility of its presence, says Uddyotakara, such a possibility can certainly be in the sapakṣa. The definition would then come to mean that the hetu is that which is indicative of the presence, in the sapakṣa, of a property which is never non-concomitant with the sapakṣa. But, then, we would have to accept visibility as a valid hetu for the proving of non-eternality of sound. (According to the Buddhist, visibility never subsists in things other than non-eternal things).

For the sake of argument let us grant, says Uddyotakara, that the word '*upadarśana*' does indicate the presence in the pakṣa of the property which is never non-concomitant with the sapakṣa. How do we then exclude that hetu which subsists in a part of the pakṣa only ? This cannot be done by the same word '*upadarśana*' ?

The Buddhists have cited two examples of the hetu: (a) the character of being produced by effort as proving non-eternality, (b) smoke as proving fire.

The first cannot be a hetu, because the property in question does not subsist in the pakṣa, sound. It is not a property of sound, as there is no sound that is produced by effort. In fact, every sound is produced by conjunction and disjunction.[5] The effort may be the indirect cause of sound, but in that way all things may be said to be the indirect cause of sound. It is therefor futile to have any such qualification as 'produced by effort'; one might as well say: 'Sound is non-eternal because it is produced'.

When the Buddhist gives 'the character of being produced by effort' (*prayatnāntarīyakatva*) in support of the non-eternality of sound, this reason is expressed by means of an abstract noun. What does this abstract noun mean ? Production or perception ? If it means production, that alone would be enough to establish non-eternality. If the abstract noun refers to perception, this alone would be sufficient to establish non-eternality; for the Buddhist does not recognize the perceptibility of any abstract object. If 'being produced' were not invariably concomitant with non-eternality, then alone would it have been useful to add the qualification 'by effort'. Things perceived are not of two kinds, as, according to the Buddhist, everything is non-eternal; nor are they of two kinds — perceived after effort and not-perceived after effort. It is not open to the Buddhist to say that there are things like '*ghaṭatva*' (jar-ness), which are eternal and also perceived after effort, as he does not accept anything as eternal. Thus the abstract noun '*prayatnānantarīyakatva*' cannot serve as a valid reason. Further, the character of being produced by effort is not invariably concomitant with the pakṣa. The term 'sound', which is the pakṣa of the reasoning in question, includes all sounds, but all sounds are not produced by effort. If, then, the reasoning is said to refer to a particular sound — and not to all sounds — the hetu, 'being produced by effort', would apply only to the first sound-unit, and not to the endless sound-units that follow each sound-unit. This means that the hetu does not subsist in the whole subject. It may be suggested that 'that particular sound which is produced by effort is certainly non-eternal'. But then we will need something other than the character of being produced, as the true hetu should subsist in the whole pakṣa.

Thus the various rival definitions of the hetu, says Uddyotakara, are defective; we must therefore accept the definition given by the sage Gautama (NV I. 1,34 & 35).

Third Member: The Example (*udāharaṇa*)

Gautama's concept of the third member of the reasoning is intimately connected with that of his fifth category 'familiar instance' (*dṛṣṭānta*). He has defined the former in the following two aphorisms: (a) The example is that familiar instance which, on account of its similarity with the probandum, is endowed with the property of that probandum (NS I. 1,36). (b) Or, the example is that familiar instance which, on account of its dissimilarity from the probandum, is not endowed with the property of that probandum (NS I. 1,37).

Gautama has defined the familiar instance as the thing about which an ordinary man and an expert entertain the same notion (NS I. 1,25).

The two kinds of the example, homogeneous and heterogeneous, are explained by the commentators as follows:

(a) *Homogeneous example*

According to Vātsyāyana, similarity with the probandum consists in the presence of the same property in both; when, on account of this similarity, the familiar instance (*dṛṣṭānta*) is found to be endowed with that same property, i.e. the property of the probandum, it constitutes the example.

In explaining the homogeneous example, Vātsyāyana says: The probandum is of two kinds: (1) in some cases it is the property as qualified by the object; e.g. the non-eternality of sound; (2) in others it is the object as qualified by the property: e.g. 'sound is non-eternal'. It is the similarity with the object as qualified by the property which converts the familiar instance into the example. For instance, in the reasoning 'sound is non-eternal because it has the property of being produced', the property of being produced implies that it comes into existence and goes out of existence and thus it is non-eternal. In this reasoning the property of being produced is the means, and the non-eternality is that which is to be proved. The relation of that which is to be proved and that which proves it between the two properties can arise only when these two are found to coexist in one thing to which these properties belong. When such a relation has been ascertained in the familiar instance, the same is inferred for the sound as well; the form that the inference takes is: Sound also is non-eternal, because it has the property of being produced, just like such things as the dish, etc. (NBh I. 1,36).

Uddyotakara explains the homogeneous example as follows:[6] The term '*sādhyasādharmya*' (similarity with the probandum) implies two restrictions: (1) the similarity should be restricted only to the probandum, and not to its negation; (2) similarity and not dissimilarity with the probandum is required. These two restrictions are implied by the term in question, because the familiar instance, by reason of the said similarity, is endowed with the property of the probandum. It is called '*udāharaṇa*', because the relation of the probandum and the probans between the two properties is indicated by it. The probandum is of two kinds: it consists of a property and an object (NV I. 1,36)

(b) *Heterogeneous Example*

As explained by Vātsyāyana, the second kind of the example consists in that familiar instance which, on account of its dissimilarity from the probandum, is not endowed with the property of that probandum; e.g. Sound is non-eternal because it has the property of being produced; things which do not have the property of being produced, e.g. the self and similar substances, are eternal. Here we have the familiar instance, 'the self and similar substances', which, on account of their dissimilarity from the probandum are not endowed with the property of the probandum, viz. the property of non-eternality. When we find, in the case of the self, the absence of the property of being produced, we infer the contrary for the sound, viz. 'because sound is endowed with the property of being produced, it is non-eternal'.

When the hetu is stated on the basis of similarity, what constitutes the example is that familiar instance which, on account of its similarity with the probandum, is endowed with the property of the probandum. When the hetu is stated on the basis of dissimilarity, the example consists of that familiar instance which, on account of its dissimilarity from the probandum, is not endowed with the property of the probandum. In the first case, the observer perceives in the familiar instance that it possesses two properties so related that the presence of one establishes the presence of the other; and from this he comes to infer that in the case of the probandum also, the presence of one should prove the presence of the other. In the second case, the observer perceives in regard to the familiar instance that there are two properties so related that the absence of one establishes the absence of another; and from this he comes to infer that in the case of the probandum also the said properties are similarly related, the absence of one establishing the absence of the other.[7] This process of proving by means of familiar instances, is not possible in the case of fallacious hetus.

The power of the hetu and the example, says Vātsyāyana in conclusion, is extremely subtle and difficult to grasp; it can be rightly understood only by the pundit (NBh I. 1,37).

Criticism of rival definitions

Uddyotakara mentions the following rival definitions of the example:[8]

Definition

(1) The example is that familiar instance which is established as such.

The definition is explained as follows: Since the example is but a familiar instance, it shows what is already proved in that instance. The dish, which is the example, shows that it has non-eternality. That non-eternality is required to be proved for the subject of the probandum.

Definition

(2) The example is that which indicates the concomitance of the hetu with what is to be proved and the non-concomitance of the hetu with the negation of the probandum.

Regarding the first definition, however much its advocates may try, says Uddyotakara in criticism, they cannot establish any relation of concomitance between the property of being a product and that of non-eternality. For according to their doctrine of momentariness there is a difference in the time at which the two properties are present; and a thing goes out of existence as soon as it is born; that is, the property of being produced is present at one point of time and non-eternality at an entirely different point; for at the time when the thing exists, its prior negation and destruction are not present. Hence the definition must be rejected (NV I. 1,37).

Familiar Instance (*dṛṣṭānta*)

Explaining the category of the familir instance, Vātsyāyana says that the instance is a thing that is directly perceived — a thing which cannot but be perceived by an ordinary man and an expert. It is an object cognized and thus is really included under the second category of object of cognition (*prameya*). But Gautama has mentioned the familiar instance as a separate category because both scripture (*āgama*) and inference depend upon it. It is only when there is an instance — and not otherwise — that there can be inference and scripture; it is the basis of all reasoning (*nyāya*).

In the Nyāya system, the instance, says Vātsyāyana, serves four purposes: First, the view of the opponent can be refuted if it is shown to be opposed to an instance. Secondly, it is through an instance that the position of the unbeliever (*nāstika*) can be demonstrated to be doubly untenable. If he admits an instance, he has to abandon his position. If, on the other hand, he does not admit an instance, he has no basis or ground to attack the position of his opponent. Thirdly, an instance is necessary to establish one's own position; in establishing one's own position, an instance has to be cited for its corroboration. Fourthly, it is only when the instance has been properly explained that the nature of the example can be understood (NBh I. 1,1).

The familiar instance, as explained by Vātsyāyana, is an object which has been cognized or perceived. If perception is understood as sense-perception, the things like the self, which are not amenable to sense-perception, would be ruled out as instances. In fact, Gautama himself has cited such instances. To meet this difficulty, Uddyotakara suggests that when an instance is said to be an object cognized or perceived, this means that it is not contrary to the perception of ordinary men and experts. The instance is included under the second category of object of cognition (*prameya*), because it is actually found to be cognized. But the instance has been mentioned as a separate category, as Vātsyāyana has remarked, because it is the basis of all reasoning. It is only when a thing has been cognized in one case that it can be inferred in another case; this shows that inference is based upon previously known instances. It is only what is known by oneself that one can speak of it to others; thus scripture (*āgama*) is based upon instances (NV I. 1,1).

Vātsyāyana's conception of ordinary men is that they do not possess superior intelligence, either by birth or by hard work. The experts, on the other hand, are different from these ordinary men; they are known as trained observers because they are capable of conducting an inquiry into things by means of the pramāṇas and disputation (*tarka*). It is when an object is known and understood by both the ordinary man and the expert that it constitutes an example (NBh I. 1,25).

In his definition Gautama says that the familiar instance is that object about which similar notions are entertained both by the average man and the expert. If the similar notion is regarded as an essential feature of the instance, then such unfamiliar things like ākāśa cannot be cited as instances. The ordinary man has no idea about such unfamiliar things. The reference to the ordinary man and the expert, says Uddyotakara, is only by way of illustration; no serious significance need to be attached to the similar notion being entertained by these two classes of men.

The utility of the familiar instance in the Nyāya system, it is objected, is questionable. Does it serve the purpose of indicating similarity ? If it does, it is not different from analogy (*upamāna*); in that case it falls within the category of pramāṇa. If it is meant to prove what is not proved, it is not different from the example, which is the third member of the reasoning. Either it is a pramāṇa or one of the members of reasoning; it cannot be regarded as a separate category.

This objection, says Uddyotakara, is based on a complete misunderstanding of the familiar instance, the example and analogy. The instance does indicate similarity; the similarity between the instance and the thing sought to be elucidated by its means consists in both being concomitant with the probans. For example, the similarity of the kitchen — the example — and the hill lies only in the fact that both contain smoke; and the comprehension of this similarity is all that is meant to be accomplished by the citing of the example. In analogy what we cognize is the relation between word and its meaning, and therefore the question of similarity is not relevant in that context. When the familiar instance is converted into the example as the third member of reasoning, as already explained, it does serve the purpose, proving of what is not proved (NV I. 1,25).

Fourth Member : The Confirmation (*upanaya*)

The fourth member of the reasoning, the confirmation (*upanaya*), is defined by Gautama as follows:

"The confirmation is the recapitulation, on the strength of the example, of that which is to be proved as being 'so' or as being 'not so' " (NS I. 1,38).

Vātsyāyana explains the confirmation: When the example cited is one which is similar to that which is to be proved, we have the confirmation in the form, 'this is so'; e.g. when the dish is cited as an example of the object which has the property of 'being produced' and is non-eternal, we have the confirmation in the form 'so is the sound', i.e. Sound has the property of being produced.

When the example cited is one which is dissimilar to that which is to be proved—e.g. when the *ātman* is cited as an example of the object which has the property of 'not being produced' and is eternal — we have the confirmation in the form 'sound is not so'.

Thus there are two kinds of confirmation based upon two kinds of example, which are, in their turn, based upon the two kinds of the hetu; these two hetus correspond to the two types of example (NBh I. 1,38).

Uddyotakara comments on the fourth member as follows: The confirmation of that which is to be established can be stated in the form 'As the example, so the summing up', e.g. 'so is sound also a product'. This formulation can be explained in two ways:

(a) By the property as perceived in the familiar instance, its invariable concomitance with the probandum having been established, the formulation serves to indicate the similarity to that property of the probandum: This, i.e. sound, is also a product.

(b) The confirmation may be regarded as indicating the relationship between the probandum and the probans in so far as the object of the proof is concerned. This relationship, it may be argued, has already been indicated in the clause 'because it is a product' (i.e. in the reasoning 'Sound is non-eternal because it is a product'). This clause, says Uddyotakara, does not furnish the required information. All that it does is to point out the mere relationship between the probandum and the probans; what the clause 'because it is a product' in the argument indicates is only the property 'being a product' in sound that would establish its non-eternality; whether this property of 'being a product' does or does not actually subsist in sound, is learnt only by means of the confirmation in the form 'the property of being a product does subsist in sound' (NV I. 1,38).

Fifth Member : The Conclusion (*nigamana*)

The conclusion is defined by Gautama as follows:

"The conclusion is the re-stating of the proposition, after the hetu has been stated" (NS I. 1,39).

Vātsyāyana explains the conclusion (*nigamana*) as follows:

(i) The conclusion is called conclusion, because it not only brings together the proposition, the hetu, the example and the confirmation, but strengthens their function in the entire reasoning.

(ii) The hetu having been stated either in its positive or its negative aspect, we have a recapitulation of the proposition in accordance with the example. This recapitulation constitutes the conclusion in the form: 'Therefore, having the property of being produced, sound is non-eternal'.

When the hetu has been stated in its positive aspect, the members of the reasoning are stated in the following forms:

(a) (1) Proposition: Sound is non-eternal

(2) Hetu: because it has the property of being produced

(3) Example: an object like the dish, etc., which has the property of being produced, is non-eternal

(4) Confirmation: sound also has the property of being produced

(5) Conclusion: therefore, having the property of being produced, sound is non-eternal.

(b) Similarly, when the hetu is stated in its negative aspect, the members of the reasoning are stated in the following forms:

(1) Proposition: Sound is non-eternal

(2) Hetu: because it has the property of being produced

(3) Example: an object like the *ātman*, etc., which has the property of not being produced, is eternal

(4) Confirmation: sound does not have the property of not being produced

(5) Conclusion: therefore, not having the property of not being produced, sound is non-eternal.

The two illustrations given by Vātsyāyana—one illustrating the affirmative and the other negative reasoning—each consisting of the five members, are entirely distinct from each other. These two reasonings, positive and negative, says Uddyotakara, are completely independent of each other; they do not constitute one single reasoning (NV I. 1,39).

In a statement (*vākya*) which is a collection of the five members mentioned above, the pramāṇas, related as they are to one another, cooperate to accomplish one object. The object of the proposition as given in the assertion of a *ṛṣi* (sage) will be regarded as proved when it is shown to be in accordance with perception and inference. In the reasoning regarding sound the object of proof is of such a character.

In (the statement of) the hetu, we have inference based upon the cognition of similarity. This has already been explained in connection with the third member, example.

(The statement of) the example is the object of perception; the unseen is established from (or on the basis of) the seen.

The confirmation is in the form of analogy, as it is expressed in the recapitulated form 'this is so' or 'this is not so'. When the property is denied of the subject, confirmation is one of that denial.

The conclusion is a demonstration of the power of all the

members to bring about the cognition of a single object.

There is also mutual relationship between the various members of the reasoning.

(a) If there were no proposition, the hetu and the other members, unsupported as they would be, could not operate.

(b) If there were no hetu, the efficacy of what could be demonstrated ? How could connection of the probandum and the example be shown ? What could be recapitulated ? On what basis could one draw a conclusion, which is a restatement of the proposition ?

(c) If there were no (statement of) the example, where would the similarity or dissimilarity with the probandum be shown ? Moreover, on the strength of what would the recapitulation proceed ?

(d) If there were no confirmation, the hetu which is put forward as the means of proof could not fulfil its function.

(e) In the absence of the conclusion there would be no indication of the mutual relationship of the various members of the reasoning, nor of the operation of the proposition and the other members towards the fulfilment of a single object. Moreover, what could be said to have been proved by the phrase 'this is so' ?

The object of each member of the reasoning is as follows:

(a) The proposition serves the purpose of indicating the relation between the property to be proved and the object.

(b) (The statement of) the hetu serves the purpose of indicating the fact of a certain property, which is either similar or dissimilar to the example, proving what is to be proved.

(c) (The statement of) the example serves the purpose of demonstrating the presence of the relation of what is to be proved and what proves it between the two properties, as manifested together (i.e. in a single substratum).

(d) The confirmation serves the purpose of indicating the coexistence of the property put forward as the means of proving, with the property to be proved.

(e) The conclusion serves the purpose of showing that it is not possible to deny, in regard to anything that is to be proved, the relation of what is to be proved and what proves it; the example shows that these properties are related to each other.

When the hetu and the example have been stated in a correct

form, there is no opportunity for the opponent to challenge such reasoning by any of the methods recognized by Gautama (NBh I. 1,39).

In his comments Uddyotakara first explains the definition of the conclusion as follows: When it is found that every one of the members stated in the reasoning is based upon a pramāṇa as bearing upon the object with which the proposition is concerned, there is a re-statement of the same proposition, for the purpose of precluding any notion contrary to that which is to be proved.

When the aphorism is thus explained, says Uddyotakara, there is really no room for any objection to the Nyāya view. Nevertheless, he then proceeds to examine the following possible objections:

(i) "The confirmation and the conclusion cannot be regarded as distinct members [of the reasoning], because their purpose is not different."

This sentence as it stands, says Uddyotakara, makes no sense at all. If the objection is that the confirmation and the hetu are the same because their purpose is not-different, this hetu put forward, 'because their purpose is not-different', is not valid. Things can be different and yet serve the same purpose. For example, two jars serve the same purpose of carrying water and yet are two distinct jars. If the opponent argues that the intention is to show that the two members serve the same purpose, then also his hetu is invalid. His proposition is that the hetu and confirmation are not different and his hetu is that the purpose is non-different. But, then, his hetu is the same as his proposition. Thus the opponent's argument is invalid.

(ii) Some philosophers maintain that 'there should be a rejection of all the members except that statement wherein the property as expressed in the hetu is shown to be concomitant with the property of the subject to be proved'.[9] The arguments which have been put forward against the first objection, says Uddyotakara, are equally valid against this view, and therefore says Uddyotakara, are equally valid against this view, and therefore this view must also be rejected.

(iii) The opponent raises an objection against the form of the confirmation — 'As that [the dish] is, so is this [sound]' (*yad api yathā tatheti*). What exactly is the significance of 'so is this' (*tatheti*) ? The property of being a product, which is the hetu for the non-eternality of sound — is this property the same in the case of both sound and the dish, or is it one for sound and another for the dish ? The expression 'this is so' is either too general or too specific. In the former case it does not convey the specific property; in the latter case it does not convey the same property.

This objection, says Uddyotakara, is not proper. The object (or purpose) of the confirmation is analogy, and the analogy does not always operate on the basis of the relation of what is to be proved and what proves it. Hence the objection has no force. Further, when the property of being a product is given as a hetu and indicated in the example, it is understood that the property has a variety of application. Hence it is quite correct to state that the subject and the example have a similar property. And this is precisely the function of analogy in the fourth member.

(iv) Another objection is that the confirmation is the same as the familiar instance (*dṛṣṭānta*). The answer to the previous objection holds good against this objection as well.

(v) On similar grounds the view that the conclusion is the same as the proposition should be rejected (NV I. 1,39).

11

THE FALLACY OF THE HETU (*hetvābhāsa*)

The hetvābhāsa *as Category*

The fallacy of the hetu, *hetvābhāsa*, is the thirteenth category in the Nyāya list, sandwiched between cavil and quibble. The categories of cavil and quibble, as Vātsyāyana has observed, are meant for the protection of the objective character of things: and he now states that the category of the fallacy is listed as one of the deficiencies, *nigrahasthāna*, which is the sixteenth category. Gautama has, however, mentioned it separately, because from among the various deficiencies the fallacies are permitted in discussion while the other deficiencies can be used only in cavil and quibble (NBh I. 1,1).

Gautama has not furnished any general definition of the fallacy of the hetu but this omission has been made good by his commentators. The fallacies of the ḥetu, says Vātsyāyana, are so called, because they do not possess the characteristics of the hetu and yet they appear like the hetu because of their similarity to it (Introductory NBh to NS I. 2,4). Or, as Uddyotakara puts it, those that are wanting in one or the other of the properties of the hetu (i.e. valid hetu) and as such are non-hetus (NV I. 1, 1).

The similarity between the hetu and the non-hetu, according to Uddyotakara, consists of the following: (i) The non-hetu, like a true hetu, is formulated after the proposition, and this constitutes a similarity. (ii) Possessing any one of the characteristics of the hetu: the hetu that is formulated for the purpose of proving the proposition is endowed with three characteristics or marks (*liṅga*); and if what is formulated happens to possess any one of these three, this constitutes a similarity. If the hetu is regarded as fulfilling two conditions as some philosophers believe, then the similarity would consist in the possessing of any one of the two characteristics.

The difference between the hetu and the non-hetu lies in the fact that while the former proves the proposition, the latter does not. And this difference is due to the fact that the former fulfils all the conditions, while the latter fulfils only some (NV I. 2,4).

The Fallacies of the Hetu

Gautama has mentioned the following five fallacies of the hetu (NS I. 2,4): (1) the inconclusive hetu (*savyabhicāra*), (2) the contradictory hetu (*viruddha*), (3) the tautological hetu (*prakaraṇasama*), (4) the unproved hetu (*sādhyasama*), (5) the mistimed hetu (*kālātīta*).

According to Uddyotakara, the purpose of Gautama in listing first the five fallacies of the hetu in the aphorism and then defining each of them separately is twofold: First, it is true that the five aphorisms which Gautama has devoted to the subject do indicate the number of the fallacies of the hetu, but this does not render the present aphorism superfluous. All that the definition does is to differentiate. It follows that all that these five definitions do is to differentiate one fallacy from another. The need for restricting their number to five remains and this is precisely what the present aphorism is meant to do. Second, even more important is the need to emphasize what is styled as restriction (*niyama*). The extent of the hetus and the fallacies of the hetu is vast; they appear in a great variety; it is therefore essential to classify them. If we take into consideration the diversities of time, of persons and of things, they are innumerable, but in a general way, if we consider the probandum and the hetu, the number of the hetus and the fallacies of the hetu, on being computed, comes to be one hundred and seventy six as follows: (a) the diversity of properties concomitant with the probandum gives sixteen; the diversity of properties concomitant with only a part of the probandum also yields sixteen; (b) so does the diversity of properties which are not concomitant with the probandum. In both of these cases the hetu may be formulated with a qualification. It then becomes necessary to distinguish between that part which is qualified and that which qualifies. This would give sixty four varieties. What is qualified or what qualifies may be ineffective in proving the proposition. And this gives another sixty four.

With this preliminary justification Uddyotakara proceeds to

deal with the various kinds of fallacies of the hetu mentioned above.

A. Diversity of properties in relation to the probandum

(i) Sixteen kinds of the hetu concomitant with the probandum.

There are the following sixteen kinds of the hetu according to the diversity of properties concomitant with the probandum. From these five are valid hetus: the third and the ninth are affirmative-negative, not concomitant with the vipakṣa at all; the tenth and the eleventh as propounded by a person entirely on the basis of his own established tenet, are affirmative; and the fifteenth is negative. The other eleven kinds are fallacious hetus (See Table I, p. 272).

(1) That which is concomitant with the probandum, the class of homogeneous objects and the class of heterogeneous objects (An object is eternal or non-eternal because it is the object of cognition).

(2) The hetu which is concomitant with the probandum, the class of homogeneous objects and partly concomitant with the class of heterogeneous objects (This is a cow because it has horns).

(3) The hetu which is concomitant with the probandum, and the class of homogeneous objects and is not concomitant with the class of heterogeneous objects (Sound is non-eternal because it is produced).

(4) The hetu which is concomitant with the probandum, not concomitant with the class of homogeneous objects and concomitant with the class of heterogeneous objects (Sound is eternal because it is produced).

(5) The hetu which is concomitant with the probandum, not concomitant with the class of homogeneous objects and partly concomitant with the class of heterogeneous objects (Sound is eternal because it is perceptible by external sense-organs).

(6) The hetu which is concomitant with the probandum, and not concomitant with the class of homogeneous objects and the class of heterogeneous objects (Sound is eternal because it is audible).

(7) The hetu which is concomitant with the probandum, partly concomitant with the class of homogeneous objects and concomitant with the class of heterogeneous objects (This is

non-cow because it has horns).

(8) The hetu which is concomitant with the probandum and the class of homogeneous objects and partly concomitant with the class of heterogeneous objects (Sound is eternal because it is intangible).

(9) The hetu which is concomitant with the probandum, partly concomitant with the class of homogeneous objects and not concomitant with the class of heterogeneous objects (Sound is non-eternal because it is perceptible by the external sense-organs.

(10) The hetu which is concomitant with the probandum and the class of homogeneous objects, and in the case of which the class of heterogeneous objects is not present. (When a person states the following reasoning entirely on the basis of his own doctrine (*siddhānta*): Sound is non-eternal because it is produced).

(11) The hetu which is concomitant with the probandum and partly concomitant with the class of homogeneous objects, and in the case of which the class of heterogeneous objects is not present (Sound is non-eternal because it is perceptible by the external sense-organs).

(12) The hetu which is concomitant with the probandum and not concomitant with the class of homogeneous objects, and in the case of which the class of heterogeneous objects is absent (Sound is non-eternal because it is audible).

(13) The hetu which is concomitant with the probandum, in the case of which the class of homogeneous objects is not present, and which is concomitant with the class of heterogeneous objects (Sound is eternal because it is produced).

(14) The hetu which is concomitant with the probandum, in the case of which the class of homogeneous objects is not present, and which is partly concomitant with the class of heterogeneous objects (Sound is eternal because it is perceptible by the external sense-organs).

(15) The hetu which is concomitant with the probandum, in the case of which the class of homogeneous objects is not present and which is not concomitant with the class of heterogeneous objects (The living body is not without soul, because [if it were] it could not be the receptacle of the sense-organs).

(16) The hetu which is concomitant with the probandum,

in the case of which both classes of homogeneous and heterogeneous objects are not present (Every thing is eternal because it is the object of cognition).

(ii) Sixteen kinds of the hetu partly concomitant with the probandum.

There are the following sixteen kinds of the hetu partly concomitant with the probandum. Since these hetus are only partly concomitant with the probandum they are all fallacies (See Table II, p. 273).

(1) The hetu which is partly concomitant with the probandum, and concomitant with the class of homogeneous objects and the class of heterogeneous objects (The earth, water, fire, air and akāśa are non-eternal because they are non-odorous).

(2) The hetu which is partly concomitant with the probandum, concomitant with the class of homogeneous objects and partly concomitant with the class of heterogeneous objects (Speech and mind are perceptible by the external sense-organs because they are non-eternal).

(3) The hetu which is partly concomitant with the probandum, concomitant with the class of homogeneous objects and not concomitant with the class of heterogeneous objects (Speech and mind are non-eternal because they are produced).

(4) The hetu which is partly concomitant with the probandum, not concomitant with the class of homogeneous objects and concomitant with the class of heterogeneous objects (Speech and mind are non-eternal[1] — because they are produced).

(5) The hetu which is partly concomitant with the probandum, not concomitant with the class of homogeneous objects and partly concomitant with the class of heterogeneous objects (Speech and mind are perceptible by the external sense-organs because they are eternal).

(6) The hetu which is partly concomitant with the probandum, not concomitant with the class of homogeneous objects and the class of heterogeneous objects (Sound is non-eternal because it originates from a non-inherent cause).

(7) The hetu which is partly concomitant with the probandum and the class of homogeneous objects and which is concomitant with the class of heterogeneous objects (Atoms are non-eternal because they are non-odorous).

(8) The hetu which is partly concomitant with the probandum,

the class of homogeneous objects and the class of heterogeneous objects (Speech and mind are non-eternal because they are non-material).

(9) The hetu which is partly concomitant with the probandum and the class of homogeneous objects and which is not concomitant with the class of heterogeneous objects (Speech and mind are non-eternal because they are perceptible by the external sense-organs).

(10) The hetu which is partly concomitant with the probandum, concomitant with the class of homogeneous objects and in the case of which the class of heterogeneous objects is not present (When the following reasoning is put forward on the basis of a particular doctrine (*siddhāntabheda*): Colour and cognition are non-eternal because they are non-eternal).

(11) The hetu which is partly concomitant with the probandum and the class of homogeneous objects and in the case of which the class of heterogeneous objects is not present[2] (The eye and cognition are non-eternal because they are non-material).

(12) The hetu which is partly concomitant with the probandum, not concomitant with the class of homogeneous objects and in the case of which the class of heterogeneous objects is not present (Sound and mind are non-eternal because they are audible).

(13) The hetu which is partly concomitant with the probandum, in the case of which the class of homogeneous objects is not present and which is concomitant with the class of heterogeneous objects (Speech and mind are non-eternal because they are produced).

(14) The hetu which is partly concomitant with the probandum, in the case of which the class of homogeneous objects is not present, and which is partly concomitant with the class of heterogeneous objects (The eye and cognition are eternal because they are material).

(15) The hetu which is partly concomitant with the probandum, in the case of which the class of homogeneous objects is not present and which is not concomitant with the class of heterogeneous objects (The body is not without soul, because [if it were] it would not be the receptacle of the sense-organs).

(16) The hetu which is partly concomitant with the

probandum, in the case of which both the classes of homogeneous and heterogeneous objects are not present (Every thing is non-eternal because it is material).

(iii) Sixteen kinds of the hetus not concomitant with the probandum

There are the following sixteen kinds of the hetu not concomitant with the probandum. Since these hetus are not concomitant with the probandum, these are all fallacies (See Table III, p. 274).

(1) The hetu which is not concomitant with the probandum and which is concomitant with both the classes of homogeneous and heterogeneous objects (The earth is non-eternal because it has odour).

(2) The hetu which is not concomitant with the probandum and which is concomitant with the class of homogeneous objects and partly concomitant with the class of heterogeneous objects (Sound is non-eternal because it is inaudible).

(3) The hetu which is not concomitant with the probandum, which is concomitant with the class of homogeneous objects and which is not concomitant with the class of heterogeneous objects (Sound is a thing because it is inaudible and because it possesses the genus of sound).[3]

(4) The hetu which is not concomitant with the probandum and the class of homogeneous objects, and which is concomitant with the class of heterogeneous objects (Sound is a thing because it has the genus of sound).

(5) The hetu which is not concomitant with the probandum, is partly concomitant with the class of homogeneous objects and is not concomitant with the class of heterogeneous objects[4] (Sound has a cause because it is a thing).

(6) The hetu which is not concomitant with the probandum and with both the classes of homogeneous and heterogeneous objects (Sound is eternal because it does not exist).

(7) The hetu which is not concomitant with the probandum, is partly concomitant with the class of homogeneous objects and is concomitant with the class of heterogeneous objects (Sound is intangible because it is a substance).

(8) The hetu which is not concomitant with the probandum, is partly concomitant with both the classes of homogeneous and heterogeneous objects (Sound has a cause because it is material).

(9) The hetu which is not concomitant with the probandum, is partly concomitant with the class of homogeneous objects, and is not concomitant with the class of heterogeneous objects (Sound has its own place of origin because it is visible).[5]

(10) The hetu which is not concomitant with the probandum, is concomitant with the class of homogeneous objects and in the case of which the class of heterogeneous objects is not present (Sound is non-eternal because it is inaudible. This reasoning is according to a particular doctrine).

(11) The hetu which is not concomitant with the probandum, is partly concomitant with the class of homogeneous objects and in the case of which the class of heterogeneous objects is not present (Sound is non-eternal because it is material).

(12) The hetu which is not concomitant with the probandum and the class of homogeneous objects and in the case of which the class of heterogeneous objects is not present (Sound is non-eternal because it does not exist).

(13) The hetu which is not concomitant with the probandum, in the case of which the class of homogeneous objects is not present and which is concomitant with the class of heterogeneous objects (Sound is eternal because it is inaudible).

(14) The hetu which is not concomitant with the probandum, in the case of which the class of homogeneous objects is not present and which is partly concomitant with the class of heterogeneous objects (Sound is eternal because it is non-material).

(15) The hetu which is not concomitant with the probandum, in the case of which the class of homogeneous objects is not present and which is not concomitant with the class of heterogeneous objects (Sound is eternal because it does not exist).[6]

(16) The hetu which is not concomitant with the probandum, and in the case of which both the classes of homogeneous and heterogeneous objects are not present (Every thing is non-eternal because it does not exist) (NV I. 2,4).

Kinds of the Hetu

Notes to Tables I-III

√in the columns probandum, class of homogeneous objects and class of heterogeneous objects indicates the total concomitance of the hetu with the term at the head of the column.

√in the columns hetu and fallacy of the hetu indicates whether the hetu is valid or a fallacy.

'Partly' in a column indicates that the hetu is partly concomitant with the term at the head of the column.

x in the columns probandum, class of homogeneous objects and class of heterogeneous objects indicates that the hetu is not concomitant with the term at the head of the column.

'No' in the columns class of homogeneous objects and class of heterogeneous objects indicates the respective absence of the hetu.

— indicates that the term at the heading of the column does not apply.

I

Sixteen kinds of the hetu concomitant with the probandum

	Probandum (*Sādhya*)	*Class of homogeneous objects* (*Sapakṣa*)	*Class of heterogeneous objects* (*Vipakṣa*)	*Hetu*	*Fallacy of the hetu* (*Hetvābhāsa*)
(1)	√	√	√	—	√
(2)	√	√	Part	—	√
(3)	√	√	x	√	—
(4)	√	x	√	—	√
(5)	√	x	Part	—	√
(6)	√	x	x	—	√
(7)	√	Part	√	—	√
(8)	√	√	Part	—	√
(9)	√	Part	x	√	—
(10)	√	√	No	√	—
(11)	√	Part	No	√	—
(12)	√	x	No	—	√
(13)	√	No	√	—	√
(14)	√	No	Part	—	√
(15)	√	No	x	√	—
(16)	√	No	No	—	√

II

Sixteen kinds of the hetus partly concomitant with the probandum

	Proban-dum (*Sādhya*)	*Class of homo-geneous objects* (*Sapakṣa*)	*Class of Hetero-geneous objects* (*Vipakṣa*)	*Hetu*	*Fallacy of the hetu* (*Hetvā-bhāsa*)
(1)	Part	√	√	—	√
(2)	Part	√	Part	—	√
(3)	Part	√	x	—	√
(4)	Part	x	√	—	√
(5)	Part	x	Part	—	√
(6)	Part	x	x	—	√
(7)	Part	Part	√	—	√
(8)	Part	Part	Part	—	√
(9)	Part	Part	x	—	√
(10)	Part	√	No	—	√
(11)	Part	Part	No	—	√
(12)	Part	x	No	—	√
(13)	Part	No	√	—	√
(14)	Part	No	Part	—	√
(15)	Part	No	x	—	√
(16)	Part	No	No	—	√

III

Sixteen kinds of hetu not concomitant with the probandum

	Probandum (Sādhya)	*Class of homogeneous objects (Sapakṣa)*	*Class of heterogeneous objects (Vipakṣa)*	*Hetu*	*Fallacy of the hetu (Hetvābhāsa)*
(1)	x	√	√	—	√
(2)	x	√	Part	—	√
(3)	x	√	x	—	√
(4)	x	x	√	—	√
(5)	x	Part	x	—	√
(6)	x	x	x	—	√
(7)	x	Part	√	—	√
(8)	x	Part	Part	—	√
(9)	x	Part	x	—	√
(10)	x	√	No	—	√
(11)	x	Part	No	—	√
(12)	x	x	No	—	√
(13)	x	No	√	—	√
(14)	x	No	Part	—	√
(15)	x	No	x	—	√
(16)	x	No	No	—	√

B. Diversity of the hetu adduced with qualifications

(1) *Unfounded qualifiers and qualificands*

The two groups, i.e. the sixteen kinds of the hetu concomitant with the probandum and the sixteen kinds of the hetu partly concomitant with the probandum, yield sixty four varieties, as each of these two groups can have a qualifier or qualificand either of which may be unestablished. This is due to the fact that both the concomitant and non-concomitant hetus are stated with a qualification.

(a) Of these examples of the hetu concomitant with the probandum are as follows:

(i) Sound is non-eternal because while being inexpressible it is an object of cognition.

In this hetu the qualifier (being inexpressible) is unfounded; (Sound is known to be something which is expressible by words).

(ii) Sound is non-eternal because while being an object of cognition it is inexpressible.

In this hetu the qualificand is 'being inexpressible' and is unfounded.

Similar varieties in regard to every one of the sixteen kinds of the concomitant hetu can be found and the same examples will serve in both cases, i.e. by reversing the qualifier and the qualificand as indicated in the examples above.

(b) The examples of the hetu partly concomitant with the probandum are as follows:

(i) The earth, water, fire, air and ākāśa are non-eternal because while being inexpressible they are non-odorous.

(ii) The earth, water, fire, air and ākāśa are non-eternal because while being non-odorous they are inexpressible.

In the first example the qualifier (being inexpressible) is unfounded; in the second example, 'being inexpressible' is the qualificand and is unfounded. Similar examples can be found of all other hetus partly concomitant with the probandum (NV I. 2,4).

(2) *Inefficient qualificands and qualifiers*

Similarly, the sixty four varieties arise because there is a diversity of the inefficient qualifiers or qualificands. For example, sound is non-eternal because while being a product it is the object of cognition; sound is non-eternal because while being the object of cognition it is a product. In the first example the qualificand (being the object of cognition) is inefficient because it has no power to prove what it sets out to prove; in the second, 'being the object of cognition', is the qualifier and it has no power to prove what it sets out to prove.

(3) *Dubious qualifiers and qualificands*

Similarly sixty four varieties can be found because there is a diversity of dubious qualifiers and qualificands. For example, we have the following two reasonings:

(i) This is the peacock's sound, because while being a *ṣaḍja*[7] it is not a phoneme.

(ii) This is the peacock's sound, because while not being a phoneme it is a *ṣaḍja.*

In the first reasoning, the qualifier, the presence of the sounds other than the *ṣaḍja,* is dubious, as the peacock's sound is believed to consist almost entirely of the *ṣaḍja* alone; in the second reasoning, the presence of the other sounds is the qualificand, which, for the same reason, is dubious.

(4) *Other diversities of qualifiers and qualificands*

The instances so far enumerated are those where both disputants agree that qualifiers and qualificands in the hetu as concomitant with the probandum are unfounded and dubious.

When only one or the other of the disputants accepts the unfounded character, this gives one hundred and twenty eight: those that are concomitant with the probandum or non-concomitant with the probandum. The same sixty four varieties again become one hundred and ninety two because there is a diversity caused by (1) the fact of the qualifiers and qualificands being incompatible; (2) the fact that the qualifiers and qualificands are dubious and (3) the fact that the qualifiers and qualificands are inefficient.

Again there are one hundred and twenty eight varieties, because there is a diversity of the qualifiers and qualificands having loci unacceptable to one or both parties. These again, as before, lead on to another group of one hundred and ninety two.[8] For example, 'this place is fiery because it is smoky'; 'the soul exists because it has the qualities of desire, etc.'

(a) The following is an instance where the qualifier is inefficient, non-concomitant and unfounded: Sound is non-eternal because while following after the effort it is a product. The qualificand in this reasoning, 'being a product', is itself capable of proving non-eternality and the qualifier, 'coming after the effort', is entirely superfluous; hence it is inefficient.

(b) The following is an instance where the qualificand is non-concomitant and inefficient: Sound is non-eternal because while differing with the causes producing it, it is apprehended. The qualificand in this reasoning 'being apprehended' belongs to eternal things also, and hence it is inefficient; non-eternality is already established by the other qualifier, i.e. differing according to the causes producing it.

(c) The following is an instance where the qualificand is not compatible with the qualifier. The primordial matter (*pradhāna*) exists because its modifications share its constituents.

(d) The following is an instance where the qualifier is not compatible with the qualificand: The words colour, etc., denote something entirely different from the word 'sandal', because while not bearing the relation between the parts and whole, they are indicated by the words 'colour, etc.'. In this reasoning, when colour is mentioned what is actually meant is the sandal, as the colour is only the sandal's constituent part.

(e) The same hetu in this reasoning when formulated inversely affords an instance of the unfounded qualificand: 'because while colour is referred to by means of the word "sandal" it does not bear the relation of parts and whole'.

(f) An instance where the hetu as formulated to prove one thing is actually known to prove also its contrary is the argument put forward by some philosophers (Mīmāṃsakas): 'Word is eternal because it can be repeated'. But according to the Naiyāyika, repetition could prove equally either eternality or non-eternality.

(g) The following is an instance where the qualifier is dubious and unfounded: 'This place has fire because while having smoke it gives light'. In this reasoning the presence of smoke has no bearing on the place giving out light. When the same reasoning is put forward in the inverse order, i.e. 'this place has fire because while giving light it has smoke', we have an instance of the dubious qualificand.

Thus we find that the dubious, the unfounded and the non-concomitant become sixty four, through the diversity caused by its being unfounded for one or both of the two parties.[9] And these, by the computation indicated above, make up the total of three hundred and eighty four. The hetus which are formulated in the manner other than those indicated above give us the same number. Similar computation applies to those hetus in which the qualifiers and qualificands are contradictory. Examples of these are given by Uddyotakara in his comments on the five fallacies of the hetu.

By the various computations indicated at various stages, the number of hetus and fallacies of the hetu, when proper distinction is made between the diversities involving the qualifiers and qualificands comes to be two thousand and thirty two. If we were to take into account all the diversities of the defects of the hetu, the varieties of such defective hetus would be beyond calculation.

The hetus not concomitant with the probandum cannot be qualified by any qualification, as they do not subsist in the probandum. Hence these have not been mentioned under the defects involved in the qualifiers and qualificands.

The hetus that have been described in full detail are those that have the property of concomitance and non-concomitance with the probanda that exist. Of these the sixteen varieties of the 'unfounded' hetu are such as are not concomitant with the probandum. The inconclusive hetus have only six main varieties; among those that are concomitant with the probandum, the number of the contradictory hetus is only four; and the fourth, concomitant with every possible probandum, is too general. The other fallacious hetus, viz. unestablished, inconclusive and contradictory, are, each of them, diversified through being non-concomitant and unfounded.[10] The examples of these are to be found amongst those which have already been cited.

According to some philosophers, the *anaikāntika* hetu amounts to a hetu which is not concomitant with its contradictory. This, says Uddyotakara, cannot be right, simply because this is an impossibility; absence of non-concomitance is not possible in referring to two contradictory things; that is to say, nothing can be concomitant with two contradictories; if, however, we do admit of such concomitance, then the number of varieties of such a hetu becomes twenty five; there are five hetus, and each of them being opposed by similar and dissimilar hetus, give rise to five pentads. Examples of every one of them is not possible. Hence these are not illustrated (NV I: 2,4).

The five fallacies of the hetu

(1) The fallacy of the inconclusive hetu (*savyabhicāra* or *anaikāntika*).

According to Gautama, the fallacy of the inconclusive hetu occurs when the hetu leads to more than one conclusion[11] (NS I. 2,5).

Vātsyāyana explains the fallacy as follows: It is known as

savyabhicāra and *anaikāntika*. (a) The term *vyabhicāra'* indicates that the hetu has not been suitably placed in the context of the proof. In the reasoning — 'sound is eternal (= proposition) because it is intangible' (= hetu), like a jar which, though tangible is non-eternal', intangibility does not prove non-eternality because it could be found in things which are eternal. The term *'anaikāntika'* can be applied in this context to two points (*anta*), viz. eternality or non-eternality (NBh I. 2,5).

Uddyotakara mentions four objections to the Nyāya definition of the fallacy and answers each of them at some length.

(i) *Objection*

The term, *anaikāntika* (not-fixed-in-one-point) is a negative term with a negative particle. The negative particle can mean either exclusion (*paryudāsa*) of what is denoted by the term following it or total absence (*prasajyapratiṣedha*) of what is denoted by that term. In the former case it has a positive meaning while in the latter case it signifies complete negation of what is denoted by that term. In the present context the former interpretation would mean that the negative particle in the word for the fallacy would exclude all the other kinds of fallacy; in the latter interpretation it would imply the total absence of all other fallacies.

Reply

Prasajyapratiṣedha, says Uddyotakara, does not mean total absence. The negative particle is a qualifier and as such it must qualify a qualificand that exists. For instance, in the word *abrāhmaṇa* (non-Brahmin) the negative particle does not mean that what is denoted by the following term Brahmin does not exist; for we know that men are Brahmins.

Thus there is no justification for saying that the negative particle in the word for the fallacy does not mean that the other fallacies are not possible.

(ii) *Objection*

The definition of the *savyabhicāra* as explained by Vātsyāyana lends itself to the interpretation that *savyabhicāraḥ* is the definiendum and *'anaikāntikaḥ'* the definiend. This interpretation is not proper, for the term *'anaikāntika'* has not been explained anywhere by the commentator and we cannot therefore understand the exact nature of the *'savyabhicāra'* fallacy. Hence it is not right to define the *savyabhicāra* as *'anaikāntika'*.

Reply

Such a definition, says Uddyotakara, is perfectly proper. What is meant by the term *'anaikāntika'* is known from ordinary usage. There is need for an explanation, in a *śāstra*, of only such things as are not known from ordinary usage; it would be absolutely futile to provide explanations of things that can be known from ordinary usage. In the case under consideration we know it from experience that the word *'anaikāntika'* signifies that which subsists in both aspects of a thing. If terms current in ordinary usage had to be explained in the *śāstra* itself, we might then be compelled to provide adequate explanation of such ordinary words as 'pain and the like'. Hence the view expressed by Vātsyāyana is quite appropriate.

(iii) *Objection*

The definition of the *savyabhicāra* is not correct, because it is not comprehensive. It does not cover all kinds of the *savyabhicāra*; for instance, the too narrow (*asādhāraṇa*).

Reply

This contention, says Uddyotakara, is not right, as this kind of hetu is actually covered by the definition. The hetu that is too narrow is actually found to be such as is found in both homogeneous and heterogeneous classes of objects, and thus can be called *'savyabhicāra'*.

(iv) *Objection*

According to some philosophers, the *prakaraṇasama* fallacy is included in the category of the *savyabhicāra*. For example, we have the reasoning: The soul is non-eternal (= proposition) because it is different from the body (= hetu). Here we find that the difference from the body is something that subsists in eternal as well as non-eternal things; thus it fulfils the condition of the *savyabhicāra*.

Reply

These philosophers, says Uddyotakara, have not really

understood the exact meaning of the diversity (*vyabhicāra*) of defining properties and the diversity of examples. When the Naiyāyika says that the *savyabhicāra* is *anaikāntika*, he is giving a definition of the *savyabhicāra* fallacy; if the characteristic mentioned in the definition is found in the *prakaraṇasama* fallacy, then alone the definition can be said to be too wide, i.e. including fallacies other than the *savyabhicāra*. The fact that a certain example of the *savyabhicāra* is found to fulfil the conditions of some other kind of fallacy does not constitute a defect in the definition of the *savyabhicāra*; for the only circumstances that can make a definition defective are when the definition does not cover all the elements that it should cover or when it includes what does not strictly belong to it. Certainly neither of these defects is found in the example given in the objection; nor can the fact that the example fulfils the condition of another fallacy constitute a defect of the present definition (NV I. 2,5).

(2) *The fallacy of the contradictory hetu* (*viruddha*)

According to Gautama, a certain *siddhānta* (established tenet) being accepted, the hetu that is opposed to it constitutes the fallacy of the contradictory hetu (NS I. 2,6).[12]

According to Vātsyāyana, the term '*tadvirodhī*' used by Gautama in the definition means 'that which opposes it', i.e. 'that which opposes the *siddhānta* (established tenet) which has been accepted'. For instance, we have the following two statements of the Sāṃkhya philosopher: (a) the modification of *prakṛti* disappears (= proposition) because it is not eternal (= hetu). (b) The modification, though it disappears, continues to exist (= proposition) because it is not totally destroyed (= hetu). In the first the argument means that no modification is eternal. This is contrary to the proposition in the second argument that the modification continues to exist.

This contradiction arises from the fact that the modification means that something new comes into existence. The disappearance of the modification means that something has gone out of existence. In both cases there is no question of eternality. Thus the hetu is contrary to the basic doctrine of the Sāṃkhya (NBh I. 2,6).

According to Uddyotakara, Gautama's definition of the fallacy may be interpreted in two ways: (a) The contradictory hetu is that hetu which contradicts the object which is accepted in the proposition, i.e. that hetu which sets aside the object of the proposition and which is set aside by the object accepted in the proposition. On this interpretation the fallacy would cover all kinds of opposition or contradiction. But the other four fallacies of Gautama have their own specific characteristics; their respective specific characteristics distinguish them from the fallacy of the contradictory hetu. In view of these circumstances it would be appropriate to give a composite name to each of these fallacies, e.g. *savyabhicāra-viruddha*. (b) The fallacy occurs when there is contradiction or opposition between the meanings of two sentences when these meanings are opposed to each other, or between the proposition and the hetu. Such opposition or contradiction subsists both in the proposition and the hetu; it may be described as subsisting in one or the other as the occasion demands.

In the reasoning 'sound is eternal (=proposition) because it is a product' (=hetu) the hetu contradicts the proposition. The property of being a product is admitted by both parties as subsisting in sound and is also confirmed by perception. Another reasoning where the hetu contradicts the proposition is: 'no single entity exists (=proposition) because the word "entity" (*bhāva*) refers to an aggregate (*samūha*) of existents' (=hetu). In this reasoning the word 'aggregate' itself stands for a single entity and thus the hetu contradicts the proposition. The example of a reasoning where there is contradiction between the proposition and the hetu is: 'substance is different from quality (=proposition) because no such thing different from quality is apprehended' (=hetu) (NV I. 2,6).

(3) *The fallacy of the tautological hetu*[13] (*prakaraṇasama*)

According to Gautama, the fallacy of the tautological hetu occurs when the hetu, though cited for the purpose of ascertainment, gives rise to suspense (anxiety) instead of ascertainment (NS I. 2,7).[14]

The fallacy of the tautological hetu is explained by Vātsyāyana as follows. The term '*prakaraṇa*' in the name of this fallacy stands for the two opposite views on a doubtful question, neither of which is definitely ascertained; the word '*cintā*' (suspense) in the aphorism, in regard to the doubtful question (or point at issue), indicates the desire to know (or ascertain) the truth — that whole process of investigation which begins with doubt and ends with ascertainment.

With this preliminary explanation, Vātsyāyana observes: the hetu which only gives rise to suspense, if put forward for the purpose of ascertainment, does not differ from the question in dispute; in this matter both parties are equally doubtful; such a hetu is tautological.

The example of this fallacy is as follows: Sound is non-eternal (=proposition) because we do not find in it the properties of eternal things and equally in objects (like a jar), no properties of eternal things have been found (=hetu).

When a property that is admitted to be common by both parties is put forward as the hetu, it is the cause of doubt; such a hetu, which is 'equal to doubt' (*saṃśayasama*), is normally known as *savyabhicāra* (i.e. it is the cause of the fallacy of the inconclusive hetu). But in the fallacy of the tautological hetu, what gives rise to the question in dispute is only that specific form of doubt which consists in the fact that there is nothing which can favour either of the two parties (NBh I. 2.7).

This hetu, it is objected, is in no way different from the unestablished hetu (*sādhyasama*). The non-perception of the properties of the non-eternal thing in sound is as much to be established as the eternality itself. And this is exactly what the *sādhyasama* fallacy stipulates. This objection, says Uddyotakara, is not valid. In the fallacy of the tautological hetu what is put forward as the hetu is that which only gives rise to a specific form of doubt, while in the *sādhyasama* the property that is put forward as hetu is as much to be proved as the proposition itself. Thus both the hetu and the proposition are on the same footing.

Another objection that is raised against this fallacy is that it is the same as the inconclusive hetu. In that case we might as well say that there is no difference between the perception, the inconclusive hetu and the tautological hetu, as perception is also a cause of doubt.

The difference between the two fallacies is this: in the tautological hetu the property that is put forward as the hetu is one of two contrary properties, both of which are equally unperceived, that is to say, when both the distinguishing properties of a thing are equally non-perceived, if one of them is put forward for the removing of the doubt, it is a case of the tautological hetu; this means that it is not possible to indicate the non-perception of both distinguishing properties as a fallacious hetu of this kind.

According to some philosophers the property of being different from the body when put forward to establish the eternality of the *ātman* is an example of the tautological hetu. This, says Uddyotakara, is not right. Even if the *ātman* were different from the body, this by itself would not prove its existence. What would prove it is that it is known by the characteristic through which it manifests itself. Therefore the hetu being different from the body is inconclusive (*savyabhicāra*) (NV I. 2,7).

(4) *The fallacy of the unproved hetu* (*sādhyasama*)

According to Gautama the fallacy of the unproved hetu occurs when the hetu itself is in need of proving (i.e. it should really function as a probandum (NS I. 2,8).[15]

Vātsyāyana explains the fallacy: In the reasoning — 'Shadow is a substance (=probandum) because it has motion (=hetu) — the hetu does not differ in its function from the probandum because it, like the probandum, is itself in need of proving. Motion as a proof for the shadow is inadequate because the motion of the shadow depends upon the continuity of the obstruction of light or of the movement of the object obstructing the light (NBh I. 2,8).

According to Uddyotakara, the hetu which is in need of proving is of three kinds: (a) That which is exactly similar to the property to be known by it (*prajñāpanīyadharmasamāna*), (b) that whose basis is unestablished (*āśrayāsiddha*), and (c) that which is otherwise established (*anyathāsiddha*). The argument — 'shadow is a substance because it moves'— illustrates the three kinds of the hetu which is yet to be proved as follows: (a) The motion of the shadow is as much in need of proof as its being a substance. (b) Shadow could be regarded as moving only if it could function like a material substance, e.g. a jar. But this is not so. (c) The movement of the shadow can be explained as absence of light caused by an obstruction or a moving object. It is the absence of light which constitutes the shadow (NV I. 2,8).

(5) *The fallacy of the mistimed hetu* (*kālātīta*)

According to Gautama the fallacy of the mistimed hetu (*kālātīta*) occurs when the hetu is adduced at the time when it is not relevant (NS I. 2,9).[16]

Vātsyāyana explains the fallacy as follows: When one part or factor of the thing adduced as hetu is found to be affected by lapse of time, it is said to be adduced at the time when it is not relevant; it is the mistimed hetu.

The example of this fallacy is the following reasoning of an opponent: 'Sound is eternal (=proposition) because it is manifested by a conjunction of the drum and the stick (=hetu), like colour; the colour that is manifested by the conjunction of light with the jar is one that was in existence before, as well as after, its manifestation; similarly, the sound also that is manifested by the conjunction of the drum and the stick, or by the conjunction of the wood and the axe, is one that is in existence before and after its manifestation; so that, being manifested by conjunction, sound must be regarded as eternal'.

This is not a correct hetu, says Vātsyāyana, because when adduced, it is mistimed. In the case of colour, the time at which the manifesting conjunction appears does not go beyond the time at which the manifested colour exists; for it is only during the time at which the conjunction of the light and the jar is present that the colour is perceived; but the colour is not perceived when the conjunction has ceased to exist. The case of sound, however, is different; for instance, it is only after the conjunction of the drum and the stick has ceased that sound is heard by the man at a distance; in fact it is heard at the time of the disjunction (i.e. at the time that the stick has ceased to touch the drum) so that the manifestation of sound is beyond the time of that conjunction; as such it cannot be caused by that conjunction; for as a rule, when the cause has ceased to exist, the effect does not appear (so that if conjunction were the cause of the manifestation of sound, the latter should cease after the former has ceased).

Thus, then, says Vātsyāyana, it is found that what is adduced as the hetu is not 'similar to the example'. It cannot therefore prove what is to be established; it is fallacious.

The definition of the fallacy as given by Gautama, says

Vātsyāyana, does not mean that 'mistiming' consists in the reversing of the order of the members of the reasoning. This interpretation is not right for the following reason: When one thing is connected with another thing, the connection subsists even when they are remote from one another; mere proximity between two things will not function as a cause when they do not possess the capacity for action. According to this law, even when the hetu is stated in an order other than the usual one, it does not lose its character of the hetu, which consists in its similarity or dissimilarity to the example. So long as it does not lose this character, it cannot be called a fallacy. Further, according to Gautama when the order of the members is reversed, it is one of the deficiencies under the sixteenth category (NBh I. 2,9).

In his comment on the reasoning — 'Sound is eternal, because it is manifested by conjunction of two things' — Uddyotakara considers an objection : The hetu — 'because it is manifested by conjunction of two things' — is none other than *anaikāntika* (i.e. the fallacy of the inconclusive hetu), as it has been found that non-eternal things also are manifested; for example, a jar (which is manifested by the conjunction of light).

This contention, says Uddyotakara, has no force. In the reasoning cited what is meant to be proved by 'manifestation by conjunction of two things' is only continuity of existence; that is to say, what is meant by the proposition is not that sound is eternal, but that it continues to exist; so that the hetu cannot be said to be *anaikāntika*; for nothing that does not continue to exist is ever found to be manifested by conjunction; and if it were so found, then alone the hetu would be *anaikāntika*.

Regarding the reversal of the order of the members of reasoning, Uddyotakara endorses the view of Vātsyāyana. The power of these members is such that just because a hetu is stated last after the other members, it does not lose the character of the hetu, which consists in 'similarity to the example'; and so long as it retains this character, it cannot be called a fallacy (NV I. 2,9).

12

DISPUTATION (*tarka*)

According to Gautama, disputation, which is the eighth category, is "that deliberation which serves, on the basis of causes, the purpose of cognizing the true nature of a thing is not known" (NS I. 1,40). Vātsyāyana explains the category: When a man does not know the true nature of a thing, he desires to know it and expresses his desire in the form "I would like to know the true nature of the thing." After this he has doubt as to whether the thing in question has one or the other of two incompatible properties and he expresses the doubt in the form: "Is this thing so or is it not so" ? He ponders over these two properties, and if he finds causes leading to one of them, he gives assent to it; his assent is expressed in the form: "a cause, a pramāṇa and a hetu are possible in favour of the property (to which the assent is being given); since there is a cause leading to the property, the thing must have this property, and not the other" (NBh I. 1,40).

Disputation is neither included under any of the four pramāṇas nor is it an independent pramāṇa. It has, however, been mentioned as a separate category, says Vātsyāyana, because it helps the pramāṇas in their operation. In discussion objects which are cognized by means of pramāṇas are questioned and this creates doubt about them. In this situation the technique of disputation enables us to test the validity of arguments and counter-arguments and remove misconceptions. Our confidence in the efficacy of the pramāṇas is again restored and what we had already known by means of the pramāṇas is confirmed. That is why Gautama says that disputation is meant to serve the purpose of attaining the knowledge of the true nature of things (NBh I. 1,1 & 40).

Uddyotakara examines the following objections raised against the category of disputation. According to some philosophers disputation is not different from the categories of doubt and ascertainment. These philosophers have been misled, says

Uddyotakara, by the fact that in these three categories we are concerned with objects whose true nature is not known. But the real point is that each of these three categories yields a different kind of cognition. Doubtful cognition is in the form of uncertainty — 'is it so or is it not so' ? Cognition resulting from ascertainment is of the very nature of determination — 'it is so'. The cognition that disputation yields is different from both these cognitions. On the one hand, it lacks the uncertainty of doubtful cognition, because the causal explanation is available; on the other hand, it lacks the certitude of ascertainment, because it does not provide the knowledge of the specific features of the object which it examines. The cognition resulting from disputation is therefore in the form of 'it may be so'. It is this absence of the recognition of the specific features of an object that marks out disputation from inference. Some philosophers hold that disputation is only a form of inference. In inference it is necessary to have recollection of the relationship between the object and its mark and also the assertion that the mark subsists in the object. But in disputation we are aware only of the object without a mark and, consequently, there is no question of any such recollection as is involved in inference. Further, it is necessary in inference to assert that the property subsists in the object, but this is not essential in the case of disputation. For instance, we say: 'There should be a human agent here, because here we find horses being driven'. What we cognise in this case is the property of being driven and not that it subsists in the subject, 'the human agent'. This argument serves the sole purpose of precluding the possibility of the agent being merely a post, and proceeds on the basis of the cognition of a property belonging to something other than the subject of inference, the human agent (NV I. 1,40).

Vātsyāyana illustrates the technique of disputation with the following two examples:

(a) *Birth*

There is doubt as to whether the birth of man is produced by a cause that is itself caused or by a cause that is uncaused. This doubt provides an occasion for resorting to disputation based upon the consideration of possible causes as follows: If the birth is brought about by a cause that is itself caused, then on the disappearance of the cause there would be cessation of the birth. Such a cause is liable to cease and when it has ceased, its effect, i.e., birth, should also cease. If, however, the birth is brought about by an uncaused cause, there would be no cessation of birth; for the uncaused cause can never cease to exist. Lastly, if the birth is produced by an accident (i.e., without cause), it would never cease to exist; hence there could be no cause for its cessation.

When this object of disputation, i.e., the birth, is cognized by means of pramāṇas, it is karma that is recognized as its cause (*nimitta*). The technique of disputation as applied to this object helps in the analysis of this object and thus confirms our cognition of its true nature (NBh I. 1,1).

According to Uddyotakara, our knowledge of the birth as due to Karma[1] is based upon the diversity of conditions,[2] good and bad. This diversity in the conditions of living beings is not possible unless there is a concomitant diversity of causes; such causes must be non-eternal and specific to each individual object and to each individual *ātmán*. The material elements cannot explain this diversity of conditions because they are common to all living beings; they cannot provide specific causes for specific effects. In fact, we do find that a specific effect is determined by a specific cause. We observe that specific conditions of living beings are determined by specific causes according to a rule; therefore the different conditions of different beings are determined by their respective karmas. Thus the diversity of birth is due to karma (NV I. 1,1).

(b) *Cognizer*

Regarding the cognizer, there is first the desire to know his real quality. This is followed by doubt as to whether he has the property of being a product or a property of not being a producer. The technique of disputation is then applied as follows: *Saṃsāra* and release would be possible for the cognizer only if he had the property of not being produced. As mentioned by Gautama in NS I. 1,2, the former consists in the successive appearance of pain, birth, activity, defect and misapprehension and in this process that which follows is the cause of that which precedes it; and release consists in the successive cessation of these in the reverse order. If the cognizer had the property of being produced, neither *saṃsāra* nor release would be possible for him. In that case the cognizer would be connected with a particular set of body, sense-organs, intellect and sensation only when he came into existence for the first time; and this would mean that the set he has acquired is not a product of his own previous actions. Further, since whatever comes into existence ceases to exist, the cognizer having come into existence would cease to exist; and this would mean that he is not available to experience the fruits of his own actions. Thus either the cognizer would not be able to have more than one body or he would not be able to separate himself from any body at all. This disputation removes misconception about the cognizer and enables us to give assent to a property for which we can find an appropriate explanation (or a cause). Obviously, the right conclusion which can explain both *saṃsāra* and release is that the cognizer has the property of not being produced (NBh I, 1,40).

13

ASCERTAINMENT (*nirṇaya*)

Ascertainment, which is the ninth category, is defined by Gautama as "determination of an object after deliberation over a view and a counter-view" (NS I. 1,41). Vātsyāyana explains the category: Ascertainment operates with reference to the object of disputation. It constitutes that knowledge of the true nature of a thing which is the fruit of pramāṇas; it is the culmination of all discussion which is conducted with the help of rejoinder and cavil. Disputation and ascertainment are the two categories involved in the conduct of all wordly business. And it is for this reason that though ascertainment is really included under the category of the object of cognition (*prameya*), Gautama has given it an independent category status (NBh I. 1,1).

According to Uddyotakara, ascertainment is sometimes the fruit of pramāṇa when it is not put forward as an instrument or means of acquiring the cognition of another object; it sometimes is a means of cognition when it leads to the cognition of something else. In fact, there is no hard and fast rule that a thing must be either a means or an outcome; it can be both (NV I. 1.1).

According to Vātsyāyana, the definition of ascertainment as that cognition which follows deliberation over two sides of a question is obviously not meant to cover all kinds of ascertainment. In discussion and scripture there is no room for ascertainment. In the former disputants are convinced of their respective positions; in the latter things are settled by reference to the scripture itself. It is only when an object of disputation is under investigation that there can be any deliberation over two sides of a question; and it is the ascertainment which follows such deliberation that constitutes the ninth category (NBh I. 1,41 also NV I. 1,41).

It is argued that the cognition which ascertainment yields is the same as the inferential cognition. Uddyotakara rejects this view on the following grounds. Inference requires the recollection of the relationship between the hetu and the probandum while the cognition resulting from ascertainment does not depend upon any such recollection. While the former is an instrument of cognition the latter is an effect, i.e. cognition itself produced by the instruments of cognition. In inference we have a definitive cognition, say of smoke, and this functions as an instrument for another cognition, i.e., cognition of fire; this is what constitutes inferential cognition. But in the case of ascertainment the cognition is of its own object and not something else (NV I. 1,41).

Explaining the definition of ascertainment, Vātsyāyana says: On any matter in dispute we have two opposite views: one seeking to establish the thing under investigation and the other seeking to disprove it. Arguments are advanced in favour of a particular view and against it. When such arguments are put forward side by side, the arguments in favour of the view are known as 'pakṣa'; the arguments against it are called '*pratipakṣa*'. It is necessary that one of these two should be proved and when it is proved, this proof is called ascertainment with reference to it.

It is argued that ascertainment is not possible in the manner envisaged above. In any discussion both disputants are equally convinced of their respective positions; there is no element of doubt in their minds. What happens in the course of discussion is: at first, one of the two disputants states a view, supports it with reasons (hetu) and rejects the objections of the second disputant. The second disputant then refutes the reasons put forward by the former in support of his view and also answers the objections raised against his own reasons. This process goes on until one set of reasons stops; where one has stopped, the other is regarded as established. It is by means of this latter set of reasons alone that the true nature of the thing in dispute can be said to have been determined; this is what constitutes ascertainment.

Vātsyāyana replies that it is only when we recognize both the possibility and the impossibility of the respective hetus that our doubt regarding the true nature of the thing in dispute can be set aside; otherwise the uncertainty continues (NBh I. 1,41).

In this connection Uddyotakara observes that if neither or both sets of arguments were rejected, doubt would not cease. It is only when one set is rejected and the other remains unshaken that doubt disappears and definite cognition arrives. That is why both the sets function jointly as the means of definitive cognition. It may be asked: At what precise stage in the deliberation does definitive cognition arrive ? Is it at the first stage when the arguments in favour of a certain view are put forward, or at the second stage when the arguments are advanced against it, or at the third stage when these arguments are answered ? Uddyotakara's reply is that while the cognition may arrive at any stage, it is more correct to say that it arrives at the third stage. When a person puts forward an argument in favour of a view, the opponent might do one of two things: if he recognizes the force of these arguments, he will not argue further; if he finds them fallacious, he will put forward arguments to refute the view. At this stage the former person either does not offer fruitless arguments if he finds his opponent's arguments sound; or, if he finds that the defects which the opponent has indicated in his arguments are not real defects, then he proceeds to point this out to his opponent; at this stage, the arguments that were urged against the first view are set aside and consequently the arguments advanced in favour of the second view are also set aside; this is the moment when definitive cognition arrives (NV I. 1,41).

The deliberation that leads to ascertainment in such matters in dispute consists in illuminating the two sides to the question and thus providing an opportunity for reasoning (*nyāya*) to operate. What Gautama has in view in this context, says Vātsyāyana, is the incompatible properties which are predicated of one and the same thing. It is quite possible that such incompatible properties may belong to similar things; if investigation does reveal such a state of affairs, it must be accepted. For instance, substance is described as that which has motion. Some substances have motion while others are incapable of motion. In such a case both views — substance has motion and substance has no motion — are quite possible. Two incompatible properties may be predicated even of the same thing if there is a clear option with regard to the time when it may or may not have such properties. For instance, the same substances may be said to have motion when it actually moves; and not to have motion at another time when it is either not moving or has stopped moving (NBh I. 1,41).

PART FOUR : TECHNIQUE OF REFUTATION

14

DISCOURSE (*kathā*)

Discussion (vāda), *Rejoinder* (jalpa) *and Cavil* (vitaṇḍā)

The tenth, eleventh and twelfth categories in Gautama's list are discussion, rejoinder and cavil. He defines them as follows:

(1) Discussion consists in the putting forward (by two persons) of a view and a counter-view, in which there is supporting and refuting by means of pramāṇas and disputations — neither of which is opposed to the established tenet, and both of which are carried on in full accordance with the five *avayavas* (NS I. 2.1).

(2) Rejoinder is that which is endowed with the said characteristics and in which there is supporting and refuting by means of quibbles, legitimate objections and deficiencies (NS I. 2,2).

(3) Cavil is that kind of rejoinder where the counter-view is not properly established (NS I. 2,3).

According to Vātsyāyana, these three categories are three kinds of discourse (*kathā*). Gautama has mentioned discussion as a separate category in order to indicate its distinctive features: so that when discussion is conducted in accordance with these features, it leads to the ascertaimnent of the true nature of things. Rejoinder and cavil are mentioned separately because they protect the knowledge of the nature of things acquired through discussion (NBh I. 1,1).

Discussion

According to Vātsyāyana, discussion consists in a number of statements put forward by various speakers, purporting to be reasons in support of various views, leading ultimately to the ascertainment of one of them as true (NBh I. 1,1).

When two contrary properties are said to subsist in the same substratum, they are called *pakṣa* (view) and *pratipakṣa* (counter-view), being, as they are, like opponents to each other; e.g.

ātman exists and *ātman* does not exist. But when the contrary properties are said to subsist in different substrata, they are not called pakṣa and *pratipakṣa*; e.g. *ātman* is eternal and *buddhi* is non-eternal.

A distinctive feature of discussion is that both the view and the counter-view are supported and refuted by means of the pramāṇas and disputations. To support is to establish and to refute is to deny or reject. Both the supporting and refuting are done in a connected or systematic manner until one of the two — the view and the counterview — is proved and the other disproved; what is proved is then accepted and what is disproved is rejected.

As a rule, deficiencies are employed in rejoinder, so that they should normally be excluded from discussion. This is generally so, but the use of some of them is mentioned. This is what is meant by the qualification, 'not opposed to the established tenet'[1] mentioned by Gautama. For instance, the fallacy of contradictory (*viruddha*) hetu can be used in discussion. Similarly, the qualification regarding the use of the five *avayavas* is meant to indicate that the use of the irrelevancy, deficiency and redundancy, are permitted in discussion.

Although the pramāṇas and disputations are reflected in the *avayavas*, Gautama has mentioned these two conditions separately. The justification for this is: (a) The pramāṇas and disputations employed by the two parties to a discussion should be inter-connected. There can be no discussion if both parties go on producing arguments which are meant only to support their own respective views, without having any bearing upon the position of the other person. (b) In some cases there can be genuine discussion if only the pramāṇas and not the five *avayavas* are employed; for such pramāṇas can lead to the ascertainment of the true nature of things. (c) The definition of rejoinder may create the impression that whenever supporting and refuting are done only by means of quibbles, legitimate objections and deficiencies, this is always rejoinder; whereas if these are done by means of pramāṇas and disputation, this always constitutes discussion. In fact, deficiencies employed in rejoinder can be used in discussion and *vice versa*. The present condition is meant to prevent this misunderstanding (NBh I. 2,1).

According to Uddyotakara, discourse is a term much wider in scope than the three categories. The threefold discourse mentioned by Gautama is concerned with the investigation into the nature of things — investigation which is carried on by means of controversy between two parties. There is discussion when an honest seeker after truth enters into a debate with his teacher and other friends; such a person has three purposes: to know what he did not know, to remove his doubts and to obtain confirmation of what he knows. The teacher in such a case has to give arguments and explanations until that person acquires the knowledge that he is seeking. Naturally, there is no room for employment of such devices as deficiencies in a friendly discussion. Rejoinder and cavil, on the other hand, are that kind of discourse which is held with ignorant persons only anxious to obtain a victory. It is therefore quite in order to use every deficiency in other forms of controversy, e.g. rejoinder (NV I. 1,1 & I. 2,1).

In discussion, disputation (*tarka*) functions as an auxiliary, for the purpose of supporting and refuting, to the pramāṇas. It helps in the investigation of the true nature of things on which the pramāṇas operate; it is not an instrument (*karaṇa*) of supporting and condemning. What is supported is the view, and what is refuted is the counter-view. But what is really refuted, says Uddyotakara, is the man who is found out or defeated. When a man describes a thing wrongly, he is defeated; so is the man who fails to understand the thing as presented to him. Misunderstanding is a property of the man, and when a counter-view is said to be refuted, it is the man who is condemned. Neither the object nor the instrument of any such operation can be condemned, because each is efficient in its own sphere. If these are found inefficient in a sphere which is not their own, the fault lies not with them but with the man who makes wrong use of them (NV I. 2,1).

Uddyotakara mentions the following definition of discussion attributed to the Buddhist philosopher, whom he names in this context Subandhu (generally known as Vasubandhu)[2] in his *Vādavidhi* in the light of the explanation given in a commentary on that work.

> "Discussion is a discourse for the purpose of proving and disproving one's own and another's views respectively (*svaparapakṣasiddhyasiddhyarthaṃ vacanaṃ vādaḥ*)."

In what follows a brief account of his criticism is given. Grammatical or exegetic comments have been omitted wherever they do not have any direct bearing on the main argument.

The terms *sva* (one's own) and *para* (another's) can be interpreted in six different ways and none of them, says Uddyotakara, can provide a satisfactory explanation in the present context. (a) If *sva* implies possessing and *para* discarding, we cannot ascertain of whom or what it is the possessing or discarding. The Buddhist says that possessing means 'making one's own' so that it would be *sva* for the man who makes it his own. When a man has the idea of 'mine' with regard to something, that is his *sva*; when he has no grounds for such an idea with regard to a thing, then that thing is *para* for him. Uddyotakara replies that this explanation is not satisfactory. In the first place, such an explanation may do for an ordinary man but not for the philosopher. Secondly, a possession always provides some benefit to its owner but the upholder of a theory cannot be said to have benefited from his theory. (b) If *sva* implies what is to be proved and *para* what is to be refuted, this would imply that one has to prove one's own view and criticize another's. There are several objections to this interpretation:

(i) The Buddhist defines *pakṣa* as that which is intended to be proved. If *sva* also means the same, we have two words saying the same thing. (ii) The phrases *svapakṣa* and *prarapakṣa* are used only for the purpose of differentiation. The *pakṣa* that is qualified by *sva* cannot be regarded as the *pakṣa* that is qualified by *para*; and if the *pakṣa* in both the phrases is the same, the qualification is useless. If the Buddhist says that a general term can denote a particular thing, Uddyotakara replies that a term that denotes a particular thing can never function as a general term; such a term is always restricted in its application because of its context and other circumstances. (iii) According to the Buddhist *pakṣa* is that which is intended to be proved. It may therefore be correct to describe it as *svapakṣa*, but criticism can have nothing to do with any *pakṣa* itself, as this is something yet to be proved. Even after effective criticism has been made of *parapakṣa*, it remains a *pakṣa* all the same. To say that the view to be proved is *svapakṣa* and the view to be criticised is *parapakṣa* makes no sense.

It may be asked: what, then, is the object of criticism ?

Uddyotakara answers: in some cases it is the object that is to be proved; in some cases the criticism is connected with one's own view or the view of another person. The proof (*sthāpanā*) is the verbal expression of five *avayavas* put forward in support of a *pakṣa*. When such a proof is fallacious and the fallacies are pointed out, the proof is the actual object of criticism. In the course of discussion other criticisms can be made — criticisms not connected with proof, one's own view or another's; e.g. legitimate objections or deficiencies.

The Buddhist argues that even though the criticism aimed at the proof of the *parapakṣa* does not wipe out of existence the *pakṣa* itself, it does serve to reject the proof for that *parapakṣa*, so that it is quite correct to say that it 'discredits', 'impairs' or 'damages' that view and hence the criticism is the criticism of the *pakṣa* in the indirect sense. Uddyotakara rejects this Buddhist argument on the ground that since the definition is meant to determine the true nature of a thing, figurative or indirect expressions have no place in it; the signification of such expressions is indeterminate.

(c) If the phrase *svapakṣa* means the earlier or wrong view and *parapakṣa* the later or right view, this interpretation would go against the Buddhist statement: All the proving should bear upon one's own view and all the criticism should bear upon another's view and not *vice versa*.

On similar grounds *svapakṣa* cannot be interpreted as a certain or first view nor can *parapakṣa* mean the contrary or second view. (d) The Buddhist offers an interpretation which is not disagreeable to Uddyotakara: *savpakṣa* and *parapakṣa* are applied to one and the same *pakṣa*; when the *pakṣa* is qualified as 'probandum', it is called *svapakṣa*; when it is qualified as 'refutable', it is called *parapakṣa*. Thus one and the same thing can have two distinguishing properties. But, then, the Buddhist should not use the dual number in the phrase *svaparapakṣayoḥ*. As a rule, when one and the same thing has several qualifications, it does not take the dual or plural number; when one observes Devadatta with an umbrella and a stick, one does not speak of him: two men, with stick and umbrella, have come. The Buddhist uses the compound *svaparapakṣa* which cannot be explained grammatically consistent with the requirements he has in view. And yet compounding of words is desirable because it leads to the economy of syllables. A treatise (*śāstra*) meant for the instruction of pupils must always economize in syllables, as that gives it brevity.

The expression '*siddhyasiddhyartham*' used by the Buddhist creates several difficulties. The word *siddhi* (proving) can mean either *utpatti* (production) or *vyakti* (manifestation). The five *avayavas* are regarded as the means of proving. They cannot be said to produce anything, because they only bring to light what already exists. But the Buddhist cannot say that *siddhi* means manifestation, as such manifestation has no proper locus. For, according to him, the umpire who is in charge of discussion is the person who receives the proofs and is convinced by them.

If the conviction is one of the umpire, we cannot say that it is a view which is proved or disproved. The view can be either something established or something yet to be established. In the former case the establishing cannot be said to consist in the convincing of the umpire; in fact, we should say that his conviction follows from the fact that a thing is as it is represented to be by the view. But the thing is ascertained to be as it is represented to be by the view only when the pramāṇas are employed. It is not therefore correct to say that the view under discussion is something already established. If, on the other hand, the view is not something established at the time when the thing is to be ascertained by the pramāṇas, then discussion is futile; for the umpire is already convinced.

There are similar difficulties in explaining what the disproving of a view really means. The Buddhist says that the criticism directly sets aside the proving of a view; it can therefore be said to set aside the view itself in an indirect or figurative sense. Figurative expressions as a contrivance, says Uddyotakara, may be useful in explaining popular parlance, but they cannot determine the true nature of a thing. And this is important in a definition. The Buddhist suggests that the disproving of a view may be said to consist in its not making known the object of that view and thus in its failing to convince. Like the previous suggestion, this is open to the same objection.

The word '*artha*' cannot be given any satisfactory interpretation in the context of the definition. It has generally three meanings, (a) aim or benefit (*uddeśa*), (b) objective (*prayojana*), and (c) meaning (*abhidheya*). (a) The Buddhist characterizes *svapakṣa* as appropriate and *parapakṣa* as inappropriate. This cannot be regarded as satisfactory. Moreover, seeming proof cannot be described as appropriate and seeming criticism as nappropriate. Appropriateness consists in being supported by proofs, and not by inappropriateness, in being open to criticism and not to seeming criticism. If, however, the former means that a thing really exists as the view represents it to be, and the latter means that a thing does not exist as it is represented to be by the view, then the thing is an object of cognition. What is an object of cognition cannot constitute conviction. This contradicts the Buddhist view that the aim of discussion is to convince the umpire. (b) *Artha* cannot mean objective because proving and disproving cannot be the purpose of offering seeming proof and seeming criticism. One who enters into a serious discussion would offer genuine proofs and genuine criticisms. (c) Neither the author of the definition nor his commentator has given a satisfactory explanation of what constitutes proving (*siddhi*) and disproving (*asiddhi*). All that he says is: what is capable of proving and of not proving; this amounts to reducing discussion to a purposeless quibble.

The explanation of the Buddhist definition offered by the commentator is equally unsatisfactory. He adds *yuktāyuktayoḥ* (appropriate and inappropriate) as qualification to *svaparapakṣayoḥ* in the original definition. What do appropriateness and inappropriateness consist in ? (a) Proof and criticism, or (b) connection with proof and criticism, or (c) the fact that a thing is or is not as it is represented to be. (a) According to the Buddhist appropriateness and inappropriateness are due to proof and criticism. This implies that they are different from the latter. (b) Proof implies the existence of that which is to be proved, and criticism implies the existence of that which vitiates what is to be criticized. But since the Buddhist does not recognize the reality of things, the question of connection with proof or criticism does not arise. (c) If appropriateness and inappropriateness consist in a thing being and not being as represented to be by a view, then these are things to be determined, i.e. they are objects of cognition. What is an object (*karma*) cannot be an instrument (*karaṇa*).

The Buddhist maintains that the purpose of discussion is to

convince the umpire.[3] The commentator has composed his work to state a correct view and remove all doubts or misconceptions. Obviously, the umpire who knows the treatise needs no convincing through discussion. It is true that people do enter into some kind of discussion with mixed motives such as reward, honour, fame, desire to prove their own view at all costs; such discussions can even develop into brawls. But this is not what Gautama means by discussion.

Even if there is an umpire, what useful rôle could he have in a discussion ? The umpire is known as *adhikaraṇa*, which means that he is a locus or receptacle (*ādhāra*). Conviction cannot subsist in the umpire, because its proper concern (i.e. abode) is with the view under discussion. Moreover, it is not necessary that in every discussion there should be an umpire, e.g. the discussion between a guru and his pupils. A discussion involves investigation, discernment of real proof or criticism from seeming proof or criticism, or establishment of a thing as it is. Both parties in a discussion are in fact entitled to prove or disprove; consequently there is no useful function for the umpire left (NV I.2,1).

Rejoinder

Explaining rejoinder, Vātsyāyana says that it has all the features of discussion; its distinctive feature is that the supporting and refuting are done not only by means of the pramāṇas and disputations but also by means of quibbles, legitimate objections and deficiencies. In the definitions of these latter Gautama states that they serve the purpose of opposing counter-views. They never, by themselves, serve as the means of supporting a view but are employed only as auxiliaries. When one's own view has been supported by means of the pramāṇas, they are useful for guarding the view. And this they do by attacking or opposing the counter-view. Similarly, when a person refutes a counter-view by means of the pramāṇas, they are useful in guarding this refutation from the attacks that might be made upon it. As Gautama has declared, rejoinder and cavil serve the purpose of safeguarding the determination of the true nature of things—just as the fencing of thorny boughs serves the purpose of safeguarding the sprouting seeds (NS IV. 2,50). However, they do function as independent means of refuting but not of supporting in rejoinder (NBH I. 2,2).

Cavil

Explaining cavil, Vātsyāyana says that the rejoinder becomes cavil when there is no attempt to establish the counter-view. A person who resorts to cavil does not seek to establish the view he puts forward but only criticizes the view of the other person. But on this ground it would not be correct to say that in rejoinder there is no counter-view. The statement that the person makes in attacking his opponent's view really constitutes his own view; it is stated only in the form of an attack on his opponent without any attempt to prove his view (NBh I. 2,3).

15

QUIBBLE (*chala*)

The fourteenth category 'quibble' is defined by Gautama as "opposition to a statement based on the assumption of an alternative meaning" (NS I. 2,10).

According to Gautama there are three kinds of quibble: quibble concerning a word (*vākchala*), quibble concerning a universal (*sāmānyachala*) and quibble concerning a metaphor (*upacārachala*) (NS I. 2,11).

The quibble in respect of a word, says Gautama, consists in "assuming a meaning other than that intended by a speaker who has not specified his meaning" (NS I. 2,12). Vātsyāyana explains: For instance, a speaker says: "*navakaṃbalo 'yaṃ māṇavakaḥ*". The compound '*navakaṃbala*' used by him can be explained either as one "who has a new blanket or one who has nine blankets". The speaker intended the compound to be taken in the former sense, but the opponent takes it in the latter sense and says: "This boy has only one blanket, where are the nine blankets ?" Thereupon the speaker should ask the opponent to give his specific reasons for assigning a meaning to the compound other than that he wished to convey. Since no such reasons can be given, the attack on the statement is unjustified. Further, there is a well known convention in the world regarding words and their meanings. A general word has a general meaning and a specific word has a specific meaning. Words are used in the sense in which they have been used before. They are used only to convey the meanings they are known to have, so that they can produce appropriate cognition of these meanings and appropriate action on the basis of that cognition. For instance, when a speaker says 'feed the Brahmin', it is clearly understood that although the term 'Brahmin' refers to all the individuals belonging to that class, only a few specially indicated have to be fed (NBh I. 2,12).

According to Uddyotakara, quibble arises not only when a sentence is misunderstood but also when a word is misinterpreted. For instance, the word '*aśvaḥ*' is both a noun and a verb; as a noun it means a horse and as a verb 'you have eaten'. The misunderstanding arises when the context in which words or sentences are used is ignored.

Whether the opponent attacks the speaker's statement knowingly or unknowingly, it is highly improper. If he knows the intention of the speaker and yet attacks the latter, he is open to the deficiency '*arthāntara*'; if he is opposing without knowing the intended meaning, he is guilty of ignorance (NV I. 2,12).

According to Gautama, the quibble in respect of a universal arises: "When a thing is possible, it is assumed to be impossible on the ground that it belongs to a universal which is very wide" (NS I. 2,13).Vātsyāyana explains: For instance, a man says: "Oh, this Brahmin is endowed with learning and character"; another man replies: "Learning and character are quite possible in a Brahmin". Thereupon the opponent attacks the latter statement in the form: "If learning and character are possible in a Brahmin, then they should also be possible in the case of a Brahmin who is delinquent". The quibble should be answered by saying that the intention of the second person in making the statement was merely to praise the particular Brahmin as having learning and character and not to give a justification (NBh I. 2,13).

According to Gautama, the quibble in respect of a metaphor consists in "denying the proper meaning of a word by taking it literally when it is used in a secondary sense" (NS I. 2,14). This quibble, says Gautama, is different from the word-quibble even though there is some similarity between them (NS I. 2,15-17).

Vātsyāyana explains: One of the properties of a word is its use according to the thing it denotes. The other property is its use in a secondary sense. The secondary meaning is indicated by such causes as association. This is what is called '*upacāra*'. For instance, when the statement, 'the scaffoldings are crying' is made, it is made on the basis that the word 'scaffoldings' is to be taken in the secondary sense of men on the scaffoldings. It is denied on the basis of the primary meaning of that word in the form: 'it is the men on the scaffoldings who are crying', and not the scaffoldings themselves. This constitutes the quibble in respect of a metaphor.

This quibble is answered: It is well known in ordinary usage that a word may be used in a primary or secondary sense; it should be understood in the sense in which it has been actually used. When any statement is made, it follows that confirmation or denial of that statement should be made in accordance with the intention of the speaker and not arbitrarily. Since in the instance mentioned above, the denial is purely arbitrary, it cannot be treated as a genuine opposition to the speaker (NBh I. 2,14).

16

LEGITIMATE OBJECTION (*jāti*)

According to Vātsyāyana the last three categories, viz. quibble, legitimate objection and deficiency, have been separately enunciated by Gautama in order to indicate their true character. It is only when their true character is clearly shown and understood that one can avoid them in one's own arguments and use them effectively to demolish the counter-arguments of one's opponent. The knowledge and understanding of this category of legitimate objection is thus essential for vindication of one's own position (NBh I. 1,1).

"Legitimate objection", says Gautama, "is that opposition which is based on mere similarity or dissimilarity" (NS I. 2,18). Vātsyāyana explains: When a hetu has been stated, the objection to it that follows is called 'legitimate objection'. This objection is of the nature of opposition, attack or denial made on the basis of similarity and dissimilarity. When the hetu is intended to prove the proposition through its similarity to the example, an objection is raised on the basis of its dissimilarity to that example. When the hetu is intended to prove the proposition through its dissimilarity to the example, an objection is taken on the basis of its similarity to that example. Such objections constitute 'legitimate objection'. They are called '*jāti*' because they are born as opponents to the original reasoning (NBh I. 2,18).

According to Uddyotakara, it is not right to restrict the scope of legitimate objection to objections raised on the basis of similarity and dissimilarity to the example. The similarity and dissimilarity may be to anything whatsoever. The legitimate objection, he says, is that hetu which is set up against the hetu to be proved but which is incapable of refuting it. The names of the various legitimate objection contain the suffix *sama* (balancing) which indicates that they are meant to balance or equalize the original argument. This equalizing may or may not be successful, but the man who puts forward a legitimate objection does so with the intention of equalizing. This is just like a man who makes efforts for the sake of his family but he may or may not be successful. Another way to look upon this equalizing function is that the legitimate objection is intended to show that both the argument and counter-argument are on the same footing; there is no special reason why either should be regarded as capable of being proved. But in no circumstances it should be understood that there is equality between the proponent of the original argument and the proponent of the legitimate objection; the former may be right or wrong but the view of the latter is always wrong. It should also be noted that a legitimate objection cannot be raised against all arguments.

The counter-argument envisaged under this category is undoubtedly a wrong argument, but it can serve a useful purpose. It can be used with force against others. It may even be used to refute a right argument. For instance, the proponent of an argument may be inclined to think that the reasoning used against him is sound, and yet being anxious to obtain wealth, honour or fame, he sets up a futile counter-argument. His motive in resorting to such a course is to confuse his opponent and, if he cannot obtain a total victory, at least to render the issue doubtful.

According to some philosophers, counter-arguments are useful in refuting unsound arguments. When a person puts forward an unsound argument it may not be possible to find a flaw in the argument, or, one may wish to place that person in an impossible position: "if my rejoinder is defective, so is yours; so that if your argument is right, so is mine". This view, says Uddyotakara, is not right. If the argument is unsound, one should naturally proceed to point out the flaw which one has detected in it. If, on the other hand, he does not detect say flaw, how could he set up any rejoinder at all ? For similar reasons, it is not right to say, as some philosophers think, that rejoinders should be set up against inconclusive reasoning.

It is argued that when a right argument is advanced by an opponent, he should be confronted with a right argument; when he puts forward a wrong argument he should be met by a wrong argument; such rejoinders constitute 'legitimate objection'. The right argument would consist in showing flaws in the opponent's argument; but such an argument, says Uddyotakara, would be a right answer and not a futile rejoinder (NV V.I,1).

Twenty-four legitimate objections

Objections raised on the bases of similarity and dissimilarity are of several kinds. Gautama has recognised the following twenty-four varieties of such objections or hetus which are set up in opposition to the hetus which are designed to prove a proposition[1] (NS V. I,1):

(1) Objection regarding the homogeneity (*sādharmyasama*)
(2) Objection regarding the heterogeneity (*vaidharmyasama*)
(3) Objection regarding an addition (*utkarṣasama*)
(4) Objection regarding a deficiency (*apakarṣasama*)
(5) Objection regarding the uncertain (*varṇyasama*)
(6) Objection regarding the certain (*avarṇyasama*)
(7) Objection regarding the alternative (*vikalpasama*)
(8) Objection regarding the probandum (*sādhyasama*)
(9) Objection regarding the co-presence (*prāptisama*)
(10) Objection regarding the mutual absence (*aprāptisama*)
(11) Objection regarding the infinite regress (*prasaṅgasama*)
(12) Objection regarding the counter-instance (*pratidṛṣṭānta-sama*)
(13) Objection regarding the non-production (*anutpattisama*)
(14) Objection regarding the doubt (*saṃśayasama*)
(15) Objection regarding the point at issue (*prakaraṇasama*)
(16) Objection regarding the hetu (*hetusama*)
(17) Objection regarding the implication (*arthāpattisama*)
(18) Objection regarding the non-difference (*aviśeṣasama*)
(19) Objection regarding the proof (*upapattisama*)
(20) Objection regarding the apprehension (*upalabdhisama*)
(21) Objection regarding the non-apprehension (*anupalabdhi-sama*)
(22) Objection regarding the non-eternal (*anityasama*)
(23) Objection regarding the eternal (*nityasama*)
(24) Objection regarding the effect (*kāryasama*)

A brief account of the twenty-four objections is given below in the light of Gautama's definitions and Vātsyāyana's comments. Uddyotakara has made no significant contribution to the subject and his comments have not therefore been given.

According to Gautama, "if against an argument based on a homogeneous or heterogeneous example opposition is offered in order to establish a property contrary to the probandum, the opposition is called 'objection regarding the homogeneity' or 'objection regarding the heterogeneity' (NS V.I,2).

Vātsyāyana explains: When an argument based on a homogeneous example is opposed by a counter-argument based on a homogeneous or heterogeneous example, in order to prove a property contrary to the probandum, we have the objection 'balancing the homogeneity'.

Argument

Ātman is active because it is a substance having a property that is the cause of activity. Every substance that has a property which is the cause of activity is active, for example, a clod of earth. Such is the *ātman*. Therefore it is active.

Counter-argument

(a) *Ātman* is inactive because it is an all-pervading substance. Every thing that is an all-pervading substance is inactive, for example, ākāśa. Such is the *ātman*. Therefore it is inactive.

(b) *Ātman* is inactive because it is a substance which is not limited in extent. Every thing that is limited in extent is active, for example, a clod of earth. Such is not the *ātman*. Therefore it is inactive.

The first counter-argument opposes the argument on the ground that *ātman* and ākāśa are homogeneous; the second on the ground that the *ātman* and the clod of earth are heterogeneous. There is no specific hetu which can determine whether the *ātman* is active or inactive.

When in order to prove a property contrary to the probandum an argument based on a heterogeneous example is opposed by an argument based on a heterogeneous or homogeneous example, we have the 'objection regarding the heterogeneity'.

Argument

Ātman is inactive because it is not-all-pervading. Every thing that is not all-pervading is active, for example, a clod of earth. Such is not the *ātman*. Therefore it is inactive.

Counter-argument

(a) *Ātman* is active because it is not devoid of properties conducive to activity. Every thing is devoid of properties conducive to inactivity, for example ākāśa. Such is not the *ātman*. Therefore it is active.

(b) *Ātman* is active because it has properties conducive to activity. Every thing has properties conducive to activity, for example a clod of earth. Therefore it is active.

The first counter-argument opposes the argument on the ground that the *ātman* and ākāśa are heterogeneous; the second on the ground that the *ātman* and the clod of earth are homogeneous. There is no specific hetu which can determine whether the *ātman* is inactive or active.

According to Gautama, the two objections should be met as follows: The original proposition would be established in the same manner as the fact of a certain animal being a 'cow' is established through 'cow-ness' (NS V.I,3).

Vātsyāyana explains: The proposition is not established on the basis of mere homogeneity or heterogeneity but of a specific property. Hence there is no question of any uncertainty at all. For instance, a certain animal is proved to be a cow because it and the cow are homogeneous, i.e. it has the specific property of 'cowness', and not because it has the dewlap. Similarly, the animal is proved to be different from a horse because it and the horse are heterogeneous; the heterogeneity consists in the fact that the animal has the specific property of cow-ness. It is the invariable concomitance of the property, positive and negative, that is decisive in such cases (NBh V.I,3).

According to Gautama, the following six objections arise when the subject and the familiar instance alternate their properties or both stand in need of proof (NS V.I,4).

Vātsyāyana explains these objections: When an argument based upon a certain property of the familiar instance is opposed by a counter-argument in which an additional property of that instance is attributed to the subject of the proposition, such opposition is called 'objection regarding an addition'. For example, it is argued that if *ātman* has the property, activity, of the instance (i.e. a clod of earth), it should also have the additional property of the instance, tangibility.

When an argument based upon a certain property of an instance is opposed by a counter-argument in which a property which is not found in that instance is attributed to the subject of the proposition, such opposition is called 'objection regarding a deficiency'. For example, it is argued that if *ātman* has the property, activity, of the instance (i.e. a clod of earth), it should also have a property not found in the inastance, e.g. not-all-pervasiveness.

If against an argument it is maintained that the property of an instance is as uncertain as that of the subject of the proposition the opposition is called 'objection regarding the uncertain'. For example, it is argued that if it is still uncertain that *ātman* is active, it is equally uncertain that a clod of earth is active.

If against an argument it is maintained that the property of the subject of the proposition is as certain as that of the instance, the opposition is called 'objection regarding the certain'. For example, it is argued that if the property of a clod of earth, e.g. activity, is certain, the property of *ātman*, e.g. activity, is equally certain.

If against an argument it is maintained that a property of the instance other than the probans belongs to the subject of the proposition, the opposition is called 'objection regarding the alternative'. For instance, a clod of earth which is active has the property of gravity while air which is active is devoid of that property. It is argued that if a clod of earth is active, the *ātman* may be devoid of activity.

The probandum is that property upon which the entire force of the probans and other members of reasoning is concentrated. When against the probandum it is maintained that the instance itself is the probandum, the opposition is called 'objection regarding the probandum'. For example, if both the clod of earth and *ātman* are substances having the properties leading to activity, the former requires proof for its activity as much as the latter does. *Ātman* is to be proved active by the instance of the clod of earth, and the clod of earth is to be proved active by the instance of the *ātman*. Thus the instance and the subject of the proposition are exactly on the same footing (NBh V.I,4).

Gautama's answer to those six objections is two fold:

(a) "There is no justification for the opposition because the confirmation is only secured on the basis of a particular similarity" (NS V. I,5). Vātsyāyana explains: The analogy between the subject of the proposition and the instance is duly established, if there is some point of similarity between them. For example, in the well-known analogy 'as the cow, so the *gavaya*', there is a similarity between the cow and the *gavaya*; it is futile to object to this analogy on the ground that there is some difference between them. Similarly, when the probans is found in the instance, it is not right to dispute its capacity to prove its presence in the subject simply because there are some differences between the instance and the subject of the proposition (NB V.I,5).

As Uddyotakara observes, in the fourth member of reasoning, confirmation, the probans is re-affirmed of the subject of the proposition. In the analogy of the cow and *gavaya* the intention is not to suggest that the cow has all the properties of the *gavaya* or *vice versa*; all that is meant is that it affirms, in regard to the two animals, just the property which is common to both (NV V.I,5).

(b) Further, the instance says Gautama, becomes an instance only because it indicates the presence of the probandum in it (NS V.I,6). What is indicated in the instance, explains Vātsyāyana, is only such an object as is not incompatible with what is agreed upon by all men, ordinary as well as learned. Since the instance becomes a true instance only because it indicates the probandum, the instance does not stand on the same footing as the probandum (NBh V.I,6).

The hetu can establish the probandum either by uniting, or not uniting, with the probandum. In the former case it becomes indistinguishable from the probandum; such opposition, says Gautama is called 'objection regarding the co-presence'. In the latter case it cannot prove the probandum, such opposition is called 'objection regarding the mutual absence' (NS V.I,7).

Vātsyāyana explains: If both the hetu and the probandum exist and are united, they would be indistinguishable from each other; we cannot say which is the hetu and which the probandum. This opposition is called 'objection regarding the co-presence'. If the hetu and the probandum are not united, the former could not establish the latter; for example, the lamp does not illumine an object unless it is united with it. This opposition is called 'objection regarding the mutual absence'.

Gautama replies to these two objections: "There is no justification for opposition because the production of jars and the oppression by means of spells are observed" (NS V.I,8). Vātsyāyana explains the reply: Effects like a jar are 'produced by the agent, instruments and receptacle only when these are united with clay. When a spell produces trouble for a person, the cause produces its effect without coming into contact with it. Thus both kinds of opposition are unjustified (NBh V.I,8).

According to Uddyotakara, if these two kinds of opposition were treated as valid, the entire fabric of hetu would be destroyed. The hetu can be either an indicator (*jñāpaka*) or a maker (*kāraka*). The twofold opposition is directed against both kinds of the function of the hetu, and thus seeks to destroy the whole causal relation. Further, such opposition is self-defeating, If the objection is valid it can accomplish its purpose either by reaching or not reaching its object. In either case the causal relation is involved. Any one who denies it cannot make his opposition effective.

When a potter uses various implements, they do come into contact with clay. But they do not become indistinguishable from the clay, nor does the causal relation between the jar and them cease; nor does the jar cease to be their effect. When the clay is turned into the jar, it does not mean that the cause operates upon something that is non-existent; in fact it operates upon the existing clay. The component particles of the clay renounce their previous pattern and assume a new one; a jar arises out of this latter pattern. This is what is meant by the clay turning into a jar. When a person is killed by a spell, the cause operates without coming into contact with its effect (NV V.I,8).

When opposition is offered on the ground that the basis (*karaṇa*) of the instance has not been stated, says Gautama, it is called 'objection regarding the infinite regress' (NS V.I,9).

The opponent asks: "What is the means of proving what is to be proved ? For example, when *ātman* is said to be active, like a clod of earth, no hetu is adduced to show why the clod of earth is active; until this is done, nothing can be accepted as true". This kind of opposition, says Vātsyāyana, constitutes 'objection regarding balancing the infinite regress' (NBh V.I,9).

Gautama's answer to this opposition is: The instance does not require a series of hetus for its establishment just as a lamp does not require a series of lamps for its illumination (NS V.I,10). People who desire to see things bring a lamp to see them. But they do not bring another lamp to see the first lamp because they can see it even without the second lamp. Similarly, the instance is stated in order to make known a thing that is not known. The instance represents a consensus of opinion amongst the learned and the unlearned; it is therefore useless to state any basis in order to make the instance known. Thus the opposition, says Vātsyāyana, should be met (NBh V.I,10).

When opposition is offered on the basis of a counter-instance, says Gautama, it is called 'objection regarding the counter-instance' (NS V.I,9). Against the argument — *ātman* is active because it has qualities conducive to action like a clod of earth — the opponent brings forward a counter-instance: ākāśa which has qualities conducive to action is actually found to be inactive, and the *ātman* should therefore be inactive like ākāśa. Such opposition, says Vātsyāyana constitutes 'objection regarding the counter-instance' (NBh V.I,9).

Gautama replies to this opposition: The instance cannot be set aside only because a counter-instance is advanced as the hetu (NS V.I,11). When the opponent states his counter-instance, he does not offer any specific hetu to show why his counter-instance should be accepted and not the instance. A mere counter-instance without an appropriate hetu cannot yield any valid conclusion. Since the original argument contains the instance with the appropriate hetu, says Vātsyāyana, the opposition has no force (NBh V.I,11). In fact the opponent, says Uddyotakara, cannot even formulate his argument without condemning his own position. If he says 'as your instance, so is mine as well', then his instance is not a counter-instance: if he argues 'just as my instance is not the right instance, so is yours also not the right instance', he is contradicting himself. In either case there is no counter-instance (NV V.I,11).

If opposition is offered on the ground that the hetu cannot subsist in the subject of the proposition before the latter is produced, says Gautama, it is called 'balancing the non-production' (NS V.I,12). Vātsyāyana illustrates the opposition: Sound is non-eternal because it comes after effort, like a jar. Against this argument the following opposition is offered: Before sound is produced, it is not present; the hetu 'because it comes after effort', cannot subsist in sound which is not present. Hence sound is eternal; that which is eternal is never produced. Such opposition is called 'objection regarding the non-production' (NBh V.I,12).

Gautama answers the opposition: The opposition to the hetu is unjustified as the hetu subsists in the subject only after it has come into existence (NS V.I,13). Sound is not even sound before it is produced; it becomes sound only after it has been pro duced. When it has been produced, the property of 'coming after effort' which is the hetu for its non-eternality, subsists in it. Thus the opposition says Vātsyāyana, is unjustified (NBh V.I,12).

According to Uddyotakara, the hetu in the argument is an indicator, not a maker. The objection applies to the hetu only in the latter capacity and not in the former. The objector argues that there is really no difference between these two capacities of the hetu as the hetu is an agent or operator in both. Uddyotakara rejects this argument: the maker is the cause of action while the indicator is the cause of indicating; the former brings things into existence while the latter brings about the cognition of things already in existence. The objector says: "Before sound is produced, the property of being produced being absent, sound comes to be that which is not capable of being produced." In saying so, says Uddyotakara, he admits the existence of sound. How can a non-existing thing have a property of being not capable of being produced ? The qualification 'before it is produced' is thus meaningless.

Some philosophers argue that the opposition under consideration is a case of 'objection regarding the implication': Before sound is produced the property of coming after effort cannot belong to it. It follows, by implication, that it is not endowed with that property: not having the property it is eternal. These philosophers answer the opposition: It is by no means necessary that what does not possess the property of coming after effort must be eternal. In fact there are three kinds of things which do not have this property: (a) some are eternal like ākāśa; (b) some are non-eternal like lightning; (c) some are absolute non-entities like sky-flower.

Uddyotakara disagrees with this answer. It is wrong to use the expression in this context, that 'things do not have the property of coming after effort'. This property really qualifies the birth of a thing; that thing is regarded as not having the property of coming after effort whose birth or production does not follow from effort. A non-entity cannot be said to have birth for the simple reason it never exists. Similarly, it is wrong to say that what is eternal has the property of not coming after effort (NV V. I,13).

Since both genus and instance are equally perceptible, there is a similarity between the eternal and the non-eternal. Such opposition, says Gautama, constitutes 'objection regarding the doubt' (NS V.I,14). Sound is non-eternal because it comes after effort, like a jar. The opponent casts a doubt over this argument: even though sound comes after effort, it is similar to the eternal genus (jar-ness) inasmuch as both are equally perceptible by the senses: sound is also similar to a non-eternal jar in this respect. This opposition, says Vātsyāyana, constitutes 'objection regarding the doubt' (NBh V.I,14).

Gautama replies to the opposition: Eternality is not established on the ground of similarity: doubt based upon similarity is dispelled by dissimilarity; doubt which is based upon both never ends (NS V.I,15). Vātsyāyana explains the answer: When we see a distinguishing feature of man,—a feature which constitutes its dissimilarity to a pillar, — we recognize that the object perceived is a man; after this there is no room for doubt on the basis of some similarity between man and pillar. Similarly, when we recognize the property of coming after effort as a distinguishing feature of sound — a feature which is its dissimilarity to eternal things, — the non-eternality of sound is duly ascertained; thereafter we can have no further doubt on the mere ground of its similarity to eternal and non-eternal things. If such a doubt were to arise, then, inasmuch as the similarity between the man and the pillar would never cease, the doubt also would never end. If even after recognising similarity and dissimilarity between things there remains a doubt about their true nature, then that doubt would never cease (NBh V.I,15).

When opposition is offered on the basis of similarity to both, says Gautama, it is called 'objection regarding the point at issue' (NS V.I,16). Sound is non-eternal because it comes after effort, like a jar. The opponent opposes this argument: Sound is eternal because it is perceptible by the auditory organ, like the universal of sound, (i.e. sound-ness). Both the original argument and opposition are based upon similarity: in the former sound is similar to non-eternal things and in the latter, to the eternal things. Thus there is doubt about the true nature of sound. Opposition which creates such suspense, constitutes 'objection regarding the point at issue'. This kind of suspense can be created by dissimilarity as well and such opposition, says Vātsyāyana, is covered by Gautama's definition (NBh V.I,16).

Gautama answers the opposition: The opposition is unjustified because it provokes a controversy which has an opposing side (NS V.I,17). Vātsyāyana explains: When the opponent says that there is suspense because of 'similarity to both', he accepts that both views, i.e. view and counter-view, are equally established. He cannot therefore question the view to which he opposes his counter-view.

The doubt which the opposition creates in this case is different from that involved in the fallacy of *prakaraṇasama*, as the doubt in the latter arises not from the counter-view but from the absence of definite knowledge (NBh V.I,17; also NV V.I,17).

If opposition is offered on the ground that hetu cannot exist at all the three times (i.e. past, present and future), says Gautama, it is called 'objection regarding the hetu' (NS V.I,18). Vātsyāyana explains: Hetu is that which proves; and this could exist only either before or after or together with the probandum. If the hetu exists before or after the probandum, inasmuch as the probandum is absent the hetu cannot be said to prove it. If both are present simultaneously, which could be the means of establishing which ? Thus the hetu cannot be distinguished from what is not hetu. Such opposition based upon the similarity to the non-hetu is called 'objection regarding the hetu' (NBh V.I,18).

Gautama answers the opposition: It is true that the hetu cannot operate at all the three times, because it is by means of the hetu that the probandum can be proved (NS V.I,19). It is a matter of common observation, says Vātsyāyana, that the accomplishing of what is to be accomplished and the knowing of what is to be known are brought about by a cause. Similarly, the hetu operates to prove the probandum which is absent; it is the means of proving what is to be proved (NBh V.I,19).

Moreover, if the contention of the opponent is right, says Gautama, his own opposition cannot operate either before or after or together with what it seeks to deny (NS V.I,20). Thus the operation of the hetu is established beyond dispute (NBh V. I,20).

The opposition to the hetu under consideration is similar to the objection raised against the operation of the pramāṇas. As already mentioned, this opposition, says Uddyotakara, is as riddled with contradictions as the objection[2] (NV V.I,20).

If opposition is offered on the basis of implication to prove a counter-view, says Gautama, it is called 'objection regarding the implication' (NS V.I,21). Vātsyāyana explains: Sound is non-eternal because it comes after effort, like a jar. The opponent opposes this argument on the basis of implication: If sound is non-eternal on the ground of its coming after effort, — this constitutes its similarity to non-eternal things, — then it follows, by implication, that sound is eternal on the ground of its similarity to eternal things, e.g. intangibility. This opposition constitutes 'objection regarding the implication'.

Gautama answers the opposition: If things unsaid could come by implication, then the opposition could itself be hurt on account of the implication being unsaid and inconclusive (NS V.I,22). Vātsyāyana explains: The opponent does not know the nature of the power of words to express things. If what is not expressly stated is regarded as implied, then the renunciation of this view by the opponent may also be taken as implied, for he has not expressly stated his own view. And in that case the original view that sound is non-eternal should be regarded as established and the opposite view as rejected. Moreover, if implication is valid for the opposition, it must be valid also for the original argument. If sound were regarded as eternal on the ground of its similarity to eternal things, it would be taken as following by implication that sound is non-eternal on the ground of its similarity to non-eternal things. Thus we would have two contrary conclusions based on implication. Further, no conclusive implication can be established on the basis of mere negation. For instance, the fact that solid gravel falls does not necessarily imply that water, which is liquid, would not fall (NBh V.I,22).

If the presence of a single property were to make two things non-different, then everything would have to be regarded as non-different, for the property of existence is present in everything. Such opposition, says Gautama, constitutes 'objection regarding the non-difference'. This opposition, he replies, is not justified because in some instances a (common) property is present while in others it is absent (NS V.I,23-24).

Vātsyāyana explains the opposition: In the argument — sound is non-eternal because it comes after effort, like a jar, — sound and jar are treated as non-different in respect of their non-eternality on the basis of their having one property in common, viz. coming after effort. If this is right, says the opponent, all things should be regarded as non-different in respect of the possession of every property; for all of them have the common property of existence. Therefore, since there is no difference between the eternal and the non-eternal, sound may be regarded as eternal. This sort of opposition is called 'objection regarding the non-difference', which aims at impairing the validity of the argument by assuming all things to be non-different (NBh V.I,23).

Vātsyāyana explains Gautama's reply: This opposition is unjustified because the property which the subject of the proposition (sound) and the instance (jar) have in common is found in some instances while it is absent in others. But even though all things have the one common property of existence, they are different in respect of the possession of other properties. Thus the opposition is unjustified.

It is argued that there can be another property common to all things, viz. non-eternality, which is indicated by the property of existence. The argument would then be: All things are non-eternal because they have the property of existence. But in that case there is nothing left to serve as example: for all things are already included under the proposition. Nor would it be right to put up as example something that is already included under the proposition; for what is yet to be proved cannot serve as an example. Moreover, things that exist are found to be both eternal and non-eternal: they cannot therefore be treated as non-eternal simply because they exist. Last but not least, if all things are non-eternal because they exist, the opponent has conceded that sound is non-eternal. Thus the opposition is unjustified (NBh V.I,24).

If opposition is offered on the ground that there are grounds for both views, says Gautama, it is called 'objection regarding the proof'. (NS V.I,25). For example, if sound is non-eternal because it comes after effort, the opponent argues that it should be regarded as eternal because it is intangible. Such opposition based upon grounds for both views, says Vātsyāyana, constitutes 'objection regarding the proof' (NBh V.I,25).

The opposition is unjustified, Gautama says in reply, because the acceptance of the grounds for both views means that the ground for the original view is admitted (NS V.I,25). Vātsyāyana observes: If, to escape from this predicament, the opponent now denies the ground which supports the non-eternality of sound, he could also deny the ground which supports the eternality of sound: for he can avoid his present difficulty by denying either of the grounds (NBh V.I,26).

If opposition is offered on the ground that we perceive a property of the subject even in the absence of the cause stated, says Gautama, it is called 'objection regarding the apprehension' (NS V.I,27). For instance, against the argument — sound is non-eternal bacause it comes after effort, like a jar, — the opponent maintains that the non-eternality of sound can be ascertained even without the hetu, viz. because it (sound) comes after effort; we perceive this non-eternality in that sound which is produced by the branches of trees broken by wind. The opposition based upon the existence of the probandum even in the absence of the hetu, says Vātsyāyana, constitutes 'objection regarding the apprehension' (NBh V.I,27).

Gautama answers the opposition: The opposition is unjustified even if the property in question can be ascertained by other means as well (NS V.I,28). In the argument under consideration all that the hetu states is that sound is produced from some cause and not that it can be produced only by one particular cause, viz. coming after effort. If non-eternality is found in sound produced from some other cause, says Vātsyāyana, this does not impair the argument (NBh V.I,28).

If against an argument proving the non-existence of a thing, opposition is offered to prove the contrary by the non-apprehension of non-apprehension, says Gautama, the opposition is called 'objection regarding the non-apprehension' (NS V.I,29).

Vātsyāyana explains: The following argument is put forward: Sound is not present before it is uttered, because the non-apprehension of obstruction is not apprehended. In the case of things like water, we find that when they are present, if they are not apprehended their non-apprehension is due to obstruction. But in the case of sound we do not find that its non-apprehension is due to any obstruction. If such an obstruction existed, it would certainly have been perceived. Hence the case of sound when not heard is not analogous to that of water.

Against this argument the opponent puts forward the following opposition: The non-apprehension of obstruction is not apprehended; from this non-apprehension of non-apprehension, it follows that the latter is not present; the non-apprehension not being present, the hetu in the first argument, viz. 'because the non-apprehension of obstruction is not apprehended', is not apprehended. Such opposition is called 'objection regarding the non-apprehension' (NBh V.I,29).

Gautama replies to the opposition: (a) Since non-apprehension is of the nature of the negation of apprehension the hetu mentioned in the opposition is not valid (NS V.I,30). Vātsyāyana explains: What exists constitutes the object of apprehension, and this object is asserted to be existent because it is apprehended. What does not exist constitutes the object of non-apprehension and this object is declared to be non-existent because it is not apprehended. Obstruction can be the object of apprehension when it is present, and if it is present, there should be apprehension of it; so that when the obstruction is not apprehended, there is the absence of apprehension that would indicate the presence of its own object. From this non-apprehension it is understood that the object in question that would have been apprehended if it was present is the object of non-apprehension; that is, it is not present. Hence the obstruction which would have explained the non-apprehension of sound before its utterance is not present. Non-apprehension is absence of apprehension and non-apprehension of non-apprehension, which signifies a mere negation of non-apprehension, cannot be interpreted to signify an existent thing. Thus the argument of the opponent — There can be no non-apprehension of obstruction because no such non-apprehension is apprehended — is not a valid argument at all because non-apprehension which is given as hetu is of the nature of mere negation of apprehension (NBh V.I,30). (b) Another argument against the opposition, says Gautama, is that there is an internal perception of the presence and absence of various kinds of cognition (NS V.I,31). Vātsyāyana explains: Every embodied person knows what cognitions are present in his body; e.g. my doubtful cognition exists, my doubtful cognition does not exist. In the case under consideration the person concerned would know whether he has or has not the apprehension of obstruction. Thus the contention of the opponent — non-apprehension of the non-apprehension of the obstruction does not exist because the non-apprehension of the obstruction is not apprehended — is not right (NBh V.I,31).

If by reason of similarity things are regarded as having analogous properties, then all things would be non-eternal; this opposition, says Gautama, is called 'objection regarding the non-eternal'. (NS V.I,32). Vātsyāyana explains: Against the argument — Sound is non-eternal because it comes after effort, like a jar — the opponent says: If sound is non-eternal because it is similar to the non-eternal jar, it follows that all things are non-eternal because they are similar to the non-eternal jar. This opposition constitutes 'objection regarding the non-eternal'.

Gautama replies to the opposition: (a) "The opposition is unjustified because nothing can be proved from a mere similarity and bacause there is dissimilarity even to that which is opposed" (NS V.I,33). Vātsyāyana explains: In the case under consideration both the argument and counter-argument consist of all the required members of reasoning, such as the proposition, etc. This constitutes the similarity between them. If similarity is a valid reason for rejection, the denial of the argument must be invalid; for it is similar to the argument. If there is a case for rejection of non-eternality of sound on the ground of its similarity to the non-eternal jar, there is equal justification for rejection of non-eternality of all things on the ground of their similarity to the jar. (NBh V.I,33). (b) Another argument against the opposition, says Gautama, is that what serves as hetu is that property which is definitely known to subsist in the instance as capable of proving the probandum; since such a hetu is capable of proving in both ways there can be no non-difference among things, i.e. all of them need not be non-eternal (NS V.I,34).

The hetu, says Vātsyāyana, can be homogeneous or heterogeneous, but the similarity or dissimilarity can function as hetu only when it is invariably indicative of the probandum. In the argument under consideration a thing is said to be non-eternal not simply because it is similar to a non-eternal jar but because there is invariable concomitance between the property of coming after effort (i.e. hetu) and non-eternality (i.e. probandum). It is therefore unjustified to conclude from the fact of mere similarity that all things are non-eternal. Thus the counter-argument cannot invalidate the original argument (NBh V.I,34).

If opposition is offered on the ground that since the property of non-eternality is eternal what is non-eternal is itself eternal, such opposition, says Gautama, is called 'objection regarding the eternal' (NS V.I,35). Vātsyāyana explains: When sound is said to be non-eternal, is this non-eternality eternal or non-eternal ? If the property of non-eternality is always present in sound, the thing to which it belongs, i.e. sound, must also be always in existence; in other words sound is eternal. If, on the other hand, the property is not always present in sound, then also sound would be eternal in the absence of non-eternality. Such opposition constitutes 'objection regarding the eternality' (NBh V.I,35).

The opposition is unjustified, says Gautama in reply, because the thing opposed is always non-eternal on account of the eternality of the non-eternal (NS V.I,36). Vātsyāyana explains: When the opponent speaks of the property of non-eternality being eternal in sound,— sound which is the object whose non-eternality he wishes to deny, — he has admitted the non-eternality of sound; he cannot now proceed to deny its non-eternality. If, however, he does not admit the eternal character of the non-eternality of sound, then he cannot offer as hetu 'because non-eternality in sound is eternal'. And in the absence of hetu the opposition cannot be proved.

What is meant by sound being non-eternal is that it is produced and ceases to exist on being destroyed. It is therefore not right to ask whether the non-eternality subsists in sound at all times or not. Sound cannot be regarded as the container and non-eternality as the contained; such a notion is self-contradictory. Moreover, eternality and non-eternality are contradictory properties; that they could belong to the same object, i.e. sound, is an impossibility. Hence the opposition is completely unjustified (NBh V.I,36).

According to Uddyotakara, non-eternality is not a distinct property. It consists in the fact that the thing is endowed with an existence which is not absolute. It is therefore wrong to ask whether non-eternality is absolute or not; for one and the same thing cannot have both absolute and non-absolute existence. But when the opponent says that non-eternality is eternal he is attributing to one and the same thing, 'non-eternality', the character of non-absolute existence which constitutes non-eternality as well as absolute existence which constitutes eternality. Since these are contradictions, the assertion of the opponent cannot be right (NV V.I,36).

If opposition is offered on the ground that there is a diversity of effects of effort, says Gautama, such opposition is called 'objection regarding the effect' (NS V.I,37). Vātsyāyana explains: The following argument is stated: Sound is non-eternal because it comes after effort. This means that the effect of the effort is such that having no previous existence, it comes into existence, e.g. a jar. On the other hand, what is non-eternal is such that having coming into existence, it ceases to exist.

The opponent puts forward the following counter-argument on the basis of the diversity of the products of effort. The product may be of the nature of something which comes into existence after effort, e.g. a jar: or it may be a manifestation of a thing concealed under some obstruction when the obstruction is removed. There is no specific reason to show whether sound is the effect of the first or the second kind: in the former case it would be non-eternal and in the latter eternal. Opposition set up on the basis of this fact of both production and manifestation being the products of effort is called 'objection regarding the effect' (NBh V.I,37).

Gautama answers the opposition: (a) Effort is not the cause of the second kind of effect, i.e. manifestation, because there is no cause of non-apprehension (NS V.I,38). (b) The same defect attaches to the opposition as well (NS V.I,39).

Vātsyāyana explains: We cannot say that sound is manifested by effort because we cannot prove that it existed already. That sound did not exist previously is proved by our non-perception of the same. The opponent cannot say that our non-perception was caused by an obstruction because no such obstruction interfered with the appearance of sound. Hence sound is an effect which is not manifested but produced (NBh V.I,38). If the hetu in the argument is inconclusive, so is that in the opposition. Just as there is no special ground to suppose that the 'effect in the argument signifies' a thing produced and not manifested, so also there is no special reason to suppose that the 'effect' mentioned in the opposition signifies 'a thing manifested and not produced'. Hence the opposition is self-destructive (NBh V.I,39).

General Principles

According to Gautama, the various kinds of legitimate objection should be met in the light of the following principles:

(i) If a specific hetu is demanded of the opponent, the same will have to be required of the original proponent. The proponent may contend that both views stand on the same footing.

(ii) Defect attaches to the opposition of the opposition just as it attaches to the opposition. If the proponent says that the hetu in the opposition is inconclusive, the opponent may retort that the opposition of the proponent to his opposition contains the same fault.

(iii) If one admits the defect of one's opposition as the consequence of one's statement — the same defect attaches to the opposition of the opposition, it is called "admission of an opinion" (*matānujñā*).

(iv) "admission of opinion" also occurs when the proponent, instead of stating hetus to rescue his view from the defect with which it has been charged, proceeds to admit the defect as the consequence of the following: 'the same defect belongs to his opponent's view as well' (NS V.I, 39-43).

17

DEFICIENCY (*nigrahasthāna*)

The last and the sixteenth category of Gautama is deficiency (*nigrahasthāna*). Like quibble and legitimate objection, it helps the disputant in formulating faultless arguments and in discovering faults in his opponents' counter-arguments; he can also use similar tactics against his opponent. The knowledge and technique of fault-finding are therefore essential. It is to meet this need, says Vātsyāyana, that Gautama has accorded the status of independent category to deficiency as well as to quibble and legitimate objection (NBh I.1,1).

According to Gautama, deficiency consists in misapprehension and non-apprehension (NS I.2,19). Vātsyāyana explains: Misapprehension is that apprehension which is either wrong or objectionable. Non-apprehension consists in not opposing what is sought to be proved by one's opponent or not answering the objections raised against one's own arguments (NBh I.2,19).

The deficiencies recognized by Gautama constitute actual occasions or grounds for defeat. They are generally concerned with the various members of reasoning; the advocates of doctrines, true as well as false, may also commit faults in their arguments (NBh V.2,1).

If fault-finding consists in misapprehension and non-apprehension, it may be asked, how can faults be said to be the faults of the *avayavas* ? This is quite justified, says Uddyotakara, because a speaker is said to be ignorant only when his speech is found faulty. Deficiencies are therefore figuratively spoken of as deficiencies of the *avayavas*. These *avayavas* as *avayavas* cannot be said to contain deficiencies; there is between them no such relationship of container and contained. The deficiencies are pointed out on the basis of the manner in which the speakers have used the various *avayavas* in their arguments.

It is understandable that the advocate of a false doctrine could be charged with various deficiencies. But how can an advocate of a true doctrine be worsted in an argument on this account ? This is quite conceivable, says Uddyotakara, because he may not realize the force of the objections raised against his own position.

Some philosophers think that it is the views which should be charged with deficiency, and not the speakers or the *avayavas.* According to Uddyotakara, these philosophers are mistaken. The views criticized remain just the same as they were prior to criticism. The *avayavas qua avayavas* cannot be said to be vitiated by any fault. It is the speakers alone who can be charged with deficiencies; for they have accepted wrong views and thus inevitably used defective arguments. This is exactly what happens in any ordinary operation. For example, in the making of a pot the potter is the agent, clay the object and shuttles the instrument. The potter is a free agent who should be able to make proper selection of his material and use of his instruments. If anything goes wrong, we complain against the potter and not against the material or the instruments for they depend upon the potter. Similarly, a speaker is a person completely free to adopt any view and use any argument according to the standard procedure. If the view which he selects is a wrong view or if he uses a faulty argument, we cannot put the blame on the view or the *avayavas* for they depend upon the speaker. However, as already mentioned, some of the recognized deficiencies which are directly concerned with the *avayavas* are figuratively spoken of as deficiencies of the various *avayavas* (NV V.2,1).

Like legitimate objection, deficiency is of several kinds (NS I. 2,20), and according to Gautama there are twenty-two such varieties (NS V.2,1).

1. Vitiating one's own proposition (*pratijñāhāni*)
2. Offering an alternative proposition (*pratijñāntara*)
3. Opposing one's own proposition (*pratijñāvirodha*)
4. Renouncing one's own proposition (*pratijñāsannyāsa*)
5. Offering an alternative hetu (*hetvantara*)
6. Offering an alternative topic (*arthāntara*)
7. Meaningless (*nirarthaka*) [hetu]
8. Unintelligible (*avijñātārtha*) [statement]
9. Incoherent (*apārthaka*) [statement]
10. Disorderly (*aprāptakāla*) [sequence of *avayavas*]
11. Incomplete (*nyūna*) [statement]
12. Containing superfluous elements (*adhika*)
13. Repetitive (*punarukta*) [statement]

14. Silence (*ananubhāṣaṇa*)
15. Ignorance (*ajñāna*)
16. Reticence (*apratibhā*)
17. Evasion (*vikṣepa*)
18. Admission of an opinion (*matānujñā*)
19. Failure to point out error (*paryanuyojyopekṣaṇa*)
20. Blaming of a faultless statement (*niranuyojyānuyoga*)
21. Deviating from *siddhānta* (*apasiddhānta*)
22. Fallacy of the hetu (*hetvābhāsa*)

According to Vātsyāyana the following six of the above deficiencies are indicative of non-apprehension: silence, ignorance, reticence, evasion, admission of an opinion and failure to point out error. The remaining deficiencies are indicative of misapprehension (NBh I.2,20).

A brief account of the twenty-two varieties of deficiency is given below. It is based upon the definitions of Gautama and comments of Vātsyāyana. Uddyotakara has generally endorsed the views of Vātsyāyana. Uddyotakara's views have been specifically mentioned wherever they appeared to be of significance.

1. 'Violating one's own proposition' occurs, says Gautama, when one admits in one's own instance the property of a counter-instance (NS V. 2,2). Vātsyāyana explains: A disputant argues: Sound is non-eternal because it is perceptible by sense, like a jar. An opponent retorts: Genus is perceptible by sense and yet eternal, and therefore the jar may also be eternal. The disputant replies: If the genus, which is perceptible, is eternal, the jar may also be eternal. In thus attributing the property of the counter-instance (the eternality of the genus) to his own example (the jar), he violates his own view down to the last *avayava*, i.e. conclusion (*nigamana*). This amounts to vitiating his own proposition upon which his view rests (NBh V.2,2).

2. According to Gautama the deficiency of 'offering an alternative proposition' occurs when one defends the object of one's own proposition by importing a new property into the instance and the counter-instance after it (object) has been denied (NS V. 2,3). For example, says Vātsyāyana, the following argument is first put forward: Sound is non-eternal because it is perceptible by a sense-organ, like a jar. An opponent offers an opposition: Sound is eternal because it is perceptible by a sense-organ, like a

genus. The author of the first argument defends himself by saying: A genus and a jar are both perceptible by sense-organs, and yet the former is all-pervasive while the latter is not. In thus defending himself he has shifted his position. His original proposition was: Sound is non-eternal: his present proposition is: sound is non-all-pervasive. Such shifting of the proposition constitutes a ground for defeat for one proposition is not proved by another; what proves a proposition are the hetu and the instance (NBh V.2,3). This manoeuvre of the person concerned, says Uddyotakara, may be due to his misapprehension or non-apprehension (NV V.2,3).

3. The deficiency of 'opposing one's own proposition', says Gautama, arises when the proposition and the hetu are opposed to each other (NS V.2,4). For instance, it is argued: Substance is distinct from quality because no object is perceived except colour, etc. If substance is distinct from quality, it is not possible that nothing except colour should be perceived; if, on the other hand, nothing except colour is perceived, then it is not possible that substance should be distinct from quality. Thus the proposition 'substance is distinct from quality' is opposed to the hetu 'because no object is perceived except colour'; such opposition is impossible (NBh V.2,4).

According to Uddyotakara, the deficiency of opposing one's own proposition arises not only when the proposition and the hetu are opposed to each other but also in the following cases:

(a) The proposition contradicts itself, e.g. A nun is pregnant.
(b) There is opposition by the hetu, e.g. Everything is distinct because positive terms (*bhāvaśabda*) are applied to an aggregate (*samūha*) of things. The hetu 'because positive terms are applied to an aggregate of things' means that they are applied to something which is one and yet applicable to many things. The proposition 'everything is distinct' means that there is no such unity in diversity. Thus the hetu contradicts the proposition.
(c) The instance contradicts the proposition.
(d) The instance contradicts the hetu.
(e) The proposition and the hetu contradict the hetu.
(f) An opponent says to a disputant that the latter's argument contains the fallacy of inconclusive hetu when such a

fallacy can only occur according to his own doctrine and not to that of his opponent (NV V.2,4).

4. The deficiency of 'renouncing one's own proposition' occurs, says Gautama, when confronted with an opposition a person disclaims the object of his proposition (NS V.2,5). A disputant says: Sound is non-eternal because it is perceptible by sense. An opponent retorts: Just as a genus is perceptible and yet eternal, so sound is perceptible and yet eternal. Confronted with this opposition the disputant says: Who says that sound is non-eternal ? This kind of retort, says Vātsyāyana, constitutes the deficiency of renouncing one's own proposition (NBh V.2,5). This shows that the disputant is not aware of the strength of his own hetu and he is defeated because of his misapprehension (NV V.2,5).

5. The deficiency of 'offering an alternative hetu', arises, says Gautama, when the hetu of a general character being opposed, one attaches a specific character to it (NS V.2,6). A disputant says: Everything that is manifested has a single origin (*prakṛti*), because modifications emanating from a single origin have a definite magnitude (*parimāṇa*), like a jar produced from clay. An opponent retorts that definite magnitude is found not only amongst modifications emanating from a single origin but also amongst those emanating from diverse origins. Confronted with this opposition the disputant replies: Everything that is manifested has a single origin, but that origin unites in itself pleasure, pain and misconception and its modifications also have within them these constituents; such modifications have a definite magnitude.

In the first argument of the disputant his hetu was of a general character, viz. modifications which emanate from a single origin have definite magnitude. He now qualifies it by saying that the modifications and their single origin have three constituents. Thus the original unqualified hetu, says Vātsyāyana, has been changed into a qualified hetu. This constitutes the deficiency of 'offering an alternative hetu'.

This deficiency is a source of defeat because the disputant cannot produce an example to corroborate his hetu; for everything that is manifested is included under the proposition. If he does produce an instance, it must be something that emanates not from a single origin but from some other origin. If he does not produce an instance at all, the hetu is uncorroborated and thus cannot prove the proposition. Thus in all eventualities the disputant cannot escape defeat (NBh V.2,6). In setting up another hetu the disputant shows its weakness. If the original hetu was capable of proving his proposition, says Uddyotakara, the second is absolutely useless (NV V.2,6).

6. The deficiency of 'offering an alternative topic' occurs, says Gautama, when the real object of an argument is opposed by one which is not connected with it (NS V.2,7). Vātsyāyana explains: A disputant says: Sound is eternal because it is intangible. Confronted by an opponent he defends his position: The word 'hetu' is derived from the root '*hi*' with the suffix '*tu*'. A word, as a part of speech, may be a noun, a verb, an indeclinable or an affix: A noun is a word with a qualified grammatical form. This form signifies that the thing denoted by the noun has its distinct action. A verb is a word which is either (a) an aggregate (*samudāya*) of the action and the agent or (b) which is simply expressed by the root and is qualified by a particular tense and number. An indeclinable is that word which, in actual usage, has no denotation apart from what is expressed by the noun or the verb. A preposition is a word which is used as an affix and serves to qualify the action denoted by the verb. Such a statement constitutes the deficiency 'offering an alternative topic' (NBh V.2,7).

7. The deficiency 'meaningless' occurs, says Gautama, when an argument is based on a nonsensical series of letters (NS V.2,8). For instance, a person says: Sound is eternal because *Ka-ca-ṭa-ta-pa* are *ja-ba-ḍa-da-śa,* like *jha-bha-ñ-gha-ḍha-dha-ṣa.* Mere letters in a series have no meaning and the person who uses them, says Vātsyāyana, deserves reproach (NBh V.2,8).

8. 'Unintelligible' is an argument, says Gautama, which, though repeated three times, is understood neither by the audience nor by the opponent (NS V.2,9). When, confronted with an opponent, a disputant is unable to defend his position, he uses words of double meaning or words not in ordinary use or words which are very quickly uttered; such words are understood neither by his audience nor his opponent, even though they are repeated three times. This sort of defence, says Vātsyāyana, constitutes the deficiency of 'unintelligible' which rightly deserves a reproach (NBh V.2,9).

9. 'Incoherent' is an argument, says Gautama, which conveys no connected meaning on account of the expressions being strung together without any sequence (NS V.2,10). Vātsyāyana explains: Confronted with an opponent a disputant is unable to defend himself and argues: (a) Ten pomegranates, six cakes. (b) Bowl—goats' skin—flesh—lump—deer-skins—of the virgin —to be drunk—her father—devoid of character. Such words and sentences have neither proper syntactical order nor connection and therefore furnish no meaning when they are taken collectively. This sort of defence is incoherent and deserves a rebuke (NBh V. 2,10). This deficiency, according to Uddyotakara, is different from the unintelligible: in the latter we have mere sound while in the former we have unconnected words (NV V.2,10).

10. The deficiency of 'disorderly' [sequence of *avayavas*] occurs, says Gautama, when the *avayavas* are stated in a reverse order (NS V.2,11). In a valid reasoning its different members are stated in a definite natural order which is based upon the nature of what is expressed by each of them. When this order is disturbed, what is expressed by the several *avayavas* does not provide a connected meaning. This, says Vātsyāyana, constitutes the deficiency of 'disorderly' [sequence of *avayavas*] (NBh V.2,11).

Some philosophers argue that this deficiency is really no ground for defeat. In the first place, even if the order of reasoning is disturbed it can still prove the proposition concerned. Second, there is no such convention that a reasoning must be stated in a particular order. Third, in all scriptures the order of reasoning is actually reversed.

Uddyotakara replies to this view on the following grounds: The first argument is analogous to the use of words in their corrupt forms. For instance, when the corrupt form of the word '*go*', *gavī*, is used, it does bring about the correct idea of the cow. But this does not mean that the rule about the correct form of the word is useless. Similarly, when the *avayavas* are stated in a wrong order, we are reminded of the reasoning in its natural order and it is this latter that gives us the correct idea of what is expressed by it; that is, the proposition is proved. This is what we find in ordinary experience; for example, when a potter is making a jar, he first takes up clay and then the implements. Similarly, the object of reasoning is a proposition to be proved and the proposition therefore comes first; then follow the instruments, viz. the hetu, the example etc.

Regarding the second argument, Uddyotakara agrees that there is no convention but it is certainly not a matter of reproach if the natural order of things is emphasized.

It is true that the scriptures do not follow the natural order of reasoning, but the reason for this is that their purpose is to provide a comprehensive account of things. But when these things are explained, one has to state arguments in their natural order. Thus the third argument has no force (NV V.2,11).

11. According to Gautama, the deficiency of 'incomplete' [statement] occurs if a reasoning is wanting even in one of its *avayavas* (NS V.2,12). Unless every *avayava* is stated, says Vātsyāyana, it cannot prove what it sets out to prove, i.e. the proposition.

Some philosophers contend that if the reasoning is stated without the proposition this constitutes no ground for defeat. Even if a person were to state all the other *avayavas* without any defect, says Uddyotakara, he would be regarded as defeated. The only justification for this defeat is that his reasoning is wanting in the proposition. If, on the other hand, he is not regarded as defeated, this would mean that even an incomplete argument proves the proposition; the proof is accomplished without the means of proving.

These philosophers argue that this difficulty is unreal because the proposition consists in the acceptance of an established doctrine (*siddhānta*). This argument, replies Uddyotakara, makes no sense. The proposition states the object of proof while the acceptance of an established doctrine consists in the acceptance of a thing which has been fully understood in all its general and special aspects[1] (NV V.2,12).

12. The deficiency of 'containing superfluous elements' occurs, says Gautama, when a reasoning contains more than one hetu and example (NS V.2,13). Since only one hetu and one example are sufficient to prove a proposition, says Vātsyāyana, when more than one hetu or example is given one or the other would be superfluous. But this would constitute a ground for defeat only if there were a rule on the subject (NBh V.2,13).

Some philosophers contend that this is no ground for defeat because it strengthens the reasoning. When several means of cognition are available they can be employed to bring about a stronger cognition of an object; for example, the hill has fire because it has smoke, like a kitchen, and also because it has light, like a furnace. And the strengthening of the cognition lies in easier understanding.

This whole idea of the strength of cognition or easier understanding, says Uddyotakara, is unsound. If these philosophers mean that more than one hetu and one example produce the necessary cognition, this is undoubtedly true. But, then, if the cognition has already been produced by means of one, the second is entirely useless; it would be like bringing another lamp when the object has already been illumined by one. Further, there would be a *regressus ad infinitum* if more than one was allowed; for in that case one could go on adding means of proof, even after the proposition had already been established (NV V.2,13).

13. According to Gautama, the deficiency of 'repetitive' [statement] occurs when words and meanings are repeated in a reasoning, except in the case of reiteration (*anuvāda*) (NS V.2,14). In reiteration there is no repetition because a special meaning is derived from the word which is repeated (NS V.2,15). Repetition consists also in mentioning a thing by name, although the thing has been indicated through implication (NS V.2,16).

Vātsyāyana explains: When a person says 'sound is eternal, sound is eternal', it is a case of repetition of words. When a person says 'sound is non-eternal; phoneme (*dhvani*) is liable to destruction', he is merely re-stating the idea of the non-eternality of sound. It is also a case of repetition of words if after having stated that 'sound is non-eternal because it is produced' the man goes on to add that what has the property of being produced is non-eternal.

Reiteration is not a case of repetition because it serves an additional purpose: for example, the conclusion of a reasoning re-states the proposition after the hetu and the example have been stated (NBh V.2,15).

14. According to Gautama, the deficiency of 'silence' occurs when a disputant fails to re-state what has been stated by his opponent three times, and understood by the audience (NS V.2,16). When the meaning of a sentence or an argument has been understood by the audience and stated three times by the opponent, the disputant should be able to re-state the opponent's

position; without such a re-statement he cannot advance argu- ments against that position. This, says Vātsyāyana, constitutes the deficiency of 'silence' (NBh V.2,17).

Some philosophers maintain that it is not necessary for the disputant to reproduce what his opponent has said. His business is to answer counter-arguments and he should be judged on the merits of his answers. The disputant may be able to meet the counter-arguments without reproducing them; he cannot therefore be said to have been defeated. In fact, when the disputant, having stated his proposition, is unable to maintain it in debate, all that we can say is that he is not good at debate, and not that his view is wrong.

Uddyotakara does not agree with this view. If the disputant does not restate the opponent's position, his answer is addressed to nothing (lit. objectless). If he is able to answer, there should be no difficulty in restating the opponents' view; if fact, it is a contradiction in terms to say that he does not restate the arguments and yet answers them. The Naiyāyika does not insist that the disputant must first restate the opponents' arguments and yet answer them. If he does answer without restating, his answer is an improper one (NV V.2,17).

15. When an argument is not understood, says Gautama, we have the deficiency of 'ignorance' (NS V. 2,18). When a disputant fails to understand an argument which is understood by the audience and repeated three times by his opponent, he is unable to refute his opponent. This, says Vātsyāyana, is a ground for defeat (NBh V.2,18).

16. The deficiency of 'reticence' arises, says Gautama, when a disputant does not know the answer (NS V.2,19). The answer consists in the refutation of his opponents' view; when the disputant does not realize this, says Vātsyāyana, he is defeated (NBh V.2,18). For example, the disputant recites verses instead of refuting the arguments of his opponent; this clearly shows, says Uddyotakara, that he is confused (NV V.2,18).

17. The deficiency of 'evasion' occurs, says Gautama, when a disputant breaks off the discussion on the pretext that he has to attend to some other work (NS V.2,20). When a disputant, having commenced a discussion, breaks it off on the pretext of some other work, and promises to resume it after he has finished that work, he is guilty of evasion. The disputant, by breaking

off in this fashion, concludes the discussion which he had commenced, and turns it into a new discussion when it is resumed after a lapse of time. This, says Vātsyāyana, constitutes 'evasion' (NBh V. 2,20). Uddyotakara mentions that the disputants sometimes pretend that they have eaten too much or have a cough which obstructs their speech. Such pretexts are given to conceal their ignorance and deserve to be condemned (NV V.2,20).

18. The deficiency 'admission of an opinion', says Gautama, consists in charging the opposite view with a defect in such a manner as involves the admission of the same defect in one's own view (NS V.2,21). When an opponent points out a defect in the view of a disputant, the latter merely says that the same defect is found in the former's view; this amounts to the admission of that defect in his own view and thus of the opinion of his opponent. This, says Vātsyāyana, constitutes a ground for defeat (NBh V.2,21). For example, when a man is charged—'you are a thief because you are a man'—he simply replies: 'You are also a thief'. If he did not wish to admit the charge, says Uddyotakara, he should have replied: 'Being a man cannot be a reason for being a thief; what makes one a thief is the connection with something belonging to another person, not freely given away by him.' If such an answer is not given, the man is defeated. Some philosophers argue that there is no ground for defeat because the disputant merely says: 'if being a man is a reason for being a thief, then, since you also are a man, you also are a thief'. In so saying he has really betrayed his ignorance of the right answer (NV V.2,21).

19. The deficiency of 'failure to point out error', says Gautama, consists in not rebuking a person who deserves a rebuke (NS V.2,22). When a person is guilty of any of the recognized faults, he should be censured explicitly: 'You have committed such and such a fault'. Such a person cannot be expected to be timid enough to say: 'I am guilty of a fault but you did not point it out to me'. In this situation, it is the duty of the audience, says Vātsyāyana, to censure him when a direct appeal is made to it: 'Who is defeated ?' (NBh V.2,22). According to Uddyotakara it is no defence in such a case that the person concerned goes on speaking and offering other answers. If there is a fault, it should be pointed out then and there (NV V.2,22).

20. The deficiency 'blaming of a faultless statement', says

Gautama, consists in charging a person with a fault when there is no such fault (NS V.2,23). It is only when a person has a wrong notion about what really constitutes the category of deficiency, says Vātsyāyana, that he would accuse his opponent of a deficiency without justification. He should then be reproached for censuring his opponent (NBh V.2,23).

21. When a person after having accepted a doctrine departs from it in the course of discussion, says Gautama, he commits the fault of 'deviating from *siddhānta*' (NS V.2,24).

Vātsyāyana illustrates the fault: A Sāṃkhya philosopher holds the doctrine: What exists does not renounce its existence; while existing there is no destruction of what now exists; what does not exist does not come into existence; nor can it be produced.

Having laid down this doctrine the philosopher proceeds to establish it: Whatever is manifested has a single origin (*prakṛti*) because modifications exhibit a homogeneous character; things like an earthen pot are all made of clay and are modifications of a single origin; whatever is manifested is found to share pleasure, pain and misconception and to have a common origin. Hence the whole universe has a single origin.

When the philosopher has thus stated his argument for his doctrine, he is asked: 'How can it be determined that a certain thing is the origin and another the modification ?' The philosopher answers: What remains in equilibrium (*vyavasthita*), while one property ceases to exist and another comes into existence, is the origin (*prakṛti*); what functions as another property is the modification.

This answer of the Sāṃkhya philosopher is contrary to the doctrine which he had previously accepted: what does not exist does not come into existence and what exists does not renounce its existence. Moreover, it is a well known fact that unless there is cessation of what has been in existence or what is coming into existence from what has not been in existence, there can be no manifestation or non-manifestation. For instance, while the clay remains constant, its own modification i.e. the jar, comes into existence; in this case the clay is said to manifest itself. When the jar has ceased to exist, the clay is said to disappear. But according to the Sāṃkhya view even such a reasonable explanation would not be right.

When such counter-arguments are urged against the Sāṃkhya

philosopher, he has two courses open to him: either he recognizes the force of these counter-arguments and admits that what exists ceases to exist and what does not exist comes into existence, or he rejects the counter-arguments. In the former case he would have deviated from his doctrine; in the latter case his doctrine would not be established (NBh V.2,24).

22. The twenty-second deficiency is 'the fallacy of the hetu'. The various fallacies which he has recognized, says Gautama, also come under the category of deficiency (NS V.2,25). According to Vātsyāyana, a question is raised: Is it because of some other characteristic that the fallacies of the hetu are regarded as deficiencies, just as the pramāṇas ? The Nyāya reply is: It is because of the characteristic of the fallacy of the hetu itself that the fallacies become deficiencies as well (NBh V.2,24).

18

DOCTRINES OF OTHER PHILOSOPHERS (*prāvāduka*)

In the first chapter of the fourth book of the *Nyāya Sūtra* Gautama examines what Vātsyāyana describes as 'doctrines of other philosophers'. As stated by the commentator the intention of Gautama is to expose these doctrines. Neither Gautama nor Vātsyāyana has named the philosophers or the systems in which these doctrines are included. The expressions the commentator uses to describe the philosophers or condemn their doctrines cannot be regarded as very polite.

This aspect has acquired some importance because one of the doctrines which figures in Gautama's review is about God. Regarding the other doctrines examined by Gautama there is no controversy; they are all considered as rejections.

Gautama has discussed the following eight doctrines: (1) Production of non-entity out of entity (2) God as cause (3) Production of entity from no cause (4) Everything is non-eternal (5) Everything is eternal (6) Everything is distinct (7) All (*sarvam*) are non-entities (*abhāva*) (8) Definite Number (*saṃkhyaikānta*).

Gautama's aphorisms on this subject are sandwiched between those on the state after death (*pretyabhāva*) and those on the result (*phala*). He has examined these doctrines in thirty aphorisms.

1. Production of non-entity (abhāva) out of entity (bhāva)

According to Gautama, some philosophers hold the view: Entity arises out of non-entity, as there is no manifestation unless there has been destruction (NS IV.1,14). Such a formulation, says Gautama, cannot be used because it involves contradiction (NS IV.1,15). The proponent of the view argues that words indicative of [Sanskrit] grammatical case-relations are applied to the past and future (NS IV.1,16). To this Gautama's answer is: (a) This is not so, because nothing is produced from things destroyed (NS IV.1,17); (b) There is no objection if sequence is mentioned (NS IV.1,18).

Vātsyāyana explains the formulation of the philosophers: Entity (*sat*) is produced out of non-entity (*asat*) because there can be manifestation only after destruction; e.g. a sprout is produced only after the seed has been destroyed. If the destruction of the seed were not the cause of the sprout, the sprout would be produced even without the destruction of the seed (NBh IV. 1,14).

Gautama's reply is explained thus: That which destroys cannot be said to come into existence after that destruction for it must have been already present to effect the destruction; if it had not already been present it could not have effected the destruction. The expression used by the proponent is therefore self-contradictory (NBh IV.1,15).

According to Vātsyāyana, Gautama's answer to this contention is: (a) The sprout is not produced out of the destroyed seed. (b) If the proponent's hetu for the proposition 'entity is produced out of non-entity is 'sequence' in the sense that destruction precedes production', such sequence is not disputed. All that Gautama wishes to maintain is that the previous pattern has ceased and another has come into existence; it is out of this latter pattern — and not out of absence — that the next substance is produced. In the case of the seed and the sprout there is a certain motion in the components of the seed owing to some cause, where upon they abandon their previous pattern and take up another; it is from this latter pattern that the sprout is produced. In fact we perceive that the components of the seed and their conjunction are the cause of the production of the seed.

Unless the previous pattern is destroyed, it is not possible for another pattern to come into existence. This is all that constitutes the sequence between destruction and production. For the production of the sprout there is no other cause except the components of the seed; it is therefore but right to treat the seed as the cause of the sprout (NBh IV.I,18). The seed, says Uddyotakara, is the material cause (*upādāna*). Hence, the hetu, viz. sequence, cannot prove the proposition of the proponent that the entity is produced out of non-entity.

2. God as Cause

Regarding Gautama's attitude towards God there is considerable controversy. Vātsyāyana introduces Gautama's aphorism on God with the remark: 'Another (philosopher) says', and characterizes the doctrine of eternality as a 'one-sided view' (*ekānta*). It is therefore obvious that the doctrines mentioned by Gautama are not his own; that is, they are not *siddhānta*. This may be borne out by the fact that Gautama's view on the subject is placed in the midst of doctrines selected for refutation. It is also significant to observe that apart from the three aphorisms on God in the present context, Gautama has not mentioned this subject in any of his other aphorisms as his own view (*siddhānta*) or as an argument in support of any of his other theories or in refutation of views with which he disagrees.

A straightforward interpretation of the three aphorisms on God would be on the following lines: God is the cause (*kāraṇa*) (= proposition) because the karma of man is observed to be without fruit (= hetu) (NS IV.I.19). There is no production of fruit in the absence of the karma of men (NS IV.I,20). It is because the production of result is due to the karma of man, that the hetu cited in support of the proposition is no hetu (NS IV.I,21). Hence God is not the cause.

On this interpretation which conforms to the text of the aphorisms the least that can be said is that the hetu has not proved the proposition. Since he has not touched upon this topic elsewhere there is no reason to attribute to the author of the *Nyāya Sūtra* any positive doctrine on God.

It is true that Vāṭsyāyana interprets these aphorisms as indicating Gautama's acceptance of God as the cause, albeit *nimitta-kāraṇa*. But he does not give any evidence in support of such a thesis. Three things should, however, be noted in this context. In the first place, the creation that is in question is the production of body, sense-organs, sensible objects, etc. and not the creation of the universe. Secondly, it is the karma doctrine which guarantees the fruits of deeds. The karma is the intermediate entity between the deed and the fruit. Thirdly, the production of the psycho-physical complex of the self is without beginning.

Regarding the purpose of Gautama in undertaking the examination of the various doctrines, Uddyotakara seems to have realized the difficulty. He introduces Gautama's discussion with the remark: "The doctrines of philosophers are exposed hereafter; some of them are rejected while others are accepted" (NV IV.I,13). Amongst the eight doctrines examined seven are treated as rejected, and one, i.e. the doctrine on God, is accepted. In his comments on the three aphorisms he follows the line adopted by Vātsyāyana. He not only comments on Vātsyāyana's views but also refutes other views on the subject. But both are agreed that God is the efficient cause. It is interesting to note here that Uddyotakara thinks that no separate investigation is necessary first to establish the existence of God, as to say that he is the cause is to say that he exists.

The interpretation of Gautama's three aphorisms (cf. above) as given by Vātsyāyana is as follows:

The doctrine mentioned by Gautama in the first aphorism is as follows: Man, desiring a certain thing, does not necessarily obtain the result of his desire; from this is inferred that his acquisition of the fruits of his actions is dependent upon some one other than himself; therefore God is the cause (NBh IV.1,19).

The second aphorism states the objection: If the production of results were dependent upon God, then such results could be accomplished even without the desire of man (NBh IV.1,20).

The third aphorism states Gautama's answer to the objection: God helps the effort of man; i.e. when man is making an effort to obtain a particular result, God accomplishes that result; when God does not accomplish it, man's karma becomes fruitless; since God accomplishes (the result), the hetu — 'the non-production of result in the absence of the karma of man'— is not a valid hetu.

On this subject of God Vātsyāyana has explained his view as follows:

God is a distinct self endowed with distinguishing properties. Since he belongs to the same category as the self, he cannot be placed under any other category. From scripture also we learn that God is the 'seer, the cognizer and the knower of all things'. But God does not have marks such as *buddhi*, etc., then how can we prove such God who has no marks ? In order to prove the existence of any object we have to depend upon such pramāṇas as perception, inference, or scripture. If God operated without regard for the results of the deeds done by selves, then this would be open to all those objections that have been raised against the view that the production of body is not due to the karma of selves.

As already mentioned, God is a distinct self endowed with distinguishing properties. These properties of God are: merit, knowledge and *samādhi* since demerit, misapprehension and defects have been destroyed; eight fold 'power' (*aiśvarya*) consisting of minuteness, etc., as the result of his merit and *samādhi*. His merit follows his volition (*saṅkalpa*). He operates the residuum of merit and demerit subsisting in each self, as also the elements (viz. earth etc.). He is omnipotent with reference to his creation but not without due regard for the results of deeds done by those whom he has created; he should be regarded as having obtained the results of his deed. He is in the category of āpta. He is to the elements what the father is to his children (NBh IV.1,21).

Uddyotakara's views on God

(A) *God as cause*

According to Uddyotakara, in order to establish that God is the efficient cause, it is not necessary to establish his existence, namely, the existence of God is established by that same proof which established that he is the cause since what does not exist can never be the cause.

The proof for God as the cause is as follows: Primordial matter (*pradhāna*), atoms and karma can act only when prior to their activity they are controlled by a conscious cause, because they are themselves unconscious, like the axe; the axe, etc., being unconscious, act only when they are controlled by the conscious carpenter.

There are numerous unquestionable proofs for God as the efficient cause. Uddyotakara explains the Nyāya view as follows:

We do not say that God is the cause independently of the karma of man, etc.; what we do assert is that God helps the karma of man. To help in this context means that God regulates each karma (of each man) in accordance with its true character and its time of fruition. If God were regarded as the cause independently of karma, there would be no possibility of release. The Nyāya view of God is free from this defect.

As one who regulates the production of the result, God is the efficient cause. 'Efficient' is a cause which helps the other two causes, viz. the inherent cause and the non-inherent cause; for example, the shuttle, which is the efficient cause of the cloth, helps the yarns which are the inherent cause, and the conjunction of the yarns which is the non-inherent cause. So far as the world is concerned God is the efficient cause helping the movement of subtle atoms to form the earth and other substances.

Uddyotakara criticizes the following two views regarding the efficient cause of the world: (a) The activity of *prakṛti* is controlled by the purpose of the *puruṣa*; (b) The activity of atoms is controlled by the karma of *puruṣa*.

(a) According to the Sāṃkhya, the activity of *prakṛti*, which is the cause of the world, is controlled by the purpose of *puruṣa*; this purpose is twofold: the perception of sound, etc., and the perception of the difference between the *puruṣa* and the constituents of *prakṛti*; neither of these purposes can be fulfilled without the activity of the *prakṛti*.

This doctrine, says Uddyotakara, cannot be accepted because the activity envisaged is not possible. There can be neither perception of sound, etc., nor perception of the difference between the *puruṣa* and the constituents of the *prakṛti* until the *prakṛti* becomes active and is modified into *mahat* (*buddhi*), etc. In the absence of these causes it is not right to say that there is any activity of the *prakṛti*.

The Sāṃkhya argues: These causes must be regarded as present for that which does not exist already can never come into existence, and that which exists can never cease to exist.

If this argument were accepted, replies Uddyotakara, it would mean that what regulates the activity of the *prakṛti* is the purpose of the *puruṣa* which is already present so that the activity of the *prakṛti* could not be for the fulfilling of the purpose of the *puruṣa*; in ordinary life one does not strive to obtain a thing which one already has.

Further, since the cause, i.e. the purpose of the *puruṣa*, is eternally there, the activity of the *prakṛti* should be unceasing. If, even though present, the purpose of the *puruṣa* does not activate the *prakṛti*, then such a purpose cannot be the cause of the activity; for that alone can be regarded as the cause of the activity of the *prakṛti*, which being present, the *prakṛti* becomes active and which being absent, it does not.

According to the Sāṃkhya, the *prakṛti* is in a state of equilibrium: this equilibrium ceases and it is followed by a state of disequilibrium; the disequilibrium is due to the relation of mutual dependence among the three constituents being unsettled.

This explanation, says Uddyotakara, does not meet the situation. How can what has been equal in the *prakṛti* (i.e. the three constituents) come to be more or less so ? For certainly there is neither an addition of anything new nor a subtraction of anything that has been there.

Further, according to the Sāṃkhya, the *puruṣa* apprehends sound, etc., not perceived before; it is the *buddhi* that makes them apprehended. When these things are apprehended, says Uddyotakara, have they any specific property ((*viśeṣa*) produced in them or not ? If specific properties have been produced in things on their apprehension, it would mean that the properties that did not exist before have been produced; this is against the Sāṃkhya view that what has not been in existence already cannot be produced. If, on the other hand, the specific properties are not produced in things on their apprehension, this is contrary to the Sāṃkhya view that it is the purpose of the *puruṣa* that activates the *prakṛti*.

The proponent of the view argues that the *puruṣa* should be regarded as the controller of merit and demerit, which belong to him. This is not possible, says Uddyotakara, because merit and demerit cannot be there before the *puruṣa* has already acquired body and sense-organs; until he has acquired them he remains without apprehension of colour etc.; and if there be no apprehension, he cannot acquire merit and demerit. Further, if the *puruṣa* were independent in his action, he could not produce pain for himself; for certainly no one wishes to have pain for oneself. Even when a person strikes his own limbs or cuts off his own head, he does so with the notion that the maiming and the dying are good for him.

(b) Some philosophers hold that the cause of the world is 'atoms as controlled by the karma of the *puruṣa*'. If atoms are active, says Uddyotakara, such activity should be unceasing. The proponents of this view argue that this contingency need not arise as the atoms operate within the framework of time. Both time and atoms are unconscious and therefore stand in need of a conscious controller.

The proponents of this view contend that unconscious things also can be active; for example, just as milk, which is unconscious, is active (i.e. flows out) for the nourishment of the calf, so also atoms, though unconscious, would be active for the fulfilment of the purpose of the *puruṣa*.

This, says Uddyotakara, is not right; for it has yet to be proved that either the atoms are active by themselves or the unconscious milk is active by itself. In fact, if the milk were active by itself, then it would flow out of the teats of the dead mother as well; it does not flow out of dead bodies; it follows that the milk is under the influence of a conscious agent. Hence it is reasonable to conclude that whenever an unconscious thing is active, it is also only under the influence of a conscious agent. The proponents argue that the atoms become active when controlled by merit and demerit. This is not right, says Uddyotakara, because merit and demerit are unconscious as well.

The proponents argue that action is produced by merit and demerit, through the atoms. No such thing, says Uddyotakara, is ever found to happen; in fact action is never produced by what is an object (*karma* = accusative) or an instrument (*karaṇa*). The *ātman* cannot be the agent (*kartṛ*) because he cannot apprehend anything before he has acquired body and sense-organs. Nor would it be right to say that the body etc., are produced without cause, as no such thing has ever been seen. And no other explanation is possible. Hence the only possible conclusion is that atoms as well as karma become active only when controlled by conscious agents.

(B) *Examination of objections*

Uddyotakara examines the following two objections raised against the Nyāya view of God as the cause:

(i) Agents like the potter are endowed with action. God is devoid of action (=hetu). He cannot therefore be the cause.

(ii) God cannot be the cause because none of the alternatives under the Nyāya theory is tenable.

Uddyotakara rejects the first objection on the following grounds: Actions are of two kinds: actions such as throwing upwards and actions which are described by means of verbs. If God is devoid of action in the first sense, this hetu is inconclusive; for we find both kinds of causes, with action and without action. For instance, when two atoms are in motion and they come into contact, their action ceases; it is only then that through their contact the two things produce other substances; this is an example of the production of things by causes without action. When two things come into contact by the action of one of them and this action comes to an end as the result of that contact, the new substance is produced simultaneously with the said cessation of the action of one of the two substances.

If it is argued that God is devoid of action in the second sense (i.e. described by verbs), this argument is not valid; for God is regarded as eternally independent. This independence of God means that he is not influenced by any agents but he influences other agents. This is the general Nyāya position regarding the case-relations (*kāraka*).

Uddyotakara explains the second objection:

(a) If God is the agent, does he act independently of some things or all things ? If he acts independently of some things, he could act independently of all things. If he acts independently of all things, there would be no result of the karma of the *puruṣa*; and this would rule out the possibility of release. And in that case this doctrine would be open to all objections raised against the view that the production of the body etc., is not due to the karma of man.

(b) If God acts in dependence of something, he cannot be the agent of that by the help of which he makes other things.

Uddyotakara answers the second objection as follows:

(a) Regarding the first alternative, the Nyāya view is not open to the objection that merit and demerit are fruitless or that the creation of the world is not dependent upon the actions of men.

(b) Regarding the second alternative, the commentator says that it is not true in all cases that one does not produce a thing by means of which one produces a different object; for instance, a man who is well-versed in several crafts produces an axe with which he produces sticks, etc. Similarly, with the help of merit and demerit God makes the body, pleasure, pain, etc.; he also brings into existence merit and demerit with the help of mind-self contact accompanied by pure and impure intentions; he also produces pure and impure intentions through the recollection of past pleasures and pains, and with the help of objects that brought about those pleasures and pains. Thus God makes things one after another.

The opponent argues that when God makes a certain thing, he is not the maker of that which helps him in the making of that thing. If this means that he cannot be the maker of the thing at the particular time, then the answer is that God does not make the things at one and the same time; he makes them one after the other.

The opponent asks: How can God make a thing in the beginning without the help of anything else ? That is, if he creates the body etc., through the help of merit and demerit, how does he produce the first thing ? The commentator's answer is that there is no such thing as the beginning of production; the *saṃsāra* is without beginning. This also explains how merit and demerit come to produce their results; merit and demerit subsisting in living beings can produce their results only if the *saṃsāra* is without beginning and the agent is dependent upon other things.

(C) *God's purpose*

In ordinary life those are agents who do a certain thing with a certain motive — 'I shall obtain this thing' or 'I shall discard this thing'. For God there can be nothing to be discarded, because he has no pain; nor can there be anything to be acquired, as he is all-powerful.

A question naturally arises: When God makes things, for what purpose does he make them? Some philosophers hold that he creates them for amusement (*krīḍā*). This cannot be right, says Uddyotakara, because God, having no pain, cannot be a seeker after joy (*rati*).

There are other philosophers who hold that God creates the world in order to make his powers known (*vibhūti*); yet others think that God creates the world in order to make known the manifoldness of the world. According to the commentator, God has nothing to gain by making his powers known nor anything to lose by not making them known. The correct view is that it is by reason of his nature (*svabhāva*) being so that God creates things; his very nature is activity (*pravṛtti*). Just as the earth upholds things because such is its very nature, so does God act because such is his very nature.

An objection is raised: If the true nature of God consists of activity then he cannot be active and inactive by turns. If the true nature of a thing is activity, it cannot cease to be active. It follows that God cannot say: 'Let this be now; let this not be now'; for out of a cause that is uniform, we do not find diversity of effects being produced.

Uddyotakara rejects this objection, as it has no bearing on his position. The Nyāya view is that the true nature of God has a qualifier, *buddhi*. His true nature thus qualified by *buddhi* and dependent upon other things can never be constantly active; it cannot produce everything at one and the same time. In fact, that alone comes into existence the causes of which happen to be in proximity with one another, while that of which the causes are not in such proximity does not come into existence. Before God does become active, he has to wait for the time of fruition of merit and demerit to arrive, and those belonging to the beings related to the things to be created, and the non-obstruction of the condition mentioned above.

(D) *God's Power (aiśvarya)*

Regarding the power of God, a question arises: Is it eternal or non-eternal ? If it is non-eternal, the cause that produces it should be indicated; in the case of the person and other beings whose powers are non-eternal, there is always a diversity of causes that produces those powers. If, however, there are diverse causes of God's powers, we would have to speak of several Gods. If two Gods, with conflicting motives, intended to undertake an activity for the production of a single thing, there would be no activity at all. If it be held that one God surpasses the other, then the one that surpasses would be the God, and not the other. If, on the other hand, the powers of God are eternal, then there would be no use for merit; for his powers, being eternal, could not be the result of his merit.

According to Uddyotakara, the correct view is that God's powers are eternal. We do attribute merit to God even though that merit does not give special powers. But it does help the individual selves in accomplishing their merit and demerit. In reality merit is not God's property.

(E) *God and selves*

It is argued that since it is not possible to determine the nature of God, there would always be a doubt as to whether God is a substance or he belongs to one of the other categories like property. According to Uddyotakara God is a substance because he is endowed with a property, viz. *buddhi*, like other substances. But he is not like other selves because he has distinct properties. Just as earth, etc., though substances, are not selves on account of their distinct properties, so also God is not just another self on account of his properties being different from those of the self; he is different from other selves.

Regarding the difference between the properties of God and those of self some philosophers maintain that the merit, knowledge, dispassion and power of God are of a superior order; and this superiority lies in their eternality.

Uddyotakara rejects this view on the ground that there is no proof for the eternality of God's merit, etc.; as there is for the eternality of his *buddhi*. The real superiority of God which distinguishes him from other selves lies in the eternality of his *buddhi*. Like ākāśa, God has six properties: number, dimension, separateness, conjunction, disjunction, and *buddhi* and all of these are eternal.

The proof for the eternality of God's *buddhi* consists in the fact that atoms are active only when controlled by an intelligent agent. It is urged that this fact only proves that God has *buddhi*, and not that his *buddhi* is eternal. The eternality of *buddhi* is evident, says Uddyotakara, from the fact that it is not restricted to only one thing, while such restriction is found only when body is present. Furthermore, it is observed that God's *buddhi* produces several effects at one and the same time. God being intelligent is not connected with body. And body itself is non-eternal.

It is argued that God's *buddhi* might be regarded as a single *buddhi* consisting of one or more series of *buddhis*. In the former case, says Uddyotakara, it would not be possible for several immovable things to come into existence at one and the same time; in the latter case we would be going against facts of perception. Any one who is prepared to hold such views might as well admit the eternality of *buddhi*.

It is argued that if God is different from other selves on account of his properties being different from those of other selves, such things as have the same properties (e.g. time, space) should be regarded as identical.

This argument, says the commentator, is not right: What the

Naiyāyika says is that from the difference in properties there follows the diversity of things, and not that from the non-difference of properties there follows the identity of things. For example, though several jars have the same properties, yet they are many; so that even though time and space have the same properties, yet they are regarded as different; for they produce diverse effects.

Unless God had intelligence the world would not come into existence. This intelligence operates on all things, past, present and future. It is perceptional, and not inferential or scriptural; for neither inference nor scripture has any bearing on it. His knowledge is eternal and there is therefore no impression (*saṃskāra*) in his case. He has no memory because his intelligence is eternal and also there is absence of impression. Recollection being absent, he has no need for inference. He has no pain because he has no demerit; having no pain, he is not disgusted with things; for that same reason he has no hatred; there is desire, but it is not tainted. His desire is unobstructed in regard to all things, just as is his intelligence.

God is not bound because he experiences no pain. Not being bound, he cannot be released. It is only the bound one that can be released.

Regarding the relation of God to the other selves, Uddyotakara criticizes the following two objections:

(a) Since there is absence of relation with the other selves, he cannot control them. The real contention, says Uddyotakara, is that since the merit and demerit inherent in the other selves are not related to God, directly or indirectly, they are not controlled by him; they are therefore not operative.

The commentator rejects this objection on the ground that the relation between God and the other selves cannot be said to have come into existence at any time (*aja*). In fact, such a view has been held by some philosophers; it may be taken as the Nyāya view as it has not been denied in the Nyāya system. These philosophers prove the timeless relation as follows: God is related to ākāśa and other all-pervading substances because he is related to corporeal substances; just as the jar, which is a corporeal substance, is related to ākāśa and other all-pervading substances.

Those philosophers who do not accept the timeless relation

will have to concede that God is related to the other selves. Every self has a mind which is atomic; all these minds are related to God; it is through this relation of God with the minds that he controls all selves; just as action is produced in the hand by the man's effort and the connection of the self with the hand, and the hand, thus rendered active, becomes connected with the pincer or some such implement, and by means of these implements he gets at the red-hot iron ball.

(b) The argument based on relationship may prove that God is the cause of production at the beginning of the world, but it seems to imply that he is not the cause of the world at present.

Uddyotakara's answer to this objection is that the arguments which prove initial production also hold good for continuous production: (a) The merit and demerit of the embodied beings who are now dead are controlled by an intelligent agent. (b) The unconscious elements are performing their respective functions of upholding objects, only because they are controlled by an intelligent agent. Similarly, grass and similar things are controlled by the intelligent agent because they are the objects of perceptions.

Apart from these arguments, there is the scriptural proof for God being the cause. The scripture says: The ordinary man, ignorant and not master of his own pleasure and pain, can go to heaven or to hell, only as propelled by God. When that God is awake, then alone is the world active; and when, with his mind composed, he goes to sleep, the whole world vanishes (NV IV. I,21).

3. Production of entity from without cause (animitta)

Gautama mentions the following view: Entity is produced without cause as we observe the sharpness of the thorn, etc. (NS IV. I,22). Vātsyāyana explains: The body etc., are produced without cause, as the sharpness of the thorn, the variegated colour of the minerals in the mountain, the smoothness of stones, etc., are found to be produced without any cause (i.e. instrumental cause) and yet each of them has a material cause (*upādāna*) (NBh IV. I,22).

Gautama refers to the following reply given by some philosophers: Entity cannot be said to be produced without cause, because the 'without cause' is the cause of its production

(NS IV. I,23). Vātsyāyana explains: The expression used by the proponent of the view is '*animittato bhāvotpattiḥ*' (production of entity without cause). The first word in this phrase ends in the suffix (*to* = *taḥ*) which has the sense of the ablative. That from which a thing proceeds is inevitably its cause; since the production of entity is said to proceed without cause, this 'without cause' is the cause of the production of entity; it follows that this production cannot be said to be 'without' cause (NBh IV. I,23).

This answer of some philosophers is no answer at all, says Gautama, because cause and 'without cause' are two different things (NS IV. I,24). That which is denied of a particular thing, says Vātsyāyana, is not tantamount to the denial of the thing itself; for example, when we say 'a pot is without water' (lit. 'with no water') what is denied is the water in the pot, and not water itself.

The commentator adds that the doctrine under discussion is not different from the view that the production of the body etc. is not caused by karma; the arguments given against that view hold good against the present view.[1]

According to Uddyotakara, it is possible to find out an instrumental cause by means of inference in the case of things where we do not perceive such a cause. Objects with shape such as a jar, have instrumental causes, and since the thorn, etc., have shape, they also have instrumental causes. Moreover, it is not acceptable to both parties that there is any object with shape but without an instrumental cause. Further, if the proponent of the view wishes to maintain that everything is produced without cause, he would be going against the position about the teacher and the taught, which he accepts: the teacher is an instrumental cause. Besides, in the case of an unrestricted generalisation like 'every thing is produced without cause', there can be no instance to corroborate it. If the generalization is meant to cover only a few things, e.g. the body etc., then whatever is cited as an instance would be wanting in one of the properties of the probandum: it would have the property of shape but not the property of being without cause.

We have two statements: (a) the production of entity is 'without cause' (i.e. 'with no cause'), and (b) 'the production of entity is 'with cause'. These two statements have different meanings. If the proponent of the view under discussion perceives the difference between their meanings, this perception of difference can only arise from the difference between the two statements; that is, he thereby accepts a cause for his perception. If, on the other hand, the proponent does not see the difference, due to the difference between the statements, then there is no point in making any particular statement; any statement might be used to convey any meaning. To assert that entity is produced without cause is to destroy the whole pattern of human behaviour (NV IV.I,22-24).

4. Everything is non-eternal

Gautama mentions the following view: Everything is non-eternal because it has the properties of being produced and being destroyed (NS IV.I,25). Vātsyāyana explains: That is called non-eternal which exists for some time. That which has the property of being produced does not exist while it is not produced; that which has the property of being destroyed is non-existent when it has been destroyed. Since every thing material (e.g. the body, etc.) and every thing non-material (e.g. *buddhi*, etc.) are known to have the properties of being produced and being destroyed, it follows that every thing is non-eternal (NBh IV. I,25).

Some philosophers refute this view as mentioned in the following aphorisms of Gautama: This is not so because of the eternality of the non-eternality (NS IV.I,26). According to Vātsyāyana, these philosophers say that if the non-eternality of every thing is eternal it cannot be true that everything is non-eternal; if, on the other hand, the non-eternality in question is not eternal, then while the non-eternality would be non-existent, everything would be eternal (NBh IV.I,25).

To this refutation of the philosophers, Gautama objects: The non-eternality is not eternal, like the destruction of fire which has destroyed the thing burnt by it (NS IV. I,27). Just as fire, after having destroyed the thing burnt by it, is itself destroyed, says Vātsyāyana, the non-eternality of every thing, after every thing has been destroyed, is itself destroyed (NBh IV.I,27).

According to Gautama, the correct position is that the eternal cannot be denied because the determination (as to whether a thing is eternal or non-eternal) must be in accordance with what is apprehended (NS IV.I,28). Explaining Gautama's answer,

Vātsyāyana observes: The view under consideration totally denies eternality, but such a total denial is wrong. When a thing is found to have the properties of being produced and being destroyed it should be regarded as non-eternal on the basis of the pramāṇa concerned; a thing that does not have these properties should be regarded as eternal. In fact these properties are not apprehended by any pramāṇa in the following: the four elements in their subtle form, ākāśa, time, space, self and mind; some of their properties, for example, universal, particular and inherence; it follows that all these are eternal (NBh IV.I,28).

According to Uddyotakara, the view under consideration is faulty for the following reasons: The proposition 'everything is eternal' cannot be proved by the hetu 'because it has the properties of being produced and being destroyed', as there are things like atoms, which are neither produced nor destroyed. Besides there can be no corroborative instance, as the subject of the proposition includes everything.

Secondly, the negative particle in a compound word like '*anitya*' signifies either the denial of what is possible or the exclusion, and in either case it presupposes the existence of what is denoted by the second member of the compound. If '*anitya*' denotes the denial of what is eternal, what is signified by the second term exists; for what is denied in one place is only what exists in another place. If it denotes what is 'other than eternal', even so what is signified by the term 'other' must exist; for unless the thing signified by the latter terms exists, there is no sense in saying that a thing is other than that.

Thirdly, non-eternality is a property. It cannot be a property if there is no object to which it can belong. If the proposition means that things which are produced and destroyed are non-eternal, this is quite reasonable. The opponent can either determine what things are actually produced and destroyed and what things are not, or prove that everything is non-eternal because it exists. The former procedure is reasonable. But if the opponent adopts the second course, he would be entitled to say that what exists is non-eternal or what exists is other than eternal. But in either case non-eternality would be possible only if what is denoted by the second term is accepted as existing (i.e. eternal). In either case the original proposition becomes faulty and has therefore to be rejected. (NV IV. I, 25-28).

5. Every thing is eternal

Gautama mentions the following view: Every thing is eternal because the five elements are eternal (NS IV. I,29). Vātsyāyana explains: Every thing in the world is of the nature of an element; since the destruction of elements is impossible such things are eternal (NBh IV.I,29).

Gautama rejects this view on the ground that the causes of production and of destruction are apprehended (NS IV.I,30). This is incompatible with the eternality of every thing (NBh IV. I,30).

Gautama mentions an objection to this argument: This is no refutation because the things which are produced and destroyed are not devoid of the character (*lakṣaṇa*) of the elements (NS IV. I,31). Gautama rejects this objection on the ground that the production and its cause are apprehended (NS IV.I,32).

Vātsyāyana explains the objection: The thing, of which the causes of production and destruction are apprehended, is not devoid of the character of the element concerned; it cannot therefore be regarded as different from the element. Inasmuch as every thing has the character of the element, Gautama's argument does not amount to a refutation of the view under consideration (NBh IV.I,31).

Commenting on Gautama's answer, Vātsyāyana gives several arguments:

(a) Both the cause and the production of the thing having properties similar to the cause are apprehended; neither of these is possible in the case of an eternal thing. On the strength of this apprehension we infer that the effect is produced as having properties similar to those of its cause; it is this effect which constitutes the objective basis of the apprehension mentioned above. No apprehension can be without an objective basis. This explains why the thing made up of an element has the character of the element concerned.

(b) In the case of the cognizer we find that he makes an effort only when he is impelled by a desire for the cause of the production of what he wishes to obtain and the destruction of what he wishes to discard.

(c) It is well known that every composite has the properties of being produced and being destroyed.

(d) The two hetus which the objector has given, i.e. because the five elements are eternal and because every thing has the character of the elements, are not applicable to sound, action, cognition, pleasure, pain, desire, aversion and effort; none of these is made of an element or has the character of an element. These hetus are therefore inconclusive.[2]

The objector argues that the apprehension of the cause and of production is a wrong apprehension, like a wrong apprehension of an object in a dream. In that case, says Vātsyāyana, the apprehension of things made of the elements might be regarded as similar to that in a dream. Moreover, this kind of argument cannot prove the proposition which the objector has in view. The atoms of elements are beyond the reach of the senses while the ordinary things of the world like a jar are not; they are neither produced nor destroyed while the ordinary things are produced and destroyed (NBh IV. I,32).

In his comment on the view of the eternalist, Uddyotakara points out that since nothing is produced or destroyed, all activity for obtaining what is beneficial and for avoiding what is harmful is futile. Since the subject of his proposition is 'every thing,' he can give no corroborative instance. Moreover, the very assertion of the statement, i.e. every thing is eternal because the five elements are eternal, is self-contradictory: Apparently, the eternalist makes the statement in order to explain his position to the other party. Either he wishes (a) to prove what is not known or (b) to disprove what is already known.

(a) In the former case, what sort of proving can the statement accomplish ? If it is the knowledge of the thing intended to be proved that is produced, this is incompatible with the thesis of the eternalist. If, on the other hand, the statement is not meant to produce the knowledge, what kind of proving has the eternalist accomplished by his statement ? Every agent (*kāraka*) is expected to accomplish something new; but this very idea is incompatible with the eternalists' view. And if nothing new is accomplished the agent loses its character.

(b) If, on the other hand, the eternalist intends to disprove what is already known, this would mean that he wishes to remove or set aside what is eternal; this is, of course, impossible. If the 'disproving' means 'disappearance' (*tirobhāva*) then also the eternalist will have to admit that when a certain thing disappears there is either something new produced, or some previously existing thing destroyed. In either case the position is self-contradictory (NV IV.I,31).

According to Vātsyāyana some philosophers argue the case for eternality: What really happens is that the original substance (*upādāna*) remaining constant, one property of it ceases and another property is produced. When a thing is said to be produced, it is something that has been already in existence even before its production; similarly, when a thing is said to be destroyed it continues to exist even after that destruction. Thus every thing is eternal (NBh IV.I,32).

According to the commentator, this view is refuted by Gautama in the aphorism: If everything was eternal there would be no arrangement (*vyavasthā*) (NS IV. I,33). Vātsyāyana explains how different arrangements would be upset if the thesis of the eternalist was valid. Since what is born and what has ceased to exist are both present, we would not be able to say: (a) this is birth and that is cessation; (b) this property is born and that property has ceased; (c) at this time there are birth and cessation, and not at that time; (d) there are birth and cessation of this property, and not of that; (e) this, not yet come, is in the future, and that is past. Thus all such expressions indicating the arrangements of thing, properties, relation and time would be meaningless.

According to the Naiyāyika, birth consists in coming into existence (*ātmalābha*) of what has not been in existence and cessation consists in the ceasing to exist (*ātmahāni*), of what has been in existence. This position, says Vātsyāyana, is free from the kind of upset which the thesis of the eternalist entails (NBh IV. I,33).

Commenting upon the argument of the philosophers, Uddyotakara asks the eternalist to explain what he really means when he says 'that which has ceased continues to exist after cessation'. If 'that which has ceased' means 'it was perceived before and is not perceived now', the non-perception of what exists has to be explained. If it were due to obstruction, then such obstruction should have been perceived. In fact when a thing, not perceived before, comes to be perceived, it has to be admitted that a new peculiarity (*viśeṣa*) has been produced in it and a previous one has dropped off. This is contrary to the thesis of the eternalist. Further, it is self-contradictory to say that a thing comes into existence and also that it exists. If 'coming into existence' means 'coming into view' (*āvirbhāva*) or manifestation' (*abhivyakti*) this implies that what was not in existence before comes into existence. And this is contrary to the eternalists' position (NV IV.I,33).

6. 'Sarvam' (all) is distinct

Gautama mentions the following view: All (*sarvam*) are diverse (*pṛthak*) because the marks (*lakṣaṇa*) of things refer to diverse entities (NS IV.I,34).[3] He rejects this view on two grounds: (a) Several marks[4] constitute one single entity (NS IV.I,35);[5] (b) The marks are restricted in their application (NS IV. I,36).

According to Vātsyāyana the view mentioned by Gautama is: (a) All are regarded as diverse because there is no such thing as a single entity (*bhāva*). (b) The mark (*lakṣaṇa*) of an entity is that which designates it, i.e. its name. The name refers to several objects; as a matter of fact, it refers to an aggregate (*samūha*). For instance, the name 'jar', is applied to an aggregate of odour, taste, colour and touch as well as to the aggregate of the bottom, sides and neck. (NBh IV.I,34).

Vātsyāyana explains Gautama's criticism of the view:

(a) It is a single entity which is produced as related to the properties of odour, etc., and to the components, the bottom, etc.; the substance is different from its properties and the composite from its components. This has already been established.[6]

The marks of things are restricted in their application; the mark of an entity, i.e. the word that is its name, for example, 'jar', is applicable to a single entity, as is evident from such expressions as 'I am touching that jar which I saw before'. Moreover, since an aggregate of atoms composing the jar is imperceptible, that which is actually perceived (i.e. the jar) must be a single entity.

(b) The argument of the proponent that there can be no single entity (= proposition) because the names of things refer to aggregates (= hetu) is doubly self-contradictory. If there is no single entity there can be no aggregate, etc., for the aggregate is nothing more than a collection of several *single* things. What is accepted in the hetu is denied in the proposition. The hetu is based upon the admission of the 'aggregate' and in denying the 'single entity' in the proposition, what can constitute the 'aggregate', viz. each component (i.e. a single entity) is denied. In view of this twofold contradiction, says the commentator, the view of the opponent must be dismissed as futile (*akiñcanavāda*) (NBh IV.I, 35-36).

The proponent's argument, says Uddyotakara, is: The name of a thing is the word, and all the names of things refer to diverse (*aneka*) objects. For example, the word 'jar' must refer to diverse objects, because it is a single word, like the word 'army', and because when we hear a word we have the cognition of several things (NV IV.I,34).

The commentator refutes this argument:

(a) There is no word that refers to diverse objects; the word 'army' refers to a single object. The hetu, i.e.. because it is a single word, is therefore not right.

(b) Since 'all names' is the subject of the proposition, there can be no corroborative instance.

(c) The fact of being a word can be explained otherwise than on the basis of the assumption that the word refers to diverse objects; in fact, colour and other properties are actually perceived as subsisting in a single entity, and this single entity is perceived to be the composite object.

(d) The word '*aneka*' (diverse) contains a negative particle which governs '*eka*' (one). Such a particle can be used only to denote either the denial of what is possible or exclusion. In the present case, '*aneka*' would mean that things are 'not-one'. This implies that what is denied (i.e. one) in one place exists elsewhere. If it denotes exclusion, *aneka* would mean 'that which is other than one'. In either case the existence of 'one' is implicitly admitted (NV IV.I,35).

The contention of the proponent, i.e. when the name 'jar' is uttered, it gives rise to the cognition of several things, is not right. The word 'jar' has a singular ending and as such cannot apply to things more than one. Moreover, when such words are used, they are understood as referring to single things.

The proponent of the view thinks that what the name of a thing denotes is its properties and components. The truth is that these do not constitute the denotation of words; they come in merely by implication (*anuṣaṅga*) as they are internal to the thing denoted.

If every thing were a mere aggregate, there could be no end to its dismemberment; hence the point where the dismemberment ceases must be the single entity. According to the proponent's view, since every object is an aggregate of components, it would not be possible to conceive of any thing becoming smaller and smaller by the process of dismemberment, as each dismembered piece would be capable of never-ending dismemberment. Such a conception would be possible only if the object could be conceived of as composed of so many component substances. If, therefore, the conception of the aggregate is to be retained, it will have to be admitted that in the case of every object, there is a point which represents the smallest dimension to which it can be reduced by dismemberment; this smallest thing would be indivisible; so that at the point where no further dismemberment is possible there must be a single entity.

Further, if the 'one' is denied the 'many' must be denied; for the 'many' is only an aggregate of several *ones*.[7]

7. All (sarvam) are non-entities (abhāva)

Gautama mentions the following view: All (things) are non-entities (*abhāva*) because it has been established that they are non-existent in relation to one another (NS. IV.I,37).

This view is not right, says Gautama, because the entities are by virtue of their own well-established nature, entities (NS IV.I, 38).

Explaining the doctrine Vātsyāyana says: The cow is non-existent in the form of 'horse', and the cow is 'non-horse'; similarly, the horse is non-existent in the form of 'cow', and the horse is 'non-cow'. We thus find that the names of things are co-substrate with the cognition of non-existence and negation; it follows that all things are non-existent (NBh IV.I,37).

In commenting upon Gautama's answer, Vātsyāyana suggests that the expression '*svabhāvasiddher bhāvānām*' (the entities are, by virtue of their own well-established nature, entities) can be interpreted in the following ways:

(a) When Gautama says that entities are entities by virtue of their very characteristic (*dharma*), he means: (i) Existence, etc. constitute the intrinsic characteristic (*svadharma*) of substances, properties and actions; (ii) Activity etc. constitutes the specific nature (*viśeṣadharma*) of substances; each of the several things in the world has such specific characteristics, which are countless (*ananta*); (e.g. the earth has several such specific characteristics); similarly, universal, particular and inherence have also their specific characteristics.

Such diversity of things would not be possible if all things were non-entities; for a non-entity is one which has no characteristic whatsoever. Since such diversity exists, it follows that all things are not non-entities.

(b) To say that it is established that an entity has its own nature is to say that it is established that it has a distinct individuality (*svarūpa*) of its own. For example, when the word 'cow' is used, what is apprehended is a particular substance qualified by (or belonging to) a particular class (*jāti*). As already explained, this is confirmed by our experience. If all things were non-entities, the cow would have been apprehended as non-entity and the word 'cow' would have denoted a non-entity.

(c) When the proponent says that the cow is non-existent in the form of the horse, he should have really said that the cow is non-existent in the form of the cow. That he does not say so clearly shows that in the form of the cow the cow is existent; this is what is meant by saying that a thing is a thing because it has its own nature well established. It follows that the proponent concedes that in its own form the substance exists.

Whenever there is denial of non-difference (*avyatireka*) — difference (*vyatireka*), in this case, consisting of the absence of relations such as conjunction, and non-difference consisting of identity (*abheda*) — even entities are spoken of as co-substrate with the notion of non-existence; for example, the jujube fruit is not in the cup.

In the case under consideration — the cow is non-existent in the form of the horse, the cow is non-horse — what is denied is the non-difference between the cow and the horse; that is, there is no identity between the cow and the horse. When this identity is denied, we get the co-substrateness of the notion of 'non--existence' with the thing 'cow'; hence we have the expression 'the cow is non-existent in the form of the horse'. This expression is on a par with the expression 'the jujube fruit is not in the cup'; the conjunction of the fruit with the cup being denied, we have the co-substrateness of the notion of 'non-existence' with the fruit, which is a real entity (NBh IV.I,38).

The statement of the opponent is wrong; because there is contradiction (i) between the two terms of the proposition and (ii) between the proposition and the hetu.

(i) In the proposition the proponent has used the term '*sarvam*' (all). It signifies many things (*aneka*) without exception (*aśeṣatā*), while the term '*abhāva*' (non-entity) signifies the negative of existence; the former (*sarvam*) has a definite nature while the latter (*abhāva*) is devoid of any nature whatsoever. How can we predicate what is devoid of any nature whatsoever of what has a definite nature ? It is therefore self-contradictory to predicate the non-entity which is devoid of any nature whatsoever of either 'several things' or 'without exception', which are the two components of the denotation of the term '*sarvam*'. Thus the proposition is self-contradictory.

The proponent argues that this is just what is meant by 'non-entity'; what the Naiyāyika considers as 'all' is precisely what is really only non-entity. Even if this were so, retorts Vātsyāyana, the charge of contradiction remains: 'many things' and 'without exception' cannot be regarded as the notion of non-entity; and yet it is just this notion that is signified by the term 'all'; it follows that 'all' cannot be a non-entity.

(ii) The proposition is: all (things) are non-entities; it denies the existence of all things. The hetu is: 'because it is established that they are non-existent in relation to one another'. On the basis of this mutual negation among things having been established, it is asserted that all things are non-entities. If all things are non-entities, it is not possible for 'things' (entities) to be the negation of one another; if 'things' are 'negations of one another', then 'all things' cannot be non-entities'. Thus there is contradiction between the proposition and the hetu (NBh IV.I,37).

Commenting on the doctrine Uddyotakara observes that the hetu on which it is based used the expression *sāmānādhikaraṇya* (having a common locus). The meaning of this expression is that when two things have a common locus the words expressing them end with case suffixes having the same meaning. It follows that the use of this expression implies that the proponent of the doctrine admits the existence of things as well as the existence of words that constitute the names of these things. The hetu is therefore contradictory to the proposition that all are non-entities.

The proposition of the proponent is really in the form 'that which we regard as 'all' must be a non-entity', as he himself does not believe in any entity whatsoever. But we can never have the notion of 'that' with reference to a non-entity; nor can the notion of 'entity' arise from it. Besides the term '*abhāva*' (non-entity) is a negative term indicating the negation of entity.[8]

Further, if all things are non-entities, the suffixes must also be non-entities; in that case the statement that 'having the same locus' (*sāmānādhikaraṇya*) consists in having the same case suffixes which have the same meaning, is contradictory in terms. The very notion of having the same locus is opposed to the notion of non-entity (NV IV.I,37).

In the statement of the doctrine the proponent first says that all are non-entities and then that there are negations of one another. The latter really means that one thing is not another (*itara*). The term 'another' is a positive term, and if all things are non-existent, there is nothing that could be affirmed and spoken of by means of the word 'another' (NV IV.I,38).

Gautama mentions what appears to be an objection to his criticism of the doctrine 'all are non-entities'. The nature of things cannot be established because they depend upon one another (NS IV. I,39).[9] Vātsyāyana elaborates the objection: 'Relative' (dependent) is that which is due to relativity (*apekṣā*); for example, a thing is spoken of as 'long' in relation to 'short', and as 'short' in relation to 'long'; neither of the two exists by itself; this is so because of the force of relativity. Hence we cannot say that things have nature of their own (NBh IV.I,39).

This objection is invalid, says Gautama, because it is contradictory (NS IV.I,40). Vātsyāyana explains: If a thing is long in relation to 'short', and if a thing is short in relation to 'long' then both 'short' and 'long' are non-relative; for what would be related to what. If the two were to depend upon each other, then the negation of one would imply the negation of another. It is not therefore right to say that the nature of 'long' should be determined with reference to 'short' or the nature of 'short' with reference to 'long'.

Further, if there were no such thing as the 'nature' of things, we would have the relative notions of length and shortness in regard to equal atoms or to any two substances of equal size. For taken relatively or non-relatively, the two substances remain the same. If the nature of things were relative, then the relativity would surely make a difference to the nature of things.

The effect of relativity is something entirely different. When we perceive two things, it is possible for us to apprehend the preponderance (*atiśaya*) of one over the other; that is, when one perceives two things and notices a preponderance in one of them, one regards it as 'long', and that which is deficient (*hīna*), one regards as 'short'. This is the real force of relativity (NBh IV.I,40).

The doctrine of non-entities, says Uddyotakara, is utterly wrong. If the proponent explains the nature of the pramāṇas, he contradicts his thesis; if he does not, he cannot prove anything. If the proponent understands the meaning of a sentence — his assertion is a sentence — he contradicts himself, if he does not, the mere uttering of sounds is futile. If he is addressing his remarks to a speaker whom he perceives, he contradicts himself. 'All are entities' and 'all are non-entities' are two distinct sentences; if the proponent sees the difference in their meaning, he contradicts himself; if he does not, the use of different words is futile. (NV IV.I,40).

8. Definite Number (saṃkhyaikānta)

In introducing Gautama's examination of the doctrine of definite number, Vātsyāyana mentions that there are various doctrines which lay down the exact number of things. Amongst these he mentions the following: (a) All are one, all being equally existent; (b) All are two, being divided into eternal and non-eternal; (c) All are three: cognizer, cognition and cognized; (d) All are four, cognizer, pramāṇa, cognized and cognition.

A definite number cannot be established, says Gautama, whether the cause is available or not (NS IV.I,41). Vātsyāyana explains: If the means of proving the probandum is something different from the probandum, then a definite number cannot be established; for the means of proving will always be different from the probandum. If, on the other hand, there is no difference between the means of proving and the probandum, then also a definite number cannot be established; for the means of proving is absent, and without such a means of proving, nothing can be established (NBh IV.I,41).

Gautama mentions an objection: The argument is not valid, because the cause is a component of the number (NS IV.I,42). Vātsyāyana explains the objection: The means is but a component of the probandum, so that it need not be anything different. It is therefore quite possible to establish a definite number; for example, there are two things (NBh IV.I,42).

Gautama replies: The hetu mentioned in the objection is not valid because there is no component available for the purpose (NS IV.I,43).

Explaining the reply, Vātsyāyana observed: The opponent first lays down the proposition that '*sarvam* (all) is one (*ekam*) without exception', and then proceeds to state in the hetu that the means of proving is only a component of the probandum; if there is nothing apart from that one — the one (*ekam*) which, as stated in the proposition, covers all things (*sarvam*), there can be no component (or means of proving) over and above that one.

Similarly, all such views which prescribe a definite number of things e.g. two, three, etc., can be shown to be faulty.

If the views which prescribe a definite number of things are based on the denial of the vast extent (*vistāra*) of diversities among things due to their distinctive properties (*viśeṣa*), they are opposed to perception, inference and scripture; they are therefore wrong doctrines. If, on the other hand, these views proceed on the basis of the admission of such diversities, then they cannot retain any fixed number; for the enumeration of things is based upon the presence of common properties, and the diversity of things upon the presence of distinct properties (*viśeṣa*). Thus any attempt to determine the number of things must be renounced (NBh IV.I,43).

In his comments on the subject, Uddyotakara remarks that if 'all things without exception' is the subject of the proposition, there is nothing which can constitute the hetu. The probandum cannot function as hetu, as a thing cannot operate upon itself; the object (*karma*) cannot be its own instrument (*karaṇa*).

The diversity among things, such as the cow and the jar, is directly perceived. It is also apprehended by inference: What is inferred is different from that by which that inference is drawn. The scripture also leads to the apprehension of diversity: one who knows the truth is the propounder of the truth while one who does not know the truth yet is the recipient of that truth from its propounder.

If it be held that there is non-difference among things because they have common properties and there is difference among things because they possess distinct properties, then, this does not militate against the *siddhānta* (i.e. the Nyāya view). In fact, there can be no room for common properties unless there is diversity of things. If common properties are admitted, diversity must also be admitted; if diversity is denied, common properties must also be denied; for common properties cannot subsist except on the basis of diversity (NV IV.I,43).

PART FIVE : OBJECT OF COGNITION (*Prameya*): SELF (*ātman*), its equipment, career and destiny.

19

SELF (*ātman*)

I. Self as object of cognition

As already mentioned, 'self' (*ātman*) is the first object of cognition in Gautama's list of *prameyas*. It is, says Vātsyāyana, the seer, experiencer, knower and indicator of everything (NBh I. 1,9). Regarding our knowledge of the self the commentator expresses different views in different contexts. In commenting on the marks or characteristics of the self he explicitly states that the self, though an object of cognition, is not an object of perception (NBh I.1,10).[1] In the context of the list of the pramāṇas he observes: we are first advised by a reliable person that the self exists; then we use inference on the basis of the various marks enumerated by Gautama. Thus our knowledge of the self is a product of two pramāṇas, word and inference. But the commentator then goes on to add that the self can be considered as perceived but not in an ordinary sense. It is perceived by a Yogin through a special kind of mind-self contact. This perception is the product of Yogic *samādhi* (NBh I. 1,3). Since the mind is recognized by Vātsyāyana as one of the sense-organs, this kind of perception can be fitted in with the definition of perception. In fact, the commentator says in another context that the recognition of the mind as a sense-organ enables us to say that the cognition of the self, pleasure, etc., is perceptual (NBh I. 1,4).

Vātsyāyana compares the combined operation of perception and inference in the case of the self to that used for the knowledge of fire. We are first informed by a reliable person that there is fire at a particular place; we then proceed to the place and if we see smoke we infer the existence of fire; and when we reach the place, we directly perceive the fire (NBh I.1,3). Presumably, the last stage in this procedure corresponds to the Yogin's perception of the self.

Characteristics of Self

According to Gautama, the marks or characteristics of the

self are: desire, aversion, effort, pleasure, pain and cognition (NS I. 1,10). It is on the basis of these marks, says Vātsyāyana, that we have the inferential cognition of the self.

The commentator explains how these various marks function to indicate the self. When the self having experienced pleasure by coming into contact with a thing of a certain kind, comes into contact with a thing of that same kind, it desires to acquire that thing; this desire to acquire originates from remembrance of the previous apprehension; and this is possible only if a single thing apprehends many things. No such desire would be possible if there were only distinct apprehensions, each pertaining to its own distinct object; for the remembrance (*pratisandhāna*) of one apprehension by another is as impossible as the remembrance arising in one body of the apprehension arising in another body. Similarly, it is only when a single entity apprehends several things and subsequently remembers the previous apprehension that it can have aversion to the thing that has been the cause of its pain.

When a thing of a certain kind has been found to be the cause of pleasure or pain, on seeing a thing of that kind, one feels pleasure or pain and makes effort to acquire or get rid of that thing. Similarly, when one wishes to know the true nature of a thing, one first ponders over it: 'What could this be ?'; having thus pondered one comes to know it: 'This is it.' In all these cases remembrance of the previous experience is essential on a subsequent occasion when a thing is apprehended, and this, in turn, is possible only if a single agent is involved in both the operations; this agent is the self.

The philosopher who does not accept the existence of the self would readily concede that if distinct apprehensions, each pertaining to its own distinct object, appear in one body, they could never be remembered in another body; similarly, apprehensions appearing in the same body could not be remembered. For him these two cases are exactly similar, as there is no single agent in either case. Thus then, if we have a single agent, we find that it can remember only what it has perceived and not what it has not perceived or what others have perceived. Similarly, if there are diverse agents, we find that one agent does not remember what has been perceived by another. These are two well known facts and the philosopher who does not accept the existence of the self cannot give any satisfactory explanation of these facts. Thus it is proved that there is self (NBh I. 1,10).

The various characteristics of the self are not apprehended. How can they prove the existence of the self? They can, says Uddyotakāra, because both these characteristics, recognition and remembrance, have the same object; it is because of this fact that all cognitions belong to a single agent. It is well known that recognition is not possible in the following three cases:

(a) cognitions belong to different agents; for example, one person cannot recognize what another person has seen;

(b) objects of cognitions are different; for example, in no case we find a recognition of the cognitions of colour, taste, touch and odour; for example, we do not have such a recognition as 'this touch that I feel is the colour that I had seen';

(c) cognitions are produced by different instruments (i.e. sense-organs); for example, 'that by means of which I see colours now is that by means of which I had felt its touch'.

According to Uddyotakara, the existence of the self can be proved with the help of the following inferences.

(i) Devadatta's cognitions of colour, taste and touch have both many causes and a single cause. They have many causes because they are produced by many objects; they have a single cause because they are all cognized by Devadatta along with the remembrance of the same objects. This is exactly like the case of a single gesture of a dancer. Several elderly persons (*vṛddha*) see the gesture simultaneously. Thus several persons have several cognitions. But these cognitions are all recognized as produced by a single cause, i.e. the single glance of the dancer. Similarly, in the case of Devadatta he has several cognitions of colour, taste and touch, but they are all recognized as having a single cause, i.e. the self. This is a positive inference.

(ii) If there were no remembrance, there could be no recognition; but recognition is a fact. Hence the agent of the recognition is something quite distinct from cognitions and series of cognitions and this is the single entity, i.e. the self. This is a negative inference.

(iii) The characteristics mentioned by Gautama are properties. They cannot be regarded as universal, particular and inherence because these characteristics are non-eternal while the universal, particular and inherence are eternal. They cannot be substance or action because they, like sound, inhere in an all-pervading substance. [Substance does not inhere in substance while action does not always inhere in all-pervading substances]. As properties, the characteristics must subsist in something other than themselves, i.e. substance which in the present case is *ātman*.

(iv) The properties that belong to the body continue as long as the body remains in existence. As the properties of desire, etc., are not found to so continue (i.e. do not perish with the body), they cannot be regarded as properties belonging to the body. Being thus precluded from belonging to the body, they can only belong to the self.

These (iii and iv) are inferences through elimination (*pariśeṣa*) (NV I.1,10).

Buddhist Objections

Uddyotakara examines six Buddhist objections to the Nyāya view of the self. The first five are primarily concerned with the existence of the self (Introductory NV III. 1,1) and the sixth with remembrance as grounds for the assertion of the self as a single agent (NV I.1,10).

(1) Objection: There is no self (=proposition) because of non-birth (=hetu), like the hare's horn (=example) (*nāsty ātmā 'jātatvāc chaśaviṣāṇavat*) (=The self is not because it is not born, like the hare's horn.).[2]

Reply:

The expression 'the self is not' is self-contradictory for the following reasons:

(a) The term 'self' denotes an entity — something existing and the term 'is not' (=*nāsti*) denotes the denial of it. Whenever and wherever the presence of a thing is denied, all that it means is that it is not present at a particular place or time; and this implies that it is present at some other place or time. It is true that the self is neither in the body nor at any other place, but nevertheless it exists. This describes exactly the self as it exists. Nor again, is it right to deny the existence of the self with reference to past, present and future; for it is eternal.

(b) There is no word without some denotation. One who

denies the self must indicate what the word denotes. If it denotes the body, then the assertion will be 'the body is not'; this is as self-contradictory as 'the self is not'.

(c) The Buddhist argues that what his denial means is that there is no such thing as the self which the Naiyāyika has assumed. This, says Uddyotakara, is completely wrong. The existence of a thing is said to be assumed when that is regarded as something which it is not, on account of its being similar to that something, and consequently, which has the properties of this latter imposed upon it. According to the Buddhist the self is a non-entity and hence to assume it as it is not, would mean that it is an entity. But since there can be no similarity between an entity and non-entity, there can be no property in virtue of which any such assumption can be made. If, however, the opponent were to suggest that there is a resemblance between them, he would have to concede that the self exists. The Buddhist contends that when he denies the existence of the self he means that the notion of 'I' (*ahaṃkāra*) which really belongs to the body is wrongly ascribed to the self. But then, inasmuch this involves the admission of something different from the body as being the object of the notion of 'I', his position remains self-contradictory.

(d) If the Buddhist tries to escape from this predicament by saying that every word need not denote an entity (e.g. *śūnya* = void, *tamas* = darkness), this would not really help him. This is not right because even words like *śūnya* have a denotation. The word *śūnya* denotes: a substance that has no one to guard or protect it becomes 'fit for dogs', and hence is called *śūnya*, which etymologically means 'fit for dogs' (*śvabhyo hitam*). The word '*tamas*' denotes such substances, qualities and actions as are characterized by non-apprehension; that is, in a place where there is absence of light, the word *tamas*[3] is used to denote these substances, etc. Further, the Buddhist himself regards *tamas* as that which comprises the four entities of colour, taste, touch and odour.

(e) The hetu 'because of non-birth (= *ajātatvāt*),' really means the denial of something totally different from the existence of the self; it merely denies the fact of birth. To be produced and not to be produced are properties of things. A thing is said to be produced if its existence is due to a cause; it is said to be not produced when its existence is not due to a cause. The hetu therefore means that the existence of the self is not due to a cause, and not that the self does not exist at all. This interpretation is based upon what the term '*ajātatva*' means. The negative particle in the term signifies the denial of production and the whole term means that the thing in question (i.e. the self) is not produced and not that it does not exist. This is like the expression 'a pot is without water' (=*anudaka*); it does not deny the existence of the pot but only the presence of water in it.

'Being produced' is a property, and no property except 'inherence' can exist by itself. The only thing in which the property of being not produced could subsist in the present argument is the self. But if the property does, the self is admitted, and this contradicts the Buddhist proposition that 'the self is not'. If the expression 'because the self is not produced' means 'the self is not born', then the hetu is impossible, for the self has its birth, i.e. the self is connected with a new psycho-somatic complex. If the meaning of the self not being produced is that it has no cause, then the hetu becomes contradictory to the proposition that the self is not; for the thing that has no cause is eternal.

(f) The example 'like the hare's horn' used by the Buddhist in the argument is impossible. The expression 'hare's horn' denotes a relationship between the hare and the horn. When the hare's horn is denied, it means the denial of the relationship and not that of the horn itself. If the Buddhist says that he would give the relationship between the hare and the horn as his example, this will not improve his position. The horn may be placed on the head of the hare and then there can be the relationship of conjunction between the hare and the horn. This is not contrary to the popular notion. What the popular notion implies is that there is no relation of cause and effect between the hare and the horn, as there is between the cow and the horn. But the denial of the causal relation does not mean that the thing (i.e. the horn) does not exist.

It may be asked: What does the expression 'the hare's horn does not exist' mean ? Does it mean universal or specific negation ? If it means a universal negation (i.e. the negation of all horns), this would mean that the horns of the cow and other animals also do not exist; this is absurd. If it means a specific negation (i.e. particular horns) the denial would mean there are no particular horns of which it can be said that they are causally connected with the animals; this would mean that the causal relation which has been observed in the case of other animals is now denied; but then, this would not be the example in support of absolute non-existence.

(g) The Buddhist position on the self is not consistent with what is said in Buddhist literature. For example, there is the following passage:[4] "O Bhadanta, colour is not 'I', nor are sensation, faculty, cognition, 'I', O Bhadanta; similarly colour is not 'you'; nor are sensations, faculty and cognition 'you'." In this passage the *skandhas* mentioned are denied as the objects of the notion of 'I' but this denial is a qualified and not an unqualified one. A philosopher who does not admit the self should express his denial in an unqualified form: "There is no 'I', there is no 'you'." The Buddhist argues that in denying the various *skandhas* one by one, it is implied that the notion of 'I' pertains to the aggregate of these *skandhas*. But if the *skandhas* are different from the aggregate, says Uddyotakara, the difference between the Buddhist and the Naiyāyika is a mere difference of names; what the Naiyāyika calls 'self' the Buddhist calls 'aggregate'. If, on the other hand, the aggregate is not different from the *skandhas*, then we cannot conceive of it in the singular form 'I'; for a singular word is never applied to several things. The fact of the matter is that the various *skandhas* are not the self either collectively or severally. Hence the notion of 'I' as applied to such *skandhas* becomes the conception of a thing as what it is not.

The following passage occurs in the Buddhist work *Sarvābhisamayasūtra*.[5] "O ye mendicants! I am going to point out to you the burden as well as the carrier of the burden: the five states are the burden and the *pudgala* is the carrier of the burden; he who holds that there is no self is a man with false notions." This implies that the self is. Thus it is difficult to know, says Uddyotakara, what the Buddhist view is.

(2) Objection: There is no self (= proposition) because of non-apprehension (= hetu) (*nāsty ātmānupalabdheḥ*) (= The self is not because it is not apprehended.).

Reply

In this argument the hetu that is given is not right; in fact the self is apprehended by perception and other pramāṇas. The cognition of 'I' (*aham*) is independent of the remembrance of the relation between the sign and the significate; it varies with the variations in the nature of the object (i.e. self); therefore it must be regarded as perceptional, just like the perception of colour. Such cognitions are regarded as direct cognitions of their objects only because no remembrance is involved.

The Buddhist argues that though there is the cognition of 'I', its object is not the self: colour and similar things are the objects of the cognition of 'I' according to the Buddhist declaration that things are called 'self' because they are the causes of the origination of the cognition of 'I'. This argument, says Uddyotakara, is contrary to the Buddhist doctrine. For example, it is said:[6] "O Bhikṣu, neither I nor you are the colour." Furthermore, we do not have such notions as 'I am colour.' The expression 'I am fair', for example, does not mean that the observer looks upon his fair complexion as his 'self'; in fact, it means 'I have a fair complexion.' It may be asked: What are the grounds for saying that the expression 'I am fair' is to be interpreted not literally (i.e. I am colour) but in the possessive sense (i.e. I possess [or have] a fair complexion) ? The reason, says Uddyotakara, is that the notion 'I am fair' represents the 'I' as coextensive with the 'my'; that is to say, the term 'I' is found to be used in reference to the body which is also regarded as 'my' (i.e. we speak of the body as 'my'; in the expression 'I am fair' the term 'I' is applied to the 'body'). Because of this coextensiveness between 'I' and 'my', instead of using 'my' one uses the term 'I'.

This may seem to be contrary to actual usage; the term 'I' is used as coextensive with 'my' even though the two refer to two different things; for example, when one person is a great benefactor of another, the latter uses the expression 'he is what I am' where 'I' is coextensive with 'he'. What he really means is 'he is *my* benefactor'. As already explained in connection with the notion of 'I' appearing in reference to the five *skandhas*, such notions of 'I' are wrong notions, apprehending one thing as what it is not.

Further, the hetu, 'because it (i.e. self) is not apprehended', is doubtful. Non-apprehension can be due to three causes: the apprehender, the apprehended object or the apprehension may be absent. If the absence of apprehension is due to the absence of the object, then the hetu is the same as the proposition; the proposition cannot prove itself. Further, non-apprehension is put forward as the hetu for proving the non-existence of the self. Non-apprehension must have a substratum. If the Buddhist says that it subsists in the self,[7] this would be self-contradictory: the self is the substratum but it does not exist. If, however, the self is not the substratum, then the hetu is useless; a hetu without a substratum cannot prove anything at all. If the Buddhist says that the non-apprehension, being merely the absence of apprehension, does not need any substratum, then there is no point in offering it as hetu; for what does not exist cannot function as a hetu. If, however, the Buddhist says that the non-apprehension is a positive property subsisting in the self, which is assumed, he should explain in what form the self is assumed: is it assumed as an entity or non-entity ? If it is assumed as an entity, then non-apprehension cannot belong to it; for example, when the post is assumed to be the man, the properties of the post are not perceived. It follows that when the non-existent self is assumed as an existing thing, there can be no conception of its non-apprehension, which is a property only of the non-existent thing. If, on the other hand, non-apprehension is the property of the self, which is assumed as a non-entity, then undoubtedly the non-apprehension can be said to be a property. But then the Buddhist theory of assumption is rendered futile for the simple reason that assumption is always false; that is, it represents a thing as what it is not. When the Buddhist says that the self is assumed as non-existent, he means that in reality it is not non-existent; but if the self is really not non-existent, then the purpose for which the Buddhist propounded the assumption is defeated. One may ask the Buddhist: what is your purpose in assuming the self to be non-existent ? If it is so assumed to provide a substratum for the hetu (i.e. non-apprehension), it may be that the hetu gets the substratum; but then, the proposition which the Buddhist wishes to prove is not proved. This is just like the case where one assumes the man to be the post and then puts forward some property of the post to prove that the man is the post. But surely, this cannot prove that the man is the post.

Thus under all possible interpretations the Buddhist hetu of non-apprehension, says Uddyotakara, cannot prove the proposition that the self is not.

(3) Objection: The living body is devoid of self (=proposition) because it is an entity (=hetu) (*jīvac charīraṃ nirātmakena pakṣayitvā sattvād iti*).

Reply

This objection is not valid because none of the alternative meanings of the term 'devoid of self' is admissible. (a) If it means that the body serves no useful purpose, no corroborative example can be given; for there is nothing that does not serve a useful purpose of the self. (b) If it means that the self is not the body, this is futile; for no one regards the body as the self. Further, the negative particle (*nir*) in the term *nirātmakam* signifies the negation of the object denoted by the second word (=*ātmakam*); and the whole term therefore means the negation of 'devoid of self'. As is known, a negative particle is never prefixed to a term denoting a non-entity, for example *nirmaśakam* (devoid of flies). (c) If the proposition is meant to deny that the self is in the body, this needs no proving; for everyone is agreed upon it. (d) If the proposition means that the body has no relation with the self, no corroborative example can be found; for there is nothing which is not connected with the self in one way or the other. (e) All the four alternative interpretations amount to the denial of nothing more than a specific property of the self; and this implies the admission of a thing (=self) of which it is the property.

(4) Objection: The term *ātman* denotes a transient object (=proposition) because it is composed of *varṇas*=phonemes (=hetu) (*ātmaśabdho 'nityaviṣayo varṇātmakatvāt.*).

Reply

The term '*nitya*' (=eternal) denotes something eternal though it is composed of *varṇas*. Therefore the hetu is inconclusive. the term *ātman* in the proposition may mean the body or something other than the body. If it means the body, then the argument only proves what is already established: the body is transient. If it means something different from the body, then this is contrary to the doctrine of the proponent of the proposition: there is no entity apart from the body, etc.

(5) Objection: The Sāṃkhya maintains that the *puruṣa* (self) exists (a) because all composite objects are for another's use, (b) because there must be absence of the three constituents of *prakṛti* and other properties, (c) because there must be control, (d) because there must be someone to experience, and because there is a tendency to emancipation; therefore, the *puruṣa* must be there. Uddyotakara has not stated this Sāṃkhya view but he examines the following Buddhist objection which is raised against the view: Inasmuch as the eye and the other organs are composite objects, they are for the use of something other than themselves; for example, the composite things like a bed or a seat. Therefore the eye and the other organs are for the use of some other composite object (and not necessarily the *puruṣa*).

Reply

This objection of the Buddhist is unfounded on the following grounds: (a) According to the Sāṃkhya doctrine the composite objects serve the purposes not of other composite objects but of the non-composite *puruṣa*. Thus the Buddhist objection is based upon a complete misunderstanding of the doctrine. If an objection based on an interpretation not intended by the author of a view were regarded as valid, then this would put an end to all inferential reasoning. Even the arguments of the Buddhists could then be rendered invalid by imposing a meaning on them which is not intended by them. (b) The Buddhist argues that while it is true that composite things exist for the sake of something other than themselves, it is only some other composite things for the sake of which such composite things exist; in the case of the bed mentioned by the Sāṃkhya, for example, it can be said to exist for the sake of the body; but the body is itself a composite thing.

This argument, says Uddyotakara, is contrary to the Buddhist view that there are no composites apart from the colour-*skandha*, etc. The body does not figure in his list of the composites. Apart from this, the Buddhist objection, if valid, would lead to an infinite regress. If one composite exists for the sake of another, and that for the sake of still another and so on, we are confronted with an infinite series of composites. But this is most unjustified. We must therefore postulate a point in the series where the series comes to an end; and that point would be a non-composite thing.

It follows from this that without the non-composite the composite cannot be explained. Thus the Buddhist denial of the non-composite is self-contradictory; for there can be no composite unless there is the non-composite.

(c) The postulation of the non-composite is undoubtedly a matter of inference. If the Buddhist were to reject such inferences because every inference can be invalidated by another, he would place himself beyond the pale of all reasoning (*nyāya*). Even then he would not be able to escape from inference altogether. If there were no inference, there would be no possibility of cognizing objects beyond the reach of the senses. It would not do to say that these objects could be known by means of scripture (*āgama*); for there are many things which can be known only by inference, but they are not dealt with by scripture; for example, the cause of the thunder of the clouds cannot be ascertained by means of perception or scripture but only by means of inference.

(6) *Remembrance*

According to the Buddhist remembrance can be explained without postulating a single self (agent). Although cognitions are distinct, they are causally connected; the earlier cognition is the cause of the later cognition. For example, the grain of paddy produces the sprout, and with the assistance of the elements the sprout, in its turn, produces the grain of paddy, and not of barley. The sprout has the power (*śakti*) to produce the paddy grain simply because the paddy grain is followed by the paddy sprout. Similarly, cognitions constitute a series in which the earlier one is the cause of the later. When cognitions belong to the same series, there is recollection of the earlier one by the later. When cognitions belong to different series, there is no causal connection between the members of one series and those of another. The presence of causal connection therefore accounts for remembrance. Hence according to the Buddhist there is no justification for invoking a single agent.

This argument, says Uddyotakara, is not sound. What is involved in the case under consideration is that the object of the earlier cognition is the same as that of the later one as well as of remembrance. Causal explanation far from proving that the cognitions are not distinct presupposes that they must be distinct. It cannot therefore explain remembrance.

The opponent contends that remembrance can be explained on the basis of the causal relation in a series of psycho-somatic experiences (*kāyācitta*): remembrance of a thing occurs in the same series of psycho-somatic experiences in which the earlier apprehension of the thing had occurred, so that the series can function as something which remembers as well as apprehends. One experience is followed by another experience, which has the potency of its predecessor. This latter experience together with the potency is called 'impression' (*vāsanā*). And this impression explains remembrance.

Uddyotakara replies: since according to the opponent all cognitions are transient, there can be no causal connection between them. A cognition that appears at any present moment appears in an immaculate form, and also disappears exactly in the same form in which it appears. Besides, such a cognition at the present moment cannot have any connection with a cognition that is yet to come.

According to the opponent the earlier sensation produces an impression which is but another sensation endowed with a certain potency. But since both the impressing sensation and the impressed sensation are momentary, there can be no connection between them. Nor can this state of affairs be properly described as impression.

Another reason why remembrance cannot be explained under the theory of momentariness is that remembrance being an action requires an agent. Becoming (*bhāva*) is an action and as such requires a becomer (*bhavitṛ*). A becomer of an action can be either an object or an agent. For example, when rice is cooked, what is cooked is the rice; the object is the becomer. When a person walks, in the action of walking it is the person who is the becomer; he is the agent. In the case of the action of remembrance we cannot say that the becomer is of the nature of the object; for things absent are also remembered. If the becomer of remembrance were its object, then at the time when one remembers an object that is not present the remembrance would be completely without any support at all. According to the opponent, remembrance is an effect, but effect is impossible without a substratum; for example, colour which is an effect has a substratum. Thus if remembrance is a form of becoming, the opponent must accept that the becomer is of the nature of an agent and not an object.

The opponent argues that this difficulty can be met if we regard the effect as becoming and the cause as the becomer; the effect-moment is the becoming and the cause-moment the becomer. And then there is no need to postulate a becomer in the shape of an agent.

This cannot be right, says Uddyotakara, because the cause and the effect which are at different moments of time cannot have the relationship of the container and the contained, as in the case of the bowl and the fruit.

The opponent suggests that the present difficulty can be met as follows: becoming is nothing more than production, and the becomer is that which is produced. In the present case remembrance is something that is produced; its production is its becoming; the remembrance itself is the becomer.

This suggestion, says Uddyotakara, is incompatible with the opponent's view. If production is something different from remembrance, its distinctive features will have to be indicated. The production of a thing can be explained only either as the connection of the thing with the existence of its cause or as the existence of the thing as qualified by the connection of its cause. This would mean that the cause and the effect have more than momentary existence. And this is against the opponent's doctrine. If, to escape from this self-contradiction, the opponent says that the production is not different from the remembrance, this makes his position even worse. It would amount to saying that the production is the becoming and the remembrance is that which is produced (i.e. the becomer); this is meaningless. This statement could, however, have some sense, if production is regarded as the becoming of remembrance; but then, they become different. And if remembrance itself is a becoming, it must have a becomer. Such a becomer, as already mentioned, can only be an agent.

In view of these considerations it is quite clear, says Uddyotakara, the opponent has no satisfactory explanation for remembrance. If there is no remembrance there can be no recognition; but recognition is a fact; hence we must conclude that what functions as the agent of this recognition is something different from cognitions and series of cognitions; and this agent is the single entity, i.e. the self. As already mentioned, this negative inference proves the existence of the self (NV I. 1,10).

II. Self as distinct from its psycho-somatic equipment.

The self is equipped with the body, the sense-organs, the mind, the intellect and the sense-experience (*vedanā*). The question that needs to be considered is: Is the self only an aggregate of these or is it something different from them ? The question arises from the fact that we have two kinds of statement. 'Statement' in this context means the expression of the relaionship of the agent with the action and the instrument of that action. The two kinds of statement are: (a) In one the aggregate is indicated by its component parts, e.g. 'the tree stands by the roots', where what is spoken of as the instrument, i.e. the roots, is a component part of the agent, i.e. the tree. (b) In the other statement we have a thing indicated by something totally different from it; e.g. 'one cuts the tree with the axe', where the instrument, axe, is different from the person who cuts it. In the case of the self we have such statements as 'he sees with the eye', 'he cognizes with the mind', 'he ponders with the intellect', 'he experiences pleasure and pain with the body'. It is not certain whether in these statements the aggregate of the body, the intellect, etc., is indicated by means of its components (i.e. the body, etc., which are spoken of as instruments, are nothing but component parts of that which sees, etc., and therefore the self is only an aggregate of the body, etc.); or, whether what is indicated is one thing (i.e. self) by means of things different from it (i.e. the body, etc., which are spoken of as instruments are different from the self).

It is this question, says Vātsyāyana, that Gautama has examined in detail. The truth is that in all such statements the agent is related to the action through the instruments as something different from them (Introductory NBh III. 1,1).

(a) *Self as distinct from sense-organs*

According to Gautama, self is different from the sense-organs because a single object is apprehended by sight and touch (NS III. 1,1). Vātsyāyana explains: when a person says 'I see the object that I had previously touched', he recognizes that the two cognitions of touch and sight are of the single object, that they have been produced by different causes (or instruments) and that they belong to a single agent. The cognitions cannot be said to have the sense-organs as their single agent, because each sense-organ is concerned only with its own object, and not that of another sense-organ. Nor can we say that the visual and tactual cognitions have the aggregate of the body, etc. as their agent. What we require in the present case is a single agent which apprehends both these cognitions produced by the different sense-organs. Such an agent must be different from the sense-organs; this is the self (NBh III. 1,1).

If we treat cognitions as actions, for instance, sight (*darśana*) as action of seeing, they would then indicate the fact that the actions are performed by an agent; for we never see an action without a substratum in which it subsists. It is true that in some cases like production, action subsists in the thing produced, but in others, e.g. remembering, the action cannot be said to subsist in the object remembered because the object may be absent.

Gautama mentions an objection to his argument. It is precisely because each sense-organ is restricted to its own object (=hetu) that this restriction cannot prove the existence of the self (NS III. 1,2). Vātsyāyana explains the objection: colour, for example, is perceived when the visual organ is present; it is not perceived when the organ is not present. The cognition should therefore be attributed to the visual organ. Hence there is no need to postulate a conscious agent (*cetana*) (NBh III. 1,2).

Gautama merely reiterates his view on the subject of the self in reply (NS III. 1,3). However, Vātsyāyana refutes the objection: In the first place the hetu mentioned above is doubtful: the fact that the presence and absence of cognitions are concomitant with the presence and absence of the sense-organs may be due to the sense-organs being themselves conscious or to their being mere instruments of a conscious being. Secondly, if each sense-organ were not restricted to its own object, it would apprehend all objects. Actually, it is the fact of restriction that leads us to infer the existence of a conscious being. Thirdly. we have actual instances to show that a conscious being is at work. On perceiving colours in an object, for example one infers the odour and taste which one had apprehended in the past. Such instances clearly show that one can apprehend various objects without any definite order. Fourthly, we can identify different cognitions as perceptional, inferential, scriptural or doubtful. For instance when a person hears the scripture, which deals with all things, he understands their meanings. These meanings cannot be said to be heard by the organ which hears the words; they are understood because the person recalls the principles of syntax and the laws governing the denotation of words (NBh III. 1,2 & 3).

According to Uddyotakara, it can be argued that consciousness must be attributed to the self because being independent it is not restricted to any particular object, like the sense-organs; the self cannot be unconscious because, if it were so, it would, like the sense-organs, not be independent. These arguments are based upon negative concomitance, but that does not make them invalid; for the force of a negative hetu lies in its invariable negative concomitance. The commentator adds that the self is different from the mind, which is also a sense-organ (NV III. 1,3).

(b) *Self as distinct from body*

[The following objection is raised: If the body were the self], there would be absence of sin (*pātaka*) in the burning of a [living] body. [There would be] this absence of sin even if the body endowed with the self were burnt for the self is eternal. [Gautama replies: This is] not so because the receptacle of effects and that which produces these effects [i.e. the body and the sense-organs] are destroyed (NS III. 1,4-6).

According to Vātsyāyana the objection mentioned by Gautama is as follows: The term 'body' denotes the 'living being' (*prāṇir*) — the aggregate of body, sense-organs, *buddhi* and feeling (*vedanā*). If the body of a living being is burnt by another living being, this constitutes 'sin' (*pātaka*) — sin arising from the killing of the living creature. If the self were not different from such an aggregate, replies the Naiyāyika, there could be no sin, for the result of the sin would not be connected with (i.e. accrue to) any agent (*kartṛ*), since there would be no such agent.

According to the aggregate theory one aggregate is produced and another destroyed and the production and destruction of aggregates constitute a series (*santati*). Since the series consists of different aggregates, the aggregate which does the killing cannot be connected with the result of that killing and what is connected with the result is not that by which the killing was done. Consequently, the two aggregates being different, it amounts to this: the aggregate which did the act becomes disconnected with the results of that act while the aggregate which did not do the act becomes connected with it: that is, two different entities are connected with the act and the result of the act. If such an entity (or living being) were subject to production and destruction, the production of such an entity could not be due to the instrumental cause (*nimitta*) of karma. And this would mean that no useful purpose is served by living the life of a religious student. This is undesirable and hence it is necessary to assert the existence of the self as distinct from the aggregate of the body, etc. (NBh III. 1,4).

It is argued that even if the body (i.e. the aggregate) as endowed with the eternal self were burnt, the burner would have committed no sin as defined above. What is eternal cannot be killed and what could be killed would not be eternal. Consequently, if on the first theory of the aggregate without the eternal self the killing produces no result, on the present theory killing itself becomes impossible.

The Naiyāyika rejects this argument on the following grounds. As already mentioned, 'killing' consists not in the destruction of the eternal entity but of the body. This body is the receptacle of effects i.e. feelings of pleasure and pain, and the apprehension of objects by the sense-organs. While the entity to which the body and the sense-organs belong is indestructible, what is destroyed in the act of killing is the body. This destruction takes the form of striking, causing pain, i.e. disorganizing, by bringing about death, or by uprooting the entity from what it is endowed with. It is this destruction of the body and the sense-organs, and not of the entity itself, that constitutes 'killing'.

Another way to look at this question of killing is this. It is only in the aggregate that the eternal self can have feelings of pleasure and pain. Hence the striking or causing pain or disorganizing of this aggregate constitutes 'killing', and not the destroying of the eternal self.

In view of this entire explanation it is not right to say that 'there could be no sin in killing if the body endowed with the self is destroyed, for the self is eternal' (NS & NBh III. 1,5 & 6).

According to Uddyotakara the Buddhist contends that if we have a single series of body and consciousness (*kāyacittasantāna*) it can be said that in the same series we have the body that does the act as well as the body that experiences the results of that act; so that since both the doing and experiencing belong to the same series, there is no such contingency as 'for the person who did the act it becomes completely lost, while it falls upon who had nothing to do with it'. Such a contingency would arise if the act is done in one series and the result accrued in another series. The Naiyāyika's reply to this Buddhist argument is that a series does not mean that the members of the series are not different. Hence to say that the doer and the experience belong to the same series does not obliterate the fact that these two are different members of the series.

The advocate of the Buddhist argument also holds that a new set of *skandhas* is produced simultaneously with the destruction of the preceding *skandhas*. It cannot therefore be said that the production of the new set is due to the karma of the preceding set; and if the production of an entity (*sattva*) is not due to karma there is no point in regarding acts as productive of good or evil (*śubhāśubhaprāpti*).

If the act is said to be done with the notion 'I shall be happy' (*sukhī syām*)—and this means that 'I perform an act with the idea that I myself may be happy', this does not improve the Buddhist position. An entity that has experienced a pleasure from a particular act also remembers the connection between the means (i.e. the act) and the effect (i.e. the pleasure); it is only then that that same entity can employ the means that had given the pleasure previously. But under the Buddhist theory the impressions are destroyed every moment and consequently the entity can have no remembrance of the connection between the pleasure and the means that produced that pleasure. An entity cannot therefore be said to perform an act with the motive of obtaining pleasure.

Under the Buddhist theory it is really not possible to make any effort for liberation (*mokṣa*). Since an entity is released no sooner than it is produced, the liberation is accomplished without any effort at all. Hence it is useless to lead the life of a religious person for liberation. Nor is there any need for such a statement: the Buddha has instructed the disciples and the latter have been properly instructed. If a person consists of entities past, present and future, none of these entities can be said to have been benefited by the Buddha's instruction. Neither the future nor the past entities exist at the time when the instruction is given; and the present entity cannot profit from the instruction for the very nature of the 'present' is such that the present being cannot be affected by any improvement. If it is suggested that

that which stimulates (*saṃskāraka*) and that which is stimulated (*saṃskārya*) are simultaneous, there will be no rule whereby we can determine 'this is what stimulates and that is what is stimulated'. It is argued that with the help of that which stimulates, that which is stimulated is enabled to produce an effect of a different character (*vilakṣaṇakārya*); it is this effect that constitutes *saṃskāra*. Unless one thing produces something specific (*viśeṣa*), in another thing, the former cannot be regarded as that which improves and the latter as that which is improved. The Buddhist cannot therefore explain the meaning of the term '*saṃskāra*'. If the Buddhist says that what the instruction does is to bring about the non-production of such '*saṃskāras*' as are yet to come (i.e. they are still in the future), this also cannot be right. Since the non-production of what is yet to be produced is already a fact (*sattva*), there is really nothing for the instruction to produce by way of any result.

In view of these circumstances it is not right for the Buddhist to say: 'the leading of the life of a religious person is for the purpose of liberation'. If there is no eternal self such consequences are inevitable (NV III. 1,4).

The opponent argues that if the term 'killing' is not used in the accepted sense, there is no justification for using it in a figurative sense. How do we then know that the term is being used in the sense of the Naiyāyika ? This is understood, says Uddyotakara, from the fact that both admit of 'killing and experiencing of results' (*hiṃsāphalopabhoga*). And this can be explained only on the basis of the eternal self.

Even for the Buddhist who believes in the destruction of *saṃskāras* every moment what is it there that could be killed ? Since the destruction is devoid of a cause (*nirhetuka*), whose work can it be regarded? If the Buddhist says that one is said to kill another when the former becomes the cause of the latter appearing in a form entirely different from his previous form (*vilakṣaṇotpattinimittatvena vyavatiṣṭhamānaḥ paro hinasti*), then this use of the term 'killing' is only figurative and not principal; for the term denotes the 'birth of another form'. The Buddhist retorts that the Naiyāyika does exactly the same: in the Nyāya theory what is killed is not the self. It is true, says Uddyotakara, that for him also the 'killing' is of the 'receptacle of effects and of that which brings about these effects' (*kāryāśrayakartṛvadha*), but there is this difference between the Nyāya and Buddhist positions: The self that undergoes the experience of the effects of an act is the same that brought about its own body, etc., and did the act; consequently, this does not involve the contingency of anyone undergoing the effects of what he had never done. The position is entirely different with the Buddhist. This view involves both the contingencies: (1) the effects of an act are lost to one who did the act; and (2) the effects of the act are visited upon one who had nothing to do with the act. Hence the only explanation that meets the situation is the acceptance of the eternal self. One is regarded as the 'agent' (*kartṛ*) of an act when cognition, the desire to act (*cikīrṣā*) and effort (*prayatna*)—all three are inherent in him; when the feeling of pleasure and pain inheres in him, he is called the 'experiencer' (*bhoktṛ*). As neither of these applies to the body, it is called the 'agent' (*kartṛ*) only because it is through the body that the agent acts (NV III. 1,6).

(c) *Recognition and remembrance*

According to Gautama recognition and remembrance clearly prove that the self is different from the sense-organs. We recognize with the right eye what we see with the left eye. This argument is concerned with the nature of the visual organ and visual perception and it has been discussed in connection with perception where it is more relevant.[8]

Another argument of Gautama of a similar type is that one sense-organ is stimulated through the operation of another. When a person has tasted a sour fruit he remembers the taste on seeing the colour of that fruit on a subsequent occasion. This is possible because the visual perception associated with the taste stimulates the organ of taste. Even if the sense-organs were themselves conscious, this would not explain the stimulation. What is seen by one could not be remembered by another. According to Gautama such remembrance cannot be explained in terms of the objects remembered. If remembrance were a property of the sense-organ, e.g. the eye, it would be impossible to remember the taste previously apprehended; for the eye is incapable of apprehending taste. If remembrance were attributed to the objects remembered, we could remember innumerable objects at a time. The fact is that we can remember only one object at a time.

Hence remembrance must be regarded as a property of a separate substance, the self.

If the sense-organs had consciousness it would mean that there are several apprehensions of objects by several agents (i.e. the sense-organs); but then, there could be no recognition at all, or if the recognition were possible the sense-organs would not be restricted to their respective objects.

Both recognition and remembrance are possible only if there is a single agent. Recognition involves present apprehension of an object and is expressed in the form: 'What I see now I had seen before'. The expression 'I had seen before' indicates past apprehension and the remembrance of that past apprehension. The expression 'What I see now' indicates the present apprehension. Thus a single act of recognition involves three different notions. These three notions cannot be attributed to several agents nor can they be said to have no agent at all; they must be attributed to a single agent.

Remembrance occurs when the object remembered is not actually apprehended. Moreover, what is remembered is not the object by itself but the object as previously apprehended by a cognizer. Remembrance is expressed in the form: 'I knew that object'. This statement clearly indicates that the cognizer, his previous cognition and the object are all involved in remembrance.

If the agent were nothing but a series of impressions (*saṃskāra-santati*), every impression would disappear as soon as it had come into existence. This would mean that at any time we have no one impression which could do all the things that we do in recognition and remembrance; nor could we have such notions as 'I' (e.g. 'I see') and 'my' (e.g. 'my cognition').

In view of these considerations the body, the sense-organs and sense-objects cannot be regarded as capable of explaining recognition and remembrance. Remembrance is a property which can be attributed to the self only. This self is the single agent who apprehends all objects, occupies the various bodies with which it is endowed from time to time, recognizes and remembers the objects previously apprehended. This single agent cannot recognize or remember experiences of other selves because it is not present in their bodies. Thus all living beings, says Vātsyāyana, depend upon remembrance in all their activities and experience (NS & NBh III. 1,13-15).

(d) *Self and Mind*

Gautama mentions the following objection : All the reasons given in support of the self are applicable to the mind (NS III. 1,16). His reply is twofold: Since there is a cognizer with an instrument of cognition, to call the mind the self is merely a difference in names (NS III. 1,17). Moreover, the objector's view is opposed to inference (NS III. 1,18). Explaining the reply Vātsyāyana says: It is well known that the instruments of cognition belong to the cognizer. The mind is as much an instrument of the cognizer as the five external sense-organs. It is an internal instrument of the cognizer (*matisādhana*) for thinking about all objects and as such, naturally operates on all objects. Thus if the objector recognizes the mind as an internal instrument of the cognizer, the quarrel is only about the name and not about the real thing. If, however, the objector wishes to maintain that the cognizer which is the thinker of all objects discharges this function without any such internal instrument as the mind, he might as well deny all the other instruments, i.e. the external sense-organs. But since the objector accepts the external sense-organs but rejects the mind, his position is thoroughly unjustified. As is known, the mind ensures that more than one apprehension does not appear at a time, because it is in contact with only one sense-organ, and not another, at one time (NBh III. 1,17 & 18).

III. Eternality of Self

Having proved that the self exists and is distinct from the psycho-somatic complex, Gautama proceeds to examine whether the self is eternal or non-eternal. This question needs examination because some things are eternal while others are not. The Nyāya view, says Vātsyāyana, is that the arguments which prove the existence of the self also prove its existence, previous and posterior to its present embodiment (NBh III. 1,18).

On birth a baby experiences joy, fear and sorrow. This is possible, says Gautama, only because it must have continuous remembrance of what it had experienced previous to its birth (NS III. 1,19). Vātsyāyana explains: It is obvious that during its current life it has not perceived any objects which could have led to its present experience. That it does have such experience is inferred from certain symptoms (i.e. overt behaviour). This experience can only be due to the continuity of remembrance, and not from any other cause. This continuity of remembrance is possible only on the basis of previous repeated experience. The previous experience could be possible only during a previous life. Thus it follows that the self continues to exist even after its body has perished (NBh III. 1,19).

It is argued that there need be no cause for the feelings of the baby; for instance, the lotus opens and closes, but such modifications have no cause (NS III. 1,20). Gautama replies: This is not right because such modifications are caused by heat, cold, rain and season (NS III. 1,21). In the case of things composed of the five physical elements—such as the lotus—their modifications appear when heat, cold, etc., are present, and they do not appear when these are not present. Thus they are not without cause. The example has therefore no relevance to the present case; in fact it supports the Nyāya argument for the eternality of the self. In the case of an adult we find that he experiences various feelings because he remembers what has roused such feelings in the past, and what is true of the adult must be true of the baby. Mere example without any valid reason cannot set aside unquestionable facts. It may also be added that the examples like the modifications of a lotus cannot be used to infer that there must be causes for the production and destruction of the self (NBh III. 1,21).

On birth a baby shows a desire for milk from its mother's breast. Such a desire can only be explained, says Gautama, if the baby had been repeatedly fed on milk in its previous life (NS III. 1,22). In the case of all embodied beings it is found that when they are hungry, they have a desire for food; this desire arises only because they remember the food they had eaten in the past. From these facts it is quite clear that one and the same self, having left its previous body, has now acquired a new body; its present experience is based upon the remembrance of its previous experience (NBh III. 1,22).

Gautama mentions an objection: A new-born baby moves towards its mother's breast in the same way as the iron moves towards the magnet (NS III. 1,23). This is not right, he answers, because there is no such activity elsewhere (NS III. 1,24). Commenting on this answer Vātsyāyana observes: It is not that any substance is attracted towards the magnet. The fact that only the iron is attracted shows that there must be a definite cause for the attraction. Similarly, in the case of the baby everyone is agreed that it moves only towards its mother's breast; this action is due to its desire for milk. The only explanation that can be given is the remembrance of its previous experience. As already mentioned, the experience of an adult amply confirms this explanation. Hence such examples like magnetic attraction are totally irrelevant; they cannot set aside undisputed facts (NBh III. 1,24).

Another argument for the eternality of the self, says Gautama, is that no one is born without desire (NS III. 1,25). Only those who have desire, says Vātsyāyana, are born. This desire, as already explained, is the result of remembrance of things previously explained; this previous experience in a previous life could not have been possible without a body. Hence the self, remembering the things it had experienced in its previous body, comes to desire them. This is what constitutes similarity (*pratisandhāna*) between its two lives. There are similar links between its previous life and its life preceding that; between that life and the life preceding it, and so on. Thus it is evident that the connection of the self with various bodies has been without beginning; without beginning also has been its connection with desire. Hence the self is eternal (NBh III. 1,25).

Gautama mentions an objection: The self is not eternal because it is produced along with its desire in the same manner as substances (*dravya*) are produced along with their properties (NS III. 1,26). He replies: This is not so because the desire, etc., are caused by an idea (*saṅkalpa*) (NS III. 1,27).

According to Vātsyāyana the objection mentioned by Gautama is: In the case of ordinary substances which have the property of being produced their properties are produced by causes like fire-contact. Similarly, it is quite reasonable to say that in the case of the self which has the property of being produced, the desire which is its property is produced by a certain cause. Gautama's answer, as mentioned before, is that the desire in the case of living beings is due to the remembrance of their previous experience; what is true of adults is true of new-born babies. Thus the self is eternal. But if the self were produced anew at each birth, it would not be possible to explain the desire as indicated above. The production of the self has not been proved nor has any other cause been found for the desire. Hence there is no justification for saying that the self and its desire are produced in the same way as other substances and their properties are produced.

As is well known, desire proceeds from complete identification (or absorption in) with the object; this identification (*tanmayatva*) is nothing but the repeated experience of the object, which leads to the notion that such and such an object is the source of pleasure or pain. The kind of desires a new-born baby has depends upon the kind of body (*jātiviśeṣa*) in which it is born. The kind of body in which the self is born is determined by tskarma. The body (or person) so born is known by a particular name by reason of the particular body in which it is born (NBh III. 1,27). It is known by a particular name, says Uddyotakara, because it serves the purpose of the self (NV III. 1,27).

Some philosophers explain desire on the basis of the 'unseen' (*adṛṣṭa*), which consists of merit and demerit. Even if this explanation were accepted, says Vātsyāyana, the connection of the self with a previous body cannot be denied; for the merit and demerit could have accrued to the self only during its previous embodiment, and not in its present life.

20

BODY (*śarīra*)

I

The body, which is the second object of cognition, is defined by Gautama as the support (*āśraya*) of actions, sense-organs and objects (NS I. 1,11). Vātsyāyana explains: (a) The self desires to obtain or discard an object; it performs an action which consists in the employment of the means for obtaining or discarding it; that in which this action is performed is the body. (b) That thing alone can be considered as the support of the sense-organs by whose benefit the sense-organs are benefited and by whose injury they are injured, and where, according to this benefit or injury, these sense-organs act upon their objects, good and bad; such a thing is the body. (c) That is to be regarded as the support of objects in which there appear the feelings of pleasure and pain produced by the contact of the sense-organs with these objects; such a thing is the body (NBh I. 1,11).

According to Uddyotakara the action that is mentioned above is strictly for the purpose of acquiring what is beneficial and discarding what is injurious: it is a movement (*parispanda*) for obtaining or discarding an object. The four sense-organs of smell, taste, touch and vision are effects, while the organs of hearing and the mind are not. The effects subsist in their causes while those that are not effects do not subsist anywhere. The body supports the sense-organs in the sense that they follow changes in the body (i.e. they are affected by the benefit and injury of the body), and not in the sense that the body is the container and the sense-organs the contained. Similarly, the body is described as the support of the sense-objects not because they are contained in the body but because they cannot function as causes of pleasure and pain except when the body is there. This is just like the relationship between the landlord and the villagers: the landlord is the support of the villagers not because the latter are contained in him, but because they can function as causes of pleasure and pain only when the landlord is there to experience them (NV I. 1,11).

According to Vātsyāyana, it is necessary to decide whether the body is composed of a single element like the sense-organs or of several elements, because there are different views regarding the number of elements involved.

According to Gautama, the body is composed of the earth, because it has the property of the earth, viz. odour (NS III. 1,28), and also because there is the authority of scripture (NS III. 1,29). If it were composed of the other elements it would not have the property of odour; for those elements are devoid of that property. But if it were built up of the earth only, without being mixed up with water, etc., it could not support action, sense-organs and sense-objects.

Bodies consisting of the elements like water, fire and air are found in other regions and they also have in them other elements by contact according to the kind of experience a person (*puruṣa*) is required to have in a particular body. Ordinary objects like a jar are also built up with the combination of various elements (NBh III. 1,28).

As mentioned by Gautama, the Nyāya view of the body is supported by scripture. According to Vātsyāyana this is confirmed by the passages from the *Ṛgveda* and the *Śatapatha Brāhmaṇa* (NBh III. 1,29).

As already mentioned, there are different views on the subject. For example, the body is composed of three elements, earth, water and fire, or four (i.e. air in addition to these three) or all the five elements, because the body has the respective properties of the elements concerned. This argument, says Vātsyāyana, is based on an inconclusive hetu; properties of elements may be present in an object because the elements are either constituents of that object or only present by contact without being constituents. The presence by contact cannot be denied; for example, a jar is composed of the earth but water, air, fire and ākāśa are all present by contact.

The human body cannot be regarded as constituted of more than one element, because if it were, it would be without odour, touch, smell and colour (NBh III. 1,28). According to Uddyotakara, the explanation for this is as follows: An object composed of earth and water, for example, would be without odour, because the odour subsisting in the single constituent atom could not produce odour in the product. No single dyad, says Vācaspati, could be produced out of one atom of earth and one atom of water; even if such a dyad were produced, it could not have odour; because in the dyad there would be a single odorous atom, that of earth, and a single atom cannot produce any effect; thus the dyad being odourless, all subsequent products would be odourless (NV & NVTT III. 1,28).

According to Vātsyāyana, there are different views regarding the formation of the body. There is therefore doubt as to whether the cause of the formation of the human body is karma or the material elements only. Gautama's answer is: the body is produced as the result of the persistence of the results of previous acts (NS III. 2,64). Vātsyāyana explains: Acts performed in the previous body of a person produce the result: merit and demerit. The result continues to inhere in the self. The body is produced out of the material elements as operated upon by the continuing merit and demerit, and not of these elements by themselves. That particular body belongs to a self in which the self regards it as 'I' (*aham*); the self remains attached to it, according to its desires obtains the various kinds of objects and acquires merit and demerit. When this body falls off, another is produced by the faculty (*saṃskāra*), in the shape of the merit and demerit mentioned above, together with the material elements. When this second body has been produced, actions are again performed for the fulfilment of the man's purpose, just as in the previous body. This phenomenon is possible only if the body is produced out of the material substances as operated upon by the acts of the self (NBh III. 2,64).

According to Uddyotakara, it is not certain whether the results of the man's acts will be experienced by him in his present or another life, or in this world or another. The reason why the results of acts do not appear at the same time as when the acts are performed lies in the mode of causal opeartion. When all the causes are present, and not obstructed in any way, their results appear immediately; when the results do not so appear, this is due to special circumstances. In the present case the delay is due to the peculiar circumstances attending the residuum of the karma (*kārmātiśaya*); the results of the residuum may not have been experienced; its results may not appear because there is obstruction caused by the maturing residuum of other living beings, whose experiences are similar to those in question; the non-appearance of the results may be due to the acts of those other human beings who share the karma of the man in question; it may be that such auxiliary causes as merit and demerit are not present at the time, or do not produce their results at all times, or are themselves obstructed by the acts of other living beings. In fact, this operation of karma, says Uddyotakara, is incomprehensive; it cannot be determined by human beings in advance; all that one can do is only to illustrate (NV III. 2,64).

II. Examination of Objections

Gautama examines the following objections to his view on the formation of the body. As already mentioned, Gautama himself has stated that the body is composed of earth. His justification for this is that there is evidence of perception regarding thep roduction of the perceptible from the perceptible (*vyakta*) (NS IV. 1,11). From the perceptible things, for instance, the material elements (i.e. the earth and the other material elements in their extremely subtle form), are produced such ordinarily known substances as the material elements in their gross form; and these latter appear in the form of the body, the sense-organs, the objects and their appurtenances. The cause is regarded as perceptible because it is similar to the perceptible thing; this similarity consists in the presence of such properties as colour, etc.

In ordinary experience we find that from the substances like clay, which are endowed with the properties like colour, are produced objects of the same kind. On this basis we can infer that the eternal and supersensuous things like atoms produce things of the same kind, i.e. having the properties of colour, etc. (NBh IV. 1,11).

(1) Gautama mentions an objection:[1] the perceptible cannot be said to be produced from the perceptible, as a jar is not produced out of a jar (NS IV. 1,12). And his answer is: a jar is actually produced from a perceptible thing (NS IV. 1,13).

This does not mean that everything is the cause of everything; all that is intended, says Vātsyāyana, is whatever perceptible thing is produced, it is produced out of a similar thing. The clay is perceptible, so is the jar produced from it. One cannot really argue, says the commentator, with a person who denied such a patent fact (NBh IV. 1,13).

(2) Gautama considers the following objection which, according to Vātsyāyana, emanates from a heretic (*nāstika*): The formation (*sarga*) of the body out of the material elements resembles that of material bodies (*mūrti*) (NS III. 2,65).

Gautama answers: (a) the proposition is still to be proved; (b) father and mother are the cause of the production of the body; (c) eating also is a cause; (d) there is result because there is no rule (*aniyama*) even in the case of union; (e) karma is the cause not only of the production of the body but also of its conjunction (*saṃyoga*) (with a self); (f) what is said (under e) explains the uncertainty (mentioned under d); (g) and the separation between the self and the body is effected by the exhaustion (*kṣaya*) of karma (NS III. 2, 66-72).

Vātsyāyana explains the objection of the heretic: From out of the material elements are produced material objects like sand, pebbles, stones, orpiment and soot, independently of karma; they are used (by men) because they are capable of fulfilling the purposes of man. Similarly, the body is produced out of the material elements, independently of karma; it is taken up by man because it is capable of fulfilling his purposes (NBh III. 2,65).

Vātsyāyana explains the reply of Gautama:

(a) The production of the material objects independently of karma is still to be proved like the formation of the body independently of karma; it cannot therefore be used as a means of proving the latter (NBh III. 2,66).

(b) The material objects are different from the body because while the former are produced without seeds (*bīja*) the latter is always produced from seeds (i.e. the ovule and semen of parents). The body is produced in the mother's womb by the karma of the self (*sattva*) which enables it to have the required experiences and by the karma of the parents which enables them to have the experiences resulting from the birth of the child (NBh III. 2,67).

(c) The food is what is eaten and drunk. The juices produced by the digestion of the food enter the seed embedded in the mother's womb; they develop along with the seed; in that seed there is as much development as suffices for the accretion of the necessary aggregate; the accretion thus formed goes on to develop into such aggregates as the cell, the foetus, embryo, etc., and ultimately into what forms the substratum of the sense-organs; when the foetus has been formed, the juices of the food are absorbed by it through the umbilical cord, and it continues to grow till it becomes fit to be born.

No such development is found in the case of food lying in a plate.

From all this it follows that the body is produced by the karma — the karma which is the cause (*nimitta*) of its production (NBh III. 2,67).

(d) Every physical connection of the parents does not lead to conception. The only explanation for this uncertainty of conception is: if the influence of karma is present, there is conception; if it is absent, there is no conception. If the material elements were independent of karma in the case of the body, there should be certainty of conception; for no element would be absent in the causes involved in the production of the body (NBh III. 2,69).

(e) The body is a pattern woven by such components as the arteries through which the bodily humours and life-breath flow; the humours of the body culminating in the semen; the tendon, skin, veins, muscles, embryo and foetus; head, arms and belly; the thighs; the wind, bile and phlegm permeating the body; and the mouth, throat, chest, stomach, intestines and bowels. Such a pattern is most difficult to produce. Hence its formation must be due to karma. Similarly, the karma is also necessary to explain how a particular self acquires a particular body. Each self has its own residuum of karma which produces a body fit for experiences of that self in which the residuum subsists and connects that body with that self. But if the elements were to produce the body by themselves, every one would have the same kind of body; this would mean that neither the bodies nor the selves would be distinguished one from the other; and this in turn would imply that all the selves will have similar experiences. But the fact is that each body is connected with one particular self only and each self has its specific experiences in an appropriate body in accordance with its own residuum of karma (NBh III. 2,70).

(f) The idea of what is called '*niyama*' (rule) in this context is that the body of one self is the same as that of all selves; *aniyama* (absence of rule) therefore means diversity, distinction, peculiarity, i.e. the idea that the body of one self is different from that of another. The fact is that there is such diversity in the birth of bodies: (1) one is born in a superior family, another in an inferior family; (2) one is praiseworthy and another blameworthy; (3) one has numerous diseases while another has none; (4) one has all his limbs while another is maimed; (5) one has plenty of suffering while another has plenty of happiness; (6) one has excellent characteristics while another has the worst; (7) one has good properties while another has bad properties; (8) one has efficient sense-organs while another has weak ones. Apart from these differences, there are others which are subtler; and these are innumerable.

(g) The possibility of the karma being exhausted creates the possibility of separating the self from the body. If the body is produced by the karma, the self can separate itself from that body when the karma is exhausted. This process of exhaustion is produced by the following cause: When right knowledge has destroyed misconception (*moha*) the self becomes free from all attachment; it performs no further acts of body, mind and speech, which could create a further body for it; the karma that the self had previously accumulated is exhausted because the self has had all the experiences resulting from the accumulated karma; thus there being no cause for the production of a further body, when the present body falls off, no further body is formed; if the formation of the body were not due to karma, there would be no possibility of the self being separated from the body; for the material elements out of which the body is produced are not subject to exhaustion (NBh III. 2,72).

(3) Gautama mentions another objection to his theory of the formation of the body: the formation of the body is due to *adṛṣṭa* (the unseen). His answer is as follows: (a) If the *adṛṣṭa* were the cause, then even after release there would be the contingency of a body being produced (NS III. 2,73).[2] (b) This is unreasonable; if the body is so produced, it would mean that the body can be produced in case of both fulfilment and non-fulfilment of its ends (NS III. 2,74). (c) There will be no cessation of the conjunction if it is caused by the karma of the mind (NS III. 2,75). (d) If there is no cause for the destruction of the body, there would be the contingency of its being eternal (NS IV. 2,76).

Gautama mentions an objection to the answer given under (d). The disappearance of the body in the state of release can be as eternal as the blackness of an atom (NS III. 2,77).

Gautama's answer is: This cannot be so because it would involve the contingency of admitting what was undemonstrable (NS III. 2,78).

According to Vātsyāyana the *adṛṣṭa* mentioned in the objection can be interpreted in two ways: The formation of the body out of the material elements is due to either (a) non-perception (*adarśana*) or (b) a specific property of an atom.

(a) *Non-perception*

(1) Non-perception: The formation of the body is due to non-perception. As long as a body is not formed, a perceiver (*draṣṭṛ*) being without an abode cannot perceive what is perceptible (*dṛśya*). The perceptible is of two kinds: (a) object (sound, colour, etc.), and (b) the diversity or difference (*nānātva*) between the *avyakta* (i.e. *prakṛti* = matter) and the self (*ātman*). The body is produced to enable the perceiver to perceive these two kinds of the perceptible. When both these have been accomplished, the material elements have done all that they were required to do for the perceiving self. Consequently, these elements do not produce any further body for the self, and thus the self can be separated from the body.

According to this interpretation of *adṛṣṭa*, the possibility of a further body being produced even after release, says Vātsyāyana, cannot be ruled out. There is one non-perception while the body is not formed, and another after the body has ceased to exist. There is no difference between these two non-perceptions. If, therefore, non-perception is the cause of the formation of the body, even after release there would be every likelihood of another body being produced.

When both the ordinary objects and the difference between the self and the *prakṛti* have been perceived, it is argued, the material elements have fulfilled their purposes; consequently, they do not proceed to form another body; thus the two non-perceptions are different because the purpose for which the body has been produced has been fulfilled.

This argument, says Vātsyāyana, is not sound. The bodies are produced again and again for the self which has not attained the release, even though the material elements have their purpose fulfilled by the self's perception of the things of the world. Further, as the bodies that are produced again and again have not brought about the perception of the difference between self and matter, the production of all these bodies must be regarded as purposeless.

In view of these considerations it is clear that if the creation of things from the material elements is not due to karma, the body cannot be said to be produced for the purposes of perception (*darśana*). But according to the Nyāya view the body can be correctly described as produced for the purposes of perception, for the Naiyāyika interprets perception as experience (*saṃvedanam*), which is the result of karma.[3]

(b) According to another interpretation,[4] *adṛṣṭa* is the name of a specific property of atoms, which is the cause of action; stimulated by this property, the atoms combine to produce the body; then stimulated by its own property of *adṛṣṭa*, the mind enters this body; when the mind has thus entered the body, the perceiver begins to have his apprehensions.

Vātsyāyana explains Gautama's answer to this objection: If the mind enters the body by virtue of *adṛṣṭa*, there should be severance of connection between the thing and the mind. If the *adṛṣṭa* which causes the entry of the mind into the body also causes its exit, this means that one and the same thing is the cause of both life and death; and this is absurd. Under the Nyāya theory this contingency does not arise: the exit of the mind from the body is due to the fact that one set of the residuum of karma to which the previous body owed its existence is exhausted and another set of the residuum of karma to which the next body owes its existence begins its fruition (NBh III. 2,75).

Another argument against the formation of the body out of the material elements independently of karma is that since death would be impossible the body would become eternal. When the results of all acts are experienced and thus the residuum of karma is exhausted, the body falls off; this is called death. And under the influence of another residuum of karma there is rebirth. In the absence of karma there would be nothing that could be exhausted; if nothing is exhausted there is no death; and if there is no death the body becomes eternal. Moreover, if death were due to mere chance (i.e. no specific cause), there would be no difference in the manner of death (NBh III. 2,76).

Gautama has argued that the *adṛṣṭa* theory implies that even after release there would be likelihood of another body being produced. To this the opponent retorts: Just as the black colour of the atom is eternal, and yet when it is set aside by fire-contact, it does not appear again, in the same manner the body though formed by the *adṛṣṭa* of the atoms would not appear again, after release (NBh III. 2,77).

According to Vātsyāyana, Gautama's reply can be interpreted in two ways: (1) The example cited by the opponent is not supported either by perception or by inference. One who believes in such an instance would be accepting something which is contrary to pramāṇa. (2) One who argues on the basis of the example that the formation of the body is not due to karma would be exposed to the contingency of the accruing of the unearned; that is, pleasure and pain accrue to the man without his having done the acts leading up to that pleasure and pain. If the opponent says that this does not matter, then he must realize that this is contrary to perception, inference and scripture.

In view of these circumstances Vātsyāyana concludes: the doctrine — "the formation of the body is not due to karma, and the accruing of pleasure and pain is not due to karma" — is clearly wrong and is maintained by the worst sinners (NBh III. 2,78).

21

BUDDHI

According to Gautama *buddhi*, which is fifth in his list of objects of cognition, is apprehension (*upalabdhi*) or cognition (*jñāna*); these three do not denote different things (NS I. 1,15). This statement is meant not only to define the *buddhi*, says Vātsyāyana, but also to indicate that this concept is opposed to that of the philosophers who hold that cognition is an operation (*vṛtti*) of the non-conscious instrument, *buddhi*, and that apprehension is an operation of the *cetana* (conscious entity or *puruṣa*) who is not an agent. Cognition cannot properly belong to the non-conscious instrument, *buddhi*; if it did, the *buddhi* would become conscious; but there is one conscious entity, different from the aggregate of the body and the organs (NBh I. 1,15).

In his detailed examination of the *buddhi* Gautama examines three main problems. (1) Is the *buddhi* eternal or non-eternal ? The discussion of this question is opened with the following doubt on the subject, which Gautama wishes to dispel. The *buddhi* resembles action (*karma*) and ākāśa in that it is intangible like them, but there is no distinguishing feature (*viśeṣa*) such as either liability to production and destruction which would determine the non-eternality of the *buddhi* or the contrary (i.e. non-liability to production and destruction) which would determine the eternality of the *buddhi*. In dispelling this doubt the Sāṃkhya concept of the *buddhi* and the Buddhist arguments are the main targets of criticism. According to Gautama the *buddhi* is non-eternal (NS & NBh III. 2,1).

(2) It is well known that the *buddhi* is a property of the self. The *buddhi* arises from contact but a specific feature of the contact is not apprehended. Hence there is doubt as to whether the *buddhi* is a property of the self, the sense-organs, the mind, or the object (*artha*) (NBh III. 2,19).

(3) The third problem discussed is: what exactly is meant by the non-eternality of the *buddhi* ? It is not certain whether the *buddhi* perishes immediately after its production like sound, or

after an interval of time like a pot. Gautama's view is that the *buddhis* follow one another in a series like sound (NBh III. 2,44).

(4) Gautama has devoted a great deal of attention to the kind of contact which recollection requires between the self and the mind. While he insists that the mind can function only inside a body, the controversy about the part (*pradeśa*) of the self and the housing of impressions which are involved in recollection throws some light on the nature of the self the philosophers had in view. A brief account of this controversy is given in this separate section.

Gautama has devoted fifty aphorisms (NS I. 1,15; III. 2,1-49) to the subject of the *buddhi* and in what follows his views as explained by Vātsyāyana are given below.

1. *Is the* buddhi *eternal ?*

According to the Sāṃkhya the *buddhi* is eternal (=proposition) because there is recognition of objects (=hetu). Recognition is that cognition which we have with regard to one and the same object in the form : 'I now cognize the same object which I had cognized before.' Such a cognition is possible only if the *buddhi* is eternal. If there were different *buddhis* capable of being produced and destroyed no recognition would be possible; for an object cognized by one cannot be recognized by another.

The Naiyāyika rejects this argument on the ground that the hetu cited by the Sāṃkhya requires proof as much as the probandum, the eternality of the *buddhi*. The *buddhi* is an instrument and the Sāṃkhya has not yet proved that recognition belongs to it.

According to the Sāṃkhya the functions of the *buddhi* are cognition (*jñāna*), perception (*darśana*), apprehension (*upalabdhi*), experience (*pratyaya*) and ascertainment (*adhyavasāya*). These are really the functions of the *puruṣa*. Only a conscious *puruṣa* can recognize what he has cognized before; so that it is to this *puruṣa*, and not to the instrument, that eternality should be attributed on the ground of recognition.

If, however, consciousness is attributed to the *buddhi*, the Sāṃkhya must state its exact nature, especially how it can be distinguished from the conscious *puruṣa*. For instance, if the *buddhi* is what cognizes, this expression is like 'the *puruṣa* cognizes'; both denote the same thing, cognition; similarly, the expressions — cognizer, perceiver, etc. — denote the same thing, the conscious being or the *puruṣa*. If the *buddhi* is 'what makes objects known', this amounts to saying that cognition belongs to the *puruṣa*, and not to the internal instrument (*antaḥkaraṇa*), i.e. the *buddhi*. If the Sāṃkhya argues that the different expressions cannot denote one and the same thing, he must give a valid hetu. If the Sāṃkhya should offer the hetu, 'the non-difference in denotation', such a hetu has already been used by the Sāṃkhya to prove its position. In the two expressions — 'the *puruṣa* cognizes' and 'the *buddhi* knows' there is no difference in the denotations of 'cognizes' and 'knows'; since both the *buddhi* and the *puruṣa* are conscious, there is no justification for predicating one of the *puruṣa*, and the other of the *buddhi*; hence one of the two must be rejected.

The Sāṃkhya argues that such difficulties can be avoided if the *buddhi* is regarded as the mind (*manas*): i.e. the instrument by means of which an object is cognized; and certainly the mind is eternal. According to the Naiyāyika, even if such a mind were eternal, recognition would not prove its eternality. For there is recognition even when there is a diversity of instruments, provided that the cognizing agent is the same. For instance, there is recognition with the right eye of what has been seen with the left eye, or recognition of an object previously seen with the help of one lamp, with what has been seen with the aid of another.

According to the Sāṃkhya, from the eternal *buddhi* proceed operations or modifications (*pariṇāma*) which constitute cognitions of objects; modification is not different from that of which it is the modification.

This view, says the Naiyāyika, is not right. If the source of the modification is not different from the modification and the source is eternal, the modification should also be eternal: that is, all our cognitions should be eternal. This means that there can be no such thing as recognition.

On the other hand, if the source is eternal but its modification is not, then the source should cease to exist whenever the modification ceases to exist. For instance, if recognition were to cease to exist the *buddhi* would cease to exist. If, however, even on the cessation of the modification the *buddhi* continues to exist, the modification should be different from the source. This means that the modification cannot be regarded as modification of the *buddhi*.

If the modification were not different from the source, apprehensions would not follow one after the other in succession; for both are eternal. Such appearance and disappearance can be explained, however, clearly within the Nyāya theory of the mind. The mind is atomic and comes into contact with the various sense-organs one after the other. Moreover, according to this concept of the mind, we can explain how an object is not apprehended. When the mind is occupied with one object another object is not apprehended.

The Sāṃkhya *buddhi* is all-pervading and cannot therefore be said to have any movement. Without movement it is not possible for the *buddhi* to come into contact with the various sense-organs and without such contact the non-simultaneous character of apprehensions cannot be explained. This argument is directed against the all-pervading character of the *buddhi* and not against its eternality. The all-pervading character cannot be established by any pramāṇa (NBh III. 2,2-8).

The Sāṃkhya argues that the notion of the difference (*anyatva*) in the case of the *buddhi* and its modification is similar to that of the difference in the case of crystal. Just as a single crystal seems to have different colours of different objects which come into contact with it, so the single *buddhi* appears to have different modifications under the influence of different objects which come into contact with it.

This contention is not right, says the Naiyāyika, because the diversity in the case of the crystal is only figurative while the diversity in the case of our cognitions is real. We have different apprehensions of really different objects. While the Sāṃkhya view is not supported by a valid hetu, the Nyāya position is well founded: the cognitions are really many, not unreal or figurative, because the cognitions of various sense-objects appear and disappear one after the other. Moreover, if there were no diversity of cognitions there could be no diversity of pramāṇas. And this would be contrary to the Sāṃkhya acceptance of three different pramāṇas, perception, inference and the utterance of *āpta*[1] (NBh III. 2,10).

According to the Buddhist who accepts the doctrine of momentariness (*kṣaṇikavādin*) the Sāṃkhya argument against the Nyāya position is not right. In the case of the crystal, in what is regarded as a single crystal several crystals appear and disappear, because such individual phenomena (*vyakti*) are momentary. That the things are momentary is evident from a series of growth and decay (*upacayāpacayaprabandha*) in the case of the body and similar things. Growth consists in the production of individual things, and decay in the destruction of individual things. The components (*avayava*) of the body undergo modification (*pariṇāma*) and the diversity of these modifications constitutes the growth of the body in course of time. Such growth is followed by decay. This is a distinguishing property of an individual (*vyaktiviśeṣadharma*); wherever there is an individual, such a property is found (NBh III. 2,11).

The Naiyāyika rejects this argument on the ground that the Buddhist has not presented a valid hetu to justify any such general rule (*niyama*). Neither perception nor inference can justify the rule. Hence the only reasonable course is to accept the Buddhist position wherever our cognition (*darśana*) warrants it. In the case of the body there is undoubtedly a continuous process of growth and decay, but there is no proof that a similar process occurs in the case of a stone or a crystal. To say that there is the production and destruction of individuals in all substances is like saying that all things are bitter because a certain plant is bitter (NBh III. 2,12).

Another version of the doctrine of momentariness is that every object is a series (*santāna*) of entities, each entity being entirely destroyed and succeeded by an entirely different entity, without any trace of the former; and each of these entities has but a momentary existence (NBh III. 2,12).

(*Yaś cāśeṣanirodhenāpūrvotpādaṃ niranvayaṃ dravyasantāne kṣaṇikatāṃ manyate*—NBh III. 2,11).

According to the Naiyāyika this Buddhist doctrine cannot be accepted because we apprehend the cause of growth and of decay. For instance, in the case of an ant-hill we see the accumulation of component particles as the cause of the growth of the ant-hill and the disruption of the particles as the cause of its destruction. But if such accumulation or disruption of the component particles were denied no cause of production or destruction could be apprehended (NBh III. 2,13).

The Buddhist argues that just as in the case of milk and curd we do not apprehend the cause of the destruction of the milk and of the production of the curd but admit such causes, the same could be said of the crystal. This argument is not right, says the Naiyāyika, because in the milk and the curd there are indicating marks whereby the causes can be apprehended while in the case of the crystal we do not find any mark indicative of the production and destruction of entities one after the other (NBh III. 2,13 & 14).

According to the Sāṃkhya the Buddhist contention mentioned above can be met in the following two ways: (a) The milk is not destroyed but modified. Modification (*pariṇāma*) means that while a substance remains the same its previous property disappears and a new property is produced. (b) There is 'manifestation of a different property' (*guṇāntaraprādurbhāva*). Since both versions maintain that while the substance remains the same, on the disappearance of its previous property a different property is produced, says Vātsyāyana, they are really based on the same doctrine (NBh III. 2,16)

2. *Can the* buddhi *be a property of the mind, the sense-organ and the object?*

Cognitions are of two kinds:

a) Cognitions produced by sense-object contact cease to exist on the destruction of the sense-organ and the object. Not can there be such cognition if the cognizer were destroyed.

b) Cognitions produced by the self-mind contact do not cease to exist even after the sense-organ and the object have been destroyed, e.g. recollection. Recollection is cognition of an object previously apprehended and if the cognizer were destroyed, what was previously apprehended could not be remembered. Cognition cannot therefore be a property of the sense-organ or the object even if the existence of the self is not admitted and the mind is regarded as the cognizer (NBh III. 2,19).

Cognition cannot be a property of the mind because the existence of the mind itself is inferred from the non-simultaneous character of cognitions of objects (*jñeya*) and also because the mind is an instrument under the control of the cognizer. If cognition were the property of the mind the mind would cease to be an instrument.

If on the basis of cognitions being produced by the sense-organs these sense-organs are regarded as instruments of a cognizing agent and on the basis of cognitions of pleasure, etc. and recollection the mind is regarded as an internal instrument of the self, then this is merely a nominal difference, not of substance. What the Naiyāyika calls the 'mind' other philosophers call the 'internal instrument'; and there is the cognizer to whom the property of cognition belongs.

Another reason why cognition cannot be the property of the mind is that the yogin has simultaneous apprehensions of objects when he occupies different bodies and thus has the use of several sense-organs in those bodies. If cognition were a property of the mind this would not be possible. For the mind is atomic and cannot be present in several bodies at one and the same time. Even if the mind were all-pervasive, this would not prove that cognition is a property of the mind; for this would mean simultaneous apprehensions of objects (NBh III. 2, 20-22).

There are two kinds of causes whereby a property may be destroyed: (a) absence (or destruction) of its substratum; (b) a contrary property. When such causes operate in the sphere of the self, since the self is eternal, the first cause cannot be said to destroy the *buddhi*. The second cause cannot be invoked for no property contrary to the *buddhi* is apprehended. If, therefore, the *buddhi* is a property of the self, it should be eternal.

The Naiyāyika's answer to this objection is that the *buddhi* is found to be non-eternal; one *buddhi* is destroyed by another as one sound is destroyed by another. Everyone knows directly from his own experience that the *buddhi* is non-eternal. That there is a series of *buddhis* (*buddhisantāna*) is also apprehended; from this we infer that one *buddhi* functions as a property contrary to another *buddhi* in the same way as from a series of sounds we infer that one sound is opposed to another (NBh III. 2,24 & 25).

It is argued that if the *buddhi* is a property of the self, recollections should be simultaneous. Innumerable impressions produced by cognitions, which are the causes of recollection, subsist in the self simultaneously. The mind-self contact, which is a cause common to all recollections, is also always present. Since the causes of recollections are simultaneously present, it follows that recollections should appear at one and the same time (NBh III. 2,25).

The answer of the Naiyāyika to the above objection is that

while the impressions and the mind-self contact are simultaneously present, there are other causes of recollection which do not operate simultaneously; e.g. attention, cognition of the mark (*liṅga*), etc. Hence the recollections do not appear simultaneously.

Generally one is not aware of all the factors that lead to recollection. When there is a series of ideas (*cintāprabandha*) about several things, a person concentrates on a particular thing and then that thing brings about a recollection. Because a person does not review his entire memory process, he thinks that his recollection is not dependent upon the various factors like attention and therefore is similar to intuition (*pratibhā*).

Even in those cases where recollection is independent of the factors enumerated above there is no possibility of several recollections being simultaneous. Neither intuitive cognitions (*prātibhaṃ jñānam*) nor recollections independent of the factors can be simultaneous.

According to the Naiyāyika the reason why even intuitive cognitions cannot appear simultaneously is not the specific karma (*karmaviśeṣa*) of a person but the capacity of the instrument that produces cognitions. An instrument can, by its very nature, produce cognitions only one by one; and several cognitions are never produced at one and the same time, either with regard to one or several objects. And it is from this observation of cognitions appearing one by one that we infer that the instrument has such a capacity.

This restriction does not hold good for the cognizer. For instance, a yogin can have several cognitions simultaneously because he can occupy several bodies and then have the use of several sense-organs in those bodies. The specific karma of man which ensures non-simultaneity of experiences (*upabhoga*) is not relevant to the question of intuitive cognitions (NBh III. 2, 34 & 35).

According to the Sāṃkhya, while cognition is a property of the self, desire, aversion, effort, pleasure and pain are properties of the internal instrument (*antaḥkaraṇa*=*buddhi*). The Naiyāyika rejects this view on the following grounds.

When a person cognizes that a certain thing is a source of pleasure or of pain, he desires to acquire it or to get rid of it; his efforts are accordingly directed towards these ends. Thus cognition, desire, aversion, effort, pain and pleasure are all connected with a single agent; they all subsist in a common substratum and are therefore properties of such an agent. These properties cannot be attributed to something that is not conscious for everyone knows from his own experience that positive and negative activity belongs to his own self and knows by means of inference that they belong to other selves (NBh III. 2,36).

According to the materialist (*bhūtacaitanika*), if desire and aversion are inferred from the marks, i.e. positive and negative activity, then those should also belong to that to which these marks belong; to that same thing should belong cognition also.[2] Since such activities are found in bodies composed of earth, water, air and fire, it follows that desire, etc., should belong to these bodies. Thus consciousness (*caitanya*) should be regarded as belonging to these bodies (NBh III. 2,36 & 37).

This argument is not valid, says the Naiyāyika, because in the case of instruments like an axe activity is not found to be concomitant with desire and aversion. Thus mere presence or absence of activity cannot prove the presence or absence of desire and aversion. What distinguishes the positive and negative activity of a cognizer due to desire and aversion is that such activity resides not in the cognizer himself but in what he operates upon; consequently, this activity is found only in such material elements as are directly operated upon by the cognizer and not in all material elements. This is what constitutes *'aniyama'*, i.e. absence of general rule. But a philosopher who does not believe in anything but the material elements has no such option open: he must say that everything — activity, desire aversion, etc. — must subsist in all material substances themselves. This is what will constitute *'niyama'* (rule) for them.

The materialist who attributes consciousness to the body is faced with the prospect of postulating several cognizers in a single body. This is not acceptable for a variety of reasons which have already been discussed in rejecting the views of other opponents.

Material elements exhibit such specific activities as belong to the instrumental cause of a quality of everything also, and on this ground we can infer the same thing in other cases also. For instance, instruments like an axe and such material elements as constitute objects like clay exhibit activity which is due to the quality of others; on this ground we can infer that the bodies of living creatures also exhibit activity under the influence of the quality of something else. This quality which produces activity subsists in the same substratum as effort and appears in the form of *'saṃskāra'*; this manifests in merit and demerit (*dharmādharma*). Like the quality of effort, it operates upon all things concerning the man and initiates activity in all material elements, for the fulfilment of that man's purpose.

The kind of activity which functions as the mark (*liṅga*= hetu) of desire and aversion is entirely different from reaction found in material elements. The former is never found in the reaction.

In addition to these objections to the materialist's view as outlined above, the Naiyāyika has other objections. As already mentioned, it is the self who is indicated by the marks of desire, aversion, etc. The material elements, the sense-organs and the mind are all instruments which operate under the influence of 'effort' and thus perform the functions of sustaining, propelling and aggregating. If these instruments were themselves conscious they would be independent. This is, however, contrary to their nature as instruments. Moreover, being conscious they would function as independent agents of activities of the mind, speech and body. Since the material elements, the sense-organs and the mind perish at death, the results of these activities in future births will have to be visited upon a cognizer who had nothing to do with these activities. On the other hand, if the elements, etc., are regarded as non-conscious, they would be the instruments of a conscious agent; it would then be quite right that the agent who has acted through these instruments should experience the fruits of acts done by himself (NBh III. 2,41 & 42).

Having thus disposed of rival views on the *buddhi*, Gautama concludes the discussion with the observation that his view is vindicated by a process of elimination and the various hetus he has previously given. According to Vātsyāyana the proposition under consideration is: 'cognition is a property of the self'. The process of elimination (*pariśeṣa*) works as follows: With regard to a property various possible substrata are considered and rejected; there is no other possible substratum except one. In the present case the material elements, the sense-organs and the mind have been rejected; there is no other substance which can be regarded as substratum; the only substance that remains is the self; *ergo* cognition is a property of the self (NBh III. 2,42).

According to Vātsyāyana Gautama has also the following in mind on the subject. The self undoubtedly is eternal. Consequently, when it has performed meritorious acts (*dharma*) in one body, on the destruction of that body it reappears in Heaven among the gods; if it has performed non-meritorious acts, on the destruction of the body it reappears in the Hells. This reappearance (*upapatti*), which consists of acquisition of a different body, is possible only if it is supported by an eternal self.

Neither *saṃsāra* nor *apavarga* would be possible without an eternal self. The *saṃsāra* which consists in conjunction (*yoga*) of a single entity (*sattva*) with several bodies and the *apavarga* (or *mukti*) which consists in the destruction of a series of bodies. (*śarīraprabandhoccheda*) are possible only if there is an eternal self. If there were a series of *buddhis,* there is nothing that could traverse the long path (of *saṃsāra*) or that could be freed from the series of bodies. And this means that there can be neither *saṃsāra* nor *apavarga*.

Further, if there were nothing but a series of *buddhis*, then each entity would consist of diverse entities. This cannot but lead to utter chaos. Another undesirable consequence of this would be the impossibility of recollection. Recollection is nothing but recognition by the same cognizer of the thing he had perceived before (NS & NBh III. 2,42).

We have a more vivid picture of this chaos in the comments of Vācaspati. Since according to the Buddhist an entity is a 'negation of the contrary' (*anyāpoha*), the following consequences are inevitable. The act begun today and finished tomorrow would be done by distinct entities; therefore it would not be recognized as the same on both days. It would not be possible to distinguish an act from what belongs to another. Similarly, there would be no distinction between the Brahmin, Kṣatriya, Vaiśya and Śūdra; for no one would have a function which he was authorized to perform according to the *varṇa* to which he belonged (NVTT III. 2,42).

3. *What does the non-eternality of the* buddhi *mean ?*

According to Gautama, a *buddhi* perishes immediately after

its production because all actions are found to be transitory. If a *buddhi* were permanent there would be only perception; for there would be absence of recollection (NS III. 2,45 & 46). Vātsyāyana explains: When an arrow is shot from a bow we apprehend a series of actions (*kriyāsantāna*) till the arrow drops down. There must be a series of *buddhis* corresponding to this series of actions for every apprehension is restricted to a single object. Even when we apprehend a durable object like a jar there is also a series of *buddhis*, which functions until we have ceased to apprehend the jar as soon as something obstructs our vision. If *buddhis* were eternal, then the perceptional cognition of the jar would continue even after the jar is hidden from our view.

If the *buddhi* were eternal we could have only perceptional cognition and not recollection. Recollection is produced by impression (*saṃskāra*) generated by the *buddhi*, and the impression is different from the *buddhi*. Moreover, if the *buddhi* were permanent, as already mentioned, it would continue even after the object of that *buddhi* had ceased to exist; and in that case there could be no recollection (NBh III. 2,45 & 46).

It is argued that if apprehension were transitory, it would not be distinct like our apprehension of colour in a flash of lightning. The advocate of the argument wants to disprove the transitory character of apprehension, says Gautama, but what he really does is to admit its transitoriness. Surely, if apprehension is not distinct it must be transitory (NBh III. 2,47 & 48).

Even though the *buddhi* is transitory, says Gautama, there is distinct apprehension as in the case of a series (*santati*) of flames of a lamp. In this series every one of the flames is transitory and so is every apprehension of every flame; but each apprehension is distinct as it pertains to its particular object (NBh III. 2,49).

The character of our apprehension, distinct or indistinct, has nothing to do with the question of permanence or transitoriness of the apprehension; it depends upon whether the causes of apprehension are transitory or durable (NBh III. 2,48).

4. *Can recollection be explained as due to the contact of the mind with a part of the self* (ātmapradeśa) *?*

According to some philosophers (i.e. *ekadeśins*) the reason why recollections appear one after the other is that the mind comes into contact with such parts of the self as house the impressions produced by cognition. The Naiyāyika rejects this explanation on the ground that the mind can function only inside the body. The mind comes into contact with the self when the latter has acquired a body; this contact appears along with such residue of karma (*karmāśaya*) as has begun to bear fruit. In fact this is what '*jīvana*' (life) means. Consequently, the mind cannot come into contact with such parts of the self as lie outside the body and may be housing impressions of previous cognitions; it can establish such contact when the self has departed from the body.

It is argued that if life consists in the fruition of the residue of karma only, the Naiyāyika has still to prove that the mind functions within the body. The reply of the Naiyāyika is that when a person recollects he is found equipped with the body. If the mind were to function outside the body, it could not establish contact with the self inside the body. Without such contact no effort would be possible, and without such effort the body would not be maintained. The effort due to the mind-self contact is of two kinds, retaining and impelling. If the mind went out of the body, the effort to maintain the body would not be made; as a result, the body of the recollecting self would collapse.

The opponent argues that no such contingency would arise for the mind is capable of swift movement. It is therefore quite possible that such a mind goes out of the body, establishes contact with such parts of the self as are outside the body and house the impressions of previous cognitions; or it goes out of the body after having produced the effort necessary for upholding the body and this would enable the body to remain intact till the mind returns after having performed its function outside the body.

The Naiyāyika replies that this explanation is not satisfactory. The process of recollection may be quick or take a long time. In the latter case the mind remains concentrated, with a desire to remember a thing, and when there appears an idea of a thing that might have a distinguishing feature of the thing to be remembered, it becomes the direct cause of the desired recollection. If the mind were to remain outside the body, such a prolonged process of recollection would not be possible.

Some philosophers argue against the view of the philosophers mentioned above: There is no reason to think that the mind can establish any contact with the self outside the body. Such specific contact can be said to be due to (a) the propulsion (*preraṇa*), of the self, or (q) chance (*yadṛcchā*) or (c) the mind functioning as cognizer. None of these alternatives is tenable in the following way:

(a) Under the first alternative the self would have to impel the mind after it has reflected thus: 'the impression which is the cause of recollection subsists in this part of the self; let therefore the mind come into contact with this part.' This would mean that the thing to be recollected is already there and does not need further stimulation. Moreover, a 'part' of the self or the impression cannot be perceptible to the self; so that such notions cannot really figure in the kind of cogitation mentioned above.

(b) The self recollects a thing only after concentrating the mind upon it for some time. The contact cannot be due to chance.

(c) The capacity to cognize does not belong to the mind at all. Hence the third alternative is untenable.

The true explanation for recollection is that even though the causes concerned are simultaneously present, the specific causes like attention, etc., do not operate simultaneously (NBh III. 2, 25-34)

22

ACTIVITY (*pravṛtti*)

The seventh object of cognition, activity (*pravṛtti*) is defined by Gautama as that which initiates the action of speech, *buddhi* and body (NS I. 1,17). In another statement Gautama confirms this definition (NS IV. 1,1).

According to Vātsyāyana, the activity mentioned by Gautama means the results of activity in the form of merit and demerit. Activity is good when it leads to merit; it is bad when it leads to demerit. The figurative use of the term is justified by common usage; for example, we speak of life as 'food' because it is the result of food.

In the sense of merit and demerit activity is the cause of respectable or disrespectable birth. And birth consists in the collective appearance of the body, the sense-organs and the *buddhi*. Where there is birth, there is pain (NBh I. 1,2).

According to Uddyotakara activity has two forms: cause and effect. As cause, it denotes the operations of speech, body and intellect; as effect, it denotes merit and demerit. As effect, (a) it subsists in the self because the effect of merit, viz. prosperity, belongs to each individual separately; (b) it is determinate (*avasthita*) because its time of fruition is fixed; (c) as subsisting in the self, it is a subordinate property, and not eternal, as is evident from the fact that there is death (NV IV. 1,1 & 2).

Activity under the influence of defects, says Vātsyāyana, leads to deeds pertaining to the body, speech and the mind. These deeds are good or bad.

Bad deeds:

(a) Body: killing,

(b) Speech: lying, rude talking, incoherent babbling.

(c) Mind: malice, heresy (*nāstikya*), desire for things belonging to others.

Good deeds:

(a) Body: charity, protecting, service.

(b) Speech: telling the truth, saying what is beneficial, study (of the Veda).

(c) Mind: mercy, faith, entertaining no desire for things belonging to other people (NBh I. 1,2).

23

DEFECT (*doṣa*)

The eighth object of cognition, defect (*doṣa*), is intimately connected with the seventh object, activity. According to Gautama, defects have the characteristic of initiating activity (NS I. 1,18). In another statement he confirms the definition (NS IV. 1,2).

Vātsyāyana explains: From wrong apprehension proceed attachment to what is agreeable and aversion to what is disagreeable, and it is under their influence that defects appear (NBh I. 1,2). In fact, attachment, aversion and misconception (*moha*) cause activity. These defects are directly apprehended by each individual self; it is the action of man acting under their influence that indicate their presence (NBh IV. 1,18).

Inasmuch as the defects subsist in the same substratum as *buddhi*, these are regarded as the properties (*guṇa*) of the self. Since they are the cause of activity and also have the power (*sāmarthya*) to bring about rebirth, they are regarded as the cause of *saṃsāra*. Since the *saṃsāra* is without beginning, the defects are regarded as operating without a beginning. Wrong apprehension ceases when right apprehension is attained; on the cessation of wrong apprehension, the whole series of attachments and aversions stops, and then follows release. It is clear, Vātsyāyana says, that defects are liable to appearance and disappearance (NBh IV. 1,2).

According to Uddyotakara, the idea of action under the influence of defects is that one is forced, helplessly to act. That one does act under the compulsion of defects one knows directly by perception: That other persons also act in a similar fashion is known by inference. This knowledge is similar to that of oneself and other persons. That the object of the notion of 'I' is the self known by each person directly by perception and not by inference or from scripture. One's own self cannot be known by inference because there is the absence of marks; it cannot be known from scripture because it is an object which cannot be known by instruction. Like colour, one's own self, says the commentator, is directly perceptible to oneself, while the self in another body is inferred from activity and the cessation of activity (NV I. 1,18).

Another observation of Uddyotakara worth mentioning is that defects are regarded as properties because while being products they are perceptible by the mind and not by the visual organ (NV IV. 1,2).

Three groups of Defects

According to Gautama, the defects can be divided into three groups, as all of them are included under attachment, aversion and misconception (NS IV. 1,3).

Vātsyāyana lists the following defects under each group:

(a) Attachment: Lust, jealousy, avarice, avidity and covetousness,

(b) Aversion: Anger, envy, malice, hatred and resentment,

(c) Misconception: Wrong apprehension, suspicion, pride and negligence (NBh IV. 1,3).

Gautama refers to the following objection to his three groups of defects: since they are all opposed by one single thing, it is not right to divide them into various groups (NS IV. 1,4). His reply is: The hetu is not valid because it is inconclusive (NS IV. 1,5).

Vātsyāyana explains the objection: All defects are opposed to or destroyed by one single thing known under different names such as knowledge of the true nature of things (*tattvajñāna*), right knowledge (*samyagjñāna*), superhuman cognition (*āryaprajñā*) and right apprehension (*saṃbodha*). Hence the defects do not denote different things.

Explaining Gautama's reply, the commentator says that the hetu is inconclusive because a single thing can oppose or destroy different things; for example, various properties of clay such as its colour, shape etc., are destroyed by a single thing, viz. fire-contact, and they are not one and the same (NBh IV. 1,5).

Vātsyāyana mentions another objection to the three groups of defects: since all defects have the same characteristic of causing activity, it is not right to divide them under three groups. This objection is not valid, says the commentator, because each group has its own characteristic. Attachment is characterized by deep involvement, aversion by resentment, and misconception by wrong apprehension. This fact is realized by every man in his own experience : for example, every embodied being knows when attachment appears, when he has the feeling that 'the property of attachment has appeared in myself'; he also recognizes the absence of such an attachment. The various feelings such as pride, etc., are all included under one or the other of the three groups; and hence Gautama has not enumerated them separately (NBh IV. 1,3).

Of the three groups of defects, misconception is the worst sin, says Gautama, because in the case of a person who is not under misconception, the other two groups of defects do not come into existence (NS IV. 1,6). When a person is under misconception, explains Vātsyāyana, attachment or aversion appears in accordance with his impressions (*saṅkalpa*). If his impression is of an object that is attractive, they produce attachment in the person for that object; if these objects are repulsive, they produce aversion. Both attachment and aversion are thus due to misconception which consists in wrong apprehension; they are nothing but misconception. When misconception is destroyed by right apprehension, both attachment and aversion cease to appear; this is the significance of the fact that all defects are opposed by one single thing, viz., knowledge of the true nature of things. It is because of this function of knowledge that Gautama has declared that after the attainment of knowledge there is a cessation of each member of the series in the reverse order (NBh IV. 1,6).

Gautama mentions an objection to his view: If there is a relation of cause and effect between ignorance on the one hand and attachment and aversion on the other, then misconception must be something different from the defects (NS IV. 1,7). His reply is: It is not so, (a) because defects already defined include misconception (NS IV. 1, 8), and (b) because there is no prohibition that things belonging to a homogeneous class should not stand in the relation of cause and effect (NS IV. 1,9).

According to Vātsyāyana the objection is : since the effect is always different from the cause, misconception, which is the cause of the defects, attachment and aversion, cannot itself be a 'defect'. To this the first answer is that since defects have been defined as having the characteristic of causing activity, misconception is included under 'defect' in accordance with the definition. The second answer is that among substances, as well as properties, of a homogeneous class, it is found that they bear to one another various kinds of causal relation (NBh IV. 1,7-9). As Uddyotakara puts it, whether a thing is as it is or as it is not is determined not by the causal relation but by its essential characteristic being the same (NV IV. 1,8).[1] For example, one apprehension is the cause of another, though they belong to the same class 'apprehension'; one substance 'shuttle' is the cause of another substance 'cloth'; the same is true of properties like contact (NV IV.1,9).

According to Uddyotakara, the various defects recognized in the Nyāya system denote different things. The names used for them are not synonyms; for things spoken of by a number of synonyms such as *Indra, Śakra, Purandara,* do not constitute a group nor are these terms used as constituting a group.

The commentator explains the specific features of the various defects as follows :

(a) Attachment (*rāga*): Lust is yearning for a woman as is shown in the saying 'unless a man is in love, he does not bedeck himself'. Jealousy is the desire not to part with a thing, even though it is inexhaustible; e.g. one wishes that people should not drink water from a large royal well. Avarice is the desire to possess what does not belong to oneself. Avidity is the desire to be born again. Covetousness is the desire for the unauthorized (*pramāṇaviruddha*) possession of what belongs to another.

(b) Aversion (*dveṣa*) : Anger is that which causes the distortion of the body and the receptacles of the sense-organs. Envy is the feeling that one has of preventing another person from having possession of what belongs to both. Malice is the feeling of being unable to bear the description of good qualities of other people. Hatred is the wish to do harm to others even when one is not able to do so. Resentment is inability to bear the harm done to oneself.

(c) Misconception (*moha*) : Wrong apprehension is the apprehension of a thing as it is not. Suspicion is the doubt in the form: 'what can it be due to ?'. Pride is the feeling of self-importance; e.g. 'How great am I'. Negligence is the failure to do what one could do.

The three groups of defects have one and the same characteristic, causing activity and they are therefore classed as 'defects'. Each group is different from the others because it has its own distinguishing characteristics. Similarly, each defect in a group can be distinguished from another, although they all have the common characteristic of the group. The fact that several things have a common characteristic does not reduce them to one and the same thing; for if this were so, there would be neither a common characteristic nor a distinguishing characteristic. The various terms for groups and individual defects are used in their distinctive senses. And this is amply confirmed from ordinary usage, e.g. when a beggar asks for alms, people do not say that he has lust for it (NV IV, 1,3).

24

STATE AFTER DEATH (*pretyabhāva*)

Connected with the second object of cognition, body, is the ninth object 'state after death' (*pretyabhāva*). According to Gautama the state after death means rebirth (*punarutpatti*) (NS I. 1,19). Having died, when the self is born again in an animated body (*sattvanikāya*), this being born again, says Vātsyāyana, constitutes the rebirth of that self, which is born. When the self is connected with the body, the sense-organs, the mind, *buddhi* and feeling (*vedanā*), this constitutes birth. To be born again is to have repeated connection with this psycho-somatic complex. This process of births and deaths is without beginning but terminable only with release (NBh I. 1,19).

How can the eternal self have rebirth i.e. birth and death ? This is possible, says Gautama, precisely because it is eternal (NS IV. 1,10). Vātsyāyana explains: It is the eternal self that departs, i.e. abandons the previous body, dies; having thus departed, it becomes, i.e. is born, it takes up another body; and it is these two — departing and becoming — that are described as 'rebirth'. This is precisely the etymological meaning of the term '*pretyabhāva*'.[1]

If rebirth were to consist of the birth of one entity and destruction of another, then we would be faced with the situation in which one entity is deprived of the effects of its acts, while another is saddled with the effects of acts done by another. Further, this would make all instruction useless; the entity which has been instructed does not last long enough to profit by it (NBh IV. 1,10).

According to Uddyotakara, the process of *saṃsāra* is an unceasing causal operation among pain, birth, activity, defect and wrong apprehension. This process is without beginning. It has no definite order of sequence, because we cannot say which comes first, and which next. If pain came first, it would not be right; for without birth there can be no pain. If birth came first, this would not be right; for there is no birth without merit and demerit. If merit and demerit came first, this would be wrong; for these are not possible without attachment and aversion. If attachment and aversion came first, this would be wrong; for without wrong apprehension they can never appear. If wrong apprehension came first, this would not be right; for without the psycho-somatic equipment there can be no wrong apprehension. Thus there is no order of sequence in this entire process.

To whom does *saṃsāra* belong ? If it means entry into and departure from bodies, it belongs to the mind; for it is the mind that actually moves. If it means the experiencing of pleasure and pain, it belongs to the self; for it is the self that experiences pleasure and pain (NV I. 1,19).

25

RESULT (*Phala*)

The tenth object of cognition is result (*phala*). It is defined by Gautama as 'the thing produced by activity and defects' (NS I. 1,20). Vātsyāyana explains: Result consists in the experiencing of pleasure and pain. Activity leads to pleasure and pain. Since pleasure and pain appear only when the body, the sense-organs, the objects of sense and apprehension (*buddhi*) are present, the result in this context means pleasure and pain along with the body, etc. Thus all of these constitute the result; it is the thing produced by activity and defects. Every time this result is received, it is relinquished; every time it is relinquished, it is again received; and there is no end or cessation of these receivings and relinquishings. It is this unceasing flow of receivings and relinquishings which constitutes the entire worldly process (*loka*) (NBh. I. 1,20).

In his comments on the subject Uddyotakara further explains the Nyāya view: Everything that is produced, e.g. the body etc., is a result, because it is produced by merit and demerit. If we regard the primary or principal result alone as constituting the present object of cognition, the experiencing of pleasure and pain is the only result; for this is what it ultimately leads to. But inasmuch as the experiencing of pleasure and pain is the final result of merit and demerit — and there is no possibility of experiencing these without the body etc. — in view of this fact, it is held that merit and demerit bring about the experiencing of pleasure and pain only after having produced the body, etc. Hence the term, fruit or result, is applied, primarily, to the experiencing of pleasure and pain, and secondarily to the body, etc. (NV I. 1,20).

(1) There is no doubt regarding the result, says Gautama, because it appears immediately as well as after a long interval (NS IV. 1,44). Vātsyāyana explains : When a man cooks rice or milks the cow, the results — the rice or the milk — appear immediately; whereas when he sows the seeds, the result — the harvest —

accrues to him after an interval of time. Now the *Agnihotra* sacrifice mentioned in the scriptural injunction — 'one desiring heaven should perform the *Agnihotra'* — is an act; with regard to the result of this act there is doubt (NBh IV. 1,44).

Gautama answers the doubt: The result is not immediate because it can be experienced only after an interval of time (NS IV. 1,45). Vātsyāyana explains: Heaven is the result mentioned in the scriptural injunction and it can only be attained when one has acquired another body after the present body has been destroyed. This kind of delayed result is also noticed in the case of actions initiated towards acquiring villages or other property (NBh IV. 1,45).

An action enjoined in a scriptural injunction, says Uddyotakara, can never be without the result mentioned therein. No one who performs a sacrifice would do so simply to obtain the heat from the sacrificial fire. From all this it follows that from the contact of the mind with the self — the contact which follows after the performance of the sacrificial acts and which is helped by pure intentions — there appears in the self merit. Since the potency of this merit is unobstructed, it yields the result under suitable conditions of place, etc; and it is only when the present body has fallen off, and the self is equipped with another body, that the result, viz. heaven, appears, and not immediately after the performance of the sacrifice (NV IV. 1,45).

(2) Gautama mentions an objection: The result cannot be produced after an interval of time because the cause (hetu) has been destroyed (NS IV. 1,46). His reply is: Prior to its production this result is like the fruit of a tree (NS IV. 1,47). Vātsyāyana explains: The objection is that since the action of performing the sacrifice has ceased to exist, in its absence no result can come about; in fact no effect is ever found to be produced out of a cause that has ceased to exist (NBh IV. 1,46). The reply of Gautama is : The analogy explains how the result can appear even when the cause has ceased to exist. The man who desires to have fruits waters the tree; when the watering has ceased the earth-particles under the roots of the tree are joined together by the particles of water; they are heated by the heat underground and produce a juicy substance; this juicy substance, as modified by the heat, comes into contact with the tree and, in a modified form (*vyūha*), enters into it and produces leaves, fruits, etc. Thus

the action of watering is fruitful, and yet the result does not quite follow from a cause that has entirely ceased to exist. In the same manner actions produce in the self a faculty (*saṃskāra*) in the shape of merit and demerit; this faculty, with the help of other causes thus produces the result after an interval of time. It is because of such continuity of the results of previous deeds that the body comes into existence (NBh IV. 1,47).

(3) Gautama mentions the following objection : The analogy to the fruit of a tree is not right because the receptacle is different (NS IV. 1,51). Vātsyāyana explains: In the case of the tree both the action of watering, etc. and the fruit appear in the same receptacle, i.e. the tree itself. In the case of the sacrifice one body performs the action of sacrificing while another body obtains the heaven; there are two different receptacles. Thus these two cases are different and the analogy therefore does not prove the point (NBh IV. 1,51).

Gautama answers that this objection is unfounded because happiness subsists in the self (NS IV. 1,52). Happiness is something, says Vātsyāyana, which is perceptible to the self; therefore its receptacle is the self. The same self is the receptacle of karma in the form of merit, because merit is the property of the self. Thus there is no possibility of the receptacles being different (NBh IV. 1,52).

(4) According to Gautama another objection is raised against his answer: The self cannot be the receptacle for the results which are mentioned, viz. a son, a wife, cattle, attendants, gold, food, etc. (NS IV. 1,53). Gautama answers: Inasmuch as the result is produced from connection with the things mentioned, it is only indirectly (figuratively) that these latter are spoken of as the result (NS IV. 1,54).

Vātsyāyana explains: What is actually mentioned as the result is the son, etc., and not happiness. It is not therefore right to say that happiness is mentioned as the result. To this objection the answer is: the true result, i.e. happiness, arises from connection with the son, etc. It is for this reason that these latter are spoken of, only indirectly, as 'result'; just as food is indirectly spoken of as 'life', in such statements as 'food is life itself' (NBh IV. 1,54).

(5) Gautama mentions the following objection of the Buddhist: The result, prior to its production, is neither existent nor

non-existent nor both, because existence and non-existence are dissimilar (NS IV. 1,48).[1] His reply is: (a) [The result, before it was produced, was non-existent] because we perceive production as well as destruction (NS IV. 1,49); (b)That it was non-existent, is proved by that very conception (*buddhi*) (NS IV. 1,50).

Vātsyāyana explains the objection: (a) A thing that is liable to production could not be non-existent before its production, because there is a restriction (*niyama*) regarding the material cause (*upādāna*). Every thing does not produce every thing; only a particular material cause can produce a particular thing. This restriction would not be there if the product were absolutely non-existent before its production. (b) Nor could the thing be existent prior to its production; for if the thing does already exist before it is produced, there is no need for a further production of the same thing. (c) The thing could not be both existent and non-existent because these two are dissimilar. The term 'existent' affirms a thing while the term 'non-existent' denies it. It is this contradictory character that is spoken of as dissimilarity (NBh IV. 1,48).

Explaining Gautama's reply, Vātsyāyana says that the thing that is liable to be produced is non-existent prior to its production because we observe the production and destruction of things. Further, the conception of restriction which the objector has cited is: 'this thing, and not all things, is capable of producing this effect': this conception clearly proves that prior to being produced, every effect is known to be capable of being produced by a particular cause. And in fact, the production of the effect is in accordance with that conception. If, however, the product is already existent, prior to being produced, then there can be no such thing as 'production' (NBh IV. 1,49 & 50).

Commenting on this subject, Uddyotakara observes that if there were neither production nor destruction, this would mean the end of all our activity. We undertake activity either to obtain or discard things. But if things were existent even prior to their production, there can be nothing to be either obtained or discarded.

Further, anyone who advocates such a view must renounce all reasoning. Reasoning is meant to produce right cognition or destroy wrong cognition, and in either case something new is produced. The position is not improved by saying that reasoning is meant to manifest an effect; for whatever interpretation may be placed on the term 'manifestation', something new is essential to make such manifestation worth-while (NV IV.1,49).

Regarding the material cause, Uddyotakara remarks that the idea of the restriction is based not upon the fact of the thing being already existent but upon its potentiality; it is the idea that 'this effect can be produced out of this cause, and it cannot be produced out of another'. It is only when a man has such a notion of the effect that he brings in, for the production of that effect, such a cause as is capable of producing it. No one brings in every cause for the production of every effect; for the simple reason that every thing is never found to be produced out of every thing.

Since the objector admits that a certain cause produces a certain effect he should explain the meanings of these two terms. He might say: the cause is that which does and the effect is that which is done. Even if such a view were right, it would be necessary to say that the effect is something new and not merely a manifestation of something already in existence. Even such expressions as 'do the hair' do not mean that what is already in existence is being manifested; for in the doing of the hair what is done is the arrangement of the already existing hair and this arrangement is not something that existed before.

If it is the non-existent thing that is produced, the objector might ask, why is it that the horn of an ass is not produced ? If there is such a thing as the horn of the ass, says Uddyotakara, it could certainly be produced. But, then, why does not the horn grow out of the body of the ass ? We do not know why it does not grow out of it; that it does not do so, says the commentator, we only conclude from the fact that we have never seen a horn being produced out of the body of the ass. The horn of the ass is not produced, not because it is non-existent, but because there is no cause that could bring it about. In fact, the non-existence of a thing cannot be regarded as a reason for its being produced; what is meant is that since what is already existent cannot be produced, it is the non-existent thing that is produced.

Further, the assertion of the objector—'the horn of the ass is not produced because it is non-existent'—goes against his own view: whether a thing is existent or non-existent, it is produced if its cause is present. Since the ass is present, its horn cannot really be non-existent. If every effect already exists, then the entire business of mankind would come to an end; nothing new is ever produced, and nothing old can be destroyed.

The objector may ask: how do we know that the effect is non-existent prior to its production ? There can be no pramāṇa, replies the commentator, for ascertaining the existence or non-existence of things. Inference is possible only when there is no difference of opinion in regard to the thing in question.[2] The dispute is not about the thing but about the properties of the thing upon which both parties are agreed. For example, in the case of the yarns and the cloth what is under dispute is not the yarns but what exactly happens when the cloth is produced out of the yarns. There are different theories on the subject and the Nyāya position is that the cloth was not existent prior to its production (NV IV, 1,50).

26

PAIN (*duḥkha*)

The eleventh object of cognition is pain (*duḥkha*). It has, says Gautama, the characteristic of distress (NS I.1,21).[1] Vātsyāyana explains: Distress in this context means affliction (*pīḍā*) and anguish (*tāpa*). This distress is mixed with, and wholly present with, pain; it is because this distress is so connected that it is known as pain itself. Realizing that everything is mixed with pain, a person wishes to get rid of pain. He realizes, therefore, that birth itself is nothing but pain, he is disgusted (*nirviṇṇa*); being disgusted he becomes free from attachment, he is released (NBh I. 1,21).

According to Gautama, birth is pain itself because it is connected with various kinds of distress (NS IV.1,55).[2] Vātsyāyana explains: The expression '*'janmotpatti'*' used by Gautama in the aphorism means the coming into existence of the body, the sense-organs, etc. in their various forms. The various kinds of distress to which Gautama has referred are the least, the medium and the greatest. The least is the lot of human beings; the medium of the lower animals; and the greatest of the denizens of hell. Gods and those who have got rid of attachment have less distress than the human beings.

When a person realizes that every form of life is beset with distress he is confirmed in his belief that pleasure and the means of obtaining it, such as the body, the sense-organs, cognitions, deserve to be regarded as pain. When he is firmly convinced in this matter, he ceases to be attached to the whole world; after he has cultivated this detachment, his longing for all worldly things comes to an end; when his longing has thus come to an end, he is released from all pain. This entire process can be compared to what a person does in the case of poisoned milk : When he realizes that by contact of poison, milk becomes poison, he does not wish to obtain the milk; not obtaining it, he does not suffer the pain of death (NBh IV. 1,55).

Vātsyāyana mentions an objection to Gautama's actual

statement on birth as pain. If Gautama did not wish to deny pleasure, he should not have said 'birth is pain itself' but, 'birth is pain'; for his statement implies that there is no pleasure at all. The reason for using the emphatic term (*eva*), says Vātsyāyana in reply, is that what is laid down is conducive to the cessation of birth; that is, birth is pain, not by its own nature, but by reason of its being beset with pain, and similarly, pleasure is pain because it is mixed with pain, and not because there is no pleasure (NBh IV. 1,58).[3]

According to Vātsyāyana, in asking us to look upon all things as pain Gautama does not wish to deny pleasure. He has stated his position as follows: (a) Pleasure is not denied because it is produced at intervals; (b) This is not opposed (to Gautama's general view on pain) because distresses do not cease to be experienced by a person on account of the fault of striving after worldly objects; (c) There is a misconception (*abhimāna*) of pleasure in what is only another name for pain (NS IV.1,56-68).

Vātsyāyana explains: (a) Every embodied person experiences pleasure even when he is tormented by various distresses; there are intervals of pleasure between distresses.

(b) When the man experiences pleasure from a certain thing, he desires that thing; sometimes this desire is not fulfilled, or if fulfilled, it is fulfilled only in part, or is fulfilled in such form as is beset with obstacles; this is what constitutes the fault of striving (*paryeṣaṇadoṣa*). It is because of this nature of the striving that the man who experiences pleasure is never free from various kinds of mental distress — the distress which is the result of the striving. This is why it is necessary to look upon pleasure as pain. It is for this reason that birth is pain, and not because there is no pleasure at all.

This idea is expressed in the following verses: (1) For the man who desires a desirable thing, as soon as that desire is fulfilled, another desire quickly gets hold of him. (2) Even though the man may obtain the entire earth surrounded by sea, along with all cows and horses, he is not satisfied with that wealth; what pleasure, then, can there be for one who seeks ordinary wealth ?

(c) The ordinary man, addicted to pleasure, regards pleasure as the highest end of man; for him there is nothing better than pleasure. When he obtains pleasure, he is satisfied that he has attained all that could be attained. Under this wrong apprehension he becomes attached to pleasure and all that produces pleasure; becoming so attached, he strives to obtain pleasure; while he is striving, he experiences several kinds of pain such as birth, old age, disease, death, contact of disagreeable things, separation from agreeable things, non-fulfilment of desires, etc.; and yet all these kinds of pain he regards as pleasure. In fact pain is an integral part of pleasure; without experiencing some pain no pleasure can be obtained; consequently, the man regards this pain as pleasure; and obsessed with this notion of pleasure he never escapes from *saṃsāra*. And it is to oppose this notion of pleasure that Gautama instructs us to look upon all this as pain (NBh IV. 1,56-58).[4]

Vātsyāyana sums up the whole Nyāya position on pain :

It is not possible to deny pleasure, to the existence of which testimony is borne by all men. The teaching that pleasure should be looked upon as pain is intended for the person who is disgusted with the pain experienced during a series of births and deaths, and is anxious to get rid of all similar experiences, so that he may be able to remove all pain. The bodies of all living beings, all the regions where living beings are born, all rebirth — every one of these is mixed with distress, being inseparable from pain. It is in view of this fact that the sages have reiterated the advice which Gautama has given — 'pain has the characteristic of distress' (NS I. 1,21); it means that all the things mentioned above should be regarded as pain. *Duḥkha* (pain) is the technical term (*saṃjñā*) for this entire complex (Intr. NBh IV. 1,55).

27

RELEASE (*apavarga*)

I

Release (*apavarga*) is the twelfth object of cognition. Gautama defines release as the 'absolute deliverance from pain'(NS I. 1,22). When there is a relinquishing of the birth that has been taken, and the non-assumption of another — this condition which is without end, says Vātsyāyana, is known as *'apavarga'*[1] by those who know it is. This condition of immortality, free from fear and imperishable, is *Brahman*; it consists in the attainment of bliss (*kṣema*).[2]

Vātsyāyana mentions the following Vedānta view: Some philosophers think that in liberation (*mokṣa*) what is manifested is the eternal pleasure of the *ātman*, just like *mahattva;* when that pleasure is manifested, the *ātman* is absolutely liberated, and becomes pleased.[3]

According to Vātsyāyana, there is no pramāṇa which can support this view; there is neither perception nor inference nor scripture to prove that like its vastness, the eternal pleasure of the *ātman* is manifested in liberation. His criticism of this concept is given below :

(1) If there is manifestation (i.e. feeling or experience) of the eternal pleasure in the state of liberation, the proponent of the view should state the cause that has produced the manifestation.

(a) If the manifestation is as eternal as the pleasure, then there would be no difference between the condition of the *ātman* when it is liberated and when it is bound: in both states the *ātman* would have both the eternal pleasure and its eternal manifestation.

If this position were accepted, we would be aware of the eternal pleasure and its eternal manifestation as concomitant and simultaneous with that pleasure and pain which, produced by merit and demerit in the substrate (viz. the *ātman*), are experienced by turns. And there would never be any substrate where either pleasure or its experience is absent; for according to the proponent's view both of these are eternal.

(b) The mind-*ātman* contact cannot function as such a cause, because it can only do so if it is assisted by other causes. If merit is treated as such an ancillary cause, it is necessary to point out the cause that has produced the merit. If the merit produced by the *samādhi* of the Yogin be the cause of the merit that produces the manifestation of the pleasure, then the manifestation must cease when the merit ceases; for what is a product must cease when its cause has ceased. When the manifestation of the eternal pleasure is absent, the eternal pleasure is as good as absent. In other words, if there is a cessation of the experience of pleasure on account of the cessation of merit, the eternal pleasure cannot be said to be experienced: there is no specific reason to determine whether the experience is absent because the pleasure is absent or that the experience is absent even though the pleasure is present.

The proponent of the view cannot escape from this predicament by suggesting that the merit produced by the *samādhi* of the Yogin be treated as imperishable. No such proposition can be proved by inference; in fact, there is a clear inference to show that what is produced is non-eternal. Only a person who has had an unceasing experience of pleasure would be justified, on the basis of his own experience, in proving by inference that the cause of that experience is eternal merit.

As already mentioned, if merit were eternal, there would be no difference between the conditions of liberation and bondage. What this means is: just as in the case of the liberated *ātman* the pleasure and the cause of the experience of the pleasure are both eternal — and there is no cessation of the experience itself, for the simple reason that the merit which causes the experience is eternal — so in the case of the *ātman* in bondage also, as its merit also would be eternal, the effect, viz. the experience of pleasure, would also be eternal. And this would mean that the eternal experience coexists with pleasure and pain produced by merit and demerit

The proponent of the view argues: In the case of the *ātman* in bondage the presence of the body and the sense-organs functions as the cause of obstruction of the experience of eternal pleasure, whereas in the case of the liberated *ātman*, the body etc., having been already shed off, there is no such cause of obstruction. This argument is not right, as the whole purpose of the body, etc. is to furnish the *ātman* with experience, and not to prevent it from having experience. There is no specific reason to prove the contrary; in fact, when the *ātman* is without the body it can have no experience whatsoever.

(2) The proponent of the view argues: The activity of man is always for the purpose of obtaining pleasure. The instruction regarding liberation and the instruction regarding the activity of men desiring liberation are both for the purpose of obtaining what is desirable; therefore neither of the two can be useless.

This argument is not right. The activity of those seeking liberation may be intended not only for obtaining what is desirable but also for avoiding or removing what is undesirable. That such activity is intended to perform the latter function is evident from the fact that there is nothing that is absolutely desirable, and not mixed up with an undesirable element; so that what is desirable also becomes undesirable. As a result, when one is engaged in an activity for removing something undesirable, one may remove or renounce also what is in fact desirable; for it is not possible to discriminate between the two in practice.

(3) The proponent of the view argues: It is observed that people renounce non-eternal pleasure and seek eternal pleasure. On this analogy it can be argued that one may renounce what is desirable but non-eternal such as the body, etc., so that eternal pleasure may be obtained.

On the analogy of this argument the proponent might as well argue that since people are observed to renounce their non-eternal body, sense-organs and intelligence, this should be taken as indicating that the liberated *ātman* has an eternal set of these. Surely, this would enable the proponent to prove the unity of the *ātman* (*aikātmyam*) in the condition of its liberation.

The proponent may object that since the eternality of the body, etc. is opposed to pramāṇa it is wrong to make such an assumption. But, then, his contention that there is eternality of pleasure is equally contrary to pramāṇa; he is therefore equally wrong in making such an assumption.

(4) All attachment or desire is considered to be a bondage. It follows that until the desire for eternal pleasure is renounced there can be no liberation. According to the proponent, since in liberation eternal pleasure is manifested, the man who engages in any activity for liberation would be doing so only under the influence of a desire for the eternal pleasure; being under such

influence he could never attain liberation nor would he deserve to attain it. If all desire is bondage, no one can be liberated while he is under bondage.

(5) Even though the scripture says that there is absolute pleasure for the liberated, there is no difficulty in reconciling such scriptural texts with the view of liberation as the absolute absence of pain experienced in *saṃsāra;* for the word *'sukham'* (pleasure) in such texts can be construed to mean 'absolute absence of pain'; in fact, in ordinary parlance people generally use the word to denote the absence of pain. (NBh I. 1,22).

Uddyotakara states the view criticized by Vātsyāyana as follows: Liberation is the absolute manifestation of pleasure. The proponent of this view argues that there is pramāṇa in support of such liberation, as there is a rule (*niyama*): that is, the inherence, in the *ātman,* of pleasure produced by several causes, is not possible unless there is a restricting agency (*niyāmaka*) which restricts a particular pleasure to a particular *ātman;* this fact proves that there is, in the *ātman,* an eternal pleasure, being determined or restricted by which the said pleasure produced by several causes comes to inhere in that particular *ātman.*

Uddyotakara rejects this argument on the following grounds:

(1) This reasoning would apply, with equal force, to all those properties of the *ātman* that are produced by several causes; so that like eternal pleasure, eternal pain, eternal desire, etc., will have to be attributed to the *ātman.*

(2) If eternal pain, etc. are not so attributed to the *ātman,* the reasoning becomes inconclusive: one property inheres in the *ātman* and is eternal while others inhere in the *ātman* but are not eternal.

(3) The proponent of the view has not explained the exact meaning of manifestation. If manifestation means cognition (*jñāna*), it is not possible to determine whether this cognition (of pleasure) is eternal or non-eternal.

(4) If the cognition of pleasure is not eternal, the proponent of the view should indicate the cause that has produced the cognition. If mind-*ātman* contact is put forward as the cause, then it is necessary to indicate an ancillary cause of that contact; for whenever products, such as substances, properties and actions, are produced by contact, this contact never operates independently by itself.

(5) The proponent argues that the mind-*ātman* contact can be said to be dependent upon pleasure. This would be against the concept of liberation. If the mind-*ātman* contact can produce the cognition of pleasure with the help of its object alone (i.e. of this pleasure), independently of other causes, then a similar contact could produce the cognition of such objects as colour, etc., with the help of those objects alone, independently of such other agencies like the sense-organs. This would mean that cognitions could be constantly crowding upon the *ātman;* this would create all sorts of difficulties for it and even do away with liberation altogether.

As explained by Vātsyāyana, the suggestion that the eternal pleasure is produced by the mind-*ātman* contact as aided by the merit produced by the *samādhi* of the Yogin is no answer to these difficulties: to say that merit is produced by the *samādhi* and is yet eternal is a contradiction in terms.

(6) If, on the other hand, the cognition of eternal pleasure be held to be eternal, this also will not be right. For the eternality of cognition of pleasure stands on the same footing as the eternality of pleasure itself: since there is no proof for the former there can be none for the latter. Moreover, this involves a number of undesirable consequences. There would be no difference between liberation and bondage. If the cognition of pleasure were eternal, it would not be possible to experience pleasure and pain by turns; nor would there be any use in striving for liberation for no one ever wishes to be delivered from pleasurable experience; if the effort is said to be made for release from pain, it would not be possible to differentiate pain from pleasure; in renouncing pain one might renounce pleasure as well. The argument that the body, etc., can prevent the eternal experience of pleasure, as already pointed out by Vātsyāyana, has no relevance in this context. It is absurd to postulate an eternal body as it is to postulate eternal pleasure; both are contrary to perception. And in any case what a wonderful release would this be for any one to strive for!

(7) The argument of the proponent that all activity is for the purpose of obtaining something desirable, as pointed out by Vātsyāyana, goes against the twofold character of activity. According to the proponents of the view mendicancy (*pārivrājyam*) is a means of liberation. It is doubtful whether this advice is

for obtaining something desirable or getting rid of something undesirable.

(8) The scriptural statement cited by the proponent in support of eternal pleasure in liberation, says Uddyotakara, needs careful consideration: does it mean the connection with eternal pleasure or the absolute separation from pain ? In fact, ordinary people who have got rid of diseases like fever say 'We are pleased and free from the disease'. Further, since all desire is bondage, the desire for eternal pleasure can only make liberation impossible. The proponent argues that if the attachment for pleasure is bondage, so is the aversion to pain. This is not right, because the aversion is not detrimental.

Uddyotakara mentions the following view of release: Attachment, etc. have influence over the *citta* only and not over the *ātman;* it is the *citta* which, under the influence of attachment, etc., comes to be produced under various conditions and in diverse substrata. It is therefore the *citta* that is released.[4]

Uddyotakara criticizes the view on the following grounds:

(1) If, according to the proponent of this view, release (*apavarga*) consists in the non-production or destruction of the *citta,* then the release would be accomplished without any effort. For, according to this view, the production of a thing is only for being destroyed, so that the destruction of that which is produced would come about without any effort.

(2) The proponent argues that the release consists not in the destruction of the *citta* but in the non-production of the series of momentary *cittas.* This is not possible, as the series is nothing but the unceasing flow of causes and effects. The proponent says: What is produced is the non-production of what has not yet been produced. But the non-production of what is not produced is already present; so that there is nothing that is produced. Under no circumstances can release be said to belong to the *citta.*

In conclusion Uddyotakara observes: release belongs to one who is released; it is the *ātman* that is released; release is separation from pain, etc. (NV I. 1,22).

II

According to Gautama, an objection is raised: There is absence of release because of the connection of debts, afflictions and activities (NS IV.1,58). Vātsyāyana explains the objection : The debts are described (in the *Śatapatha Brāhmaṇa* I.7,2,1) as follows :

(A) *Debts*

When a Brahmin is born, he is born under three debts: from the debt owing to the sages he is released by leading the life of a religious student; from the debt owing to the gods he is released by the performance of sacrifices; and from the debt owing to the ancestors he is released by begetting children.

The connection of these debts consists in the relation of acts connected with the debts. That it is necessary to perform these acts is described as follows (in the Veda): "The sacrifice known as the *Agnihotra* and the *Darśapūrṇamāsa* should go on till old age or death; it is only either by old age or by death that one is released from the necessity of performing these sacrifices." In view of this the connection of these three debts persists till one has reached old age or died, and as a result there is no time left for the performance of acts conducive to release. Hence there is absence of release (i.e. there is no opportunity for release).

(B) *Afflictions*

Man is born with afflictions and dies with afflictions; he is therefore never free from the connection of these afflictions.

(C) *Activities*

From birth till death, man is never free from activities of speech, mind and body. In view of this the statement which Gautama has made — "Pain, birth activity, defect and misapprehension — on the successive annihilation of these in the reverse order, there follows release" (NS I. 1,2) — cannot be true (NBh IV. 1,59).

Reply to the Objections

(A) *Debts*

Gautama answers the first part of the objection regarding the three debts: (1) If a word cannot be taken in its primary sense, it should be taken in its secondary sense, so that the sense of praise and blame can be obtained (NS IV. 1,60). (2)An injunction must be appropriate to the topic (under which it is mentioned), as is the case with other branches of learning (NS IV. 1,61). (3) Release cannot be denied, because there is transportation [of the Fires] (NS IV. 1,62).

Vātsyāyana explains the answer of Gautama: The phrase '*ṛṇa*' in the primary sense means that one gives to another something that has to be repaid and another receives such a thing. This phrase as used in the *Śatapatha Brāhmaṇa* cannot be interpreted in this way. The phrase has to be understood in the secondary sense: if a person fails to perform the acts mentioned, he is to be blamed in the same manner as the debtor who does not repay his debts: and if he performs the acts, he should be praised in the same manner as the debtor who honours his debts.

Similarly, the phrase '*jāyamāna*' (when he is born) in the passage is also used in the secondary sense. It is obvious that when a person is actually born he cannot be expected to perform the acts mentioned; nor can he be authorized to do so. Only those persons can perform the acts who wish to obtain the results following from the acts, are capable of performing the acts and are authorized to do so. Such persons are the Brahmins who have entered the stage of householder. The reference to old age and death in the passage is also to be understood in the secondary sense: since the desire for the results accruing from the acts does not come to an end till old age and death, one should continue to perform the acts till one has reached the last stage of life, the renunciation.

The opponent argues: The text under consideration directly refers to the stage of the householder, but there are not direct references to the other stages of life in the *Śatapatha Brāhmaṇa*, such as the renunciation. It follows that there are no other stages except the householder.

Vātsyāyana replies: In the first place, there is no direct injunction saying that there are no other stages except the householder. Secondly, that the injunction under consideration directly refers to the householder is based upon the fact that it is this stage that constitutes the subject of discussion. This is exactly what is done in other branches of learning; the fact that each scripture directly lays down certain things only is due to those things alone being connected with its own subject-matter. Thirdly, there are several *Ṛk* verses and *Brāhmaṇa* texts which speak of release (*apavarga*) along with the means of attaining it and the four stages of life (NBh IV. 1,60-61).[5]

The passages which speak of the sacrifices continuing till old age and death actually refer to the man that desires the results following from the act. For example, there is a Vedic injunction that having offered the *Prājāpatya* sacrifice, having offered the libations of all his belongings, and having transported the Fires into his *ātman*, the Brahmin should go out as a renunciate. This injunction clearly shows that the Fires are meant only for the man who has risen above all desires for children, wealth and fame and whose desire for the results of the sacrifices also has entirely ceased (NBh IV. 1,62).[6]

If the performance of the acts till old age and death were taken as referring to all men, then the after-death rites ending with the 'collecting of sacrificial vessels' would also have to be performed for all men. This is quite clear from the passages where it is stated that such rites are not necessary for those Brahmins who have risen above all-desires.[7]

Apart from these textual arguments, the four stages of life are stated in the *Itihāsas*, the *Purāṇas* and the *Dharmaśāstras*. These scriptures are authoritative on he following grounds: (1) Their authoritative character is vouched for by authoritative texts. The *Brāhmaṇa* texts testify to the authoritative character of the *Itihāsas* and the *Purāṇas*; in fact they are described as the fifth of the Vedas.[8] As regards the *Dharmaśāstras*, if these were not authoritative, this would put an end to all business among living beings; this would mean the end of the world. (2) The 'seers' and 'speakers' of these scriptures are the same as those of the *Mantra* and *Brāhmaṇa* texts of the Veda. (3) The authority of each scripture is restricted to its own subject-matter. The subject-matter of the *Mantra* and *Brāhmaṇa* texts is 'sacrifice'; the *Itihāsas* and the *Purāṇas* deal with the doings of men; the *Dharmaśāstras* are concerned with the 'regulation of men's business'. Since no single one of these scriptures controls all the subjects, every one of them must be regarded as authoritative in regard to its own subject; just as every one of the sense-organs is an authoritative means of the cognition of its own special object of perception (NBh IV. 1,62).

(B) *Afflictions*

Gautama answers the second part of the objection regarding the afflictions: Release is possible, as there are no afflictions in the case of a person who is in deep sleep and sees no dreams (NS IV. 1,63).

Vātsyāyana explains the answer: It is observed that when a man is in deep sleep and sees no dreams, there is an end of attachment with the world, as also of all connection with pleasure and pain. Exactly in the same way there could be an end of all such afflictions in release as well. In fact, those who know the *Brahman* describe the condition of the released *ātman* as similar to that of deep sleep. (NBh IV. 1,63).

(C) *Activities*

Gautama's answer to the third part of the objection regarding activities is: For the man who has got rid of the afflictions, activity does not lead to recrudescence (*pratisandhāna*) (NS IV. 1,64).

Vātsyāyana explains the answer: When attachment, hatred and misconception are destroyed, activity does not lead to recrudescence. Recrudescence means rebirth at the end of the previous life; this rebirth is always produced by the *adṛṣṭa* (the unseen force); when the *adṛṣṭa* has been destroyed, there is no further birth after the previous life has come to an end; this is what is meant by non-recrudescence; and this is release.

This should not be understood to imply that actions are without their appropriate results. All that is meant is that the previous life comes to an end, there is no further birth; and since the results of all one's acts have been experienced in the birth preceding release, there is no result left to be experienced (NBh IV. 1,64).

According to Gautama an objection is raised against this view: There can be no end to the series of afflictions, as it is natural (NS IV. 1,65). According to him, some philosophers answer the objection: Even what is natural is non-eternal like the absence that was prior to production (NS IV. 1,66); Or it may be non-eternal like the blackness of an atom (NS IV. 1,67). According to Gautama the correct reply to the objection is: Attachment, etc. are due to wrong notion ((*saṅkalpa*) (NS. IV. 1,67).

Vātsyāyana explains: The objection is that since the series of afflictions is without beginning, what is without beginning is natural and therefore cannot be destroyed (NBh IV. 1,65). Some philosophers reply to the objection: The absence of things prior to their production has had no beginning, and yet it is set aside by the existence of things when they are produced. Other philosophers reply: The dark colour of an atom is without beginning, and it is destroyed by contact with fire. Similarly, the series of afflictions can be said to be destroyed even though it has no beginning.

Vātsyāyana rejects the answer of these philosophers on two grounds: (1) Eternality and non-eternality are properties and these can be present in positive entities only; to negative entities they can be attributed only in an indirect or figurative sense. (2) There is nothing to prove that the black colour of an atom is without beginning; it is not therefore right to put the blackness of the atom as a hetu in support of the proposition; nor can we give 'not liable to production' as a hetu to prove non-eternality (NBh IV. 1,65-67). It will be noted that Gautama has not mentioned the arguments given by Vātsyāyana.

Explaining the answer given by Gautama, Vātsyāyana observes: (a) Attachment, hatred and misconception proceed respectively from such wrong cognitions as actually lead to delight, anger and misconception. (b) Action also produces the bodies of living beings, and gives rise to attachment, hatred and misconception within well-defined limits; that there are such limits is evident from the fact that in some bodies attachment preponderates while in others misconception may preponderate. (c) Attachment, hatred and delusion appear as a result of one another; that is, it is the man under misconception who desires things or is impelled by hatred; the man under the influence of desire falls into misconception; the man under the influence of hatred falls into misconception.

All wrong notions cease to appear as soon as the knowledge of the true nature of things appears; and inasmuch as on the cessation of the cause (i.e. wrong notions) the effect cannot appear, attachment, hatred and misconception cannot appear at all.

Further, the contention of the objector that the series of afflictions is without beginning has no point at all. All such things are related to the self and are without beginning. The whole psycho-somatic complex proceeds in a series which has no beginning. There is no member of this series that is produced without another individual having gone before it. There is only one exception: the knowledge of the true nature of things which is produced once only for a self.

This Nyāya doctrine, says Vātsyāyana, should not be understood to imply that things that have the property of being produced have the property of being destroyed. As soon as wrong notions are destroyed by the knowledge of the true nature of things, karma also, which produces the body of each living being, ceases to be productive of attachment, hatred and misconception. However, the karma does continue to produce its result in the form of experience of pleasure and pain (NBh IV. 1,68).

PART SIX : SOURCE OF *SAMSĀRA*

28

MISAPPREHENSION (*mithyājñāna*) AND KNOWLEDGE OF THE TRUE NATURE OF THINGS (*tattvajñāna*)

I

According to the Naiyāyika misapprehension or wrong notion is responsible for the involvement of the self in *saṃsāra* and the remedy for it is the knowledge of the true nature of things (*tattvajñāna*). The result of this knowledge is supreme felicity (*niḥśreyasa*) which is equated with release (*apavarga*).

According to Gautama the final result follows the successive annihilation of the five properties, in the reverse order of pain, birth, activity, defect and misapprehension. The first four of these are included in the twelve objects of cognition (*prameya*). Misapprehension is neither an object of cognition nor is it one of the sixteen categories. It is, however, interesting to note that the fallacy of the hetu (*hetvābhāsa*) has been accorded category status by Gautama.

Gautama and his commentators have given considerable thought to the various aspects of misapprehension and the procedure for the attainment of knowledge. In what follows a brief account of their position is given.

In the opening aphorism of the *Nyāya Sūtra* Gautama states that supreme felicity (*niḥśreyasa*) is attained by the knowledge about the true nature of his sixteen categories (NS I. 1,1). According to Vātsyāyana this is the purpose for which Gautama has composed his treatise. He then goes on to add that the object of the whole treatise is that the supreme felicity is attained by the knowledge of the twelve objects of cognition (*prameya*) recognized by Gautama. And this object is reiterated in the next aphorism where Gautama states how release is attained on the successive annihilation, in the reverse order, of pain, birth, activity, defect and misapprehension (wrong notion). The significance of this aphorism is that supreme felicity is attained when one has rightly understood the true nature of the following four classes of things: (a) that which should be rejected (i.e.

pain) along with its causes, (b) that which is absolutely destructive (of pain, i.e. knowledge of the true nature of things), (c) the means of destroying (a) and (b) (i.e. *śāstra*), (d) the goal to be attained (i.e. supreme felicity). These are the four kinds of objects dealt with by the *śāstras*.

According to the commentator, there are four *vidyās* (i.e. four branches of learning) which have been propounded for the good of living beings, and amongst these is the Nyāya. Each of these four branches deals with a distinctive subject of its own and has its own method of treatment appropriate to its subject-matter. Each of the four branches contains the knowledge of the true nature of things within its competence and provides for the attainment of supreme felicity (*niḥśreyasa*) by means of such knowledge. The Nyāya, which is the queen of all branches of knowledge, deals not only with the sixteen categories — this distinguishes it from the *Upaniṣads* which deal with the *ātman* only — but also with *adhyātmavidyā* (knowledge of *ātman*). (NBh I. 1,1).

According to Uddyotakara, the four branches of learning mentioned by Vātsyāyana are: *trayī* (Vedic triad), *vārtā* (agriculture), *daṇḍanīti* (science of polity) and *ānvīkṣikī* (epistemology and logic).

The Vedic triad provides knowledge of such things as sacrifices (for example, *Agnihotra*), the proper method of obtaining materials for the sacrifices. The supreme felicity the triad offers is the attainment of heaven; this is described as the fruit. Agriculture provides knowledge of plough, cart, soil, etc. The supreme felicity it offers is the harvest resulting from agricultural operations. The science of polity furnishes knowledge of such things as the distinction between the king and the minister, the employment of conciliation, gifts, punishment and dissension, at the right time and place, and in accordance with one's strength. The supreme felicity the science offers is the conquest of the earth. *Ānvīkṣikī* provides knowledge of the various categories like doubt. It is the spiritual science which provides knowledge of the self and the supreme felicity it offers is the attainment of release (NV I. 1,1).

Commenting upon the four classes of things the knowledge of which is necessary for supreme felicity, Uddyotakara lists the following items included under each of them: (a) That which is to be regarded as pain; the causes of pain are ignorance (*avidyā*) and desire (*tṛṣṇā*), as also merit and demerit; (b) that which destroys pain is knowledge of the true nature of things; (c) the means of destroying pain is *śāstra;* (d) the goal to be attained is release.

Vātsyāyana describes these four classes as *'arthapadāni'* (objects dealt with). These are so called, says Uddyotakara, because it is these which are described by the preceptors (*ācārya*) in all spiritual learning (*adhyātmavidyā*) (NV I. 1,1).

Uddyotakara begins his *Vartika* on the *Nyāya Sūtra* with a statement about his own purpose in undertaking the enterprise: his purpose is to eradicate the misrepresentation fostered by bad logicians about the *śāstra* composed by Akṣapāda (i.e. Gautama) for the benefit of the world. The commentator then proceeds to explain the purpose Gautama has in composing his *Nyāya Sūtra.*

The *śāstra* is a specifically arranged collection of words which describes the various categories. The special characteristic of the *śāstra* is that it explains the true nature of such things as cannot be cognized by perception and inference. And the man who is entitled to study the *śāstra* is that disciple who is endowed with inner strength.

Uddyotakara then proceeds to divide men into four categories: (a) those who have knowledge of the truth; (b) those who do not have it; (c) those who are in doubt; and (d) those who are perverse. Only those in the first category can teach; those in the other three categories are men to be taught because they are in need of knowledge. Amongst those to be taught those who depend upon the sense-object contact learn through perception; those who depend upon the perception and recollection of certain marks learn through inference; those who need instruction (*upadeśa*) learn through the *śāstra.*

The felicity (*śreyasa*) of man is of two kinds: pleasure and cessation of pain. Each of these two kinds is of two kinds: seen and unseen. The cessation of pain is absolute and non-absolute. The non-absolute cessation of pain is that which is brought about by the removal of such causes as thorns. The absolute cessation of pain is brought about by the removal of the twenty-one kinds of pain. These twenty-one kinds of pain are: the body, the six sense-organs, the six objects, the six kinds of cognition, pleasure and pain. The body is pain because it is the abode of pain. The sense-organs, the sense-objects and cognitions are pain because they are the causes of pain. Pleasure is pain because it is mixed with pain. Pain is pain by its very nature. Pain is removed when the causes of pain, merit and demerit, are abandoned. Merit and demerit which are not yet produced are ignored because they have not been produced. Merit and demerit that have been produced are abandoned through exhaustion which results from experiences of pleasure and pain (*upabhoga*).

Uddyotakara divides men into two categories: those who have attachment and those who are free from attachment. Attachment consists in the desire for objects, and non-attachment (*vairāgya*) in the absence of desire for objects. According to this twofold division of men, human activity also is twofold: the activity of men with attachment and the activity of men without attachment. The former is of two kinds: for the obtaining of the desirable thing and for the avoiding of the undesirable thing. The latter is of only one kind, viz. for the avoiding of the undesirable thing. All activity of men without attachment arises from the motto expressed in the form 'may I avoid the undesirable'.

The activity of men with attachment is further divided into two categories: effective (*samartha*) when they succeed in obtaining what they desire and not effective (*asamartha*) when they do not.

There is another classification of activity: when pramāṇa leading to the activity is rightly effective or when pramāṇa leading to the activity is not rightly effective. This aspect of activity is important in the context of the Nyāya theory of pramāṇa and is therefore explained in the chapter of the pramāṇa (Introductory NV).

According to Uddyotakara some philosophers hold that the knowledge of the sixteen categories cannot lead to supreme felicity; on the contrary, the knowledge of categories is the cause of pride and arrogance. The commentator rejects this objection on two grounds: In the first place, these philosophers have not understood the meaning of the aphorism: no one would interpret the aphorism to mean that the supreme felicity results from the knowledge of the sixteen categories. In fact it is the knowledge of the twelve objects of cognition (*prameya*) that leads to supreme felicity. Secondly, there is no causal connection between the knowledge of the categories concerned on the one hand and pride and arrogance on the other. As a matter of fact, we find that pride and arrogance are present when the knowledge of the categories is absent, and they are absent when this knowledge is present. For instance, the impertinent servant has no knowledge of the categories but he has pride and arrogance; even though the philosopher who knows the truth has the knowledge of categories, he may be completely free from pride and arrogance (NV I. 1,1).

Vātsyāyana raises a question: Does the supreme felicity appear immediately after the knowledge of the true nature of things? His answer is : No, after the knowledge.

According to Uddyotakara, the question raised by Vātsyāyana is a fully-fledged objection: In whatever way we look at this matter, there are insuperable objections. If release were to follow immediately after the knowledge, those who have attained release would not be alive. But we do find such people living even after the attainment of release. This is quite evident from the continuity of scriptural tradition (*śāstrasaṃpradāya*); such tradition consists in the handing down of the scripture from the preceptor to the pupil, without a break. If release were to follow immediately after the attainment of the knowledge, this continuity of the tradition would be disrupted at that point; for as soon as a person would attain knowledge he would become released. If, to avoid this difficulty, it be held that the person who has attained the knowledge does continue unreleased, then the knowledge cannot be regarded as the cause of release; for the release would be present when the knowledge is present; and there must be something else the absence of which is responsible for the release not being present, even though the knowledge is present. The real cause of a thing is that being present, the thing is present, and being absent, it is absent. Then again, if release were to appear immediately after the knowledge, the scripture would be something not previously known; that is, it would be a mere 'castle in the air', not preceded by any vision of the truth.

According to Uddyotakara, there is really no difficulty in solving the problem as to whether or not release follows knowledge immediately. There are two kinds of supreme felicity: higher (*para*) and lower (*apara*). It is the lower kind that follows immediately after the knowledge. As it is said, the learned man, while he still lives, becomes freed from pain and pleasure. This lower kind is the basis of scripture. The higher kind of felicity, on the other hand, comes about gradually after the knowledge; and it is this process of gradual succession (*krama*) which is described in the second aphorism of Gautama (NV I. 1,1).

According to Uddyotakara the supreme felicity can also be regarded as 'seen' (*dṛṣṭa*) and 'unseen' (*adṛṣṭa*). The former follows from the knowledge of the sixteen categories and the latter from the knowledge of the twelve objects of cognition (*prameya*).

Whenever any of the categories is truly known, the seen variety of the supreme felicity is quite evident; for the knowledge of any one of the categories brings about the idea of acquiring, rejecting or indifference. But if this were so, says the objector, the knowledge of all the categories would be required for the attainment of the supreme felicity. Why should there be only one of the categories, i.e. *prameya,* singled out as the category the knowledge of which is necessary for the supreme felicity ? The commentator's answer is: the seen variety results from the knowledge of the various categories but the unseen results from the knowledge of the twelve objects of cognition (i.e. the category of *prameya*).

An objection is raised: it is true that we do find the seen variety resulting from the knowledge of the various categories, but there is no pramāṇa to prove that the unseen variety is the result of the knowledge of the twelve objects.

Uddyotakara replies that there is a pramāṇa which can prove the unseen variety. It is a fact that the supreme felicity is attained through the knowledge of the twelve objects of cognition; and conversely, when these objects are wrongly apprehended, the *saṃsāra* cannot be averted. There is no person who does not have knowledge of the various categories mentioned by Gautama, but if release were to follow from such knowledge, then such people could also obtain release. If supreme felicity could be attained by the knowledge of the sixteen categories only, Gautama would not have mentioned specifically in another aphorism the various objects of cognition; it would indeed have been foolish of the author to have mentioned first all the objects of cognition in the first aphorism and then proceed to specify in another aphorism only a few things as the 'objects of cognition' (Introductory NV).

II

Release, says Gautama, follows on the successive annihilation, in the reverse order, of pain, birth, activity, defect and wrong notion (NS I. 1,2). Vātsyāyana explains: These five properties (*dharma*) when operating continuously, constitute *saṃsāra*. When knowledge of the true nature of things is attained, wrong notions disappear; when the wrong notions disappear, defects disappear; when the defects disappear, the activity disappears; when birth disappears, pain disappears; when pain has disappeared absolutely, there is release, which is the supreme felicity (*niḥśreyasa*) (NBh I. 1,2).

According to Vātsyāyana, there are various kinds of wrong notions regarding the twelve objects of cognition (*prameya*) recognized by Gautama. From among these objects the commentator mentions wrong notions about the following: self, activity, defects, transmigration and release. In addition he mentions wrong notions about other objects (NBh I. 1,2).

Object	*Wrong notion*	*Right notion*
1. Self	The self does not exist.	The self exists.
2. Non-self	The non-self is self.	The non-self is non-self.
3. Pain	Pain is pleasure.	
4. Non-eternal	The non-eternal is eternal.	
5. Non-safe	The non-safe is safe.	Each of these should be known according to the object concerned(*yathāviṣayam*).
6. Fearful	The fearful is free from fear.	
7. Disgusting	Disgusting is agreeable.	
8. That which should be rejected	That which should be rejected should not be rejected.	
9. Activity	Karma does not exist, nor does the fruit of karma.	Karma exists, so does the fruit of karma.
10. Defects	*Saṃsāra* does not have defects as its cause.	*Saṃsāra* has defects as its cause.

Object	Wrong notion	Right notion
11. State after death.	(a) There is no animal, or creature, or an embodied self (*jīva*) or an entity, or a self, who could die, or having died, could be born again.	There is an animal, or a creature, or an embodied self, or an entity, or a self who having died, is born again.
	(b) Birth is without cause.	Birth has a cause.
	(c) Cessation of birth is without cause.	Cessation of birth has a cause.
	(d) State after death has beginning but no end.	State after death has no beginning but an end in release.
	(e) State after death does not have karma as its cause even though it has cause.	State after death, having a cause, has activity as its cause.
	(f) State after death is without self because it exists in the destruction (at death) and restoration (at birth) of the series of body, sense-organs, *buddhi* and sensation (*vedanā*).	State after death is with self, (i.e. connected with self) because it operates through destruction (at death) of the series of body, sense-organs, *buddhi* and sensation.
12. Release	(a) Release is terrible as it involves cessation of all activity.	Release, involving as it does separation from everything and cessation from all activity, is peaceful: much that is painful, frightful and sinful disappears on release.
	(b) In release which consists in separation from everything many good things are lost.	
	(c) How can any intelligent person like release in which all	How can any intelligent person fail to like release, consist-

Object	*Wrong notion*	*Right notion*
Release (*Contd.*)	pleasure is destroyed and there is no intelligence.	ing as it does in the destruction of all pain, and devoid of all consciousness of pain ? Release is free not only from pain but also from pleasure, because pleasure is mixed with pain and as such should be avoided, in the same manner as food mixed with honey and poison is avoided.

In his comment on release following the successive annihilation of the five properties, Uddyotakara explains the *saṃsāra* as consisting in the causal operation among the five properties. This operation is without beginning. There is no such rule (*niyama*) that one of these must appear before and the others after; for instance, there is no such rule either that pain, etc. must always precede wrong notion or that wrong notion must always precede pain, etc.

When knowledge appears wrong notion disappears. This happens because there is opposition between them when they are about the same object; one and the same object cannot have two characters (*rūpa*).

How can a wrong notion, which appears first, be set aside by a true notion which appears later ? This is due to the fact that the wrong notion is devoid of support while the right notion has the support of the object. This is so: (a) because the true notion is the notion in accord with the object as it is; (b) because the true notion has the assistance of pramāṇas.

With the continued assistance of scripture and inference we form a notion of an object; we then ponder and meditate over the object; this gives us a cognition of the object as it is, which is intuitive. Thus the knowledge of the object as it is comprehends what has been cognized by perception, inference and scripture. Once a wrong notion has been set aside by such knowledge, it can never arise again. The two are opposed to each other; it is impossible for them to co-exist (NV I. 1,2).

As mentioned by Vātsyāyana, the wrong notion about the self is that the self does not exist. Since the self is cognized, on the strength of pramāṇas, as something existing, the notion that it does not exist must be regarded as a wrong notion.

Uddyotakara considers the following objection to this view : No such wrong notion is possible because there is no similarity between what exists and what does not exist.

According to the commentator, because there is a similarity between what exists and what does not exist: they can both be cognized by pramāṇas. But they do differ in this: what exists has activity and properties while what does not exist is devoid of them (NV I. 1,2).

The wrong notion about the self arises because we impose upon the self the properties of the non-self, i.e. being devoid of activity and qualities. Similarly, the wrong notion about the non-self in the body is that 'the body is the self'. The similarity between the self and the non-self which leads to mistaking the latter for the former consists in the fact that both the self and the body are the objects of the notion of 'I'. But there is a difference between them: the self is the support of desire and other properties while the body is not.

The body is the object of the notion of 'I' because the word 'I' is actually used in the same case as, and co-ordinated with, words signifying the body; for example, the statement 'I am fair': what is fair is the body. This is the point of similarity between the non-self (i.e. body) and the self. But there is a difference between them; it is only the self, and not the body, which has the properties of desire, etc. When we impose the properties of the self on the body we have the wrong notion 'I am the body' (NV I. 1,2).

When wrong notion disappears, defects disappear, for there is a causal relation between them. Wrong notion is the cause of defects and without the cause the effect cannot appear. It may be asked: The defects that have not appeared may not appear on account of the disappearance of the cause; but how can the disappearance of wrong notion produce the cessation of the defects that have already appeared ? These disappear, says Uddyotakara, on account of dispassion (*vairāgya*). Dispassion is defined as non-attachment to enjoyment, and non-attachment must set aside attachment which is the core of all defects. And this dispassion is produced by the recognition of defects in the objects of enjoyment and by the knowledge of the true nature of things.

When defects disappear, activity ceases. Activity mentioned by Gautama does not mean action (*kriyā*) but merit and demerit. The reasons for this are: (a) these latter function as the means (*sādhana*) of producing birth; (b) all action is momentary and could not function as a means of producing birth.

An objection is raised: As regards the merit and demerit that have not yet come into existence, it is reasonable that they should not appear in the absence of defects; but this could not be the case with the merit and demerit that are already in existence, because they are found to be present in men who are entirely free from defects; in fact we often find that the man who is entirely free from defects continues to live and experience the fruits of merit and demerit.

This objection, says Uddyotakara, has no force. What is meant is not that the merit and demerit already in existence cease to exist on the disappearance of defects, but that all merit and demerit that have not yet come into existence will not be produced because the cause of their production is absent. The merit and demerit that are already in existence will be destroyed only through the exhaustion of their effects; that is, all merit and demerit produce some sort of effect, and when all the effects have been produced, they cease to exist. What keeps the body in existence is the *saṃskāra*, called by the name of '*dharma* and *adharma*' (merit and demerit). When this *saṃskāra* is exhausted the body drops off.

When there is no birth there is no pain; for the simple reason that there can be no pain without a body; until there is a receptacle for it no pain can appear. As is said, "so long as there are merit and demerit in the self, there are also life, body, sense-organs and objects".

A man is said to be 'released' only when he has become free from every one of the group consisting of wrong notion, etc., mentioned by Gautama. The man is free not only from pain but also from pleasure. When Vātsyāyana says that all pleasure is invariably connected with pain, and as such should be renounced, what he means is this: It is not possible to exercise any discrimination (*viveka*) at the time of renouncing; we cannot renounce pain after having properly discriminated it from pleasure; as a result, when one seeks pleasure, one experiences pain also along with it; and when one renounces pain, one must renounce pleasure also along with it. The connection (*anuṣaṅga*) to which Vātsyāyana refers means: (a) invariable connection (*avinābhāva*), the one being present wherever the other is present, or (b) both have the same causes (*sādhana*), or (c) both have the same support, pain subsists where pleasure subsists, or (d) both are apprehended by the same agent (*samānopalabhyatṛ*) (NV I. 1,2).

III

Vātsyāyana raises the following question: Is the knowledge of the true nature of things that is required in connection with release meant to be of all things that there are or only of some of them? It would not be possible to have such knowledge of every one of the knowable things that there are, because they are innumerable. Nor would it be right to say that such knowledge is only of some of the things; for this would mean that with regard to those things of which the knowledge has not been acquired, one's misconception has not ceased, so that there would still be a residue of misconception left behind. Nor would it be possible to say that misconception in respect of one thing could be removed by knowledge in respect of another thing.

Vātsyāyana answers the question: misconception is undoubtedly wrong notion, and not mere non-production of knowledge. The knowledge that has to be sought for is the knowledge of that object the wrong notion of which is the seed of *saṃsāra*. This wrong notion is the notion of what is self as non-self, expressed as 'I am'; this is the notion of 'I' (*ahaṃkāra*), and this is misconception. When one looks upon the non-self as 'I am', this is the perception (*dṛṣṭi*) that is called *'ahaṃkāra'*. And this notion is misconception.

This notion of 'I' arises in respect of the body, the sense-organs, the mind, sensation and *buddhi*. It functions as the seed of *saṃsāra* as follows:

When a man looks upon the body, etc., as 'this is I', he regards a destruction of body as one's own destruction; so that he becomes imbued with a longing (*tṛṣṇā*) for the non-destruction of the body, etc., and as a result, acquires them over and over again; having acquired them, all his efforts tend to bring for him births and deaths; so that not having been separated from these births and deaths, he is never released.

On the other hand, the man who looks upon pain, abode of pain (body), and pleasure mixed with pain as pain — he is the man who recognizes the true nature of pain; when he has so recognized pain, he does not have it; it comes to be abandoned, just like poisoned food. Such a man looks upon defects and action (*karma*) also as causes of pain; until the defects have been renounced, there is no possibility of the cessation of the continuity of pain; hence the man renounces the defects; and when the defects have been renounced, activity does not lead to the state after death.

In this manner the man comes to the conclusion: (a) state after death, result and pain are things to be known; (b) action and defects are things to be abandoned; (c) release is a thing to be attained; and (d) the knowledge of the true nature of things is the means of attaining it: When the man attends to, repeatedly looks upon and ponders over, the four objects of cognition as grouped under the four categories mentioned above, there comes to him right perception (*samyagdarśana*) — the cognition of things as they are, i.e. *tattvajñāna* (knowledge of the true nature of things) (Introductory NBh IV. 2,1).

It is in this context, according to Vātsyāyana, that Gautama says: Through knowledge of the true nature of the causes of defects, there is cessation of the notion of 'I' (NS IV.2,1). The commentator explains: The following objects of cognition are the causes of defects: body, sense-organs, objects of sense, *buddhi,* mind, activity, defects, rebirth, result, state after death and pain; they are the causes because they are the objects of wrong notions. When the knowledge of the true nature of these objects appears, it sets aside the notion of 'I' regarding them; for knowledge of the true nature of objects is opposed to the wrong notions about the same objects.

What Gautama has said in the present aphorism, says Vātsyāyana, is only a re-affirmation of what he has stated in his aphorism on release following the annihilation in the reverse order of the series of pain, birth, activity, defect and wrong notion (NS I. 1,2); it is not meant to be a new doctrine (NBh IV. 2,1).

According to Vātsyāyana, Gautama has laid down in the following aphorism the order in which the knowledge mentioned above is to be attained: Colour and other objects, when they are the objects of wrong notion, become the causes of defects (NS IV. 2,2).

Vātsyāyana explains: The sense-objects to which Gautama has referred here are the objects of desire. When they are wrongly conceived, they lead to attachment, aversion and misconception. It is therefore necessary that man should seek to know these objects first of all. When he has acquired this knowledge, his wrong notion about them disappears; he should then proceed to acquire knowledge about the true nature of such objects as are directly concerned with the self: e.g. the body, etc., and when this knowledge has been attained, the notion of 'I' in regard to the objects directly concerned with the self ceases. Thus the man, acting with his *cit* (consciousness) wholly unattached either to external objects or to objects directly concerned with his self, comes to be called 'released' (NBh IV. 2,2).

On this subject Uddyotakara has made an interesting observation. The wrong notions about the sense-objects consist in their being regarded as the exclusive possession of one's self-expressed in such words as 'these are mine only'. These should be looked upon as 'common' to others belonging, in common, to such others as gods, thieves, fire and relatives. When the man looks upon things in this manner, his misconception ceases.

With regard to release, the commentator quotes with approval the passage: 'While still living, the wise person becomes released from joy and sorrow' (NV IV. 2,2).

According to Vātsyāyana, in the following aphorism Gautama lays down his instruction as to which aspects of things should be ignored and which aspects pondered over; it has nothing to do with either acquiring or discarding things (NBh IV. 2,3): The obsession (*abhimāna*) with the object as a whole is the cause of defects (NS IV. 2,3).

Defects are produced when one looks upon an object as a whole, as an embellishment (*pariṣkāra*). For instance, if the male looks upon the female in this fashion, this becomes a cause of his defects; if the female looks upon the male in this manner, this becomes a cause of her defects. And there are two aspects of conceiving an object: parts and secondary marks (*anuvyañjana*).

The parts are teeth, lips, eyes and nose. The secondary marks of these parts, teeth for instance, are that the teeth are the part, and are beautiful (= secondary marks). These ways of looking upon objects increase passion and other defects dependent upon it. Such defects have to be avoided.

In order to avoid such defects, it is necessary to conceive of objects in terms of their component parts. For instance, the female should be conceived as only composed of hairs, flesh, blood, bones, tendons, arteries, phlegm, bile, ordure, etc. This is what is called 'disagreeable' (*aśubha*) aspects of things, when one ponders over this aspect, one's desire and attachment for it cease.

In view of the fact that every object has two aspects, agreeable and disagreeable, Gautama's advice is that the agreeable aspect should be ignored and the dis-agreeable pondered over. This advice is just like what one is expected to do in the case of the poisoned food: we should ignore the agreeable aspect of the object, food, and ponder over the disagreeable aspect, poison (NBh IV. 2,3).

The next question considered by Gautama is: How does the knowledge of the causes of defects which sets aside the notion of 'I' arise? This, he says, arises from the practice of a particular form of *samādhi* (NS IV. 2,38).

Vātsyāyana explains: When the mind is withdrawn from the sense-organs and kept steady by an effort, a contact, the distinguishing feature of which is the eagerness to find the true nature of things, takes place between the mind and the self; this contact is what constitutes *samādhi*. During this *samādhi*, no cognition is produced in respect of the sense-objects. And from the practice of such *samādhi* is produced the knowledge of the true nature of things (NBh IV. 2,38).

Gautama mentions an objection to this concept of *samādhi*: The *samādhi* is not possible on the following two grounds: (a) Certain objects are extremely powerful (NS IV. 2,39). It is found that even when one may not have any desire to have cognition, explains Vātsyāyana, the cognition is produced; for instance, one hears the thunder of clouds in spite of oneself (NBh IV. 2,39). (b) Hunger, etc. impel us to action (NS IV. 2,40). As explained by Vātsyāyana, hunger, thirst, heat, cold and disease produce cognitions even against our wishes, and therefore concentration is not possible (NBh IV. 2,40).

Gautama's answer to the objection is : *Samādhi* arises through connection (*anubandha*) with results of what was done previously (NS IV. 2,41). It is possible that the man may renounce *samādhi*, and there may also be causes which produce such agitation as constitutes an obstacle to *samādhi*. But even so, merit and wisdom acquired in previous lives serve to produce knowledge of the true nature of things. And the yogic practices have the necessary power to bring about *samādhi*. If such practices were barren of results, no one would take notice of these practices; even in the case of worldly acts, it is found that constant practice has the power of producing a certain result (NBh IV. 2,41).

According to Uddyotakara, a particular kind of *samādhi* has been practised in the preceding bodies; its result is merit; and this merit produces another kind of *samādhi;* this *samādhi* leads to the suppression of external objects. Even in the case of the ordinary man when he is rapt in *samādhi*, even though the external objects may surround him, he has no cognitions of them; how much more so should this be the case with the yogin. If cognitions were to be produced simply because there are external objects gathering round the man, then such cognitions would also be produced after he has attained release. This is absurd (NV IV. 2,41).

In order to remove the obstacles to *samādhi*, his advice is, says Gautama, that *samādhi* should be practised in places such as a forest, a cave or on a sand-bank (NS IV. 2,42).

In his comment on this aphorism Vātsyāyana observes: The merit produced by the practice of yoga follows the self in other births as well. When the merit that produces knowledge of the true nature of things has reached a high stage of development, and the exercise of *samādhi* has assumed great proportions, knowledge is produced. It is actually observed that *samādhi* can suppress the force of even the most powerful objects; as for example, even the ordinary man says: 'My mind was elsewhere, or I did not hear this' (NBh IV. 2,42).

According to Gautama, the opponent argues that if the cognitions can be produced even against one's wishes when there are powerful objects,[1] this contingency would arise even in release (NS & NBh IV. 2,43).

Gautama answers: This contingency cannot arise because cognition can appear only in a body that has already been formed and also because there is absence of body in release (NS IV. 44-45).

In order to attain release it is necessary to purify the self, says Gautama, by means of restraints (*yama*), observances (*niyama*) and such other methods and injunctions regarding internal discipline as are found in the yoga (NS IV. 2,46).

Vātsyāyana explains: Restraints are the means of acquiring merit, common to men in all stages of life. Observances are prescribed for each stage. The purification of the self consists in the destruction of demrit and the accretion of merit. Injunctions regarding internal discipline should be learnt from the *Yogaśāstra.* Internal discipline consists of penance, control of breath, abstraction of the mind, contemplation and concentration of the mind (NBh IV. 2,46).

In order to secure release, it is also necessary, says Gautama, to study and understand continually the nature of knowledge (*jñāna*) as well as to hold discussions with those equipped with knowledge (NS IV. 2,47).

According to Vātsyāyana, the purpose of friendly discussion with persons learned in the *śāstra* about the self is to bring about the maturation of the knowledge acquired. This maturation consists in the destruction of doubt, the knowledge of things not already known, and confirmation of (or consent to) the conclusions already arrived at. The friendly discussion (*saṃvāda*) serves to bring about an agreement (NBh IV. 2,47).

In order to clarify the scope of the friendly discussion mentioned above, Gautama says that the discussion should be conducted with disciples, preceptors, fellow-students and those who seek specific felicity; such persons bear no malice (NBh IV. 2,48).

In case a seeker after the truth finds it necessary for the fulfilment of his purpose, says Gautama, he may hold discussion even without an opposing side (NS IV. 2,49).

Vātsyāyana explains: It might be thought that theories and counter-theories, if put forward in discussion, would be unpleasant to the other party. The seeker after the truth who simply expresses a desire to learn the truth, without trying to prove any theory of his own, clarifies his own system (*darśana*) (NBh IV. 2,49).

According to Vātsyāyana, through excessive partiality to their own views, some people transgress all bounds of reasoning. In such cases Gautama's advice is: Rejoinder and cavil should be employed to keep up one's determination to get at the truth, just as the hedge of thorny branches is put up for the protection of sprouting seeds (NS IV. 2,50).

According to the commentator, such devices are meant only for those persons who have not acquired knowledge of the true nature of things, whose defects have not been removed, and who are still making effort in those directions (NBh IV. 2,50).

An opponent may be rude and it may not be possible to find a right answer to his unfounded allegations. In that case Gautama's advice is that one may quarrel with the opponent and employ rejoinder and cavil (NS IV. 2,51). Such extreme measures are meant to defeat the opponent, and not to get at the truth. But this should be done, says Vātsyāyana, only for the purpose of defending the true learning (*vidyā*) and not for the purpose of obtaining wealth, honour or fame (NBh IV. 2,51).

PART SEVEN : REFLECTIONS ON THE NYĀYA SYSTEM

29

REFLECTIONS ON THE NYĀYA SYSTEM

According to the commentators a *śāstra* is expected to follow the following method of treatment: enunciation (*uddeśa*), definition (*lakṣaṇa*) and examination (*parīkṣā*). The *Nyāya Sūtra* being a *śāstra* broadly conforms to this method.

The work is divided into five books (*adhyāya*) and each book is divided into chapters (*ānhika*). The first book and its chapters contain the enunciations and definitions of the sixteen categories and the sub-categories of some of the categories. The second book and its two chapters deal with the examination of the first category, pramāṇa. The third book and its two chapters are concerned with the examination of the second category, *prameya*. This is continued in the first chapter of the fourth book; this chapter also contains the examination of the doctrines of other philosophers. The second chapter of the fourth book deals with the examination of the true nature of things and its opposite and of the categories of discussion, rejoinder and cavil. The first chapter of the fifth book contains the examination of the category of legitimate objection and the second chapter of the same book of the category of deficiency.

Gautama has not followed strictly the prescribed method outlined above. For instance, he has merely listed the pramāṇas but not defined the category itself. The commentators frequently confuse the division of a category with its definition with a view to showing that the author has not actually departed from the method. A category of *hetvābhāsa* is itself listed as one of the sub-categories of the category of deficiency. Apparently the writers were not quite sure about the logical nature of definition, division and classification. This lack of clarity is quite evident in the exposition of one of the objects of cognition, defect. If a category is meant to have an ontological status of a high order, such demotion should not have been tolerated. It is therefore not inappropriate to treat the categories first and foremost as topics selected by Gautama as a subject of his work.

It is customary among the system-makers to state the purpose of their works and the means of accomplishing it. *Vaiśeṣika Sūtra* as we have it now opens with the declaration that the author intends to explain *dharma*. *Dharma* is then defined as that which leads to the accomplishment of prosperity (*abhyudaya*) and of the supreme good (*niḥśreyasa*). The supreme good is then said to be the result of the knowledge of the true nature of the categories of substance, property, action, genus, species and inherence and this result is produced by a specific *dharma*, by means of their similarities and dissimilarities.[1] Īśvarakṛṣṇa declares that he intends to investigate in his *Sāṃkhya Kārikā* the remedy for the termination of affliction by three-fold suffering and lays down discriminative knowledge of the manifest, the unmanifest and the knower as his prescription.[2] Patañjali begins his *Yoga Sūtra* with a modest statement that his work is a revised text (*anuśāsana*) of Yoga which is said to be the restraining of modifications of consciousness (*cittavṛttinirodha*).[3] Jaimini promises to investigate *dharma* in his *Mīmāṃsā Sūtra*. *Dharma* is described as an objective (*ārtha*) defined by Vedic injunction.[4] Bādarāyaṇa proposes to investigate *Brahman* in his *Brahma Sūtra*. And this *Brahman* is the source of the world.[5]

According to this general convention amongst the system-makers, Gautama also first declares his purpose in undertaking the composition of the *Nyāya Sūtra*. This purpose is to enable us to acquire the supreme good (*niḥśreyasa*) through the knowledge of the true nature of his sixteen categories. The commentators are somewhat perplexed that the author has not proclaimed his purpose to be release (*apavarga*). Release is mentioned in the second aphorism only as something which follows the successive annihilation, in the reverse order, of pain, birth, activity, defect and misapprehension. What is even more surprising — and this is not suggested by the commentators — is that while the fallaacy of the hetu is accorded category status by Gautma, misapprehension (*mithyājñāna*), which is far more serious in all conscience, occupies no such pride of place. Surely, in the Nyāya system misapprehension deserves a better deal.

It is customary to describe a school of Indian philosophy as system (*darśana*). The *Nyāya Sūtra* has undoubtedly a central theme, viz., the categorical structure, and within this theme Gautama has produced a theory of cognition, a doctrine of objects of cognition, a concept of proof and a technique of refutation. The theory of cognition is intended to establish the objects of cognition (*prameya*). The concept of proof is meant to confirm *siddhānta* and the technique of refutation is designed to demolish what may be described as heresy. Thus Gautama has undoubtedly given us a set of co-ordinated doctrines.

As already mentioned, the theory of cognition is tailored to demonstrate the objects of cognition. Within the theory of cognition itself the first three pramāṇas, perception, inference and analogy, present a coherent empirical theory of knowledge. But the fourth pramāṇa, *śabda*, does not really tally with that theory. Moreover, while the nature and characteristics of *ātman* are undoubtedly important for any philosophical system, it seems that the other so-called objects of cognition, which represent the incidents in the career of the *ātman* and its destiny, cannot really be established by the first three pramāṇas. Thus the Nyāya explanation of the physical world and even of the *ātman* is based on the first three pramāṇas, but the incidents and destiny of the *ātman* must be regarded as based on the fourth pramāṇa. Strange as it may seem, the former can be constituted as a respectable empirical system while the latter rests almost entirely on the authority of āpta. Though Gautama is deeply interested in this problem, this aspect of his system is its weakest part. Such a principle of authority may be relevant to a theological system but it cannot be reconciled with an empiricism which claims to be founded on a sense-object theory of perception. In this sense there is a logical wedge between the theory of cognition and the doctrine of the objects of cognition with the exception of the nature and characteristics of *ātman*.

The Naiyāyika is engaged in giving an empirical account of various philosophical problems. This account is not only consistent with his premises but also recognizes no frontiers to the search for knowledge or explanation. The Nyāya system is founded on a firm belief in our capacity to explain the universe with the help of the four pramāṇas. It is therefore surprising that in one of his central notions the Naiyāyika is prepared to tolerate an element of inexplicability. The relation between substance and its properties is one of inherence (*samavāya*), but the Naiyāyika frankly confesses that he cannot explain what it is. Surely, such a notion cannot be used in a system which prides itself on making everything intelligible. Atoms and selves are substances in the Nyāya system and they have certain properties. But the manner in which they are related is left mysterious. If this argument were pressed to its logical conclusion, it would make the Nyāya system a bundle of mysteries. But if we were to leave out this notion, the system can still be salvaged as an empirical philosophy comparable to modern schools of empirical thought in Western philosophy.

Another feature of the Nyāya system which obscures its significance is the concept of hetu. This concept is central to its scheme of proof. By and large, the Nyāya hetu is a real element in a real universe and what the Naiyāyika wants to show is that the hetus which are known by means of the pramāṇas can be demonstrated. Logicians have looked with disfavour upon induction and even baptized it into a problem of induction. Leaving aside these controversial problems, the Naiyāyika can be said to have formulated a logic of discovery. His discoveries lay in a sphere not easily amenable to the canons of cumulative evidence as enshrined in his pramāṇa doctrine and if these two aspects are separated, we can appreciate the tremendous significance of Gautama's contribution. As I have said elsewhere, Gautama was an Indian version of Mill in a scriptural and social environment. But then, like other Indian philosophers he was a product of an ethos of conformity without any social compulsions. Even when Indian philosophers were doing theology rather than philosophy they were doing so as empiricists and pragmatists.

It is often suggested that Indian philosophy is based on intuition rather than reason. 'Mystical philosophy, in all ages and in all parts of the world, is characterized,' says Russell, 'by certain beliefs which are illustrated by the doctrines we have been considering'.[6] [These doctrines represent the views of Parmenides, Heraclitus and Plato.] He lists four main characteristics of mystical philosophy: (a) the belief in insight as against discursive analysis: the belief in a way of wisdom, sudden, penetrating, coercive, which is contrasted with the slow and fallible study of outward appearance by a science relying wholly upon the senses; (b) the belief in unity and the refusal to admit opposition or division anywhere; (c) the denial of the reality of time;

(d) the belief that all evil is mere appearance, an illusion produced by the divisions and oppositions of the analytic intellect.[7]

So far as the Nyāya system is concerned, these four characteristics of the mystical philosophy cannot be said to hold good in any strict sense. The Naiyāyika does not believe in a contrast between sense and intellect. In fact the analytic part of the system is meant to be firmly rooted in sense experience. Even more so, mental experience and its expression in language are said to reflect what there is. There is a kind of direct experience which is said to reveal directly the whole of the Nyāya system, but this experience is more in the nature of direct acquaintance as visualized in the Nyāya theory of perception. In any case this experience can be verified by evidence or what are called pramāṇas. This direct acquaintance is the foundation of the fourth pramāṇa, *śabda*. In the basence of any direct revelation from a divine agency it is difficult to say that the Nyāya categories require any direct insight or revelation. Of course, there is the doctrine of salvation, which is common to all systems of Indian thought except the Cārvākas. The fact that it is something which happens to the self at the end of its prolonged journey through the *saṃsāra* — it does not constitute any essential part of the philosophical aspects of the Nyāya system.

The Naiyāyika firmly believes in the plurality of ultimates in his universe and he does not deny the reality of time. In fact, it is difficult to believe how any system which accepts unequivocally the fact of *saṃsāra* and advocates its termination can deny time or evil. The karma doctrine permits no escape from the total settlement of accounts in terms of what is due to oneself, whether it be pleasure or pain.

Another striking feature of the Nyāya system, as perhaps of other systems, is that the philosopher is deeply interested in communication. To ensure that the communication is both truthful and effective, the Naiyāyika goes as far as to believe in a sort of pre-established harmony between what is, what we experience, what we say about that experience, and what those who receive the communication understand from that communication. There is no room in this picture for any radical challenge to the inherent harmony between all the elements as mentioned above. Even the language which the philosopher speaks and the language which the layman hears is not divided by any psychological, semantic, or even social barriers; every word is tied to its object by conventions established by the grammarian. The grammarian is placed on the same pedestal as the authors of the Vedas. In this connection it is worth noting that while the Naiyāyika is irrevocably committed to the *varṇāśrama* system with all that it involves by way of privileges, immunities and obligations of different classes or castes, he seems to be prepared to relax that system in favour of the privileged communication (*āptavacana*). Like almost all philosophers, he holds that there are two classes, the philosophers and the others, and that the former are superior because of their acquisition of insight, but that has really no bearing on the fundamental questions of pre-established harmony. This does involve certain difficulties for the composition of a *śāstra*, but as we shall see, the difficulty is solved by a simple device of classification.

If we look at the *Nyāya Sūtra* itself and the explanations given by the commentators, the system seems to fall into two main parts: one is predominantly philosophical and the other is concerned with matters which can best be characterized as factual. In the first part we can include the theory of cognition, the concept of proof and the technique of refutation. In this part it would be quite legitimate to include the nature of the self. The second part can be said to cover the process of successive annihilation, in reverse order, of pain, birth, activity, defect, and misapprehension.

So far as the first part is concerned, there is nothing which the most hard-headed empiricist or analytic philosopher could not have established on the bases of perception and reasoning founded upon, and confirmed or confirmable by perception. It is true that while Gautama has explicitly stated the self to be an inferential object, the commentators wish to bring in an āpta to cite as evidence of his direct acquaintance with the self. This contention seems somewhat arbitrary. If there is the self—and if everyone is or has the self—there is no reason why we have to depend upon indirect evidence. Surely, we can be acquainted with our selves if there are such entities. In any case such an experience is not so extraordinary as to be taken into the realm of mysticism. If the self is an object, we can be acquainted with it in the same way as we are said to be acquainted with other objects.

The Naiyāyika wants us to believe that we are directly aware of our defects (*doṣa*) and their decisive influence on our lives and experiences stretching across eternity. Surely, this is merely an attempt to introduce a doctrine of *saṃsāra* and karma in a manner in which the Naiyāyika cannot prove to the satisfaction of anyone who would like to accept only that which is strictly warranted by the Naiyāyika's more rational canons of evidence. The Naiyāyika subscribes to the correspondence theory of truth and we can safely say that such beliefs do not correspond to empirical phenomena. We must remember that different philosophers hold different views, and if we were to accept the claims of all such doctrines to correspond to the facts, we would land ourselves in a mass of contradictions. Faith may offer a way-out of such an impasse, but when it comes to rational assent, we cannot accept such contradictory propositions. Nor, strange as it may seem, would the Naiyāyika like us to do so.

The philosophical part of the Nyāya system is straightforward reasoning; we do not need any intuition nor has the Naiyāyika in his explanation made much use of it. All that he would claim is that somehow the structure of categories has been discovered by Gautama or his predecessors, and all that intuition could add to it is to impress his contemporaries. It is really in the second part, which is factual and practical, that it looks as though intuition has come into its own. Here we have the full dominion of an āpta. To assign such a role to intuition or āpta is really to introduce in a system the least examined part of the attitudes of the philosopher, without a shred of evidence. That is why even in the sphere of revelation or morality the function of intuition is increasingly found to be the rationalization of what one wishes to believe. If there is such a 'will to believe'[8] irrespective of evidence, there is nothing that can stop such a belief. Such beliefs may even seem acceptable because they are found to give immense satisfaction, but for the Naiyāyika, if he were true to his basic tenets, such an option would not really be available. He is committed to a theory of pragmatic truth and therefore it must be founded on cognition, and cognition is cognition in so far as it reveals a thing that is as it is, and a thing that is not as it is not.

As an empiricist the Naiyāyika laboured under certain limitations. First, he did not have at his disposal sufficient factual or scientific knowledge. The only science of an empirical character which was widely spread in ancient India was medicine. This science could never shake off the legacy of the Atharva Veda nor could it utilize all the resources of our five senses. In its therapy it depended on the sense of taste — a sense which does not offer exciting opportunities for the exploration of the universe.[9] But the philosopher took over the corpus of medical knowledge and on this foundation built up his edifice of psychosomatic equipment of human beings. His main resource of information was language, but this too became progressively divorced from the vital currents of society.

Like the medical knowledge, he seems to have taken over not only the heritage of the *Dharmaśāstras* but the pattern of society which they depicted. The authors of these *śāstras* were concerned with the most far-reaching regulation of individual and social behaviour, developed an elaborate framework of a theoretical kind for the purpose, and in the process created — what must be regarded in a broad sense a social morality. Like the Āyurveda, they too were tied to certain basic doctrines like salvation.

It was on such slender foundations that the Naiyāyika built quite a remarkable system of thought which could be compared with the modern empirical philosophical systems. Its besetting sin was its extra-ordinary reverence for the principle of authority. In the West the principle was gradually eroded by the impact of scientific knowledge and movements for the emancipation of the oppressed classes. Once again, however, we find that the Western empiricists are busy reconciling empiricism with theology.[10] The Indian theology was always deeply embedded in empirical tradition with the added assurance of a deep-seated belief in the efficacy of remedies for what seemed like ordinary problems, for instance, *duḥkha* (suffering). The concept of such an ordinary fact of life as *duḥkha* was identified with psychosomatic endowment of human beings and with the concentration on two dramatic points of life, birth and death, and thus the path was opened for imaginary extensions of the human predicament backwards into the past and forwards into the future. The cause of suffering was shrouded in mystery and the end of it was promised on the basis of strict conformity to the instruction of the philosopher. Such an end could be most tantalizing. For instance, if there is no psychosomatic endowment it is obvious there can be no experience in an ordinary sense. If there is no such experience, the question of suffering does not arise. Hence salvation becomes the total absence of pain: that is *apavarga* (release). First, this is expressed in the visualizing of a chain or a series of births and deaths; and then this chain is said to be destroyed. What can be easily forgotten is that what can be destroyed in the first instance is not the chain but the links of the chain; but the links of the chain being birth and death, the first, birth, cannot be destroyed if it has occurred and at most, it can be prevented, and the second, death, can never be ignored. A proposition of this kind has however been invested with such intricate machinery of sanctions and communication that it has come to be accepted as a gospel truth. What is really important is the experiential suffering and the remedy for its eradication within one's own life.

The philosopher in India was not only a learned and well-educated person, but he had cultivated a mode of life which gave him considerable detachment from the ordinary affairs of society. This gave him a prestige which eventually made him into a holy person. The philosopher had thus power of an unrivalled character to influence the mind of man but with no regular source of authentic information about the problems or difficulties of ordinary men and women and without any genuine responsibility. It is not unlikely that his major contact point must have been the establishment. And the establishment acted under the strong influence of the social engineers, the thinkers of its age.

The impression that the Indian philosopher was not concerned with moral philosophy is only partly true, and this would depend upon what one regards as moral problems. They have varied from society to society and in the Indian context they appear in different forms. This only means that the kind of moral philosophy which the Indian philosopher practised was different from what it is often thought to be in the West. But this does not mean that the Indian philosopher was not concerned with morality. He was deeply concerned with the problems of individual and social morality.

Indian theories of knowledge are presented in the form of pramāṇas. All schools of philosophy generally recognize perception and inference as pramāṇa but they differ about other sources of knowledge. Formal recognition or non-recognition does not mean that the philosophers actually accept only those pramāṇas which they recognize or reject those which they do not. For instance, Gautama recognizes only four pramāṇas, but has incorporated four other pramāṇas in his scheme as variations of one or the other of his four pramāṇas. The Buddhist rejects the *śabdapramāṇa* in the sense that it is only a modified version of inference, but by the time this controversy had arisen he had accepted the authority of the Buddha and the *āgama*. This repudiation of the Vedic authority is not necessarily the repudiation of the principle of authority but only of a particular authority.

Indian philosophers generally philosophize in the third person rather than in the first person. This is inevitable because they philosophize in a representative capacity. There is either a canonical text or an author who had the insight of truth at some time or other. All that a subsequent writer has to do is to communicate what he had heard from the person who had the insight or from the person who had heard from the person who had the insight. His problem is to communicate to those who have had no such insight but are otherwise eligible to acquire that insight and to induce a correct attitude towards the communication. His main concern is to translate his own or someone else's insight which is incorrigible into a language suitable for the purpose.

The Indian philosopher speculates as a spectator and not as an agent. Since the philosopher is concerned with an incorrigible psychological experience, the third person approach tends to obscure the presentation of the issues involved.

According to the Naiyāyika the pramāṇa is what gives the cognition of a thing as it is and the *apramāṇa* (non-pramāṇa) is what gives the cognition of a thing as it is not. This is a correspondence theory of truth. Coupled with this is the Nyāya view that a pramāṇa is meant to be effective, that is, it enables us to accept, reject or treat with indifference the object cognized. On the one hand, this view appears to imply that a pramāṇa compels us to give our assent or dissent or to suspend judgment; on the other it seems to suggest practical action. A pramāṇa enables us to acquire or discard an object of cognition or look upon it with indifference. This amounts to a pragmatic theory of truth. But the Nyāya concept of the pramāṇa is bound up with the specific objects of cognition enunciated by Gautama. What the author would really like us to do is not only to accept his pramāṇas but his set of objects of cognition. Of course, these objects are concerned with the self, its equipment, career and destiny. But this is a doctrinal prescription for suitable action. Similarly, it is intended that once the Nyāya pramāṇas are accepted other doctrinal prescriptions would be automatically condemned as heresies.

The Nyāya concept of pramāṇa is based on the logical grammar of instrument (*karaṇa*). An instrument is defined by the following characteristics. It is something which is operated by an agent upon only one object at a time and which cannot operate by itself. In the theory of knowledge this concept means that there is a cognizer who operates a pramāṇa on an object; the operation represents cognition. This concept is used in various contexts. For instance, the sense-organs and the mind (*manas*) are declared as instruments with the necessary implications. The significance of the characteristic, i.e. not operating by itself, is that the instrument must always serve the purpose of something other than itself. The entire psychosomatic equipment is an instrument, and, consequently, it must serve the purpose of something else, i.e. the agent. Thus the notion of instrument is interpreted as a kind of teleology.

This view of instrument is different from our modern view. In scientific investigation we use instruments to increase the range and accuracy of our observation. In life machines are used to multiply goods and services or mitigate drudgery. The grammatical notion of instrument has none of these dynamic or utilitarian aspects. It represents a moribund view of the world.

The central problem of modern philosophy has been the problem of knowledge. There is no general agreement as to what precisely is the problem of knowledge. One of the well-known statements on the subject is that of A. J. Ayer: 'I conclude then that the necessary and sufficient conditions for knowing that something is the case are first that what one is said to know be true, secondly that one be sure of it, and thirdly that one should have the right to be sure."[11] As the three conditions are treated as fulfilled in the Nyāya system *ab initio* because either Gautama or some predecessor of his had the incorrigible insight, all that is necessary for us is to follow the text and implement the recipe. The system thus proceeds on the assumption that we know that there is a real world of things and persons; a philosopher has merely to give a reasonable and persuasive account of this world.

To use Professor Strawson's expression, philosophical theory of knowledge is intended to be descriptive and not revisionary.[12]

The Naiyāyika affirms his complete confidence in the faculties of man to know the world. He even goes further and asserts that not only is there nothing which is unknowable, but also, given a proper method of knowing, there is nothing which cannot be known by men. In this context I include an āpta as a human being. A sceptic who questions our capacity for knowledge or the very possibility of knowledge, says the Naiyāyika, is not entitled to borrow the conceptual framework of one who is not a sceptic and then proceed to demolish that framework; he must find his own means and then proceed to establish his scepticism. In the Nyāya idiom, a pramāṇa can only be repudiated by means of another pramāṇa; if the sceptic cannot adduce any pramāṇa to prove his position, there is no reason for any rational person to give his assent to the sceptic's views. This is the real significance of the debate between the Buddhist and the Naiyāyika and the essence of the deadlock which in some important cases is found in their disputations.

According to the Naiyāyika the method of acquiring knowledge of the world of things and persons is the method of cumulative evidence. The foundation of this method is perception and on this foundation we can raise a pyramid of knowledge with the help of inference, analogy and verbal testimony. This method demands that whatever passes for knowledge must be confirmed or confirmable by perception, and underlies the doctrine of the convergence of pramāṇas. The opponents of this view were apprehensive lest this doctrine would lead either to confusion in the operation of the pramāṇas or even to the complete eclipse of the pramāṇas. Their fears were more doctrinal than epistemic.

It is thus obvious that the Naiyāyika is an empiricist. The problems of knowledge begin with perception and are resolved by perception. Since our knowledge depends upon cumulative evidence every aspect of evidence must be carefully scrutinised before it is accepted. We have sense-experience, we base our inferences on that experience, we discover similarities between things and learn relations between words and meanings. But all our sense-experiences, inferences, discoveries of similarities and acquaintances with words and their meanings — these are not in themselves knowledge; they are the raw material of our knowledge. For each one of these sources of knowledge we need criteria so that we accept the right things and reject the wrong things. The doctrine of pramāṇas is the doctrine of criteria for this purpose. Our ordinary beliefs about things and persons would become knowledge only when they stand the test.

As an empiricist, the Naiyāyika is fully aware that the empirical knowledge cannot claim the certainty of demonstration of formal logic. This knowledge must necessarily consist of restricted generalizations which are warranted by evidence. Every such generalization must be based upon perceptual data and confirmed or confirmable by perceptual experience. But this does not mean that such generalizations do not hold good for all times, present, past and future. What the Naiyāyika strongly objects to is the kind of unrestricted generalizations which some philosophers are fond of making; for example, everything is eternal. Since such a generalization covers everything, according to the Nyāya theory of proof, no fresh evidence can be offered in supprot of the generalization. In the technical language of the Nyāya such a proposition cannot be supported by a valid hetu because no example lying outside 'everything' can be cited in support of the hetu; and an unsupported hetu is invalid.

The Nyāya view can be compared with the classical attack of Mill on syllogistic reasoning of Aristotle and the falsifiability criterion of Sir Karl Popper. According to Mill, 'It must be granted that in every syllogism, considered as an argument to prove the conclusion, there is a *petitio principii*. When we say,

All men are mortal,
Socrates is a man,
therefore
Socrates is mortal;

it is unanswerably urged by he adversaries of the syllogistic theory, that the proposition, Socrates is mortal, is presupposed in the more general assumption, All men are mortal.[13]

From the second assertion Mill draws the conclusion that syllogistic reasoning cannot be inference, properly so called: 'All inference is from particulars to particulars: General propositions are merely registers of such inferences already made, and short formulae for making more: The major premise of a syllogism, consequently, is a formula of this description: and the conclusion is not an inference drawn *from* the formula, but an inference drawn *according* to the formula: the real logical antecedent, or premise, being the particular facts from which the general proposition was collected by induction. Those facts, and the individual instances which supplied them, may have been forgotten; but a record remains, not indeed descriptive of the facts themselves, but showing how those cases may be distinguished, respecting which the facts, when known, were considered to warrant a given inference. According to the indications of this record we draw our conclusion; which is, to all intents and purposes, a conclusion from the forgotten facts. For this it is essential that we should read the record correctly: and the rules of the syllogism are a set of precautions to ensure our doing so.[14]

According to Karl Popper, '... *the criterion of the scientific status of a theory is its falsifiability, or refutability, or testability*.'[15] 'Assume that we have deliberately made it our task,' says the philosopher, 'to live in this unknown world of ours; to adjust ourselves to it as well as we can; to take advantage of the opportunities we can find in it; and to explain it, *if* possible (we need not assume that it is), and as far as possible, with the help of laws and explanatory theories. *If we have made this our task, then there is no more rational procedure than the method of trial and error — of conjecture and refutation*; of boldly proposing theories, of trying our best to show that these are erroneous; and of accepting them tentatively if our critical efforts are unsuccessful.'[16]

In these comparisons we must remember that Gautama or his commentators were not preceded by an Aristotle nor did they have the rich background of modern science. What the Naiyāyika is really saying is that if a philosopher starts with an empirical proposition — and we must treat the propositions selected by Gautama as empirical or factual — then the authors of such propositions have debarred themselves from proving these propositions. They can offer no confirmatory proof. This is similar to the doctrine of estoppel in law.[17] The only legitimate propositions that can be derived from experience or empirical evidence are the propositions in the nature of *niyama* (rule). Though these are generalizations of a sort they cannot be regarded strictly as universal propositions; they are particular propositions relevant to particular facts. The Naiyāyika knew only of causal laws and grammatical rules and their sphere was the nature which they explained without observation and with the grammar of the Sanskrit language which they took for granted. Moreover, they were not really involved in the kind of debate about *a priori* and *a posteriori* or experience versus reason in the context of mathematical knowledge and empirical or factual knowledge. They had the assurance of certainty based on incorrigible intuitive perception, but this assurance is very much similar to the immediacy and certainty of ordinary sense-perception.

The Nyāya strategy is quite simple. First, if there were no such thing as a physical object which we perceive, the problem of perception could not arise at all. It is precisely because what we perceive is a single object that we begin our investigation. Secondly, in perception it is the object with which our senses are in direct contact; it is the object which produces sense-experience. Thirdly, even though an object is a product of atoms it is not just an aggregate of the atoms but a new product with a numerical identity.

This kind of theory can be broadly described as naïve realism. Such naïve realism is open to what is considered to be an effective argument against it. 'Naïve realism,' says Russell, 'leads to physics, and physics, if true, shows that naïve realism is false. Therefore naïve realism, if true, is false; therefore, it is false.'[18] This argument may be effective against modern naïve realism but has no bearing on the Nyāya position. There is no gap between the Nyāya physics and the Nyāya theory of knowledge, nor is there any reason for general 'scepticism of the senses'; the four elements, the physical objects and the four sense-organs — these have four qualities. Only ākāśa, sound and the auditory organ have a privileged position. But throughout there is a pre-established harmony between them. This Nyāya physics has no provision for the distinction between primary and secondary qualities — a distinction which led many Western philosophers to reduce the physical object to something mental or neutral between the physical and the mental. This shows how a problem is set for the philosopher and how the direction of his explanation is determined in the light of the factual knowledge available at the time.

Amongst the pramāṇas Gautama has devoted considerable attention to perception and *śabda*. The basic problem of perception is that of justifying our belief in the existence of the physical object which it is commonly taken for granted that we perceive. The Naiyāyika defends this belief against the Buddhist, and, given the premises with which the debate is conducted, one can say that the Naiyāyika has made a good case for his position.

Both the Naiyāyika and the Buddhist are agreed upon the atomic structure of the physical object. According to the former, the task of the philosopher is to analyse the complex into the simple. Taking the physical object as complex we analyse it into its simplest components and this gives us four kinds of atoms corresponding to the four qualities of objects, colour, taste, smell and touch. Secondly, since a physical object is a product of the simple elements, it must have cause. And this cause is the component atoms.

There are two questions that arise in this context. First, since the atoms are imperceptible, how can we say that the object made of imperceptible atoms is perceptible ? Second, since the object consists of atoms, how can we say that what we perceive is a simple object ? It will be noted that the first question is exactly the reverse of what the modern philosophers deal with: how can a perceptible object be said to consist of or explained in terms of scientific objects ?

The Naiyāyika is a thorough-going empiricist. All our knowledge, whether of persons or of things, is derived from and confirmed or confirmable by perceptual experience. The whole concept of the second and third pramāṇas, inference and analogy, is empirical. The Nyāya theory of inference is primarily psychological in the sense that it emphasizes what we had perceived before and what we remember now. It is a theory of invariable concomitance previously perceived and now remembered, but throughout it is tied to what was perceived and what is perceived. Memory is nothing but reproduction of what was previously perceived. The kinds of inference mentioned by the Naiyāyika are from cause to effect, effect to cause and the extension of the similarity observed to a new phenomenon. Similarly, analogy is based on observed similarity between two objects or the learned relation between a word and an object denoted by it to the identification of a new object. The latter amounts to what is called 'ostensive definition'.

The Naiyāyika accepts the principle of causation without any reservation. Every event has a cause and the connection between cause and effect is uniform. The main preoccupation is with what is known as material cause in the terminology of Aristotle. Such causes need prodding and we have therefore the notion of efficient cause. The notion of cause as a law of change is modern and it is not surprising that it does not play any important part in the Nyāya scheme. Moreover, the philosophers are really concerned with the metaphysical formulation of the causal principle. The debate between the Naiyāyika and the Buddhist is not about the fact of causation but how best to describe it in language. If a thing is said to be produced, what is the meaning of production ? According to the Nyāya view, what is produced cannot be said to have existed before production. According to the eternalist, what is produced must have existed in some form before it was produced. This is largely the view of the Mīmāṃṣaka and the Sāṃkhya. The Buddhists do not deny the fact of production but contend that no reasonable explanation can be given for the fact. Their problem is to reconcile momentary existence with causation. The metaphysical characterization of production as real or unreal does not eliminate the fact of production.

The Naiyāyika has not really considered the problem of causation in a systematic manner, though his theory of inference is primarily based on causation. Nor has the Naiyāyika raised the question of justification for extending our knowledge of causal connection from the past to future. The psychological justification, that is, we remember the concomitance previously observed, merely states the fact of remembrance and not its validity. Moreover, it is equally important to have some justification for our belief that causal connections based on past or present experience will hold good in future.

As is well known, this is the familiar problem of induction which was raised by Hume in Western philosophy. As far as I am aware, no Indian philosopher of repute had raised the question of guarantees for extending our knowledge from the past or present to the future or from the present to the past. It is a striking fact in the history of philosophy that only certain questions are raised or even can be raised only at certain times. In the Indian context the major reasons why such an awkward question could not have been raised are mainly two. The quest for certainty in knowledge was stifled if not killed by a general belief in the factual premises of the karma doctrine and by the surrender of one's own judgment to an external authority. The whole concept of *saṃsāra* and salvation depends upon an unquestioning belief in the efficacy of karma and remedial measures. If the demand for the justification of the factual premises had been made, it would have required factual evidence and not logical arguments. No such evidence could have been easily produced. This would have meant a severe setback to the vast enterprise of the communication system. Similarly, if everyone had set himself or his experience or reason as the final arbiter of truth, many awkward questions about the kind and content of authority would have to be answered. It is one of the great paradoxes of Indian thought that those who took upon themselves the responsibility of defending common sense or ordinary human experience did not raise the kind of questions we can now raise. The development of thought takes different turns according to the questions that are put. In a sense the job of a philosopher is first to ask a right question, even if he has no ready-made answer.

According to the Naiyāyika there can be only one apprehension at a time. Each apprehension denotes or refers to an object and since each sense-organ is concerned with only one kind of sense-experience, there is no difficulty in saying that the cognizer has one apprehension connected with one object at a time. This gives a criterion for determining the numerical identity of cognitive apprehension. The same thing is done for our desires and experiences of pleasure and pain. Thus we have one object correlated with one mental occurrence. The only relation that can be established between them is one of association. As in the case of the structure of the world we have an indefinite number of particulars, each logically distinct and independent and therefore only one kind of relation between the ultimate particulars, contact (*saṃyoga*), so in the context of mental life there can only be laws of association. The atomic structure of the external world is related by the atomic structure of mental life. The interpolation of the mind (*manas*) between the cognizer and the sense-organs, which is itself atomic, guarantees the atomic structure of mental or conscious life.

While the reference to the numerical identity of the object guarantees the numerical identity of mental occurrences the qualitative differences between mental occurrences are guaranteed by the qualitative differences between the objects or the manner of their presentation in experience. In the case of perception there is direct sense-object contact and the object must therefore be present. In the case of inference we can deal with objects past, present and future. In analogy we have reference to two objects, one present and another not present but expected to be present or the relationship between word and meaning previously learnt and ready for application to the future case. But there is a distinct object all the same.

When we come to the *śabdapramāṇa* it would seem as if the Naiyāyika is not sure whether such a criterion can be used. To say that there are two kinds of objects, perceived and unperceived, is not really adequate for the purpose. The general Nyāya position is that the *śabdapramāṇa* is radically different from the other pramāṇas, particularly inference. Since perception can deal with objects present, inference with objects absent, and analogy with the relationship between word and meaning, the original criterion of objective relation cannot ensure the independence or integrity of the *śabdapramāṇa*. It must also be remembered that there is some overlap between analogy and the *śabdapramāṇa*, for the latter is also concerned with the problem of word and meaning. In so far as this aspect is concerned, there is no doubt that the naming of an object is an important part of a theory of knowledge. And the Nyāya discussion has considerable philosophical significance. I am therefore inclined to think that the part of the *śabdapramāṇa* concerned with authority is not logically connected with the Nyāya theory of the pramāṇa.

The Naiyāyika has met this difficulty by invoking the authority of a person (āpta). In the case of the other pramāṇas there is some attempt to offer criteria which are sufficiently intelligible and can be applied to individual instances. For example, the Naiyāyika has disposed of questions about erroneous perception consistent with his general definition of perception and his overall argument that if there is an error it can only be discovered by comparing it with what is not an error. To use a simile of Ryle's, 'There can be false coins only where there are coins made of the proper materials by the proper authorities.'[19] This is the Nyāya distinction between the principal and the subordinate, the original and the counterfeit or the primary and secondary meaning. Invariable concomitance is a dependable criterion for determining the validity of causal inferences. The grammatical conventions about words and meanings, if one has learnt them well, may also be a sufficient guide. But in the case of the *śabdapramāṇa* the criteria offered by the Naiyāyika are not only psychological but somewhat vague.

An āpta is said to be a person who has had direct experience of truth, is honest or has no reason to be dishonest and is actuated by a desire to share his insight with ordinary human beings because he wishes to help them who are otherwise utterly helpless. Apart from the condescending attitude and poor estimate of ordinary human beings, the Naiyāyika has not given any reasonable explanation of these three conditions. It may be argued that this is because there was a generally accepted view of the holy man or the sage, but the crucial question is how to determine that a particular person is an āpta. Take first the criterion of direct experience. During the period when the Nyāya system was formulated there were rival claimants to the privileges and immunities of such outstanding men. In fact, the seers or their spokesmen claimed precisely this direct acquaintance, but they had not reached anything like consensus on what the so-called truth was. It is precisely because of this kind of conflict between warring philosophers that Gautama had set out to create a code for discourse and its conduct. The Naiyāyika has himself called others in the field a variety of names including charlatans or demented fellows. What these conditions came to is that everyone who had the upperhand in the philosophical establishment could declare himself or any one of his choice as an āpta. And this is what actually happened. Each school of philosophy had its own canonical texts and āptas.[20]

The handling of the problem of authority in the Nyāya systems shows a brilliant strategy brilliantly executed. First, the Naiyāyika gives the merit award to almost everyone who could have written anything. The whole corpus of literature available at the time becomes authoritative and their authors āptas. To the privileged few who are authorized to study the Veda and benefit from the study he gives a comforting assurance that they should find no difficulty in following the rituals and thus profit from their compliance. The Naiyāyika goes even further and gives this testimonial to anyone in a village who might be able to guide a villager to the place where there is a fire. The Buddhist would not be too unhappy because the sacred authority is no longer the monopoly of a particular canon but depends upon a human being. Thus the entire establishment, sacred and secular, is mobilized behind the principle of authority.

But the Naiyāyika had his own scores to settle. He enlists the grammarian, the medical practitioner and even the layman to join in his battle against the Mīmāṃsakas. The grammarian has given us the conventions whereby we connect words with objects and if there were really any intrinsic or natural connection between them, there would have to be some kind of contact between them. This of course is absurd. Moreover, the language of the learned is no different in this respect from that of the layman. The ritual part of the Veda with which the Mīmāṃsaka is really concerned, assures the Naiyāyika, remains intact because the injunctions are as successful as the medical prescriptions. To cap it all, he declares that in any case the affairs of men shall continue to be regulated by the system of do's and dont's or rewards and punishments, which has already been devised and which nobody has challenged. Any alteration in the intellectual foundations of the principle of sacred authority would not upset the established *varṇāśrama* system and the beneficiaries of that system could therefore take such minor deviations into their stride.

In retrospect one would think that the transfer of allegiance from scripture to man amounts to a veritable intellectual revolution with the possibility of far-reaching impact on the whole fabric of society. Nothing of the sort happened. Those who could have challenged the principle of authority had themselves accepted it in their own thinking. Even the logicians failed to notice the flaw in the revised version of the principle. In effect the Naiyāyika says that a person is an āpta if he has seen the vision of the truth, is honest and well-disposed and he is all these because he is an āpta. Nor did the opponents urge that what is true of part of the canon cannot be true of the entire canon. The real point about the *śabdapramāṇa* is not whether it is an independent pramāṇa or a variation of the pramāṇa of inference; of course, it is an inference. What is vital is whether or not reason or argument should remain tied to the holy strings. Whether the strings are canonical or human, they are nonetheless strings. Even now it cannot be said that we have emancipated ourselves from the stranglehold of authority. The Nyāya effort to undermine one kind of authority produced only another kind, without altering the habits of thought or behaviour.

The second aspect of the *śabdapramāṇa* is of considerable philosophical interest. In dealing with the Vedic injunctions the Naiyāyika is really arguing for the three current theories of meanings: the use or contextual theory, the verification theory and the emotive theory. First, the Naiyāyika recognizes that the purpose of the speaker and the context in which he uses words are important in determining their meanings. Second, the meaning of every Vedic injunction can be verified in the same way as the meaning of Āyurvedic injunctions can be verified by their results. The Vedic injunctions represent not only a command structure but also an elaborate machinery for inducement. The hopes and fears or rewards and punishments are enshrined in the Vedic texts and their function is to induce compliance with the commands by all possible emotional appeals. The positivists, the linguistic philosopher and the followers of Wittgenstein will find one thing or another here to suit their tastes.[21]

The grammarian is placed on a very high pedestal in the entire theory of language.[22] It is he who decides what word should mean what, and he decides this not only for the learned but also for the laity. After all, grammar is canonical and the grammarian an āpta. As it has happened in Western theories of meaning, a noun-word is said to denote an object. This concept is eventually extended to every sentence or an argument. We have already seen how every mental occurrence is said to denote an object. In the absence of any reasonable system of determining what can be broadly called facts this word-object theory led to an apotheosis and reification of linguistic entities. Even a philosopher who claims to be an empiricist bound by the canons of evidence is tempted to forget the dictates of common sense or ordinary observation. The universe is crowded with entities which are no better than linguistic inventions. Causal explanations which are meant to explain things or events take the form of linguistic devices. If an inventory of the hetus used by the philosophers is taken it will be found that these hetus have little relevance to the world of nature or society as we know it. In the Indian context it seems that the reification or apotheosis of linguistic expressions has led not only to the neglect of the obvious and the commonplace but also handicapped factual investigation of nature and society.

The Naiyāyika has also a compromise theory of meaning in conventional terms. It is the theory that a noun-word denotes universal, individual and configuration. But an even more important aspect of this discussion is the Nyāya criticism of the Buddhist theory of meaning. The Naiyāyika holds that a noun-word must denote an object or refer to something positive. If it did not, no discourse, logical or otherwise, would be possible. That is why the Naiyāyika insists that since a statement or an argument must be about something that really exists, it is self-contradictory to disprove such an object. A well-established ontology is open only for confirmation, and not for disconfirmation. As elsewhere, the fundamental argument of the Naiyāyika is that if no expression or statement has a meaning, this cannot even be said in language. The Buddhist must either abandon his *apoha* theory of meaning or abandon speech altogether.

The Nyāya theories of meaning, if applied to their own views on other themes, would lead to consequences that the Naiyāyika would not readily accept. For instance, the Sanskrit words *ātman* and *apavarga* are both noun-words. It is difficult to imagine what configuration they could have. The notion of *apavarga* is altogether negative in the sense of a total absence of pain. It would not make sense to say that *apavarga* denotes or refers to something positive. Much the same difficulty can be noticed in the context of the Nyāya pramāṇas and objects of cognition, (*prameya*). The Nyāya does not recognize *abhāva* as an independent pramāṇa, but *apavarga* is one of the objects of cognition, and rather an important one for the whole Nyāya system.

The Naiyāyika is concerned with terms (or noun-words) and objects rather than propositions. That is why he has difficulties in dealing with the problem of negation. The Naiyāyika goes to the farthest limits in explaining negative terms like the hare's horn. He says that what is intended in such terms is not that the hare or the horn does not exist, but rather that the hare does not have the horns. This means that negation as understood in logic is not only impossible in the world but also in language. And yet the Naiyāyika is prepared to concede that absence can be apprehended. Like the composite theory of meaning, the positive theory of meaning creates complications for other Nyāya themes. It is really not convincing to say, to take the example of *apavarga* again though it is not strictly a negative term, it cannot denote or refer to a total absence. In this context what is important is not the pain we have had in life but an entirely different state of affairs. The Naiyāyika has argued against the Buddhist, not without some sarcasm, that even the term *śūnya* has a positive meaning. If so, then the term *apavarga* should have even more positive meaning. It would have been interesting to see how the Naiyāyika and the Buddhist sort out this tangled skein of *apavarga, nirvāṇa* and *śūnya* purely in the context of their linguistic and logical theories.

As an empiricist, the Naiyāyika's main justification must be that the āpta pramāṇa is based upon direct experience which has the same intuitive certainty as ordinary perceptual experience. But in the case of perception the Naiyāyika has definitely laid down sense-object contact as part of the definition. Since the Naiyāyika takes this stand on perception as the foundation of all knowledge, it is quite obvious that the direct experience of truth by an āpta cannot be equated with the kind of perceptual experience permissible under the Nyāya theory. The Naiyāyika therefore adopts a tactic which is really not straightforward. He first declares the mind as the sense-organ and substitutes the mind-self contact for the sense-object contact of the ordinary kind. He then proceeds to confine this contact and experience to a Yogin and we are in the field of Yogic practices like *samādhi*. This is certainly an unjustified extension of the basic empiricism of the Naiyāyika. Moreover, it substitutes what must be regarded as an exceptional or extraordinary psychological experience as an incorrigible experience for its standard theories of truth, the correspondence and pragmatic theories.

The philosophical significance of the *śabdapramāṇa* for an empiricist like the Naiyāyika can only be that whatever evidence is cited must be translated in appropriate language. It is only when perceptual experience is expressed in statements that it can be put to the test of confirmation, whether it be by correspondence or by practical efficiency. There are philosophers who consider the correspondence theory dead[23] and the pragmatic theory as something that merely works like a motor car,[24] but if there is anything like truth as a property of propositions or statements, there must be something extra-linguistic with which they can be compared. If a proposition cannot be confirmed by experience and if it is an empirical proposition, its logical merits would not compensate for its failure in practice. In any case this attitude is foreign to the Indian tradition. It claims that the knowledge it offers is meant to have tremendous bearing on one's life.

As the reader must have noticed, I have grouped together the seven categories of doubt, the objective, established tenet, *avayava*, the fallacy of the hetu, disputation and ascertainment under the common heading 'concept of proof'. Amongst those seven categories the *avayava* has received a great deal of attention and it is even suggested that Gautama's reputation as a logician depends upon this part of the Nyāya system. This seems to me to be a somewhat one-sided view of Gautama's contribution to the logic of proof. To appreciate his concept of proof as he viewed it we need to look at all these categories as an inter-connected programme of proof.

The doubt recognized by Gautama is different from the well-known Cartesian doubt. According to Descartes he was in search for that kind of certainty and validity which would leave no shadow of doubt. 'So, on the grounds that our senses sometimes deceive us,' says Descartes, 'I wanted to suppose that there was not anything corresponding to what they make us imagine. And, because some men make mistakes in reasoning—even with regard to the simplest matters of geometry—and fall into fallacies, I judged that I was as much subject to error as anyone else, and I rejected as unsound all the reasonings which I had hitherto taken for demonstrations. Finally, taking account of the fact that all the same experiences which we have when we are awake can also come to us when we are asleep without there being one of them which is then veridical, I resolved to pretend that everything which had ever entered into my mind was no more veridical than the illusions of my dreams. But at once I noticed that while I was wishing in this way to think in this way that everything was false it followed necessarily that I who was thinking must be something. And I observed that this truth, *I think, therefore I am,* was so solid and certain that all the most extravagant suppositions of the sceptics were unable to upset it. I judged that I could receive it without hesitation as the first principle of the philosophy which I was seeking.'[25]

Neither Gautama nor his commentators are willing to entertain such a universal doubt or even to pretend to do so. This kind of scepticism and individualism is totally foreign to the Nyāya concept of doubt which marks the beginning of investigation. The Naiyāyika is mainly concerned with perceptual doubt which arises from lack of uniformity in observation or non-observation and doctrinal doubt which arises from conflicting views on one and the same subject. The perceptual doubt is removed by the discovery of distinguishing properties of an object and in the last resort, this question can be settled only by appeal to perceptual evidence. In fact Gautama has provided for such evidence in his definition of perception. Regarding the conflicting views, the Naiyāyika is quite aware of the logical aspect. If there are two contradictory propositions — or as the Naiyāyika would say, if two contradictory properties are attributed to one and the same object this is either logically impossible or there is really no contradiction. One and the same thing cannot have contradictory properties at one and the same time or in one and the same sense. And yet there are philosophers who hold diametrically opposed views. For instance, one party says that the *ātman* exists while the other holds that it does not. Even though the Naiyāyika cannot be said to be aware of the distinction between analytic and synthetic propositions or whether or not existence can be logically predicated of a subject, he knows that the question of existence or non-existence cannot be settled by formal logic. And what he is primarily interested in is not logical objects or logical possibilities but the real entities such as the self or the incidents in its career.

Secondly, his whole concept of investigation is to establish such entities. The reason for this is that the Naiyāyika expects us to act upon our beliefs. Whatever we do or we do not do has a purpose, and he has even conceded a category status to the objective (*prayojana*).

Thirdly, the mission of Gautama was to establish positive truth and eradicate error or heresy. He himself has a system of such truth to offer and knowing as he does that numerous philosophers inside or outside the Hindu fold are opposed to him in one respect or another, he is anxious to prove that what he believes in is right while all of his opponents are wrong. But he knew far too well how far he could go in establishing his own system without making too many enemies. He had already made the most generous gift of the āpta status to the entire establishment; he now invites his fellow-thinkers to join together as āptas and sort out their intellectual differences without making too much noise. I am reminded of what a distinguished Indian philosopher said about himself: 'I am a philosopher among statesmen and statesman among philosophers.' Neither Plato nor Kṛṣṇa would object to such a role to the philosopher. It is not surprising that India could produce a Mahatma who was both a saint and a liberator of modern India.

A modern reader is tempted to treat the arguments cited by the philosophers as mere paradigms. Paradigms undoubtedly they were, but in the philosophical and cultural tradition of India some of them can be aptly described as 'life and death' problems. For instance, the debate about the eternality or non-eternality of sound seems to us divorced from common sense or ordinary experience, but the conclusion that one may reach in this controversy can make or mar the entire corpus of a system of thought as orthodox as the Pūrva Mīmāṃsā.

Fourthly, when we come to the category of disputation (*tarka*), we have an even more explicit indication of the Nyāya concept of proof. In the first place, unlike the category of *avayava*, it does not proceed on the basis vouched for by the pramāṇas. The category begins to operate with an object about which the philosopher has doubt, but the object does not command the initial certitude of objects which are subjected to the rigorous procedure of proof, i.e., the *avayava*. It is therefore quite reasonable to conclude that what the category of disputation yields is not knowledge but mere opinion; one could even go as far as to say that it yields a proposition having a high degree of credibility.

The second aspect of this category is its exclusive domain of operation: it is concerned with causality. When the Naiyāyika is confronted with two opposite views about the nature of an object — in the light of what is said above these views must be treated as hypotheses — he wishes to settle the conflict by appeal to a specific cause which can corroborate one of the two hypotheses and reject the other. The Naiyāyika has used the category to establish the cause of a specific phenomenon like the *saṃsāra*, in which he is deeply interested. It is true that the argument given by the Naiyāyika to illustrate the operation of the category has the logical flavour of a *reductio ad absurdum:* we assume that a proposition is true in order to show that its truth would imply a proposition to be true which is known to be false; from which it would follow that the proposition assumed to be true is false. But the way the Naiyāyika has used this category clearly shows that his main interest lies in the elimination of possible causes but one, by showing that the various alternatives would lead to impossible consequences. The significance of this category in the Nyāya system lies not in its logical character but in the deliberate effort to instal a current opinion, which is of greater social than logical interest, in the portrait of the universe. Categories of this kind can be truly described as 'cultural posits'.[26]

Last but not least, there is the category of ascertainment (*nirṇaya*). Like the category of disputation, this category is not rooted in the pramāṇas: it does not begin with the initial certitude guaranteed by the pramāṇas and cannot therefore yield any certitude through its operation. This is quite evident from the fact that its domain of operation consists of objects which are subject to disputation. When what is disputed is ascertained, what we obtain is not knowledge but opinion thoroughly investigated and strengthened. Since the objects disputed and ascertained are not intended to be subjected to rigorous proof, i.e., the *avayava,* they cannot be said to be even proved according to the standards of the Naiyāyika. To say that these categories assist the pramāṇas does not add to the logical or epistemological merits of the pramāṇas.

The function of this categorical framework can best be described as psychological. The doubt as visualized by Gautama has not only to be resolved but the audience is to be thoroughly convinced about the outcome. The entire process is intended to induce a firm conviction in the minds of men that what they had heard from their masters must be irrevocably fixed in their minds. What the Indian philosopher asks of his readers from his logic or theory of knowledge is not so much rational assent based on canons of evidence but a total and final commitment. From those who have the privilege of being educated by him he demands not only personal loyalty and acceptance but also a solemn promise to propagate the truth. One of the aims of Gautama is to produce the weapons of philosophical warfare for the wholesale demolition of heresy. From the ignorant and illiterate public the philosopher demands nothing more than appropriate behaviour which will show conformity both in thought and action. As Vātsyāyana repeatedly emphasizes, the pramāṇas are meant to regulate the lives of men and animals; without such regulation the system of society as he knew it would end in chaos and disaster. The pramāṇas and the logic of proof are instruments of this vast intellectual and social enterprise.

As already mentioned, the *avayava* is the better known of the aspects of Gautama's concept of proof. In order to determine the precise character of the proof it is necessary to take into account the following features of the Nyāya discussion of the subject.

The first thing to note is that according to the Naiyāyika the four pramāṇas recognized by him are not only logically prior to the *avayavas* but the *avayavas* are in fact the explication of the results of the different pramāṇas. This means that what is stated in each of the five *avayavas* is known to be true or certain. The five *avayavas* collectively constitute a statement (*vākya*) and the statement refers to a single object. This is exactly the counterpart of the doctrine which is central to the Nyāya theory of cognition, the convergence of pramāṇas on a single object.

This raises the question as to why what is known to be true or certain should be subjected to the logical torture of proof. In fact the Buddhist has raised this precise question in a manner which puts the Naiyāyika on the horns of a dilemma.[27] Apart from the purely linguistic aspects of the controversy, the Buddhist question is: if knowledge and proof are logically equivalent, it is absurd to say that one should be supplemented by the other; but if they are not, the so-called knowledge can be regarded as nothing better than mere opinion or unestablished belief. This objection is aimed at both the doctrine of pramāṇas and more importantly, at scripture. The Naiyāyika cannot easily answer this objection for he is not only committed to the doctrine of the four pramāṇas but also to the view that in so far as the proof is concerned with the *siddhānta*, what is expected of the proof has already been accomplished by the pramāṇas and this accomplishment has the imprimatur of an *āgama* (scripture).

The most dramatic point of this controversy is about the nature of the first *avayava*, the proposition. If the proposition is not only known to be true or certain with the help of the pramāṇas but also incorporated as a *siddhānta* in the *āgama*, how can the Naiyāyika offer it for further scrutiny ? That there are different types of *siddhānta* is merely a diversionary move. Even the question as to whether it is the object to be proved or the property of the object to be proved or the object as qualified by the property to be proved is primarily an ontological and not a logical question. According to the Naiyāyika, if there is a substance, it must have a property and if there is a property it must be the property of a substance: these are logically equivalent propositions. For the Buddhist there is no enduring entity and he is therefore primarily interested in pinning down the Naiyāyika to the admission that in the doctrine of proof one must be concerned with the properties only.

By rejecting the five of the ten members of the ancient reasoning the Naiyāyika has destroyed the possibility of defending his theory with psychological, semantic or linguistic arguments. The only answer that is open to him—and this is what seems to be the upshot of the debate—is that it so happens that there are conflicting views on identical subjects. Each claims to be established by a set of pramāṇas recognized by its protagonist and to have the sanction of his canon. Two such conflicting views cannot be said to be true and this dispute is therefore beyond the reach of formal logic. The formal logic of any kind can only tell us that if two propositions are contradictory, one must be true and the other false and both cannot be true together. Moreover, both the protagonists of the two conflicting views have no doubt in their mind about the truth of their positions for both are bound by their doctrinal commitments.

Thus there is a complete deadlock in the philosophical discourse. There are two possible solutions. One is to throw open the views of the philosophers to a public scrutiny and let them decide. But this will be merely passing the buck. If the public is to decide upon the rival claims on any reasonable grounds, it will need an organon for its use. Hence the only course left open is to appeal to facts. Such a course can satisfy the *amour propre* of both the committed protagonists. Both claim to be concerned with questions of fact and in all fairness, questions of fact must be settled by ordinary canons of evidence.

At this stage, if there had been a body of empirical knowledge in the form of natural and social sciences, their compulsion would have transferred the controversy from the metaphysical heights to the scrutiny by proper standards of evidence. But then philosophy would have been assimilated to the natural and social sciences. And in fact it would seem as though when Gautama was elevating the physician to the highest status, he was planning to create a science out of philosophy. This is a dream which many modern philosophers have had, partly because they have been impressed by the prestige, results and methodology of modern science and partly because they have been distressed by the poor results achieved by the philosophers over the centuries and even more by the lack of consensus on the nature, scope and method of their study. Even if Gautama had cherished such a dream the climate for its fulfilment was not there. The only observational science which the Indians had widely cultivated, Āyurveda, was mixed up with the Vedic heritage and tied to the sense of taste which had very limited possibilities in the exploration of the world.

What actually happened was that the concept of proof which is meant to be empirical was a still-born child. The philosophers returned to their old habit and instead of seeking fresh evidence or applying any rigorous canons of evidence converted the concept of proof into a pale imitation of what they had done with the help of the pramāṇas and scriptural authority. This of course prevented the refinement of the pramāṇas themselves, and certainly any viable relationship between the pramāṇas and the world. India was big enough to provide an opportunity for philosophising in many ways and if only philosophers kept up a gentleman's agreement to let the sleeping dogs lie undisturbed, they would not only be able to play the game according to certain rules but also find a sufficient clientèle which would give them sustenance as well as reverence. Thus the theory of proof became the theory of communication in two senses: it established reasonable communication between the contending philosophers and between the philosophers and the public. On the intellectual plane this link between the philosopher and the public was forged by the Epics, the *Purāṇas*, the *Dharmaśāstras*, etc. Incidentally, this is the essence of the classical notion of live and let live in the ancient intellectual establishment.

In view of the close connection between the pramāṇas and the *avayavas* — in fact one could say that they are logically equivalent — it is not surprising that the nub of the proof lies in the hetu and the example. In the formulation of the proof the Naiyāyika has separated the proposition from the hetu but in fact the probandum and the hetu are meant to be invariably concomitant. This invariable concomitance is causal. In doing so the Naiyāyika has severed the cause from the effect. In the third member, the example, the invariable concomitance is fully expressed but the concomitance is highlighted and the object in which the concomitance is said to be found is tacked on to this concomitance. But what is explicitly asserted is that there must be similarity or dissimilarity between the hetu and the homogeneous or heterogeneous example. This is indeed an odd way of comparison. Either we should say that two instances are similar or dissimilar in a particular respect, that is, in respect of invariable concomitance or causal relation, or the concomitance or causal relation is similar or dissimilar (hetu is present or absent) in two instances. The Naiyāyika is always expressing himself in the object language and this kind of clarity in expressing relations of concomitance cannot be expected. In the fourth *avayava* again, it is because of this object language we are told 'this is so' or 'this is not so'. What is really intended is to emphasize that there is a causal relation present because it is either invariably present in a positive instance or invariably absent in a negative instance. The fifth *avayava* merely repeats the proposition, though the procedure is said to increase our confidence in the certitude of the proposition on account of its having been subjected to the intermediate steps.

In this context we must also remember the psychological approach of the Naiyāyika to the problem of inference. He believes that in an inference we first perceive the concomitance of cause and effect and then remember it when we perceive one of the pair which is said to be concomitant. There the psychological process begins with perception, passes through memory and again ends with perception of the object presented in the example. When the procedure is completed we are said to have the requisite inferential cognition. In the concept of proof the account of this process is not given as a temporal process but as a finished product. In this sense it is a logical explanation. What is already known by this process is first announced but the announcement is left incomplete; it should really be restated as the connection of the probandum with the hetu in a positive instance or the absence of the connection with the probandum in a negative instance. On the basis of the presence or absence of the connection as exemplified in the instances we can assert that the connection has been proved. Since the Naiyāyika is preoccupied with positive confirmation and does not even contemplate the possibility of disconfirmation, I have confined the formulation to confirmation procedure, but there is no logical reason why it should be so restricted. If this restriction is removed, the position can be even clearer. We can then begin with an hypothesis, draw certain consequences from it and indicate the evidence for confirmation or disconfirmation. In fact the Naiyāyika should really have no objection to treating his proposition as hypothesis. After all, on the present interpretation even though he may be absolutely convinced about its truth, he is placing it before the public for scrutiny. There is no reason why we should only nod to the Naiyāyika's proposition and not withhold our assent if he has not proved his case. We can still allow the Naiyāyika the freedom to cite his facts from whatever source he might select, provided he does not take away our freedom to assent or dissent from his hypothesis or facts. This will only enhance the credibility of the Nyāya and induce a more solid approval of it.

Whatever metaphysical views the Indian philosophers held about causation, there is no doubt that this principle was the pivot of their conceptual framework. And the Naiyāyika is no exception. But his main interest is to establish specific individual causal connections. In this respect he often speaks in the idiom of a modern professional scientist. He is against unrestricted generalizations which are not warranted by empirical facts. But his notion of generalization is largely based on the grammatical and religious notion of rule (*niyama*). In the former sense it is cited to explain a particular case; in the latter it is meant to regulate one's conduct. In either case it means to the philosopher something like a constricting bow. Moreover, while he does believe in what can loosely be called causation in the sphere of ethics, he is most anxious to ensure that every individual as an individual reaps the entire harvest of his deeds. In a sense this is a generalization about the individual's life, past, present and future. But even here he wants to provide for a loophole so that his own prescription for the termination of *saṃsāra* is not contaminated by any doubt about its efficacy. Moreover, he is interested in the causation of an individual's psychosomatic equipment. Last but not least, he has to provide for two different classes of people, the Yogin and the laity. This kind of approach to causation creates a good many gaps in the causal framework.

Such a notion of causation is far too anthropomorphic to allow for its refinements into the kind of explanation which a scientist gives for events in nature or society. Moreover, the notion of causation is deeply embedded in what is known as the material cause. While the important aspect of causal relation is temporal succession the concentration on the material cause is liable to reduce causation to one of co-existence. That is why the notion of invariable concomitance in the Nyāya system partakes of the character of both succession and coexistence depending upon the context. This is also inherent in the notion of substance and property and what is known as *sāmānādhikaraṇya* (community of locus). A substance is a locus of properties and while the substance continues its properties change. But the properties are the properties of substance and therefore the notion of change fades away in subsistence in a locus (*adhikaraṇa*). According to the Naiyāyika, substance and its property or relation and the universals are all objective and are parts of the universe. In a broad sense one could call them 'natural kinds' in Mill's sense. 'Among the uniformities of coexistence which exist in nature, may hence be numbered all the properties of Kinds. The whole of these, however, are not independent of causation, but only a portion of them. Some are ultimate properties, others derivative; of some no cause can be assigned, but others are manifestly dependent on causes.'[28] He also observes: '... there must be one class of coexistences which cannot depend on causation; the coexistences between the ultimate properties of things — those properties which are the causes of all phenomena, but are not themselves caused by any phenomenon, and a cause for which could only be sought by ascending to the origin of all things. Yet among these ultimate properties there are not only coexistences, but uniformities of coexistence. General propositions may be, and are, formed, which assert that whenever certain properties are found, certain others are found along with them. We perceive an object; say, for instance, water. We recognise it to be water, of course by certain of its properties. Having recognized it, we are able to affirm of its innumerable other properties; which we could not do unless it were a general truth, a law or uniformity in nature, that the set of properties by which we identify the substance as water, always have those other properties conjoined with them.'[29]

Even without the scientific background of Mill, it seems the Naiyāyika was much closer to Mill's position than one might suspect. The discussion as to how to identify an object by a distinguishing property in the context of doubt and the kind of example which is required to support a valid hetu in the Nyāya proof reminds us forcibly of Mill's formulation of inductive inference. The Naiyāyika is concerned with invariable concomitance but concomitance both in succession and coexistence. The example which renders the hetu valid is an example of homogeneous or heterogeneous class. An example is an example because it belongs to such a class. The inference that is drawn is explicitly based on the recognition of resemblances. In an inductive inference both the enumeration of instances and the recognition of important resemblances are important. And this is what is contemplated in the Nyāya proof.

It is unfortunate that the Naiyāyika should have underestimated the importance of the number of hetus or examples. If a number of hetus can be entertained, there is room for examining alternative hypotheses. Similarly, if a number of examples is allowed, the range of observation would have increased. In inference as a pramāṇa the Naiyāyika seems to be content with an example and this is reflected in the proof. Perhaps, if the Naiyāyika had recognized the importance of the variety of examples, he would have hit upon the importance of a counter-example. In the case of the disputation category there is something in the nature of counter-example but it is used only to prove that if the counter-example is true we find ourselves in a false position. It is a serious omission that a genuine counter-example is neither searched for nor accepted; in fact, it is explained away. In the long run this must have created a bias in favour of merely finding favourable evidence for whatever is believed. In this connection it is not out of place to mention that this attitude of the Naiyāyika is diametrically opposed to their general acceptance of cumulative evidence or convergence of the pramāṇas on a single object.

Mill was interested in the social sciences and in modern times he was really the first to have formulated in a systematic manner the methods for causal determination as 'methods of proof'. His account has been criticised by modern writers on various grounds but this need not concern us here. What is important is how far the Nyāya concept of proof can be regarded as essentially inductive in character.

Scientific analysis of a causal situation is really based upon two principles: (1) Nothing is the cause of an effect which is absent when the effect occurs; (2) Nothing is the cause of a given effect which is present when the effect fails to occur. Accordingly, when we seek for the cause of an event or occurrence, we look for cases where the causal factor concerned is present and cases where it is absent. The analysis may involve actual physical separation or isolation only in thought.

The two principles mentioned above are the basis of the rules which Mill lays down for investigation: (1) compare different instances in which the event or phenomenon under investigation occurs; (2) compare instances in which the event or phenomenon occurs with instances in other respects similar in which it does not occur. From these two principles Mill formulates his four methods. Each method is formulated hypothetically in what he calls a 'canon'. The Naiyāyika was no natural scientist and though he was interested in nature, man and society, he was not a social scientist either. Even when the Naiyāyika is said to have been influenced by the Āyurveda, he has no obvious scientific interest in that science. He had really no notion of experiment, though in his discussion of doubt and perception he seems to be aware of some of the problems of observation. He was not therefore aware of the problems of physical isolation in any profound sense but he was analytic enough to have realized the importance of isolation in thought. He believed in particulars and their actual relations. Above all, as we have seen, he was committed to causation.

In view of these general observations it is worth while comparing the Naiyāyika concept of proof to Mill's methods.

According to Gautama the hetu is the means for proving what

is to be proved on the basis of homogeneity or of heterogeneity of the example; and the example is that familiar instance which, on account of its similarity with the probandum, is endowed with the property of that probandum or the example is that familiar instance which, on account of its dissimilarity from the probandum, is not endowed with the property of the probandum.

Let us compare this statement of Gautama with that of Mill regarding the first three methods.

1. The Method of Agreement.

Canon: *'If two or more instances of the phenomenon under investigation have only one circumstance in common, the circumstance in which alone all the instances agree, is the cause (or effect) of the given phenomenon.'*[30]

2. The Method of Difference.

Canon : *'If an instance in which the phenomenon under investigation occurs, and an instance in which it does not occur, have every circumstance in common save one, that one occurring only in the former; the circumstance in which alone the two instances differ, is the effect, or the cause, or an indispensible part of the cause, of the phenomenon.'*[31]

3. The Indirect or Joint Method of Agreement and Difference.

Canon : *'If two or more instances in which the phenomenon occurs have only one circumstance in common, while two or more instances in which it does not occur have nothing in common save the absence of that circumstance; the circumstance in which alone the two sets of instances differ, is the effect, or the cause, or an indispensible part of the cause, of the phenomenon.'*[32]

4. The Method of Concomitant Variations.

Canon : *'Whatever phenomenon varies in any manner whenever another phenomenon varies in some particular manner, is either a cause or an effect of that phenomenon, or is connected with it through some fact of causation.'*[33]

Let us compare this with Gautama's argument in connection with *sandhi*.

According to Gautama the following argument is not right: If phonemes (*varṇas*) were subject to modification an increase in the original would be attended by a corresponding increase in the modification.

According to some philosophers there is no evidence for this argument because modification is found to be less than, equal to, or greater than the original. Gautama disagrees with these philosophers and says that the modification may undergo variations corresponding to the variations in the original but this has nothing to do with the grammatical argument about the modification or substitution in *sandhi*.[34]

5. The Method Residues.

Canon: '*Subduct from any phenomenon such part as is known by previous inductions to be the effect of certain antecedents, and the residue of the phenomenon is the effect of the remaining antecedents.*'[35]

Let us compare this statement with the following Nyāya view of the *śeṣavat* kind of inference.

Gautama has not defined the three kinds of inference he has in view.

According to Vātsyāyana one of these '*śeṣavat*' means *pariśeṣa* (residue). With regard to an object some of the possible properties are denied; this denial does not apply to the other possible properties; we have then the inferential cognition of those that remain. This is the *śeṣavat* inference. For example, with regard to sound, we know that it is an entity and that it is non-eternal. Further, these two properties, i.e. being an entity and being non-eternal, are known to be common to substances, qualities and actions only, and these two properties of sound distinguish sound from the other categories of universal, individuality and inherence (all of which are entities and eternal). In view of this we have a doubt as to whether sound is a substance, a quality or an action. We resolve this doubt as follows:

(a) Sound cannot be a substance, because it inheres in a single substance (i.e. ākāśa). (This hetu is based on the view: There is no substance which inheres in one substance only; all substances either inhere in more than one substance, e.g. the jar, or do not inhere in any substance, e.g. the atom.)

(b) Sound is not an action, because it is the cause (or originator) of another sound. (Sound produces something that is of its own kind; action never produces an effect of its own kind, i.e. another action.)

Having thus eliminated substance and action, what remains is quality. It is therefore concluded that sound must have the character of quality (*guṇatva*) i.e. it is a quality.

Amongst the arguments in support of *buddhi* as a property of the self Gautama refers to *'pariśeṣa'*. He has not defined this term, as he has not defined the *śeṣavat* inference. Vātsyāyana has explained this argument as follows:

The term *'pariśeṣa'* means: when something is denied and there is no possibility of its being elsewhere, we have a definite cognition of what remains (*pariśeṣo nāma prasaktapratiṣedhe anyatrāprasaṅgāc chiṣyamāṇe sampratyayaḥ*).

The question under investigation is: Cognition is a property of the self (*ātmaguṇo jñānam*). It cannot be a property of the material elements, the sense-organs and the mind (*manas*). There is no other substance of which it can be a property. What remains is the self. Therefore cognition is the property of the self (or, as it is put by the commentator, cognition is therefore cognized as the property of the self).

The commentator further adds that the hetus which Gautama has given elsewhere also make the *pariśeṣa* known and also leads to the proving of what was intended to be proved and to cognition (as the property of the self).[36]

According to Mill, even though the Method of Residues is not independent of deduction, like his other methods it also requires specific experience; it may therefore be regarded as a method of direct observation and experiment. He is of the view that this method with all its limitations is 'one of the most important among our instruments of discovery. Of all the methods of investigating laws of nature, this is the most fertile in unexpected results; often informing us of sequences in which neither the cause nor the effect were sufficiently conspicuous to attract of themselves the attention of observers.'[37] If we substitute the objects and laws which the scientist discovers in nature, then it will be obvious that the Naiyāyika has used his method to build up his ontology and causal connections.

As already mentioned, the Nyāya inference depends upon instances and resemblances. The Naiyāyika undoubtedly knew what number or quantity meant, but in the absence of interest in or knowledge of mathematics or experimental science, such problems did not seem to have occurred to the Naiyāyika. And yet he had in the etymology of the pramāṇa itself a sufficient pointer to the importance of measurement. Similarly, he had considered the pramāṇa of inclusion (*saṃbhava*) and also used the analogy of the weighing balance. But the standard he was interested in was a standard for the measurement of cognitive occurrences. Obviously, such occurrences cannot yield to quantitative application and what was gained for the theory of knowledge was lost for quantitative sciences.

Even the pramāṇa of analogy (*upamāna*) — one of the recognized four pramāṇas and reflected in the fourth *avayava* of proof — has received scant attention either as a pramāṇa or as an *avayava*. For instance, in answer to the objection that partial, considerable or complete similarity cannot yield a valid cognition, all that Gautama says is that the pramāṇa of analogy does not operate through varying degrees of similarity but from a well-known similarity capable of proving the probandum.[38] The commentators do not throw any further light on the matter. The one point that they seem to make is that if two things resemble in every respect, there would be no analogy at all. This is an important problem which is known as the 'Identity of Indiscernibles'[39] but the Naiyāyika has not examined this logical problem nor has he realized the nature of resemblance that is required in a sound analogy. It is not surprising, therefore, that the philosophers are impressed by very weak analogies.[40] Incidentally, it is interesting to note that while rejecting the principle of varying degrees of similarity the Naiyāyika is not averse to using the principle of concomitant variations in another context. The non-recognition of a principle does not bind the author not to use it when it is expedient.

As in the case of the first *avayava*, the Naiyāyika and his opponents are occupied with questions of lesser importance. According to the official view what is well known (*prasiddha*) means that both the expert and the laymen are willing to accept it as relevant to the proposed proof of a proposition. This notion is really not capable of being made precise and in a society where only a few have an access to formal education, this provision gives a *carte blanche* to the philosopher to use whatever examples he may like, without any check. For instance, the kind of paradigms which are used to create an imposing edifice of metaphysics or ethics seems often so remote from what is sought to be proved. The fire and smoke in the kitchen, the proverbial lamp and its capacity, or the seed and the plant are the stock-in-trade of the philosopher.

Since it seems that the general stock of empirical knowledge of nature or society remained much the same, the same examples keep on repeating, though they are used for different purposes by different authors at different times. What is well known can thus be nothing more than what the philosopher declares to be so. And the philosopher's magnanimous gesture of an honoured place for the populace in the heart of the proof does not bring the experience of ordinary people to bear on the proof itself, nor does it help the populace in knowing what the philosopher is doing in its name. If the smoke and fire argument were accompanied with some thought of extinguishing the fire — and this is reasonable to expect from the doctrine of the effectiveness of the pramāṇas — the populace would have honoured the philosopher as the creator of a modern fire-brigade.

Another problem which needed consideration was the exact significance of the knowledge which is said to be obtained by various pramāṇas or what the proof actually contributed to this knowledge. The Naiyāyikas have used a variety of terms like *upapatti, saṃbhava, yukta* and *siddha.* While it is rightly emphasized that the argument must be free from the recognized fallacies of the hetu, this still leaves open the question of the degree of credibility which should be attached to the outcome of various pramāṇas or even of the proof itself. If the doctrine of cumulative evidence is properly understood, it would need something in the nature of the theory of probability for all empirical investigation. This is all the more necessary in the Nyāya system where the incorrigible character of an intuitive experience is combined with ordinary perceptual evidence as the hallmark of knowledge or certainty. It seems that the kind of terms used in different contexts is capable of such construction. The term *siddha* or *upapatti* could be distinguished from the other terms; the former seems equivalent to certainty or conclusive proof and the latter to varying degrees of certainty or, more precisely, the varying degrees of probability.[41] The whole question of revising the terminology in a philosophical discourse required serious consideration, but it seems as though the sanctity of the original text and its language must have been a bar to such an enterprise.

All along I have argued that the Nyāya proof or inference is basically inductive in character. Whether or not inductive inference should be recognized in a system of logic is a controversial question. Similarly, what relation or relations should hold between propositions so as to constitute deductive inference is a complex question discussed by modern mathematicians and logicians. According to Russell the relation in virtue of which it is possible for us validly to infer is 'material implication'[42] while Moore considers the relation of entailment to be essential for deductive inference.[43] For our purpose what is important is that in such inference we should be able to say 'p implies q'.

In trying to determine the character of the Nyāya proof the first thing to note is that the Naiyāyika is not considering any formal relation of implication or entailment between propositions. Although we have translated *'pratijñā'* as 'proposition', it is evident that the logic of propositions is not what Gautama had in view. The Nyāya proposition is not a premise from which a conclusion is derived, for the proposition and the conclusion are identical. As previously indicated, if we consider what is really the import of the first *avayava,* the proposition, and the second, the hetu, or the third *avayava,* the example, they state a causal connection and in the fourth *avayava* this connection is confirmed. It is not easy to characterize this whole process as one of implication or entailment. Hence it is reasonable to characterize the Nyāya doctrine of *avayavas* as one of proof or inductive inference. This is in general agreement with the overall position of the Naiyāyika on the various themes which he has discussed.

In spite of the limitations of the intellectual and social environment in which the Nyāya system grew up there is no doubt that Gautama's contribution to logic and epistemology is outstanding. He was the first to formulate a formal theory of proof in a systematic manner and his followers made their own contribution to the theory. Gautama evolved a system which would fit with the requirements of scientific investigation but without the background of science or the advantage of Aristotelian legacy. To sum up, Gautama was an Indian version of J.S. Mill. Like Aristotle, Gautama dominated subsequent developments and he has therefore the same place in the history of Indian philosophy.[44]

The Nyāya system is often described not only as *'pramāṇa-śāstra'* but also as *'hetuvidyā'*. Both descriptions are fully justified. The character of the Nyāya proof is essentially one of a search for valid hetu. The valid hetu is primarily a genuine cause. This cause may be physical, psychological or social, but it is the actual or real cause which the Naiyāyika seeks to discover and having discovered, to prove it to the satisfaction of his contemporary philosophers. The overwhelming impression one gathers from the Nyāya discussion of valid and invalid hetus is that the term 'hetu' for the Naiyāyika denotes a natural cause rather than a logical reason or ground. The Nyāya procedure of proof is the procedure of confirmation or verification. Of course, a hetu is accepted or rejected according to the current conventions. Such conventions may be concerned with facts or doctrines. These reflect the contemporary consensus in the philosophical establishment.

What the Naiyāyikas have given us is a conceptual framework for much of Indian thought. It has many features which may seem strange to us. But if we treat this framework as a creation of a community with certain formal education, attitudes, beliefs and conventions, we can appreciate its true significance not only for the ancient Indian thought but also for modern India. In recent years we have gone through an agonizing reappraisal of our Indian ancient heritage and of Western Thought and whatever may be said by the orthodox revivalists, things can never be the same in India again.

The kind of approach which is being suggested for the study of the Nyāya system can be compared to the attitude which some of the modern thinkers are adopting towards ontological speculations and scientific explanation. If we could imagine ourselves living in a world based on our experience derived from only one of our senses, say hearing, our auditory universe and our conceptual framework would be different from the one which is largely based on sight, touch and hearing. Such an auditory world, says Strawson, would be a 'No-Space world' though he makes it quite clear that the idea of a purely auditory world is the only possible model for a 'No-Space world'.[45] The Indian philosopher lived primarily in such an auditory world. His sources of knowledge and communication were based on hearing. But the Naiyāyika was convinced that this is the world he had discovered and was real. To this world he added the sense-experience of taste largely based on the current medical science. Between these two sources of his experience, one direct and another indirect, the philosopher created a conceptual framework which seemed to be adequate to his needs.

Another well-known thinker, Quine, has argued that the kind of conceptual framework which we accept depends upon our interests and purposes. According to him we have two competing conceptual schemes: one phenomenalistic and another physicalistic. Each has its advantages; each has its special simplicity. Each deserves to be developed. 'Let us by all means see,' says the philosopher, 'how much of the physicalistic conceptual scheme can be reduced to a phenomenalistic one; still, physics also naturally demands pursuing, irreducible *in toto* though it be. Let us see how, or to what degree, natural science may be rendered independent of platonistic mathematics; but let us also pursue mathematics and delve into its platonistic foundations.'[46] This still leaves the question open of what ontology to adopt and the 'obvious counsel is tolerance and an experimental spirit.'[47]

As is well known, Thomas S. Kuhn and Sir Karl Popper hold different views regarding science and scientific explanation. I have had occasion to refer to the views of Popper. In the present context I would like briefly to refer to the views of Kuhn which are relevant to the approach I have suggested before: 'A scientific community consists,' says the author, 'on this view of the practitioners of a scientific speciality. To an extent unparalleled in most other fields, they have undergone similar educations and professional initiations; in the process they have absorbed the same technical literature and drawn many of the same lessons from it.'[48] 'A paradigm is what the members of a scientific community share,' says the philosopher, 'and, conversely, a scientific community consists of men who share a paradigm'[49] This definition is undoubtedly circular but for that reason it is not, says the philosopher, a case of vicious circularity. He defines the paradigm in two ways: 'On the one hand, it stands for the entire constellation of beliefs, values, techniques, and so on shared by the members of a given community. On the other hand, it denotes one sort of element in that constellation, the concrete puzzle-solutions which, employed as models or examples, can replace explicit rules as a basis for the solution of the remaining puzzles of normal science.'[50]

In a recent symposium on *Criticism and Growth of Knowledge* Kuhn clarified his position in the light of the criticism levelled against his views as given in his book *The Structure of Scientific*

Revolutions (the extract cited above is from this book) as follows:

In a new version of his *Scientific Revolutions* the philosopher would open with 'a discussion of community structure. Having isolated an individual specialists' group, I would next ask what its members shared that enabled them to solve puzzles and that accounted for their relative unanimity in problem-choice and in the evaluation of problem-solutions. One answer which my book licenses to that question is 'a paradigm' or 'a set of paradigms'. (This is Miss Masterman's sociological sense of the term.) For it I should now like some other phrase, perhaps 'disciplinary matrix' : 'disciplinary', because it is common to the practitioners of a specified discipline; 'matrix', because it consists of ordered elements which require individual specification. All of the objects of commitment described in my book as paradigms, parts of paradigms, or paradigmatic would find a place in the disciplinary matrix, but they would not be lumped together as paradigms, individually or collectively. Among them would be: shared symbolic generalizations, like '$f=ma$', or 'elements combine in constant proportion by weight'; shared models, whether metaphysical, like atomism, or heuristic, like the hydrodynamic model of the electrical circuit; shared values, like the emphasis on accuracy of prediction, discussed above; and other elements of the sort. Among the latter I would particularly emphasize concrete problem solutions, the sorts of standard examples of solved problems which scientists encounter first in student laboratories, in the problems at the ends of chapters in science texts, and on examinations. If I could, I would call these problem-solutions paradigms, for they are what led me to the choice of the term in the first place. Having lost control of the word, however, I shall henceforth describe them as exemplars.'[51]

As is well known, the Indian philosopher was preoccupied with the problem of suffering, its identification with *saṃsāra,* the search for a remedy which would eliminate suffering through the elimination of *saṃsāra,* salvation, and a theory of knowledge and proof adequate for the solution of these problems. He had developed a reverential pattern of authority and a distinctive mode of life. Last but not least, he remained convinced that the essence of morality was the preservation of the kind of society which he knew best, though he preferred to believe that he had actually and irrevocably opted out of the society to which he always returned as a saviour if not a participant. It therefore seems to me that the kind of approach which these philosophers have developed for different purposes could profitably be used, with suitable modifications, in the study of Indian thought.

According to the pattern of exposition I have adopted in this book, I have grouped together the categories of discussion (*vāda*), rejoinder (*jalpa*), cavil (*vitaṇḍā*), — these three have been put under the general heading of discourse (*kathā*) — quibble (*chala*), legitimate objection (*jāti*) and deficiency (*nigrahasthāna*) as well as the doctrines of other philosophers (*prāvāduka*) refuted by Gautama, under the general heading of technique of refutation. Although the category of the fallacy of the hetu (*hetvābhāsa*) was dealt with in connection with the Nyāya concept of proof, Gautama has himself included this category as one of the deficiencies; it is obviously involved in the Nyāya technique of refutation. What is somewhat odd in Gautama's list of the categories is that while the author is prepared to give the category status to the fallacy of the hetu and even to the not very respectable tricks of discussion, he has not accorded this honour to misapprehension (*mithyājñāna*). And yet, if the commentators are to be believed, the entire business of involvement in *saṃsāra* and liberation rests on the notion of misapprehension. Gautama has specifically mentioned this notion only once, and that too in his opening statement on the successive annihilation of the elements involved in *saṃsāra*. Other references to wrong apprehension (*mithyopalabdhi*) are in the context of the defence of the pramāṇas and of what must be treated as questions connected with veridical and erroneous perception.[52] In fact, the entire notion of misapprehension has to be collected from the various stray references in the discussion of the Naiyāyikas.

Another question of a somewhat general character is the place of the fifth book of the *Nyāya Sūtra*. It has been argued that this book is in the nature of interpolation. But what is important is that neither Vātsyāyana nor Uddyotakara refused to acknowledge these as part of the *Nyāya Sūtra*, though the latter does not seem to be much interested in these topics. It is therefore reasonable to assume that in their times the *Nyāya Sūtra* was regarded as being more or less in the form in which we have it now. Moreover, the technique of refutation is based upon the categories recognized by Gautama in his opening aphorism.

Besides, Gautama states explicitly at the end of the fourth book that rejoinder and cavil are essential for the protection of what has been determined as the true nature of things (*tattvādhyavasāyasaṃrakṣaṇa*). The seed that has been planted has to be protected from the thorny boughs. This is exactly what Uddyotakara proposes to do at a later stage, though his attack is directed against different targets. The Nyāya system is not only an embodiment of truth but also a technique of its defence. And as in war so in philosophy, the best defence is often the offensive against the enemy. Neither the Western nor the Indian philosophy can tolerate peaceful coexistence of truth and untruth.

'A pattern of argument which is proper and even proprietary to philosophy,' says Gilbert Ryle, 'is the *reductio ad absurdum.* This argument moves by extracting contradictions or logical paradoxes from its material.'[53] 'On first consideration it will seem,' continues the philosopher, that such arguments 'can have only a destructive effect. They may be effective in demolishing silly theories and thus possess, besides the pleasing property of defeating opponents, the useful one of clearing the site for subsequent constructive theory. But it will be felt that no demolition can result in the erection of a new dwelling. I hope to disarm any such objection by showing that (to use another metaphor) *reductio ad absurdum* arguments are neither more nor less nihilist than are threshing operations. Or, to change the picture again, the position will be maintained that philosophical arguments of the type described above have something in common with the destruction-tests by which engineers discover the strength of materials. Certainly engineers stretch, twist, compress, and batter bits of metal until they collapse, but it is just by such tests that they determine the strains which the metal will withstand. In somewhat the same way, philosophical arguments bring out the logical powers of the ideas under investigation, by fixing the precise forms of logical mishandling under which they refuse to work.'[54]

Every philosopher imagines that this is what he does in his occupation and Indian philosophers are no exception to this general practice. If we could find a body of philosophers without any initial commitment to any dogma or doctrine who would sit in judgment on what are known as *pūrvapakṣa* and *uttarapakṣa* (i.e., view and counter-view), then it would be possible for us to determine what was demolished and what was constructed by our philosophers. In the Nyāya system the technique of refutation is primarily aimed at the opponents of the official view and to that extent its scope is limited. The concept of the disputation category, to which reference has already been made in the context of proof, may seem to be an exception, but in the context in which Vātsyāyana and Uddyotakara have used it, it seems to be designed as a weapon against the opponents of the karma and *saṃsāra* theory. Refutation is an essential part of the philosopher's occupation, and to reject this part of the *Nyāya Sūtra* is to mutilate his treatise and categorical framework. Gautama and his followers are pledged to defend *siddhānta* and the technique of refutation is an essential part of its defence. The path of the *siddhānta* is strewn with thorns and the philosophers wish to remove them so that the followers of the system have no difficulty in following the path cleared by the philosophers.

In order to judge the merits of Gautama's technique it is first necessary to look at the problems or tasks he had set for himself. These are stupendous and a philosopher of lesser ability or ambition would have left them alone. The technique that Gautama has actually evolved is meant to demolish the scriptural, ontological, epistemological and logical structure of the systems of all his opponents. This technique is basically logical in character because it is intended to demolish every other possible doctrine, provided, of course, the fundamental premises of these doctrines are the same or shown to be the same by the Naiyāyika.

The most difficult and delicate problem for Gautama is: how to maintain the principle of authority in philosophical discourse and yet to demonstrate that the doctrines of all his opponents are erroneous in spite of the authority they all claimed to possess. At an elementary level it is of course not difficult to dispose of this question: one could say that one's own authority alone was totally and absolutely right and that everyone else's totally and absolutely wrong. But this would invite a simple rebuff: the opponents, singly or collectively, could retort that their own authority is totally and absolutely right. This leads to a total deadlock; the philosophical game cannot even start. Moreover, if Gautama was the sole representative of a particular authority, his task would have been simpler. Unfortunately, he had to contend not only with several representatives of what was regarded as a single authority — generally known under the rubric of the Vedic authority — but also divergent interpretations each of which was said to be authoritative. Even more serious was the nature of authority. Every contestant in the field claimed that his authority was based on direct experience. That they differed about the nature or upshot of this experience makes no logical difference: all contestants were empiricists of one sort or another. And as we have seen, the foundation of the Nyāya system is empiricism. To add to the complexity of his task, he had virtually set himself or his *Nyāya Sūtra* as an authority: he had a system to offer.

It is in this perspective that we must view Gautama's enterprise. His solution for the clash of authorities is disarmingly simple. In the concept of proof he invites all philosophers to state their respective doctrines on the bases of their respective authorities. The *siddhānta* of every one can be proved. This is where the whole procedure of proof commences: that is, the first *avayava*. But before the *siddhānta* is subjected to this procedure, there are certain preliminary conditions to be fulfilled. The *siddhānta* must be such that it corresponds to objective fact (*dṛṣṭānta*) in the universe and this correspondence must itself be an outcome of a legitimate purpose and doubt of the contestant concerned. What is even more important is that the *siddhānta* must have been established by the pramāṇas. What is implied in this procedure but not expressed in so many words is that a *siddhanta* is a *siddhānta* in so far as it conforms to the Nyāya concept. Of course, it is recognized in another context that there are different kinds of *siddhānta* and what is to be subjected to proof is not what the philosophers are agreed upon but what they are divided on. This is an ingenious compromise: a philosopher can not only have his cake but eat it too. There are two serious objections to this approach. First, to rule out *ab initio* the application of the proof procedure in any sphere is to reject out of hand what is perhaps the most important task of a philosopher: examination of every one of his premises, whether there is a consensus or not. Second, the condition that the proof is meant only to confirm a *siddhānta* destroys the very possibility of its being disproved. In the context in which the theory of proof is developed it is undoubtedly argued that the entire proof procedure is preceded by epistemological scrutiny but for the Nyāya kind of proof this is not sufficient. If the ultimate sanction of proof is perceptual evidence, the possibility of any *siddhānta* being falsified must be kept open. It may be said in defence that formal logic deals only with the problems of validity and not invalidity for it starts with premises which are true or known to be true. This defence is not of much use to the Naiyāyika for his entire proof is only a translation of the pramāṇas; for him the question of validity is in the last resort a question of truth and falsity.

Nor can the doctrine of the fallacious hetu resolve this difficulty. The hetu in the Nyāya system is primarily ontological or objective. The hetu represents a causal connection or invariable concomitance and for the Naiyāyika every relation or connection belongs to the structure of the universe; it is not a mental addition or construct. The proof is undoubtedly concerned with invariable concomitance and every such concomitance is or is meant to be part of the universe. The hetu that we consider fallacious is spurious not because any hetu can itself be spurious but because it is used in a wrong way. The category of the fallacious hetu (*hetvābhāsa*) refers to objects and their connections and represents what must be regarded as a distortion of the basic structure of the universe. If we look at this category along with misapprehension, it will seem as though this category is a mild variety of the deadly misapprehension. And in a theory of salvation based upon the recipe of knowledge error is no ordinary intellectual aberration; it borders on moral turpitude. One who misconceives a hetu is therefore guilty of this offence.

According to the Naiyāyika the most important fallacy is the contradictory hetu (*viruddha*). It is a hetu which is contrary to the authority of the proponent of the proposition. Nothing would have frightened such a person more than this veiled suggestion. In the climate of that age even a suspicion of this kind would have damned any philosopher beyond any hope of redemption. After all, one of the greatest crimes of the Cārvākas was their alleged defiance of traditional authorities.

The fallacy of the contradictory hetu is a double-edged weapon. Having asked the philosopher to argue on the basis of his own authority he is now told not to depart from it on the pain of being convicted as a bad logician. In the interest of his intellectual and moral reputation the philosopher would therefore fall for the Nyāya concept of proof. But what he has not quite realized is that he has accepted a fundamental conceptual framework. And in doing so he has reaffirmed his faith in the principle of authority, though he might differ from everybody else on matters of the nature of authority or doctrine. Within the same framework it is not impossible to arrive at divergent doctrinal positions. As we know, the Western thinkers swore allegiance to Aristotle till the middle of the nineteenth century and yet evolved divergent doctrines. It was only when the mathematician and the logician arrived on the scene that the Aristotelianc onceptual framework has been radically revised. And this challenge along with the tremendous possibilities of science for good or evil have only added to the uncertainties of our age.

That the fallacious hetu is but a distortion of ontology can also be seen from the kind of the fallacies recognized by Gautama. These clearly indicate the considerations one must keep in mind in offering a proof. For instance, the invariable concomitance must be properly verified and there must be no time-lag between cause and effect. If the Nyāya hetu is basically causal, it is obvious that the fallacies are also fallacies of proof rather than the fallacies of a deductive inference.

It is not only the concept of proof that is put in an epistemological straightjacket. The whole philosophical discourse is placed in an equally tight fit. According to Gautama the discourse must be conducted not only in accordance with the pramāṇas but also be not opposed to *siddhānta*. This means that the parties to a discourse know what is true or certain and are armed with an appropriate authority and this, in turn, implies that they cannot go back upon their respective positions without self-contradiction. In fact, deviation from a *siddhānta* is against the code of philosophical discourse; it is not sanctioned as a separate fallacy in the context of proof, but it is recognized as a source of defeat (*apasiddhānta*). The philosophical discourse is not therefore a midwife of truth but a rubber-stamp procedure. This is the logical characteristic of the discourse.

But the philosophical discourse involves views which are different or sometimes mutually opposed. In fact it is frequently concerned with propositions which are logically contradictory. The manner in which such propositions are stated does not indicate any logical defect; for example, the soul exists or the soul does not exist. Both parties can advance equally cogent hetus supported by appropriate examples; they are therefore fully authorized to draw their respective conclusions. If we were to treat this as deductive inference, there is no ground for condemning either proposition as invalid. But the real purpose of the discourse is not only to show that one is right but also that the other is wrong.

Thus if the discourse is treated as an exercise in formal logic, while confirmation of one's own position is possible refutation of one's opponent is logically impossible. This logical deadlock can be noticed in various contexts. For instance, it is argued that if one person maintains that sound is eternal because it is a product, the entire fabric of inference would disintegrate. It is obvious that whether sound is eternal or not, this has no conceivable bearing on the nature or validity of inference, deductive or inductive. The threat this holds out is not to logic but to the entire structure of authority. The crucial question for the Naiyāyika is: having thrown the *siddhānta* open for discussion, how to maintain one *siddhāntá* and refute another which is diametrically opposed to the first, even though both are equally valid and authoritative ?

It is obvious that this question cannot be settled within the confines of formal logic. Like the Nyāya concept of proof, the Nyāya scheme for refutation depends upon appeal to facts — or evidence. The crux of the refutation scheme is to exhibit the hetu as unfounded, and this, in its turn, depends upon the inability of the third *avayava*, the example, to corroborate the hetu. In fact, this is no more than showing that the invariable concomitance invoked by one's opponent has no foundation in fact. If the Naiyāyika had realized what was actually involved in genuine refutation, he would have stated in simple terms that counter-example is the *sine qua non* of such refutation; all other refutation is spurious.

But what the Naiyāyika says is that the example cited by the opponent does not corroborate the hetu and consequently his proposition is not established. Another line pursued by the Naiyāyika is what I have described as the doctrine of estoppel.[55] It seems that none of the contestants was really aware of the difference between a universal proposition and a generalization. If it is a proposition in formal logic, it can be invalidated only if it is self-contradictory; or, if its implication or entailment is contradictory. For example, the proper objection to the argument — sound is eternal because it is a product — is to say that sound cannot be a product if it is eternal or sound cannot be eternal if it is a product. Either it amounts to tautology or what would now be recognized as self-contradiction. In either case it is not relevant whether or not the hetu is supported by the example.

What the Naiyāyika is telling his opponent is that his view is in the nature of enumerative generalization. Such a generalization must be supported by the well-known canons of evidence. It is the lack of this evidence that vitiates the opponent's view. When a philosopher says that everything is eternal or non-eternal he has to produce the requisite evidence. This evidence is already contained in the generalization. Consequently, the opponent has deprived himself of the opportunity of presenting a well-reasoned proof. This is a legal approach rather than an approach of a formal logician. The prosecutor has no case and therefore the defendant is not required to substantiate his innocence.

This attempt to bypass logic by a legal device was perhaps dictated by the reverential attitude towards all forms of authority current in a philosophical discourse. The Naiyāyika could not say that a *siddhānta* was not corroborated by evidence without contradicting himself, for the discourse is itself based upon the pramāṇas. Nor could he tell the opponent that his *siddhānta* is not properly authenticated for he would then also contradict himself. Moreover, he was always anxious to preserve the principle of authority. The Naiyāyika therefore says that the opponent should shut up. Thus in silence all the serious issues involved are altogether muffled. One of the ways in which an opponent can be regarded as defeated is silence in the progress of a controversy. In fact, one of the difficulties recognized by the Naiyāyika in the procession of arguments and counter-arguments is the question of decision: how and precisely at what stage can one of the parties be declared defeated ? The answer of the Naiyāyika is that one should see for oneself where the force or the strength of a hetu or the corroborating capacity of an example lies; it is at that stage that the thesis of an opponent can be regarded as rejected. It is not surprising that Vātsyāyana declares the whole doctrine of hetus and examples to be extremely difficult. There is an air of mystery about the whole concept of proof.

As Wittgenstein remarked, 'we have the idea that the meaning of a word is an object'. This idea is based on the belief that objectivity requires an object, which is shared by conflicting parties in many philosophical disputes. Such disputes depend upon something assumed as obvious by both the disputants; these disputes can be settled only if we reject the shared assumption. As F. P. Ramsey observes, 'most of us would agree that the objectivity of good was a thing that we had settled and dismissed with the existence of God. Theology and Absolute Ethics are two famous subjects which we have realized to have no real objects.'[56]

In India also we have such controversies among philosophers. All of them accepted perception as pramāṇa and so far as the Naiyāyikas are concerned, they hold that in perception there is an object with which our senses are in direct contact. In fact the Nyāya universe is populated with objects of cognition (*prameya*).

Like these epistemic objects, the Naiyāyikas have another set of objects which are primarily linguistic. A noun-word denotes an object and it follows that there must be at least as many objects as there are noun-words in the Sanskrit language. By the time Gautama had arrived on the scene, Sanskrit had become the official language of the Indian philosophical world. These philosophers also used noun-words and they would therefore be entitled to a set of their own objects on this basis.

This linguistic ontology had a special flavour in India. Every *śāstra* (scripture) represented, as the Naiyāyika puts it, a collection of objects. We would be justified in saying that such objects were the objects denoted by the noun-words in the *śāstra*. But every system had its own *śāstra* and consequently, it would be entitled to have a scriptural ontology of its own.

Such ontologies may be capable of ostensive definition when they are first formulated. The authors may be able to point to the objects they have in view; but as time goes by, the relation between words and their meanings or objects becomes increasingly difficult to identify. This difficulty is partly resolved by the belief that grammar decides such questions. The Naiyāyikas believe, for example, that Sanskrit grammar is as sacred and authoritative as the Veda, because, like the Veda, it is designed by āptas. And whatever an āpta says is authoritative. But the actual relation between words and meanings is a matter of convention. We learn the language from our elders who are āptas and thus we know what a word denotes. Moreover, both the philosopher and the laymen are bound by such conventions made by the grammarian āptas. Hence there need be no doubt that words must denote objects. This explanation is meant only to reinforce the credibility of the scriptural ontology.

If the philosophers were content with laying down general theories, this kind of approval might be regarded as satisfactory. But the Indian philosophers were interested not only in abstract theories but their practical application. While these philosophers did not attempt to map out a complete inventory of the objects in the universe, they did select a few which they considered to be of paramount importance. Since both the words and the corresponding objects had an ancient history, the question of connecting a particular word with a particular object was none too easy. Most of such objects were of a character that made direct identification impossible. For instance, the self in the Nyāya system is an inferential object and it is obvious that we cannot point out to it and say that this is the self. However, the self is, after all, not such a strange object. We can find some physical and psychological criteria by which we may identify the self. But there are objects like heaven or *saṃsāra* which cannot be easily located.

In the third pramāṇa, analogy (*upamāna*) and the fourth *avayava* in the concept of proof we have an attempt to meet the difficulties of identification. An āpta may have directly perceived either an object or its properties or both — in the Nyāya terminology these are all objects. According to the Naiyāyika, if an āpta who has perceived two objects and their similarity, he can tell an ignorant man how to identify one of the two objects which he has not perceived on the basis of the similarity which the āpta has communicated. This is what is also provided in the fourth *avayava*.

Having made available to everyone the procedure for proof, every philosopher can use it to prove his own set of objects. But as elsewhere, there is no consensus on the nature or number of objects among philosophers. The Naiyāyika has himself a set of his own objects and he is interested in showing that all other sets are the wrong sets. And this calls for refutation.

Since such objects are regarded as existing concrete entities, no appeal to formal arguments or consistency in arguments of this kind can settle such questions of fact. Of course, this does not mean that such devices are to be shunned or rejected out of hand. But in the last resort questions of fact can only be settled by appeal to evidence. The meaning of word lies in its verification or verifiability.

In view of these considerations it is obvious that the Naiyāyika needs a well-formulated scheme of refutation and this scheme has to be complementary to his concept of proof. When we look at the kind of the elements provided in the scheme, the character of the Nyāya theories becomes even more explicit.

Let us look at the category of legitimate objection (*jāti*). The most striking feature of this category is equality; even the name of each legitimate objection contains a reference to this aspect. The entire debate between the two disputants arises because the nature and scope of the probandum, the capacity of the hetu to prove the probandum and of the example to support the hetu are cogently questioned. It is argued that the scope of the original probandum should be expanded or contracted. The hetu cannot be distinguished from the probandum or it is altogether impossible to cite a hetu because it just cannot be said to exist at any time. The kind of similarity or dissimilarity between the hetu and the example, i.e. the presence of invariable concomitance between the probandum and the hetu in the positive instance or the absence of the concomitance in a negative instance can be confronted with another kind of similarity or dissimilarity which can show that it can either disprove the original probandum or prove an entirely different probandum. There can be no distinction between the hetu and the probandum or the hetu cannot be properly formulated. The example cited cannot be said to be capable of supporting the hetu or is itself in need of proving; it may be confronted with a counter-example.

The overall impression one gathers from the debate is that the disputants are in search of factual or empirical considerations to prove or disprove a probandum. They are in search of facts in the universe they knew. The issues are undoubtedly framed in the context of doctrinal views and controversy, but the whole temper is empirical. Have we got hold of real causes and effects, similarities or dissimilarities, hetus, examples or counter-examples, objects of a real homogeneous or heterogeneous class ? These are all questions of fact and the so-called scheme of refutation is nothing more than the confrontation of which the disputants consider as facts. It is assumed that the first disputant is in full possession of all the evidence while the opponent has either misunderstood the facts or cited what cannot be regarded as facts.

These are all issues which every empiricist must face. It cannot be said that the Naiyāyika or his opponents have faced up to the implications of their empiricism. For example, if objections are raised on grounds of what is perceived or not perceived, these cannot be dismissed in the way in which the Naiyāyika has done. The universe in which the disputants were searching for facts was crowded with things somewhat remote from the world in which we live. Consequently, their whole concept of fact was different from what we expect from a good empiricist. This debate reveals rather sharply that the disputants were really not interested in evidence which might go against their own position; they were looking for evidence which would be favourable to themselves. The summary rejection of the counter-instance is a serious lacuna in the whole discussion. If the Naiyāyika had considered this matter carefully, he could have urged a genuine counter-instance against the unrestricted generalizations of the philosophers. And this would have really disproved the generalizations. An empiricist has to keep his feet firmly planted on the earth, even if his mind is in the clouds.

When we come to the last category of deficiency, the position becomes even clearer. Gautama says that the argument is deficient because it is either not understood or misunderstood. The deficiency category must therefore be regarded as psychological, epistemological and linguistic. For instance, the faults of the first *avayava* — these are the first four deficiencies — are not really logical faults of the argument; they arise because a proponent concedes to the opponent what he should not. But this concession, if it is considered purely in a logical context, is quite legitimate. For according to the Nyāya requirements all the arguments are either valid or capable of being formulated as valid arguments. There is no fallacy in the Nyāya sense, certainly no fallacy in terms of formal logic. The proponent of an argument does not realize the merits of his own argument and may put forward revised arguments, but even so, none of these original and modified arguments need be regarded as invalid by the Naiyāyika.

The same can be said about the hetus. To advance more than one hetu or example or to omit one or the other is a defect only because the Naiyāyika says that a particular number of hetus and examples is sufficient. If the hetus are logical and not causal, there should be no objection in increasing or decreasing the number of hetus or even omitting the hetu. Every such argument can be correctly formulated. What the Naiyāyika says is that one should stick to the original argument when confronted by an opposition. But that does not mean that the proponent's revised argument is invalid or that the opponent's counter-argument is wrong. It is not out of place to mention here that in this discussion the Naiyāyika seems to have forgotten his own doctrine of cumulative evidence.

The same can be said about the manner in which the *avayavas* are to be stated. The Naiyāyika defends the Nyāya order of the *avayavas* on the ground that a change in the order complicates the task of understanding. This again is a matter which raises no serious difficulty in formal logic. Every student of elementary logic knows how ordinary arguments can be reformulated to satisfy the requirements of the logician. When we come to symbolic logic, even arguments become irrelevant; what we need is a system of notation.

Perhaps by far the most serious defect is when a proponent of an argument departs from a *siddhānta*. It may be desirable that one should stick to one's own credal doctrines, but conformity to a doctrine has no logical value. Formal Logic is concerned with the logical structure and character of inference and every doctrine, good, bad or indifferent, can be given a formally valid structure. That is why theology is sometimes hailed as deductive logic *par excellence*. Once the premises are granted to be true or certain a perfectly valid conclusion can be drawn, and one can choose any premises one may like. The defect of deviation (*apaṣiddhānta*) from a credal doctrine is the most heinous crime in the Nyāya vocabulary. In fact, every argument is expected to begin with an *avayava* which states the doctrinal position of the proponent of an argument and a departure from it constitutes a major defect of any argument. The first *avayava*, i.e. the proposition, the fallacy of the contradictory hetu and the deviation from a *siddhānta* belong to the same family. We must not forget in this context that all fallacies of the hetu are included in the category of deficiency.

In this category of deficiency the Naiyāyikas have also provided for sense and nonsense. Unfortunately, he has concentrated on the ordinary faults of a poor arguer rather than the examination of the entire question of meaningfulness. For example, the Naiyāyika could have clarified what is now recognized as a distinction between sense and reference. If this had been done, the Nyāya ontology would have been reduced to size; or at best we would have learnt to appreciate the character of ontology. As empiricists, the Naiyāyikas could have developed what is called the verification theory of meaning. The whole concept of *saṃsāra* is essentially incapable of being verified in an ordinary way. If it has no cognitive meaning, it cannot make sense. That would leave us still free to accept such notions, but the grounds of our acceptance would not be those of truth or intelligibility but of passions and sentiments or what you like.

Another important element in the Nyāya scheme of refutation is the category of quibble (*chala*). Like the category of deficiency, the important characteristic of this category is psychological or subjective. An opponent does not really comprehend the intention of the speaker who puts forward a statement and argues on the basis of wrong interpretation. Of course, this is highly undesirable. If there are two parties to a dispute, they must first settle the precise forms of their dispute. There is one variety of the quibble that deserves special mention, the quibble regarding metaphor (*upacāra*). What the Naiyāyika insists on is that if a word is intended to be understood metaphorically it should not be taken literally. There can be no quarrel about this. But even more important is the question: if a word has one literal or cognitive meaning, are we entitled to use its metaphorical meaning to build up a system of beliefs meant to be accepted as true or at least important enough to be commended for acceptance ? For instance, if the word 'pleasure' denotes pleasure and we then proceed to describe pleasure metaphorically as pain, we are then not describing pleasure truly; this kind of description is found throughout the Nyāya view of *saṃsāra* and even liberation. This is not a quibble, but it does raise serious issues regarding true and false description. I shall revert to this subject in my comments on the objects of cognition.[57]

The main logical interest of the refutation of the various contrary views or heresies, as we have already noticed, lies in the nature of the main doctrine as stated and the proof offered. While the refutation has a close affinity to Mill's classic attack on syllogistic reasoning of Aristotle, we must resist the temptation to identify the two. What the Naiyāyika says is quite clear: if the doctrine is stated as it is, its proponent cannot even offer a proof; for the evidence that he can produce cannot be cited because there is nothing left. With the heavy ontological bias of the Naiyāyika it is not difficult to appreciate his line of refutation.

The Naiyāyika could have also argued that since the number of things in the universe is beyond enumeration, by no stretch of imagination could one ever include a complete inventory of the objects in the universe under the proposition offered for proof. To say everything is eternal or non-eternal is to achieve the impossible. A somewhat better formulation would have been: if the universe is infinite, infinity would cease to be infinity if it could be completed. This formal argument cannot be rebutted.

Such an argument could have been given against the doctrine under which a definite number of objects is postulated. Instead, Vātsyāyana merely confines himself to the number of *avayavas*.[58] It sounds convincing if we think in terms of an object-language.

In the context of this technique of refutation it must be stated that the Naiyāyika tends to dismiss whole doctrines of other systems by bringing them under one or the other of the varieties of legitimate objection and deficiency. This builds up an atmosphere in which a dispassionate discussion is not possible. For instance, the whole doctrine of the eternalist or the non-eternalist is treated in this fashion. It seems as though these varieties have been manufactured to give the views of the opponents a bad name before they are refuted. It is a well-worn procedure to give a dog a bad name and then hang it.

It is still mentioned in the east and the west that the entire philosophical establishment in India consisted of men of irreproachable character or extra-ordinary gifts. Since we do not have much biographical evidence about individual philosophers it is difficult to judge them individually. But what can be reasonably said from the Nyāya account of the philosophical discourse and the devices actually used or sanctioned is that every member of the establishment cannot be said to have lived up to this public image.[59] Perhaps their contemporaries were more discriminating in their judgment than their modern image-makers. Unfortunately, they too have left no reliable evidence of what they thought about them. Maybe, it is because of this that the philosophers have seldom if at all, been cast in stone or bronze!

As the reader must have noticed, I have included the categories of disputation and ascertainment under the concept of proof. The exposition of the category of disputation is somewhat ambiguous. The Nyāya proof is based upon the pramāṇas and the pramāṇas are designed to give true cognitions. If this is so, the cognitions so yielded cannot be regarded doubtful at all. And yet, it is suggested that there is doubt because what is cognized is infested with doubt in discussion. Of course, this doubt is set at rest with the help of disputation. All this has psychological significance and cannot impair the logical character of the pramāṇas.

Disputation is not a pramāṇa and therefore cannot yield valid cognition. If the object of disputation were the same as that of the pramāṇa it would have been proper to subject it to the procedure of proof. In that case there would be no need for a separate category. If the role of disputation is merely clarificationary, it has no place in the list of categories. In fact, an important characteristic of a category should be at least something in the nature of an independent function. And as we know from the discussion of the pramāṇas, the Naiyāyika is not prepared to give the pramāṇa status to minor instruments of cognition such as implication (*arthāpatti*).

It seems that the category of disputation is designed to deal with objects other than those of which we have cognition by the various pramāṇas. It deals with objects which are not capable of being duly ascertained. The illustrations given by the commentators strengthen this impression. For instance, Vātsyāyana raises a far-fetched doubt about birth. Since the Naiyāyika is committed to the causal explanation, what he has to find out is not whether there is an uncaused or caused cause or an accident but the specific cause of birth. This is exactly what he finds at the end; karma is the instrumental cause of birth. It is really not necessary to mix up an ultimate justification with a specific investigation into a specific event. This is what is brought out even more clearly in the illustration of Uddyotakara. A specific event needs a specific cause.

The examples given by the commentators remind us of *reductio ad absurdum*. In the context of the problem raised these seem to indicate the elimination of various hypothetical causes except one which is to be treated as the efficient cause.

If we were to look at the progress of the arguments and their upshot, it seems that the fact of birth can be explained in perfectly biological or natural terms and the so-called diversity of birth by social, political, economic and biological factors. If there is any absurdity, it is certainly not logical. A causal explanation is quite legitimate for the Naiyāyika and he has himself laid down a procedure for the determination of invariable concomitances. It is not so much the procedure that is at fault but the kind of events selected for explanation and of the causes that are accepted as explanation. In the climate of that age such explanations were acceptable to the learned minority. But these learned people took a very heavy responsibility when they lent the prestige of their authority and wisdom to such explanations. Prejudices or superstitions often have a learned ancestry!

The category of the so-called ascertainment is meant for the object of disputation. If we keep the objects actually discussed in view, it seems as though these objects are the objects cognized. What is somewhat disconcerting is that the philosophical discourse commences with properly ascertained and established subjects. Like proof, discussion is meant to affix the seal of approval on such themes. In a sense the categories up to discussion (*vāda*) have a private use; when this process is completed, the conclusions are exposed to public view. But the differences are seldom settled in private. They are often settled with every conceivable device ranging from a logical argument to what Francis Bacon called 'Idols'.

Discussion is said to be conducted according to the pramāṇas and disputation. It is not therefore out of place to insert these remarks in this context.

In the development of the concept of mind in Western philosophy we find 'a complex pattern, comprising, in addition to variations on one central theme, a number of 'counter-themes', and variations on them.'[60] The Cartesian notion of substance constitutes this central theme. The counter-themes are provided by concepts of mind put forward as alternatives to Descartes' notion of mind as one of two kinds of substances. Amongst the counter-themes two views deserve special mention. According to one view the mind is '*subject*', as opposed to what is the *object* of its activities. According to the second view the mental is something *private* as opposed to what is *public*. 'The peculiarity of the soul,' says one of its advocates, Wisdom, 'is not that it is visible to none but that it is visible only to one.'[61] A variation on the theme of the privacy of the mental is that of the mental as what is known 'directly' or 'without inference'.

During the last 300 years or so, one of the problems in this field, which has occupied the attention of the philosophers, is the problem of the relation of body and mind. And the roots of this problem lie in the philosopher's concepts of mind, of matter and of causality.

In recent years the philosophy of mind has received a great deal of attention among the philosophers. It is felt that normative ethics need to be based upon clear and comprehensive analysis of mental concepts. Within ethics and the theory of knowledge some of the specific questions subjected to critical examination are: the ascription of responsibility; intersubjective comparisons of feelings and mental states; the notion of character and of character traits, and of human dispositions and their differences from the causal properties of physical objects; the relation of pleasure to the activities; and the limits within which one is immune to error in describing one's own sensations. And there are the philosophers who have been greatly concerned with toothache.

Our attitudes to the external world and our own thoughts and feelings are different. We are prepared to ignore the questions of value in our treatment of the external world; but when we are dealing with ourselves, we are vitally concerned with our place in nature and society. In an unfriendly environment, we wish either to come to terms with it on a rational basis or on a basis which opens up attractive prospects of deep emotional satisfaction. In this way the philosophy of mind is bound up with our social and intellectual background and even a philosopher is, after all, a human being susceptible to the influences of his environment. It is therefore not surprising that the philosophers reared in different cultures pose different questions and find different answers. Take, for example, the problem of God. Philosophers all over the world have discussed it, but the manner in which they have dealt with it differs not only from philosopher to philosopher but, more importantly, from one culture to another. This is true not only of Western philosophy but perhaps more so of Indian philosophy. And this makes it difficult to say where theology ends and philosophy begins.

As is known, the philosophers generally deal with what are described as 'perennial problems'. The problems in the philosophy of mind have an ancient lineage. Soul, immortality and god are the traditional and perennial problems in the philosophy of the mind. The philosopher is not only concerned with the external world but also with the place of man in nature and society. This concern takes many practical forms. According to Plato justice is always to the advantage of the man who acts justly but inevitably the emphasis was placed on the everlasting character of the benefits. This practical concern can be seen in modern philosophy. According to Locke, virtue, which, for the classical philosopher, had, beauty, becomes 'the most enriching purchase, and by much the best bargain'.[62] And this morality is to be found in the gospel of Christ.

Immortality in the sense of survival after death has been the main interest of philosophers. 'If the soul, or the Universe, or God, or anything else, is thought to be everlasting,' as A. N. Flew says, 'then, surely, the presumption, in default of positive reason to the contrary, should be what will be without end was also eternally without beginning; and the other way about likewise.'[63] For those brought up in a Christian or post-Christian culture the problem of pre-existence and not the immortality in the sense of survival after death, the philosopher continues, may seem outlandish, but pre-existence and immortality are really two complementary aspects of one and the same doctrine.

In this perspective the Nyāya doctrine of the objects of cognition can be seen as a contribution to the philosophy of mind. These objects centre round the self, which, in the Nyāya theory of cognition, has already an important function as the cognizer. In fact, in the fourfold scheme of knowledge — the cognizer, the object of cognition, instrument of cognition and cognition — the commentators treat the cognizer as the most important factor. This epistemological notion of the cognizer is now given the ontological status in the doctrine of the objects of cognition. The epistemological concept of objectivity in the Nyāya is virtually the notion of the accusative and, as is known, it is customary among philosophers to think that objectivity requires an object. The grammatical objects are now treated not only as elements or parts of the structure of the objective universe but also as objects of human endeavour. Thus epistemology, ontology and ethics are in a way coordinated to present a unified picture of what is ultimately real..

According to the Naiyāyika the universe contains an indefinite number of distinct objects which have certain properties in common and other properties which distinguish one object from another. A philosopher who wishes to explain the entire universe will, therefore, be confronted with an impossible task. Consequently, Gautama has selected, so the justification runs, a few of these objects for special treatment. The more specific reason is said to be his desire to enable us to attain supreme felicity or release. In a sense, the theory of the pramāṇas may, therefore, be regarded as designed to establish the twelve objects of cognition (*prameya*).

It will be helpful at this stage to refresh our memory. According to Gautama there are the following twelve objects of cognition:

(1) self (*ātman*), (2) body (*śarīra*), (3) sense-organ (*indriya*), (4) object (*artha*), (5) apprehension (*buddhi*), (6) mind (*manas*), (7) activity (*pravṛtti*), (8) defect (*doṣa*), (9) state after death (*pretyabhāva*), (10) result (*phala*), (11) pain (*duḥkha*), (12) release (*apavarga*).

These twelve objects really fall into two main categories:

(a) *artha* (object) and (b) the self, its psychosomatic equipment, career and final destiny. The former can be said to correspond broadly to the external or physical world and this we have discussed under the Nyāya theory of the pramāṇas. As already remarked, the second category revolves round the self. It is therefore necessary first to look closely at this object of cognition (*prameya*).

The main difference between the Nyāya theory of knowledge of the external world and the doctrine of the objects of knowledge is that, in the Nyāya theory, the āpta does not have any significant function, while, in the doctrine, it seems as though the āpta is of paramount importance. One could go even further and say that the *śabdapramāṇa* comes into its own really in the realm of the self and all its works. Much depends upon the meanings of words and in this sphere the meanings acquire the status of objectivity. Hence they become objects in the same fashion as we treat material things as objects.

According to Gautama the self as an object is inferential and is established on the basis of the inferential marks or signs. The inferential marks are perceived or perceptible and since they are present where the self is present and since they are absent where the self is absent, the self is proved to be an inferential object. This is a proof based on invariable concomitance. These inferential marks are strictly non-eternal. Though the involvement of the self in *saṃsāra* is a product of a mistake (*mithyājñāna*), no explanation of this mistake can be given because the involvement of the self in *saṃsāra* has no beginning. This really amounts to saying that the Naiyāyika is not prepared to give the causal explanation as he is bound to give in all cases of invariable concomitance. Nor can the mistake be said to constitute the essential characteristic of the self for then the elimination of the mistake would mean, not liberation or perfection of the self, but its essential mutilation. It is logically conceivable that the self should be without any involvement in the *saṃsāra* for it is capable of being free from *saṃsāra*. Hence the explanation has the ethico-physical character. But the question that the Naiyāyika cannot effectively answer is: if the self is established on the basis of invariable concomitance lasting over a finite period, its existence as an inferential object cannot be known on the termination of that concomitance. Moreover, if there is genuine possibility of liberation, it cannot be argued that there is invariable concomitance except for a limited period.

In the wider context of the Nyāya doctrine of pramāṇa and *prameya* the Naiyāyika has a similar difficulty. The Nyāya pramāṇas are designed to establish the twelve *prameyas*. But since misapprehension (*mithyājñāna*) is not classed as one of the *prameyas*, it cannot be said to be known by any of the pramāṇas; consequently it cannot be said to be proved by the Nyāya procedure of proof. If we do not know the nature of a thing, our action cannot be successful. Hence whatever we do about this misapprehension cannot be successful. If the knowledge of the true nature of the sixteen categories is meant to eradicate misapprehension and ensure liberation, it follows that on the present ground this is impossible. The pramāṇas are thus bereft of their effectiveness in a sphere where the Naiyāyika needs them most. Incidentally, misapprehension is the one characteristic which can help us in identifying the self in the midst of *saṃsāra* and yet strangely enough, it is not even listed as one of the characteristics of the self.

As it is customary among philosophers, the Naiyāyika treats the self as substance. According to him, a thing can be a substance if and only if it has a property and a thing can be a property if and only if there is a substance to which the property can belong. The relation between substance and property is thus logical. Such a relation cannot obtain between the self and the properties listed by the Naiyāyika; for these properties belong to the self only till it is liberated. It is also not inconceivable that the self could have been without such properties, though misapprehension is said to be without beginning; for to say that a thing's cause cannot be given because we cannot find it out and therefore the thing is without a beginning (=cause) is only a contingent fact. Strictly speaking, the Naiyāyika is not entitled to offer such an explanation, because he believes that there is nothing which cannot be known by his set of pramāṇas.

Moreover, the properties of the self cannot be regarded as the essence or even the true nature of the self. A thing that is merely temporary or just a product of contamination of *saṃsāra* cannot be regarded in this fashion. In fact the Naiyāyika has described these properties as merely signs or marks (*liṅga*). It is not therefore surprising that the commentators feel no compunction in adding characteristics to the original list of Gautama. Even *adṛṣṭa* (unseen) is sometimes described as a property of the self. Such an open-texture concept of the self cannot really be reconciled with the nature of substance.

The Nyāya theory of the physical world is free from a difficulty of this kind. The four kinds of atoms and ākāśa are substances and they always have their qualities. In all physical objects produced out of the atoms the qualities of the atoms remain intact and ākāśa retains its property even when it constitutes our hearing organ. It is somewhat startling to arrive at such a conclusion: the Nyāya account of the physical world is more consistent with its central thesis of substance and property than the doctrine of *prameyas*. In fact, these two parts of the system can be easily separated without any damage to the Nyāya view of the physical world.

The Naiyāyika subscribes to the correspondence theory of truth and pragmatic theory of truth, but the latter is strictly based upon the former. A pramāṇa is a pramāṇa first because it reflects a thing that is, as it is and a thing that is not, as it is not, and such a pramāṇa must be effective (*arthavat*) because it represents the true nature of things. As already mentioned, the Naiyāyika has not listed misapprehension as one of the properties of the self. It is therefore no part of our knowledge of the self that it had had misapprehension without beginning. If, therefore, misapprehension is the cause of the involvement of the self in *saṃsāra*, we have no knowledge of such involvement. If there is no such involvement liberation is superfluous. If the Naiyāyika wanted to save all the paraphernalia of *saṃsāra* and liberation, misapprehension should have been listed as the property of the self as knowledge (*jñāna*) has been listed.

In the course of the explanation of the remedy for salvation the Naiyāyika observes: (a) pleasure is a fact which cannot be disputed; (b) pleasure should be regarded as pain. If the first statement is true, then what we are asked to do in the second statement is to treat the thing that is as it is not, not as it is. According to the correspondence theory of truth this amounts to asking us to act upon what is not true. According to the pragmatic theory of truth such action is doomed to failure for it is not based upon the true state of affairs. It is quite open to the Naiyāyika to ask us not to cultivate pleasures but to do so on such grounds is not consistent with his theory. What the Naiyāyika needs is something in the nature of an emotive theory of meaning or the Platonic noble lie.

Much the same can be said about desire, aversion and activity. If these are the properties of the self, it is not quite right to ask us to desist from disliking the things or from desiring the things we like or from activity simply because all such activity is due to defect (*doṣa*).

In these matters tnere is really no point in invoking the aid of any of the pramāṇas. Perception, inference and analogy have been fully utilized in establishing the existence of the self and its properties. The *śabdapramāṇa* cannot be called in to convert what is a true state of affairs into something different for the logic of this pramāṇa is that the āpta is an āpta if and only if he reflects the true state of affairs. An untruthful āpta is a contradiction in terms.

The Naiyāyika has used the notion of *upacāra* (metaphor)[64] to tide over this difficulty. If metaphor describes a thing that is as it is not, or a thing that is not as it is, it cannot be used for a philosophical purpose. Of course, a philosopher may not always be doing philosophy and in that capacity he is free to resort to any devices which he may like. The Naiyāyika has himself rejected such a procedure in his controversy with his opponents. Besides, metaphor can have no place in philosophy if it is meant to function as a substitute for the search for truth.

Another point deserves mention. The Naiyāyika insists that pain is pain and that it cannot be anything else. It is quite legitimate to ask us to rid ourselves of pain not only because it is pain but also because that is what everyone desires. Since the *saṃsāra* involves the experience of pleasure and pain, it follows that in getting rid of the *saṃsāra* we are not only getting rid of pain but also of pleasure. If *saṃsāra* is nothing but pain — and this it is not — it would be quite correct to say that to rid ourselves of *saṃsāra* is to rid ourselves of pain. But since the *saṃsāra* is a mixture of pleasure and pain — and this is the essence of the *saṃsara* according to the general moral principles of the system — in ridding ourselves of the *saṃsāra* we must say that we are ridding ourselves both of pleasure and pain. But then liberation cannot be described as merely absence of pain. Of course, the Naiyāyika has introduced the notion of mixture: if pleasure is mixed with pain, it ceases to be pleasure. Here again, what the Naiyāyika is asking us is to adopt a particular attitude. If the Naiyāyika had worked upon an undiluted pragmatic theory of truth such as is said to be envisaged by William James,[65] this may not be an inconsistent course of action. But the basic foundation of the Nyāya theory of pramāṇas is the correspondence theory and the pragmatic theory derives its validity directly from that foundation. On these grounds the Nyāya concept of *apavarga* (release) is strictly not equivalent to the elimination of pain. Mixture, like metaphor, is no substitute for truth or action based upon truth. As already mentioned, if the Naiyāyika had taken his stand only on the pragmatic theory or developed some kind of emotive theory of meaning,[66] he could have quite a respectable way-out of this impasse.

According to the Naiyāyika salvation depends upon the knowledge of the true nature of things and this knowledge is the knowledge of the categorical structure of Gautama as given in his Nyāya system. This knowledge was obtained by an āpta and communicated by him to others. The āpta belongs to the category of self and has the standard psychosomatic endowment. The difficulty that the Naiyāyika faces here is as follows: the attainment of knowledge must historically coincide with the attainment of liberation for otherwise the efficacy of such knowledge would be in question. If the āpta would attain his own liberation with the knowledge he has acquired, he would certainly have realized his own purpose. But then we who are not āptas are deprived of the only means by which we can attain our own liberation. For if the āpta were to attain his liberation simultaneously with the attainment of knowledge, he would be bereft of his psychosomatic endowment and thus of any means of communication. In simple words we would be deprived of the Nyāya system as a panacea for salvation.

Uddyotakara recognizes this difficulty and meets it by introducing what really amounts to a doctrine of degrees of salvation, *para* and *apara*. In the former the āpta has knowledge but only partial salvation. Thus he retains the means of communication and the Nyāya system can be delivered by him. Presumably, when he has done this, he is free to attain his final liberation. In that state there is no communication from the āpta nor do we need it. Thus the difficulty is solved by introducing a classification. This may be regarded as quite satisfactory in practical terms, but the reasonable course would have been to say that the āpta has done better than other ordinary human beings and that in view of this accomplishment we should follow his lead. But that would mean that the āpta has ceased to be what the Naiyāyika has made him to be: a person who is in possession of the whole truth. The difficulties of this kind only go to illustrate how awkward it is for an empiricist to maintain dogmatic positions. What a theologian or a philosopher of that persuasion can do the empiricist of the Nyāya type cannot easily do. The god of the Naiyāyika is busy with operating the karma system of rewards and punishments and he cannot strictly assume the role of the āpta nor can the āpta elevate himself to the status of god.

It may be argued that when the Naiyāyika is talking about the self and the incidents in its career or ultimate destiny he is really dealing with an empirical self. We are then confronted with the prospect of two selves: the self as it is itself and the self as found in *saṃsāra*. Since the self is involved in *saṃsāra* without beginning, because of the misapprehension being without beginning, it follows that the self that we encounter till it attains liberation is the empirical self. It is obviously impossible for us to know this self except through the *śabdapramāṇa*. But this can only mean that the āpta who has attained partial salvation can tell us about the self as it will be when it has attained salvation. When the āpta has attained salvation, he cannot communicate with us. This is not a very satisfactory position for any system which prides itself on our capacity to know everything by means of the pramāṇas. Moreover, there is the logical question of identity: are the empirical self and the liberated self two or one. The Naiyāyika has not shown any concern for this problem and we must therefore leave it as an unsolved question of the Nyāya system.

Perhaps the difficulties of this kind have led the Naiyāyikas to offer more secure arguments for the existence of the self. The first step in this direction is to exploit the possibilities of the doctrine of the convergence of the pramāṇas on a single object. According to Vātsyāyana we first hear about the existence of the self from an āpta. This communication is veridical because it is based upon his direct acquaintance with the self in a manner in which ordinary people cannot claim to have such acquaintance, as they have to depend upon inference based upon sense-organs and the perceptual data listed by Gautama, viz., desire, aversion, etc.

This entire argument rests on the credibility of the āpta, or, more precisely, as the Naiyāyika should have said, the credibility of the memory of the āpta. But this still leaves open the question: how to select such an āpta. There are at least two main parties who hold exactly contradictory views on the existence of self or soul. And here the Naiyāyika has really no convincing guidelines. To say that the communication of the āpta regarding the self is like that of the āpta informing the villager about the fire does not really add to his credibility on the subject.

In this matter, therefore, as in many other Nyāya doctrines, the question of memory crops up. Even if the āpta has direct experience he must be able to remember the experience and express it sufficiently accurately. In any system which depends upon such basis the believers have to determine the full meaning of the original communication. With the passage of time, problems become more difficult as different interpretations are offered. Students of Indian philosophy need no reminder of these problems. In fact, one of the perennial problems of Indian philosophy which has consumed the intellectual energies of our learned men over the centuries is precisely how to determine what the original authors must have meant. The basic issues can only be clarified when such problems are completely isolated and settled.

Another argument of the Naiyāyika is based upon recognition and recollection. Every apprehension or mental occurrence is distinct, having its own distinctive object. Recognition is possible only if the previous apprehension is recollected at the time of the present apprehension. This means that there is a common agent to whom both apprehensions belong. The pramāṇas were one of the criteria by which we determine the qualitative difference between the apprehension which we can regard as knowledge and the apprehension which cannot be so regarded. In that context also, recollection was found necessary to obtain inferential, analogical and verbal cognitions. Thus knowledge depends upon recollection and recollection means the unity and continuity of an agent to whom distinct apprehensions belong. This argument looks like the Cartesian argument: I think; therfore I am. The Nyāya version would be: I remember; therefore I am. As A. J. Ayer has pointed out, this is really not an argument. This argument from recollection is of course subject to the same criticism as the memory of the āpta mentioned earlier.

Another argument worth mentioning is a logical or semantic one. If there is a noun-word, it must denote a thing; we have such a word, '*ātman*'; therefore, there is a thing denoted by the word; hence there is *ātman*. In fact the Naiyāyika holds that no intelligible statement can be said to be about nothing. And this argument is implicit in the *śabdapramāṇa*. But to found the case for the existence of the self on a purely denotative basis would not satisfy the kind of self which the Naiyāyika has in view. There are objects of all kinds and if the self were just like any of them, it would not have the privileged position which the Naiyāyika has given to the self either in his epistemology or in his ontology. Perhaps the present argument, if it can be rigorously formulated, may be compared to the well-known ontological argument for the existence of God in Western philosophy.

A striking feature of the Nyāya case is its attempt to decide the logical grammar of the self on the basis of the paradigm: 'One sees colour with the eye'. Here the self is the agent = nominative; 'sees' is the verb = action; 'with the eye' is the instrument—instrumental. In the context of substance and property the substance is that on which or in which rests the property; it is the locus of the property = locative. The logic of these paradigms is that without the notion of the agent all such expressions cannot be explained. In this way the self is *kartṛ* = agent. This grammar of the various cases is intended not only to establish the basic character of the self as agent but also its distinction from all other things or their combinations. The self has a body, sense-organs and mind, but it is not an aggregate of these. In a sense all that the self can do depends upon the tool kit that is placed at its disposal. The creativity of the self seems to be exhausted in getting equipped for the tasks ahead set up for it by the original mistake (*mithyājñāna*)--a mistake really not of its making.

The real interest of the Naiyāyika in the problem of the self is revealed in the manner in which he seeks to prove its eternality. It is obvious that philosophical investigation of the nature of mental life begins from human experience. And the Naiyāyika is no exception. The Naiyāyika starts with what he finds in a human being. The body, sense-organs and mind are meant to be the structure of a human being. The concept of the body is derived from current Āyurvedic themes and the sense-organs are far too well-known to require any special pleading. Of course, Gautama has taken some pains to prove that the criteria for the numerical identity of the sense-organs are mainly spatial and functional and that they cannot be reduced to a single sense-organ. Incidentally, the Western philosophers have generally ignored this problem.[67] The mind is a connecting link between the sense-organs and the self and is also a part of the structure of the human being. Activity, defect, result and pain are distinctively human. The state after death represents the result of one's deeds and release is the highest objective which one could possibly have. The fact that the Naiyāyika actually proceeds from the human predicament needs to be emphasized for it is often forgotten that all the paraphernalia of *saṃsāra* are based on the paradigm of human experience and equipment, as understood by the philosophers. What they have done is to run off carbon copies of the human predicament and spread them backwards and forwards, without showing how this process began but with the promise of a future radically different from the past and the present. In a sense this is a recovery of the original by the original; only the embodiments are thrown by the roadside.

Like most philosophers, the Naiyāyika is aware that if the self or soul were to come into existence with the present body and perish with it, it would be reduced to being merely a product of the working of that body. It will be, in the words of T. H. Huxley, 'as completely without any power of modifying that working as the steam-whistle which accompanies the working of a locomotive engine is without influence upon its machinery.'[68] A conscious automaton is the bugbear of most philosophers. That is why Gautama first carries out what is virtually an elimination-contest for the true nature of the self; it is not the sense-organ, the mind, the body or the physical object for it has what none of them has, consciousness. If the self is an aggregate of physical or physiological things, it will be impossible to resist the temptation of reducing it to a material entity.

Similarly, the Naiyāyika sees clearly that if the self is reduced to a bundle of apprehensions, his battle against the materialist will be lost. This offensive, too, is aimed at the Buddhist, but it would not be unfair to say that the target is the materialist. However, the Naiyāyika is particularly vulnerable to the Buddhist attack for he has agreed to treat apprehensions as transient as sound itself. Each apprehension is distinct and temporary. He has even accepted the basic concept of a series in his explanation of sound. If the phenomenon of sound and its transmission can be explained in this fashion, it is quite legitimate to ask: why not mental life ? Similarly, both the Naiyāyika and the Buddhist are prepared to concede that what comes later can be explained with reference to what comes earlier. And this is at least one of the aspects of causation. If the self were reduced to a series of apprehensions, then the Naiyāyika would be reduced to the position held by Hume in modern times. And then, the traditional theology and ethics would be in jeopardy. But even in this respect the real opponent is the full-blooded materialist.

As in the case of the external world, the Naiyāyika is most anxious to preserve the integrity of the most important object of cognition, the self. His arguments for the defence of the self are two: psychological or epistemological and ethico-social If there is no recollection, there can be no reasonable explanation of mental life which consists of ephemeral apprehensions. And recollection requires a single agent. If there is no single agent, there will be no reasonable way of ascribing moral responsibility. There must be an agent or doer so that we can not only hold him responsible for his deed but make sure that it is the same doer who is visited with the consequences of his deed. Thus far, the Naiyāyika is doing philosophy as any other respectable philosopher. This way of presenting the problem of moral responsibility and deserts has the sternness and harshness of a judge who is anxious to keep law and order rather than promote a climate where people follow a code of conduct with full freedom of choice.

But when the Naiyāyika throws his net across eternity he has problems. Even here, he is not that isolated. As Socrates says in the *Phaedo*, 'The theory of learning and recollection has, however, been established on a sound foundation. For it was agreed that our souls existed even before they entered the body, just as do the realities to which we give the name of Forms.'[69] It is well known that Plato toyed with a doctrine of metamorphosis or the transmigration of souls, which is a combination of the two complementary notions of pre-existence and immortality. Of course, the Naiyāyika was not concerned with the mathematical notions or Forms of Plato; he was arguing in the context of the prevailing scientific or common sense beliefs of his time. More specifically, he was arguing against the materialists who had no better ideas of nature or society and its workings. It is not therefore surprising that the Nyāya arguments appear to be somewhat crude and bizarre.

What the philosopher who subscribes to such a doctrine of immortality does is to mistake the logically prior for the temporality prior. Moreover, it is one thing to explain mental occurrences with reference to the preceding ones provided they fall within one's present life span but quite another to invoke pre-existence on the present model and then proceed to explain the earliest occurrences from one's birth with reference to the mental occurrences prior to the birth. Similarly, there is a case for moral responsibility in one's present life and in relation to other human beings in a society; but to say that the pleasures and pains of the present life are first the consequences of one's deeds in one's previous existence is something which requires substantial evidence. Apart from the question of the eternality or non-eternality of the self, such a theory really amounts to a reproduction in the past of the current state of affairs. So far as the future is concerned, it will be sheer twisting of our usage and common sense to use the device of memory for explanatory purposes. It may be argued that our attitude towards the future is determined by our experience of will or capacity to influence our environment; but to argue on this basis that the future will repeat the present will need a great deal of convincing. As in the case of the past, we will need the reproduction in the future of the current state of affairs. This undoubtedly sound like the classical problem of induction. It may be asked: if we can give scientific explanation on inductive grounds, why should we not treat such proposition in the same way ? The simple reason is that the paradigm of explanation for the world is increasingly regarded as the laws of nature or scientific theories. Natural and social sciences have established a pattern of explanation which we find credible or acceptable. The kind of propositions to which we will have to assent in this sphere does not command confidence or credibility.

The Nyāya case for the eternality of the self, everlasting in time and not in the sense of timeless eternality, rests largely on the psychological theory of memory and the doctorine of moral responsibility and deserts. In the actual exposition psychological, ethical and social arguments are mixed up. Let us take, for instance, recollection. It is said that a new-born baby sucks milk from its mother's breast because it had done so in its previous life. Adults do what pleases them and avoid what pains them on the basis of their previous experience. If this doctrine were isolated from the pre-existence of the self or its moral associations, it could be regarded as a respectable theory of learning by experience.

Even if the facts of memory were adequate for establishing pre-existence, they cannot help in establishing survival after death. Here comes ethical hedonism which can be used to explain the present with reference to the past and the future with reference to the present and the past. In simple terms the Nyāya view is that a good deed produces pleasure and a bad deed pain. It is then suggested that the pleasures and pains we have in our present life can be explained with reference to previous deeds. But it so happens that in practice this does not work out as expected. Besides it is not unlikely that all the consequences of one's deeds in previous lives might not have been realized even uptodate. But it sounds rather incredible to say that the consequence of a deed performed a long time ago should appear now or in the remote future. In order to ensure the purity of the causal principle—the effect must follow immediately the cause—an entity is manufactured to function as an intermediary between the deed and the result. This is the classical karma. The good deed produces merit (*dharma*) and the bad deed demerit (*adharma*) and the karma doctrine is tantamount to a store-house of merit and demerit. It will be noticed that one and the same moral concept is repeated in the evaluation of deed and creation of the entity, karma. This moral concept is then tied to pleasure and pain. Thus hedonism is the crux of the karma theory.

It is absolutely essential that the law of karma should be allowed to operate without let or hindrance. To ensure this two conditions are necessary: first, the doer of all his deeds must be available at all times to have the experience due to him; second, in order to have the experience the doer must have the requisite endowment. The whole idea of such experience is obviously modelled on human experience and we know that in order to have the experience we need a body, the sense-organs, the mind and the *buddhi*. This pattern of endowment must therefore be always available to the self. It would be simply incredible even to suggest that once the self has entered a particular body it will continue to occupy it indefinitely. Death is far too serious business to be ignored. The best solution therefore is to acquire the requisite endowment and abandon it from time to time. If we were to say that this endowment will always be human, it would look like a cheap imitation of our present life; and to repeat it would not be exciting enough. It is therefore better to use our knowledge of the living beings that now exist or can be invented with a judicious combination of what we know and what can look credible. Such living beings can be shown to be the worst possible or the best possible and they can be housed appropriately in different parts of the universe. There are such regions easily available for occupation, heaven, hell and earth. This picture can be varied to suit the taste and ability of the authors concerned, but the basic framework remains much the same.

If this was all that the philosopher offered, the prospects would not inspire sufficient confidence. Several basic notions are therefore introduced in the scheme. Everyone knows that pain is pain and what is pain cannot be transformed into something which is not pain. The philosopher recognizes this brute fact and he therefore explores other avenues. Contrary to his basic hedonistic thesis he now fiddles first with the notion of pleasure and transforms the notion of pain beyond all recognition. It is well known that we cannot go on enjoying a thing indefinitely. Besides, there are always unfortunate experiences round the corner, either in one's own life, or in the life of near and dear ones or of neighbours. If nothing else is available, there are the constant episodes of life like birth, sickness, old age and death. Each one of them has its painful aspect. The first step in this enormous transformation is to characterize pleasure itself as pain because it does not last indefinitely; the second step is to concentrate on the episodic aspects of pain; the third step is to identify the entire complex with the psychosomatic endowment which alone can make the whole complex possible. It is logically impossible to have any experience without such endowment.

The second basic notion is the identification of the recurring psychosomatic endowment with the original hedonistic concept of morality but with a radical alteration. From the pleasure-pain principle pleasure has either been so modified or suppressed altogether that its elimination is hardly noticed. Here some elusive analogies like poisoned milk are used to increase the credibility of this silent elimination. After all, no one wants to drink poison. And when all that is offered is poison, one can easily forget that there is wholesome milk available somewhere.

In this context one must remember that the Naiyāyika insists that he does not deny the fact of pleasure; all that he wants us to do is to regard all such pleasures as pain. It is almost like throwing the baby with the bath-water.

Now the picture has become sufficiently grim. If it was left here, one would be so frightened that one might get used to it like the pictures of horror or violence on modern television or just reject it as a pure fabrication. The stick alone seldom produces all that one may wish for. It is the combination of the stick and the carrot that works. Again contrary to the hedonistic thesis, pleasures are promised for good behaviour and the element of pain is either reduced or almost eliminated. But the threat of painful existence is kept up. Even if a person had all the pleasures he could think of, say in heaven, he has still the psychosomatic endowment which holds out the threat of painful experiences. For those who are allotted all the pain one could possibly conjure up, say in hell, some encouragement is necessary. Obviously, what he would like most is first to get rid of his enormous pain. Thus both the good man and the bad man can be persuaded to agree upon the total liquidation of pain. Of course, there is this difference: one who had the pleasures in this life and next on account of his good deeds is only deprived of the possibility of pain; but one who had all the misery in this life and next will have experienced the misery but will have the comforting assurance that if only he behaved himself he may be spared all the miseries in future.

We now reach the culmination of this complex pattern. This is the doctrine of liberation. The prospectus varies from philosopher to philosopher, but they are all agreed that liberation means the end of psychosomatic endowment, and thus there is a cast-iron guarantee that the kind of experience one can ever have with this endowment can never occur. The Nyāya concept of liberation (*apavarga*) is total absence of pain. It says what one will not have but it is silent on what one will have. But one will always be what one had always been: the original self will recover itself, without so much as a trace of all that has happened to it since it was thrown into the orbit of *saṃsāra*. The beginning may be shrouded in mystery but the end is crystal clear.

This is the kind of pattern that emerges from the Nyāya *prameyas*. The problems of moral philosophy as practised in the

West—such as moral judgment, moral discourse and its language or logic, freedom of will versus determinism, nature of influence exercised by mind on body and *vice versa*—do not figure in this pattern. In recent years moral philosophers have urged that their predecessors could not answer the questions which they posed satisfactorily, because they were not clear about the questions themselves. Some of the contemporary philosophers recognize that moral concepts change as social life changes. As Alasdair MacIntyre syas, 'Moral concepts are embedded in and are partially constitutive of forms of social life. One key way in which we may identify one form of social life as distinct from another is by identifying differences in moral concepts.'[70] It is not therefore surprising that the Indian philosopher was said to have ignored moral problems; for the manner in which the Indian philosopher framed moral questions and sought to answer them was deeply rooted in his social life.

The Indian philosopher begins to do philosophy with the unshakable assurance that either he has acquired the moral truths himself or obtained them from someone who had acquired them. His main task is therefore to explain the acquisition. Even more important is his concern for what he considers to be fallen humanity. He is anxious to persuade people that they should accept the technique which he has himself found effective and thus profit from his experience. It is practice rather than theory that is important in the moral sphere. Moreover, he knew that the authors of the *Dharmaśāstras* had established a pattern of individual and social behaviour. The philosopher belonged to the same intellectual establishment as those authors and he just took over the finished products of their labour.

It is often said that the Indian philosopher being a holy man or a sage had completely opted out of society. This is undoubtedly true to the extent that he did not have to work for his living or, generally, he did not occupy any office. But he could not dispense with society altogether. In his early childhood he received some kind of formal education. After he had finished education he had to depend upon society for sustenance. But he needed society—or, society needed him—because he was deeply interested in sharing his wisdom with his receptive fellow-men.

The philosopher was undoubtedly detached in his attitude towards the ordinary affairs of men but he could not have closed his mind to the intellectual and social influences of his times. The classical example of this is the manner in which he imbibed and utilized the ethos of his society. The moral philosophy of the *Dharmaśāstras* provided a basis for his metaphysic and thus remained the least unexamined part of his philosophical discourse. The so-called consensus among the Indian philosophers is precisely this unexamined part of their philosophy. The arguments about the merits of different techniques of salvation cannot be said to have departed from this consensus. These are far more relevant to the kind of objective which a technique might accomplish rather than to the clarification of moral issues as understood in moral philosophy. In order to do full justice to Indian philosophy it is necessary to assess the contribution of the *Dharmaśāstras* and bring them in line with the strictly philosophical speculations. This problem would require a separate study.

As already mentioned, there is at present a debate about moral problems not only among philosophers but also among those who are concerned with the management of society. It is therefore necessary to have a fresh look at the ethical part of the Nyāya framework.

This Nyāya framework is based upon the following notions: *dharma* and *adharma, saṃsāra* and karma.

It is well-nigh impossible to render the Sanskrit terms *dharma* and *adharma* in any foreign language. The etymology of the term *dharma* suggests that which upholds, supports or sustains. It has undoubted associations with the Vedic injunctions and rites or rituals. It is concerned with the well-known *āśramas* and *varṇas*. Eventually, the most prominent significance of the notion, in the words of P. V. Kaṅe, came to be 'the privileges, duties and obligations of a man, his standard of conduct as a member of the Āryan community, as a member of one of the castes, as a person in a particular stage of life'.[71] According to him, the term was used in this sense in the *Dharmaśāstra* literature.

In the realm of morals this type of doctrine is not unique. Plato had his three classes depending upon which part of the soul in dominant; this division is based upon the tripartite soul. Into which class a man falls may in part be a matter of his early training, but cannot fundamentally be so determined. Plato believes that there are born shoemakers and born rulers. Justice in the state is a matter of everyone knowing his place. Plato's morals were intimately connected with his political *weltanschauung*.

In the Indian context the politics of the philosopher cannot be unravelled because he has officially opted out of society. To understand his politics we have therefore to look towards his mentors in the *Dharmaśāstras*. But the Indian philosopher is quite convinced that the social order that he knows is a moral order and any attempt to change it amounts not only to the subversion of society but also to the collapse of the moral order. When the moral and social order are integrated with the order in the universe, we have really a complete picture of a collective disaster of cosmic dimensions. The prophets of the heat-death or the ecological doom have a very distinguished pedigree.

The concept of *dharma* is a concept of the *status quo* and the concept of *adharma* is that of rebellion against the *status quo*. It is a prescription for perpetuating a particular kind of society. The most convincing answer to this kind of *dharma* and *adharma* has already been given in the Indian Constitution. The Constitution is a complete repudiation of such doctrines.[72]

Looking at such doctrines, we have to raise some pertinent questions: First, there is a question of fact: are there such social institutions as envisaged by the *Dharmaśāstra* writers, and if so, do they reflect the kind of morals postulated? The second question is whether morality based on a society which is ceasing to exist or has ceased to exist can be given assent ? The third question is: if a new code of morals is publicly proclaimed, can we accept a society which is incompatible with that code ?[73]

Such questions are undoubtedly important for sociologists, moral philosophers and all those who have taken upon themselves the responsibility for creating a new social order in India. What is of immediate concern to us in the evaluation of the Nyāya system is what the Naiyāyika has done with these questions. Even a cursory glance at the exposition of the system given in this book will show that our philosophers have accepted wholesale the finished products of external origins and thus sanctioned morals without proper scrutiny. They cannot therefore be said to have performed their essential task as moral philosophers. But even more serious is the manner in which they have used such unexamined doctrines to create a portrait of the universe. The eternality of the self, its involvement in *saṃsāra,* constant emphasis on the preservation of the social order and the fear of chaos resulting from any disturbance of that order, as well as acceptance of all kinds of literature as authoritative—these are but a few of the examples of this uncritical acceptance. The fusion of the social order with the order of the universe has been an obsession with many thinkers in the East and the West, but it rests on very slender foundations. Anthropologists commonly assert that myths express social structures and this fusion may be just one of such myths. So far as the Naiyāyika is concerned, he really does not have any grand vision of the moral order pervading the entire universe, and even the divine agency which the followers have found for it amounts to no more than the role of *deus ex machina.* In the everyday world there is a hiatus between the deed and its moral desert in terms of pleasure and pain: a confirmed sinner often goes unpunished and the best of saints remains unhonoured in his own life time. It is the function of the divine agency to ensure that what seems to have failed in the past is made good in the present or the future. This may sound like delayed-justice but its utility in present life is elusive.

Another important question in moral philosophy is: what do we judge when we pass a moral judgment ? In this context we have first to define the area of our life with which moral judgment can be properly said to be concerned. If we were to make moral discourse coterminous with the entire gamut of our life, it is obvious that the moral discourse ceases to be meaningful. Another way of saying the same thing is that if my moral responsibility covers everything I do or feel or think, then every aspect of my life becomes an object of moral judgment. This really destroys the notion of moral responsibility. If my sneezing is as much an object of moral judgment as my hitting someone, then there is nothing distinctive left for the moral discourse or moral responsibility. Hence the problem of freedom of will versus determinism or the controversies about mechanism versus teleology or rival theories about the justification of punishment are important for any moral philosophy. A moral philosophy tied to the basic doctrine of individual salvation really skirts such issues and concedes the underlying assumptions of its morality, which are founded in the social order.

Another question which must be raised in the context of morality based on caste or class and stage of life (*varṇāśrama*) is: Must we accept that we belong to a particular caste or class, and if we do, must we always do so ? It is obvious that in the context of the *varṇa* system this is no longer acceptable. A modern untouchable refuses to connive at a moral code which degrades him to the status of less than a human being. Mahatma Gandhi has already baptised him into a Harijan and thus subverted at least one part of the theoretical structure.

Even more important is the question: can we really accept the so-called stages of life ? Unless the entire span of life as visualised in the *āśrama* system is guaranteed in advance, this kind of morality cannot be practised except by the centenarian. There is of course the additional question of eligibility in the traditional structure of the *varṇa* system. If a particular kind of morality depends upon a particular class or a stage of life, it has become thoroughly relativistic; even more, it is virtually impossible of attainment. Those of us who cannot live to the stipulated period of life cannot hope to fulfil the moral code. If this difficulty is met by a promise of some future life, our moral life becomes a hostage to the karma doctrine. And this doctrine has been the bane of the Indian society for centuries.

The karma doctrine is undoubtedly concerned with such moral issues. Take, for example, the area of moral discourse. According to the Naiyāyika, activity (*pravṛtti*) is due to defect (*doṣa*). Activity is defined as that which initiates speech, corporeal and mental action. If this is taken literally, every aspect of one's life becomes an object of moral judgment; and what is even more serious is that every moral judgment is reduced to moral disapproval. This view destroys at one stroke both the possibility of a well-defined moral discourse as well as the distinction between good and bad, or right and wrong, which must be the very foundation of any moral philosophy. If every thing is good or bad, surely, there is no point in using any moral terms. Of course, it is suggested that the philosopher is concerned with that activity which can be brought under the blanket pejorative term *doṣa*, but the fundamental assumption of the karma doctrine is its claim to govern every aspect of life and even the psychosomatic apparatus. Even the so-called virtues must ultimately be reduced to some kind of *doṣa*.

Another complication in the Nyāya moral discourse is the mysterious mistake (*mithyājñāna*). This mistake has no beginning and the Naiyāyika really has no explanation why there should be such a mistake or if there is one, why it should launch the self in the orbit of *saṃsāra*. The doctrine of knowledge as virtue is of distinguished lineage, but the doctrine of error as the source of all that we are or do must inevitably lead to the belief that those who are ignorant are not only intellectually inferior but also morally corrupt. A society, where education and knowledge have been regarded as the birthright of some and denied to others on grounds of birth, is one which can only perpetuate the knowledge of those who had always had it, and the ignorance of the many to whom that knowledge was denied. There can be no social or spiritual justification for keeping any part of society away from the secrets of the universe.

What is often not realized in the context of that mysterious error is that the philosopher is really concerned with something in the nature of the monopoly of truth. A heresy is a heresy in so far as it is a departure from a particular doctrine and in practice it means nothing more than the doctrine of the opponent. There is a temptation to confuse *mithyājñāna* (erroneous apprehension) with heresy, as there is a definite effort to identify the *tattvajñāna* (knowledge of the true nature of things) with the system the Naiyāyika has himself formulated. When we are thinking of the different paths to salvation—*jñāna* (knowledge), *karma* (action) and *bhukti* (devotion), or even such classifications as the *pravṛttimārga* (the path of activity) and *nivṛttimārga* (the path of renunciation)—we must always bear in mind this underlying assumption of such doctrines. It seems as though religious or theologically inclined thinkers were prepared to combine divergent theories while the philosophers were unable to recognize that ways of reaching the supreme objective of salvation may vary. Religions normally claim to have the monopoly of truth and have always distinguished between two classes of people; 'us' and 'them' is not only a social reality but also a hard spiritual doctrine.

If every aspect of life is an object of moral judgment or if every moral judgment is nothing but moral disapproval, it follows that Nyāya morality cannot be given the kind of justification to which the Naiyāyika is committed. He has thus deprived himself of the opportunity of being a moral philosopher. Such morality as the Naiyāyika has laid down can therefore be accepted if we take him on trust. If we do so, we have of course his word for the rewards for our good conduct and for the suffering for our bad conduct. But, then, we are asked to subscribe to morality without justification. To say that the Naiyāyika is himself an āpta is really to beg the whole question.

According to the Naiyāyika, there can be no valid proof if the proposition to be proved covers everything, for there can be no valid hetu supported by an example. The essence of this notion is that we should not indulge in an unrestricted generalization, not supported by evidence. But in his speculations about the self and other objects of cognition (*prameya*), the Naiyāyika seems to have departed from his basic concept.

The karma doctrine has several aspects. Essentially, it is an essay in physical, physiological, biological and social engineering. It is a doctrinal expression of a social system generally described as *varṇāśrama*. This system is an ingenious justification for a non-egalitarian society.[74] According to the standard exposition of the system, there are four permanent classes with permanent privileges, immunities and obligations. At the apex of the system is the class concerned with learning and education. Learning is sacred if not secretive, and both learning and education are strictly meant for this class. This class is expected to be supported and revered by the other classes. The second class in order of merit is that of the warriors. This class is expected to wield political and military power. The third class is concerned with money-making. It is the class of merchants and bankers. These three classes constitute the privileged and honoured sections of the community. The fourth class at the bottom of the *varṇāśrama* system is that of the peasants. It is the class concerned with the production of food and other goods and services. There is a fifth class which is outside the system which must perform manual and dirty work which no other class will.

The outstanding merit of the system is that it created such a mental and social climate that those who prospered under the system seldom if at all questioned the injustice of the system while those who were the victims of the system hardly realized the nature and scope of the injustice. The karma doctrine killed at one stroke intellectual and social protest. As already mentioned, such theories of society are not uncommon amongst philosophers. It is sometimes said that all Western philosophy is a series of footnotes to Plato. Perhaps one could say that a hierarchical system could not have found a more brilliant theoretician in the Western thought. But what the generation of philosophers and writers of the *Dharmaśāstras*, the Epics and the *Purāṇas* have accomplished must be regarded as a monument to the contribution of the learned and privileged classes to the bondage of human beings and their minds. It is often said that the philosopher who propagates a myth or superstition does so only because he has succumbed to the pressures of his less educated fellowmen. This must be one of the noblest alibis of which even Plato would be proud. After all, he sanctioned the 'noble lie' in his Republic.

Like the classes and their roles, we have another classification of objectives to be pursued by the different classes and types of people. There are some whose objective is *dharma*; some whose objective is wealth; some whose objective is erotic pleasure (*kāma*); some whose objective is salvation.

The Naiyāyika has given us still another classification on the basis of his pramāṇa doctrine. This classification is not only dubious but even contrary to its basic tenets. There are some who depend for knowledge on perception: some who acquire knowledge through inference; some through analogy; some through the *śabdapramāṇa*.

In similar vein we have a classification of activity: some activity is always successful, like that of those who follow the prescribed path of salvation and some activity can never be successful or only partially successful, like that of ordinary people. Success is the hallmark of spiritual activity while failure or partial success is the fate of all worldly activity. The Naiyāyika has also labelled men according to their capacity for understanding or comprehension. Students of philosophy are familiar with the ancient distinction between knowledge and opinion or the wise man and, to use an expression of a modern philosopher, 'the mob'.

This grand pattern of individuals, classes, mental capacities, traits of character, occupations, objectives and success and failure in the order of hierarchy or order of merit, secular as well as spiritual — this is said to be the actual framework of the Indian society from the earliest times. Such a comprehensive generalization of an empirical character is sometimes offered even in our age with all the prestige of social science. The natural scientist is beginning to shy away from such generalizations or if he does offer them, he claims for them nothing more than a certain degree of probability. But in the context of he Indian philosophical and religious speculations the karma theory claims for itself absolute and unquestionable truth. Dogma is an essential feature of this doctrine. If it were treated as an empirical proposition, it could be judged by the ordinary standards of empirical investigation. And then it will be found to contain a mass of unverified and unverifiable assumptions.

What has puzzled many observers of the Indian scene is not that such a scheme governing every aspect of life stretching across eternity was fabricated but that it has survived over the centuries, apparently without dissent or revolt. It is even suggested that the survival is itself the criterion of its great merit. It is obvious that this system could not have survived by brute force alone. Like the British Raj, it may be said to have survived because it appeared to be better than what actually obtained. Its theory was more attractive than the reality. In this process of orientation the elaborate machinery of communication worked out over the centuries must have penetrated the innermost recesses of the minds and the hearts of the people. Those who have watched the prayer meetings of Mahatma Gandhi would testify how powerful such a medium can be. Even the television spectacular conducted with a satellite could not have matched the range of this communication medium. Myths or superstitions travel faster than reason and these grow on what they feed.

History has given us two outstanding examples of comprehensive conformity of thought and behaviour: The Catholic Church[75] and the *varṇāśrama* system. In recent years we have seen how even the most highly educated community can be harnessed in the service of a ruthless and scientific tyranny. Social engineering has now become both a science and an accomplished art, and it has raised questions not only of our value systems but also the survival of the human race. Power, whether intellectual, economic, political or spiritual, corrupts, and absolute power corrupts absolutely. A change in the Indian society, as in any other society, must mean the redistribution of this power.

The process of annihilation, in reverse order, of pain, birth, activity, defect and erroneous apprehension, which Gautama has mentioned in his opening statement, is a complicated causal operation. The Naiyāyika who believes in a regular causal order in other spheres frankly says that in this sphere there is no such order. In most of Indian thought there is such a chain but the remedy for destroying the chain varies from philosopher to philosopher. This means that different causes produce the same effect: this would amount to a plurality of causes. On a strict application of the plurality doctrine the value of the causal principle for explanation is substantially reduced. If there is not the same cause for the same effect, it is difficult to pin down specific effects to specific causes. The Naiyāyika who is concerned with a design of the conceptual framework seems to have ignored this problem in handling the question of causality. Perhaps no other Indian philosopher has viewed this question in this context.

Another aspect which the Naiyāyika should have considered is the nature of the series (*santāna*) which seems to me nothing but a universal (*jāti*). If this is so, such a universal is a permanent fixture of his universe. The universals in the Nyāya system are indestructible. If, then, pain, birth, activity, defect and erroneous apprehension constitute a series, this series cannot but be a universal. Nothing can therefore destroy the series. It is difficult to understand how if a series is indestructible the members of that series can be destroyed without destroying the series itself; that is, there is no such series. But, then, we are confronted with a very difficult situation. Since the *saṃsāra* is the series, either there is no *saṃsāra* or if there is one it cannot be destroyed. If the *saṃsāra* cannot be ended, there can be no liberation. Consequently, whatever remedy may be prescribed, it cannot be effective; this means there can be no liberation.

It would seem more reasonable to say that if the series is to be destroyed its individual members should be destroyed. But it is difficult to imagine how the kind of members that there are in the chain can be destroyed. It is obvious that once one is born what can be destroyed is not birth for that is an event that has already occurred; what can be destroyed is life itself; but this would amount to killing and no one would suggest such a course. It seems impossible to destroy death; no one has been able to avoid death as it is generally understood. The Naiyāyika recognizes death explicitly in his discussion of the object of cognition, state after death (*pretyabhāva*). Death can be postponed, but the doctrine of rebirth requires that one should be born and die according to the dispensation of one's karma. Strictly speaking, any programme of birth-control and of medical treatment calculated to prolong life or avert death would be logically incompatible with the karma doctrine and its counterparts, *saṃsāra* and liberation. The Naiyāyika could say that the series is itself a metaphor, and when the series is said to be destroyed, all that is meant is a metaphorical description. This is inherent in the Nyāya concept of pain. But then what weight can be given to what the philosopher regards as nothing more than metaphor ? It is of course possible to say that if birth itself is prevented death cannot follow. In fact this often seems to be the nub of the doctrine. This is undoubtedly true but then what we are destroying is not the series. If this referred to the first ever birth, the series has not even begun. It is of course possible to interrupt the series at any intermediate stage and this would be liberation.

In all theories of the Naiyāyika the basic relations are contact, causation and inherence. Since the universe consists of distinct particulars spread all over in ākāśa, the most important relation between them is one of contact. This relation of contact is used not only in the ontology of the Nyāya but also in its epistemology. The qualitatively different atoms, when in contact, produce the physical world. They also produce the body and the sense-organs and even though the position about the mind is confused, we must treat the mind as part of the material world. The selves are the occupants of the corporeal bodies. But the kind of bodies they have are determined by their merit and demerit or karma. Thus the atoms are the material cause while the karma is the instrumental cause.

The notion of causation is the notion of things producing things. The ultimate constituents of these things are indestructible and unchangeable and the entire variety of the physical world is thus predetermined by the original pattern of the four kinds of atoms. Of course, the Naiyāyika insists that there is real production of new things in the universe, but if *qualitative* differences are first determined in the atomic constitution, there cannot be genuine novelty in the universe. That is why the debate between the Buddhist and the Naiyāyika as to whether the object is merely an aggregate or a new product — is primarily metaphysical; it is a matter of giving a proper description. But with the kind of the theory of the physical universe which they both shared there can only be stale repetition or recurrence. If this theory is also applied to the evolution of life, it cannot but lead to a similar result. If everything is as it was except in detail, there cannot be much of the sense of wonder which is associated with the Greeks. Moreover, there is always someone who knows all that is to be known; in fact, since the philosophical discourse begins with this initial assumption, there is no need for adventure of ideas. In this connection it is worth recalling the observation of Whitehead on the Greeks and the Chinese who 'achieved certain perfections of civilization — each worthy of admiration. But even perfection will not bear the tedium of indefinite repetition. To sustain a civilization with the intensity of its first ardour requires more than learning. Adventure is essential, namely, the search for new perfections.'[76] If perfection is already ingrained in one's self there can be not much of adventure in discovering the original perfection. Human endeavour is deprived of the exhilaration of achievement.

The notion of causation in terms of things makes it a static notion. If eternal things are the important causes, they must always be there. And then what happens to them afterwards can only be in the nature of a creation in spatial terms. The atoms and the selves are such eternal entities. When they function as causes, their effects can only be added on to them. In this context the cause becomes the support of the effect and continues throughout the process of effectuation. With this notion, apprehensions, merit and demerit, results of merit and demerit — these are all given a resting place in the self. The physical world rests on the atoms; the living world rests on the selves. The distinction is blurred. In this sense the causal relation becomes one of inherence. It may not be far wrong to say that the relation of contact is transformed through causation into inherence. And this relation, says the Naiyāyika, is inexplicable.

If we look at the Nyāya doctrines from the point of view of the relation of inherence, the system is exposed to the charge of inexplicability. Its main doctrines revolve round the notion of substance and property. The self is a substance and it has the properties mainly connected with consciousness. The atom is a substance and each one of the four kinds of the atoms has a property. The relation between substance and property is one of inherence. Since this relation is not considered as explicable, we are really reduced to the position of saying the same thing about the doctrinal structure of the system itself. If we were to pursue this line, to the bitter end, we would have to say that even knowledge or proof in the Nyāya system is inexplicable.

The notion of substance is often described as one of the container and the contained. In this context it means that the properties are contained in the substance to which they belong. But a substance also functions as a cause. In this context the properties are said to be produced from the substance, but then what is produced will have to be treated as contained in the cause. That is to say, the effect is contained in the cause. The relation of the container and the contained is really non-temporal. As the Naiyāyika insists, if there is to be the relation of the container and the contained, the container must be present to hold the contained. This relation can therefore be regarded as spatial. If this is so, any change in the world can be nothing more than a re-arrangement of things which are indestructible. Another way by which this relation is described is one of the principal and the subordinate. The substance is the principal and its property the subordinate. Inherence can also be viewed as the relation of the agent and its action. The self is an agent and its actions consist of apprehensions. The agent is eternal but its actions are ephemeral. In this way even the atoms must be regarded as agents and the actions of the atoms give us the things of the world.

The whole pattern of explanation is deterministic. What was before or happened before determines what is now or happens now; what is now or happens now determines what will be in the future or will happen in the future. In this pattern there is really not much room for any genuine teleology. If teleology means a purpose towards which we strive and which we eventually accomplish, so far as *saṃsāra* is concerned, we cannot say that the self gets involved in *saṃsāra* with the end or purpose of involvement in view. In fact, this involvement is entirely foreign to its essential nature or purpose. Hence the misapprehension (*mithyājñāna*) must be located in the past to account for the involvement of the self in *saṃsāra*. To say that this process has no beginning really explains nothing. Even salvation is in the nature of the correction of a past error. It acquires something of a presence because the error is expressed in psychosomatic terms. All the same, the correction of a mistake is important enough an achievement. Even the process of correction — in the Nyāya language, the annihilation of pain, birth, activity, defect and erroneous apprehension — loses any semblance of an order in the hands of the commentators. It is said that there is no such rule that one must precede the other. This amounts to a breakdown of the law of karma. If the law of karma means anything, it means a definite order of good and bad deed — merit and demerit — pleasure and pain — psychosomatic equipment. We may start at the beginning or at the end, but once we have decided upon a starting-point there must be some regularity in the process. Otherwise, like the relation of inherence the notion of the annihilation becomes inexplicable. The gloss of the commentators is certainly not an improvement on Gautama's position.

In this connection we must remember the extraordinary concern of the Naiyāyika for order or lack of order. In the context of the doctrines of his opponents the Naiyāyika protests vigorously against the reign of rule (*niyama*). He wants the rule to say no more than what is actually observed. But he is equally apprehensive about the lack of uniformity or even of rule in other contexts. The argument from chaos and the argument from the obstruction are regular features of the Nyāya exposition. If one sound did not produce another sound and the last member of such a series did not reach our ear, there would be chaos in what we hear; so also in nature. If words were not related to objects as the grammarians have decided, there would be chaos in all discourse and communication. If we did not act upon the pramāṇas — and it is not easy to see how one can really act upon such things — there would be chaos in human affairs. More specifically, if we did not accept the authority of the āptas and their outpourings, the whole society would go to the dogs. If our sensations were not filtered through the mind, one by one, there would be utter confusion in our conscious life. Last but not least, if the karmic order were disturbed there would be complete moral anarchy. The whole concept of chaos is rooted in the concept of the four orders of society and the four stages of life (*varṇāśrama*). In fact, it is the fear of disturbing this pattern that is at the root of the argument from the chaos.

Every breakdown of rule or its application to a concrete situation can be explained by reference to an obstruction. This is the argument from obstruction. If there were no obstruction, we would apprehend what we do not apprehend. This opens up vast possibilities of asserting the existence of anything even if one does not see it: not to be is not to be apprehended. This is almost the obverse of Berkeley's dictum: *Esse est percipi*. While the Naiyāyika is no subjectivist, he is prepared to say that a thing need not be dismissed as non-existent if it is not apprehended. After all, the Naiyāyika has recognized the distinction between the perceived and the unperceived objects in the context of the *śabdapramāṇa*. And the unperceived objects — the objects which the humans are debarred from perceiving — are the objects like heaven or the remote consequences of good or bad deeds. If the Vedic injunction says that on the performance of a sacrifice a son will be born and if it so happens that the performer is not blessed with the son, this is explained with reference to obstruction or deficiency somewhere amongst the factors involved in the sacrifice. As a safeguard, the Naiyāyika declares that it is impossible to say when, where and how the fruit of our actions will appear or even will not appear. Thus, as in the case of inherence we have the spectre of inexplicability.

Such arguments from the chaos and the obstruction are also used in the context of the hetu and the corroborating example, positive or negative. If a particular cause does not produce a particular result or if a particular hetu seems to be incapable of being corroborated by an example, it can be said that there was some obstruction why the effect did not appear or the example does not seem to support the hetu. What is to be regarded as apprehended or non-apprehended or what precisely constitutes a reliable apprehension or non-apprehension is itself so vague that anyone who is determined enough can declare anything as the case, to suit his convenience or argument. That is why the Naiyāyika leaves such matters to conventions set up by āptas or covenants or agreements between the experts and the laymen; in practice this really means the covenant among the philosophers to agree or to disagree. And they agree upon matters concerning the society in which they live but disagree on doctrinal creeds. Their real battle is not so much a battle for truth but a battle for the minds of men who are not really involved at any stage in the making of their views. There is not only an impenetrable iron curtain between the learned and the ignorant but even more so it is reinforced by the sanction of holiness. There is no dialogue between the philosopher and the community.

One of the ways in which the Naiyāyika could have escaped from this charge of inexplicability would have been to stick to his basic thesis: there are distinct particulars; the relation between them is one of contact or of causation. Though the Naiyāyika has planted the universal in the structure of the universe, he is really interested in similarities. Even his similarities sometimes look like the family resemblances of Wittgenstein. Instead of using the relation of inherence in the sphere of mental life he could have used the principle of association, which, in a way, would be a counterpart of contact. But this would have meant partial or complete abandonment of the notions of substance and agency. If the relation between substance and property is mysterious, so must be the philosophy which rests on such a relation. The Aristotelian notion of the material cause is really of what constitutes what. To understand the changing universe we need a different notion of cause: an event leading to another event or as it is sometimes put, event-particle to event-particle.

The controversies between the Naiyāyika, on the one hand, and the Buddhist and the Sāṃkhya, on the other, rest on the nature of communication in language. The debate between the Sāṃkhya and the Naiyāyika regarding the nature of the *buddhi* is really conducted from different premises. The Nyāya *buddhi* is a mental event which becomes conscious because of the agency of the self, while the Sāṃkhya *buddhi* is an element partaking of the character of the *prakṛti* but its specific function being converted into one of conscious experience because of its contact with the *puruṣa* or the reflection of the *puruṣa* in the *buddhi*.

The debate between the Buddhist and the Naiyāyika about the self, recollection or generally mental life is conducted on the basis of their respective metaphysical positions regarding the nature of change and causation. Although the philosophers have generated a great deal of heat in these controversies, it does not appear that they have produced commensurate illumination. This is largely because they shared a common mode of training and life, common attitudes towards the society in which they lived and loyalties to certain basic presuppositions. They differed on ultimate questions such as perfection or salvation and the way to attain it. No one could have interfered with their objectives and their ways of life did not provoke any dissent or revolt; on the contrary, they commanded all the reverence and admiration they could have asked for. But perhaps there was always a respectable distance between the philosophers and the public. The Indian establishment and the populace cast their gods in stone or bronze and worshipped them in temples. Somehow their private love for the wisdom of the philosopher was seldom expressed in stone or bronze, where both the establishment and the populace could give him public homage in recognition of his gifts. Is anonymity of the philosopher the expression of private admiration and public non-recognition ? If gods were worshipped, why were not the philosophers reverenced in the customary manner ? In fact, the gods were active all the time, but the philosophers have been resurrected only now. And the process of discovery is still not complete.

As I have remarked earlier, philosophy and theology cannot be easily separated. Some philosophers treat natural theology, i.e. the knowledge of God as gained from his works by light of nature and reason as part of philosophy. In any case those who are reckoned as philosophers have been deeply concerned with the problem of God and all that it involves. The story of the ontological argument, the cosmological argument and the physico-theological proof or the argument from design for the existence of God is far too well known to dissolve the relation that has existed between theology and philosophy. Even some of the most modern empiricists have found enough justification in their empiricism for the belief in God.[77] If the Indian thinkers have discussed god and his works without using the notions of natural light or reason, this does not necessarily mean that they were not using arguments to justify what they believed on faith or they did not reach their faith after having exhausted the whole range of arguments they were accustomed to. Here as elsewhere, the basic problems raised and answers given were largely determined by the cultural complex to which the philosopher belonged. What is really striking about Indian thought is, not whether theology should be part of philosophy, but that India has produced religions without God. These thinkers have examined the problem in its various aspects and have not found it necessary to found their faith or religion on the existence of God. What is even more striking is that within the Hindu thought a dominant trend was away from, not towards, God. Amongst the six systems of Hindu philosophy at least four — Pūrva Mīmāṃsā, Sāṃkhya, Vaiśeṣika, and Nyāya — were originally non-theistic if not atheistic in temper. The Pūrva Mīmāṃsā is known to be the defender of the Vedic religion, but it too had no pretensions to theism. Even though some of the commentators ushered in God into their respective systems, this was more in the nature of accretion. Whether or not the belief in God was incorporated in the earlier formulations of the systems or added on to the systems by later commentators, it really makes no difference. In the structure of these systems as we know them there is really no reasonable basis for incorporating it in their systems. And I must emphasize that this is meant to be, not an historical argument but the logical or philosophical one. The *Brahman* doctrine must be distinguished from the doctrine of God and it is not therefore surprising that in the Vedānta of Śaṅkara God has a somewhat inferior position.

According to the Naiyāyika God belongs to the same category (*kalpa*) as the self. If this is so, God would be, as is the self, subject to the same misapprehension, *saṃsāra* and liberation. To say that God has more or better of what the self has cannot alter the fact that they both belong to the same category. If, however, the properties of God are fundamentally different from those of the self, it is not reasonable to say that God belongs to the same category as the self; for such an identification would amount to what may be called a 'category mistake'.[78]

The Nyāya universe consists of eternal selves and eternal atoms: these cannot therefore be created or destroyed. The kind of relations that the Naiyāyika has recognized cannot really be established between God and the universe. Contact, causation, agency and inherence are the recognized relations and these cannot be said to subsist between God and the universe or its main components. His only function is to regulate the karma system of rewards and punishments.

In the Nyāya system the self has two basic problems: involvement in *saṃsāra* and liberation. The former is explained as due to misapprehension (*mithyājñāna*) which has no beginning. The latter is due to the knowledge of the true nature of things (*tattvajñāna*) as provided by Gautama in his Nyāya system. God is not one of the Nyāya sixteen categories nor does the Nyāya system claim to be a divine revelation. All that it claims to be is the revelation of truth as vouched for by an āpta. Thus God has no significant part in the Nyāya scheme of *saṃsāra* and liberation. In liberation, as in *saṃsāra*, the Naiyāyika insists that the self must maintain its distinct individuality, identity and continuity. The self cannot be merged in any other agency. The self is self, whether bound or free.

In *saṃsāra* the Naiyāyika has one difficulty for which he has no satisfactory explanation. In the world in which we live it is not uncommon to find that the saints are not always rewarded nor are the sinners always punished. This discrepancy between the theory of the moral governance of the universe and the actual facts in the universe has exercised the minds of theologians and philosophers both in the West and in the East. The specific problem that worries the Naiyāyika is how to reconcile this discrepancy with his view of causation. He believes that a proper cause must produce its effect immediately and as contiguously to the empirical self as possible. The Naiyāyika could have remained content with the kind of explanation which he has frequently given in such matters. He could say that the discrepancy is no real discrepancy but is due to merely our errors of observation or some defects of the individuals concerned. For instance, he has argued that if a son is not born even when a person has performed a sacrifice, it can be explained by saying that something went wrong with the performance. Or, he could say, as he has done sometimes, that these are matters which are beyond our comprehension. But it seems that he is not prepared to depend upon such explanations for the discrepancy is far too serious to be explained away in this fashion. The Naiyāyika wishes to preserve the undisputed rule of the moral or karmic principle for he is convinced that once the faith in this system is undermined there will be nothing but chaos. In the last resort this chaos could only be the disruption of the social order he saw around him. The Naiyāyika therefore has found in God the saviour of the moral order of his conception and the society with which he was intimately acquainted. It is God who ensures that before any self attains its liberation it has settled its moral account. It must have experienced every pleasure and pain due to it before it can be eligible for salvation. In this picture what can be easily forgotten is that some people must have their full share of suffering on moral grounds while others must have their full share of their pleasures on the same grounds. This would be justifiable because the pains are due to bad deeds as pleasures are due to good deeds. In this kind of moral dispensation those who suffer are not only condemned to their unenviable lot but also are deprived of any concrete remedy to alleviate their suffering in this life. Their only hope lies in relief in the hereafter. This moral dispensation equally makes sure that those who have pleasures in this life must have them and they have an additional advantage that this is what is due to them. Apart from those who opted out of society for one reason or another, this moral dispensation means that the haves should remain haves and the have-nots have-nots. This is the price of maintaining a theory or principle in the face of evidence to the contrary. This may satisfy the conscience of a dogmatic theologian but certainly cannot appeal to any sensible moral philosopher or lover of humanity. The Indian philosopher rightly says that suffering is his concern and that it must be eradicated. The only question is: which suffering and how ? The empiricist, if he is true to his basic canons of evidence, can only give an answer which most people would give. And that is to create conditions on this earth where all avoidable suffering is dealt with sympathy and compassion.

The problem of personal identity is of great importance both for the philosophers and practical men. Even the most extreme idealist or materialist has to give some account of how to determine personal identity. Moral philosophy is vitally concerned with this question. In practical life much depends upon the determination of personal identity. For instance, the State needs a working concept of individual or person in order to confer privileges or inflict punishments.

In a system like the Nyāya, this question becomes rather complicated, because its notion of personal identity extends backwards to eternity and forwards to an indefinite future. This range is the range of the travels of the self in a variety of manifestations. When the self has attained liberation and has shed all the psychosomatic paraphernalia except some kind of nondescript or indescribable consciousness, the difficulties become almost insuperable. And then, we have another problem: how to distinguish God from other selves.

In solving this problem it is obvious that the common properties allotted to the self by Gautama can only define what the self is, not who he is. This enables us to say that there is a class of entities characterized by consciousness and that this class is different from the class of those entities which do not have consciousness. To say that the self is a kind of eternal substance with consciousness is really no answer to the problem; it merely records the fact that one has somehow been identified but does not explain why a self is the self that it is. In the case of an eternal self the physical or psychological criteria cannot account for the personal identity, because they are really intended to function as common properties. Moreover, it is impossible to compile the entire history of the self for by definition the self is eternal and eternity cannot be completed. This may be possible for an omniscient God, but what we are concerned with is how we as human beings can determine personal idenuty, not how this can be done by any other agency including divine agency.

In view of these difficulties it is not surprising that the Naiyāyika ultimately rests his case for personal identity on the criterion of the karma of the self. Even here, he is forced to bring in God because it is not easy to connect the deed with the fruit in the sense of the cause immediately being followed by the effect. But the operation of karma, as Uddyotakara confesses, is something of a mystery which no philosopher has been able to fathom. In another context it is also said that it is impossible to say why a particular cause produces a particular effect; we can only say that it does so in the light of our experience. But the real significance of this for the Naiyāyika is that this apparently scientific presumption helps him to meet the inscrutable character of the operation of karma.

That the karma criterion is not of much help can be seen from the fact that the Naiyāyika eventually translates it into worldly terms, like birth in a particular family, defects or excellences of body or intelligence. The criteria of personal identity become physical, psychological or social, but always with a strong moral flavour.

The criteria of such character can only be applied in a particular culture complex. In this sense they are sociological and it is for the sociologists to determine their value and validity. What is obvious is that these criteria cannot be treated as logical. We now know that different societies evaluate different characteristics differently; what may be considered important in one sciety, say colour, may not be so considered in another society, even in the same society at different times. Here as elsewhere, it is important to bear in mind that the Indian philosopher was always a sociologist, sometimes conscious and sometimes unconscious of it. That is why philosophers like Gautama or Vātsyāyana are most anxious to convince the Brahmins how the acceptance of his doctrine of knowledge as a remedy for salvation can be combined with the performance of the Vedic ritual, in fact he seems to say that there is enough time in the life of a Brahmin for such varied pursuits and yet obtain the results he wants most. Similarly, Vātsyāyana insists that the pramāṇas and disputation govern the affairs of men and animals; and this means that every. one should do what he is authorised to do.

NOTES

(The first figure indicates the number of the note; the second figure indicates the number of the page. For instance : 1.237 means Note 1 on page 237.)

INTRODUCTION

1. XXXVIII Flew, Anthony: *An introduction to Western philosophy*, Thames and Hudsons, London, 1971, p. 36.

2. XXXVIII Guthrie, W. K. C. *A history of Greek philosophy*, Vol. II, Cambridge at the University Press, 1965, p. 53.

In this footnote the author is mainly concerned with the doctrine of *Māyā* and Brahmanism as outlined by S. Radhakrishnan and C. A. Moore in their '*A source book in Indian philosophy*' ('The power of illusion, Māyā', pp. 589-97) and by H. Zimmer in his *Philosophies of India*, p. 380.

The author holds that 'India and Parmenides are poles apart', but he is prepared to compare Heraclitus with the ideas in such Indian systems as the Sāṃkhya and Pātañjala Yoga.

PART ONE : CENTRAL THEME

1

CATEGORIES

1.3. Cf. Introduction

PART TWO : THEORY OF COGNITION

2

PRAMĀṆA

Introductory

1.9. The various pramāṇas recognized by different systems are well summed up in the quotation from *Tārkikarakṣā* of Varada Rāja reproduced by Randle in his ILES, n., p. 305.

Pratyakṣam ekaṃ cārvākāḥ kaṇādasaugatau punaḥ anumānaṃ ca; Tac cātha sāṃkhyāḥ śabdaṃ ca te api; Nyāyaikadeśino 'py evam, upamānaṃ ca kecana. Arthāpattau sahaitāni catvārya āha prabhākaraḥ, abhāvaṣaṣṭhāny etāni bhāṭṭā vedāntinas tathā saṃbhavaitihyayuktāni tāni paurāṇikā jaguḥ.

The Nyāya school which recognizes only three pramāṇas is represented by the followers of the *Nyāyasāra* of Bhāsarvajña. Varada Rāja refers to this school (See HIL, p. 358).

Among the Buddhists, a Hīnayānist preceding Nāgārjuna, admits four pramāṇas as maintained by the Naiyāyikas, and the older school of Yogācāras excludes analogy (*upamāna*) therefrom, without giving any reason (See Hattori, Notes, p. 78).

2.9. For the Jain view, see *Tattvārthādhigama Sūtra* of Śri Umāsvāti Ācārya, Sacred Books of the Jainas, Vol. II, Arrah: India: The Central Jaina Publishing House, 1920, Sūtras I.1.9-11 and nn. pp. 21-23.

I. The nature and scope of the pramāṇa

3.11. "Dignāga's statement that a clear understanding of *prameya* (=*artha*) depends upon pramāṇa (*pramāṇādhigamaḥ prameyādhigamaḥ*) has an affinity with the opening statement of the *Nyāya Bhāyṣa-pramāṇato 'rtha pratipattau pravṛtti sāmarthyād arthavat pramāṇam.*" The Naiyāyikas and the Vijñānavādins differ regarding the nature of pramāṇa and *prameya.* Dignāga shares the Vijñānavādins' view that they are of ideational character (See Hattori, Notes p. 76).

4.13. *Pratyakṣānumānānadhigatavastutattvānvākhyānaṃ śāstradharmaḥ tasya viṣayaḥ pratyakṣānumānānadhigatavastutattva ādhyātmikaśaktisampadyukto 'ntevāsī* (Introductory N.V).

5.17. The objection as stated by Uddyotakara applies to all pramāṇas, but he answers it with reference to perception only. The answer to the objection when taken in reference to all pramāṇas, according to Jha, should be that the pramāṇa is not brought into existence by the cognizer and the object of cognition; these latter only serve to set it into activity towards the production of cognition (See Jha, Vol. I, n. p. 19).

II. Validity of the pramāṇas

6.25. The polemic in NS II. 1,8-12 and II. 1,16-18 is similar to that between Nāgārjuna and a Nyāya opponent in the *Vigrahavyāvartanī.*

According to Vācaspati the objection based on the inapplicability of the pramāṇas to three times, past, present and future, which is embodied in NS II. 1,8-11, emanates from the Mādhyamika Buddhists. The Mādhyamika view is as follows:

"We hold that nothing can be established and that this is true of pramāṇas. But since other philosophers accept pramāṇas, we will show that on the basis of their own pramāṇas they melt away by their own inner contradictions. And this is no fault of ours. The argument against the pramāṇa doctrine may be thus formally stated:

'Perception and other pramāṇas cannot be regarded as pramāṇa, because they cannot prove or indicate the presence of objects at any time; anything that does not prove its object at any time is not regarded as pramāṇa; for instance, the conception of hare's horns; perception and other pramāṇas are such; therefore they cannot be regarded as pramāṇa'" (NVTT II. 1,8).

7.28. The illustration of the hidden musical instrument is given in NBh II. 1,25.

8.29. The argument as formulated by the opponent is faulty in its structure. The hetu, viz. the impossibility of connecting the pramāṇas with three times, is heterogeneous in that it has no relation to the subject of the proposition.

III. Status of additional four pramāṇas

9.42. According to Vācaspati, the denial would be certain only if it were in the form 'there is no such thing as presumption'.

But the denial of the existence of a thing, on the basis of its being uncertain, would not be true. For certainly what is not certain does not cease to exist.

10.42. With regard to this objection, Uddyotakara says that it is not non-existence which is a pramāṇa but its conception. The objection, according to him, is this: Non-existence cannot be treated as a pramāṇa, as it can have no object; that which has no object cannot be a pramāṇa, e.g. the word 'cow' is not an instrument of the cognition of the 'horse', simply because the horse is not its object; thus non-existence has no object and cannot, therefore, be treated as a pramāṇa. It is not non-existence that is a pramāṇa, says the commentator, but it is the conception (*pratipatti*) of non-existence that is the pramāṇa as by means of this conception, things are cognized. The object of this conception is non-existence (NV II. 2,7).

3

PERCEPTION (*pratyakṣa*)

I

1.47. *Indriyārthasannikarṣotpannaṃ jñānam āwyapadeśyam āvyabhicārī vyavasāyātmakaṃ pratyakṣam* (NS. I. 1,4).

2.47. According to Uddyotakara the explanation of the word '*pratyakṣa*' given by Vātsyāyana is not meant to be a grammatical explanation of that compound but only to convey the sense intended by Gautama in his aphorism: perception consists in the action of each sense-organ upon a particular object (*akṣasyākṣaya prativiṣayaṃ vṛttiḥ pratyakṣam-iti*). He has taken the compound as *avyayībhāva* but the derivation does not conform to the strict grammatical form, which is *akṣaṃ akṣaṃ prati vartate*; i.e. which would not allow the use of the genitive '*akṣasya*'. The compound '*pratyakṣa*' has to be explained as '*pratigatam akṣam*' (pertaining to the sense-organs) (NBh & NV I. 1,3).

The etymological explanation of *pratyakṣa* as given by Dignāga is *akṣaṃ akṣaṃ prati vartata iti pratyakṣam*. *Pratyakṣa* is so named because it occurs in close connection with ([*prati*] each sense faculty [*akṣa*]) (See Hattori, pp. 76-77).

3.48. See II·Cognitive Apparatus, B Mind, pp. 111-32.

4.49. The objection and answer as given by Vātsyāyana are similar to those mentioned by Śabarasvāmi (See ILES, pp. 80-83).

5.51. The explanation of the Buddhist definitions is based on Hattori, pp. 82-86, 117-19. Dignāga has a section on the *Vādavidhi* definition. Dignāga is sceptical about Vasubandhu's authorship, as it appears faulty to him. Hattori says that this work can be safely ascribed to Vasubandhu, *ibid.*, pp. 117-19.

In stating the explanation of the Buddhist definitions what Uddyotakara has said has also been incorporated. His account appears to be reasonably faithful to the views of the authors of the definitions.

The instance of wrong cognition, cognition of shell as silver, is mentioned in Uddyotakara's criticism of the *Vādavidhi* definition.

Uddyotakara does not mention either the philosophers or their works in this connection but at one place he mentions Bhadanta.

6.54. See ILES, pp. 107-10.

II

1.55. For the various views of Indian philosophers on sense-organs see: J. Sinha, *Indian Psychology*, pp. 1-29.

2.68. Regarding the aphorisms NS II. 1,20-32, there is a great deal of confusion as to which aphorism represents the objector (*pūrvapakṣa*) and which Gautama's view (*siddhānta*). This is due to the manner of exposition adopted by Uddyotakara. But the position of Gautama and his commentators on the various contacts involved in perception is quite clear. Dr. Jha thinks that the word '*lakṣaṇa*' used in aphorism II. 1,20 is confusing. Vātsyāyana, Uddyotakara and Vācaspati take it to mean 'cause'. Uddyotakara, however, is prepared to take it to mean 'definition'. The question under discussion is whether or not sense-object contact alone is the cause or the mind-sense and mind-self contacts are also to be included as cause.

The aphorism regarding place, etc. (NS II. 1,22) is interpreted by the commentators as an objection. Gautama has not specifically answered this objection.

The entire debate between Gautama and his opponent is conducted on the basis of the former's basic assumptions regarding the sense-object contact, and the role of the mind and self in perception. It raises the important question of causation and the kind of factors or conditions which should be included in the statement of the cause of any occurrence. While Gautama describes sense-object contact as efficient cause (*nimitta*) the commentators use both the words *kāraṇa* (cause) and *nimitta* without discrimination.

3.70. Uddyotakara gives several reasons for not mentioning mind-sense contact and for mentioning sense-object contact in the definition. (a) Since sense-object contact is sufficient to distinguish perception from other cognitions, this contact need not be mentioned. All distinctive features need not be enumerated. (b) Only sense-object contact is mentioned because this forms the distinctive feature of every individual perception; when one perception differs from another, the difference does not consist in mind-sense contact, i.e. individual perceptions are not spoken of in terms of the mind-sense contact. The perception of colour is never called 'mental perception'. Everything is named after that which is peculiar to it, e.g. barley-sprout. (c) Some Naiyāyikas say that the mind-sense contact is not mentioned because it is a factor common to all perceptions which are otherwise different; that is to say, the mind-sense contact remains the same in different perceptions while the sense-object contact varies with each perception. If this reasoning was right, the sense-object contact would also have to be omitted; for all perceptions obtained through any one sense-organ remain the same. The commentator rejects this and maintains that it is sufficient to say that Gautama is not enumerating all that produces perception. (d) The mind-sense contact is not mentioned because it is similar to the mind-self contact. This similarity can be explained in several ways. Both contacts subsist in a substratum that is not perceptible; neither of the two belongs to the object perceived; both contacts subsist in the mind (NV I. 1,4).

4.71. According to Vācaspati one thing cannot be the cause of another simply because one is found to occur while the other is present; the negative concomitance has to be ascertained. (NVTT I. 1,41).

5.71. The use of the word '*pradhāna*' (principal) used by Vātsyāyana in this context does not make it quite clear as to how the sense-object contact is a principal cause or factor; for according to his explanation it is a subordinate factor in some cases. The meaning is, however, clear. Whatever may be the varying importance of the different contacts, there can be no perception unless there is sense-object contact.

6.72. According to the Nyāya theory, at the beginning of creation in each *kalpa*, an activity arises among the permanent atoms of earth, fire, water and air in their subtle form. This activity is in the form of motion. As a result of this motion, the atoms proceed to combine in various ways and thus evolve into several physical objects. Similarly, there is activity in the minds of selves. This activity brings about several qualities and from these follow the experiences — happy and unhappy — of the selves. All this is due to the unseen force attendant on each self, as the effect of its good and evil deeds in the past *kalpa*; so that each self becomes endowed with such bodies and organs as would provide him with happy and unhappy experiences in accordance with his past deeds.

7.73. Uddyotakara makes two different observations on the question of the perception of pleasure, etc. In one place he says the word cognition included in the definition is meant to exclude pleasure and similar things. At another place he mentions that the cognition of pleasure and other qualities of self is produced by the contact of the sense-organ with the object. The pleasure and other qualities are not apprehended by inference as there is no inferential mark; they are not amenable to pramāṇas other than perception. Hence there is no alternative but to accept pleasure and other qualities as amenable to perception (NV I. 1,4).

Dr. Jha says that Uddyotakara seems to have in mind a distinction between pleasure and cognition of pleasure. The real difficulty is that if every cognition must have an object, it is a little awkward to treat the quality of the cognizer himself as an object (Jha. Vol. I, p. 133 n.).

8.73. VS III. 2,1 argues that the mind exists on the ground

that when there is contact of object, organ and soul, knowledge sometimes arises but sometimes does not — which implies a fourth factor. In both arguments the mind stands for 'attention'. The argument from non-simultaneity of cognitions and volitions is used in VS III. 2,3 to prove that there is only one 'mind' in each body: and similarly in NS III. 2,59. VS VII. 1,23 says that *manas* is atomic not pervading like the soul: similarly NS III. 2,62.

It is interesting that VS III. 1,18 omits the mind in its list of factors of the contact from which external perception arises, just as NS I. 1,4 does. In both VS and NS there is no explicit mention of the mind as a sense-organ. The motive for calling the mind a sense-organ in both systems is that both systems class psychical processes and states among the 'qualities': and a sense-organ is required for the perception of these qualities. Vātsyāyana and Praśastapāda both call the mind a sense-organ.

The occurrence of *manas* in VS V. 2,13 proves nothing, since that sūtra is defining the apprehension of pleasure and pain, in which *manas* is concerned in its special 'inner-sense' function.

Vidyabhusana says that Dignāga in quoting VS III.1,18 inserts *manas* into the formula (HIL p. 279 n.) He may have inserted it as representing the doctrine of the Vaiśeṣika school of his day.

On these various grounds Randle thinks that the omission of the mind in these contexts in VS and NS shows that this is a later development. The explicit notion of *catuṣṭaya* of factors comes after the sūtra period; though already present in Vātsyāyana and Praśastapāda (See ILES, pp. 102-03 nn.).

In this connection two things are significant. While the mind is not mentioned either in the definition of perception or the list of sense-organs Gautama has no doubt brought the mind into the picture in his discussion of the various objections to his sense-object contact theory. Secondly, the mind, though not a sense-organ, has a higher status in his view, as he has included it in the list of objects of cognition. It would have been interesting to hear the commentator on the demotion of the mind rather than its elevation to the status of sense-organ.

9.73. *Paramatam apratisiddham anumatam.* '*Anumata*' is the name given to one of the *tantra-yuktis* both in Kauṭilya's and in Suśruta's lists: and it is defined by them in exactly the same words here used by Vātsyāyana.

Dignāga in his *Pramāṇasamuccaya* ridicules Vātsyāyana's use of the principle in this passage, saying that if acceptance of doctrines follows from not rejecting them, the other sense-organs need not have been mentioned by Gautama; for these are also mentioned in VS. Dignāga seems to point out that the admission of *manas* to the status of organ of perception is in fact implied in including psychical states such as pleasure and pain among the objects of cognition (*prameya*). His point against the sūtra apparently is that it ought to have mentioned *manas* as an organ but failed to do so ("Either psychical states are not objects, or else mind is an additional organ.") (See ILES, p. 102 nn.).

Vidyabhusana quotes the following verse from Dignāga's work mentioned above : *Na sukhādi prameyaṃ vā mano nāstīndriyāntaram aniṣedhād upāttaṃ ced anyendriyarutaṃ vṛthā* (HIL. p. 280 n). The first line is quoted by Vācaspati (NVTT I. 1,4).

Uddyotakara observes on this subject that unless a philosopher lays down certain doctrines, there can be no such distinction for him between 'one's own view' and 'another's view'; that is to say, he will have to give up his own views simply because other philosophers may have propounded them.

The comment of Vācaspati is more instructive. Every theory is mentioned in some system or the other, being mentioned in some philosophical work, or current among the common people. What the view held by a certain philosopher is cannot be known unless he expresses it in words; and it cannot be known if he confines himself to denying the views he does not hold, and does not propound any positive views.

The so-called methodological device (*tantra-yukti*) is an open sesame for borrowing without acknowledgment. How much effort, time and talent would have been saved if the philosophers had acknowledged their sources! Incidentally, the point raised by Dignāga is missed altogether.

10.77. The objection to sense-object contact in visual and auditory perception is raised by Dignāga (See Hattori, pp. 37-38).

11.80. Uddyotakara seems to have been the first to have developed the sixfold contact theory. Four kinds of contacts are mentioned by Praśastapāda, and Jinendrabuddhi mentions five varieties. It is not certain whether the fivefold contact theory as held by some Naiyāyikas or Jinendrabuddhi omitted the sixth variety (*op. cit.*, pp. 120, 137).

IV

1.87. The Buddhist contention as stated by Uddyotakara is : The cognition of the jar, etc. are wrong cognitions (*mithyāpratyaya*). That is to say, these cognitions are not right cognitions (*saṃyakpratyaya*). They are wrong cognitions produced by disposition to use words (*śabdavāsanā*).

Uddyotakara's exact answer is : This contention is not appropriate, as all wrong cognitions have the resemblance of right cognitions. Whenever a wrong cognition appears in the world, it always bears resemblance to right cognitions. But (for the Buddhist who does not admit any such things as the jar) there can be no basis for any cognitions of the jar, etc., all of which are regarded (by him) as wrong cognitions; (so that there is no right cognition to which these wrong cognitions can bear the resemblance); all these wrong cognitions can never appear without some such basis. From all this the conclusion follows that the cognitions (of the jar, etc.) are not wrong. Further, that the cognitions of the jar, etc. are wrong can be proved only after it has been proved that the jar, etc. are not something distinct from the qualities, colour, etc. (NV I. 1,13 & 14).

With regard to Uddyotakara's contention that an erroneous cognition of a substance presupposes a right one, Vācaspati suggests that this argument could be raised only in the case of a chain of errors having a beginning, but in the case of an error without beginning, it could be said that it was based on a prior erroneous notion, and that erroneous notion on a still prior one, and so on (NVTT I. 1,12).

V

1.88. Aphorism NS IV.2,26 resembles the verses in LS II.175, p. 116; II.198, p. 132; *Sagāthakam,* verse 167, p. 287 and 374, p. 312.

Aphorism NS IV. 2,32 is similar to MK VII.34. The dream argument mentioned in the aphorism NS IV. 2,31 is similar to the view expressed in LS II. 2-4, p.22 and MK VII, 34.

(See ILES pp. 85-86 nn; pp. 90-91 nn. Also HIL pp. 46-47 nn.)

2.89. This may refer to the *Sarvāstivāda* school (See ILES p. 91 n.).

VI

1.94. See pp. 51-53.

2.97. The problem of variegated colour which is described by Uddyotakara as *citravivāda* has engaged the attention of later commentators. The question that naturally arises is : how can the contradictory qualities, blue, yellow, etc., produce one colour, called variegated colour. The Buddhist view that the colours, like blue, yellow, are in the form of negation of one another (*itaretarābhāvātmaka*) is not acceptable to the Nyāya-Vaiśeṣika, as these colours are perceived to be of a positive nature. If these were accepted to be in the form of negation of one another, it would involve the flaw of interdependence. The opponent points out that there would still be contradiction on account of the difference in the nature (*svarūpa*) of the various colours. The Nyāya-Vaiśeṣika rejoins : True, this contradiction is there, but there is no impropriety in holding variegated colour as one, because, being produced by the power of manifold causes, it is established as one by common experience.

The theory of variegated colours was rejected by Navya-Nyāya. It holds that an object having many colours possesses them in a non-pervasive manner (*avyāptavṛttitvena*), like the qualities of contact, etc., which are confined to one part of an object, and do not pervade it wholly. It abandoned the principle of the early Nyāya that qualities like colour pervade their substance wholly, which was an essential part of the doctrine of the composite. If different qualities resided in different parts of an object, it would not be one object but an aggregate of different parts. This is what the Buddhist held.

Vācaspati remarks that the whole episode of variegated colour has been cited only as a joke. The Buddhists ridiculed the theory of variegated colour: What can be more queer than to call variegated colour as one colour. There is a pun on the word *'citra'* which means variegated colour as well as queer.

3.104. According to the Vaiśeṣika, sound is produced not only from ākāśa, but also from such conglomeration of material substances as the cloth; so that sound is only a conglomeration of many things. Hence the notion of one in regard to sounds would not be a correct prototype for the unitary notion of one in regard to the many atoms. According to the Nyāya also, unity, which is a quality, can subsist in another quality. Thus according to the Nyāya and Vaiśeṣika the unitary notion in regard to sound, says Vācaspati, is as secondary or indirect as that in regard to the atoms.

4.106. In his comment on the community of locus (*sāmānādhikaraṇya*) Uddyotakara gives another illustration. When we say 'the lotus is blue', the notion of 'blue' has the same substratum as the notion of 'lotus'; these two notions belong to a thing which has both these characters (*dharma*) — being blue and being a lotus (NV II. 1,36).

4

INFERENCE (*anumāna*)

1.118. If inference is defined as that which is preceded by perception, it is objected, the definition becomes too wide. It covers both impression (*saṃskāra*) and ascertainment (*nirṇaya*); for the faculty which brings about remembrance is preceded by perception; so also ascertainment which, in the case of perceptional cognition, would be preceded by perception. Thus the definition becomes too wide.

This objection, says Uddyotakara, is unjustified. Impression is not a cognition and what we are concerned with in the definitions of pramāṇas is forms of cognition. Ascertainment is sometimes a means of cognition, sometimes a result of cognition. When it is in the form of the cognition of a thing — affording an idea of that thing, it is only a result; in this case it is obviously not a pramāṇa. But when ascertainment leads to the further cognition of something else, it does become a pramāṇa; and there is nothing wrong in this.

2.119. The consideration of the sign (*liṅgaparāmarśa*) as aided by the recollection of the relation between the sign and the significate brings about inferential cognition. It is this consideration which explains the presence of *upanaya* as one of the members of reasoning (NV I. 1,5).

3.119. The first definition is attributed to Dignāga. The third definition is in the nature of his explanation of the first definition. Vācaspati attributes both to Dignāga. Vidyabhusana has not mentioned the first but gives the Tibetan version of the second as from Chapter II of the *Pramāṇasamuccaya* of Dignāga. Randle thinks that the latter may be from Dignāga's *Vṛtti* on his work mentioned above.

(See H.N. Randle : *Fragments from Dignāga,* Sections 10 and 11, pp. 21-23; Also HIL, n.2, p. 288.)

4.130. According to Uddyotakara the *pūrvavat* and *śeṣavat* inferences have four characteristics and *sāmānyato dṛṣṭa* has five. He has not listed these characteristics but Vācaspati has given the following explanation: All inferences have three common characteristics: not contradicted, not neutralized and concomitant with the probandum. The *pūrvavat* has three characteristics. The *śeṣavat* has an additional fourth characteristic, concomitant with the probandum and with homogeneous objects. The *sāmānyato dṛṣṭa* has an additional fifth characteristic, not observed anywhere else except in the subject. Thus the *pūrvavat* has three characteristics, the *śeṣavat* four and the *sāmānyato dṛṣṭa* five.

In this connection Vācaspati observes that he has expressed his own opinion on Gautama's aphorism on the subject in accordance with the views of Vātsyāyana.

The Sanskrit text of Vācaspati's comment is as follows :

Etad uktam bhavati : abādhitaviṣayam asat pratipakṣaṃ pūrvavad iti dhruvaṃ kṛtvā śeṣavad ity ekā vidhā sāmānyato dṛṣṭam iti dvitīyā śeṣavat sāmānyatodṛṣṭam iti tṛtīyā tad evaṃ trividham anumānam. Tatra caturlakṣaṇaṃ dvayam. Ekaṃ pañcalakṣaṇam iti. Tad evam svamatena sūtraṃ vyākhyāya bhāṣyakṛn matena vyācaṣṭe (NVTT I. 1,5).

5.135. *Bhaviṣyati bhūtā veti kālasyāvivakṣitatvāt. Yaḥ kaścit kāla upādeya iti* (NV I. 1,5).

6.136. The text *'na punar deśāntaraprāptir nityāndriyatvāt'* is defective. The reading should be *na punar deśāntaraprāptir ity atīndriyatvāt* (NV I. 1,5).

5

ANALOGY (*upamāna*)

1.143. Neither Vātsyāyana nor Uddyotakara has explained clearly whether inference is or is not for the benefit of another person (*parārtha*). It is quite clear that a man who makes the analogical statement has nothing to gain from it. The same could be said of inference when expressed in words. Uddyotakara says that analogy is entirely for the benefit of another person and this is not the case with inference.

2.144. According to Jha the text is defective. The proper reading should be to place the words *parārthatvāc ca parārthaṃ copamānaṃ bhavati* lower down after *bhavitum arhati.* This gives better sense (See Jha, Vol.II, n. p. 236-37). This amended reading makes better sense but it has no bearing on the question. However, I have followed Jha's reading in giving Uddyotakara's explanation of analogy as a pramāṇa distinct from perception and word.

6

WORD (*śabda*)

I

1.146. The text of NS I. 1,7 is : *āptopadeśaḥ śabdaḥ*. According to Vācaspati, the word *'upadeśa'* stands for advice for the benefit of others. It applies to a sentence containing words as well as what is expressed by it. When the sentence is regarded as a pramāṇa, the result brought about by it is the cognition of what is expressed by it; when this latter is the pramāṇa, the result consists in acquiring or discarding the thing expressed by the sentence.

2.147. According to Vācaspati, non-perceptible things have been mentioned in order to include the Veda under the word pramāṇa, as the Veda does speak of such non-perceptible things. The Veda, being without an author, is free from all those defects that can vitiate the reliability of assertions. In the case of ordinary human beings, they are reliable when they have the sanction of other pramāṇas. For instance, even a robber can be a reliable person if he correctly points out a way to a certain place. It is not necessary for ordinary persons to be free from all defects to function as āpta for purposes of the present pramāṇa.

3.149. According to Vācaspati, the contact theory has been selected as a target for criticism for the following reasons: the natural (permanent) relation between a word and its object can be only one of three kinds: identity, relation between denoter and denoted (i.e. that which makes cognizable and that which is cognized) and contact. The first is not possible because object is different from cognition. The second is acceptable, but it is not eternal as believed by the Mīmāṃsā school. Thus the relation can be one of contact only.

4.153. The theory of *apūrva* as propounded in the Pūrvamimāṃsā system is described by S. Dasgupta in his *History of Indian Philosophy* I, p. 405 as follows :

"When a sacrifice is performed according to the injunctions of the Vedas, a capacity which did not exist before and whose existence is proved by the authority of the scriptures is generated either in the action or the agent. This capacity or positive force called *apūrva* produces in time the beneficent results of the sacrifice (e.g. leads the performer to Heaven). This *apūrva* is like a potency or faculty in the agent which abides in him until the desired results follow."

5.153. According to Vidyabhusana, the Buddhist argument mentioned by Uddyotakara was advanced by Dignāga in his *Pramāṇasamuccaya* (See HIL p. 288). Vācaspati attributes it to Dignāga. The argument as explained in the text is based upon the account given by Uddyotakara and Vācaspati. Uddyotakara says that the definition of word as given by Gautama means *'śabdollekhena pratipattiḥ'* (NV I. 1,7).

II. Specific Word

1.157. According to Vācaspati, the contradiction does not lie among the three *mantras* themselves, which prescribe the time for the offering of oblations but among these *mantras* and corresponding deprecatory texts. The contradiction is not an actual contradiction, but incompatability (*sahāsaṃbhava*) as Uddyotakara has mentioned. As an alternative explanation, Uddyotakara also suggests the contradiction among the texts laying down the three times for the offering. According to Jha, in view of the term used by the *Bhāṣya, 'anyatarat'*, it is best to take the contradiction as between the two texts in each pair of the texts as suggested by Vācaspati. (See Jha, Vol. II, p. 263 n.)

2.158. According to Uddyotakara, the arguments in support of the character of pramāṇa may be formulated as follows:

(a) Vedic texts are pramāṇa because they have been asserted by a special person (*puruṣaviśeṣa*) as are the statements in the *mantras* and the Āyurveda.

Or

The *mantras* and the Āyurveda are the work of a special person, because they deal with supernatural things and are accepted as pramāṇa (by all qualified persons); the texts which are not composed by a special person do not deal with supernatural things and are not accepted as pramāṇa, just like other assertions of other philosophers.

Having thus proved the character of pramāṇa in the case of *mantras* and the Āyurveda, the Vedic texts are proved to have this character as follows : All Vedic texts are pramāṇa because they are the assertions of a special person, as are the *mantras* and the Āyurveda.

Uddyotakara's arguments given above have been given in the light of Vācaspati's comment. Vācaspati introduces an omniscient person in the argument and mentions the Buddhist assertions as unreliable because they are not made by an omniscient person (NV II. 1,69; Also NVTT II. 1,69).

Uddyotakara has also formulated two arguments on this subject first taking particular Vedic texts as the subject and then the Vedic texts as a whole.

(1) The Vedic texts laying down the performance of sacrifice for the birth of a son, etc., are pramāṇa, (a) because they are parts of the Veda, as are such texts as 'the earth is a vast field'; (b) because there is a restriction in regard to their words, etc., e.g. 'the year consists of twelve months'; (c) because they are asserted by a special person, as is the assertion 'fire is the antidote of cold'.

In this argument particular Vedic texts are the subject.

(2) Vedic texts are pramāṇa, because they are divided according to the purposes they serve; just as are the texts of Manu and other authors. In the case of the latter we find that they serve a diversity of purpose, and serving such diverse purposes, they are pramāṇa; since the Vedic texts serve a diversity of purpose, they are also pramāṇa (NV II. 1,62).

3.159.

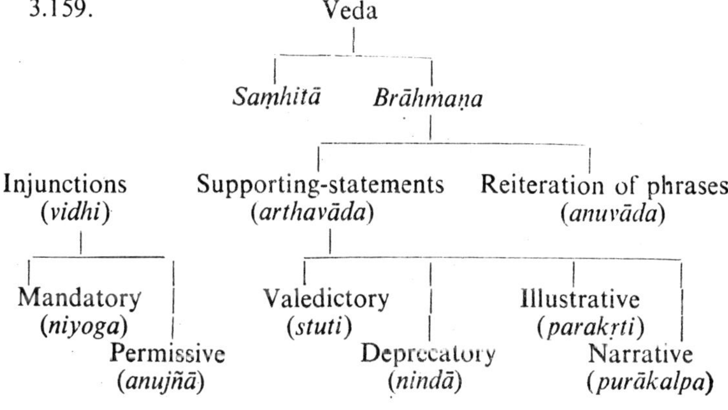

III. Non-Eternality of Sound

1.174. According to one view, there is only one sound pervading over the entire ākāśa. This all-pervading sound is heard only when it is manifested by the agency of conjunction and disjunction.

If this view is right, every sound would be manifested by conjunction occurring anywhere in the world, and as such, would be heard by all men. If only a part of sound is manifested, no cognition of the thing denoted by the whole sound could arise. That part of sound is just like a single syllable of a word, and a single syllable cannot signify what is signified by the whole word.

Can we say that since a single *varṇa* cannot signify anything, a number of *varṇas* should be able to do so ? If several *varṇas* subsist in ākāśa at one and the same time, whatever manifests one of these sounds would manifest all the sounds that coexist with that sound. This will produce a tremendous uproar (*kolāhala*), just like the chatter of several performances in a gathering of acrobats or of various musical instruments in an assembly of dancers.

If we postulate several sounds subsisting in ākāśa simultaneously, there would be no reason why one particular sound should be manifested. In fact, whatever manifests one sound should manifest all sounds. In ordinary experience we find that when a number of visible things are in one place and if a lamp is lighted, it illumines all of them. If this were true in the case of sound, we might hear the braying of an ass when a lute is being actually played.

Can we say that the case of sound is like that of a universal (*sāmānya*) ? A universal is related to things belonging to it only and not to things belonging to different universals. The universal of cow — 'cow-ness' — is related to cows. There is no similarity between this concept of the universal and sound.

Some philosophers hold that sound is manifested by a certain quality of air, vibration (*nāda*). This is not right, as we hear sound at a distance. For even when one perceives a vibration at a distance, one does not hear the sound at the start where the vibration has been perceived; besides neither the air nor its vibration is present at the place where one may be standing.

The notion of direction we have regarding sound is due to the source and not to the sounds themselves. These sources are located in different directions and this explains the cognition of direction in the cognition of sound. If the notion of direction were due to sounds themselves, it should be the same in regard to all sounds. This is not so.

2.174. Uddyotakara explains the grammatical arguments as follows : According to Pāṇini abstract affixes denote the character *of* something. The genitive case is used only with reference to that which exists. *Anityatā* is an abstract noun which denotes the character of being non-eternal (*tasya anityasya yo bhāvaḥ sā anityatā*). It has therefore a positive character.

If *anityatā* were not a positive character, it would have been wrong to use an abstract noun; it cannot be used to denote mere absence (*abhāva*).

In the expression *vināśavac charīram* (the body has the character of being destructible), the possessive affix is used in relation to the body that exists; it is the body which has the character of being destructible. It is true that the words like *vināśavat* or *vināśī* are used as synonymous with the word *adhruva* (impermanent) — *vināśy etac charīram* and *adhruvā ete viṣayāḥ*, but the meanings are different. When the body is said to be *vināśī*, the term is applied to the body figuratively or in a secondary sense; that is, 'the destruction will certainly come about'. The use of the genitive in 'having destruction', when destruction does not exist, indicates the certainty of destruction. But the term *adhruva* directly denotes non-eternality.

Anityatā is different from *pācaka* (cook). Personal nouns like *pācaka* actually apply to all the three times, past, present and future; we have such expressions as this man is a cook; he was a cook; he will be a cook. Nouns like *anityatā* do not apply to all the three times; for instance, the adjective *anitya* is not applied to a thing not existing at the time of the application (NV II. 2.14).

V. Word and Meaning

1.179. NS II. 2,60 is aimed at the *sphoṭa* theory of the grammarians. Vācaspati describes the theory as follows: Things are not signified by *varṇas*, either singly or collectively. They cannot pe signified by the *varṇa* as aided by the impressions left by the preceding *varṇas* for the following reasons: Impressions can pertain to their own objects, and not to other things; in the present case impressions of *varṇas* can bring about the cognition of *varṇas* only, and not of things.

But the fact is that when the *varṇas*, say *ghaṭaḥ*, (jar), are uttered, there is a cognition of the jar. It follows that the *varṇas* concerned produce the manifestation of an entity in the shape of *sphoṭa* — a kind of conglomerate sound — which in its turn brings about the cognition of the jar. That several *varṇas* should produce one *sphoṭa* is just like several words constituting a sentence. Hence it is not the word which signifies a thing.

In answer to this view of the grammarians, Gautama says that the 'word' by which things are denoted consists of *varṇas* themselves, and not of any such things as *sphoṭa*. When a thing is spoken of by means of a word, we do not perceive anything except the *varṇas*. Hence the name 'word' applies to the *varṇas*. Since the *varṇas* are many and the word is one only, the name applies to the *varṇas* on the basis of the fact that though many, they produce the cognition of a single thing. So long as the phenomenon of verbal expression can be explained on the basis of the directly perceived *varṇas*, there is no justification for postulating a super-natural and a purely hypothetical entity like the *sphoṭa* (NVTT II. 2,60).

2.179. The grammatical criteria for words as discussed by Vātsyāyana, Uddyotakara and Vācaspati are briefly summarized below.

Words are of two kinds: nouns and verbs. The noun is *varṇas* ending with noun-affixes (e.g. *brāhmaṇa*) and the verb is *varṇas* ending with verb-affixes (e.g. *pacati*). When what is denoted by the word becomes qualified by association with a particular action, the word is called 'noun'; e.g. the word *brāhmaṇa* represents a conglomeration of an action of being or existing and an agent (i.e. one who is or exists), and is qualified by the Number of the Agent (i.e. one in this case). That which signifies the duration of action (*kriyākāla*) and of which action constitutes the principal factor, is called the 'verb', e.g. *pacati* ('cooks').

According to Vācaspati, the noun, though it signifies an action, does not signify duration; e.g. *pākaḥ* denotes the action of cooking, but not its duration, which is signified by only the verb 'cooks'. Thus while the verb signifies action resting in itself, the noun implies action of something else. In this sense action is said to constitute the principal factor in the verb.

The definition of the noun is meant to include infinitives and participles. Their denotation is not complete except through qualification by an action; they always require another verb to complete their sense.

It there are only two kinds of affixes, how can prepositions and indeclinables be treated as words since they do not end in such affixes ? These are words as is evident from Pāṇini's rule, II. 4,82: There is *luk*-elision of *āp* (the feminine termination) and *sup* (the case affixes) after an indeclinable (*avyayādāp supaḥ*).

There is a convention that only words can signify things. This is another reason for treating them as words (NBh, NV &.NVTT II. 2,60).

3.182. *Vyakti* is that which is manifested or apprehended by senses (*vyajyata iti vyaktiḥ*). A substance of limited dimension is known as *mūrti*, because it is composed of components *mūrtiḥ mūrchitatvāt* (NV II. 2,69).

4.183. *Samānaprasavātmikā jātiḥ* (NS II. 2,71). *Yā samānāṃ buddhiṃ prasūte bhinneṣv adhikaraṇeṣu yayā bahūnītaretarato na vyāvartante yo 'rtho 'nekatra pratyayānuvṛttinimittaṃ tat sāmānyam. Yac ca keśāṃcid abhedaṃ kutaścid bhedaṃ karoti tat sāmānyaviśeṣo jātir iti* (NBh II. 2,71).

PART THREE : CONCEPT OF PROOF

7

DOUBT (*saṃśaya*)

1.198. *Vimarśa iti nānārthāvamarśanaṃ vimarśaḥ. Ubhāv arthau mṛṣatīva saṃśītīḥ, saṃśaya iti bhāvasādhanam. Karaṇasādhanaṃ vā, Saṃśayyate 'nenātmā supta iva bhavati* (NV I. 1,23).

2.198. *Samānānekadharmopapatter vipratipatter upalabdhyanupalabdhyavyavasthātaś ca viśeṣāpekṣo vimarśaḥ saṃśayaḥ* (NS I. 1.23).

3.202. Regarding the validity of the argument in the *pratitarka* reasoning Uddyotakara says that this is according to the principle: 'things are designated according as they are well known' (*prasiddhena vyapadeśā bhavanti*) (NV I. 1,23).

4.206. The Vaiśeṣika definition of doubt is: *Sāmānyapratyakṣād viśeṣāpratyakṣād viśeṣasmṛteś ca saṃśayaḥ* (VS II. 2,17): 'Doubt arises from the perception [of the objet] having the general characteristic, the non-perception of the specific characteristic and the remembrance of the specific characteristic.'

In Gautama's definition the expression used is *viśeṣāpekṣaḥ* and not *viśeṣasmṛteś ca*. Vātsyāyana says at the end of his explanation of the definition that doubt arises from the cognition of the similar characteristic depending upon remembrance (*samānadharmādhigamāt samānadharmopapatter viśeṣasmṛtyapekṣo vimarśa iti*). Apart from this reference to remembrance the commentator has not referred to this aspect in his explanation.

Uddyotakara says that the expression *viśeṣasmṛti* should be taken in a general sense; so should be the expression *viśeṣāpekṣa*. When the doubt pertains to a thing already known, its distinguishing characteristics are also known, so that their remembrance is not impossible. When, however, the doubt pertains to a thing which is not previously known but resembles something known, the distinguishing characteristics of the thing known can be recalled on account of the similarity of two things.

The commentator adds that the non-apprehension of the distinguishing characteristics mentioned by Kaṇāda as one of the sources of doubt is really covered by Gautama's definition, although he has not specifically mentioned it. Similarity is regarded as a source of doubt, because it is not invariably present; specificity is also a source of doubt, because it is not invariably present. The latter can therefore be regarded as implied by the former (NBh & NV I. 1,23).

5.206. *Sādharmyadarśanād viśeṣopalipsor vimarśaḥ saṃśayaḥ* (NV I. 1,23)

6.207. The reading of NS II. 1,6 is not correct. It should be *yathoktādhyavasāyād eva tadviśeṣāpekṣāt saṃśayo nāsaṃśayo nātyantasaṃśayo vā.*

9

ESTABLISHED TENET (*siddhānta*)

1.214. The word '*siddhānta*' consists of two words: *siddha* and *anta*. The former denotes an object about which we have the notion '*idam itthaṃ bhūtam*' ('this is so'); the latter denotes the conviction one has about that particular object. A statement of the object asserted in the form 'this is so' constitutes '*siddhānta*' (NBh I. 1,26).

10

AVAYAVA (*member*)

1.220. The ten members of reasoning as illustrated in the *Daśavaikālikaniryukti* of Bhadrabāhu are as follows: (1) *pratijñā* (proposition), (2) *prātijñāvibhakti* (limitation of the proposition), (3) *hetu* (reason or probans), (4) *hetuvibhakti* (limitation of the hetu), (5) *vipakṣa* (heterogeneous example), (6) *vipakṣaprātiṣedha* (denial of heterogeneous example), (7) *dṛṣṭānta* (familiar instance), (8) *āśaṅkā* (doubt of the validity of the familiar instance, (9) *āśaṅkāprātiṣedha* (denial of the doubt), and (10) *nigamana* (conclusion).

Bhadrabāhu's illustration of the ten members mentioned above is quoted by I. M. Bochenski in his *History of Formal Logic*, pp. 423-25. From the illustration the exact nature of the members seems to be as follows : The first member is the proposition as generally understood. The second member merely states the proposition as based on scriptural authority. This aspect of the proposition is covered by the Nyāya explanation of the proposition. The third member gives a number of hetus and the fourth states that the hetus are to be found in the sapakṣa only. The fifth member is a statement of a heterogeneous example which is meant to disprove the proposition. It is thus different from the Nyāya heterogeneous example which is a negative instance but is meant to prove the proposition. The sixth member questions the validity or propriety of the heterogeneous example. The seventh member is really a homogeneous example and corresponds to the Nyāya example of this kind. The eighth member questions the propriety of this example and the ninth meets this objection. The tenth member states the conclusion and the hetus previously stated. The Nyāya conclusion merely restates the proposition. What is actually missing in the ten members is any precise member corresponding to the fourth member of the Naiyāyika. However, the refutation of the objections would seem to provide this aspect of the Nyāya reasoning. In this connection it may be mentioned that *dṛṣṭānta* is one of the categories of Gautama.

According to Vidyābhusana Vātsyāyana refers to the Jain reasoning of Bhadrabāhu (See HIL, n. p. 122). From what has been said above it is obvious that the five members of Gautama are a simplified version of the Jain ten members. Of course, the Naiyāyikas have given a rigorous formulation.

2.235. *Yadi punaḥ sādharmyaṃ hetur ityetāvanmātram ucyeta bhavaty evaṃ vivakṣitārthasiddhiḥ* (NV I. 1,34).

3.242. Obviously the reference is to the atom of earth.

4.246. The Sanskrit text is obscure. It has been freely translated. The passage quoted is: *Saptikāsaṃbhave ṣaṭpratiṣedhād ekadvipadaparyudāsena trilakṣaṇo hetur iti tad apy ayuktaṃ dvipadalakṣaṇayuktayor hetutvāt tatra kila saptikā saṃbhavati* (NV I. 1,35).

5.252. According to the Naiyāyika, sound is produced by conjunction and disjunction. A sound thus produced is followed by another sound until it reaches the sense-organ or obstacle.

6.254. Uddyotakara has mentioned several objections to the interpretation of NS I. 1,36, which are purely linguistic and grammatical. These have therefore been omitted.

7.255. Uddyotakara has made no significant comment on the heterogeneous example.

8.255. Uddyotakara mentions the criticism of a logician that Gautama has created confusion about the three members of reasoning. He replies: In fact, Gautama has given a correct definition of each of the members; it is the logician who has done the confounding. *Tad etsaminn avayavatraye evaṃ lakṣaṇenopapādite teṣām trayo durvibhāvā iti* (NV I. 1,37). According to Vācaspati the logician mentioned by Uddyotakara is Vasubandhu (NVTT I. 1,37).

9.262. *Pakṣadharmatvasaṃbandhasādhyokter anyavarjanam* (NV I. 1,39).

11

THE FALLACY OF THE HETU (*hetvābhāsa*)

1.268. Jha suggests that the reading should be *nitya* in place of *anitya* as that would not give a fallacy (See Jha, Vol. I, n.p. 986). This argument is doubtful depending upon the assumptions and therefore the present reading is kept.

2.269. Read *vipakṣa* for *sajātīya* in the text.

3.270. According to Vācaspati, if mere audibility were given as hetu it would apply to genus (*sāmānya*), etc. According to VS VIII. 2,3, '*artha*' stands for substance, quality and action.

4.270. The text is defective. It should read: *sādhyatajjātīyaikaaeśāvṛttirvipakṣāvṛttiḥ* (NV I. 2,4).

5.271. According to the Vaiśeṣikas inherence is not visible, being beyond the reach of the senses, and knowable only by inference. This meets the objection that inherence is visible and yet without its own place of origin and thus visibility is not non-concomitant with the class of heterogeneous objects (See Jha, Vol. I, n.p. 489).

6.271. The example has been supplied by the Benares edition.

7.275. *Ṣaḍja* is the name of the first or (according to some) of the fourth of the seven *svaras* or primary notes of music (so called because it is supposed to be produced by six organs, viz. tongue, teeth, palate, nose, throat and chest; the other six *svaras* are *ṛṣabha, gāndhāra, madhyama, pañcama, dhaivata* and *niṣāda*) (See Monier-Williams, *Sanskrit-English Dictionary*, p. 1109).

8.276. According to Jha, a whole line after *dvānavaśatam* is missing from the Bibliotheca Indica edition:
Evam aprasiddhāśrayobhayānyatarapakṣāprasiddhyā dvātriṅśakaṃ śataṃ te punaḥ pūrvavad eva dvānavataṃ śatām (See Jha, Vol. I, n.p. 492).

9.277. The reading in both editions is corrupt. The reading is according to the explanation given by Vācaspati in his commentary: *Ye sandigdhāsiddhāvyāpakabhedena dvātriṅśat ubhayānyatarāsiddhyā catuḥṣaṣṭir bhavanti* (See Jha, Vol. I, n.p. 494).

10.278. This rendering is according to the text in the Benares edition which is better than that in the text in the Bibliotheca Indica edition (See Jha, Vol. I, n.p. 495).

11.278. *Anaikāntikaḥ savyabhicāraḥ* (NS I. 2,5).

12.281. *Siddhāntamabhyupetya tadvirodhī viruddhaḥ* (NS I. 2,6).

13.282. Jha calls this fallacy 'neutralized' and Vidyabhusana 'the equal to the question'. Since neither of these names fits with the explanation it has been called 'the tautological hetu'.

14.282. *Yasmāt prakaraṇacintā sa nirṇayārtham apadiṣṭaḥ prakaraṇasamaḥ* (NS I. 2,7).

15.284. *Sādhyāviśiṣṭaḥ sādhyatvāt sādhyasamaḥ* (NS I. 2,8).

16.285. *Kālātyayāpadiṣṭaḥ kālātītaḥ* (NS I. 2,9).

12

DISPUTATION (*tarka*)

1.289. The diversities mentioned by Uddyotakara are given in the chart on page 603.

2.289. Vācaspati explains the characteristics of the cause required to account for the diversity of birth as follows:

(1) The cause must be manifold because, if it were single, then there would be uniformity, and not diversity.

(2) It cannot be momentary, as it could not bring about the diversity long after its own existence; yet such is to be found to be the actual case.

(3) It must be non-eternal; as, if it were eternal, the resulting pleasure and pain would also be eternal; but neither pleasure nor pain is eternal.

(4) It must pertain to one individual object because, if the same cause affected several objects, then there would be no variety among these objects.

(5) It must pertain specifically to each individual *ātman*; as otherwise there would be no variety in the conditions under which several souls are born. (NVTT. I. 1,40).

PART FOUR: TECHNIQUE OF REFUTATION

14

DISCOURSE (*kathā*)

1.298. Uddyotakara does not accept this interpretation. According to him, it is meant to exclude *apasiddhānta*, which is one of the deficiencies. This consists in not arguing according to a tenet once accepted. Vātsyāyana says that Gautama has included this qualification in order to exclude the fallacy of the contradictory hetu (*viruddha*). This explanation is not right, says Uddyotakara, because the reference to the five *avayavas* which is also included in the definition can take care of this (NV I. 2,1).

2.299. Uddyotakara says that the definition of discussion

BEINGS

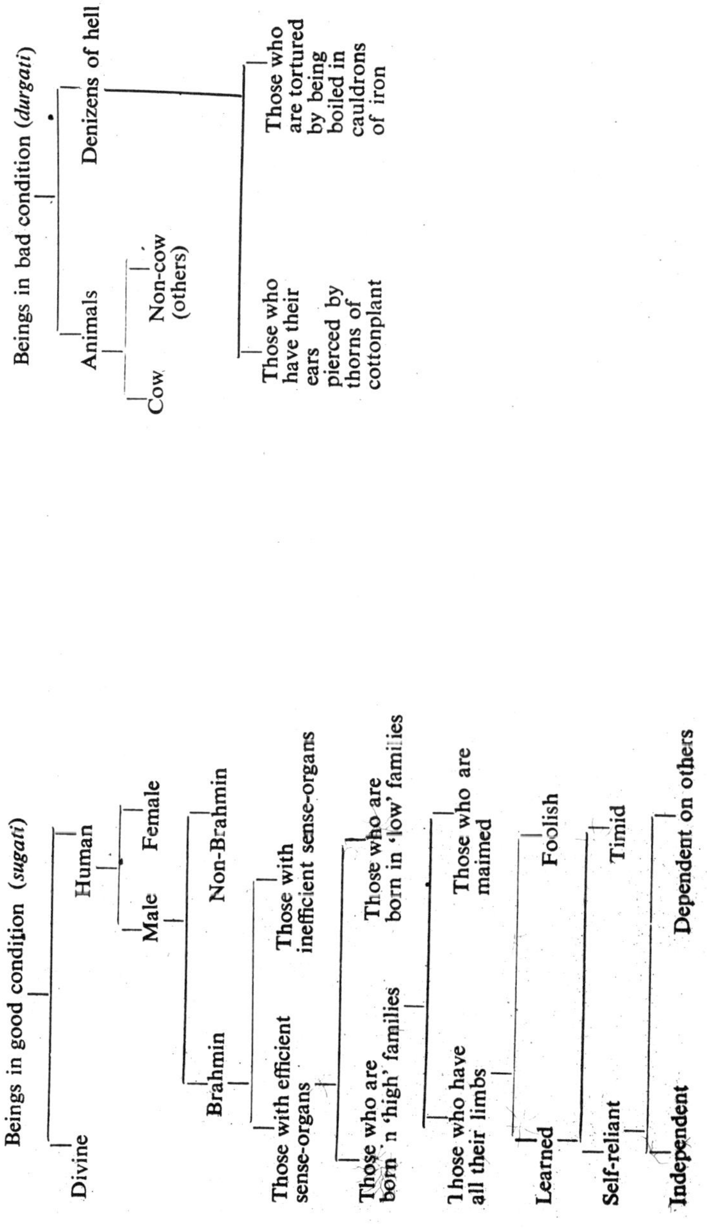

- Beings in good condition (*sugati*)
  - Divine
  - Human
    - Male
      - Brahmin
        - Those with efficient sense-organs
          - Those who are born in 'high' families
            - Those who have all their limbs
              - Learned
                - Self-reliant
                  - Independent
                  - Dependent on others
                - Timid
              - Foolish
            - Those who are maimed
          - Those who are born in 'low' families
        - Those with inefficient sense-organs
      - Non-Brahmin
    - Female
- Beings in bad condition (*durgati*)
  - Animals
    - Cow
    - Non-cow (others)
  - Denizens of hell
    - Those who have their ears pierced by thorns of cottonplant
    - Those who are tortured by being boiled in cauldrons of iron

originates from others (*apare*). He also refers to an author of the work in which the definition is given (*granthakāra*) and a commentator on that work (*bhāṣyakāra*). According to Vācaspati, the author of the definition is Subandhu. His work is *Vādavidhi* or *Vādavidhāna*.

3.304. According to the commentator on Vasubandhu's work, the term '*pakṣasiddhi*' indirectly indicates the conviction with regard to the establishing of the view, just as the contemplation of the object '*śūnya*' is indicated indirectly by the term *śūnya*. This, says Uddyotakara, is not right, because indirect construction is not necessarily justified; it is permitted only when the expression is one that is met with in common usage, and yet its literal meaning is found to be untenable. Further, it is not right to use indirect expression in a definition (NV I. 2,1).

.16

LEGITIMATE OBJECTION (*jāti*)

1.311. Uddyotakara answers several objections to the doctrine of legitimate objection:

(i) The first five legitimate objections should be set up against arguments containing the fallacy of inconclusive hetu.

This objection is not valid, he says, because if the argument is fallacious the relevant fallacy should be pointed out. If one does not detect a fallacy, one cannot say anything relevant to the issue.

(ii) Some philosophers maintain that the legitimate objections are fourteen and not twenty-four as there is needless repetition of certain objections. For example, objection regarding the co-presence and objection regarding the mutual absence, objection regarding the doubt and objection regarding the homogeneity, objection regarding the point at issue on the one hand and objection regarding the doubt and objection regarding the homogeneity on the other, objection regarding the non-difference and objection regarding the homogeneity, objection regarding the proof and objection regarding the point at issue, objection regarding the non-eternality and objection regarding the non-difference, objection regarding the effect on the one hand and objection regarding the doubt and objection regarding the homogeneity on the other — these are not really different.

Objection is also raised against the inclusion of objection regarding the non-production and objection regarding the perception in the list of legitimate objections. Uddyotakara's answer is: the twenty-four legitimate objections enumerated by Gautama represent different ways in which opposition can be formulated: each of them represents a distinctive formulation. It is true that they all share an essential characteristic, but that does not mean that they are one and the same; to regard them as one and the same would itself be of the nature of the legitimate objection of balancing the non-difference.

(iii) Regarding the legitimate objections, objection regarding the co-presence and objection regarding the mutual absence, Uddyotakara observes: One may speak of them as two or one objection according to one's point of view. For example, in the case of the forest and the trees, if one wishes to emphasize diversity, one speaks of them as many trees; if one wishes to lay stress on their forming a single entity, one speaks of them as the forest. Attempts to formulate other objections like *traikālyasama* on the basis of the opposition envisaged under these two objections must be rejected (NV V. I, 1, 6, 7, 13, 14, 16,17, 23, 25, 28, 32 & 39).

2.320. Cf. pp. 30-34.

17

DEFICIENCY (*nigrahasthāna*)

1.336. *Yat tu bravīṣi siddhāntaparigraha eva pratijñā etad api na buddhyāmahe karmaṇa upādānaṃ pratijñā. Sāmānyaviśeṣavato 'vadhāritasya vastunaḥ parigrahaḥ siddhānta iti* (NV V. 2,12).

18

DOCTRINE OF OTHER PHILOSOPHERS (*prāvāduka*)

1.356. Cf. NBh IV. I, 24; also NS & NBh IV. I, 64-78

2.360. Commenting on the remark of Vātsyāyana that the hetu given by the eternalist is inconclusive (*anekānta*), Uddyotakara explains the inconclusiveness as follows: The subject subsists in both ends of it (*pakṣasyāntadvaye 'vasthānāt*). The subject of the proposition — 'every thing is eternal' — is 'every thing' (*sarvam*); this includes both things having the character of elements and things other than those things. In this sense the hetu is non-pervasive (*avyāpaka*).

According to Vācaspati, the text *'pakṣasyāntadvaye 'vasthānāt'* should be interpreted as *hetor antadvaye sattvāsattvarūpe pakṣasyāvasthānāt*. Of the hetu — 'possessing the character of elements'— there are two ends, existence and non-existence; the subject 'every thing' (*sarvam*) is concomitant with both, since 'every thing' includes 'elements' which co-exist with the existence of the hetu, and non-elements which co-exist with the non-existence of the hetu; so that it is not right to say that every thing possesses the character of elements.

This interpretation is not quite in keeping with the text. The natural meaning is that the hetu subsists in both ends of the subject. But this makes the hetu valid as it subsists in all conditions of the subject. If by 'two ends' are meant 'existence and non-existence', then it would be true to say that the hetu co-exists with the existence and non-existence of the subject 'every thing'; for as a matter of fact, 'possessing the character of elements', which is the hetu, is never co-existent with the non-existence of 'every thing'. Jha therefore recommends the acceptance of Vācaspati's interpretation (See Jha Vol. IV n.p. 72).

3.362. According to Vidyabhusana, the doctrine mentioned in NS IV. L, 34 refers to the Buddhist doctrine which denies the existence of substance apart from qualities and the existence of whole apart from its component parts. This is evident from the writings of Nāgārjuna, Ārya Deva and others. He cites the following (See SBH nn.p.115): MK. Chapter I, p.64; MK Chapter I, p. 71; *Śataka* quoted in MV, Chapter I, p.71.

4.362. According to Vātsyāyana, the compound *'anekalakṣaṇaiḥ'* used in NS IV. I, 35 should be treated as one that has the middle word eliminated; it stands for *'anekavidhalakṣaṇaiḥ'* (marks of several kinds of marks (NBh IV. I, 35).

5.362. According to Vidyabhusana, the Buddhists oppose the Nyāya view as stated in NS IV.I,35 on the ground that the substance independent of its qualities, and the whole independent of its parts as advocated by the Naiyāyika are opposed to reason and cannot be accepted as real; however, there is no harm in acknowledging them as appearances for the fulfilment of our practical purposes (See SBH, nn.p.116). He cites the following: MV Chapter I, pp. 66-67, 70.

6.362. Cf NS & NBh II. 2, 31-33.

7.364. Regarding the one and the many, Uddyotakara mentions another view of the Buddhists: (a) The so-called indivisible atom is only an aggregate of colour, etc. (b) The four substances, the earth, etc., are composed of the atom.

The commentator criticizes the view: If the properties combine to constitute the atom, it has to be explained: to what belongs the colour, etc. that are found in the atom. Further, if the four substances (viz. earth, air, water and fire) combine to constitute the atom, this means that the quartet is an aggregate; in that case the Buddhist must explain: of what things each one of the four substances singly is the aggregate. If he wishes to postulate an endless (*ananta*) series of aggregates, his *śāstra* is violated: 'Verily, the atom consists of eight substances, and is without sound (*Kameṣṭadravyakoṇuṛ aśabda iti*).

Thus, if there is no single entity, there cannot be many entities. The commentator therefore rejects the whole theory of the Buddhist (NV IV. I 36).

8.367. Cf above

9.367. According to Vidyabhusana, NS IV. I,39 refers to the Mādhyamika doctrine of relation : "all things are inter-dependent and nothing is self-existent". He gives the following (See SBH, nn.pp.117-18) MK, Chapter XV, p. 259; Āryaratnākara quoted in MV, Chapter I, p. 90; MK, Chapter XV, p. 267.

PART FIVE : OBJECT OF COGNITION (*Prameya*) SELF: (*ātman*) its equipment, career and destiny

19

SELF (*ātman*)

1.373. According to Uddyoṭakara, the aphorism of Gautama is intended to serve three purposes : (a) to differentiate the self from what is similar to it, i.e. other objects of cognition (*prameya*), (b) to strengthen by inference what is already known by means of scripture (*āgama*), (c) to illustrate the joint operation of several pramāṇas (NV I. 1,10).

2.376. According to Uddyotakara, the arguments he has given in refutation of this objection also hold good against the following hetus, given in support of the proposition 'the self is not' : (a) because it (self) has no hetu, (b) because no cause of its birth can be indicated, (c) because it is not an effect and (d) because it has no cause (*etena nirhetukatvāj janmahetvanupādānād akāryatvād akāraṇatvād ity evam ādayas tulyadoṣā iti pratyuktāḥ*) (Intr. NV III. 1,1).

3.377. Uddyotakara puts forward the following argument in favour of the self: the notion of 'I' must pertain to an object distinct from colour, etc., like the notion of a jar. For the Buddhist the instance of the jar, says Uddyotakara, is not a correct instance because for him the jar is not anything distinct from colour. But for the Naiyāyika it is quite correct because for him the thing possessed of the quality is distinct from the quality itself.

The Buddhist argues: the term 'darkness', for example, is a single word and also not the same as the colour-state, etc., and yet it does not denote anything at all. Uddyotakara points out that this is contrary to the Buddhist view of darkness as containing colour, taste, odour and touch. However, for the Naiyāyika darkness does denote something and is quite in order. This view is in no sense contrary to the Vaiśeṣika concept of darkness: darkness is absence (of light) because it is different in production from substance, quality and action (vide VS V. 2,19). The Vaiśeṣika view is that the word 'darkness' denotes such substances, qualities and action as are devoid of all connection with light.

4.379. *Katham iti rūpaṃ bhadanta nāhaṃ vedanā saṃskāro vijñānaṃ bhadanta nāham iti evam etad bhikṣo rūpaṃ na tvaṃ vedanā saṃskāro vijñānaṃ vā na tvaṃ iti.*

Ta ete skandhā rūpādayo 'ahaṃviṣayatvena pratiṣiddhāḥ (Intr. NV III. 1,1).

5.379 ....*sarvābhisamayasūtre 'bhidhānāt . . . Tathā bhāraṃ vo bhikṣavo deśayiṣyāmiṣ bhārahāraṃ ca bhāraḥ pañcaskandhā bhārahāraś ca pudgala iti. Yaś cātmā nāstīti sa mithyādṛṣṭiko bhavatīti sūtram* (Intr. NV III. 1,1).

6.380. *rūpaṃ nāhaṃ evaṃ etad bhikṣo rūpaṃ na tvam iti* (Intr. NV III. 1,1).

7.381. *ahaṃkārālaṃbanotpattinimittatvād ātmety ucyate* (Intr. NV III. 1,1).

8.393. Cf. pp. 61-63.

20

BODY (*śarīra*)

1.402. Gautama mentions this objection in connection with his examination of the ninth object of cognition, state after death.

2.405. According to Uddyotakara this objection comes from the Sāṃkhya.

3.407. According to Uddyotakara the *adṛṣṭa* theory criticized by Gautama is that of the Sāṃkhya.

4.407. According to Jha this objection comes from the Jain view. It is answered by Gautama in NS III. 2,75.

21

BUDDHI

1.412. Vātsyāyana has not directly referred to the Sāṃkhya pramāṇas.

2.417. According to Uddyotakara this refers to the system of Cārvāka (NV III. 2,40).

23

DEFECT (*doṣa*)

1.428. Na *kāryakāraṇabhāvena padārthānāṃ tathābhāvo 'tathābhāvo vā siddhyati kintu lakṣaṇasyābhedād* (NV IV. 1,8).

24

STATE AFTER DEATH (*pretyabhāva*)

1.430. Vātsyāyana takes the compound as *dvandva.*

25

RESULT (*phala*)

1.435. According to Vidyābhusana, the view mentioned in NS IV. 1,48 refers to the *Mādhyamika* Buddhist philosophy which maintains that the effect, before it is produced, is neither existent nor non-existent, nor both. The effect was not both existent and non-existent prior to its production because existence and non-existence are incompatible with each other. He gives relevant extracts (See SBH. p. 120 nn.) as follows:

(1) Nāgārjuna, MK, Chapter VII, p. 162
Sataśca tāvad utpattir asataś ca na yujyate. Na sataścāsataś ceti pūrvam evopapāditam. Naivāsato naiva sataḥ pratyayo 'rthasya yujyate. Na san nāsan na sad asan dharmo nirvartate sadā.

(2) Ārya Deva's *Śataka* quoted in MV, Chapter I, p. 16
Sad asat sad asac ceti yasya pakṣo na vidyate Upārambhaś cireṇāpi tasya vaktum na śakyate.

2.437. *Athāsatkārye kiṃ pramāṇaṃ na sattve na cāsattve 'numānam asti dharmiṇy avipratipatteḥ kva tarhi vivādaḥ yad ubhayapakṣasaṃpratipannaṃ tasya dharmeṣu tad ubhayapakṣasaṃpratipannāḥ.* (NV IV. 1,50).

The idea is that if the thing, which would be the subject of inference, is non-existent, it cannot form the subject of any inference at all, so that any inference regarding such a thing would be baseless (*āśrayāsiddha*).

3.437. Uddyotakara illustrates the dispute between the two parties with the case of the yarns and the cloth. Both parties admit the things, viz. the yarns, and the dispute is about the relation of the yarns to the cloth. Regarding this relation, there are several theories:

(i) The cloth is only the yarns (i.e. non-different from the yarn) (*tantumātraṃ paṭaḥ*).

(ii) The cloth is the yarns arranged in a certain form (*tantavaḥ saṃsthānaviśeṣeṇāvasthitāḥ*).

(iii) It is the yarns alone that appear in the form of the product or effect, the cloth (*tantava eva kāryātmanā 'vatiṣṭhante*).

(iv) One character or property (*dharma*) of the cloth disappears and another appears. (*eṣāṃ dharmādharmāvirbhāvatirobhāvau*).

(v) The cloth is only the yarn endowed with a peculiar potency (*śaktiviśiṣṭās tantavaḥ paṭaḥ*).

The first theory is wrong, as the cloth is undoubtedly different from the yarns.

Against the second theory, it can be argued that prior to the time when the cloth is perceived as a finished product, the yarns were devoid of that particular form, because they are the cause of the cloth, like the loom, etc. The same argument holds against the third and fourth theories.

Regarding the fifth theory, it undoubtedly involves the admission that prior to the causal operation that brought about the cloth, the yarns have existed as endowed with another potency. This does not militate against the Nyāya view. To say that the cloth is the yarns endowed with a peculiar potency, is exactly what Gautama has asserted, namely, 'that the product is non-existent is clearly proved by that very conception' (NS IV. 1,50). Under every one of the first four theories, it is impossible to have the notion of the cloth ((*paṭabuddhi*) without the production of something that did not exist before and hence they are all self-contradictory (NV IV. 1,50).

26

PAIN (*Duḥkha*)

1.438. *Bādhanālakṣaṇaṃ duḥkham iti* (NS I. 1,21).

2.438. *Vividhabādhanāyogād duḥkham eva janmotpattiḥ* (NS IV. 1,55).

3.439. *Janmavinigrahartho yo vai khalvayam eva śabdaḥ kathaṃ na duḥkhaṃ janma svarūpataḥ kiṅtu duḥkhopacārād evaṃ sukham apīti etad anenaiva nirvartyate na tu duḥkham eva janmeti* (NBh IV. 1,58).

4.440. *Tad asyāḥ sukhasaṃjñāyāḥ pratipakṣo duḥkhasaṃjñābhāvanam upadiśyate duḥkhānuṣaṅgād duḥkhaṃ janmeti na sukhasyābhāvāt* (NBh IV. 1,58).

27

RELEASE (*apavarga*)

1.441. *Tadatyantavimokṣo 'pavargaḥ* (NS I. 1,22).

2.441. *Tadabhayamajaramamṛtyupadaṃ brahma kṣemaprāptir iti* (NBh I. 1,22).

According to Vācaspati, free from fear means absence of fear of *saṃsāra*; the adjective 'imperishable' is meant to deny the view that the *Brahman* evolves itself into diverse names and forms; the phrase 'condition of immortality' is meant to exclude the Buddhist theory that liberation (*mokṣa*) consists in the absolute cessation of *citta* (NVTT I. 1,22).

3.441. *Nityaṃ sukham ātmano mahattvavan mokṣe vyajyate tenābhivyaktenātyantaṃ vimuktaḥ sukhī bhavatīti kecin manyante* (NBh I. 1,22).

4.446. *Cittam vimucyate ity anye rāgādināṃ tatra sāmarthyāt. Yadrāgādivaśaṃ cittam ālaṃbanāntaragatyantareṣūtpadyate na punarātmani rāgādināṃ sāmarthyam asti* (NV I. 1,22).

5.449. Vātsyāyana quotes passages from *Taittirīya Āraṇyaka*, *Vājasaneyī Saṃhitā*, *Chāndogya Upaniṣad*, *Bṛhadāraṇyaka Upaniṣad*, *Taittirīya Saṃhitā*. In none of these passages the word '*apavarga*' occurs, but there are references to the various stages of life.

6. & 7.449. Vātsyāyana quotes passages from the *Bṛhadāraṇyaka Upaniṣad.*

8.449. Vātsyāyana quotes passages from the *Chāndogya Upaniṣad.*

PART SIX : SOURCE OF *SAMSĀRA*

28

MISAPPREHENSION (*mithyājñāna*) AND KNOWLEDGE OF THE TRUE NATURE OF THINGS (*tattvajñāna*)

1.470. Cf. NS IV. 2,39.

PART SEVEN : REFLECTIONS ON THE NYĀYA SYSTEM

29

REFLECTIONS ON THE NYĀYA SYSTEM

1.476. VS I. 1,2 & 4. The introduction of the concept of *dharma* has no bearing on the ontology of the Vaiśeṣika system.

2.476. Sāṃkhya Kārikā 102, *The Sāṃkhya Kārikā of Īśvara Kṛṣṇa*, ed. and trans. by Suryanarayana Sastri, Madras: University of Madras, 1935.

3.476. Yoga Sūtra I. 1 & 2, *The Yoga Sūtras of Patañjali*, with the *Yoga-bhāṣya of Vyāsa and the Tattva-Vaiśāradī of Vacaspati Miśra*, trans. by Rama Prasad, SBH vol. IV., Allahabad: The Panini Office, 3rd ed. 1924.

4.476. Pūrva Mīmāṃsā Sūtra I. 1,1 & 2, *The Pūrva Mīmāṃsā Sūtras of Jaimini*, trans. with an original commentary by Ganganath Jha, SBH vol. X., Allahabad: The Panini Office, 1916.

5.476. Brahma Sūtra I. 1,1 & 2, *The Brahma Sūtra:The philosophy of spiritual life*, trans. with an introduction and notes by S. Radhakrishnan, London: George Allen & Unwin Ltd., 1960.

6.478. Bertrand Russell, *Mysticism and logic and other essays:* London: Unwin Books, George Allen & Unwin Ltd., 1963, p. 14.

7.479. *Ibid.*, pp. 14-16.

8.481. The lecture of William James on '*The will to believe*' was published in the *New World* in 1896 and a collection of his addresses was published under the same title in 1897.

In his lecture on *Pragmatism* James observed: '... the history of Philosophy is to a great extent that of a certain clash of human temperaments.' (Quoted by A. J. Ayer, *The origins of pragmatism*, London: Melbourne: Toronto: Macmillan, 1968, p. 191).

James has given different statements regarding his pragmatic theory of truth. In brief the theory is: A proposition is to be accepted as true if and only if it works.

A. J. Ayer has discussed the philosophy of William James in *The origins of pragmatism*. See also Bertrand Russell, *History of Western philosophy*, London: George Allen & Unwin Ltd., 1962, Chapter XXIX, William James, pp. 766-73); and *Philosophical essays*, London: George Allen & Unwin Ltd., 1966, Chapter IV. Pragmatism, pp. 79-111 and Chapter V. William James's conception of truth, pp. 112-30.

9.482. Amongst the historians of Indian philosophy S. N. Dasgupta is the only Indian historian to have included a comprehensive account of Āyurveda. Chapter XIII. 'Speculations in the medical schools', in *A history of Indian philosophy*, Vol. II (Cambridge: The University Press, 1965), pp. 273-436.

Regarding tastes in the Āyurveda Dasgupta observes in this chapter on p. 357: 'The theory of *Rasas* or tastes plays an important part in Āyur-veda in the selection of medicines and diet and in diagnosing diseases and arranging their cures. In I.26 of Caraka we hear of a great meeting of sages in the Caitraratha Forest ... for the purpose of discussing questions of food and tastes.'

10.482. In the symposium on 'Theology and falsification' Anthony Flew puts forward a general principle: an assertion, in order to be an assertion, must rule out some conceivable state of affairs. This poses a dilemma for the theologian. Either theism is meaningless because it is unfalsifiable or it is meaningful but in fact falsified. R.H. Hare seeks to escape between the horns by suggesting that what the religious believer does is not to make assertions but to adopt a principle; he lives by a principle and adopts it for interpreting experience. It is more fundamental than assertions and cannot be refuted by evidence, because it determines what shall count as evidence. Basil Mitchell rejects the second horn of the dilemma and maintains that the theist can and does cite the evidence that would count against his assertion, e.g. the occurrence of evil. This argument is carried forward by I.M. Crombie and John Hick. Crombie says that 'suffering that was utterly, eternally and irredeemably pointless' would decisively go against the assertion that God is merciful. Hick claims that theism cannot be falsified; it is possible to conceive experiences after death which, if they occurred, would verify it.

R.H. Braithwaite develops something like Hare's proposal for dealing with Flew's dilemma. The previous discussion proceeded on the assumption that religious beliefs claim to be true. In 'An empiricist's view of the nature of religious experience' Braithwaite avoids the difficulties associated with this claim of religious beliefs. 'A religious assertion, for me, is the assertion of an intention,' says Braithwaite, 'to carry out a certain behaviour policy, subsumable under a sufficiently general principle to be a moral one, together with the implicit or explicit statement, but not the assertion, of certain stories.' (p. 89). The 'stories' of Braithwaite are not concerned with truth or falsehood; they are meant to illustrate the moral policies which are fundamental to religious belief.

This empiricist's view is not quite palatable to the ordinary Christian view. According to D.Z. Phillips criteria of meaning in religion must be intrinsic to religion itself. This amounts to a repudiation of the critical claims of philosophers in relation to religious belief. If religious belief, like a language-game having its own internal criteria of meaning, is totally impervious to criticism, then religion cannot be shown to be meaningless or false nor is it capable or in need of being verified or falsified by reference to any kind of evidence. Phillips' analysis of religious belief seems to have been influenced by Wittgenstein's philosophy. According to Wittgenstein religious beliefs are like our believing in a picture. 'Believing in the picture means, for example, putting one's trust in it, sacrificing for it, letting it regulate one's life, and so on. . . . Beliefs, such as belief in the Last Judgment, are not testable hypotheses but absolutes for believers' (p. 130).

(This account is based on the Introduction of the Editor and papers published in Basil Mitchell, ed., *The philosophy of religion*,

London : Oxford University Press, 1971. Quotes are from this publication).

In his book on *Belief* H.H. Price has analysed the nature of belief and discussed the pros and cons of what he calls 'the Traditional Analysis' and 'the Occurrence Analysis'. He distinguishes beliefs into two kinds: belief-in and belief-that. The belief-in is evaluative while belief-that is factual. 'Belief in God', says Price, is 'the most important of all the varieties of evaluative belief-in'. The author has sketched an 'Empiricist view of religion' which differs considerably from Professor Braithwaite's, one which does not part company so decisively with traditional conceptions of Theism: ' I have suggested that the Theistic world-outlook lays itself open at one crucial point to an empirical test. This is because an assertion about human nature is an essential part of it.. The assertion is that every human being has spiritual capacities, latent in most persons and partially developed in some; and moreover that when and if these capacities are developed, or freed from the inhibitions which keep them in a latent state, experiences will be forthcoming which will support the basic Theistic propositions themselves, the propositions concerning the being and attributes of God and God's relations to us upon which the Theistic way of 'viewing the world' depends. This assertion about human nature and its latent spiritual capacities can be empirically tested. Moreover, Theists themselves recommend a procedure for testing it. The procedure is difficult to carry out; but though difficult, it is not in principle impracticable. It is open to anyone to try it and see for himself whether it does produce the effects it is alleged to produce. 'Try it and see for yourself' is one way of formulating the 'empirical principle'. (H.H. Price, *Belief*, London: George Allen & Unwin Ltd., New York, Humanities Press, 1969, pp. 487-88).

11.485. A.J. Ayer, *The problem of knowledge*; London; Penguin Books Ltd., 1964, p. 35.

12.486. 'Metaphysics has been often revisionary, and less often descriptive. Descriptive metaphysics is content to describe the actual structure of our thought about the world, revisionary metaphysics is concerned to produce a better structure.'

P.F. Strawson, *Individuals: An essay in descriptive metaphysics,*

London: University Paperbacks, Methuen & Co. Ltd., 1965, p. 9.

13.487. John Stuart Mill, *A system of logic: Ratiocinative and inductive*, Two volumes, Sixth edition, London: Longmans Green and Co., Mdccclxv, vol. I, p. 205.

14.488. *Ibid.*, pp. 216-17.

15.488. Karl R. Popper, *Conjectures and refutations: The growth of scientific knowledge*, London: Routledge and Kegan Paul, 1965, p. 37.

16.488. *Ibid.*, p. 51.

17.488. In Halsbury's *Laws of England*, Third edition, (Simonds edition), Vol. 15, London: Butterworth Co. Publishers Ltd., 1956, the doctrine of estoppel is explained as follows (p. 168):

'334. Meaning of estoppel. There is said to be an estoppel where a party is not allowed to say that a certain statement of fact is untrue, whether in reality it is true or not. (a) Estoppel, or "conclusion" as it is frequently called by the older authorities, may therefore be defined as a disability whereby a party is precluded (b) from alleging or proving in legal proceedings that a fact is otherwise than it has been made to appear by the matter giving rise to that disability. Estoppel is often described as a rule of evidence (c), but the whole concept is more correctly named as a substantive rule of law (d).

'335. Kinds of estoppel. Estoppel properly so called is of three kinds, namely, estoppel by matter of record or quasi of record, estoppel by deed, and estoppel *in pais*. There is also a doctrine, whose scope is yet undermined, which is known as promissory estoppel (e)'.

18.489. Bertrand Russell, *An inquiry into meaning and truth*, London: George Allen and Unwin Ltd., 1940, p. 15. This argument of Russell is said to have impressed Einstein.

19.493. Gilbert Ryle, *Dilemmas*: The Tarner lectures, 1953, Cambridge: University Press, 1964, p. 94.

20.494. In his book on *Belief* (*op. cit*), H.H. Price has discussed the distinction between belief 'in', which is an attitude to a person, whether human or divine, and belief 'that', which is just an attitude to a proposition. Many philosophers think that belief-in is in one way or another reducible to belief-that. That is why epistemologists seldom thought it necessary to discuss belief-in very seriously. Those who hold religious beliefs are inclined to think that the belief-in cannot be reduced to belief-that. Price discusses the arguments for the 'reducibility thesis' of the philosophers and the 'irreducibility thesis' of the religious thinkers (pp. 427-59).

The *Śabdapramāṇa* has undoubted similarity to belief-in. Such belief-in is regarded as equivalent to belief-that. That is, belief-in is reduced to belief-that, and thus given the truth value of the belief-that. However, if the belief-in admits of degrees, it would be tantamount to a doctrine of degrees of probability. This would be a reasonable formulation but it would then be open not only to assessment according to the theories of probability but it would never reach the certainty which the *Sabdapramāṇa* stipulates.

21.496. In Western philosophy there are at present numerous theories of meaning and each theory has the support of some distinguished thinker. In a recent publication on the subject H.G.R. Parkinson has classified the current theories under the following heads:

(1) denotative theory, (2) image theory, (3) causal theory, (4) picture theory, (5) verification principle, (6) verification theory, and (7) use theory. (G.H.R. Parkinson, ed., *The theory of meaning*, London: Oxford University Press, 1968, Bibliography pp. 183-86; see also Introduction, pp. 1-14.)

Another writer, William P. Alston, has grouped the theories of meaning into three types: referential, ideational and behavioural. The writer observes: 'If the referential theory of meaning is based on the fundamental insight that language is used to talk about things, the ideational and behavioural theories are based on an equally fundamental insight — that the words have the meaning they do only because of what human beings do when they use language.' (William P. Alston, *Philosophy of language*, Englewood Cliffs, New Jersey: Prentice Hall, Inc., 1964, p. 19.)

In his *Language, truth and logic*, A.J. Ayer classified judgments as logical, factual and emotive. In the logical class he included truths of logic and mathematics, which are analytic; in the factual class the empirically verifiable or falsifiable truths of the sciences and of common-sense knowledge; in the emotive class judgments of value. Ethical judgments express feelings about certain objects, not assertions about them. The meaning of the various ethical words can be defined in terms 'both of the different feelings they are ordinarily taken to express, and also the different responses which they are calculated to provoke: that is, they have "emotive" meaning.' According to Ayer ethics, theology and metaphysics fall within the third class. (A. J. Ayer, *Language, truth and logic*, London: Victor Gollanz Ltd., 1962, pp. 102-20.)

The most powerful exponent of emotivism has been C.L. Stevenson. According to him, broadly speaking, we use language for two purposes. 'On the one hand we use words (as in science) to record, clarify, and communicate *beliefs*. On the other hand we use words to give vent to our feelings (interjections), or to create moods (poetry) or to incite to actions or attitudes (oratory).' The first use of words is 'descriptive'; the second 'dynamic'.

The primary function of moral words, according to Stevenson, is to redirect the attitudes of others so that they accord more fully with our own. Moral words have this dynamic function, because they are emotive. The emotive meaning of a word is the tendency of a word, arising through the history of its usage to produce affective or emotional responses. (C.L. Stevenson, 'The emotive meaning of ethical terms', in A.J. Ayer, ed., *Logical positivism*, The Free Press of Glencoe, U.S.A.: 1969, pp. 264-81.)

22.496. Modern philosophers have adopted different attitudes towards grammar. Russel observes: 'The study of grammar, in my opinion, is capable of throwing far more light on philosophical questions than is commonly supposed by philosophers. Although a grammatical distinction cannot be uncritically assumed to correspond to a genuine philosophical difference, yet the one is *prima facie* evidence of the other, and may often be most usefully employed as a source of discovery.' (Bertrand Russell, *The principles of mathematics*, London: George Allen & Unwin Ltd., 1964. p. 42.)

We have now what is called generative grammar. According to Chomsky it means 'simply a system of rules that in some explicit and well-defined way assigns structural descriptions to sentences.... Any interesting generative grammar will be dealing, for the most part, with mental processes that are far beyond the level of actual or even potential consciousness; furthermore, it is quite apparent that a speaker's reports and viewpoints about his behaviour and his competence may be in error. Thus a generative grammar attempts to specify what the speaker actually knows, not what he may report about his knowledge.' (Noam Chomsky, *Aspects of the theory of syntax*, Cambridge, Massachusetts: The M.I.T. Press, Massachusetts Institute of Technology, 1965, p. 8.)

For Wittgenstein 'distrust of grammar is the first requisite for the philosophizing'. (Quoted by Max Black, *A companion to Wittgenstein's 'Tractatus'*, Cambridge: University Press, 1964, p. 26.)

The Naiyāyika placed the grammarian on the same pedestal as the authors of the Veda and accepted the current grammatical views without any critical examination. The theory of noun-words, cases and tenses are merely accepted and the grammatical notions involved are converted into philosophical doctrines with justification.

23.498. P.F. Strawson makes the following observation on the correspondence theory:

'Mr. Austin offers us a purified version of the correspondence theory of truth. On the one hand he disclaims the semanticists' error of supposing that "true" is a predicate of sentences; on the other, the error of supposing that the relation of correspondence is other than purely conventional, the error which models the word on the world or the world on the word. His own theory is, roughly, that to say that a statement is true is to say that a certain speech-episode is related in a certain conventional way to something in the world exclusive of itself. But neither Mr. Austin's account of the two terms of the truth-conferring relation, nor his account of the relation itself, seems to me satisfactory. The correspondence theory requires, not purification, but elimination.'

("Truth", Proceedings of the Aristotelian Society, Supp. Vol. XXIV [1959] reprinted in *Truth*, ed. by George Pitcher, Englewood Cliffs, New Jersey: Prentice Hall, Inc., 1964, p. 32).

24.498. Russell sums up the philosophy of pragmatism in the following definition: 'A truth is anything which it pays to believe.'

(Bertrand Russell, *Philosophical essays*, London: George Allen & Unwin Ltd., 1966, p. 118).

25.499. Quoted by Anthony Flew, *An introduction to Western philosophy*, *op. cit.*, pp. 280-81.

26.502. This phrase 'cultural posits' is used by Quine. The following observation is worth mentioning:

'As an empiricist I continue to think of the conceptual scheme of science as a tool, ultimately, for predicting future experience in the light of past experience. Physical objects are conceptually imported into the situation as convenient intermediaries — not by definition in terms of experience, but simply as irreducible posits comparable, epistemologically, to the gods of Homer. For my part I do, qua lay physicist, believe in physical objects and not in Homer's gods; and I consider it a scientific error to believe otherwise. But in point of epistemological footing the physical objects and the gods differ only in degree and not in kind. Both sorts of entities enter our conception only as cultural posits. The myth of physical objects is epistemologically superior to most in that it has proved more efficacious than other myths as a device for working a manageable structure into the flux of experience.' (W.V.O. Quine, *From a logical point of view: Logico-philosophical essays*, Cambridge, Massachusetts: Harvard University Press, 1964, p. 44).

If we substitute the ontology of the Naiyāyika for the ontology of Quine but without reference to the mythical aspect and with the addition of *siddhānta* we have a very close parallel to the Nyāya speculations. Prediction is an important part of the Nyāya theory and even previous experience is involved but only of an āpta. There is of course the future experience of a sort in all doctrines of salvation with or without a permanent soul.

27.503. cf. Uddyotakara's examination of objections to the Nyāya definition of the proposition pp. 416-25.

28.508. Mill's *System of logic*, *op. cit.*, Vol. II, p. 111.

29.509. *Ibid.*, p. 110.

30.511. Mill's *System of logic*, *op. cit.*, Vol. I, p. 430.

31.511. *Ibid.*, p. 431.

32.511. *Ibid.*, p. 437.

33.511. *Ibid.*, p. 443.

34.512. Vide NS II. 2,42-44.

35.512. Mill's *System of logic, op.cit.* Vol. I, p. 439.

36.513. Vide NS & NBh III. 2,42.

37.513. Mill's *System of logic, op. cit.*, Vol. I, p. 439.

38.514. Vide NS II. 1, 44-45.

39.514. 'It [the Identity of Indiscernibles] asserts "that there are not in nature two indiscernible real absolute beings" (D. 259; G. VII. 393), or again that "no two substances are completely similar, or differ *solo numero*" (G. IV. 433).' (Bertrand Russell, *A critical exposition of the philosophy of Leibniz*, London: George Allen & Unwin Ltd., 1964, p. 54.)

40.514. 'We are all at times apt to be impressed,' says Miss Stebbing, 'by weak analogies owing to the fact that a resemblance that is *interesting* or emotionally satisfying will seem to be significant if we are not on our guard. The greater our ignorance of the subject-matter, the more likely we are to be misled by a weak analogy. ... That *some* likenesses are important is the logical foundation of argument from analogy. The distinction of those likenesses that are important from those that are not emerges slowly as our knowledge of natural occurrences increases. Hence we should not find it difficult to understand that, as Mr. Keynes points out, 'the common sense of the race has been impressed by very weak analogies." (L. Susan Stebbing, *A modern introduction to logic*, London: Methuen & Co. Ltd., 1961, p. 254).

41.515. Where probability is definite, says Russell, the frequency theory is applicable. But there is 'another conception, misleadingly called by the same name, to which something more like Keynes's theory [of probability] is applicable. This other conception I called 'degree of credibility' or 'degree of doubtfulness.' It is obvious that we are much more certain about some things than we are about others, and that our uncertainty has often no statistical aspect.' (Bertrand Russell, *My philosophical development*, London: George Allen & Unwin Ltd., 1959, p. 192).

42.516. 'The relation in virtue of which it is possible for us validly to infer is what I call material implication. We have already seen that it would be a vicious circle to define this relation as meaning that *if* one proposition is true, *then* another is true, for *if* and *then* already involve implication. The relation holds, in fact, when it does hold, without any reference to the truth or falsehood of the propositions involved.' (Bertrand Russell, *The principles of mathematics, op. cit.*, p. 33.)

43.516. 'We require, first of all, some term to express the *converse* of that relation which we assert to hold between a particular proposition *q* and a particular proposition *p*, when we assert that *q follows from or is deducible from p*. Let us use the term "entails" to express the converse of this relation.' (G.E. Moore, *Philosophical studies*, London: Routledge and Kegan Paul Ltd., 1965, p. 291.)

44.516. Although I have mainly referred to Mill with regard to the inductive character of the Nyāya proof, the following observations of Braithwaite will be found of interest. It seems to me that they reinforce the interpretation which I have stressed.

According to R.B. Braithwaite everyone agrees that 'it [a scientific law] always includes a generalization, i.e., a proposition asserting a universal connexion between properties. It always includes a proposition stating that every event or thing of a certain sort either has a certain property or stands in certain relations to other events, or things, having certain properties. The generalization may assert a concomitance of properties in the same thing or event, that everything having the property A also has the property B; e.g. that every specimen of sugar is soluble in water. Or it may assert that, of every two events or things of which the first has the property A and stands in the relation R to the second, the second has the property B; e.g. that in every case of every pair of free billiard balls of which the first is moving and strikes the second, the second will move. Or it may make more complicated but similar assertions about three or four or more things. The relationship between the things may be a relationship holding between simultaneous events in the things, or it may hold between events in the same thing or in two or more things which are not simultaneous. ... All these types of generalization may be brought under concomitance generalizations — that everything which is A is B — by allowing A and B to be sufficiently complex properties.' (R. B. Braithwaite, *Scientific explanation: a study of the function of theory, probability and law in science*, Cambridge: University Press, First paperback edition, 1968, pp. 9-10.)

45.517. P.F. Strawson has discussed this problem in the chapter on Sounds in his *Individuals, op. cit.*, pp. 59-86.

In this connection the following observation of Strawson is worth noting:

'Claiming a special status for one class or category of entities as opposed to others is very common in philosophy. It is the philosophical phenomenon of category-preference. I have been exhibiting category-preference in claiming that certain material bodies are, in a certain sense, basic in relation to other categories of particulars. But I should like to emphasize the point that there are certain ways in which category-preference may be exhibited, in which I am not exhibiting it' (*ibid.*, p. 59).

The ontology of the Naiyāyika can be regarded as exhibiting his category-preference.

46.518. W.V.O. Quine, *From a logical point of view, op. cit.*, p. 19.

47.518. *Ibid.*, p. 19.

48.518. Thomas S. Kuhn, *The structure of scientific revolutions,* Second edition enlarged, Foundations of the unity of sciences, Volume II-Number 2, Chicago: The University of Chicago Press, 1970, p. 177.

49.518. *Ibid.*, p. 176.

50.518. *Ibid.*, p. 175.

51.519. Imre Lakatos & Alan Musgrave, ed., *Criticism and the growth of knowledge: Proceedings of the inter-national colloquium in the philosophy of science,* London: 1965, volume 4, Cambridge : The University Press, 1970, pp. 271-72.

52.520. Vide NS I. 1,2; IV. 2,35 & 37.

53.521. A.J. Ayer's *Logical positivism, op. cit.*, Philosophical arguments by Gilbert Ryle, p. 330.

54.521. *Ibid.*, pp. 330-31.

55.526. See note 17.

56.528. F.P. Ramsey, *The foundations of mathematics*, London: Routledge & Kegan Paul Ltd., 1965, pp. 288-89.

57.534. According to Aristotle's statement in the *Poetics* 'Metaphor consists in giving the thing a name that belongs to something else; the transference being either from genus to species, or from species to genus, or from species to species, or on grounds of analogy.' (Quoted by Max Black, *Models and meta-*

phors: Studies in language and philosophy, New York : Cornell University Press, 1966, p. 36n.)

'To draw attention to a philosopher's metaphors,' says Max Black, 'is to belittle him — like praising a logician for his beautiful handwriting. Addiction to metaphor is held to be illicit, on the principle that whereof one can speak only metaphorically, thereof one ought not to speak at all.' (*Ibid.*, p. 25).

Black's own view is different from the old formula of 'saying one thing and meaning another.' 'A memorable metaphor has the power,' says Black, 'to bring two separate domains into cognitive and emotional relation by using language directly appropriate to the one as a lens for seeing the other; the implications, suggestions, and supporting values entwined with the literal use of the metaphorical expression enable us to see a new subject matter in a new way. The extended meanings that result, the relations between initially disparate realms created, can neither be antecedently predicted nor subsequently paraphrased in prose. We can comment *upon* the metaphor, but the metaphor itself neither needs nor invites explanation and paraphrase. Metaphorical thought is a distinctive mode of achieving insight, not to be construed as an ornamental substitute for plain thought.' (*Ibid.*, pp. 236-37.)

For the Naiyāyika metaphor is one of the varieties of quibble (*chala*). Though quibble has a category status, it is not one of the pramāṇas. It has therefore no cognitive value. Nor has it any place in the Nyāya scheme of proof. It is only a device for use in discussion primarily for the exposure of an opponent. Thus metaphor for the Naiyāyika cannot be 'a distinctive mode of achieving insight.' But it is the basis of the Nyāya speculations about the career and destiny of the self.

58.534. Cf. NS & NBh IV.1, 41-43.

59.535. Cf. NS & NBh V.2,8-10, 17, 20.

60.536. G.N.A. Vesey, ed., *Body and mind,* London : George Allen & Unwin Ltd., 1964, p. 12. The Western position as outlined is based on Vesey's Preface (*Ibid.*, 1-21).

61.537. *Ibid.*, p. 14.

62.538. John Locke, *The reasonableness of Christianity,* quoted by Anthony Flew in his *Introduction to Western philosophy, op. cit.*, p. 126.

63.538. Quoted by Anthony Flew in his *Introduction to Western philosophy, op. cit.*, pp. 126-27.

64.543. Cf. *upacāra* p. 306. See also note No. 57.

65.543. See Note no. 8.

66.544. See Note no. 21.

67.547. In the article on 'Distinguishing the senses' in *Mind*, vol. LXXIX, No. 316, October 1970, J. W. Roxbee Cox observes on p. 530:

'(1) By what criteria are the senses distinguished from one another ? (2) How is it that, when one sees something, one is able to say that one *sees* it, as opposed to hearing or feeling it, for example, that when one hears something one is able to say that one hears it, etc. These questions ... have seldom been directly discussed.'

The writer also points out in a footnote on p. 530 that H.P. Grice has discussed these questions in his paper 'Some remarks about the senses' (in R.J. Butler, ed., *Analytical philosophy*, Oxford, 1962.)

68.548. Quoted by N.A. Vesey in his Preface, *Body and mind, op.cit.*, p. 11.

In recent years the philosophers have been concerned with what is known as the Mind-Brain Identity Theory or more briefly the Identity Theory. According to this theory 'mental states are quite literally identical with brain states: any given mental state is, roughly, a brain state, brain process or feature of a process in the central nervous system. However, what is distinctive about the currently canvassed Identity Theory is that the proposed identity is put forward as a scientific discovery — or at least potential scientific discovery — and not as a truth concerning the meaning of mental terms or concepts' (Editor's Introduction, C.V. Borst, *The mind-brain identity theory,* London: Macmillan St Martin Press, 1970, p. 13.)

As is known, Descartes introduced a fundamental distinction between mind and matter. The problem then arises as to how the two can be related. Among the traditional answers have been epiphenomenalism, parallelism, and interactionism. The first of these says that consciousness is some sort of result or property of a certain sort of material thing, but it is incapable of any reciprocal effect on matter. One of the analogies used is phosphorescence on water or 'the halo on the saint'. The second claims that mental and physical states run parallel with one another but with neither affecting the other. The traditional analogy here is that of two ideal clocks, each keeping perfect time, but neither having the slightest effect on the other. The third is that the two interact, each one upon the other. Descartes was in favour of a two-way interaction.

It is to this problem set by Descartes that the Mind-Brain Identity Theory is meant to offer a solution. (See A.N. Flew's Foreword, *Ibid.*)

Such problems do not really bother the Naiyāyika. Body and mind — body and self — are interlocked from time immemorial. The karma of the self fashions the body out of matter and the body functions throughout as an instrument of experience and action. The self is different from the body or matter but their relationship presents no problems. In a sense it may be said that the radical Cartesian distinction between mind and matter is foreign to the Nyāya way of doing philosophy — or it is lost in ethical or pseudo-ethical doctrines.

69.549. Quoted by Anthony Flew in his *Introduction to Western philosophy; op. cit.*, p. 140.

70.554. Alasdair MacIntyre, *A short history of ethics : a history of moral philosophy from the Homeric age to the twentieth century*, London: Routledge & Kegan Paul, 1968, p. 1.

71.555. P.V. Kane, *History of Dharmaśāstra*, Vol. I, Poona: Bhandarkar Oriental Research Institute, 1930, p. 2.

72.556. See Part III, Fundamental Rights and Part IV, Directive Principles of State Policy, *The Constitution of India*, New Delhi : Government of India Press, 1960, pp. 7-28.

73.556. According to some philosophers the central problem in moral philosophy is the 'is-ought' problem: 'How is what is the case related to what ought to be the case — statement of fact to moral judgment ?' This is the classical problem posed by Hume and there is a great deal of controversy about its precise meaning or implications. 'All morality,' says Hume, 'depends upon moral sentiments.' According to Anthony Flew the central insight of Hume was: moral judgments are not statements of either logically necessary truths or facts about the natural (supernatural) universe.

G.E.M. Anscombe suggests that since we do not have at present adequate philosophy of psychology, moral philosophy should be laid aside. She also maintains that the concepts of moral obligation and duty should be jettisoned because these are survivals from an earlier conception of ethics which no longer survives.

The Indian concept of 'ought'=*dharma* is derived from 'is'= *varṇa* and *āśrama*. This 'ought' represents the feelings of those who produced the *Dharmaśāstras* and the 'is' is the traditional Hindu society. This society is ceasing to exist and consequently the morality of that society cannot be accepted. If, however, the 'ought' should be derived from the 'is', then this 'ought' can only be based on a new pattern of society now emerging in India. (See A.G.N. Flew, On the interpretation of Hume, pp. 64-70, Miss G.E.M. Anscombe, Modern moral philosophy, pp. 175-95, in W.D. Hudson, ed., *The is-ought question: A collection of papers on the central problem in moral philosophy,* London: Macmillan & Co. Ltd., 1969.)

74.560. 'Of all systems of human inequality, the Indian is the most ancient, the most highly systematized, and the most complex.' Philip Mason, *Patterns of dominance,* Institute of Race Relations, London. New York. Toronto : Oxford University Press, 1970, p. 137. See also Chapter VII, India: Traditional structure and Chapter VIII, India: The discovery of self, pp. 137-90.

75.562. William Sargant has examined in his book *Battle for the mind* (Pan Books Ltd., London: Richard Clay (The Chaucer Press), Ltd., Bungay, Suffolk, 1970) problems connected with influencing the minds of men by a variety of methods such as stirring up anxiety, exciting stimuli to the brain, prolonging tension to a point where the brain becomes exhausted and trans-marginally inhibited, the role of protective inhibition in producing temporary disturbance of normal judgment and greatly increased suggestibility, the bombarding of the brain with the variety of stimuli in the form of ever-changing attitudes and questions. It would be worthwhile examining the techniques of influencing the minds of men in the Indian context with the help of all such scientific disciplines.

The whole enterprise of social engineering is involved with the question of distributing rewards and inflicting punishment. The philosophers have been concerned with these problems not only in the context of ethical philosophy but also in connection with political philosophy. The arrival of the welfare state has reopened questions of human interest and some thinkers have been concerned with such questions. The karma doctrine needs first to be isolated from the narrow confines of philosophy or religion as it is understood in India and then subjected to a rigorous analysis with the resources of the modern social sciences. This would no doubt prove the whole doctrine unfounded.

76.565. A.N. Whitehead, *Adventures of ideas,* The Free Press, New York; Collier-Macmillan Limited, London, 1967, p. 258.

77.570. See note no. 10.

78.571. 'The theoretically interesting category-mistakes are those made by people,' says Ryle, 'who are perfectly competent to apply concepts, at least in the situations with which they are familiar, but are still liable in their abstract thinking to allocate those concepts to logical types to which they do not belong.' (Gilbert Ryle, *The concept of mind,* Penguin Books, Reprinted 1966, p. 19.) According to Ryle, the official philosopher's (Descartes') dogma of 'the Ghost in the Machine' 'is not merely an assemblage of particular mistakes. It is one big mistake, and a mistake of a special kind. It is, namely, a category mistake. It represents the facts of mental life as if they belonged to one logical type or category (or range of types or categories), when they actually belong to another. The dogma is therefore a philosopher's myth' (*Ibid.,* p. 17).

APPENDIX

Uddyotakara's comments on noun functions (*kāraka*)

1. Nominative

The tree stands: In this sentence the tree is called the nominative because it is independent in its own action of standing. The meaning of independence (*svātantrya*) is as follows :

While it stands the tree does not require the operation of any other agency except itself. The word 'stands' expresses absence of motion. When the same word expresses mere existence (i.e. 'the tree stands' means 'the tree exists'), the word means 'the tree exists standing', i.e. the tree manifests itself. Existence always implies the manifestation of the thing. Here also the tree is used in the nominative.

When the verb 'stands' is expressive of connection with a particular house, e.g. Devadatta stands in the house, the verb 'stands' denotes neither mere existence nor absence of motion, but connection with the house. Here also, in the action of standing Devadatta does not require the operation of any other agency save himself and thus he is independent.

When the verb 'stands' denotes 'unbroken' (*abhagna*), i.e. 'the tree stands' means the tree stands unbroken, in this case also the tree, in its own act of standing, does not require the operation of any agency other than its own component parts, e.g. 'the tree stands by its roots' or 'the house stands by its pillars'.

'Standing' (*sthiti*) may also mean 'being the object of cognition at two different times' (*pūrvāparaprațyaikaviṣayaṭā*) (i.e. continuity of existence). That is to say, a thing which, perceived at some previous time, may be perceived again at a later time constitutes the object of more than one perception appearing at different times, and this is what is meant by its 'standing'. In this action of standing, the operation of auxiliary agencies like the eye is needed — agencies which perceive the thing at different times. Such an agency is called 'instrument' (*karaṇa*). But even in such cases the tree would be the nominative, as it is the tree, independently by itself, that sets into operation those contributory agencies (*sahakārisādhana*).

In this connection it is argued that our notion of recognition must be wrong, as we find in the case of the revolution of the wheel and of the lamp. When a wheel is revolving, all revolutions are so alike that there is a notion that it is one and the same revolution which is appearing. Similarly, when a lamp is burning, there is a quick succession of numerous flames. Each of the flames has but a momentary existence but we have an idea that the same flame is continuing. If no single thing can form the object of more than one cognition, says Uddyotakara, we cannot explain such well-known conceptions as 'that same tree is standing.' Certainly, the very first sight of a tree cannot give rise to the conception that 'this is that same tree standing.'

The opponent continues that we do find such a conception of standing, even when the two things are entirely different, e.g. we say that the wheel continues to revolve (*cakraṃ bhramat tiṣṭhati*) or 'the lamp continues to burn' (*pradīpo jvalan tiṣṭhati*). In these cases the notion of identity (*tadbhāva*) appearing as it does with regard to several non-continuous revolutions and lamp flames, must be regarded as wrong, as it apprehends a thing as that which apparently it is not. Similarly, such a notion must be wrong in cases like 'the tree stands.'

Uddyotakara rejects this contention, as there are no pramāṇas in support of it. No pramāṇa is available for saying that there is multiplicity in a tree succeeding one another in rapid succession. Further, all wrong notions are but a resemblance of right cognitions (*mithyāpratyayāś ca samyak pratyayānukāreṇa bhavanti*).

Apart from these objections, there are positive proofs for the notion of continuity, i.e. the same thing exists at different points of time. When we have various cognitions of qualities of an object like colour, taste and touch, we recognize them as belonging to one and the same object. Another proof is the well-known fact that, being the substratum of the effect, the cause must continue to exist at the time of the manifestation of the effect. A thing that is a receptacle or substratum of another is always found to exist at the time of the existence of the latter, e.g. the jujube berry lying in the bowl. Since the cause is the substratum of the effect, it follows that it should exist at the time when the effect appears.

The opponent might argue that the effect is without a substratum (*anādhāra*). This contention cannot be right for the following reasons: That the container and the contained are coexistent in time is a fact vouched for by ordinary experience. There is no instance of any effect existing without a substratum admitted by both the parties (viz. the opponent and the Naiyāyika), which can corroborate the contention of the opponent. On the other hand, we have such assertions as 'the jewel is the receptacle of light' (*maṇiḥ prabhāyā āśrayaḥ*); 'the bowl is the receptacle of the jujube berry'. If colour, taste, touch, etc., did not subsist in a common substratum, then each of them should be perceived entirely apart from the other; we should perceive them as so many distinct substances as we do perceive the sesame, beans, etc. As a matter of fact, these are never perceived apart from one another and it therefore follows that they are dependent upon something else, i.e. their common substratum. Thus we can say that what is meant by a certain thing standing may also be that it constitutes one common object of past and present cognitions together with the remembrance of the thing as cognized in the past.

2. Accusative (*karma*)

An object can function as a noun (*kāraka*) also in the sense that it is the object of action (*kriyāviṣaya*). This definition includes even those objects which, even though not desired, retain the function of the accusative. The tree is the object, as it is desired to be got at by the act of seeing.

3. Instrumental (*karaṇa*)

The instrumental, being the most efficient cause, means that it is the most immediate antecedent of action, e.g. 'He indicates the moon by the tree.' The sense of this expression is that the person sees the moon immediately after he has seen the tree. Hence the expression 'by the tree' is called the 'instrumental'.

4. Dative (*saṃpradāna*)

The dative is that which is intended to be reached by means of an object, e.g. 'He pours water for the benefit of the tree.'

5. Ablative (*upādāna*)

The ablative is that which remains fixed while something else is moving. For instance, in the expression 'falls from the tree' (*vṛkṣāt patati*), the tree is called the ablative.

6. Locative (*adhikaraṇa*)

The locative is that which is the cause of upholding (*dhṛtihetu*). When a thing is contained in or rested upon another thing, the latter is the cause of the upholding of the former. Hence it is called the 'locative'. For instance, in the expression 'the birds on the tree' (*vṛkṣe vayāṃsi*), the cause of the counteracting of the force of gravity in the birds is their connection with the tree, which, on that account, is spoken of as the 'locative'. In this connection it may be mentioned that according to Vācaspati, the instance is only a particular case of upholding. It is not the same in all cases. When we speak of the substance containing a quality, the quality is upheld by the substance; but there is no counteracting of gravity in this case. The actual definition of the 'locative' is simply 'that which upholds'. In view of this explanation the term 'noun function' (*kāraka*) is applied neither to mere substance nor to mere action. It is only when one perceives the action in its relationship to a substance that one speaks of them by the common name 'noun function'. The character common to all noun functions is that they are the cause of action (*sāmānyaṃ ca kārakāṇāṃ kriyānimittatvam*). When one wishes to speak only of this fact of being the cause of action but does not wish to speak of a particular form of relationship, one applies the generic term 'noun function'. When one wishes to speak of a particular form of relationship, one applies the specific term such as nominative, accusative, etc. Every noun function is self-contained with reference to the sphere of its own function. It is only in relation to some other primary action that each of them comes to be known by a specific grammatical case, e.g. nominative. What the scripture (*śāstra*) means by the term 'noun function' is 'producer' or 'agent'. According to this principle, the several grammatical case names are used. Hence what is said in this context refers, not to mere action in general (such as belongs to every one of these agents, individually), but to a primary action towards whose accomplishment all the agents contribute their activity. In regard to this primary action, one thing may give only a remote aid, while another might render more approximate and immediate aid; still another might give some sort of help in some way or other. It is according to the character of aid afforded that the names of cases such as nominative, etc. come to be applied.

It may be urged against this concept of the case names that if the application of these names is due to the relation they bear to an action, then the word 'cook' (*pācaka*), which denotes the nominative of the action of cooking, would apply only to one who is actually doing the cooking at that time; we cannot have such expressions as 'the cook will cook' or 'the cook has cooked'; for at the time when the expressions are used the man is not doing the act of cooking. This objection is not valid, says Uddyotakara, as the capacity (*śakti*) continues at all the three times. We can therefore use the nominative name 'cook', for instance — in connection with the verb in all the three tenses.

If the capacity remains at all the three times, it is urged, it is not proper to express the three tenses at all. Just as the substance is there at all the three times, so is the capacity; consequently, just as the three tenses are not used in connection with the substance, they should not be used in connection with its capacity. In that case we cannot speak of a man as 'he cooks', even when he is not doing any cooking at all; nor can we use such expressions as 'the cook will cook' or 'the cook has cooked', as the capacity being always present, it would be wrong to connect it with the past or the future.

According to Uddyotakara, this objection does not affect the Nyāya position. What brings out and manifests the existence of the capacity of a thing is its relation to action. The word 'action' expresses what is denoted by the verbal root; that which is the principal agent of that action is the nominative; it is only when this nominative agent is related to the action that it brings out or manifests its capacity.

This capacity, in the case of the cook for example, is a property of the cook as distinct from the person and his cooking. It shows his ability to use the necessary means connected with the act of cooking. This property is manifested by relationship to an action. Thus the nominative, in this case, the cook, is directly applicable only where all the three conditions are fulfilled, viz. the knowledge of the means, the power, and the relationship to the action, as we have in the case o. the expression 'the cook is cooking.' In a case where the relationship to an action is not present and only the power and the knowledge of the means are present, such use can only be indirect or secondary. For example, in the expressions 'the cook will cook', 'the cook cooked', one of the three conditions is absent and the use of the nominative 'cook' can only be regarded as indirect or secondary.

The names 'pramāṇa' and *'prameya'* are words denoting active agency. They are related to a particular action. Just as words like 'cook' are used only in relation to a certain action, so are the words 'pramāṇa' and *'prameya'*. The word 'pramāṇa' signifies the instrument for the action of cognizing and the word *'prameya'* the object of cognizing (NV & NVTT II. 1,16).

SELECTIVE BIBLIOGRAPHY

(Works with asterisk are those cited in the text)

Alston, William P., *Philosophy of language,* Englewood Cliffs, New Jersey : Prentice Hall Inc. 1964.*

Athalye, Yaśavanta Vāsudeva, and Bodas, Rajaram Mahadev, ed., *The Tarka-sangraha of Annambhatta,* Bombay Sanskrit Series 55, 2nd ed., Bombay, 1930.

Atreya, Bhikan Lal, *The elements of Indian logic, with the text and Hindi and English translations of tarkasangraha (Buddhikhaṇḍa),* 2nd ed., Benares : The Indian Bookshop, 1934.

Ayer, A. J., *Logical positivism,* The Free Press of Clarence, U.S.A. 1963.*

———, *Language, logic and truth,* Fifteenth Impression of the second edition, London: Victor Gollancz Ltd., 1962.*

———, *The problem of knowledge,* London: Penguin Books Ltd., 1964.*

———, *The origins of pragmatism,* London: Melbourne: Toronto: Macmillan, 1968.*

Bagcchi, Sitansusekhar, *Inductive reasoning, A study of Tarka and its role in Indian logic,* Calcutta: Calcutta Oriental Press Ltd., 1953.

Barlingay, S.S., *A modern introduction to Indian logic,* Delhi: National Publishing House, 1965.

Bhaduri, Sadananda, *Studies in Nyāya-Vaiśeṣika metaphysics,* Poona: Bhandarkar Oriental Research Institute, 1947.

Bhāsarvajña, *Nyāyasāra,* ed. S.C. Vidyabhusana, Bibliotheca Indica, Calcutta, 1910: V.P. Vaidya, Bombay, 1910.*

Bhattacharyya, D.C., *Bange Navya-nyāya Carcā,* Calcutta: Bangīya Sāhitya Parishat, 1952.

———, *History of Navya-nyāya in Mithilā,* Darbhanga: Mithila Institute of Postgraduate Studies and Research in Sanskrit Learning, 1958.

Bhattacharyya, Gopikamohan. *Studies in Nyāya Vaiśeṣika theism,* Calcutta Sanskrit College Research Series, No. XIV, Calcutta: Sanskrit College, 1961.

Black, Max, *A Companion to Wittgenstein's 'Tractatus',* Cambridge: University Press, 1964.*

———, *Models and metaphors : studies in language and philosophy,* New York: Cornell University Press, 1966.*

Bochenski, I.M., (trans. and ed. by Ivo Thomas), *A history of formal logic,* Notre Dame, Indiana: University of Notre Dame Press, 1961.*

Bodas, Rajaram Mahadev, See Athalye, Yaśavanta Vāsudeva.

Borst, C.V., ed., *The mind-brain identity theory,* London: Macmillan St Martin's Press, 1970.*

Braithwaite, R.H., *Scientific explanation: a study of the function of theory, probability and law in science,* Cambridge: University Press, First paperback edition, 1968.*

Brough, John, "Audumbarāyaṇa's theory of language", *BSOAS* (London), 14 (1952), 73 ff.

———, "Some Indian theories of meaning", *Transactions of the Philological Society* (Oxford), 1953, pp. 161-79.

——— "Theories of General Linguistics in the Sanskrit Grammarians", *Transactions of the Philological Society* (Oxford), 1951, pp. 27-46.

Burrow, T., "Indian theories of meaning (summary)", *Transactions of Philological Society,* London, 1936.

Chakravarti, Rai Manmohan Bahadur, *History of Navya Nyāya in Bengal and Mithila,* Journal and Proceedings of the Asiatic Society of Bengal (new series), XI (1915), pp. 259-92.

Chatterji, J.C., *The Hindu realism; being an introduction to the metaphysics of the Nyāya-Vaiśeṣika system of philosophy,* Allahabad: The Indian Press, 1912.

Chatterjee, S.C., *The Nyāya theory of knowledge, a critical study of some problems of logic and metaphysics,* 2nd ed., reprinted, Calcutta: University of Calcutta, 1965.

Chi, R.S.Y., *Buddhist formal logic, Part I, A study of Dignaga's hetucakra and K'uei,-chi's great commentary of the nyāyapraveśa,* Dr B.C. Law Trust Fund, Vol. I, London. The Royal Asiatic Society, 1969.

Chomsky, Noam, *Aspects of the theory of syntax,* Cambridge, Mass.: The M.I.T. Press, Massachusetts Institute of Technology. 1965.*

Dasgupta, Surendranath, *A history of Indian philosophy,* Cambridge: University Press (Vol. I), 1963; (Vol. II), 1965.*

Datta, D.M., *The six ways of knowing : a critical study of the Vedanta theory of knowledge,* London: George Allen and Unwin Ltd., 1932.

Dharmakīrti, *Pramāṇavārttika,* ed., Rahula Sankrityayana with the commentary of Manorathanandin, Patna: Bihar and Orissa Research Society, 1938-1940. The same, with the commentary of Prajñākaragupta, called *Pramāṇavārttikabhāṣya,* Patna: K. P. Jayaswal Research Institute, 1953.

———, *Nyāyabindu,* ed. D. Malvania, with *Nyāyabindu-ṭikā* and *Dharmottarapradīpa* of Durvekamiśra, Tibetan Sanskrit Works Series, Vol. II, Patna, 1955.

Dhruva, A. B., ed., *Mallisena's syādvāda-mañjarī with anyayoga-vyavaccheda-dvātriṃśikā of Hemacandra,* Sanskrit and Prakrit Series LXXXIII, Bombay: S.K. Belvalkar, Bhandarkar Oriental Research Institute, 1933.

———, *Nyāyapraveśa,* Sanskrit text with commentaries, GOS, Baroda: Oriental Institute, 1939.

Dignāga: See Tucci; also Randle.

Dvivedin, Manilal Nathubhai, See Laugāski Bhāskara.

Flew, Anthony, *An introduction to Western philosophy,* London: Thames and Hudson, 1971.*

Foucher, A., *Le compendium des topiques d'Annambhaṭṭa,* Paris: Adrien-Maisonneuve, 1949.

Frauwallner, Erich, *Materialien Zur āltesten erhenntnislehre der karmamīmāṃsā,* Österreichische Akademie d. Wissenschaften, Phil-Hist-Kl., 250 Bd., 2. abh., Vienna, 1968.

———, *Raghunātha Śiromaṇi,* Vienna: WZKSO, 1966, 1967, 1970.

Gadādhara Bhaṭṭācāryya, *Gādādharī. A commentary on tattva-cintāmaṇi-dīdhiti.* See Raghunāth. Edited with *tattvacintāmaṇi* and *tattvacintāmaṇidīdhiti* by Pandit

Bamacharan Bhattacharyya and others. Chowkhamba Sanskrit Series, 42. Benares; Chowkhamba Sanskrit Series Office, 1913-1927.

———, *Viṣayatāvāda,* Benares Sanskrit Series: Benares: Braj B. Das, 1886.

———, *Nañvādavivṛtti.* A commentary on Raghunātha's *Nañvāda,* included in *tattvacintāmaṇirahasya,* Part IV: see Mathurānātha.

Gaṅgeśa Upādhyāya, *Tattvacintāmaṇi,* Edited with *Māthurī* in *tattvacintāmaṇirahasya:* see Mathurānātha. The same edited with *gādādharī* and *dīdhiti* in *gādādharī:* see Gadādhara. The same edited with *Jāgadīśī* and *dīdhiti* in *gādādharī:* see Jagadīśa. Also see Goekoop, C.

Gautama, *The Nyāyasūtras with Vātsyāyana's Bhāshya and extracts from the Nyāyavārttika* and the *Tātparyaṭīkā,* ed. G.S. Tailaṅga, VSS, Volume II, Benares: E.J. Lazarus & Co., 1896.*

———, *Nyāyasūtra of Gautama : A system of Indian logic, with the Nyāyabhāṣaya of Vātsyāyana, the Nyāyasūcī and the Ṭippaṇī of Ganganath Jhā,* Poona: Oriental Book Agency, 1939.*

Goekoop, C., *The logic of invariable concomitance in the tattvacintāmaṇi : Gaṅgeśa's anumitinirūpaṇa and vyāptivāda, with introduction and translation,* Dordrecht : D. Riedel Publishing Company, 1967.

Guha, D.C., *Navyanyāya system of logic,* Vārāṇasī: Bhāratīya Vidyā Prakāśan, 1968.

Guthrie, W.K.C., *A history of Greek philosophy,* Vol. II, Cambridge: University Press, 1965.*

Halsbury, *Laws of England,* Third. Edition (Simonds edition), Vol. 15, London : Butterworth Co. Publishers Ltd., 1956.*

Hamblin, C.L., *Fallacies,* London: Methuen & Co. Ltd., 1970.

Hattori, Massaki, *Dignāga, On Perception, being the pratyakṣapariccheda of Dignāga's pramāṇasamuccaya from the Sanskrit fragments and the Tibetan versions :* translated and annotated. Cambridge, Mass.: Harvard Oriental Press, 1968.*

Hudson, W.D., ed., *The is-ought question : A collection of papers on the central problem in moral philosophy*, London: Macmillan & Co. Ltd., 1969.*

Imre Lakatos & Alan Musgrave, eds., *Criticism and the growth of knowledge : Proceedings of the international colloquium in the philosophy of science*, London: 1965, Cambridge : The University Press, 1970.*

Ingalls, D.H.H., *Materials for the study of Navya-nyāya logic*, Harvard Oriental Series 40, Cambridge, Mass.: Harvard University Press, 1951.*

———, "The Comparison of Indian and Western Philosophy", *Journal of Oriental Research* (Madras), Vol. 22, parts i-iv (1954), pp. 1-11.

Īśvara Kṛṣṇa, *The Sāṁkhya Kārikā of Īśvara Kṛṣṇa* (ed. and trans. by S.S. Suryanarayana Sastri, Madras: University of Madras, 1930.*

Jacobi, Hermann, "Indische Logik", *Nachrichten der Göttingen Gesellschaft der Wissenschaften*, Göttingen: Philologisch-historische Klasse, 1901.

Jagadīśa Tarkālaṅkāra, *Jāgadīśī*. A commentary on *tattvacintāmaṇidīdhiti*, Edited with *tattvacintāmaṇi* and *tattvacintāmaṇidīdhiti* by Pandit Somanatha Nyayopadhyaya and others. Chowkhamba Sanskrit Series 29, Benares: Chowkhamba Book Depot, 1906-1908.

Jaimini, *The Pūrva Mīmāṃsā Sūtras of Jaimini*, trans. with an original commentary by Ganganath Jha, SBH vol. X, Allahabad : The Panini Office, 1916.*

Jaini, J. L., ed. and trans., *Tattvārthādhigama Sūtra* (*A treatise on the essential principles of Jainism*) *by Śri Umāsvāti Ācārya*, The Sacred Book of the Jainas, Vol. II, Arrah: The Central Jaina Publishing House, 1920.*

Jayanta, *Nyāyamañjarī*, Ed., G. Sastri Tailanga, VSS 10. Benares: E.J. Lazarus and Co., 1895.

Jha, Ganganath, trans., *The Nyāyasūtras of Gautama with Vātsyāyana's Bhāṣya and Uddyotakara's Vārttika*, The Editor, Indian Thought, Allahabad, Vol. I, 1915, Vol. II, 1917, Vol. III, 1919, Vol. IV, 1919.*

Jha, Ganganath, trans., *The tarkabhāṣā* (*by Keśavamiśra*) *or*

Exposition of reasoning, 2nd rev. ed., Poona: Oriental Book Agency, 1924.

Jha, Ganganath, trans., *The tattvasangraha of Śāntarakṣita*, GOS, Vol. LXXX (1937), LXXXIII (1939), Baroda: Oriental Institute.

———, *The Nyāya philosophy of Gautama* (*Sadholal lectures*), Allahabad: Allahabad University, n.d.

Jwala Prasad, *Indian epistemology*, The Punjab Oriental Series, No. XXV, Lahore: The Punjab Sanskrit Book Depot, 1939.

Kamalaśīla, *Tattvasaṃgrahapañjikā*. Edited with the *tattvasaṃgraha* of Śāntarakṣita by E. Krishnamacharyya. 2 Vols., GOS 30, 31, Baroda : Central Library, 1926.

Kaṇāda, See Sinha, Nandalal.*

Kane, P.V., *History of Dharmaśāstra*, Vol. I, Poona: Bhandarkar Oriental Research Institute, 1930.*

Kavirāj, Gopināth, *Gleanings from the history and bibliography of Nyāya-Vaiśeṣika Literature* : The Princess of Wales Saraswati Bhavana Studies III, pp. 79-157; IV, pp. 59-70; V, pp. 129-62.

Keith, Arthur Berriedale, *Indian logic and atomism, an exposition of the Nyāya and Vaiśeṣika systems*, Oxford: The Clarendon Press, 1921.

Krishnamacharyya E. See Kamalaśīla.

Kuhn, Thomas S., *The structure of scientific revolutions*, Second edition enlarged, Foundations of the unity of sciences, Volume II - Number 2, Chicago : The University of Chicago Press 1970.*

Kunjunni Raja, K., *Indian theories of meaning*, The Adyar Library Series, Vol. 91, Madras: The Adyar Library and Research Centre, 1963.

Kunst, A., *Probleme der Buddhistischen Logik in der Darstellung des Tattvasaṅgraha*, Cracow, 1939.

Laṅkāvatāra Sūtra, See Nanjio, Bunyiu.*

Laugāski Bhāskara, *Tarkakaumudi*, Bombay Sanskrit Series XXXII, Edited with English notes by Manilal Nathubhai Dvivedin, Bombay Sanskrit Series, 1886.

MacIntyre, Alasdair, *A short history of ethics : a history of moral philosophy from the Homeric era to the twentieth century*, London : Routledge & Kegan Paul, 1968.*

Mādhavāchārya, *Sarvadarśanasaṁgraha:* Edition by Vāsudeva Śāstri Abhyankar, Government Oriental Series, Poona, 1924. Translated by E.B. Cowell and A. E. Cough, Trübner Oriental Series, 1882 [2nd ed. 1894].

Malvania, D., See Dharmakīrti.

Mason, Philip, *Patterns of dominance,* Institute of Race Relations, London, New York, Toronto: Oxford University Press, 1970.*

Mathurānātha, *Māthurī or tattvacintāmaṇirahasya.* A commentary on *tattvacintāmaṇi* BI 98. Edited by Pandit Kamakhyanatha Tarkavagisha 4 parts. Calcutta: Asiatic Society of Bengal, 1884-1901. See Gadādhara Bhaṭṭācāryya; also Gaṅgeśa Upādhyāya.

Matilal, Bimal Krishna, *The Navya-Nyāya doctrine of negation,* Cambridge, Mass.: Harvard University Press, 1968.*

———, *Epistemology, logic and grammar in Indian philosophical analysis,* The Hague-Paris : Mouton, 1971.

McDermott, Senape A.C., *An eleventh-century Buddhist logic of 'exists'. Ratnakīrti's Kṣaṇabhaṅgasiddhiḥ vyatirekātmikā,* Dordrecht: D. Reidel Publishing Company, 1969.

Mill, John Stuart, *A system of logic : Ratiocinative and inductive,* Two volumes, Sixth edition, London : Longmans Green and Co., 1865.*

Mishra, Umesh, *Conception of matter according to Nyāya-Vaiśeṣika: with a foreword by Ganganath Jha and an introduction by Gopinath Kaviraj,* Allahabad : M.N. Pandey, 1936.

Mitchell, Basil, ed., *The Philosophy of religion,* London: Oxford University Press, 1971.*

Mookerjee, Satkari, *The Buddhist philosophy of universal flux, an exposition of the philosophy of critical realism as expounded by the School of Dignāga, Calcutta:* University of Calcutta, 1955.

Moore, Charles A., See Radhakrishnan.

Moore, G.E., *Philosophical studies,* London: Routledge and Kegan Paul, Ltd., 1965.*

Musgrave, Alan, See Imre Lakatos.*

Murti, T.R.V., *The central philosophy of Buddhism,* London: George Allen & Unwin Ltd., 1955.

Nāgārjuna, *Vigrahavyāvartanī,* ed. E.H. Johnston and A. Kunst, Melanges chinois ed bouddhiques, IX (1951), 99-152.*

——, *Mūlamadhyamaka kārikās* (*Mādhyamikasūtras*) with the commentary of Candrakīrti, *Prasannapadā:* edited by Louis de la Vallée Poussin, Bibliotheca Buddhica, St Petersburg, 1908.*

Nanjio, Bunyiu, ed., *The Laṅkāvatāra sūtra,* Kyoto: The Otani University Press, 1923. Also see *Laṅkāvatāra Sūtra.**

Parkinson, G.H.R., ed., *The theory of meaning,* London: Oxford University Press, 1968.*

Patañjali, *The Yoga Sūtras of Patañjali, with the Yoga-bhāṣya of Vyāsa and the Tattva-Vaiśāradī of Vācaspati Miśra,* trans. by Rama Prasad, SBH Vol. IV, Allahabad: The Panini Office, 3rd ed., 1924.*

Pitcher, George, ed., *Truth,* Englewood Cliffs, New Jersey : Prentice Hall, Inc., 1964.*

Popper, Karl R., *Conjectures and refutations : the growth of scientific knowledge,* London: Routledge and Kegan Paul, 1965.*

Price, H.H., *Belief,* London: George Allen & Unwin Ltd.; New York : Humanities Press, 1969.*

Quine, W.V.O., *From a logical point of view : Logico-philosophical essays,* Cambridge, Mass.: Harvard University Press, 1964.*

Radhakrishnan, S., *Indian philosophy,* Vols. I & II, London: George Allen & Unwin Ltd., New York: The Macmillan Company, Vol. I, 1923; Vol. II, 1927, rev. second edition, 1931.

——, *The Brahma sūtra, the philosophy of spiritual life,* London : George Allen & Unwin Ltd., 1960.*

Radhakrishnan, S. and Moore, Charles A., eds., *A source book in Indian philosophy,* Princeton: Princeton University Press, 1957.*

Raghunātha Śiromaṇi, *Nañvāda* Printed as an appendix to the *tattvacintāmaṇi* of Gaṅgeśa in the Bibliotheca Indica edition, edited by Pandit Kamakhyanatha Tarkavagisha, Part IV, vol. II, pp. 1010-86: see Mathurānātha. The same printed in the *Vācaspatya* of Taranatha Tarkavacaspati under the word *'Nañ'* see Taranatha.

Raghunātha Śiromaṇi, *Padārthatattvanirūpaṇa.* Edited with the commentaries of Raghudeva and Rāmabhadra by Vindhyeswaraprasad Dvivedin. The same reprinted from the 1903-1905 issues of *The Pandit*, Benares: E. J. Lazarus and Co., 1916.

——, *Tattvacintāmaṇidīdhiti.* A commentary on the *tattvacintāmaṇi* of Gaṅgeśa. Edited with *jāgadiśī;* see Jagadīśa. The same edited with *Gādādharī,* see Gadādhara.

Ramsey, F. P., *The foundations of mathematics,* London: Routledge & Kegan Paul Ltd., 1965.*

Randle, H. N., *Fragments from Diṅnāga,* The Royal Asiatic Society, Prize Publication Fund, Vol. IX, London: The Royal Asiatic Society, 1926.*

——, *Indian logic in the early schools. A study of the Nyāyadarśana in its relation to the early logic of other schools,* London: Humphrey Milford, Oxford University Press, 1930.*

Robinson, Richard H., *Early mādhyamika in India and China,* Madison, Milwauki and London: The University of Wisconsin Press, 1967.

Ruben, Walter, *Zur indischen Erkenntnistheorie: die Lehre von der Wahrnehmung nach den Nyāyasūtras.* III. I. Leipzig: O. Harrassowitz, 1926.

Russell, Bertrand, *An inquiry into meaning and truth,* London: George Allen and Unwin Ltd., 1940.*

——, *My philosophical development,* London: George Allen & Unwin Ltd., 1959.*

——, *History of Western philosophy,* London: George Allen & Unwin Ltd., 1962.*

——, *Mysticism and logic and other essays,* London: Unwin Books, George Allen & Unwin Ltd., 1963.*

——, *A critical exposition of the philosophy of Leibniz,* London : George Allen & Unwin Ltd., 1964.*

——, *The principles of mathematics,* Eighth impression, London : George Allen & Unwin Ltd., 1964.*

——, *Philosophical essays,* London : George Allen & Unwin Ltd., 1966.*

Ryle, Giblert, *Dilemmas,* The Tarner lectures, 1953, Cambridge: University Press, 1964.*

———, *The concept of mind,* Penguin Books, Reprinted 1966.*

Sanghvi, Sukhlalji, *Advanced studies in Indian logic and metaphysics,* Reprint, Calcutta: Indian Studies, Past and Present, 1961.

Sankrityayan, Rahula, See Dharmakīrti.

Śāntarakṣita, *Tattvasaṃgraha,* see Kamalaśīla.

Sargant, William, *Battle for the mind,* Pan Books Ltd., London: Richard Clay (The Chaucer Press), Ltd., Bungay, Suffolk, 1970.

Sastri, Gaurinath, *The philosophy of word and meaning: some Indian approaches with special reference to the philosophy of Bhartṛhari,* Calcutta Sanskrit College Research Series, No. V, Studies No. 2, Calcutta: Sanskrit College, 1959.

Śāstri, Hari Prasad, *Six Nyāya Buddhist tracts*: Bibliotheca Indica, Calcutta, 1910.

Sastri, S. Kuppuswami, *A primer of Indian logic according to Annambhaṭṭa's tarkasaṃgraha,* Madras: P. Varadachary & Co., 1932.

Schayer, S., "Studien zur Indischen Logik I, II", *Bulletin internationale de l'Académie polonaise des Sciences et des Lettres.* Classe de philologie, classe d'histoire et de philosophie (1932), pp. 98-102; and (1933), pp. 90-96.

———, "Über die Methode der Nyāya-forschung", *Festschrift Moriz Winternitz,* Otto Stein und Wilhelm Gampert, Leipzig: O. Harrassowitz, 1933.

Seal, Sir Brajendranath, *The positive sciences of the ancient Hindus,* London, New York: Longmans Green & Co., 1915.

Sen, Saileswar, *A study on Mathurānātha's tattvacintāmaṇirahasya,* Wageningen: H. Veenman en Zonen, 1924.

Shastri, Dharmendra Nath, *Critique of Indian realism: A Study of the conflict between the Nyāya-Vaiśeṣika and the Buddhist Dignāga School,* with a Foreword by Dr. S. Radhakrishnan, Agra: Agra University, 1964.

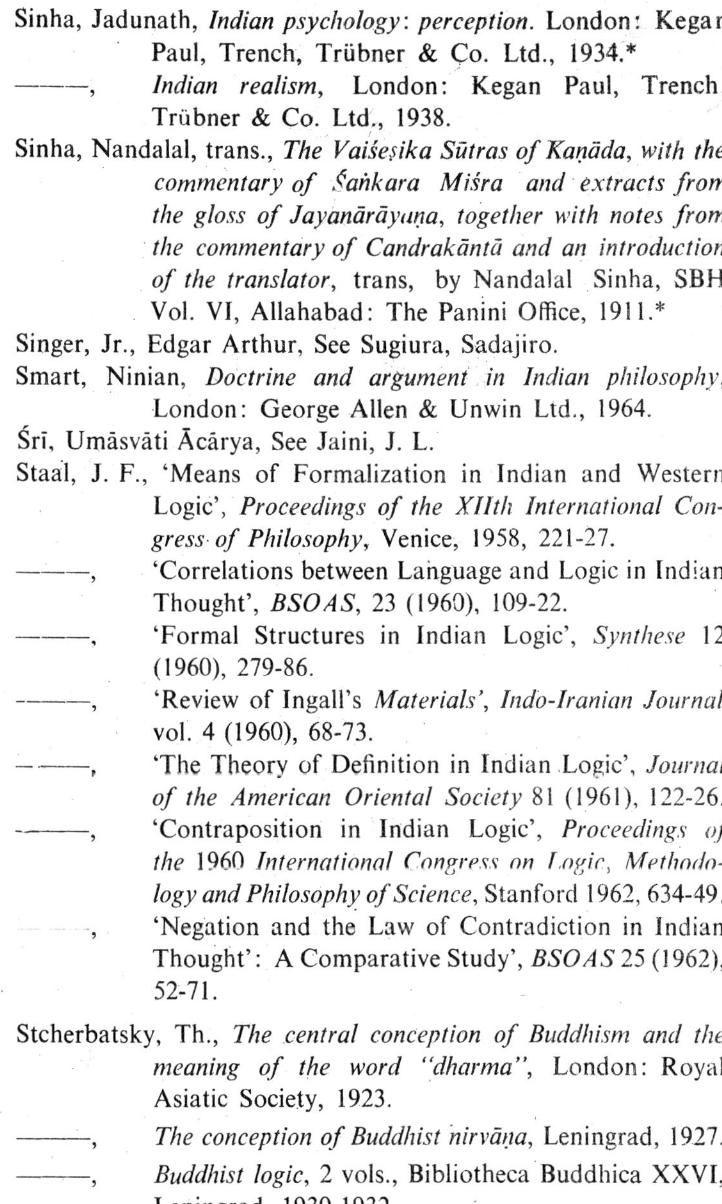

Sinha, Jadunath, *Indian psychology: perception*. London: Kegan Paul, Trench, Trübner & Co. Ltd., 1934.*

———, *Indian realism*, London: Kegan Paul, Trench, Trübner & Co. Ltd., 1938.

Sinha, Nandalal, trans., *The Vaiśeṣika Sūtras of Kaṇāda, with the commentary of Śaṅkara Miśra and extracts from the gloss of Jayanārāyaṇa, together with notes from the commentary of Candrakāntā and an introduction of the translator*, trans, by Nandalal Sinha, SBH Vol. VI, Allahabad: The Panini Office, 1911.*

Singer, Jr., Edgar Arthur, See Sugiura, Sadajiro.

Smart, Ninian, *Doctrine and argument in Indian philosophy*, London: George Allen & Unwin Ltd., 1964.

Śrī, Umāsvāti Ācārya, See Jaini, J. L.

Staal, J. F., 'Means of Formalization in Indian and Western Logic', *Proceedings of the XIIth International Congress of Philosophy*, Venice, 1958, 221-27.

———, 'Correlations between Language and Logic in Indian Thought', *BSOAS*, 23 (1960), 109-22.

———, 'Formal Structures in Indian Logic', *Synthese* 12 (1960), 279-86.

———, 'Review of Ingall's *Materials*', *Indo-Iranian Journal*, vol. 4 (1960), 68-73.

———, 'The Theory of Definition in Indian Logic', *Journal of the American Oriental Society* 81 (1961), 122-26.

———, 'Contraposition in Indian Logic', *Proceedings of the 1960 International Congress on Logic, Methodology and Philosophy of Science*, Stanford 1962, 634-49.

———, 'Negation and the Law of Contradiction in Indian Thought': A Comparative Study', *BSOAS* 25 (1962), 52-71.

Stcherbatsky, Th., *The central conception of Buddhism and the meaning of the word "dharma"*, London: Royal Asiatic Society, 1923.

———, *The conception of Buddhist nirvāṇa*, Leningrad, 1927.

———, *Buddhist logic*, 2 vols., Bibliotheca Buddhica XXVI, Leningrad, 1930-1932.

Stebbing, L. Susan, *A modern introduction to logic*, London: Methuen & Co. Ltd., 1961.*

Strawson, P. F., *Individuals: An essay in descriptive metaphysics*, London: University Paperbacks, Methuen & Co. Ltd., 1965.*

Sugiura, Sadajiro and Singer, Jr., Edgar Arthur, *Hindu logic as preserved in China and Japan*, Philadelphia: University of Pennsylvania, 1900.

Suzuki, D. T., *Studies in the Laṅkāvatāra sūtra, a Mahāyāna text*, trans. for the first time from the original Sanskrit, London: George Routledge and Sons Ltd., 1932

Taranatha Tarkavacaspati, *Vācaspatya*. An encyclopaedic dictionary of Sanskrit terms. First published in Calcutta. Reprinted in Chowkhamba Sanskrit Series 94. Benares : Chowkhamba Office, 1927.

The Constitution of India, New Delhi: Government of India Press, 1960.*

Tucci, G., *Pre-Diṅnāga Buddhist texts on logic from Chinese sources*, GOS, No. XLIX, Baroda, 1929.*

———, *The Nyāyamukha of Dignāga, the oldest Buddhist text on logic after Chinese and Tibetan materials*. Materialien zur Kunde des Buddhismus, 15 Heft, Heidelberg: Kommission bei O. Harrassowitz, 1930.

Uddyotakara, *Nyāyavārtika*, ed. Vindhyeśvarī Prasāda Dvivedin (Dube), Bibliotheca Indica, Calcutta, 1907.*

Vācaspati Miśra, *Nyāyavārtikatātparyatīkā*, ed. R. S. Dravida, Kashi Sanskrit Series, 24, Benares: Chowkhamba Sanskrit Series Office, 1925.*

Varadarāja, *Tārkikarakṣā*, ed. (in the *Pandit*) by Vindhyeśvarī Prasāda Dvivedin, Reprint, Benares, 1903.*

Vesey, G. N. A., ed., *Body and mind*, London: George Allen & Unwin Ltd., 1964.*

Vidyabhusana, S.C., trans., *Nyāyāvatāra: the earliest Jaina work on pure logic (by Siddhasena Divākara)*, Calcutta: Indian Research Society, 1909.

———, *A history of Indian logic (ancient, mediaeval and modern schools)*, Calcutta: University of Calcutta, 1921.

———, trans., *The Nyāya Sūtras of Gotama*, SBH, Volume, VIII, Allahabad: The Panini Office, 1930.*

———, see Bhāsarvajña.

Whitehead, A. N., *Adventures of ideas*, The Free Press, New York, London; Collier-Macmillan Limited, 1967.*

GENERAL INDEX

abhagna 631
abhāva, absence 9 10, 39, 42, 81, 111, 342, 343, 364, 366, 367, 497, 595n.2
abheda 201, 365
abhibhava 168
abhidheya 303
abhimāna 90, 439, 468
abhivyakti 362
abhyudaya 476
abhyupagama 216
abrāhmaṇa 279
ācārya 457
adarśana 406
ādeśa 176
ādhāra 97, 304
adharma, demerit 14, 465, 551, 555, 556
ādheya 97
adhigantavya 23
adhika 330, definition 336-337
adhikaraṇa 34, 216, 508, 634; see also umpire
adhruva 595n.2
adhyavasāya 207, 410
adhyātmavidyā 456, 457
āgama, *śāstra*, scripture xl, 4, 9, 13, scriptural objects 13, 16, 24, 25, 35, 63, 89, 115, 116, 122, 123, 126, 130, 144, 157, 160, 169, 197, 203, 212, 218, 219, 228, 232, 256, 257, 280, 291, 302, 335, 336, 345, 354, 355; see also *prāvāduka*. God as cause; 369, 384, 388, 400, 408, 425, 444, 448, authority of various scriptures 448-449, 456, 457, scriptural tradition 459, 463, 471, method of treatment 475, purpose and means 476, 480, 482, 484, 495, 503, 504, 505, 528, 607 n.7, 608n. 1, 634
Agnihotra 24, 156, 159, 433, 447, 456
aham 380, 401
ahaṃkāra 377, 466
aikātmyam 443
aiśvarya 346, 352
aitihya, historical tradition 9, 10, 38, 39-40
aja 354
ajñāna 331, definition 338
ākāra 87
ākāśa 56, auditory organ 60, 61, auditory organ distinct from other sense organs 60-61, 62, 63, 69, 70, 71, 78, 81, 99, 100, auditory perception 110, 111, 128, 135, 140, 150, 154, 164, 165, 168, 169, 173, 184, 235, 257, 268, 275, 312, 313, 317, 318, 346, 353, 354, 358, 400, 409, 489, 512, 541, 564, 588n. 3
akiñcanavāda 363
ākṛti, configuration 3, 179, 183
akṛtsna 85
Akṣapāda, Gautama 457
Alston, William P. 618n. 21
anādhāra 633
ananta 364, 607n. 7
ānantya 189
ananya 172
anaikāntika see *savyabhicāra*
ananubhāṣaṇa 331, definition 337-338
anavadhāraṇajñāna 207
anavasthā, infinite regress, objection to pramāṇa 35-38, 86, 101, 125, *prasaṅgasama jāti* 311, 316-317; 337; Sāṃkhya objection 383-384
Anscombe, G. E. M. 628n. 73
aneka 199, 201, 363, 366
anekadharma 198, 200, 201, 202, 206
anekārthasamavāyi 185
āhnika, xl, 13, 475
animitta 355
anitya 358, 594-595n. 2, 600n. 1
anityasama 311, definition 325
anityatā 174, 594-595n. 2
aniyama 178, 417, in context of formation of body 402-405; see also *śarīra* (body) and *niyama* (rule).
annihilation, of series 5, 427, 455, 461, causal operation 463, 562-564, second part of Nyāya system 480, 482-483 destruction of series 562-564
anta 279
antaḥkaraṇa 411, 415, 416
aṇu, atom, mind as 68, indivisibility of 99-102; ultimate constituent and substance 109-113, as pramāṇa 117, 163, controlled by Karma: cause of world 348-350; see also God as cause 489-490, substance and property 541-542, 556
anubandha 470
anudaka 378
anujñā 593n. 3
anumāna, inference xxxiv, 4, 9, 24, definition of, 114; 117-119, Buddhist

and Sāṃkhya definitions 119-122, as instrument 117f.; three kinds of: *pūrvavat*, *śeṣavat* and *sāmānyato-dṛṣṭa* 114, interpretations 127-131, objections 114, 131-140, three kinds of: *anvayi* (positive), *vyatireki* (negative) and positive-negative (*anvayavyatireki*) 129ff., relation to other pramāṇas 122-124, difference between perception and inference 124, objections 124-127, different from *tarka*: see *tarka*; inference by elimination (*pariśeṣa*), 63, 418
anupalabdhisama 311, definition 323
anuṣaṅga 363, 466
anuśāsana 476
anutpattisama 311, definition 317
anuvyañjana, 468
anvayi, *anvaya* 129, 131, 200
anvayavyatireki 129, 131
ānvīkṣā 115
ānvīkṣikī 115, 116, , 456
anyāpoha 419
anyathābhāva, difference 172; see also *śabda*
anyathāsiddha 284
anyatva 412
apakarṣasama 311, definition 313-314
apara 459, 544
aparisaṃkhyeya 12, 21
apārthaka 330, definition 335
apasiddhānta 331, definition 340-341, 525, 532, 602n. 1
apavarga, *mokṣa*, release, liberation, emancipation, salvation, xxxv, 4, 5, 6, 109, 213, 419, definition of, 441, Vedānta view 441-446, release of *citta* 446, objections: debts, afflictions and activities 446ff.; 448-449, 455, 456, 461, for exact timing: see *niḥśreyasa*; yoga recommended 471, protection of truth 471f., 476, absence of *duḥkha* 482-483,497, meaning of *apavarga* 497-498 539, 544, degrees of salvation 544, 553; see also critique of moral philosophy and karma 551-561, 612n. 5.
apekṣā 367
apoha 191, 192, 193, 497
aprāptakāla 330, definition 335, objections 335-336
aprāptisama 311, definition 315
apratibhā 331, definition 338
āpta, role in cognition of self and fire 116, characteristics of 147; 148, 152, function in *nantras* and Āyurveda 160-162, 164, 346, Sāṃkhya pramāṇa 412, 477, role in second part of Nyāya system 480-483, 486, 494, 495, 528, 529, 539, 543, 544, 545, credibility of, 545, 546, 560, 568, 572, 621n. 26
āptavacana 480
āptopadeśa 24, 36
apūrva 153, 591n. 4
argument, from: instrument (*karaṇa*), purpose (*prayojana*), object (*artha*) 58; chaos 567-569; obstruction *ibid.*, ontological argument 547, 570; physico-theological proof and cosmological argument 570
Aristotle 6, 487, 488, 491, 516, 525, 534, 569, 624n. 57
arthāntara 307, 330, definition 334
artha, object, xxxv, 4, kinds of, 11f., 14-15, object of cognition 206; see also pramāṇa 20-21, 23, 52, 53, 54, 57, 58, 109, 213, meanings of *artha*: Buddhist definition of *Vāda* 302-303, 409, 476, 539, 578n. 3, 600n. 3
arthapadāni, see *tattvajñāna*
arthāpatti, implication 9, 10, 38, 39, 40, 41ff, 535
arthāpattisama 311, 318, definition 321
arthaśūnyaśabda 54
arthavāda 593n. 3
arthāvadhāraṇa 207
arthavat 12, 542
arthavijñāna 12
ārya 147, 152, 555
Ārya Deva 606n. 3, 610n. 1
āryaprajñā 426
Āryaratnākara 607n. 9
asādhāraṇa 19, 280
asādhāraṇadharma 200, 201, 240
asādhya 225
asamānadharma 200
asamartha 458
asarva 193
aśeṣatā 366
asiddha 227
asiddhi 29, 303
āśrama 555, 558, 628n. 73
āśraya 399
āśrayāsiddha 284, 611n. 2
assumption, definition 188, Buddhist view *ibid*; Buddhist theory 380-381
aśubha 469
asya idam 149
atiśaya 19, 106, 368
ātman, self, xxxv, xl, 4, 5, 6, 45, 48, argument from double visual organ 61, *adṛṣṭa* as quality of 72f., qualities as perishable 112, ultimate constituent and substance 111-113, 116, cognition of self

through combined operation of pramāṇas 116; peculiar mind-self contact *ibid.*, *sāmānyatodṛṣṭa* inference 129, 139-140, perception of qualities by internal organ 140, 198, 204, 210, 231, 234, 237, 238, 258, 284, 289, 298, 312, 313, 314, 317, 349, evidence for existence 373f., role of inference in evidence 375-376; Buddhist objections 376-386, distinction from psychosomatic equipment 387-389: recognition and remembrance as proof 393-394, body and sin: Buddhist objection 389-393; reasons for self, not mind 395, eternality and baby 395-397, 406, 441, 442, 443, 444, 445, 446, 449, 450, 456, 477, 497, 500, critique of self: *prameya* doctrine 536 ff., 608n. 2
ātmahāni 361
ātmalābha 361
ātmapradeśa 420
attachment 425, 426, 431, 443, 446, 451, 452
atyanta 174, 212
Austin, John 620n. 23
authority principle of, 477; 482, 484; see also *śabda* 493-499; reverential pattern of, 519; role in refutation 522-527
avadhi Jain pramāṇa 9
āvaraṇa 36
avarṇyasama 311, definition 314
avasthita 423
avayava, member, xxxvi, 3, 4, 10, Gautama's statement on five *avayavas*: *pratijña*, hetu, *udāharaṇa*, *upanaya* and *nigamana* 217f., justification for separate enumeration 218-220, three and ten members of reasoning 220-222, 226, formal statements on five member reasoning: positive and negative 259-260; fulfilment of object 261f., mutual relation 261, purpose of each *avayava* 261, objections 262f., 297, role in discussion 298-299, 301, 302, 329, 330, 331, disorderly sequence of: see *apārthaka* 335-336, see also *nyūna* and *adhika*; 413, 499, 501, 502, critique of 503-511; comparison with Mill's methods 511-513, 516, 523, 526, 529, 531, 532, 534, 602n. 1
avayavin 94
aversion 426, 427, 431
avidyā 16, 456
avijñātārtha 330, definition 334
aviparīta 12
āvirbhāva 362
aviśeṣaṇasama 311, definition 321-322
aviśiṣṭadharma 208
aviṣṭambha 100
avīta 238
avyakta 406
avyabhicāri 49
avyabhicāridharma 202
avyapadeśya 48
avyāpaka 606n. 2
avyatireka 365
avyūha 100
Ayer, A. J. 485, 546, 618n. 8, 616n. 11, 618 and 619n. 21, 624n. 53
Āyurveda 156, similarity to Veda 160-162; see also *śabda*; empirical science 481-482, 505, 510, 547, 592n. 2, 614n. 9

Bacon, Francis 536
Bādarāyaṇa 476
bādha, *bādhā* 203, 239
Berkley 568
Bhadanta 379, 581n. 5
Bhadrabāhu, ten members of reasoning 598-599n. 1
bhākta 165
bhakti 103, 169, 559
bhāktapratyaya 103
Bhāsarvajña 578n. 1
Bhāṣya 592n. 1
bhāṣyakāra 604n. 2
bhāva 89, 282, 362, 385
bhāvaśabda 332
bhavitṛ 385
bheda 95, 96
bhedaśabda 190
bhoktṛ 393
bhūtacaitanika 417
bīja 403
Black, Max 620n. 22, 624n. 57
Bochenski, I. M. 599n. 1
Borst, C. V. 626n. 68
Brahman 441, 450, 476, 571, 612n. 2
Brāhmaṇa 158, 159, 160, 180, 447, 448, 449, 593n. 3
Brahmin, *Brāhmaṇa*, Brahmanism 55, 180, *Brāhmaṇa*-hood 183, 226, 229, 279, 306, 307, 419, 447, 448, 575, 577n. 2, 596n. 2, 603n. 1
Brahma Sūtra purpose 476, 613n. 5
Braithwaite, R. N. 615 and 616n. 10, 623n. 44
Bṛhadāraṇyaka Upaniṣad 612n. 5, 613n. 6 and 7
British Raj 562
Buddha 39 , 484
buddhi, xxxv, 4. 26, 34, 165, 198, 298, 345, 347, 348, 352, 353, 357, 389; definition of, 409; non-eternal

property of self 415, 419; Sāṃkhya, Buddhist and Materialist views: see Chapter 21; *Buddhi* 409-422, 423, 425, 430, 432, 435, 462, 466, 467, 512, 539, 551, 569

buddhisantāna 415

Buddhist 9, 45, 46, 52, 53, 55, 74, 86, 87, 95, 96, 101, 102, 103, 104, 105, 106, 107, 137, 138, 146, 152, 153, 154, 165, 186-193 *passim*, 203, 206, 214 215 245-252 *passim*, 299-304 *passim*, 376-384 *passim*, 390, 391, 392, 393, 409, 412, 413, 414, 419, 434, 484-504 *passim*, 548, 564, 569, 578n. 1, 579n. 6, 581n. 5, 586n. 1, 587n. 2, 591n. 5, 592n. 2, 606n. 3. 607n. 5, 607n. 7, 608n, 3, 610n. 1

Butler, R. J. 626n. 67

caitanya 417

candra 229

Caraka 614n. 9

Cārvāka materialist 9, 418, 479, 524, 549, 609n. 2

Catholic Church comparison with Varṇāśrama system 562

catuṣṭaya 584n. 8

cause most efficient 19, principal-predominant 19, general and specific 19, causal juxtaposition 83, resemblance 143; see also *upamāna*; non-eternality 165-166, God, *prakṛti* and atoms 346-370; see also *prāvāduka*: God as cause: production of entity without cause; instrumental cause 355-356, kinds of causal relations 427-428, causal process of *saṃsāra* 430-431, material cause 435, implications of causation 490-495, function of causation in *avayava* 507-511, 548, notion of things in causation 564-566

certainty, xl, of formal logic 487

cetanā 388, 409

chala, quibble, xxxvi, 3, 4, 127, 264, 297, 298, 304, definition 306, three kinds and their definitions: concerning word (*vākchala*), universal (*sāmānyachala*) and metaphor (*upacārachala*), 306-308, 309, 520, 533, role of metaphor 543-544, 625n.57

Chāndogya Upaniṣad 612n. 5, 613n. 8

chedana 215

Chinese 565

Chomsky, Noam 619 and 620

Christian 538, 615n. 10

cikīrṣā 393

cintā 282

cintāprabandha 416

cit 468

citra, citrarūpa, citravivāda, variegated colour 97-99, 587 and 588n. 2

citta 93, 446

class, classes of men on different bases 13-14, 457-458; *varṇas* and *āśramas* 454-455; of philosophers 480; Plato's classes 555-556, inegalitarian society 560-562

Clay-cow 181, 184, 187

cognitive apparatus 45-46, 55; see also sense organs, mind and contact 45, 46, 55; see also *indriya, manas* and contact under relation

communication significance of, 479-483; 492, proof as theory of, 505; machinery of, 562; Buddhist and Sāṃkhya views 569

composite and component objections 94-99; substratum (*ādhāra*) and superstratum (*ādheya*) *ibid.*'; also justification for indivisible atom; Buddhist objections 101-109, Sāṃkhya view 412-413; see also *buddhi*; inherence 112

conceptual framework, xl, 6, 486, role of causation 507-508, comparison with modern approach 517-520, 525

Constitution of India 556, 627n.72

counter-instance, importance of, 526; 530, 531

cow 180, 181, 182, 184, 185, 186, 192, 193

credibility of proof and pramāṇa 501, 515, 529, 545

Crombie, I. M. 615n. 10

cowness 181, 183, 184, 185, 186, 187

Cox, J. W. Roxbee 626n. 67

cultural posits 502, 621n. 26

dadhi 176

daṇḍin 54

daṇḍanīti 116, 456

darśana 388, 407, 410, 413, 471, 476 (system)

Darśapūrṇamāsa 447

Dasgupta, S. 591n. 4, 614n. 9

Daśavaikālikaniryukti 598n. 1

definition 73-74

deity 152

deśa 64, 218

Descartes, R. 113; see also *manas*; Cartesian doubt 499, 536-537 Nyāya version of Cartesian argument 546, 626-627n. 68

determinism, pattern of explanation 566-569
Devadatta 244
dharma, merit 14, 29, relation to objects of apprehension 93f., 140, 160, 177, 179, 213, 364, *pravṛtti* as product of *dharma* and *adharma* 418, 419, 423; see also *buddhi* 419, figurative use 423, pleasure and pain as result 432, 433; see also *phala* 432, 434; purpose of *Vaiśeṣika Sūtra* and *Mīmāṃsā Sūtra* 476, 551, 555, 556, 561, 588n. 4, 613n. 1, 628n. 73
dharma, property 5f, 29, 124, 137; true nature of things: āptas' intuitive perception 160-161
dharmādharma 418
Dharmaśāstra 449, role in Nyāya system 476, 482, 505, 554, 555, 556, 561, 628n. 73
dharmin 137, 206
dhṛtihetu 634
dhvani 337
Dignāga 54, 55, 119, 144, 578n. 3, 581n. 5, 584n. 8, 585n. 9, 585n. 10, 589n. 3, 591n. 5
dik 69, 79, 140
discourse 4, 297, 299, 525, 526, 554, 558, 559
disproof, nature of, 209-304; see also Buddhist definition of *vāda* and proof
Ḍittha 54; 234
doṣa, defect, xxxv, 4, 5, definition 425, three groups 426-427, *moha* (misconception) 427, objections 427-428, specific features 428f., direct awareness of, 481; 539, 542, 558
dravya, see substance
dream 88ff, 92, 93
draṣṭṛ 406
dṛṣṭa 460
driṣṭi 466
dṛśya 406
dṛṣṭānta, familiar instance, xxxvi, 3, 10, 224, 227, 253, definition and utility of, 256-258, objections 257-258, 263, role in *jāti* (legitimate objection) 313-318, 599n. 1
dravyaśabda 54
duḥkha, pain, xxxv, 4, involvement in *saṃsāra* 5, member of series 5, 6, relation with good of man 13-20, 355 definition of, 438; as birth *ibid.*, analogy of poisoned milk 438, objection to birth as pain 438ff., pleasure affirmed *ibid.*, technical term 440, kinds of, 457-458 connection with pleasure 465-466; kinds of connection *ibid.*; 480, ordinary fact 482-483, 539, critique of, 552-553, 557, 573; see also critique of *prameya* under *prameya*; 615n. 10
duḥkhahetu 12
durgati 603n. 1
dvandva 610n. 1
dveṣa 428, 451 (hatred)
dvitva 107

Einstein 617n. 18
eka 95, 363, 369
ekānekapratyayahetu 201
ekadeśa 83, 95
ekadeśin 420
ekānta 344
empiricism 5, logical wedge 477; role of āpta and *śabdapramāṇa ibid.*; see also proof 480-484 *passim*; 490, 498-499, 523, 530, 531, 544-545, justification for God 570-571, 573, 614-615n. 10
entity 342, 355, 356, 357, 364
epistemology, Indian xli, 4, 11 (epistemic problem), notion coordinated with ethics, grammar and ontology 538-539, 547
error, doctrine of, see *mithyājñāna*; also *avyabhicāri*
establishment 483, 534-535, 570
estoppel doctrine 488, 526, 617n. 17
eva 120, 244, 439

Flew, Anthony, xl, 538, 577n. 1, 614n. 10, 621n. 25, 625n. 62, 626n. 63, 627n. 68, 627n. 69, 627n. 73

Gandhi 558, 562
Ganges 180
Gautama, similar to Aristotle 6, Indian version of J. S. Mill 478, 516, see also Akṣapāda
gavaya 141, 142, 143, 144, 314
gavī 335
generalization 356, comparison with Mill and Popper 486-489, notion of rule (*niyama*) 507-508, 526-527, 531, empirical generalization about society 561-562
ghaṭa, *ghaṭatva* 190, 252
God 419, 428, 528, 538, 544, 547, divine agency 556, critique of, 569-574, 616n. 10; see also *prāvāduka*: God as cause
grahaṇa 93
grammar, convention 480, rule 488,

495, 496, 528, logical grammar of self 547, 619-620n. 22
granthakāra, 604n. 2
Greek, xl; see also philosophy; 565
Grice, H.P. 626n. 67
grīṣma 75
go 54, 335; see also cow
guṇa, *guṇatva* 20, 111, 198, 425, 512
guṇaśabda 54
guṇāntaraprādurbhāva 414
Guthrie, W. K. C., xl, 577n. 2

Halsbury 617n. 17
hāna 23
hānopāya 16
Hare, R. H. 614n. 10
Hattori, M. 578n. 1, 578n. 3, 581n. 2, 581n. 5, 585n. 10
hedonism, crux of Karma theory 551, 552
hemanta 75
Heraclitus 478
hetu, definition and kinds of, 217, 219, 234-235; components of definition 235-237, objections 237-241, Buddhist definitions 241-253, 316, legitimate objection (*jāti*) regarding hetu 311,320, objection similar to that against pramāṇa 320; see also pramāṇa; derivation of, 334; see *hetvantara* 330, 333-334; role in proof 478
hetusama 311, definition 320
hetuvidyā 516
hetvābhāsa, fallacy of the hetu, xxxvi 3, 4, 10, 236, definition of, 264; five kinds of: *savyabhicāra*, *viruddha*, *prakaraṇasama*, *sādhyasama* and *kālātīta* 265; see under each head; justification for restriction to five 266, classification and computation of hetus and fallacies 266-278, 455, category status 476 520, 524 *nigrahasthāna*: 331, 341
hetvantara 330, definition 333
heya 16, 23
Hick, John 615n. 10
hiṃsāphalopabhoga 392
hīna 368
Hīnāyanist 578n. 1
Hudson, W. D. 628n. 73
Hindu 500, 570, 571
Hume, David 491, 627n. 73
Huxley, T. H. 548

I, *ittva* 176, 177
immortality 538
identity, 56, 365, numerical 492-493; logical question 545, criterion for numerical, 547-548; problem of personal, 572, 573-574; identity theory 626-627n.68
Identity of Indiscernibles 514, 622 n. 39
Idols 536
individualism 500
Indra 428
indriya, see sense-organ
indriyasaṃplava, convergence of sense-organs, 111; see also *pramāṇasaṃplava*
induction, problem of, 478, 550, inductive character of proof: see critique of proof under proof
instrument, *karaṇa* 16, 34, 58, nature of, 66, 67; of self 112, 113; operation process 117f.; see also *anumāna*; *upamāna* as instrument 141; see also *upamāna*; *siddhānta* as instrument 215, 226, 292, 299, 303, 315, 316, 330, 335, 344, 349, 356, 369, 387, 388, 395, 410-418 *passim*; see also *buddhi*; logical grammar of instrument 485, 535, 631, 633, 636
intuition, illumination, *pratibhā* xli, 160, 416, role of intuition in philosophy 478-482; see also mysticism
iṣṭa 227, 228, 229, 231
Īśvarakṛṣṇa 476, 613n. 2
itara 367
itaretarābhāvātmaka 587n. 2
Itihāsa 449

Jaimini 476, 613n. 4
Jain 9; see also pramāṇa; 578n. 2, 599n. 1
jalpa, rejoinder, xxxvi, 3, 4, 214, 218, 220, 291, definition 297, 298, 299, explanation of, 304, 520
James, William 613-614n. 8
janma, birth 5, of son by sacrifice 171, illustration 288-289; see also *tarka* 423; as pain *ibid.*; rebirth defined 430; see also *pretyabhāva*; 535-536
janmotpatti 438
jāti, legitimate objection xxxvi, 3, 4, 103, 298, 301, 304 definition 309, significance of counter-argument 310, twenty-four kinds of *jāti* 311, definitions and examples 311-327, principles of answering legitimate objections 327-328, 475, 520, 530, universal: 2, 183, 193, 365, 563
jātimat 189
jātiśabda 54

jātiviśeṣa 398
Jha, G. 579n. 5, 581n. 2, 583n. 7, 590n. 2, 592 n. 1, 600n. 1, 601n. 8, 601n. 9, 601n. 10 601n. 13, 606n. 2, 606n. 4, 613n. 4
Jinendrabuddhi 586n. 11
jīva 200, 238, 462
jīvana 421•
jñāna 93, 409, 410, 444, 471, 542, 559
jñāpaka 316
jñeya 414
Jyotiṣṭoma 159

kadamba 167
kālātīta, fallacy of the mistimed hetu 265, definition 285-286, reversal of order of reasoning 286; see also *nigrahasthāna*; different from the inconclusive 286
kalpa 571, 583n. 6
kāma 561
kalpanā 51, 53
Kaṇāda 229, 598n. 4
Kane, P. V. 555, 627n. 71
Kāraka, noun function 18, 34, Buddhist view 215, 316, 631ff.
kāraṇabahutva 85
karma 9, 46, 56, 60, 74, role in visual perception 78, 91, 110, 111, 112, 113, force driving self's toolkit 113, 289, 344, 345, 346, 347, 348, 349, 350, 356, 390, 391, role in determination of body of self 397 f., 401, incomprehensive operation 401, 402, 403, 404, 405, 407, 408, 416, 421, 434, 452, 461, 462, 479, 481, 492, 522, 535, 544, 551, criterion of personal identity 574, critique of 551-561, 567, 627 n. 68, 629n. 75
karma, accusative 226, 349, 633
karma, action 409, 467, 633
karma, object 34, 93, 303, 349, 369 633
karmāśaya 421
karmātiśaya 401
karmaviśeṣa 416
kartṛ 34, 349, 389, 393, 547, nominative 631-633
kartṛtva 19
kāryasama 311, definition 327
kāryāśrayakartṛvadha 392
kathā, 212, 297, 520
Kauṭilya 584n. 9
kāyācitta 385
kāyācittasantāna 390
Keynes, J. M. 622n. 41
kevala, Jain pramāṇa 9
Khyātinimitta 126
knowledge 6, central problem of, 485; pyramid of, 486, see generalization and *pramiti*
kolāhala 594n. 1
krama 460, *kramabhāva* 26
krīḍā 351
kriyā 64, 67, 93, 118, 192, 465
kriyākāla 596n. 2
kriyāśabda 54
kriyāsantāna 420
Kṛṣṇa 501
kṛtsna 85, 95
kṣaṇikavāda, momentariness, Buddhist interpretations 412-413; see also *buddhi*
Kṣatriya 249, 419
kṣaya 403
kṣema 441
Kumārila Bhaṭṭa 9
Kuhn, Thomas S. 518, 624n. 48

Lakatos, Imre 624n. 51
lakṣaṇa, xxxix, 359, 362, 475, 581n. 2
lakṣaṇasāmānya 37
lamp 12, analogy of, 22; 35-38 *passim*, 90, as pramāṇa 154, 163, 315, 316, 411, 514
Leibniz 622n. 39
Locke, John 538, 625n. 62
liṅga 84, 130, 264, 416, 418, 541
liṅgaparāmarśa 589n. 2
locus, community of (*sāmānādhikaraṇya*), 106; 366, 367; see also *prāvāduka*: all are non-entities; coextensiveness 187-191 *passim*; see also paradigm of *sat* 187-191
Logic, Indian xli, 5, of discovery 478, technique of refutation 523-524, 531-536 see also induction
loka 205, 432

MacIntyre, Alasdair 554, 627n.70
Mādhyamika 579n. 6, 607n. 9, 610n. 1
Mahābhāṣya 54
mahat 106, 154, 347
Mahatma 501
mahattva 85, 441
Manaḥparyāya, Jain pramāṇa 9
manas, mind 45, ghost in atomic machine 46, 113, basis of misery and liberation 46, mind-sense contact 45, 63, mind-self contact 45, 63, 409, 421-422, 433, 442; existence and marks 63-68, double of self 113, distinction of mind from self 87, 395; 399, entry into body and *adṛṣṭa* 407f., 431;

Sāṃkhya view: buddhi as mind 411-414, 419, bad deeds 423-424, 431, 492, 548, 564, 581n. 3, 583-584n. 8, 585n. 9
manda 107
mantra 156-160 *passim*, 449, 592n. 1, 592n. 2
Manu 593n. 2
mark 42, 43, 44
Mason, Philip 628n. 74
matānujñā 328, *nigrahasthāna*: 331, definition of *matānujñā* 339
Materialist 9, 10, 417, 418; see also *buddhi* as property under *buddhi*, 548
mati, Jain pramāṇa 9
matisādhana 395
Māyā, xl, 88, 577n. 2
Meru 143
Methods of Mill, Agreement, Difference, Joint Method, Concomitant Variations and Residues 511-513; see also Mill, J. S.
Mill, J. S., Gautama as Indian version of Mill 516; comparison with Mill's attack on syllogism and Popper's falsifiability criterion 487-488, Nyāya proof compared with Mill's views 509-513; also with Mill's Methods 511-513; 617n. 13, 621n. 28, 621n. 30, 622n. 35 and 37, 623n. 44
Mīmāṃsā Sūtra dharma as purpose 476
Mīmāṃsaka, Pūrva Mimāṃsā 9, 152, 162, 163, 164, 165, 277, 491, 495, 501, 571, 591n. 3, 591n. 4
Mind 626n. 67
mirage 49, 88, 90, 91, 204
Mitchell, Basil 614-615n. 10
mithyājñāna, misapprehension, xxxvii, 5; 430, 431, responsibility for *saṃsāra* 455; neither category nor *prameya ibid.*; 476, see also 519-520; 455, wrong notion of 'I' 466-468; annihilation affirmed *ibid.*; aspects of objects 468, 476, 520, 540, original mistake 547, 559, 566, 567, 571
mithyopalabdhi 520
mithyāpratyaya 586n. 1
mleccha 147, 152
moha, misconception 405, 425, 426, 427, 428, 451, 452
mokṣa, *mukti* 391, 612n. 2; see also *apavarga*
Moral philosophy, morality, role in Indian philosophy 483, moral responsibility 549-552, Western view and critique of, 553-56
Moore, C. A. 577n. 2
Moore, G. E. 516, 623n. 43
mūrti 28, 597n. 3
musical instrument, analogy 28
Musgrave, Alan 624n. 51
Mysticism, mystical philosophy, xl, xli, Russells' characteristics 478-479, 481

nāda 594n. 1
Nāgārjuna 578n. 1, 606n. 3, 610n. 1
Naive realism 489
nānātva 406
nāntarīyakārtha 119
Nārikeladvīpa 119, 164
nāstika, heresy 4, 256, 423, objections 403-406; see also *śarīra*; 477, 500, 502, 534, 559
navakaṃbala 306
Navya-Nyāya 587n. 2
negation, universal and specific 378-379, see also *ātman*: Buddhist objections; Buddhist view 419; see also *buddhi* as property 414-419; problem of negation 497-498
nigamana, conclusion, definition and kinds of, 218; 219, 259, 260, 261, 262, 331
nigrahasthāna, deficiency, xxxvi, 3, 4, 264, as reversed order of reasoning 286; see also *kālātīta* 285-286 *passim*; definition and category status of, 329f; speaker's responsibility 330, figurative use 330, twenty two kinds of, 330-331; also twofold classification *ibid.*, 475, 520, meaningfulness and reference 533
nīlotpalam 193
nimitta 48, 63, 69, 211, 289, 390, 404, 582n. 2
nimittakāraṇa 344
nindā 593n. 3
niranuyojyānuyoga 331, definition 339-340
nirarthaka 330, definition 334
nirhetuka 392
nirātmaka 246, 382
nirmaśakam 382
nirṇaya, ascertainment, xxxvi, 3, 4, 115, 197, different from *tarka* 287f., scope of, 291ff.; critique of, 502, 536; 588n. 1
nirvāṇa 498
nirviṇṇa 438
nitya 382, 600n. 1
nityasama 311, definition 325-326
nivṛttimārga 559
niyama 265, 404, 413, 417, 435, *niyāmaka* 444, 463, 471, 488, 507, 567

niyoga 593n. 3
non-cow, non-cowness 186, 192, 193
No-Space world 517
notion, concept, figurative 103, analogical 103f., unitary, 106-107, comprehensive 172-173, uniform *ibid*, open-texture 541, mixture 543-544, mathematical-forms of Plato 549, notions in Karma doctrine 551-554, is=*dharma* and ought=*varṇa* and *āśrama* 556, 627n.73, eternality and non-eternality: see *prāvāduka*: everything is eternal and non-eternal 357-362; see also *nityasama* and *anityasama*: distinct (*pṛthak*): see *prāvāduka*: everything is distinct 362-364, number: see *prāvāduka*: definite number 368ff.
nyāya 55, 114, 115, 203, 215, 256, 293, 384, 456; see also reasoning
nyāyābhāsa 122
Nyāyabhāṣya, xxxix
Nyāya Sūtra, xxxix, 455, 457, supreme good as purpose 476, 480, 520, 522, 523
Nyāyasāra 578n. 1
Nyāya System, xl, xli, distinction from *Upaniṣads* 456, *darśana* status 476-477, 478, 479, two parts: factual and philosophical 480-483, inexplicability 565-567, 568-569
Nyāya-Vaiśeṣika 587n. 2
Nyāyavārtika, xxxix, 457
Nyāyavārtikaṭīkā, xxxix
nyāyavidyā 115
nyāyaviplava 122
nyūna 330, definition 336

ontology 4, ontological status 4, 5, 475, 497, linguistic 496, 528, scriptural 529, 533, ontological argument 547
opposition, contradiction, nature of, 202-203; Buddhist view *ibid.*
ostensive definition 490, 528
outfit 5

pācaka 18, 54, 595n.2, 635
pada 179
padārtha, category, categories, xxxiv-xxxvi, 3; significance 3-6, separate enunciation for distinction of Nyāya from *Upaniṣads* 114ff., topics of Gautama 475, category status 3, 500, *hetvābhāsa* and *mithyājñāna* 475, 520; structure-framework 475, 502, 544; God and self 352-355, 371; mistake 571, 629n. 78; preference 624n. 45
pāka 596n. 2
pakṣa 214, 215, 227, 230, 231, 232, 233, 240-252 *passim*, 292, 297, 300 Buddhist definition 300; see also *pratijñā*
pakṣasiddhi 604n. 3
Pāṇini 594n. 1, 596n. 2
para 300, 459, 544
paradigm, of *sat* 187-191, 501, 514, definition 518, of visual perception 547, 548, of explanation 550
parakṛti 593n. 3
paramanyāya 218
parāmarśa 118
parapakṣa 300, 301, 303, need for scrutiny 521-522
parārtha 590n. 1
paraśu 215
parīkṣā, xxxix, 212, 475
parimāṇa 106, 154, 333
pariṇāma 411, 413, 414
pariśeṣa 60, 63, 376, 418, 512, 513
pariṣkāra 468
parispanda 399
parivrājyam 445
Parkinson, G. H. R. 618n. 21
Parmenides, xl, 478, 577n. 2
parokṣa, indirect pramāṇa (Jain) 9
paryudāsa 202, 279
paryanuyojyopekṣaṇa 331, definition 339
paryeṣaṇadoṣa 439
pātaka 389
paṭabuddhi 611n. 3
Patañjali 54, 476, 611n. 3
Paurāṇika 9; also see pramāṇa
phala, result, xxxv, 4, 432, definition 432-433; objections 433ff.; Buddhist objection *ibid.*
phalānubandha 11
Phaedo 549
Phillips, D. Z. 615n. 10
Philosophy, Eastern, Western and Greek xl, Indian xl, xli, 4, methods and manners 483-495, *prameya* doctrine and Western philosophy of mind, 536-554, society and ethos 553-558, 569-570; relation to theology 570-571, Indian philosophers as sociologist 575
Pitcher, George 620n. 23
pīḍā 438
Plato 478, 501, 538, 542, 549, 561
Popper, Karl 487, 488, 518, 617n. 15
Prabhākara 9; see also Pūrva Mīmāṃsā
pracaya 85
pradeśa 165, 168, 185, 410
pradhāna 88, 92, 104, 277, 346, 583n. 5

prādhānya 16, 19
Prājāpatya 449
prajñā 63
prajñāpanīyadharmasamāna 284
prakaraṇa 13, 282
prakaraṇasama jāti 311, definition 319-320
prakaraṇasama, fallacy of the tautological hetu 208, 265, 281, definition 282f.; different from: the inconclusive and the unproved 283f., 282n. 13
prakṛti 175, 281, 333, 340, 347, 348, 383, 406, 569
pralaya 99
pramāṇa, recognition of number and kinds of, 9ff.; *pratyakṣa, anumāna, upamāna* and *śabda ibid.*, status of: not recognized 9-10, 38-40; Jain distinction between direct and indirect pramāṇas 9 definition 11; analysis and interpretations of the definition 11-20, distinct from other factors of cognition 17; see also *pramiti*; Buddhist objection 19-20, as cause-instrument 16f; as noun-function (*kāraka*) 18, 33-35; see also *prameya*; process of operation: convergence (*pramāṇasamplava*) 20, 23-25, 111; illustrations: cognitions of fire and self; analogy of lamp 12, 22, 35-37, 116; objections to validity of, 25-33; similarity with objection to *jāti* of *hetusama* 320, objection: infinite regress (*anavasthā*) 35-38; see also *prameya*; collective operation in reasoning 116f., significance of recognition of pramāṇas 483-484 logical grammar of instrument 485, cumulative evidence and criteria 486-487, 515-516; 531; social engineering 502-503, critique of pramāṇa doctrine 538ff., see also critique of *prameya ibid.*
pramāṇābhāsa 10, 20
pramāṇaphala 48
pramāṇasamplava, convergence of pramāṇas 20, 23-25; see pramāṇa and *indriyasamplava*
Pramāṇasamuccaya 144, 585n. 9, 589n. 3, 591n. 5; see also *vṛtti* 589n. 3
pramāṇaśāstra 10, 516
pramāṇatva 29
pramāṇaviruddha 428
prāmāṇya 160
pramātṛ, cognizer 12, 18, , independence of 21; illustration ir *tarka* 289f., see also *tarka*
prameya, object of cognition, xxxv, xl, 3-6 *passim*, 10, 12, 18, 23, 26, 27, 28, 30, 33-38 *passim*, 88, 114, 197, 214, 256, 291, 373, 455, 458, 460, 475, 476-477, 497, 528, critique of *prameya* doctrine 538ff.; see also critique of pramāṇa doctrine *ibid.*, 578n. 3, 585n. 9, 608n. 1, 636
pramiti, cognition, theory of, xxxix; 4, 12, factors of: *pramātṛ*, *artha*, pramāṇa and *pramiti* 21, dependence of *tattva* 21, entity and non-entity in relation to categories and supreme felicity 21-23, difference between *śabda* pramāṇa and inference; see *śabda*; 117, comparison with empiricism 477-483
prāpti 107
prāptisama 311, definition 315-316
prasajyapratiṣedha 279
prasaṅgasama 311, definition 316-317
Praśastapāda 54, 584n. 8, 586n. 11
prasiddha 514
pratighāta 107, 170
pratidṛṣṭāntasama 311, definition 317
pratijñā, proposition, definition of, 217, 218, 219; significance of *sādhya* 222, obections 222-227, see also *āgama* 218f.; also *siddhānta* 225f., 232-233, rival definitions 227-234, *nigrahasthānas* (deficiencies) of, 330-333; analytic and synthetic propositions 500, 516, 598-599n. 1
pratijñāntara 330, definition 331f.
pratijñāhāni 330, definition 331
pratijñāsannyāsa 330, definition 333
pratijñāvirodha 330, definition 332-333
pratipatti 580n. 10
pratipakṣa 292, 297
pratisandhāna, similarity, 397
pratitantra 215
pratitarka, see reasoning
pratyakṣa, perception, xxxiv, 4, 9, Jain direct pramāṇa 9, see also pramāṇa, basis of all pramāṇas 10, 45, 47, 486, definition 47-51, Buddhist definitions 51-55, different from: *śabdapramāṇa* 48; inference 85f.; non-inferential characters of, 81-86; object (composite) of, *ibid.*; physical object 489
pratyanīkabhāva 40
pratyāsatti 83, 107
pratyaya 198, 410
pratyayānuvṛtti 107
prāvāduka, doctrine of other philosophers, xxxvii, eight doctrines 342; production of non-entity (*abhāva*)

out of entity (*bhāva*) 342-343; God as cause: controversy and Nyāya view 343-346, Sāṃkhya objections 346-351, purpose 351-352, power 352, God and selves 352-355; production of entity without (no) cause 355-357; everything is non-eternal 357-358; everything is eternal 359-362, 606n. 2; *sarvam* (all) is distinct 362-364, 606-607ns. 3-7; all (*sarvam*) are non-entities 364-368, 607ns. 8 and 9; definite number (*saṃkhyaikānta*) 368-370
pravṛtti, activity, xxxv, 4, 5, 11, kinds of 14-15; regulated by pramāṇas 147, 351, definition 423; figurative use *ibid.*; deeds resulting from, 423-424; see also *doṣa*; 539, 558
pravṛttimārga 559
prayatna, 72, 393
prayatnāntarīyakatva 252
prayojana, xxxvi, 3, 4, 21, 58, 115, 213; basis of reasoning 115, 213; definition 213, pleasure and pain as objective, 213, 220, 500
preraṇa 422
pretyabhāva, state after death, xxxv, 4, 342, meaning of *pretyabhāva* 430, relation to eternal self 430, 539, 563
Price, H. H. 616n.10, 617-618n. 20
probability 6, theory for cumulative evidence 515, 562, 622n. 41
proof, xxxix, xl, 4, nature of, 297-298; see also Buddhist definition of *vāda* and disproof 299-304; critique of, 499-517; see also hetu 478, 623n. 44, 625n. 57
pṛthak 362
pṛthakpravāda 210
psychology 4, 506
pudgala 379
punarukta 330, definition 337
punarutpatti 430
pundit 255
Purandara 428
purākalpa 593n. 3
Purāṇa 449, 505, 561
pūrva 130, 133
pūrvapakṣa 521, 581n. 2
puruṣa 347, 348, 349, 350, 383, 400, 409, 410, 411, 569
puruṣaśreya 13, two kinds 14
pūrvavat, see *anumāna* 114-139, 511-513, 589n. 4

Radhakrishnan, S. 577n. 2, 613n. 5

rāga 428
Rāma 143
Rama Prasad 613n. 3
Ramsey, F. D. 528, 624n. 56
Randle, H. N. 578n. 1, 584n. 8, 589n. 3
rati 351
Rāvaṇa 143
reasoning, collective operation of pramāṇas; see pramāṇa; process 115ff., inherence based on reasoning 124-127; see also *samavāya*; role of doubt: see *saṃśaya*; *pratitarka* reasoning 202, 597n. 3
recognition, definition 61 role in inference 117-119, argument for existence of self 373-376, 393-395; see also remembrance; Sāṃkhya view 410-412, 420-422, critique 545-551; see also remembrance *ibid.*
reiteration, *anuvāda*, distinguished from repetition 160, 337, 593n. 3
relation, as quality 97-98, 188, contact (*saṃyogasannikarṣa*) 45, role in perception: see *pratyakṣa*: definition; kinds of contact 80-81, 100, 102, 106, 124-126, role in verbal cognition 148-151, association 492, 569; substance and property 566; causation: see cause; inherence: see *samavāya* critique of relations 563-566
religion 4, 559, without God 570-571, 629n. 75
remembrance, memory, *pratisandhāna*, definition 83; role in inference 116-119, argument regarding self 373-376, 384-386; see also Buddhist objections under *ātman*; mind-self contact 410, 420ff., 450, 490, critique 545-556, argument from remembrance *ibid.*; see also Descartes; Plato's theory *ibid.*
repetition, distinguished from *anuvāda* 160, argument for eternality of sound 171-172; see also non-eternality of sound 337
Ṛgveda 400
Ṛk 448
ṛṇa, debt 446, 447, 448
Roxbee, J. W. 626n. 67
rūpa 202, 463
Russell, Bertrand 478, 516, 613n. 6, 614n. 8, 617n. 18, 622n. 41, 623n. 42
ṛṣi 260
Ryle, Gilbert 493, 521, 617n. 19, 624n. 53, 629n. 78

Śabarasvāmi 581n. 4

śabda, verbal testimony, word, śabdapramāṇa, xxxiv 3, 9, 24, 39, 48, 128, aspects of: nature, specific (śabdaviśeṣa), non-eternality, modification (śabdavikāra), meaning 146; definition and kinds of, 146f.; objections: word as inference 147-152, 154f.; cognitive process and conventional connection *ibid.*; Mīmāṃsā and Buddhist objections 152-154, pramāṇa status 154, indictment of Veda 155-158, Veda as *śabdapramāṇa* 158-164, comparison of Vedic *mantras* and Āyurveda 160-162, conventional denoting power of Veda 162-164; Mīmāṃsā concept of eternality of Veda *ibid.*; eternality as continuity of tradition 162-163, non-eternality (*anityatā*) of sound: Mīmāṃsā, Sāṃkhya, Vaiśeṣika and Buddhist theories 164-174; three hetus for non-eternality 174-175, series of sounds 165-167, Sāṃkhya theory of modification of *varṇas* and Nyāya theory of substitution in *sandhi* 175-178, argument from absence of rule (*aniyama*) 178, definition of *pada* (word) 179; explosion (*sphoṭa*) theory *ibid.*; theories of meaning: individual (*vyakti*), configuration (*ākṛti*) and universal (*sāmānya*) 179-183; comprehensive notion as basis of universal 183-184, universal apart from individual 184-187, Buddhist objection 186f., paradigm of *sat* 187-191; Buddhist objection *ibid.*; Buddhist theory of *apoha* 191-194, cow and clay-cow 183-187, critique of *śabdapramāṇa* 493-499, 618n. 20; word: meaning of, xl; etymology of *padārtha* 3, kinds of: according to Dignāga, Patañjali and Praśastapāda 54; meaning: direct (*tattva*) · and figurative (*bhākta*) 165f., basis of figurative meaning 169; 'part' as figurative *ibid.*; definitions of different kinds of word 334, denotation 376, primary and secondary sense 448, see critique of *śabdapramāṇa* 493-499
śabdollekha 25
sacrifice, scriptural guarantee for result 433-434; see also objections under *phala*
sadbhāva 64
sādhaka, sādhakatama 18, 32
sādhana 14, 465, 466
sādhāraṇa 199
sādhāraṇadharma 198, 199
sādharmyasama 311, definition 311-312
sādhya 222, 224, 225, 226, 227, 233, 234, 272, 273, 274
sādhyasādharmya 254
sādhyasama, fallacy of the unproved hetu, 265, definition, 284
sādhyasama jāti 311, definition 314
ṣaḍja 276, 601n. 7
Sagāthakaṁ 586n. 1
sahakārisādhana 631
sahāsaṃbhava 202, 592n. 1
sāhacarya 138
sajātīya 600n. 2
Śakra 428
śakti 384, 635
sama 309
samādhi 345, 346, 373, 442, 445, 469, 470, 498
samāna 199
samānadharma 198, 200, 201, 206, 208
samānānekadharma 200
sāmānādhikaraṇya 187, 193, 366, 367, 508, 588n. 4
samānapratyaya 183
samānāsamānadharma 200
samānopalabhyatṛ 466
sāmānya 15, 19, 163, 167, 173, 177, 199, 200, 215, 245, 594n. 1, 600n. 3
sāmānyachala, see *chala*
sāmānyatodṛṣṭa 40, see *anumāna* 114-140, 589n. 4
samartha, *sāmarthya* 11, 18, 204, 425, 458
samavāya, inherence 81, relation between: atoms and products 111; composite and components 112; object and quality 124-127; cause and effect *ibid.*; universal and individual 186; superstratum and substratum *ibid.*; see also paradigm of *sat* 187-191; not based on faith 126, inexplicability of *samavāya* 477-478, 601n. 5
samavetasamavāya 81
samaya, convention 148, 151, 162, denotation 162; see also *śabda*; grammar 528-529
saṃbhava, inclusion, possibility 9, 10, 30, 39, 513, 515
saṃbodha 426
saṃcaya 102
sāmīpya 141
saṃjñā 440
Sāṃkhya 9, 119, 164, 173, 175, 281, 340, *prakṛti* as efficient cause 346-348; see also *prāvāduka*: God as cause 343-346; 383, 410,

411, 412, 414, 416, causation 491, 569, 571, 577n. 2, 609n. 2, 609n. 3, 609n. 1
Sāṃkhya Kārikā, remedy for suffering as purpose 476, 613n. 2
saṃpradāna 34, 633
saṃpratipatti 211
saṃsāra, xl, 5, 6, 289, 290, 351, 419, 425, causal process related to mind and self 430f., 440, 444, 455, 460, 461, 463, 466, 479, 481, 492, 501, 508, 519, 520, 522, 529, 533, 540, 541, 542, 543, 545, 548, 553, 555, 557, 559, 563, 564, 566, 571, 572, 612n. 2
saṃśaya, doubt, xxxvi, 3, 4, 50, role in reasoning 115; in categories 197-198; definition and kinds of, 198-206; Vaiśeṣika and Buddhist definitions 206, objections 206-212, different from *tarka*: see *tarka*; 220, Cartesian doubt 499-501
saṃśayasama 283, 311, definition 318-319
Saṃhitā 159, 593n. 3
saṃskāra 72, 74, 182, 354, 392, 401, 418, 420, 434, 465, 588n. 1
saṃskārasantati 394
saṃsthāna 87, 100
samudāya 107, 163, 193, 334
samūha 13, 101, 282, 332, 362
saṃvāda 471
saṃvṛtijñāna 52
samyagjñāna 426
Samyagdarśana 467
samyakpratyaya 586n. 1
saṃyuktasamavāya 81
saṃyoga see relation
saṃyuktasamavetasamavāya 81
sandhi 175, 511; see also Methods of Mill: concomitant variations
saṅkalpa 88, 346, 397, 427, 450
Śaṅkara 571
sannikarṣa, see relation
santāna, see series; also annihilation
santati, see series; also annihilation
sapakṣa 241-251 *passim*, 272-274 *passim*
sarga 403
Sargant, William 628n. 75
śarīra, xxxv, 4, definition 399, scriptural authority for composition of *śarīra*; also evidence of perception 402; objections 402ff.; karma as cause *ibid.*; *adṛṣṭa* as cause 405-406, 539
sārūpya 207
sarva, *sarvam* 193, 362, 364, 366, 606n. 2
sarvagata 184
Sarvajit 159
sarvapramāṇavilopa 35
Sarvāstivāda school 587n. 2
sarvatantra siddhānta 215, 226
śaśi 229
śāstrasaṃpradāya, see *āgama*
Sastri, S. 613n. 2
sat, existence 4, 6, 11, 12, 13, 22, 128; see also paradigm of, 187-191 *passim*; 187, 188, 189, 190, 191, 342
Śataka 606n. 3, 610n. 1
Śatapatha Brāhmaṇa 400, 447, 448
sātatya 207
sattā 20, 111, 186, 188, 189, 190, 191
sattva 391, 392, 403, 419
sattvanikāya 430
Sautrāntika 245
savikalpakapratyakṣa 54
savyabhicāra, *anaikāntika*, fallacy of the inconclusive hetu 236, 265, definition 278f., objections 278-281, 282, 283, 284, 286, 606n. 2
scepticism 46, Buddhist and Naiyāyika debate 486, scepticism of senses 489, 499, 500
sense-object contact 45, 47-48, 74, Buddhist and Jain views 74, existence of visual ray 74-77, contact of visual organ 77-80, six kinds of contact 80-81, 166; see also relation
sense-organ, *indriya*, xxxv, 4, 45, proofs for five sense-organs 55-61, double visual organ 61-63, coalescence of sense-organs (*indriyasaṃplava*) 111; see also *pramāṇasaṃplava*
series, *santati*, *santāna*, series of sounds: see non-eternality of sound 164-168, aggregate and Buddhist theory 389-392, of buddhi 409-410, Buddhist view 412-414, 419-420, 548-549; 416, destruction of series 562-564; see also annihilation
śeṣa 130, 134
śeṣavat 114, 128, 130, 132, 134-135, 139, 512, 513, 589n. 4; see *anumāna*
siddha 225, 227, 515
siddhānta, established tenet, xxxvi, 3, 4, 127, 214, justification for category status 214-215, definition of 214; kinds of, 214-215f.; Buddhist view 214-215, 217, as embodied in *pratijñā* 225f.; see also *pratijñā*; 281, 297, 298, 336, *apasiddhānta* 331, 340, see *prāvāduka*: God as cause 343-346; 370, role in proof 476-477, 503; 504, 522-533 *passim*; 581n. 2, 598n. 1, 621n. 26
siddhāntabheda 269

siddhi 302, 303
similarity, *sādṛśya*, basis of analogy 141-144; see also *upamāna*; neither quality nor universal 198-199
Sinha, J. 581n. 1
śiśira 75
skandha 379, 380, 383, 391
sociology 556, critique for identity of self 574f., 628-629n. 75; see also Philosophy
Socrates 549
soul 9, 113, 239, 538, 548, 550
spanda 106
spells 315, 316
sphoṭa 179, 595-596n. 1
spirituality, xli
śreyasa 457
Śrughna 224
śruti, Jain pramāṇa 9
Stebbing, Susan 622n. 40
Stevenson, C. L. 619n. 21
sthāpanā 301
Strawson, P. F. 486, 517, 616n. 12, 620n. 23, 624n. 45
stuti 593n. 3
sthiti 631
Subandhu 299, 604n. 2
śubhāśubhaprāpti 391
substance, *dravya* 45, 48, 54, distinct from quality 86-87; Buddhist view *ibid.*; 187, 188, 397, 478, 566
sukhahetu 12
Śūdra 419
Suez, xl
sugati 603n. 1
sukha, pleasure, cognition of pleasure and its cause 12, good of man 14-15, 443
śukla 54
śūnya 377, 498, 604n. 3
Suśruta 585n. 9
svabhāva, *svābhāvika* 152, 205, 351
svadharma 364
svapakṣa 300, 301, 303, need for scrutiny 521-522
svaparapakṣa 303
svarūpa 14, 202, 205, 365, 587n. 2
svatantra, *svātantrya* 21, 34, 631
śyāmaka 117

tadbhāva 632
tadvat 20
tadvirodhi 281
Taittirīya Āraṇyaka 612n. 5
tamas 377
tanmayatva 398
tantrārtha 34
tantrayukti 73, 585n. 9
tāpa 439
tarka, disputation, xxxvi, 3, 4, 197 217, 257, definition 287, not pramāṇa but aid 287f., different from *saṃśaya*, *nirṇaya* and inference 287-288, technique of, 288-290; 291, 297, 298, 299, critique of, 501-502, 535-536
Tārkikarakṣā 578n. 1
tat 52, 53
tatheti 142, 260 ('this is so')
Taittirīya Saṃhitā 612n. 5
tattvādhyavasāyasaṃrakṣaṇa 521
tattva, true nature of things 11, 21, 22, 88, 92, 165
tattvajñāna, knowledge of true nature of things, xxxvii, 6, 16, 426, four classes of things (*arthapadāni*) 23, 456-457; knowledge of some or all things 466, *samādhi* as means 469; objections 469-471; see also *mithyājñāna*
tattvaṃbhāva 126
Tattvārthadhigama Sūtra 578n. 2
technique of refutation, xl, demolition of heresy 477, inclusion in first part of Nyāya 480, critique 534-536, Mill's attack on syllogism 534
teleology, see determinism 566-569
time, reality and function in *saṃsāra* and Karma 479
theism 571
theology xli, 477, 478, Indian and Western 481-483, 532, 544, 549, relation to philosophy 570, 572, 614n. 10
tirobhāva 360
tīvra 107
toolkit, of self 113, 547
traikālya 29
traikālyasama 605n. 1
traikālyasiddhi 28, 29
trividham 127
tṛṣṇā 16, 457, 467
trayī 115, 456
truth 4, pragmatic theory 481, 484, 542, correspondence theory 484, 542; Nyāya concern with truth, not validity 524, 543

udāharaṇa, example, 31, 234-241 *passim*, definition and kinds of, 217 253-255; rival definitions 255f., connection with familiar instance (*dṛṣṭānta*) 256-258, 259, 260, 261, 315-317 *passim*
udāharaṇasādharmya 235
udāharaṇavaidharmya 237
udbhava 75
uddeśa, xxxix, 302, 475

ūhā 63
Umāsvāti 578n. 2
umpire, *adhikaraṇa*, Buddhist view 303-304
untruth 4; see also truth
universe, 111, contents 109-113, justification for selection of twelve *prameyas* 539-540; see also *prameya*
Untouchable 558
upabhoga 416, 458
upacāra, metaphor, see *chala*
upacayāpacayaprabandha 413
upādāna 34, 343, 355, 361, 435, 633
upadarśana 251
upadeśa 457, 590n. 1
upalabdhi 94, 409, 410
upalabdhihetu 17, 27
upalabdhisama 311, definition 323
upalabdhiviṣaya 27
upamāna, analogy, xxxiv, 4, 9, 25, 123, definition 141f., different views 141-142 objections 142-145, different from: inference 143f., perception and word 144-145; for benefit of another (*parārtha*) 143, 257, 263, 314f., critique of, 513-515; 529, 590n. 40, 590n. 2, 622n. 40
upamānapratyaya 103
upanaya, confirmation, definition and kinds of, 218, 219, 258-259; 260, 261, 262, 589n. 2
Upaniṣad 114, 116
upapatti 419, 515
upapattisama 311, definition 322-323
upāya 23
utkarṣasama 311, definition 313
utpatti 235, 302
utpattidharma 235
uttarapakṣa 521

Vācaspati, xxxix, 172, 419, 579n. 6, 579n. 9, 581n. 2, 584n. 4, 585n. 9, 586n. 1, 587n. 2, 588n. 3, 589n. 3, 589n. 4, 590n. 1, 591n. 2, 591n. 3, 591n. 5, 592n. 1, 592n. 2, 600n. 8, 602n. 2, 604n. 2, 606n. 2, 612n. 2, 613n. 3
vāda, discussion, xxxvi, 2, 4, 197, 214, 215, 218, 220, definition 297-299, Buddhist definition 299-304, 475, 520, 536
Vādavidhānaṭīkā 232
Vādavidhi 233, 299, 581n. 5, 604n. 2
vaidharmyasama 311, definition 311-312
vairāgya 458, 464
Vaiśeṣika Sūtra, purpose as *dharma* 476
Vaiśeṣika 9, 54, 165, 184, 206, 228, 236, 571, 584n. 8, 588n. 3, 597n. 4, 601n. 5, 608n. 3, 613n. 1
Vaiśya 419
Vājasaneyī Saṃhitā 612n.5
vākchala, see *chala*
vākya 218, 260, 503
Varada Rāja 578n.1
varṇa, phoneme 13, 163, 170, 176, 177, 178, 179, 382, 511, 594n. 1, 595n.1, 596n.2
varṇa, class 419, 555, 558, 628n. 73; see also *Varṇāśrama*
Varṇāśrama 558, 560, comparison with Catholic Church 562-563, 567
varṇyasama 311, definition 314
vārtā 115, 456
Vārtika 245, 457
vāsanā 91, 385
vasanta 75
Vasubandhu 299, 581n.5, 600n. 8, 604n.3
Veda 24, 114, 115, 116, 123, 155-164 *passim*, 400, 447, 449, 480, 484, 494, 495, 496, 523, 528, 555, 568, 571, 591n. 2, 591n. 4, 592-593n. 2, 593n. 3, 620n. 22
vedanā 93, 387, 389, 430, 462
Vedānta, xli, 9; also see pramāṇa; 441, 571
Vesey, G. N. A. 625n. 60, 626n. 68
vibhūti 351
vidhi 593n. 3
vidyā, learning, apprehension 94 (*upalabdhi*) four branches 114, 456-457, 472
Vidyabhusana, S. C. 584n.8, 585n.9, 589n. 3, 591n. 5, 599n. 1, 601n. 13, 606n. 3, 607n. 5, 607n. 9
Vigrahavyāvartanī 579n. 6
vijñāna 53
Vijñānavādin 578n. 3
vikalpasama 311, definition 314
vikāra 176
vikṣepa 331, definition 338-339
vilakṣaṇakārya 392
vipakṣa 120, 236, 241-251 *passim*, 266, 272-274, 600n. 2
viparyayahetu 236
viruddha, fallacy of the contradictory hetu 202, 265, definition 281-282, 298, 524, 602n. 1
viruddhārthasādhakatva 202
viṣāṇa, *viṣāṇin* 54
viṣaya, object, individuality and generality 19-20, 21, 59, Buddhist objections 86-94
viśeṣa 19, 102, 163, 198, 199, 200 203, 205, 207, 208, 209, 210, 211, 212

245, 348, 361, 369, 392, 409
viśeṣaṇa 54, 139
viśeṣadharma 201, 364
viśeṣaṇaviśeṣyabhāva 81
viśeṣaviśiṣṭadharma 208
viśiṣṭaviṣaya 19
vistāra 369
vīta 238
vitaṇḍā, cavil, xxxvi, 3, 4, 213, 214, 218, 220, 264, 291, definition 297, 304, 305, 471, 472, 520
viveka 466
vṛtti 81, 409, 589n. 3 (commentary)
vyabhicāra 201, 239, 281
vyadhikaraṇa 29
vyakta 402
vyakti 3, 179, 302, 413, 497n. 3
vyaktiviśeṣadharma 413
Vyāsa 613n. 3
vyatireka, vyatireki 129, 131, 365
vyavacchedahetu 199
vyavasāyātmaka 50
vyavasthā, vyavasthita 340, 361
vyūḍha 13
vyūha, vyūhana 67, 433

weltanschauung 556
Whitehead, A. N. 565, 629n. 76
Wisdom, John 537
Wittgenstein 496, 528, 615n. 10 620n. 22

yadṛcchā, yadṛcchāśabda 54, 422
Yajñadatta 244
yama 471
yathākāmam 152
yathā tathā 144
yava 152
yoga, yogin 24, 66, 373, 415, 416, 419, 442, 445, 470, 471, definition of yoga 476 and 498, 508, 577n. 2
Yogācāra 578n. 1
yogasamādhi 24
Yogaśāstra 471
Yoga Sūtra revision as purpose 476, 613n. 3
yukta 515

Zimmer, H. 577n. 2